To David Bentley Hart

with warm wishes

Bernie

MYSTICISM IN THE
GOLDEN AGE OF SPAIN
(1500–1650)

A multi-volume series

THE PRESENCE OF GOD:
A HISTORY OF WESTERN CHRISTIAN MYSTICISM

MYSTICISM IN THE GOLDEN AGE OF SPAIN (1500–1650)

Vol. VI, Part 2 of
**The Presence of God:
A History of Western Christian Mysticism**

by
Bernard McGinn

A Herder & Herder Book
The Crossroad Publishing Company
New York

A Herder & Herder Book
The Crossroad Publishing Company
www.CrossroadPublishing.com

In continuation of our 200-year tradition of independent publishing, The Crossroad Publishing Company proudly offers a variety of books with strong, original voices and diverse perspectives. The viewpoints expressed in our books are not necessarily those of The Crossroad Publishing Company, any of its imprints or of its employees, executives, or owners. Although the author and publisher have made every effort to ensure that the information in this book was correct at press time, the author and publisher do not assume and hereby disclaim any liability to any party for any loss, damage, or disruption caused by errors or omissions, whether such errors or omissions result from negligence, accident, or any other cause. No claims are made or responsibility assumed for any health or other benefits.

Book design by The HK Scriptorium

Library of Congress Cataloging-in-Publication Data
available from the Library of Congress.

ISBN 978-0-8245-0090-0

Books published by The Crossroad Publishing Company may be purchased at special quantity discount rates for classes and institutional use. For information, please e-mail sales@CrossroadPublishing.com.

Contents

Preface

THE GENESIS OF THIS BOOK in relation to the other two parts of Volume VI of my ongoing history of Western Christian mysticism, *The Presence of God*, has been partly explained in the "Preface" to Volume VI, Part 1, *Mysticism in the Reformation (1500–1650)*. I originally conceived of this as a single volume covering this century and a half, but over several years of research and writing it gradually became clear to me that it would not be possible to do justice to the richness of early modern mysticism, among both Catholics and Protestants, in a single book. Hence, in mid-2016, with the writing of VI, Part 1 complete, and well launched into the treatment of Spanish mysticism (partly due to the inspiration of the five hundredth anniversary of the birth of Teresa of Avila in 2015), I realized that Volume VI needed to be divided. The shape that I eventually decided on was not just a division between Protestant and Catholic mysticism but, rather, as this volume will make clear, a tripartite structure. Protestant mysticism demanded a book of its own, so my treatment of mysticism in the early Reformers (VI.1) appeared at the end of 2016. I then realized that two substantial books (VI.2 and VI.3) would be required to do justice to the richness of Catholic mysticism in the era of the dividing of Christianity. The first of these (VI.2), the present volume, deals with Spain in its Golden Age between 1500 and ca. 1650. Volume VI.3 will treat developments in Catholic France, Italy, and Germany in the same period.

For more than a century a powerful impetus in the Catholicism of the nineteenth and twentieth centuries, especially its attempt to advance a counternarrative to secular modernity, sought to identify key figures in Catholic history whose teaching could serve as both guides and bulwarks for the defense of the church against its opponents, intellectual and political. From the perspective of doctrinal theology, the rise and triumph of neo-Thomism in the nineteenth century was the preeminent example of this impetus. Leo XIII's encyclical *Aeterni Patris* of 1879, as well as many subsequent papal, curial, and academic statements in support of the neo-Thomist position, made "Thomism" (this variety of it at least) a central aspect of Catholic thought for almost a century. A second, if less widespread, endeavor was to identify the "Catholic" view of mysticism. Here the writings of the Spanish Carmelites Teresa of Avila and John of the Cross were often advanced as enjoying an authority in mystical teaching analogous to that of Thomas in doctrine. The historical channels by which the emphasis on these Spanish mystics as dominant authorities was effected are not entirely clear, but a survey of much of the neo-Scholastic and even post-neo-Scholastic study of mysticism shows that Teresa and John were often held to be *the* mystical teachers against whom all others were to be measured. There were good reasons for this concentration on the two Carmelites. Few figures in the history of Christianity had left such an extensive corpus of properly mystical writings, and even fewer had explored the mystical element of Catholicism in such detail and with comparable penetration and insight. This is why the mysticism of Spain's Golden Age, especially of Teresa and John, will always remain central to any account of Western Christian mysticism.

In the chapters of this volume I try to give a just appreciation of the achievement of Teresa and John—always a difficult task—while at the same time questioning views that would make them cynosures of the highest point of mystical teaching in Christian history. Both Teresa and John insisted that there were many ways to God and that they spoke only out of their own life experiences insofar as this might prove helpful to others. I believe that we should take them at their word. No single figure or group of figures, however great, can exhaust the riches of the great symphony of Christian mysticism in its historical development. A second misperception that I am trying to overcome in this volume is the notion that the Carmelites represent the essential contribution of the mysticism of Spain in its Golden Age. We need to remember that during this period Spain witnessed an outpouring of mystical writings and hagiographical accounts of ecstatic mystical women that was almost unrivaled in Christian history. The other chapters in this volume try to give some sense of the variety and wealth of Spanish mysticism without pretending to exhaust it.

Just as the release of the historical Thomas Aquinas from the "house arrest" of neo-Thomism has led to a new flowering of study of the great "Common Doctor" of the church, I also believe that contemporary recognition of the symphonic nature of the Christian mystical tradition, with its many instruments, parts, and voices, is encouraging a renewed and deeper appreciation of Teresa of Avila and John of the Cross, as well as of the many other Spanish mystics of early modernity, and of their place both in the mysticism of Spain's Golden Age and in the wider mystical tradition.

CHICAGO
FEBRUARY, 2017

Abbreviations

DIP	*Dizionario degli Istituti di Perfezione.* Edited by Guerrino Pelliccia and Giancarlo Rocca. 10 vols. Rome: Edizioni Paoline, 1973-2003.
DS	*Dictionnaire de spiritualité: Ascétique et mystique, doctrine et histoire.* Edited by Marcel Viller et al. 17 vols. Paris: Beauchesne, 1937–97.
The Dionysian Corpus	The writings ascribed to Dionysius the Areopagite are found in the critical edition of Beate Regina Suchla, Günter Heil, and Adolf Martin Ritter, *Corpus Dionysiacum.* 2 vols. Berlin: Walter de Gruyter, 1990–91. The following abbreviations will be used:
CH	*De coelesti hierarchia (The Celestial Hierarchy)*
DN	*De divinis nominibus (The Divine Names)*
EH	*De ecclesiastica hierarchia (The Ecclesiastical Hierarchy)*
Ep	*Epistulae (Letters)*
MT	*De mystica theologia (The Mystical Theology)*
McGinn	Bernard McGinn, *The Presence of God: A History of Western Christian Mysticism.* New York: Crossroad Herder, 1991–. The previous volumes in the series will be abbreviated as follows:
Foundations	*The Foundations of Mysticism: Origins to the Fifth Century* (1991)
Growth	*The Growth of Mysticism: Gregory the Great through the Twelfth Century* (1994)

Flowering	*The Flowering of Mysticism: Men and Women in the New Mysticism, 1200–1350* (1998)
Harvest	*The Harvest of Mysticism in Medieval Germany, 1300–1500* (2007)
Varieties	*The Varieties of Vernacular Mysticism, 1350–1550* (2012)
Reformation	*Mysticism in the Reformation, 1500–1650* (2016)
Peers, *Studies*	E. Allison Peers, *Studies of the Spanish Mystics*. 3 vols. New York: Macmillan, 1927–36. Revised edition, New York: Macmillan, 1951.
PL	*Patrologia cursus completus. Series Latina.* Edited by J.-P. Migne. 221 vols. Paris: J.-P. Migne, 1844–64.
STh	Thomas Aquinas, *Summa theologiae* (cited by part, question, and article; e.g., Ia, q. 3, a. 1).
Vg	*Biblia Vulgata (Vulgate Bible)*

MYSTICISM IN THE GOLDEN AGE OF SPAIN (1500–1650)

"The Most Catholic Kingdom":
The Place of Spain in Early
Modern Catholicism

Spain and Spanish Catholicism in the Golden Age

IN ORDER TO BEGIN TO UNDERSTAND the remarkable phenomenon that is Spanish, or Hispanic, mysticism,[1] it is necessary to make a few brief remarks about the historical
position and religious situation of the Kingdom of Spain
between 1500 and 1650.[2] At the beginning of the fifteenth century, Spain was divided into a number of competing kingdoms
and did not have much weight in European politics. With the
unification of Aragon and Castile under the Catholic monarchs
Ferdinand (ruled 1479–1516) and Isabella (ruled 1474–1504),
the successful conclusion of the *Reconquista* with the fall of
Granada in 1492, and the Spanish discovery of the New World
and the wealth it brought to the kingdom, the situation was
dramatically reversed at the outset of the sixteenth century.
Under the first two Hapsburgs, Charles V (Charles I in Spain,
1516–56) and Philip II (1556–98), Spain reached its acme as the
great power of the day and the staunchest defender of Roman
Catholicism in divided Europe—"the Most Catholic Kingdom."
The reign of the pious Philip III (1598–1621) marked the beginning of the decline of Spain's prosperity and hegemony in the
Catholic world, a process accelerated under the rule of Philip
IV (1621–65). As Stephen Haliczer noted, "The Spain of the late
sixteenth and seventeenth centuries, when mysticism reached
its peak as a social phenomenon, was also a society in crisis,

wracked by wave after wave of epidemic disease and an economic depression that placed families under stress as never before."[3]

Spain's form of national Catholicism was exceptional.[4] According to Stanley G. Payne, "The most distinctive historical traits of Spanish Catholicism were acquired during the fifteenth and sixteenth centuries, a time of fundamental change in religious policy and emphasis."[5] Some of these traits were traditional, rooted in the Middle Ages and the long struggle to free the peninsula from Islamic control. Among these were the aristocratic emphasis on honor and the insistence on purity of doctrine. Other developments were new, such as the emergence of what Christian Hermann called "a papal-royal co-government of the Hispanic churches" between 1480 and 1520.[6] Although the interests of the papacy and the Spanish crown sometimes clashed, Spain's support of the papacy during the crisis of the early Reformation prompted the popes to give the Spanish kings special rights over the church in Spanish domains, effectively making the king the papal vicar for his lands. In turn, the Spanish crown guaranteed the rigorous unity of faith that gave Spain a religious stability lacking in other realms where the Reformation led to divisions and armed conflicts, as can be seen in Hapsburg Central Europe, in France in the second half of the sixteenth century, and in England. As is often the case, Spain's political preponderance produced a burst of cultural achievement in literature, art, and religious life. The "Golden Age" was a time of great accomplishments, not least in religion, but also of significant limitations.[7]

Prominent among the limits were the rigidity and formalism of Spanish religion and society that became increasingly evident in the seventeenth century. Again to cite Hermann, "Two movements shaped the country's religious evolution: one animated by the demands of Christian perfection, the assimilation of modernity, and intellectual and moral courage; the other marked by fanaticism, exclusivist rejection, and repressive dogmatism."[8] Both were products of the same spiritual climate, however much we see them as scarcely compatible today. The negative pole of this situation expressed itself in terms of the kingdom's treatment of its Jewish and Muslim minorities, in the establishment of the Spanish Inquisition, and in disputes over the legitimacy of interior religion.

During the Middle Ages there was considerable religious warfare in the Spanish peninsula as the Catholic kingdoms conducted the long struggle of Reconquest against the Muslim states. The expanding Catholic realms not only gained many Muslim subjects but also had substantial Jewish minorities. Although far from perfect, there was a measure of "coexistence" (*convivencia*) among the three faiths, at least in the late Middle Ages. Beginning around 1400, as part of the nation-building process, toleration of Muslims and Jews weakened, as rulers began to adopt a policy of forced conversions (i.e., either baptism or exile) in order to solidify the Christian character of their realms. This culminated in 1492 in the expulsion of the Jews who refused to convert.

The converted Muslims (*moriscos*) and especially the converted Jews, called "New Christians" (*conversos*), were looked down upon by the "Old Christians," not least because they were suspected of continuing Jewish practices in secret, thus becoming formally heretics. In order to bring these Jewish "heretics" to heel, in 1478 Ferdinand and Isabella received permission from Pope Sixtus IV to set up an Inquisition under the control of the crown.[9] The Spanish Inquisition was thus different from its medieval predecessors due to its royal control and original focus on suppressing latent Judaism. The scope of the Inquisition, however, was expanded in the sixteenth century to include any form of deviance against the Spanish church-state order. Thus, the Inquisition was the key component in the repressive state-church structure of sixteenth-century Spain, although other forms of societal control, such as the establishment of lists, or indices, of forbidden books, played a role.

After the outbreak of Luther's protest against the papacy in 1517, growing fear not only of Jews but also of "Lutherans" (often meaning any and all forms of heresy), increased exponentially in Spain. These fears encouraged the repressive tendencies in Spanish society that strengthened under Philip II, who sought to close off Spain from the dangerous tendencies, political and religious, that were disturbing Europe. Teófanes Egido describes the religious situation of Spain in Philip's time as "closed to Europe, open to heaven."[10] The paradox of the situation was that such a repressive religious realm, one dominated by suspicion of interior spirituality and mysticism, also produced so many major mystics.

Spanish fear of aliens and outsiders, especially Jews and heretics, heightened the social and cultural dominance of the notion of "honor," that is, public reputation based on sexual purity for women and "purity of blood" (*limpieza del sangre*) for the family. In the fifteenth century, the church resisted laws of purity of blood that restricted the social mobility of converted Muslims and Jews, arguing that all Christians were equal in God's sight. By the sixteenth century, however, especially in the second half of the century, guarantees of purity of blood came to rule in both church and society. To have an ancient lineage of "Old

Christian" stock, free from any hint of Jewish or Muslim impurity, was to belong to the dominant class of the nobility (*hidalguía*), even if a person's official patent of *hidalguía* was purchased or gained by dissimulation, as was the case with many upwardly mobile *conversos*, such as Teresa of Avila's father. Given their ambiguous and often dangerous position in society, it is no surprise that the *conversos* sought to counter their alien status by covering over the stain of their Jewish blood in order to gain social integration.

Religious Reform

Like the rest of Western Europe, Spain confronted the issue of religious reform in the late fifteenth and first half of the sixteenth century. As Alastair Hamilton says, "The [late fourteenth-century] vision of Spain as a world power was accompanied by plans for a widespread and thorough reformation of the Spanish Church."[11] Spain's reformist movements, which antedated Luther's protest by several decades, took distinctive forms. Three of these reform tendencies are of importance for understanding sixteenth-century Spanish mysticism: the reform of religious orders;[12] the spiritual reform associated with Cardinal Francisco Jiménez de Cisneros (1436–1517); and the new emphasis on interior prayer.

In the late fourteenth and throughout the fifteenth century widespread movements of "Observant" reform—that is, the desire to return to a stricter and more authentic mode of living the original charism of a particular form of religious life—percolated across Europe, affecting the Benedictine, Franciscan, Dominican, Cistercian, and Carmelite orders. Tension and conflict between Observants and "Conventuals" (those who were content with the approved mitigations and their rules and way of life) were frequent. King John II of Castile (ruled 1406–54) supported Observant reform in his domain. Though some popes were unhappy with these religious reformers, they received strong support under Ferdinand and Isabella. Alexander VI allowed the monarchs to appoint commissioners to further the Observant reforms in the Franciscans and the Dominicans. Fra Diego Deza was the Dominican commissioner; the Franciscan commissioner was Jiménez de Cisneros.

Cisneros was a high clerical official who resigned his benefices to become an Observant Franciscan and hermit. In 1492 he became the confessor of Queen Isabella of Castile and soon was an important advisor to her and her husband, Ferdinand, eventually becoming archbishop of Toledo and briefly regent after Ferdinand's death. Cisneros spread the Franciscan Observant reform in Spain, but he also played an important role in wider reform currents through his patronage of religious humanism, especially biblical scholarship, and his interests in interior prayer and the devotional and mystical literature that fostered it.[13]

At the beginning of the sixteenth century, Cisneros established a new university at Alcalá de Henares, where all three major schools of Scholasticism (Nominalist, Scotist, Thomist) had equal footing and where humanistic studies of ancient languages and critical biblical scholarship were pursued. With his support, in 1522 a team of scholars at the university produced the great six-volume *Complutensian Polyglot*, the first critical edition of the Latin Vulgate, the first edition of the Greek Septuagint, and the first printing of the Hebrew Bible by Christians. The works of the Dutch scholar Desiderius Erasmus (1466–1536), the most famous humanist of the age, began to spread in Spain at the beginning of the sixteenth century.[14] In 1516 Cisneros even invited Erasmus to collaborate on the *Complutensian Polyglot*, but he was turned down. Erasmus was deeply influential in Spain for more than a decade, but a reaction to his ideas began in 1527, and some of his disciples were eventually brought before the Inquisition. What is most important about the reforms of Cisneros for our interests was his fostering of the publication of religious literature, especially relating to interior prayer and mysticism. Cisneros was a great patron of publications in many fields—biblical, humanist, liturgical—but, to cite Felipe Fernández-Armesto, "in terms of numbers of volumes, Cisneros's devotional library was on a vastly greater scale than his other projects."[15]

Cisneros's publishing activities with regard to devotional literature were a vital part of the background to the flourishing of the mysticism of Spain's Golden Age.[16] Cisneros was a Franciscan, and most of the sixteen spiritual works he sponsored represented late medieval mendicant piety, which he helped make available in the new world of early modern Spain. These works include central books of Franciscan mysticism, such as the *Book of Angela of Foligno*, which came out in Latin in 1505 and in Castilian in 1510. A patristic text used by many Spiritual Franciscans, the *Ladder* of John Climacus (d. 649), was published in 1504. Cisneros was interested in the lay Franciscan mystic Ramon Llull, and had his *Book of the Lover and Beloved* published in 1516, although in Latin. Cisneros was also instrumental in putting some Dominican mystics into Spanish, such as Raymond of Capua's popular *Life of Saint Catherine* in 1511, and the saint's own *Book of Letters and*

Prayers in 1512. An edition of the Dominican Vincent Ferrer's *On the Spiritual Life*, emphasizing the mystical elements, appeared in 1510, while a translation of Cistercian Mechthild of Hackeborn's *Book of Spiritual Grace* came out in 1505.

Other spiritual literature was also made available to the Spanish public, whether published before the time of Cisneros's editorial efforts or issued independently in the two decades when he controlled the Spanish church. The *Imitation of Christ* was translated into Spanish as early as 1490 and often reprinted. A Spanish version of the *Life of Christ* by the Carthusian Ludolph of Saxony (d. 1378) appeared in four volumes between 1502 and 1503. Translations were made of patristic classics, like Jerome and Gregory the Great. Among the most important of the medieval works of spirituality made available was the 1514 publication of *Light of Contemplatives* (*Sol de contemplativos o mística teologia*), a version of Hugh of Balma's handbook, *Viae Sion lugent*, often ascribed to Bonaventure in the late Middle Ages. If we consider the mystical element in Christianity as fostered by a tradition of texts designed to both inspire and guide deeper contact with God, the presence of this remarkable translation effort is of major significance.[17]

Cardinal Cisneros himself was seen by his contemporaries as a mystic, but his surviving writings are official in nature. We do know that he was a strong supporter of ecstatic women and apocalyptic prophets, such as the controversial Dominican Sor María de Santo Domingo (see chap. 1), whom he defended when she was under suspicion by the Inquisition and by the Dominican authorities in Rome. In short, the Cisnerian Reform was decisive in setting the stage for a new mystical tradition in Spain, one that did not directly come into conflict with the repressive state-church system during his own lifetime (Cisneros himself was the head of the Spanish Inquisition). After the Cardinal's death, however, suspicion of mysticism and interior prayer began to grow.

A Forerunner: García Jiménez de Cisneros

A final aspect of the era of Cisneros deserves note. The cardinal's cousin, García Jiménez de Cisneros (1455–1510), produced the first mystical handbook in Castilian, presumably with the encouragement of his powerful relative.[18] García Cisneros was a Benedictine reformer, who, as abbot of the ancient house of Montserrat in Catalonia (1499–1510), not only revived this monastic center but also installed a printing press to publish spiritual and mystical treatises. His career is further testimony to the religious revival sweeping Spain at the time and to the links between late medieval and early modern mystical traditions. The *Ejercitatorio de la vida espiritual* (*Exercises of the Spiritual Life*), published anonymously in 1500, was an anthology of mystical texts on methodical prayer. Cisneros's main sources were the *devotio moderna*, the writings of Bonaventure and Pseudo-Bonaventure, Jean Gerson, and the late medieval Carthusian writers, such as Hugh of Balma and Nicholas Kempf.[19] The *Ejercitatorio* was widely diffused, not only in Cisneros's reformed Benedictine Congregation of Valladolid but also throughout Spain in the sixteenth and seventeenth centuries in both Spanish (three editions) and Latin (nine editions). It was translated into French and Italian.[20]

A brief look at this treatise provides a sense of how Spanish mysticism of the early sixteenth century was shaped by the mystical traditions of the late Middle Ages. Cisneros divides the book into four sections. After an introduction (chaps. 1–9), the first section deals with the purgative way (chaps. 10–19), whose principal exercise is repentance. The second section concerns the illuminative way (chaps. 20–25), with the main exercise being thanksgiving, while the third part deals with the unitive way and praise (chaps. 26–30). This progression in the spiritual life is described as a passage from "servile fear" (*temor servile*), through the "initial fear" (*temor inicial*) of gratitude to God, to the goal of pure "filial fear" (*temor filial*).[21] The final part of the book (chaps. 31–68) completes the third part in treating more questions concerning contemplation,[22] before the concluding chapter 69, which is in the form of a spiritual alphabet.

Like many late medieval mystical anthologists, Cisneros chose his sources with care and wove them together, along with his own comments, into a useful handbook on the practice of prayer as the path to union with God. It is well known that Ignatius of Loyola used his visit to Montserrat in March of 1522 to deepen his conversion to the interior life of prayer and contemplation. His confessor, the Montserrat monk John Chanones, appears to have given him a copy of Cisneros's *Ejercitatorio* in preparation for his general confession. Ignatius found the book helpful, and there has been some discussion about how far the volume may have influenced his own *Spiritual Exercises*, which he began developing at Manresa as early as fall of 1522 but published only much later. The judgment of Terence O'Reilly is that, while both the audience and the purpose of Ignatius's *Exercises* were different from Cisneros's monastic anthology, important structural aspects of the *Ejercitatorio,* such as the transition from servile to filial fear and the three ways of contemplating Christ, show that some of Cisneros's favored mystical themes were taken up in a transformed way in the Jesuit founder's famous work.[23]

Notes

1. In recent years scholars have begun to use the term "Hispanic mysticism" in order to embrace mystics not only in the Kingdom of Spain but also in Portugal and the New World; see, e.g., Hilaire Kallendorf, ed., *A New Companion to Hispanic Mysticism,* Brill's Companions to the Christian Tradition 19 (Leiden: Brill, 2010).

2. Classic histories include John H. Elliot, *Imperial Spain 1469–1716* (London: Penguin, 2002; first published in 1963); and John Lynch, *Spain 1516–1598: From Nation State to World Empire* (Cambridge, MA: Blackwell, 1992). For a brief sketch, see Christian Hermann, "Settlements: Spain's National Catholicism," in *Handbook of European History, 1400–1600: Late Middle Ages, Renaissance, and Reformation*, ed. Thomas A. Brady, Heiko A. Oberman, and James D. Tracy, 2 vols. (Grand Rapids: Eerdmans, 1996), 2:491–522.

3. Stephen Haliczer, *Between Exaltation and Infamy: Female Mystics in the Golden Age of Spain* (Oxford: Oxford University Press, 2002), 155.

4. A helpful account is Stanley G. Payne, *Spanish Catholicism: An Historical Overview* (Madison: University of Wisconsin Press, 1984), chaps. 1–2.

5. Payne, *Spanish Catholicism*, 25.

6. Hermann, "Settlements: Spain's National Catholicism," 511.

7. See the summary in Payne, *Spanish Catholicism*, 44–61.

8. Hermann, "Settlements: Spain's National Catholicism," 516.

9. See Henry Kamen, *Inquisition and Society in Spain in the Sixteenth and Seventeenth Centuries* (Bloomington: Indiana University Press, 1985).

10. Teófanes Egido, "The Historical Setting of St. Teresa's Life," in *Spiritual Direction*, ed. John Sullivan, Carmelite Studies 1 (Washington, DC: ICS, 1980), 128.

11. Alastair Hamilton, *Heresy and Mysticism in Sixteenth-Century Spain: The Alumbrados* (Toronto: University of Toronto Press, 1992), 1.

12. For a brief survey, see Adolfo de la Madre de Dios, "Espagne, III: L'Age d'Or, C: Réformes Religieuses et nouveaux Ordres," DS 4:1136–46.

13. For an overview of the role of interior prayer in Spain at this time, see Melquíades Andrés Martín, "Alumbrados, Erasmians, 'Lutherans,' and Mystics: The Risk of a More 'Intimate' Spirituality," in *The Spanish Inquisition and the Inquisitorial Mind*, ed. Angel Alcalá, Atlantic Studies on Society in Change 49 (New York: Columbia University Press, 1987), 457–94.

14. On Spanish Erasmianism, see especially Marcel Bataillon, *Erasme et l'Espagne*, ed. Daniel Devoto and Charles Amiel, 3 vols. (Geneva: Jérôme Millon, 1991; reprint of the 1937 original with additions and corrections).

15. Felipe Fernández-Armesto, "Cardinal Cisneros as a Patron of Printing," in *God and Man in Medieval Spain: Essays in Honour of J. R. L. Highfield*, ed. Derek W.

Lomaz and David Mackenzie (Westminster: Aris & Phillips, 1989), 149–68, here 159.

16. There is no up-to-date full survey of Spanish mysticism in English, though many helpful individual volumes will be listed below. Although old, there is much of value in E. Allison Peers, *Studies of the Spanish Mystics*, 3 vols. (New York: Macmillan, 1927–36; rev. ed., New York: Macmillan, 1951). In French, see Adolfo de la Madre de Dios et al., "Espagne, III: L'Age d'Or," DS 4:1127–78. There is a large literature in Spanish. Two important works are Melquíades Andrés Martín, *Historia de la mística de la Edad de Oro en España y América* (Madrid: Biblioteca de Autores Cristianos, 1994); and Eulogio Pacho, *Apogeo de la mística cristiana: Historia de la espiritualidad clásica española, 1450–1650* (Burgos: Monte Carmelo, 2008). For a theoretical overview, see Macario Ofilada Mina, "Between Semiotics and Semantics: An Epistemological Exploration of Spanish Mysticism and Literature and Its Contribution to Spirituality in the Academy," *Studies in Spirituality* 22 (2012): 69–88.

17. There is a helpful list of "Early Translations of Mystical Writers into Spanish," in Peers, *Studies,* 3:255–61.

18. Mateo Alamo, "Cisneros (Garcia ou Garzias de)," DS 2:910–21; Peers, chap. 1, "The Dawn of the Golden Age: García de Cisneros," in *Studies,* 2:3–37; and Terence O'Reilly, "The Structural Unity of the Exercitatorio de la Vida Spiritual," in O'Reilly, *From Ignatius Loyola to John of the Cross: Spirituality and Literature in Sixteenth-Century Spain,* Collected Studies 484 (Aldershot: Variorum, 1995), 287–324.

19. Of the sixty-nine chapters of the work, twenty-seven are drawn from writers of the *devotio moderna* (Gerard Zerbolt van Zutphen, Thomas à Kempis, and Jean Mombaer); ten chapters come from Bonaventure and Ps.-Bonaventure; and eleven chapters are from Carthusian authors (Hugh of Balma, Ludolph of Saxony, Nicholas Kempf). Cisneros also makes use of Jean Gerson and Richard of St. Victor. On Cisneros's sources, see Pierre Groult, *Les mystiques des Pays-Bas et la littérature espagnole du seizième siècle* (Louvain: Librairie Universitaire, 1927), 92–100.

20. The critical edition of the text is by C. Baraut, OSB, *García Jiménez de Cisneros, Obras Completas,* 2 vols. (Montserrat: Monastery of Montserrat, 1965), vol. 2. There is an English version from an earlier edition by E. Allison Peers, *Cisneros: Book of Exercises for the Spiritual Life* (Montserrat: Monastery of Montserrat, 1929).

21. See O'Reilly, "Structural Unity of the Exercitatorio," 293–311.

22. Part 4 has three sections: chaps. 31–43 on contemplation; chaps. 44–60 on preparing for contemplation, especially by meditating on the life of Christ; and chaps. 61–68 on perseverance in contemplation.

23. Terence O'Reilly, "The Exercises of Saint Ignatius Loyola and the Exercitatorio de la Vida Spiritual," in O'Reilly, *From Ignatius Loyola to John of the Cross,* 303–23.

CHAPTER 1

Spanish Mysticism: The Early Stages

URING THE MIDDLE AGES, especially the twelfth and the thirteenth centuries, the Iberian peninsula was the home of some of the greatest representatives of Jewish and Islamic mysticism, the land of Sufi masters like Ibn al-'Arabi and major Kabbalists like Moshe de Leon. It is puzzling, then, to consider why there was little Christian mystical writing produced in the kingdoms of medieval Spain. The only important medieval mystic from Iberian lands was the Catalan Franciscan layman Ramon Llull (1232–1316), a polymath who wrote in Latin and Catalan. Llull was a visionary, a missionary, and an idiosyncratic philosopher who had a significant impact in some later circles of thought. A prodigious author of about 250 works, he wrote a good deal about contemplation, but mostly as a tangential aspect of his project to create a new form of logic and philosophy. His central mystical work is *The Book of the Lover and Beloved* (*Lo libre d'amich e amat*) written in 1283 as part of his large romance called *Blanquerna*.[1] Some of his writings were available in sixteenth-century Spain, but it is difficult to discern any pronounced influence on later Spanish-language mysticism.

The roots for the growing interest in interior prayer in Spain and the emergence of mystical writings in Spanish after 1500

I am very grateful to Gillian T. W. Ahlgren, Professor of Theology at Xavier University, for her careful reading of this chapter and many helpful suggestions.

are difficult to uncover, at least in a fully satisfactory way. This new chapter in the story of Western mysticism was certainly connected to the issue of reform, both the reform of the religious orders and the broader reform program of Cardinal Cisneros briefly discussed in the introduction. It also reflected Spain's new position as a world power and the role of Catholicism as the cultural cement of the newly unified kingdom. The rise of the Reformation would soon give Spain the role of the guarantor and defender of the "true Catholic faith." Spanish hunger for mystical literature, both from Italy (e.g., Angela of Foligno and Catherine of Siena) and from northern Europe (the *devotio moderna* and the Germanic mystics), was a factor, but more as a sign of Spanish interest in mysticism than as a precipitating element. There were doubtless many contributing factors in what during the course of the sixteenth century was to grow into a veritable flood of mystics and mystical writings.[2]

This chapter will look at three aspects of the earliest stage of Spanish mysticism from its origins down through the middle of the sixteenth century. The first is the role of female visionaries and holy women (*beatas*), who were already active in Spanish domains in the fifteenth century but became particularly important in the early decades of the sixteenth century.[3] The second is the Franciscan Observance and its practice of the inner prayer of "recollection" (*recogimiento*). The third is the question of the "Enlightened, or Illuminated" (*Alumbrados*), that is, the individuals condemned by the Spanish Inquisition as mystical heretics, beginning in the third decade of the sixteenth century. This last issue overlaps with the previous two, since many of the *Alumbrados* were *beatas*, and some Observantine Franciscans, at least in the early stages, were connected to the groups and individuals subsequently condemned.

Visionaries and *Beatas*

The visionary explosion of the late Middle Ages, beginning toward the end of the twelfth century and growing over the next three centuries and more did not bypass Spain.[4] Late medieval visionaries, often but not always women, had repeatable manifestations of God, Christ, Mary, and the saints, sometimes by going up to heaven, at other times by showings here on earth. These seers were often given messages to convey to the world, sometimes to specific people, including popes, kings, and other sacred and secular leaders. At times the visions were written down by their recipients (e.g., Hildegard of Bingen, Hadewijch, Henry Suso, Julian of Norwich); at other times confessors and clerical advisors wrote accounts of the showings given to their penitents and advisees. Ecclesiastical suspicion of this visionary flood produced investigations, inquisitorial proceedings, and even condemnations, as well as the growth of a specialized literature on the "discernment of spirits" (*discretio spirituum*), providing guidelines for distinguishing true visions sent from God from false ones that were either a product of the imagination of the visionary, or (what is worse) diabolical deception.[5] Medieval religion, especially late medieval religion, was a religion of visions, as well as suspicions of visions.

"Visionary" and "mystic" are sometimes seen as interchangeable terms—all visionaries are mystics and all mystics receive visions from God. The relation of the two modes of religious life, however, is actually more complex, especially if we advert to the personally transformative aspect of the mystical element of Christianity. From this perspective, the decisive issue is not so much the claim to have seen a heavenly figure, or even to have received a message from on high (messages that were of many kinds—admonitory, consoling, didactic, reformative, and so on), but rather the effect a divine manifestation has on transforming the consciousness of the recipient to a deeper awareness of God's action in one's life and an impetus for spreading this message through either oral or written teaching. This is why important mystical teachers, even those who were gifted with visions like Julian of Norwich and Teresa of Avila, insisted that visions were secondary aspects of their deepening sense of God's presence. Many mystics, of course, did receive visions or celestial apparitions as a part of their special graces; others did not. Not all visionaries, however, need to be counted among the mystics, given the political, didactic, and localized message that they received from their heavenly visitors, as well as their lack of interest in personal and social transformation.

An example of the difference can be found in the Marian visions of fifteenth- and early sixteenth-century Spain, especially in Castile, as described by William Christian Jr.[6] These visions of Mary (e.g., Santa Gadea in 1399, Jaen in 1430, Cubas in 1449, Escalona ca. 1490) feature the appearance of the Virgin to a poor person (shepherd boy, laborer, laborer's wife, etc.), instructing them to tell the local authorities about the need to build a shrine, monastery, or church on the location of the apparition. In other visions the message is an assurance to the neighboring population of the Virgin's protection or an announcement of plagues and other coming catastrophes. Such manifestations were obviously important for local piety, but scarcely for the story of mysticism. Once the Inquisition began to widen its scope beyond pursuing backsliding *conversos* in the early sixteenth century, Marian visionaries became subject to greater oversight and often condemnation by the official church. Beyond the illiterate visionaries, however, we can ask about the female authors from the fifteenth century. Were there mystics among them?

Teresa de Cartagena (ca. 1420–ca. 1470) was a Franciscan nun from a well-known *converso* family who produced two prose writings, the *Grove of the Infirm* (*Arboleda de los enfermos*)—she herself suffered from deafness—and *Wonder at the Works of God* (*Admiración operum Dey*).[7] Teresa showed herself an able apologist for the role of women as writers and interpreters of scripture, but she had no interest in mystical themes. The same is true of the princess Constanza de Castilla (ca. 1390–1478), who, for political reasons, was compelled to enter the Dominican convent of Santo Domingo el Real in Madrid, where she had a long career as abbess. Constanza wrote a series of prayers, meditations, and devotional works for her nuns, but these were scarcely mystical.[8]

María de Ajofrín (d. 1489) was a *beata*, a woman who made a private vow of chastity (which could be temporary) and wore a religious habit but who was not formally associated with a particular order. Such women might live under the protection of a male religious house and could be cloistered or not. Some lived alone; others in a community, a *beaterio*,[9] not unlike the Beguines of northern Europe in the late Middle Ages. The *beata* María had visions of Mary and the Christ child, as well as other heavenly figures. In later years she became famous for her prophecies predicting divine vengeance on Spain due to the immorality of the clergy and the spread of heresy, prophecies that won the support of Cardinal Pedro González de Mendoza, the archbishop of Toledo and primate of Spain. Some of María's visions involve a sharing in the sufferings of Christ and in the *compassio* of Mary, but, as Ronald Surtz remarks, even when María took on the maternal role of the Virgin, "There is no caressing, no tenderness; holding Christ does not produce a moment of mystical union."[10] María's visions, at least as described in the *Life* written about her by her confessor Juan de Corrales, are different from those of Angela of Foligno, the nuns of Helfta, and other late medieval visionaries, due to their lack of engagement with an interior transforming union and the kind of exterior, often public, vocation it gives to the recipient.

There were, however, some figures active in the first two decades of the sixteenth century who provide evidence for an explicit mystical role for women in the early stages of Spanish mysticism. These women were also *beatas*, usually with some association with the mendicant orders. Neither the Franciscan Juana de la Cruz (1481–1534) nor the Dominican Sor María de Santo Domingo (1486–1524) was a fully professed nun. Following a pattern often seen in the late Middle Ages, the two *beatas* did not write their own accounts (they were probably functionally illiterate). What we know about them comes from their clerical supporters or from literate members of their religious houses.

The visionary and prophet Juana de la Cruz was born of a peasant family and ran away at the age of fifteen disguised in men's clothing to join the community of Franciscan *beatas* at Santa María de la Cruz in Cubas.[11] Famed for her asceticism and ecstatic visions, she was elected leader of the community, which Cardinal Cisneros supported and regularized under the Rule for Third Order Franciscan women. In 1510 the Cardinal took the unusual step of giving the convent and its prioress rights over the local parish at Cubas, with regard to both revenue and the presentation of the pastor. Having a woman in control of an ecclesiastical benefice was controversial and would come back to trouble Juana and the community after Cisneros's death in 1517. (During the quarrels over this issue Juana was briefly deposed in 1527, but she was then reinstated and served as prioress until her death in 1534.) From 1505 to 1518 Juana delivered a series of ecstatic sermons to her community related to the feasts of the liturgical year. Her amanuensis, Sor María Evangelista, recorded a number of these in a book called *The Consolation* (*El Conhorte*), which is our main source for Juana's visionary mysticism.[12] The two other sources for Juana's life and mystical ecstasies are the hagiographical *Life*, which she partly dictated, and a historical account of her monastery "Nuestra Señora de la Cruz."[13]

Juana was controversial. After her death, several readers left comments on the manuscript of *The Consolation*, some attacking and some defending her views. In the early seventeenth century several biographies of Juana appeared, and in 1621 her cause for beatification was introduced in Rome. In 1666–67 both the *Life* and *The Consolation* were submitted to the Holy Office for investigation. *The Consolation* was examined by the Jesuit Martín de Esparza Artieda (1606–1689), who was obviously not happy with the claims for the superiority of the Franciscan order made in the book, while the *Life* was given to the well-known theologian and spiritual writer Giovanni Cardinal Bona (1609–1674) for investigation. Both men found serious doctrinal errors in the works and Juana's cause came to a halt. That was not the end of the story, however. In the eighteenth century, Spanish supporters pushed to have the cause reopened, claiming that the two works submitted were not Juana's, but this ploy did not work and again the cause was ended, only to be reopened once again in 1986.

Ronald E. Surtz has analyzed a number of Juana's sermons delivered in ecstasy. He describes their general format as follows: "The sermons normally consist of a novelesque retelling of the gospel episode followed by a description of the allegorical pageants [she calls them *figuras*] that take place in Heaven to celebrate the major feasts of the liturgical year. Juxtaposed with these pageants are such spiritual and tropological interpretations as are relevant to the salvation of humankind."[14] Juana knew that it was dangerous for a woman to take on a preaching office and that her imaginative additions to the scriptures might be questioned. Hence, *The Consolation* adopts an authorizing technique found in a number of texts by and about women—the claim that the Holy Spirit speaking through Jesus is the real author of the book, so that Juana merely channels what the Spirit says. *The Consolation* is presented as a heavenly book, that is, one actually written on the walls of the celestial city. Its additions to the biblical account are defended because God alone knows all the details of the events of sacred history.[15]

An example of Juana's sermonic style and its mystical dimensions can be found in the Sermon for the Feast of St. Francis (October 5), which picks up on a theme also found in the *Life*, that is, how Francis and his daughter Juana serve as co-redeemers with Christ in their ability to rescue souls from purgatory. Both Francis and Juana are imaged as hens who gather and protect their brood following the example of Jesus, who before the passion spoke of himself as a mother hen (Matt. 23:37). According to the *Life*, in imitation of Christ, Juana took upon herself the sufferings of the souls in purgatory and made this concrete by having the nuns bring both heated and frozen stones in which souls had been imprisoned (!) into her bed so that she could suffer along with them and hasten their departure for heaven.[16] Co-redemption, especially with regard to the souls in purgatory, is a theme found in other late medieval and early modern mystical women, but Juana's adaptation is very much her own.[17] Another sermon that treats the souls in purgatory is dedicated to St. Clare (August 11), the co-patron of Juana's order.[18]

The theme of suffering with Christ is given a special emphasis in a series of visions and locutions recounted in the *Life* that employ musical instruments to describe the visionary's relation to Jesus. It was commonplace to speak of preachers as trumpets or flutes of God, and since

Juana was preaching, she too is said to be a trumpet. In one vision, her guardian angel, St. Laruel, announces that God wills to send her such trials and tribulations "to break that organ or trumpet through which he spoke and he wished to change and transform it into another state so that it would appear scorned and sickly. . . ." This happened in a vision on the Vigil of the Feast of Saint Achatius and his Companions (June 21), when the suffering Christ embraced Juana, pressing all the parts of his body against hers, so that she experienced both intense pain and heavenly sweetness:

> Then the Lord embraced me and placed his feet on my feet and his knees on my knees—he purified them completely—and his palms on mine and his head and body against mine. And when he did this, what I felt was so intense that it seemed there was a multitude of very sharp, burning nails piercing me. And there sounded a din all around as when they perform a Passion Play, striking blows with a hammer. It [my body] was filled with his presence and with the taste and sweetness of his love.

These and other experiences of direct contact with the crucified Christ are described as a temporary reception of the stigmata. At such moments Juana feels her body transformed into a new instrument of God, a guitar: "I seem to see all the limbs and veins and joints of my body transformed into the strings and keys or pegs of a guitar and Our Lord playing on them with his most holy hands, playing on them as upon an instrument or guitar and making a very sweet and gentle harmonious sound."[19] Christ as the supreme musician, and even Christ as a harp hanging on the wood of the cross making music for the salvation of the world, were motifs found in earlier mystics, such as Bonaventure. Juana takes these a step further in describing her own sharing in Christ's redemptive suffering.[20]

The sometimes disturbing character of Juana's mysticism is evident in her Sermon for the Nativity of the Blessed Virgin (September 8).[21] Marian devotion was central to Juana—her message is as much mariological as it is christological, if not more so.[22] Like most of Juana's sermons, recounting the Gospel story and its reenactment in the liturgy on earth (*hic*) leads on to what takes place in the heavenly realm, the goal of contact with God in the life to come (*ibi*). Juana proleptically participates in this celestial reward, and, because these sermons were preached to her community, she is inviting the sisters to begin to share here and now in the final union with Christ the Divine Bridegroom.[23] Extrapolating on accounts of the infancy of Mary in pseudepigraphal

Gospels and the notion of the Virgin as being foreordained from all eternity in the deliberations of the Trinity,[24] Juana's narrative has the infant Mary taken up into heaven to enjoy converse with the Father and be received into his arms. Throughout the sermon Mary appears as the new Eve, reversing the damage done to humanity in the Fall. The unusual elements in the narrative begin as the angels disrobe the infant Mary so she can be naked in heaven. Nakedness is a symbol of Mary's Adamic purity and freedom from sin, but it becomes the focal point of the vision in an insistent way. Mary desires to be naked on earth until she is presented in the temple. In the allegorical pageant set in heaven, Mary continues naked, even dancing before God as her breasts begin to grow in adolescence. After she is commanded by all three persons of the Trinity to dance naked before all the angels and saints in heaven, she says, "My Lord Father and my almighty God, it pleases me to dance naked not only before all the inhabitants of heaven, but I am even disposed to obey if your Majesty ordered me to go now to earth and to walk among all the people as naked as I was born." God the Father, struck with the beauty of her breasts, says, "Climb up here, my beloved daughter, and give me your breasts, for you are lovely and more perfect than all the daughters of Sion and Jerusalem." The Father then praises the beauty of Mary's naked body as she starts to dance again. After this, the Father requests, "Give me your breasts, for I wish to play with them." Mary refuses, saying that she will only do so in the "flowery garden," language recalling the Song of Songs and indicative of her inner union with the three persons of the Trinity.[25] The vision goes on to talk about how Mary conceives and bears Christ in the Trinity within her virginal belly, as well as how the Father clothes Mary with his own mantle of protection for humanity. In this vision Mary is an ideal more than a model for Juana or her sisters, who cannot share in the Virgin's sinless status. Despite the modern mammary fixation, we should beware of oversexualizing this account, but I cannot share Ronald Surtz's attempt at a reductionist psychological interpretation (Juana as a victim of child abuse), nor do I agree with his claim that "what redeems the Blessed Virgin is the special nature of her seductiveness: she can play the meretricious role for a worthy purpose, while retaining her exemplary chastity. Ironically, this notion of Mary as a kind of divine seductress—even a holy prostitute—redeems all women."[26]

A comparable ambiguity can be found in the case of Juana's contemporary, Sor María de Santo Domingo. As a proponent of Dominican reform in Spain, María was opposed by the Conventual Dominicans and even by the Dominican general in Rome, the influential Tommaso de Vio, Cardinal Cajetan (1480–1547). Nevertheless, she found strong support not only among the Dominicans influenced by the reforms of Girolamo Savonarola (d. 1498) in Italy but also with important clerical and lay leaders in Spain. As Jodi Bilinkoff has shown,[27] through her prophetic and mystical gifts María was able to gain the assistance of her local lord, the duke of Alba, in a way similar to how some contemporaneous Italian *sante vive* were backed by Italian dukes and princes. María, however, went them one better by obtaining the support of Ferdinand, the embattled king of Aragon, and even Cardinal Cisneros, ever on the lookout for divine approbation for his political and religious projects. María de Santo Domingo profited much from such weighty supporters, but they too gained something from having a noted mystic and prophet proclaim that God was on their side.

María was born into a peasant family in a village not far from Avila, probably in 1486.[28] She received the habit of the Third Order Dominicans about 1503 in Piedrahíta, but as a *beata* ("the *beata* of Piedrahíta") María never took formal vows. By 1507 she had moved to live near the male Dominican convent of Santo Tomás in Avila, which was becoming known as a center of the Dominican reform. María soon undertook travels to spread the reform, and her prophecies began to attack the Conventual (i.e., unreformed) Dominicans. The first of María's influential supporters was her local ruler, the duke of Alba, Don Fadrique Álvarez de Toledo, heir of one of the most powerful families in Spain and a friend of the Dominicans. It appears to have been the duke who brought her to the attention of his cousin, King Ferdinand, who, since the death of his wife Isabella in 1504, had been struggling to assert his influence in Castile (by law he could not ascend to the throne). María was summoned to the royal court at Burgos in 1507–8, where her ecstasies and prophecies won the support of the king because they fit in well with his own messianic expectations of becoming the predicted Last World Emperor. Here she also came into contact with Cardinal Cisneros, ever a supporter of ecstatic and prophetic women. María won his favor in part by predicting his unexpected triumph over the Moors at Oran in 1509.[29]

María had enemies as well. The Dominican provincial, Diego Magdaleno, originally supportive, turned against her, and Cajetan, the master general, strongly opposed her. Four investigations conducted over several years witnessed a back-and-forth movement of condemnation and support, but, given the influence of her powerful backers, it was a foregone conclusion when María was finally exonerated in

1509. Nonetheless, damage had been done, and the holy woman had to retreat to the new convent the duke of Alba had built for her in her hometown of Aldeanueva, where she remained until her death in 1524. The orders of the Dominican general about restricting her contact with the friars seem to have had little effect on her supporters in the reform movement, but her fame in life did not outlive her death.

As in the case of Juana de la Cruz, we are dealing not with a female author but with someone whose work was written down by her supporters, male supporters in this case, probably her confessor, Diego de Vitoria, O.P., and/or her defense counsel, Antonio de la Peña. The text, composed between about 1512 and 1518 at the request of Cisneros, was published in 1518 under the title the *Book of Prayer* (*Libro de la oración*). It was dedicated to Cardinal Adrian of Utrecht, at that time Grand Inquisitor of Spain, but soon to be elected for a brief reign as Pope Adrian VI. The *Book of Prayer* is of a mixed genre—partly a defense of the nun against her attackers, and partly an account of some of her ecstatic visions.

Based to some degree on the investigations to which María was subjected, the first part of the *Book of Prayer* deals with three attacks on her featured in the 1509 examination: (1) her severe fasting, (2) her claims to the stigmata, and (3) accusations of worldliness. In each case, the author emphatically rejects the accusations, but at times in ways that test the credulity of the reader. For him there was no middle ground when it came to the *beata* of Piedrahíta.[30] With regard to María's reputation for not eating, the author has ample material for his rebuttal, namely, biblical prototypes for severe fasting and more recent examples like Catherine of Siena. Similarly, he attacks those who could deny the possibility of María's stigmata, stating, "We know that St. Francis's side opened, as did that of the blessed St. Catherine of Siena."[31] The third accusation is more troubling. María's defender does not deny that she often dressed in rich clothing and jewels and that "she rides a mule and amuses herself with worldly but decent pleasures and pastimes." She also eats extensively after her fasts. But, insists her defender, María's rich clothes are worn only for the sake of humility, so that others may think less of her due to her weakness (!). Her eating is for the same purpose, because she vomits afterwards: "For since she does not need nor does she take natural sustenance besides the food of his grace, she eats to receive suffering and persecution for having eaten by throwing up when she does eat."[32] The *Book of Prayer* gives a long, convoluted defense of María's worldly behavior,[33] but it does not go into the more troubling issue raised at her trial regarding sexual impropriety with her Dominican confessor. The investigation records indicate that María admitted that her confessor and sometimes other supporters would stay in her room overnight close to her bed or even lying on it in order to prevent attacks by the devil. Once, rescuing her from such an attack, her confessor had embraced her and kissed her; at other times, her followers would hold her in tight embraces. At the hearing, all the witnesses insisted that these activities were conducted with the purest of intentions and without the slightest taint of lasciviousness.[34]

The history of modern Catholicism shows more than a few examples of claims to mystical exception for what can only be judged as unacceptable sexual behavior. Some of God's "favorites" seem to have lived by other rules. Close to Juana's own time was the case of Benedetta Carlini (1590–1661), the abbess of the Convent of the Mother of God in Pescia, Italy, who acquired a reputation for visions, ecstasies, and the stigmata (as well as diabolical temptations) before being married to Jesus in 1619. An investigation by a papal nuncio in 1622 proved that it was all a hoax and Benedetta admitted to having conducted a lesbian affair with another nun for some years, acting in the person of her alter ego, the angel Splenditello.[35] Closer to the details of María's case were the events that unfolded in mid-nineteenth-century Rome, when the young and attractive novice mistress of the convent of Sant'Ambrogio acquired power over the house and many curial officials due to her claims of mystical contact with the heavenly world and her prophetic abilities.[36] Like María, Sr. Maria Luisa was sorely tried by demons, who even sometimes took on her own appearance to do evil things in the convent. Hence, her confessor, the noted Jesuit neo-Scholastic theologian Johannes Kleutgen (hiding under the pseudonym of Fr. Peters) had to spend nights alone in her cell, often in her bed, protecting her from demons. When the case was investigated by the Holy Office in 1861, both Sr. Maria Luisa and Fr. Kleutgen finally admitted to sexual contact but denied that any lustful intention was involved! Of course, we can never really know about Sor María and her unusual behavior. Was she a holy woman who did unusual things? Or was she a sham who was protected because her interests matched those of the most powerful people in Spain?

María's *Book of Prayer* portrays her as a visionary mystic and ecstatic. It also shows that the view of some that she was an *Alumbrada*, or sympathizer with the "Enlightened" who were becoming active in the second decade of the sixteenth century, is far from the truth. The three contemplative raptures described in the *Book of Prayer* are filled with erotic language, as the author explicitly notes, advising the reader

not to let "your heart be disturbed if you encounter words expressing amorous passion spoken in the mystical sense," because "many
excellent contemplatives" have used such language.[37] María's ecstasies have a distinctive flavor that Mary E. Giles describes as essentially
theatrical, "Sor María's contemplations were an 'ecstatic theatre' in
which she was at once author, text, and actor."[38] Unlike Juana de la
Cruz, whose sermons were delivered primarily to her nuns in the
third person, María's raptured contemplations were delivered publicly before a large audience, ecclesiastical and secular, and spoken
in her own voice.

The "Contemplation While Enraptured on Easter Sunday" starts
with an impassioned prayer: "Oh, my God. Oh, my God. Oh, my God.
Oh, woe is me. Oh, woe is me who is not resurrected with you. When will
I be resurrected in your love and fear?" After briefly praying to Mary
Magdalene, María continues, "When will I be received in your arms
so that my soul may be quieted with him and gladdened by him? My
God and my Savior, when will I rest sad in your sweet arms? When will
my soul be inebriated in your love and unable to leave you?" Although
it is the feast of the resurrection, the cross and passion are never far
away. Complaining about "the crude body" that she is still slave to, she
addresses her soul, saying, "In order to conquer and avenge yourself of
it [the body], when will you embrace with the cross the One who resur-
rects by opening up the road I closed? I closed it, my God, with my sins
and disobedience; your delicate flesh, your delicate limbs all bruised
and broken, they opened it up."[39] These passages give a sense of the
dramatic quality of María's ecstatic contemplations in which different
voices and characters appear to have been acted out by the visionary.

As the drama proceeds, different biblical figures are introduced and
take their respective roles. María thanks Christ for giving happiness
to his mother and mercy to his disciples by the resurrection in a long
introductory prayer to Mary—"Oh most kind and sweet Mother of God
and Mother of sinners!" As with many mystics, María's central desire
is for a share in Mary's suffering: "Oh devout Queen, give me some
little bits of the pain and love with which to weep."[40] Soon Jesus enters
the scene and there is a dialogue between Jesus and Mary that María
reports, occasionally adding her own editorial comments. Mary and
Jesus want to share the richness they have experienced with his followers, so Mary Magdalene is brought in to converse with Jesus as she
did in the garden at the tomb (John 20:11–18). This prompts a didactic
section in which María invites the hearer to imitate the Magdalene in
total surrender to Christ. "Oh sister, see how our Beloved comes with

hoe in hand for us to till the soil! Behold the task he assigns us!" That task is to clear the garden of conscience with the hoe of penitence so that the water of divine grace can flow through the channel of our wills in perfect conformity with Christ, who makes the flowers and grasses of virtues beautiful.[41] Later María introduces Peter and John running to the tomb (John 20:2–10) and provides a dramatic dialogue between the two apostles. When they arrive at the tomb, they fall on their faces and Jesus appears, raising them up and conversing with them. As the miniature play draws to an end, María once again becomes didactic, emphasizing the message of embracing the crucified Christ so that the garden of the soul will be well kept. She ends with a prayer to the "Most kind Father" and to Mary, God's mother and the mother of all.

The other two contemplations found in the *Book of Prayer*, one "While Enraptured Hearing Music" and the other on the "Feast of the Discovery of the Cross" (September 14), are shorter than the Easter Contemplation and are directly concerned with Sor María's mysticism of the passion with its emphasis on the blood of Christ. On listening to a clavichord being played on December 10 in Piedrahíta, María went into rapture and in the presence of all the religious of the house began a fervent prayer to Jesus, whose blood knows how to tune the instrument of the soul that sin has put out of tune. María speaks of this in terms of a deep inner loving union with Christ: "When the soft hand of your love and fervor touches and enflames my soul, what harmony and knowledge of you and me you place in my understanding." She goes on to describe the happiness she has from and in Jesus and his blood: "It is not that anyone can give you more joy than what you have in yourself and for all, but it still pleased you to receive what you give me, not because I made you happy, but because when I am happy in you the happiness of you in me lives and is happy."[42] Christ's blood puts everyone in tune, but the "adversary" (i.e., the devil) tempts the soul into sin, which causes the disharmony that can be healed only by the confession of sins. María desires to be bound to Christ with such love that she is overcome with desire to succor sinners: "Bind me to you, my Love, and let the binding be with the delicate chain of your charity and love, so that when I am tied and bound to you and see your fallen children, I will be able to go down and take them in my arms and bring them to your loving lap." This is the source of María's apostolic vocation, which is, as Richard of St. Victor would put it, "the insanity of love": "My God, tie me to you like a crazy woman, so that I may be mad in your love."[43]

Like the mysticism of Catherine of Siena, María's mysticism focuses on the blood of Christ and the Eucharist, in which we eat his body and blood; but she adds a musical dimension, one originating in Jesus and sent down to our world by the ministry of the four angels God sent to Mary and to others in scripture. She says, "Then two of the four who heard the music took it from the others. For that reason music is a delicacy drawn from your heart, issuing forth from those who were nearest to you and are one with you." At the passion, Christ's two hands and two feet function as another four mediators: "The delicate song of these four is your most sacred Blood, which invites us with its most sweet melody to harmonize our souls with you so that you may tune us with your Blood and play and dwell in us."[44] María de Santo Domingo's final contemplation, the "Contemplation on the Feast of the Discovery of the Cross," features a brief conversation in which she asks the Lord if his revelation had been given "before now on the islands which Columbus recently discovered." He assures her that it had, but it had not taken root due to the evil lives of the inhabitants.

Juana de la Cruz and María de Santo Domingo are early examples of the role of women in the mysticism of Spain's Golden Age. Some of the later women, most notably Teresa de Jesús, wrote accounts of their lives and mystical teaching, but most of the *beatas* and nuns were rather written about in hagiographical accounts and reports of their visions and miraculous gifts. For all the fascination and support they sometimes gained, women mystics remained a sign of contradiction in the Spanish patriarchal church and society—always subject to the need for the "discernment of spirits" and often under investigation by the Inquisition. Some women gained approval; many did not.[45] Without denying the importance of the large numbers of women who were reported to have received mystical gifts as a historical phenomenon, from the viewpoint of the theological significance of mysticism, the following chapters will concentrate on those women whose stories and/ or writings have had a significant ongoing impact, or who have had a revival in modern study.

Recogimiento and the Observant Franciscans[46]

The term *recogimiento*, usually translated as "recollection," is central to the understanding of sixteenth-century Spanish mysticism.[47] This rich word and its relatives (*recogido-recoger*) were used both in the broad sense of a spiritual way of life based on withdrawal, interiorization, and silence and in the more restricted sense of a method of interior mystical prayer at the center of such a way of life. Melquíades Andrés Martín defines it as follows: "The way of recollection is a methodical spirituality, or prayer, or art of love. It requires, then, labor and technique. It is a complete life treating of the lifting up of a person from the depths of sin to the sublimity of mysticism."[48] Angelo DiSalvo notes that "[t]he Spanish word *recoger* implies not simply a withdrawal or retiring, but also a collecting together, which also includes a reformation." Hence, he emphasizes the multifaceted nature of the process of "recollecting," noting that "it is a physical withdrawal of the individual to a quiet and secret place, but at the same time it is a gathering within of the powers of the soul as well as a holding (possession) or a contemplation of God in this profoundest and most intimate part of the soul."[49] Within this penumbra of meaning, different authors gave their own understandings of the term and its relation to other key words in Christian spirituality and mysticism. Because the English "recollection" captures only a part of the meaning of the Spanish, in what follows I prefer to use the Spanish *recogimiento*.

Although the prayer of *recogimiento* became widespread in sixteenth-century Spain among many religious and laity, it was Observant Franciscans who initiated the practice and who popularized it through their teaching and writing in the first third of the century.[50] Institutionally this mode of prayer was rooted in the small communities, hermitages, and houses of prayer described by terms like *casa de recolección/recoleta/ retiro* that had been set up by Franciscans of the Observance from the early fifteenth century onward. Following an old Franciscan custom, the friars in these houses lived a life of silence, strict asceticism, poverty, and intensive prayer, both liturgical and private.[51] Important leaders of the movement included Pedro de Villacreces (d. 1422) and Juan de la Puebla (d. 1495). Some of the more noted houses of recollection were found in Castile at places like La Salceda, Alcalá, and Torrelaguna. This movement, as we have seen, formed the spiritual context of Cardinal Cisneros, who had lived in such a hermitage before being called to the positions of authority that made him the leader of Spanish Catholicism. It was in this context from about 1480 that some friars began to practice the interior affective prayer that came to be called *recogimiento*. The first stage of the *recogimiento* movement falls into two parts: (1) ca. 1480–1523, when the houses of recollection were consolidated under the new minister general Francisco de Quiñones; and (2) 1523–1559, the period when the major *recogimiento* authors issued their treatises. This period ended with the publication of the Index of Fernando de Valdés, which forbade many vernacular spiritual works, including some of the *recogimiento* books.

The friars who began this way of prayer were heirs to a variety of mystical traditions, and sources marked by late medieval "affective Dionysianism" were among the most important, especially the Flemish Observantine Hendrik Herp (d. 1477), whose Dutch *Mirror of Perfection* was available in Latin from 1509 and later translated into Portuguese and Spanish.[52] Along with classics of medieval monastic mysticism, works of the *devotio moderna*, such as the *Imitation of Christ* and Jean Mombaer's *Rosetum*, were also influential. This form of prayer soon spread widely, even among the laity. Evidence for the emergence of the movement comes from Francisco de Osuna, the foremost proponent of *recogimiento*. In his *Third Spiritual Alphabet* (1527) Osuna speaks about an old man who once told him about his mystical gifts: "An old man whom I confessed—he had practiced these spiritual things for more than fifty years—told me in great confidence that among other mysteries it often happened [that] . . . his understanding was so stilled and occupied from within that nothing of creation could take form in it."[53]

As heirs to the treasury of medieval spiritual literature, the *recogimiento* authors employ much of the language and themes of late medieval mysticism. Nevertheless, the movement of *recogimiento* was not just a repetition of the past but was a distinctive product of early modern Spain, not least by using *recogimiento* as a focus to organize mystical teaching. The *recogimiento* writers adapted the traditional schema of the three stages of the mystical life,[54] but they employ this threefold pattern (beginners–progressives–perfect) with their own accents. The beginning stage of purgation and vocal prayer stresses knowledge of self and self-annihilation through profound humility. The progressive stage of illumination and meditation is deeply christological, marked by meditation on the passion and *imitatio Christi*. The final stage of perfection and contemplation is that of the transforming union of love.

The practice of this form of mysticism in the first decades of the sixteenth century soon produced introductions and handbooks, written mostly by Franciscans, although religious of other orders also made contributions.[55] Some of the Franciscan devotional works of the first two decades hint at the practice of *recogimiento* without giving the term central importance. For example, Jaime de Alcalá's *Book of Christian Knighthood* (*Libro de la caballería Cristiana*) first published in 1515, a devotional manual in three treatises, touches on mystical themes in the third treatise but does not use the word *recogimiento*.[56] Alonso de Madrid published his *Art of Serving God* (*Arte de servir a Dios*) in 1521. The first part sets out rules for the spiritual life, while the second deals with spiritual exercises and virtues in nine chapters. The four chapters of part 3 concern the love of God. Here Alonso says that one can serve God anywhere through *recogimiento*, but he does not describe the practice in detail.[57] Between 1525 and 1535, however, three Franciscans produced spiritual treatises that highlighted *recogimiento*: the lay brother Bernabé de Palma (ca. 1469–1532); another lay brother, the doctor and pharmacist Bernardino de Laredo (1482–1540); and the priest Francisco de Osuna (1492–1540).

Bernabé de Palma's *Way of the Spirit* (*Via Spiritus*), published posthumously in 1532, is less well known than the other two books.[58] The work is divided into five parts and features four movements toward union with God that always remain active in the mystic's life. Bernabé laments that for more than twenty years he got nothing out of the usual ascetical and devotional practices until he found what he calls "mental prayer" (*oración mental*), which, as he describes it, is clearly what others called *recogimiento*. The first movement involves the ascetical practices of the recollected way of life; the second is an inner evaluation of our sinfulness and recognition of our nothingness, that is, "annihilation or knowledge of our own nothingness" (*aniquilamiento o conocimiento de nuestra propia nada*). The third is gazing on God's greatness, which leads to what he calls "squared knowing" (*concimiento cuadrado*), that is, knowing God's height, depth, width, and length (see Eph. 3:18). Finally, we come to quiet rest in God, where the intellect is emptied and we are filled with divine love. Despite Bernabé's Franciscan status and orthodoxy, the *Way of the Spirit* was put on the Valdés Index of 1559.

Bernardino de Laredo was an influential mystical author, who has seen a revival of interest in the past century.[59] Bernardino was born in Seville in 1482 to a prosperous *converso* family and studied medicine. He practiced as a physician before entering the Franciscans in 1510. Bernardino remained a lay brother at the recollect house of Villaverde del Río down to his death in 1540, serving as both an apothecary and a doctor. He wrote several respected medical works, and Jessica A. Boon has argued for a strong influence of his medical knowledge and outlook on his spiritual writing. His major mystical work was the *Ascent of Mount Sion* (*Subida del Monte Sión*) in three books. It was first published in 1535; but Bernardino, partly as a result of reading Hugh of Balma and Henry Herp, recast book III of the *Ascent* in the second edition put out in 1538.[60] Unlike some of the other *recogimiento* authors, Laredo's work did not run afoul of the Inquisition and did not appear on the Valdés Index of 1559. The third book was read and praised for its teaching on union by Teresa of Avila (*Life* 23.12).

The structure and sources of Laredo's *Ascent* give a sense of its con-

tribution. Although as a lay brother Laredo had not received an education in theology, he was learned and widely read, as his use of many
sources from the mystical tradition indicates. In chapter 1 of part III,
he says that, because "this third book is beyond the author's powers
and capabilities, it is taken and compiled from the sentiments and
judgments of the contemplative doctors and explained with the help
of figures from Holy Scripture."[61] Part III directly cites many sources
but also makes tacit use of a wide range of authorities.[62] In the 1535
version of book III, Richard of St. Victor is the major authority cited,
but in the version of 1538 the affective Dionysianism of Herp comes
to the fore. Herp's *Golden Directory* is quoted more than any other text
(sixteen times). Along with Herp, whom Laredo describes as "a theologian excellent and enlightened as regards pure contemplation" (chap.
11), Hugh of Balma's *Sun of Contemplation* (Latin, *Mystica Theologia*,
and sometimes *Viae Sion Lugent*) is also an important source. Laredo
references Dionysius (I count ten times), as well as standard writers
such as Ambrose, Augustine, Jerome, Gregory the Great, Bernard,
Bonaventure, Henry Suso, and Gerson.[63] He is also aware of contemporary Spanish mystical writers, such as García de Cisneros, Bernabé
de Palma (e.g., chap. 3), and Francisco de Osuna (e.g., chap. 4). Thus,
the *Ascent of Mount Sion* is in part a compendium of traditional mystical
teaching, although, as Fidèle de Ros insists, "the originality of *Mount of
Sion* is not in question."[64]

The first two parts of the *Ascent* remained substantially unchanged
in the first and second editions.[65] Part I deals with the self-knowledge,
or annihilation, necessary for beginning the ascent of the mountain
of contemplation. Laredo gives a concrete program for the spiritual
exercises of this stage, envisaging the would-be contemplative as a rider
ascending the mountain and providing allegorical interpretations of
his equipment as signifying the virtues needed for the climb.[66] Part II
treats of the humanity of Christ, especially meditation on the passion.
Devout dwelling on the passion had been a feature of late medieval
spirituality and mysticism since the thirteenth century, especially in the
Franciscan tradition, and was widely practiced in Spain in the fifteenth
and sixteenth centuries. It was an integral part of mystical ascent to
God, and, as Boon has argued, Laredo gives the embodied practices
of passion meditation a more important role in his presentation of
recogimiento than do writers such as García de Cisneros or Francisco
de Osuna, especially by inviting his readers to "envision the Passion
transcribed onto their own souls and bodies."[67] The second part of the
Ascent contains fifty-three chapters. The first twelve deal with the incar-

nation and construct a picture of the flowing out of the persons of the Trinity as three rivers and the overflow of the rivers from the "ocean of Divine Love" (II.1–10) into the Incarnate Son of God. The soul is meant eventually to flow back into the divine ocean so that it will "find itself at length engulfed in Him in such a way that it will be no longer able to name itself, but will be wholly in God."[68] Chapters 13 through 36 form a succession of meditations on Christ's passion, death, and resurrection. Here Laredo makes use of late medieval mnemonic and optical science to construct a new variant of traditional forms of passion piety.

In the prologue to part III, Laredo insists on the integral connection of the three books of the *Ascent*. If the reader has sowed the seed well in part I, and "threshed your wheat well in the school of Christ and imitating his cross [part II], you must know that what you read in this third book represents for you the granary of the great King, where the grain is stored after being purified and cleansed of the chaff." He goes on: "We may now conclude that, however completely the soul is immersed in quiet contemplation, yet, for as long as it is on earth—that is to say, in this body—it must never forget self-knowledge and the following of the Cross of Christ, for that is the first step and the means whereby it may come to this end."[69] There seems to be no overarching structure to the forty-two chapters of part III, which feature a digressive consideration of key themes concerning the sublimity of quiet contemplation seen as the inner spiritual meaning of Mount Sion (III.1–2). Chapter 1 equates the three parts of the work with the traditional tripartite understanding of the mystical path—purgation, illumination, and "the heights of quiet contemplation by means of the juncture of love, which is called the Unitive Way."[70] The threefold division is central to Laredo's presentation, but this does not preclude him from also offering fourfold divisions, such as in chapter 3, which talks about the four ages of human life (infancy, childhood, adolescence, manhood) as illustrative of the path to perfection. Chapter 26 distinguishes four kinds of love in the ascent of the mountain: *amor operativo*, which befits beginners when they are first aroused to love; *amor amigable*, or friendly love, which belongs to those who have made progress in contemplation; *amor esencial*, where the soul "feels that its love is like a drop of water falling into the boundless sea," characteristic of those approaching perfection; and finally *amor unitivo*, which belongs to those who are perfect in quiet contemplation.[71]

Bernardino de Laredo's favorite description of the summit of Mount Sion is "the quiet of contemplation," but this phrase is also equated with *recogimiento*, union, mystical theology, and the height of love.

Chapter 22 deals with "The Manner wherein the Faculties [of the Soul] are to be recollected and the Soul is to be uplifted to God." Here Laredo talks about how the soul must enter into itself and be recollected in his presence, which affectively and effectively raises the soul above all that is not God.[72] He brings together all the main terms of his mysticism in describing the summit of the mountain:

> It must be noted, therefore, that in this recollection or gathering-in [*recogimiento o recolección*] of our own souls it behooves us to make a reflection [*reflexión*] of all thoughts and of the entire operation of our faculties. So that in quiet contemplation [*quieta contemplación*], or in Mystical Theology [*Mística Teología*], nothing must be admitted other than the soul's essential substance, so that it alone may occupy itself in pure, naked and unitive love [*unitivo amor*], not in operable love [*amor operable*]. . . . [T]here must be a reflection of all dispersed thoughts and wandering fancies and operations of the understanding, . . . and all your faculties must be drawn closely in and gathered together in your own soul.[73]

This returning to "the secret place within" is the essence of *recogimiento*.

Like the other *recogimiento* authors, Laredo distinguished between mystical theology and scholastic theology. In chapter 9 he speaks of "the path most commonly taken," namely, that of Scholastic theology, by which humans communicate to each other in describing contemplation, distinguishing it from "the delectable science, or wisdom, or mystical theology, which God teaches within the soul, . . . raising it up on an instant by the path of aspiration."[74] He illustrates the God-given nature of this gift by referring to a woman of his acquaintance who was enraptured as a child and now, fifty years later, knows many divine truths without ever having studied. Laredo uses the term mystical theology almost twenty times, often referring to the Dionysian corpus.[75] His understanding of mystical theology is essentially affective, as found in Balma, Herp, and Gerson. He says that "infused science, or hidden wisdom, or secret or mystical theology, or the practice of aspiration, is to be understood as signifying a sudden and momentary uplifting of the mind, wherein, by divine instruction, the soul is raised up suddenly, through pure love, by the affective way alone, to union with its most loving God, without the intervention of any thought, or operation of the intellect, or understanding, or natural reasoning."[76] Thus, it is not surprising that the Franciscan brother insisted on the purely operative, or infused, nature of the grace that achieves full stilling of the faculties.[77]

Following his affective Dionysian sources, Laredo insists that this rising up is without intellectual operation, "that is not knowing how to understand anything communicable even of the things we contemplate, having no awareness of ought save love" (chap. 15). Nonetheless, chapter 12 talks about the "two eyes of the soul," that is, will and understanding, and gives understanding a preparatory role in gazing on God in the mirror of creatures, while insisting that it is only the eye of love operative in the will that can be penetrated by God's uplifting ray. In this chapter Laredo identifies the *synderesis*, or highest power of the soul, not with an intellectual faculty but with an affective one, citing Song of Songs 4:9: "This vivacity of the affective nature, which demands ever to be carried upward to its God, is a most living spark, called by the theologians *synderesis*, or *synteresis*—a word meaning a quick and complete attentiveness which soars aloft, through long habit, to the Sovereign Good."[78] The *Ascent of Mount Sion* has many striking passages on love, such as in chapter 10, which speaks of "the touches of love" and "the wound of love" (both terms that will recur in Teresa of Avila and John of the Cross).[79] A good idea of Laredo's view of love can be gained from chapter 40, an exposition of the twenty-four verses on love set down originally in the first edition and here explained in response to the requests of his readers.[80] Bernardino de Laredo's hortatory mode of presentation, however, does not allow for any in-depth discussion of the relation of knowing and loving, or of love as a form of understanding.

Bernardino's thoughts on the role of Christ's humanity in the third part of the *Ascent of Mount Sion* have been somewhat controversial. Whatever may be said about the first edition, the second edition gives devotion to Christ's humanity, especially in the passion, an ongoing and important role. As he puts it in chapter 28, "In truth, there is no open road to the most quiet contemplation of the incogitable and inaccessible Divinity, nor is there any entrance so sure as meditation on the mysteries of our Jesus Christ, founded on a lively sense of our own humility deriving from our own knowledge of our annihilation."[81] Nevertheless, Laredo seems to hold, following Christ's saying about depriving the apostles of his bodily presence when he returns to the Father (see John 14:28), that the highest form of perfection does not consist in such meditation. Chapter 4, for example, states, "So we have learned here that love in perfection does not consist in meditation on the Sacred Humanity, but in quiet and perfected contemplation of the inaccessible Divinity."[82] It is not that the mysteries of Christ are forgotten, but they are remembered in a nondiscursive way, according to chapter 13: "They that are perfect must not forget the mysteries of Christ Jesus, our Lord and Redeemer, but they must remember when they meditate upon them, to remain in the state of quiet. For this reason they must not think upon aught that is corporeal, or admit it into the plan of their meditations."[83]

The ongoing role of Christ is also emphasized in one of the major additions to the second edition, the treatise on the reception of the Eucharist found in chapters 32–39. Based in part on Henry Suso's *Clock of Wisdom* (*Horologium Sapientiae*), this eucharistic section summarizes the importance of receiving Christ for attaining union. Laredo introduces the treatise with the following words:

> Since the whole aim of this third book is to unite the soul with its God by way of unitive love, and the most perfect union that is possible or can be attained in this hard exile consists in communion through grace in the Most Holy Sacrament, for this cause and for the recreation of the souls that are most full of love, we intercalate the material which follows, in the name of Jesus.[84]

The unitive love that leads to quiet contemplation and perfect *recogimiento* involves the cessation of the activity of the faculties, most especially understanding, as we have seen (e.g., III.19–20). Like other authors of the school of *recogimiento*, Laredo sometimes describes this by using the phrase *no pensar nada*. For example, in explaining a passage from Richard of St. Victor's *Mystical Ark*, Laredo says, "If, then, the perfection of every contemplative consists in the love of our Christ Jesus, which is impeded by thought, we must needs grasp the meaning of the author who said that in quiet contemplation it is best to think nothing [*no pensar nada*]."[85] Speaking of the limitations of academic theologians in analyzing the inner motions of the soul, Laredo tells of how he consulted about "withdrawals of the soul" (*encerramientos*) with a poor woman of deep spiritual insight who told him, "At a time like this the soul finds it has knowledge of that which it understands not and understands that which it knows not."[86] The apophatic dimension of Laredo's teaching fits in quite well with the affective Dionysianism to which he was heir.[87]

Suspension of the faculties can sometimes involve rapture, to which Laredo devotes a whole chapter, although he says, "I confess that I know it otherwise than from my own experience."[88] In this chapter Laredo defends the importance of rapture against its opponents, though he admits that some people experience false raptures. His teaching largely depends on the testimony of others about their states of rapture and the incommunicable knowledge of divine things they received. Laredo does provide theological background for understanding these experiences when the soul's "understanding [*discurso*] fails and recedes from itself and is transformed into pure intelligence [*pura inteligencia*]." Perfectly quiet and withdrawn, "this soul has soared above itself; we say 'above itself' because it surpasses and transcends the natural limits which it can set for itself. All that it achieves in this state is wholly supernatural."[89] Laredo says that it is possible for a soul to soar above itself and still be in possession of its senses and faculties, but at other times the soul not only soars above itself but is raptured out of itself. Laredo goes on to claim that, in the case of a soul who continues to soar above itself, "only one thing can happen, namely, that it will lose all sense and movement, be entirely alienated from itself, and fall into an ecstasy, that is, it will go where its mind cannot follow, or, as one says, become enraptured."[90] He says that he once spoke for five days with a man who had frequent experience of such raptures and who told him "that true alienations brought such satisfaction that a single one of them was more than sufficient to compensate for all the tribulations which in a long life he had offered to God and suffered for his sake."[91]

As will be evident even from this brief account, Bernardino de Laredo has a rich teaching on uniting with God, although he did not set forth union as the discrete topic of any of the individual chapters, but rather intermingled it with various discussions throughout the *Ascent*.[92] The Franciscan did not wish to construct a detailed account of the forms of union but wanted to show how the quiet contemplation of *recogimiento* makes the soul one with God insofar as that it possible in this life. Letter XI, published with the *Ascent of Mount Sion*, summarizes his teaching on union. Comparing the soul to a spark consumed in a roaring fire, he says:

> The same comes to pass with the soul that is made one spirit with God (1 Cor. 6:17), by God and with God. While not ceasing to be a soul, it is so completely infused in God, so entirely transformed in him, so like to God in the one will which is between them, that there is one act of willing [*querer*] in them and between them. In this act of willing the two things are only one, in one will enamored, converted, infused, engulfed and transformed in very refined love, wherein the soul is absorbed and made one with love that transformed it into itself.[93]

This passage provides an insight into the core of Bernardino's mystical teaching.

The most widely read of the Franciscan writers on *recogimiento* was Francisco de Osuna, whose work ranks among the greatest writings of Spain's Golden Age of mysticism.[94] Osuna was born in 1492 and entered the Franciscan order about 1513. His eight to ten years of training included theological studies at the University of Alcalá, but he also lived for some years in the Observant *recoleta* of La Salceda. A prolific author in both Latin and Spanish, Osuna was advanced to positions of authority in the order and elected as commissary general for the Franciscan mission in the New World, a position he never actually filled. He also traveled to France, the Low Countries, and Italy on the business of the order, before returning to Spain and dying about 1542.

It appears to have been between 1520 and 1530 that Osuna worked on the massive six-part spiritual compendium he called the *Spiritual Alphabets*, because most of the sections are presented as commentaries on two-line poems, or distichs, arranged according to the alphabet. It is difficult to know if the alphabets were written in order, but their publication history did not follow numerical order.[95] The *Third Spiritual Alphabet* (*Tercer abecedario espiritual*) was the most mystical and the most widely read.[96] It first appeared in 1527 and was reprinted four times in the sixteenth century and once in the seventeenth. It has been translated into five languages.

The *Third Spiritual Alphabet* is a lengthy and often prolix compendium of all aspects of *recogimiento*, connecting the term to the main themes of Christian mysticism.[97] Osuna never defines *recogimiento* in a precise way, but in a noted section he gives a detailed description. Chapter 2 of Treatise 6 says, "[T]his devotion bears many names in Sacred Scripture and the works of holy, learned doctors because of its excellence. Some call it mystical theology."[98] After contrasting mystical theology with speculative or analytical theology, Osuna gives a series of other names for his subject. "This kind of prayer is also called wisdom, because as you can see, it is delectable knowing." This prayer is also called "the art of love," and "It is called union because the person who attains to God in this prayer is made one spirit with him by an interchange of wills." He concludes, "This exercise is known as profundity (*profundidad*) with respect to the depth and darkness of devotion, for it originates in the depths of man's heart."[99] Chapter 3 broadens the picture. Scripture calls this exercise "concealment, because God hides in the secret recesses of the heart." But it is also called "abstinence" in the sense that the person who practices it must abstain not only from sin but also from human love and consolations and even thought. The scriptural names pile up (forty in all)—drawing near (Num. 6:1–4; Exod.

20:18–21), enkindling (Luke 12:49), welcome and consent (Job 22:21), marrow and fat (Lev. 3:16–17), attraction and adoption (Esth. 2:7), as well as the arrival of the Lord to the soul, the height that raises up the soul, spiritual ascension with Christ, and "the third heaven where contemplatives are enraptured" (2 Cor. 12:2). Even more scriptural names are laid out before Osuna finally summarizes:

> It seems to me that the most suitable name for this exercise and that which most clearly reflects something of its nature is *recogimiento*. . . . No one of them [the other names] clearly suits this holy devotion as does *recogimiento*, however, for the purpose of this exercise is to bring together and collect what has been dispersed, and because this devotion collects and brings together so much, the exercise itself is called *recogimiento*.[100]

Osuna emphasizes that *recogimiento* is not a solitary exercise but is rather the cement of the community of those earnestly seeking God: "We note that the devotion is called *recogimiento* because it gathers together those who practice it and, by erasing all dissension and discord, it makes them of one heart and love. Not content with just this, *recogimiento* . . . has the known, discernible property by which someone who follows it can be greatly moved to devotion when he sees another person also recollected."[101]

This exposition of the nature of *recogimiento*, its cognates, and biblical basis provides insight into the sources of Osuna's book. The Bible read in the tradition of spiritual interpretation is paramount. The Franciscan cites texts and images from the whole of the Old and New Testaments on every page. He also makes use of the *Glossa ordinaria* to elucidate many passages. As far as theological and mystical authorities are concerned, his favorite authors (at least insofar as explicit naming is concerned) are not surprising. Bernard of Clairvaux (49 citations) and Augustine (43 citations) are the most popular, followed by Gerson (37), Gregory the Great (35), and Jerome (21). Richard of St. Victor (13), Bonaventure (9, but some of these references are actually to Hugh of Balma), Francis (7), and Dionysius (7) also appear, as do a number of other writers. Jean Mombaer is mentioned explicitly only once (Tr. 13.3). Osuna was well read and traditional in his authorities.

Given the length and digressive character of the *Third Spiritual Alphabet*, some might imagine it to be poorly organized, but such is not the case. The twenty-three treatises commenting on the alphabetical distichs fall into two large sections: (1) Treatises 1–12 on the preparation for (Tr. 1–5) and progress of *recogimiento* (Tr. 6–12); and (2) Treatises 13–23 on the spiritual exercises of those advanced in the practice. Each of the treatises is divided into from four to ten chapters, treating a large number of issues, often in considerable detail.[102] It will not be possible to give a full account of this long book, but a look at the major themes of Osuna's understanding of the practice and meaning of *recogimiento* will demonstrate the book's importance in the story of Spanish mysticism.

In his *Los recogidos* Andrés Martín gives lists of both Osuna's favorite terms and his major modes of expression. The terms he notes are *meditación, contemplación, unión*, as well as *noche, oscuridad, alumbramiento* (illumination), *caligine* (cloud), *ocio y silencio* (rest and silence), *experiencia*, and *noticia amorosa* (loving knowledge).[103] Among Osuna's favored expressions are *no pensar nada* (thinking of nothing), *atento a solo Dios* (attention to God alone), *atento a solo Dios y contento* (attention to God alone and contentment), *puro amor/solo amor* (pure love/love alone), and *Dios solo y alma sola* (God and the soul alone).[104] These will be touched on in what follows.

Osuna was a trained theologian, but he was not writing a work of speculative theology. Hence, there is no extended discussion of the divine nature or the triune God in the *Third Spiritual Alphabet*. Given the practical and mystagogical nature of the work, Osuna does touch on theological anthropology. He affirms in a number of places the traditional view of humans as created in the image and likeness of God and discusses the inner and outer powers of the soul. The First Treatise speaks of the four principal passions of the soul (Tr. 1.3), and the difference between spirit-conscience-reason and person-sensuality (Tr. 1.4–5). Osuna asserts that the soul possesses inner senses matching the external senses (Tr. 3.1), and he adheres to the traditional Augustinian tripartite view of the soul's higher powers as consisting of memory, understanding, and will (e.g., Tr. 2.8, 3.3, 4.3, 10.7, 12.1). The purification of these three powers is an integral part of the path of *recogimiento*.[105] In line with most mystics, Osuna emphasizes the role of the will empowered by love in attaining God, though he allows for a role of affective knowing in union, as we will see below. One passage provides a more theoretical treatment of the power of understanding. In Treatise 21.1 Osuna says we can speak of understanding in two ways: first, as practical in the sense of directing us to what must be done or not done; and, second, as speculative "insofar as we scrutinize secret hidden mysteries." The practical aspect is the conscience, which is naturally ordered to the good and will continue to exist even in hell. Osuna identifies it with "synderesis, . . . the spark of conscience that never dies," claiming that "synderesis is the spirit that intervenes for us with unutterable groanings (Rom. 8:15)."[106] Even here, however, Osuna is interested not in clarifying the relation between the two aspects of understanding but only in the need for quieting the conscience.

An overriding theme in Osuna, as it was to be later for Teresa of Avila, is the insistence on the need for *experiencia*, lived knowledge, rather than mere book learning of the realities of the mystical life. Experience is not feeling but is an integral way of knowing, even of things that cannot be put into words.[107] This conforms to the Franciscan's teaching on the two modes of theology, speculative and mystical. As we have seen, Treatise 6, chapter 2, contrasts the speculative theology pertaining to the intellect, which requires much learning and will vanish when we see God in heaven, with the hidden, that is, mystical, theology, which is attained through "pious love and exercising moral virtues" and which grants an "infused knowledge" (*infusa ciencia*), what he elsewhere calls "experiential knowledge" (*noticia experimental*; e.g., Tr. 21.3, ed., 558). Hidden theology is more desirable than speculative, but, insists Osuna, "[i]f we could have everything, it would be best to have two right hands [i.e., both kinds of theology], the first of gold, the second gold overlaid with precious stones."[108] For Osuna, experience is needed throughout the course of the process of purgation, illumination, and uniting with God. Experience appears in two contexts. The first is the insistence that one needs to seek out experienced spiritual directors and teachers, as we see especially in Treatise 8, chapters 6–7.[109] The more frequent context is the appeal to the reader to come to know by experience the truth of the spiritual matters about which Osuna writes. The Franciscan appeals to tradition here, especially Bernard of Clairvaux and his insistence on learning from "the book of experience." "According to St. Bernard," he says, "experience alone teaches wisdom of the heart, which is attained only through prayer. . . . Those inexperienced in such matters will not understand them unless they read them more clearly in the book of experience."[110] Speaking of the grace of perfect prayer in Treatise 18.3, he says, "In this experience the understanding is so illumined and instructed that it seems to have been given the key of wisdom itself. . . . The spirit is enlightened in such a fashion that when those who experience this speak or write of God, they immediately utter profound truths with no effort at all."[111] Nevertheless, there are limits to how much the deep experience of God can be transmitted to others. Treatise 17.6 expresses this in commenting on Philippians 3:12–14: "In this last sentence the Apostle warns all those who follow the way of perfection to experience this matter, and he clarifies that he addresses the perfect rather than the imperfect. We are to experience rather than explain this, for the experience can be felt very keenly but never adequately described."[112] Almost every treatise of the *Third Spiritual Alphabet* speaks of the experience of those acquainted with the various stages of the spiritual path and invites the reader to strive for a similar experiential knowledge.[113]

The protean word *recogimiento* appears throughout the *Third Spiritual Alphabet*.[114] As noted above, Treatise 6, especially chapters 2–3, shows how *recogimiento* is the hidden meaning of many biblical images and the equivalent of phrases and words that express the central issues of Christian mysticism, such as mystical theology, wisdom, and union. In Treatise 15.2 Osuna says there are two kinds of *recogimiento*: general, which is "our way of going continuously alert with our hearts pacified and sealed, caring not for human things"; and special, which is "when you retire secretly to pray silently to the Lord, leaving aside absolutely every other occupation and business."[115] The special form of *recogimiento* seems to involve two modalities, not unlike what will later appear in Teresa of Avila, that is, an interior recollection primarily based on our own effort in cooperating with grace (later called acquired contemplation) and a deeper *recogimiento* that is the result only of God's action (later called infused contemplation). Thus, speaking of contemplation (= *recogimiento*), Osuna says, "We have by nature some capacity for contemplating the Divinity of Our Lord God, but it is necessary that the Sun of Justice revitalize and move us."[116] Treatise 11.5 expands on this in its discussion of how the soul is called by God, noting that some who use the exercise of *recogimiento* "desire fervently without knowing why these profound sighs issue from their hearts." Although they call out to God, "it might be better to affirm that God calls them to follow him into the desert of contemplation." Although these desires arise in the heart, the heart is not their primary cause, because the heart is moved by God.[117] Later Osuna concludes, "[I]t seems evident that the sigh that lifts to God should be called divine."[118]

Recogimiento has both negative and positive aspects. Negatively, *recogimiento* functions something like the Eckhartian notion of detachment. Discussing the third letter of the *Spiritual Alphabet*, Osuna says, "Thus our letter says you are to clear your heart of all vice and human obstacles and empty it of everything created, for the less company God has, the more easily he fits within you." This guard over the heart "consists of emptying the heart of every created thing so that all life, which is God, can better issue forth."[119] This message is repeated throughout the *Third Spiritual Alphabet*. Fundamental to the emptying process is the profound humility by which we recognize our own nothingness, what Osuna and the other *recogimiento* authors sometimes call "annihilation" (*aniquilación*).[120] Transposing a common apophatic expression into a different register, Osuna says the best kind of humility, which is the humility that does not recognize itself ("since the height of pridefulness is to judge ourselves humble"), can be described as "learned ignorance" (*docta ignorancia*).[121] Among the distinctive ways the negative aspect is expressed is by the expression "the no of *recogimiento*" (*no del recogimiento*). As Osuna puts it in Treatise 7.8: "The no of *recogimiento* rejects everything created that pushes through the portals of the senses, and it opens our hearts to God, for the 'no' does not renounce God but rather rejects everything else so that we can be with him alone."[122] The "no of *recogimiento*" is an activity of the first stage of the mystical life, though it continues during the advanced levels. This is true of another feature of the negative aspect of *recogimiento*, that is, the way it serves as the most effective safeguard against temptation and the attacks of the devil (e.g., Tr. 7.8 and 20.3). The emptying process is the necessary condition for the positive aspect of *recogimiento*, that is, the divine filling of the soul of which Osuna speaks in many ways—union with God, perfect contemplation, mystical theology, and so on.

Osuna provides some practical guidelines for the practice of *recogimiento*. Commitment to this form of life demands separation from the world and enclosure in a cloister, so the *Third Spiritual Alphabet* has a chapter on the cell as the best place to practice *recogimiento*. However, the essential cell, he insists, is the cell of the heart—"every soul practicing the devotion will be a recluse in the cell of his heart, the door to which is the *recogimiento* whereby we are to enter into ourselves."[123] In line with an old theme in Christian mysticism, to go within is also to go above, that is, to ascend to God: "No one can rise to God if he does not first enter into himself" (Tr. 18.1); and "In order to go above ourselves, we must first retire within to find and make of ourselves a ladder for going higher" (Tr. 19.4). In other places Osuna links these two movements to both human effort and divine operation, as in Treatise 9.7, where he says, "the soul equally prepared and inclined to both [movements] should first enter into itself, since rising above is the result of the former, which is to go into yourself, while rising above will occur without your endeavor and is thus the purer and the more spiritual of the two."[124]

Interiorization entails stilling the noise of the world, the clamor of the senses, and even the whispers of the higher powers of the soul. Citing Lamentations 3:26 ("It is good to wait for God's salvation in silence") and before discussing what Dionysius and Bonaventure (really Hugh of Balma) have to say about the need for the "blindness, deafness, and dumbness" of the understanding, will, and memory, Osuna says, "All these words admonish us to quiet our hearts and to observe perpetual silence if we wish to ascend to high contemplation."[125] Treatise 21.4 lays out three kinds of silence pertaining to *recogimiento*: the silence when all fantasies, imaginations, and visible things cease in the soul; the silence in which the soul is quieted in itself waiting for a word from the Lord; and "the quiet of the understanding . . . accomplished in God when the soul is entirely transformed in him and tastes his sweetness abundantly."[126] Osuna discusses this last at some length, citing Richard of St. Victor's *Twelve Patriarchs*, chapter 84. These three silences parallel other triple formulas used of *recogimiento* in the *Third Spiritual Alphabet*, such as *no pensar nada* for the level of purgation, *atenta a solo Dios* for that of illumination, and *sola amor* for the stage of perfection (see Tr. 21.5).

The emphasis on enclosure and silence might incline one to think that *recogimiento* was meant only for clergy and religious, but this is not the case, as numerous passages show. "The main reason I decided to write this book," says the Franciscan, "was to inform everyone about the devotion of *recogimiento* and thus I included in the letter [H that begins the distich being explained] the word 'everyone' in order to demonstrate that we are not to be selective but rather to teach all people how to approach our universal Lord who wishes to be served and loved by all."[127] Furthermore, *recogimiento* can be practiced anywhere—"Experienced people are just as recollected and occupied in God while doing manual chores around the house as are beginners kneeling in a secluded spot" (Tr. 6.5). All people, therefore, are called to embark on the path of *recogimiento*, which, as noted above, comprises the three traditional levels of beginners, proficient, and perfect. Osuna describes the three levels in a number of ways. Among the most important is the linking of the three levels to three stages of prayer.

Treatise 13.1–4 treats the three stages of prayer in correspondence with the three states of those who practice it. Chapter 1 deals with vocal prayer, either the prayer of those who recite the divine office, or any prayer pronounced with the mouth, especially "the most blessed prayer of the *Pater Noster*." (Chapter 2 deals with Francis of Assisi's prayer inspired by the Our Father.) Chapter 3 treats the prayer we pray within our hearts without outward expression, especially meditation on the passion,[128] while chapter 4 concerns "the prayer called mental or spiritual in which the highest part of the soul is lifted more purely and affectionately to God on the wings of desire and pious affection strengthened by love."[129]

The second stage of this itinerary, meditation on Christ's passion, raises an important issue in evaluating Osuna's mystical teaching—to what extent is it christological? There is no question that the passion was of great importance to Osuna, as can be seen from the fact that he devoted two of his six "alphabets" to passion meditation. Christ and the passion have a significant role throughout the *Third Spiritual Alphabet*. Especially important in this connection is Treatise 17, which speaks of the need for meditation on the sacred humanity of the Savior, insisting that the recollected person must continue to follow Christ's humanity with his body and Christ's divinity with his soul (Tr. 17.1–6). In this treatise Osuna insists that both practices remain essential, however much imitation of Christ's divinity is superior to imitating his humanity (Tr. 17.5–6). As long as we are in this life, both in body and in soul, we need to practice both. Corporeal imitation of Christ is not so much in imagination (i.e., meditation) as in practice of the works of mercy (Tr. 17.4), while imitation of Christ's divinity seems to involve ceasing "to follow the holy Passion in meditation," which Osuna admits that some people find difficult. Certainly, the Franciscan never abandons the centrality of Christ, but his distinction between imitation of the humanity and imitation the divinity of Christ may have led some of his followers to relegate Christ's sacred humanity to a secondary level.[130] This was to be an issue that Teresa of Avila had to confront.

Osuna illustrates the nature of the third level of affective prayer conducted without words, images, or even thoughts by citing Song of Songs 2:16 ("My Beloved to me and I to my Beloved"), noting that "God's greatest gift to his friend is himself and man's greatest gift to God is himself." Therefore, "man's giving himself to God and God himself to man is such a perfect exchange of gifts that when one gives himself, it seems that God is in the person totally and entirely." This is the prayer of union in which "recollected people" (*personas recogidas*) reserve nothing for themselves, so that "they remember God and give themselves so completely to him that they forget themselves as totally as if they did not exist." It is important to note that Osuna qualifies these strong expressions of union by invoking "it seems that" (*parece que*).[131]

The three stages of the spiritual life, expressed in various ways and tied to many other aspects of his teaching, appear throughout Osuna's *Third Spiritual Alphabet*.[132] Among the longest of these is the treatment in Treatise 18.1–4 of water as an image of the increasing role of God's grace in the transition from the lower to the higher stages (a presentation that may have influenced Teresa of Avila). Beginners draw water from a cistern, while proficients are served by a flowing well when God fills the heart with "the plenitude of grace." The perfect "enjoy streams supplying others." Osuna admits that it is difficult to distinguish the proficient from the perfect, although the proficient retire into themselves in silence, while the perfect retire above themselves into union with God (Tr. 18.3).[133] Another threefold pattern (Tr. 10.3–5) employs three forms of the tears of *recogimiento*. Beginners weep for the absent Bridegroom (Tr. 10.3); the proficient shed tears even in their *recogimiento* (10.4); the perfect continue to shed tears of joy that will be consummated in heaven. In one of the most striking passages in the *Third Spiritual Alphabet*, the Franciscan waxes eloquent on the biblical prototypes for these tears:

> If you wish to be raised above the earth to the heights of contemplation like the ark of Noah, the waters must multiply in you, and the fountains of the sea, which are wounds of your Bridegroom, Jesus Christ, must burst forth in your heart, and the channels of the heaven of Divinity must open in you so that you will have in perfect abundance the whole deluge in which you are to be saved and be like the Bride in the Canticle who is called a well of living waters rushing from the mountain Libanus (Song 4:15).[134]

Perfect *recogimiento* is the height of contemplation, the fullness of the union possible in this life, as well as a form of transformation into God, though the Franciscan rarely employs this language. It can also involve rapture, although here too Osuna tends to be moderate in his language.[135] Discussions of contemplation abound in the *Third Spiritual Alphabet*, despite the fact that Osuna does not try to construct a theory of the various kinds of contemplation.[136] Like his confrere Bernardino de Laredo, he speaks of contemplation as a mountain: "Whoever ascends the mountain of contemplation will undergo more than he effects, be moved more than he moves, and not profit at all from the knowledge and understanding that were the soul's eyes for seeing things."[137] Since "high contemplation" deals with divinity, it is inaccessible to both the outer and inner senses. Like the prophet Elijah and Moses, our eyes must be covered and blinded if we are to recover "the primal knowledge of God in the soul" that Adam possessed but lost by sin. If we become blind to everything that is not God, the "Sun of Justice" will revitalize our natural capacity for contemplation by the grace of the Holy Spirit so that it can contemplate the divinity of Our Lord God.[138] The flight to the repose of contemplation that takes place "in the solitude of *recogimiento*," as we are told in Treatise 12.1, demands the use of the two principal wings of the soul, that is, both understanding and will. "Even though understanding may discover and analyze numerous sublime matters," Osuna continues, "there is good reason for you to believe that complete fulfilling repose is not to be found through the functions of the intellect and that ultimately the least part of what we do not know exceeds everything we do know."[139] The power to understand will never be satiated in this life, but only in heaven. Thus, understanding is needed but not sufficient—charity alone unites us to God, both here and hereafter. Osuna explains:

> The understanding bears God to us so that we may know him. But since it cannot bring him to us in his naked essence, but only according to our fragile understanding and in the manner whereby we are capable of receiving him, clearly we must know him through other things. Love, however, takes us out of ourselves to place us in what we love; love goes and enters into that which is most secret, leaving understanding outside with creatures.[140]

Although love active in the will is the motive force for high contemplation and union, Osuna has a role for a new kind of understanding in the higher stages of *recogimiento*, as suggested above. In discussing "The Excellence of the Tears of Recollection" (Tr. 10.2), he provides his most detailed exposition of this new knowing. The devout person must close the windows of his senses so that his intellect is in darkness. In this *recogimiento*, continues the Franciscan, he "will receive that excellent gift, that perfect present from above that descends from the Father of Lights (Jas. 1:17), and the darkness that was in him previously and negated his own understanding will be transformed into the clarity of midday where the Bridegroom will instruct him spiritually." This "higher form of knowing" (*conocimiento más alta*) is described as being halfway between our ordinary way of knowing and the knowledge of the blessed in heaven, as well as being both sublime and incommunicable. "[S]uch great things are understood in such a lofty way that neither that which is understood nor the manner of doing so can be explained, nor can any person capture in words what he has felt and understood."[141] Osuna is once again traditional in preferring the contemplation figured in Mary to the action represented by Martha (see, e.g., Tr. 12.7, 14.3), but he also recognizes that both forms of life are necessary here below: "He who perseveres in contemplation preserves his spirit and, not forsaking what he can do in the active life, preserves his soul, and being constant in doing penance preserves his body."[142]

Osuna recognizes that God bestows various spiritual gifts and special graces on those practicing *recogimiento*, but he does not give these gifts undue emphasis. One thing he does insist on is that there is no reason to be suspicious of, or fearful of, such gifts. If God sees fit to send them, we should welcome them in his name (Tr. 12.3–7). He says that those who "dare to say we should not seek divine consolation or taste spiritual things" are really doing the work of the devil.[143] Among the favors the Franciscan mentions are "divine locutions" (Tr. 12.2) and the "wound of love" (Tr. 11.4, 12.5). He also discusses rapture in a number of texts. Osuna does not side with those who condemn all raptures (Tr. 5.2), but rather he says that God is free to give a foretaste of the delectable honey of heaven to those who are meritorious and pray for it (Tr. 5.3). He compares this to a liquid heated in a container over a fire that "begins to bubble and boil" and cannot be held in the container, "but when the spirit of love is conceived in the fervor of the heart, in some way the soul goes jumping outside of itself and flying above itself."[144] Osuna, however, also recognizes the danger of those who simulate holiness and pretend to be enraptured (Tr. 18.4).

Recogimiento is mystical theology, wisdom, the height of contemplation; it is also union with God.[145] We have already seen a number of the passages where the Franciscan talks about union (e.g., Tr. 6.2, 13.4, 21.3). Once again returning to the important Treatise 6 on *recogimiento*, especially chapters 3–4, we find a rich development in which Osuna notes that "the truest and oldest meaning [of *recogimiento*] expresses a state similar to that suggested by the word union, which term is not used in human, physical matters but in those divine and spiritual."[146] In Treatise 6.4 the tenth and final effect of *recogimiento* is to recognize "how it gathers God and the soul that has been so greatly drawn to itself into one. . . . Then occurs the most perfect *recogimiento*, which unites and recollects God with the soul and the soul with God. The soul participates in the Lord himself and is perfectly recollected in him."[147] Treatise 21.3 implicitly cites two of the traditional biblical texts for union, Song of Songs 5:2 and 1 Corinthians 6:17, when it says, "Her [the soul's] heart keeps vigil because love does not slumber in peace in one who loves. The understanding sleeps and the will rests because the soul is united with God and made one spirit with him. Then the Sabbath of Sabbaths reigns."[148] Chapter 5 of Treatise 22 lays out a general understanding of uniting with God in a series of practical maxims directed to all the faithful. We can be perfectly united to God, he says,"if we contemplate the Creator in all creatures." "Also," continues Osuna, "you will unite perfectly with God if you give him a part in everything you do." Yet more, "You can also unite with God in all things if you credit him as principally responsible for all that happens." "Also, you will join perfectly with God when you receive everything as from his hand." Finally, "you will unite with God even through evil if you remember that he permits it in order to test your love for him."[149] Osuna's wise spiritual advice reminds the reader that the truest form of union we can attain in this life is always based on love and humility.

Union with God, though realized in the detached and God-centered life of *recogimiento*, also has notes of transformation and erotic ecstasy, at least in some of its manifestations. Osuna does not much employ the language of deification, perhaps because of the suspect *Alumbrados*, though one prayer addresses God as follows, "O adorable friend of my soul, most beneficent goodness of all who seek you, comfort and security of my soul, God deifier of those devoted to you" (*Dios deificador de los que se dan a ti*).[150] It is interesting to see the Franciscan using the image of the silkworm transformed into the butterfly to describe the transformation of *recogimiento* (Tr. 16.6), though he does not give this the prominence it later acquired in Teresa of Avila. Finally, Osuna does not shy away from the language of love in describing the transformation process, especially as found in the Song of Songs. Speaking of the "bed of *recogimiento*" in Treatise 12.2, he weaves together many of the verses of the Song into a rich tapestry describing the delights of a soul lost in love of God.[151]

Spanish Mystical Heresy: The *Alumbrados*

Spain's emergence as a center for mystical teaching, not surprisingly, also meant that suspicions about mysticism soon arose. Since the late thirteenth century, tensions between the church's teaching, on the one hand, and some representatives of the "New Mysticism," on the other, had become a feature of the story of mysticism.[152] These tensions often involved questions of clerical authority, as well as doctrinal issues. What constituted "mystical heresy" was highly contextual and continued to be debated, but a series of ecclesiastical condemnations from the early fourteenth century on shaped how suspicious groups came to be viewed by clerical authorities.

The similarity between the accusations directed against a number of mystics and groups of mystics between roughly 1250 and 1700 points to the inherited weight of tradition in creating "mystical heresy," even when there was no intention of conscious dissidence and rejection of doctrine on the part of those judged heretical. Prominent among these accusations were claims that some of the devout thought they had attained such a close union with God that they were released from the constraints of the moral law (antinomianism) and from obedience to the church and its sacraments (anti-ecclesiasticism). Such mystics were also often accused of attacking the clergy and their learning, as well as claiming an inner divine enlightenment about the true meaning of scripture. Did these "dangerous" mystics really hold such views over many centuries and in such diverse contexts? Or did the guardians of orthodoxy resort to earlier condemnations, especially the decree "Ad Nostrum" issued against the Beguines and Beghards at the Council of Vienne in 1312, to form a kind of Procrustean bed to fit dissidents into categories that had already been judged wanting? Answers are not easy to come by.

Down to Vatican II most Catholic theologians and many Catholic and non-Catholic historians were convinced that there was indeed a tradition of mystical heresy (often an underground one) that accounted for the similarities in reports about the heretics. In the past half-century historians and theologians have been more inclined to question what is "mystical heresy," and whether it can be considered as representing a tradition, even one with considerable variety. It is within this contestation that the Spanish mystical heresy called *Alumbradismo* (i.e., Illuminism) becomes an issue, not only in the sixteenth and seventeenth centuries, when it was so much feared, but also in modern study, as scholars try to determine what *Alumbradismo* really was and, indeed, whether "it" was a single phenomenon.[153]

The origins and sources of *Alumbradismo* have been much debated. Among the theories put forth have been those of Islamic roots, of the influence of northern European medieval mysticism, of Erasmianism, and of Lutheranism. Noting that many of the Enlightened came from *converso* background, some scholars (e.g., M. Bataillon, S. Pastore) have searched for Jewish roots of the movement. The sources seem too sparse to provide an account that will be convincing to all,[154] but it seems likely that *Alumbradismo* sprang, in good part, from the combination of the movement for church reform evident in Spain at the beginning of the sixteenth century and the closely allied desire for a more interior spiritual life widespread throughout the peninsula at the time.[155] Concern about locating religious and doctrinal authority in such an interior realm substantially increased after 1520, when the growth of the Protestant Reformation became increasingly seen as a threat to Spain's civil and religious order.[156] After the death of Cisneros, fears of "Lutheranism" (meaning anything that threatened the Spanish understanding of Catholic orthodoxy) gained strength, and the Spanish Inquisition, designed as a weapon against Jewish converts, began to turn its attention to a wide variety of other dangers, including the *Alumbrados.*

This complex situation raises another question, that of the relation between the *Alumbrados* and the Franciscan practitioners of *recogimiento,* especially in the early stages of the movement. Both the *Alumbrados* and the Observant Franciscans were devoted to interior prayer. A number of the men and women accused of being *Alumbrados* in the third decade of the sixteenth century were connected with Franciscan *recogimiento* circles. At least one Franciscan friar, Francisco Ortiz, a friend of Francisco de Osuna, was said to be an *Alumbrado.* Nonetheless, the fact that there were links between the Observant Franciscans and those accused of *Alumbradismo* does not lead to the conclusion that the phenomenon had a Franciscan origin.

The earliest center for *Alumbradismo* was in the area of Toledo about 1510–12. This was prior to both the wave of Erasmianism and the possible influence of Lutheranism. Three key figures of the Toledo groups shared a *converso* background.[157] Isabel de la Cruz, a Franciscan tertiary, began preaching in the Guadalajara region about 1512, but we know little about her and her message. More important is the layman Pedro Ruiz de Alcaraz, an accountant who worked for some of the major nobility of the area. Although not university trained, Alcaraz had an impressive library of spiritual works and was a figure with some charism. His theological views, which can be partially pieced together from the documentation of his trial, include a strong emphasis on human sinfulness and the need for justification, an insistence on total abandonment to the love of God, a suspicion of ecstasies and visions, as well as a desire for a simple religion based on scripture. Alcaraz attached himself to Isabel de la Cruz and began to help spread her message. He was investigated by the Inquisition in 1519 and was reprimanded, but he continued to preach down to his arrest in 1524. The third figure was María de Cazalla, a laywoman who moved in aristocratic circles and whose brother Juan de Cazalla (d. 1530) was a Franciscan, chaplain to Cardinal Cisneros, and eventually a bishop. These three interrelated figures were often at odds with other neighboring *beatas* who preached a similar message, such as Mari Núñez and Francisca Hernández.

The three early leaders were said to have called themselves "enlightened, abandoned, and perfect" (*alumbrados, dexados, e perfectos*). Such claims to special enlightenment later became the catchphrase for this chapter in the story of mystical heresy, but in the debates of the 1520s the term *dejamiento*, that is, abandonment, was actually more central. *Dejamiento* was seen as both a form of prayer and an inner state characterized by absolute surrender to God, perfect stillness, and eschewing all activity, outer and inner. The twelfth condemned proposition of the Inquisitorial list of 1525 put it as follows:

> In the state of *dejamiento* they should not act because they should not put an obstacle to what God wished them to perform, and they should not think of any created things, and even to think of the humanity of Christ impeded abandonment to God, and they should reject all thoughts which presented themselves, even if they were good, since they should search for God alone. The labor involved in rejecting such thoughts was meritorious and in that state of quiet in order not to be distracted it was a temptation even to remember God.

The decree denounced this proposition as "false and erroneous, and scandalous and heretical."[158]

When tortured by the Inquisition, Pedro Ruiz de Alcaraz said that Isabel de la Cruz had created the doctrine of *dejamiento* out of the Franciscan practice of inner prayer (i.e., *recogimiento*). There are, to be sure, affinities between *recogimiento* and *dejamiento*, especially the stress on the superiority of mental prayer. The two terms may well have been used together in the Franciscan houses of recollection in the early years of the sixteenth century. By the time that *recogimiento* authors like Bernardino de Laredo and Francisco de Osuna put pen to paper in the 1520s, however, clear differences between the two styles of prayer and their consequences had emerged as the Franciscans sought to distance themselves from what they saw as the dangers of *dejamiento*. Prominent among these problems was the "proto-Quietism" reflected in Proposition 12, that is, the claim to have achieved a state of abandonment so total that it barred all good thoughts and actions as distractions. Although Alcaraz claimed that *recogimiento* and *dejamiento* meant the same thing, even his testimony from the trial indicates that there were some real differences in the circumstances and practices of the two forms of prayer.[159] The Franciscans soon began to draw a clear line between their prayer practices and those devoted to *dejamiento*. In 1524 the Franciscan Provincial Council held at Toledo condemned the practice of *dejamiento* and deprived Isabel de la Cruz of her Franciscan habit. The arrest of the Toledo leaders by the Inquisition began a few months afterwards. As we have also seen, Osuna explicitly attacked the *Alumbrados* in his *Spiritual Alphabets.*

The arrest of Isabel, Alcaraz, and one of their clerical followers in 1524 was partly due to the accusations of their rival, the *beata* Mari Núñez, who accused them of such things as denying the existence of hell, not following church rules about fasting, and mockery of the sacraments. Some of these accusations echoed those against Judaizers, but the Inquisitors found little evidence of this, nor of the "Lutheranism," or Erasmian tendencies, which were seen as current dangers. Indeed, both the trial documents and the eventual punishments meted out suggest that the key issue was not so much doctrinal error as the reassertion of clerical authority. We get some sense of the social makeup of the early followers of *dejamiento* from a list given to the Inquisition in 1527, which contains forty-six names, of which eleven were friars and thirteen were women. In the long run the Inquisitors were not overly harsh, at least because no one was executed. In 1529 Alcaraz was publicly flogged and Isabel de la Cruz had to do public penance. Their property was confiscated and they were sentenced to perpetual imprisonment, but in a few years were given their freedom. The third early figure, María de Cazalla, was arrested in 1532 and, unusually in the case of a woman, was subjected to torture in 1534. She was eventually released after doing public penance.[160]

On September 23, 1525, the Inquisitor General Alonso Manrique issued the "Edict on the *Alumbrados* of Toledo," containing forty-eight condemned propositions. This document was a touchstone for later disputes over mystical heresy in the Hispanic world, especially the outbreaks of *Alumbradismo* at Llerna in 1570–79, and the pursuit of the so-called *Alumbrados* of Seville (1622–28). A number of the condemned propositions show similarities to the teaching of the *recogimiento* authors, which comes as no surprise because the adherents of *dejamiento* had connections with the world of the Franciscan houses of recollection. Authors such as Osuna and Laredo, of course, had already corrected the presentation of teachings they shared with the *dejamientos*, such as on the meaning of pure love.[161]

The 1525 Edict follows no particular order. The central propositions Nos. 10–12, as well as 19, 23, and 43, concern *dejamiento* and its indifference to external works, prayer, and even to thoughts of God. Proposition 10 says that "in this *dejamiento* there is no need for prayer, or *recogimiento*, or special place, or anything else."[162] A number of propositions are denounced as "Lutheran" (e.g., Nos. 8, 26, 28); others deal with errors about the sacraments (e.g., Nos. 4–7, 19), the denial of hell (No. 1), and attacks on sacred images and the cult of the saints (e.g., Nos. 15, 18, 24, 26). Some, such as No. 45, concern the interpretation of scripture. Nos. 20–22 condemn those who say there is no value in oral prayer, while Nos. 29 and 33 address errors regarding pure love. Also important is the claim to sinlessness found in Proposition 9: "The love of God in man is God and whoever gives himself to this love of God orders persons in such a way that they cannot commit either mortal or venial sins."[163] A number of the issues first ventilated in this 1525 Edict were to remain under discussion and subject to debate down to the Quietist condemnations at the end of the seventeenth century. This trajectory demonstrates the significance of the first Spanish clash between mystics and ecclesiastical magistrates.

To what extent can the *Alumbrados* be considered mystics?[164] In the first place we need to note that the term *Alumbrados* was a creation of the Inquisitors, not a self-identification of the teachers of *dejamiento*. In the absence of their own writings, we can have questions about the teachings of the handful of *Alumbrados* known from the Inquisitorial documents, but many of the things for which they were condemned and to which they seem to have admitted at their trials fit within the penumbra of the mystical errors that had been under attack since the late thirteenth century. The Spanish religious world in the second and third decades of the sixteenth century was highly diverse with many spiritual currents. A number of the mystical and/or prophetic *beatas* encouraged by Cardinal Cisneros, as well as the spirituality of the Franciscan houses of recollection, originally nurtured styles of prayer that later became suspect. The *Alumbrados* of Toledo may not have been all that important in themselves, but their condemnation had a significant effect in helping establish an atmosphere in which interior prayer and mysticism became suspect, as we shall see in the cases of Ignatius of Loyola (chap. 2), Teresa of Avila (chap. 3), and others.

Notes

1. For more on Llull's mysticism, see McGinn, *Flowering*, 133–36.
2. Stephen Haliczer, speaking of the sixteenth century, goes so far as to say, "But nowhere in Europe did mysticism come to play such a dominant role as in Spain, where it was not limited to a comparatively small number of devout individuals but took on the character of almost a mass movement, at least among the urban middle and upper classes" (*Between Exaltation and Infamy*, 8).
3. Although he treats primarily of the later sixteenth and seventeenth cen-

turies, Haliczer's *Between Exaltation and Infamy*, dealing with thirty biographies and autobiographies of women mystics and fifteen Inquisitorial investigations of "false mystics," is a rich source for the study of female Spanish mystics. See also Gillian T. W. Ahlgren, "Negotiating Sanctity: Holy Women in Sixteenth-Century Spain," *Church History* 64 (1995): 373–87. On the early *beatas*, see Geraldine McKendrick and Angus MacKay, "Visionaries and Affective Spirituality in the First Half of the Sixteenth Century," in *Cultural Encounters: The Impact of the Inquisition in Spain and the New World*, ed. Mary Elizabeth Perry and Anne J. Cruz (Berkeley: University of California Press, 1991), 93–104. The general survey by Milagros Ortega Costa, "Spanish Women in the Reformation," in *Women in Reformation and Counter-Reformation Europe: Public and Private Worlds*, ed. Sherrin Marshall (Bloomington: Indiana University Press, 1989), 89–119, treats many of the women mentioned in this chapter.

4. The literature on medieval visions is large. A fundamental account remains that of Peter Dinzelbacher, *Vision- und Visionsliteratur im Mittelalter*, Monographien zur Geschichte des Mittelalters (Stuttgart: Hiersemann, 1981); see also his *"Revelationes,"* Typologie des sources du Moyen Âge occidental 57 (Turnhout: Brepols, 1991). For a brief characterization of the "visionary explosion," see McGinn, "Introduction," in *Flowering*, 24–30.

5. On the issue of diabolical deception, see Moshe Sluhovsky, *Believe Not Every Spirit: Possession, Mysticism, and Discernment in Early Modern Catholicism* (Chicago: University of Chicago Press, 2007).

6. William A. Christian Jr., *Apparitions in Late Medieval and Renaissance Spain* (Princeton: Princeton University Press, 1981).

7. Teresa's writings have been translated by Dayle Seidenspinner-Núñez, *The Writings of Teresa de Cartagena*, Library of Medieval Women (Rochester: Boydell & Brewer, 1998). See also Ronald E. Surtz, *Writing Women in Late Medieval and Early Modern Spain: The Mothers of Saint Teresa of Avila*, Middle Ages (Philadelphia: University of Pennsylvania Press, 1995), chap. 1.

8. See Surtz, *Writing Women in Late Medieval and Early Modern Spain*, chap. 2.

9. J. A. Salazar, "Beaterio," DIP 1:1153–54.

10. On María de Ajofrín, see Surtz, *Writing Women in Late Medieval and Early Modern Spain*, chap. 3 (quotation from 74–75).

11. On Juana de la Cruz, see Ronald E. Surtz, *The Guitar of God: Gender, Power, and Authority in the Visionary World of Mother Juana de la Cruz (1481–1534)*, Middle Ages (Philadelphia: University of Pennsylvania Press, 1990); and more briefly Surtz, "Juana de la Cruz and the Secret Garden," chap. 5 in *Writing Women in Late Medieval and Early Modern Spain*, 104–26. See also Mary E. Giles, "Spanish Visionary Women and the Paradox of Performance," in *Performance and Transformation: New Approaches to Late Medieval Spirituality*, ed. Mary A. Suydam and Joanna E. Ziegler (New York: St. Martin's Press, 1999), 273–97; and Jessica A. Boon, "Mother Juana de la Cruz: Marian Visions and Female Preaching," in Kallendorf, *New Companion to Hispanic Mysticism*, 127–48.

12. Juana de la Cruz, *El Conhorte: Sermones de una mujer, La Santa Juana (1481–1534)*, ed. Inocente García de Andrés, 2 vols. (Madrid: Fundación Universitaria Española, 1999). There are two manuscripts, one in the Vatican and one in the Escorial. Surtz provides excerpts from four of the seventy-two sermons in the "Appendices" to *The Guitar of God*. There is also a new translation of six full

sermons in Ronald E. Surtz and Jessica A. Boon, eds., *Mother Juana de la Cruz, 1481–1534: Visionary Sermons* (Tempe: Arizona Center for Medieval and Renaissance Studies, 2016).

13. The *Vida y fin de la beinaventurada virgen santa Juana de la Cruz* is unedited, as is the *Libro de la casa y monasterio de Nuestra Señora de la Cruz*. The *Vida* has a number of texts describing Juana's ecstasies, which are said to have begun when she was a baby (see Surtz, "Juana de la Cruz and the Secret Garden," 124).

14. Surtz, *Guitar of God*, 6.

15. On these authorizing techniques, see Surtz, *Guitar of God*, 110–17. Juana's additions to the biblical narrative are sometimes based on materials found in familiar sources such as the Pseudo-Bonaventuran *Meditationes Vitae Christi* and Ludolph of Saxony's *Vita Christi*, but many of them come from her own fertile imagination.

16. This complex of ideas and texts to illustrate them are presented in Surtz, "The Mother Hen," chap. 2 in *Guitar of God*, 37–62.

17. See Barbara Newman, "On the Threshold of the Dead: Purgatory, Hell, and Religious Women," chap. 4 in Newman, *From Virile Woman to WomanChrist: Studies in Medieval Religion and Literature* (Philadelphia: University of Pennsylvania Press, 1995), 109–36, who mentions Juana on 121.

18. This sermon is analyzed by Surtz in "The Chosen Vessels," chap. 4 in *Guitar of God*, 87–107.

19. These texts from the *Life*, ff. 59r–60r, are found in Surtz, *Guitar of God*, 67–68. A number of passages in the *Life* speak of Juana as the bride of Christ; here the marital union is given a direct expression.

20. The text from Bonaventure's *Mystical Vine (Vitis mystica)* is cited by Surtz, *Garden of God*, 72, along with other relevant texts about the use of musical analogies regarding the passion.

21. Once again, I depend on the analysis and texts of Surtz, this time from chap. 5, "Juana de la Cruz and the Secret Garden."

22. See Boon, who says, "Juana understood the trajectory of her own career primarily in relation to Mary, not Christ, the Trinity, or the Church" ("Mother Juana de la Cruz," 138).

23. On the transformative intention of Juana's sermons, see Jessica A. Boon, "Introduction," in Surtz and Boon, *Mother Juana de la Cruz*, 30–33.

24. The theme of the Trinity conversing about (and sometimes with) Mary in eternity, what has been called the *consilium trinitatis*, is found in a number of women mystics, such as Mechthild of Magdeburg (see McGinn, *Flowering*, 232–34). There is another passage on the *consilium trinitatis* in Sermon 1 on the Incarnation (Surtz and Boon, *Mother Juana de la Cruz*, 46–47). Other sermons contain unusual descriptions of or analogies for the Trinity, for example, the three suns analogy in Sermon 2 on the Nativity (Surtz and Boon, *Mother Juana de la Cruz*, 92–94).

25. The image of the garden is frequent in the Song of Songs (e.g., Song 4:12, 15–16; 5:1; 6:1, 10; and 8:13), and there are also references to breasts in Song 7:8 and 12. The erotic aspect of this vision is a refashioning of Song of Songs texts, which, as Juana would have known, were applied to Mary in Marian feasts.

26. Surtz, *Women Writing in Late Medieval and Early Modern Spain*, 118.

27. Jodi Bilinkoff, "A Spanish Prophetess and Her Patrons: The Case of María de Santo Domingo," *Sixteenth Century Journal* 23 (1992): 21–34.

28. On María, see Mary E. Giles, *The Book of Prayer of Sor María of Santo Domingo: A Study and Translation* (Albany: State University of New York Press, 1990). See also Surtz, "The New Magdalene: María de Santo Domingo," chap. 4 in *Writing Women in Late Medieval and Early Modern Spain*, 85–103. On the relation of María to the broad currents of early modern mysticism, see Rebeca Sanmartín Bastida, *La representación de las místicas: Sor María de Santo Domingo en su contexto europeo*, Propileo estudios 1 (Santander: Real Sociedad Menéndez Pelayo, 2012).

29. The mutual interests of María and her supporters are well laid out by Bilinkoff, who concludes that, in María's case, "[c]harismatic spirituality served to subvert or even invert the boundaries of class and gender in a traditional society. This meant that an illiterate peasant woman had access to a form of spiritual authority that a duke, a king, and a cardinal of the church might only envy" ("Spanish Prophetess," 34).

30. In the "Summary of Her Virtuous and Perfect Life" at the outset of *The Book of Prayer*, the author says, "Speaking with fear and caution about the matters of the Madre Beata Sor María of Santo Domingo, I maintain that there is no middle ground between two extremes, for either these matters are the most perfect and holy that we know in the world or the worst and most imperfect" (Giles, *Book of Prayer*, 129; subsequent references to the *Book of Prayer* are to the page numbers in the translation by Giles).

31. *Book of Prayer*, 136.

32. Ibid., 138.

33. Ibid., 138–44.

34. For a summary of the allegations of sexual impropriety, see Giles, *Book of Prayer*, part 1, 17, 32–36.

35. See Judith C. Brown, *Immodest Acts: The Life of a Lesbian Nun in Renaissance Italy*, Studies in the History of Sexuality (New York: Oxford University Press, 1986).

36. For an account, see Hubert Wolf, *The Nuns of Sant' Ambrogio: The True Story of a Convent Scandal* (New York: Alfred A. Knopf, 2015).

37. *Book of Prayer*, 145.

38. Giles, *Book of Prayer*, 102. Giles develops this further in her essay "Spanish Visionary Women and the Paradox of Performance."

39. *Book of Prayer*, 147–48.

40. Ibid., 150–51.

41. Ibid., 158–59. The motif of the garden of the soul, which goes from 158 to 161, is reminiscent of Teresa of Avila's famous four waters account in her *Life* (chaps. 11–22).

42. *Book of Prayer*, 170.

43. Ibid., 172.

44. Ibid., 175.

45. On the ambiguous position of women mystics and the processes that influenced their acceptance or rejection, see Haliczer, *Between Exaltation and Infamy*, esp. chaps. 3–6, and 11.

46. For the sake of convenience I am talking about the Observantine Franciscans as if they were one thing, but there were actually several groups and currents among the "Observantines," who were all dedicated to returning to a more original and austere form of Franciscan life. For a sketch of the evolution and many forms of the Franciscan life, see the multiauthor article "Fratri Minori," DIP 4:823–911.

47. The essential work on recollection and those who practiced it is Melquíades Andrés Martín, *Los recogidos: Nueva visión de la mística española (1500–1700)* (Madrid: Fundación Universitaria Española, 1975). For a brief overview, see Saturnino López Santidrián, "Recueillement, II: Dans la spiritualité classique espagnole," DS 13:255–67. In English, see Angelo J. DiSalvo, *The Spiritual Literature of Recollection in Spain (1500–1620): The Reform of the Inner Person*, Texts and Studies in Religion 84 (Lewiston, NY: Edwin Mellen, 1999); and William J. Short, "From Contemplation to Inquisition: The Franciscan Practice of Recollection in Sixteenth-Century Spain," in *Franciscans at Prayer*, ed. Timothy J. Johnson (Leiden: Brill, 2007), 449–74.

48. Melquíades Andrés Martín, *La teología española en el siglo XVI*, 2 vols., Biblioteca de Autores Cristianos, Serie Maior 13, 14 (Madrid: Biblioteca de Autores Cristianos, 1977) 2:202.

49. DiSalvo, *Spiritual Literature of Recollection*, 99.

50. A number of these writings are available in the three volumes edited by Juan Bautista Gomis, OFM, *Místicos franciscanos españoles*, Biblioteca de Autores Cristianos, Sección 4: Ascética y mística 38, 44, 46 (Madrid: Biblioteca Autores Cristianos, 1948–49), as well as in the more recent two-volume collection, Pedro M. Cátedra et al., eds., *Místicos franciscanos españoles* (Madrid: Biblioteca Autores Cristianos, 1998).

51. Such houses had a long history in the Franciscan order; see Costanzo Cargnoni, "Houses of Prayer in the History of the Franciscan Order," in *Franciscan Solitude*, ed. André Cirino and Josef Raischl (St. Bonaventure, NY: Franciscan Institute, 1995), 211–64, who discusses the "Spanish Hermitages" on 224–28.

52. The Latin version of the *Mirror of Perfection* was called *Directorium contemplativorum*, or sometimes *Directorium aureum contemplativorum*. In 1538 the Cologne Carthusians published several of Herp's works under the title *Theologia Mystica*, a work that was also influential in Spain. On Herp, see McGinn, *Varieties*, 130–36. Another key source was the Carthusian Hugh of Balma's *Viae Sion Lugent* (ca. 1290), also known as *De mystica theologia*, and *De triplici via*. This often circulated under Bonaventure's name and was translated into Spanish as the *Sol de contemplativos* in 1514; see Andrés Martín, *Los recogidos*, 70–76. There is an English translation in Dennis Martin, *Carthusian Spirituality: The Writings of Hugh of Balma and Guigo de Ponte*, Classics of Western Spirituality (New York: Paulist Press, 1997).

53. Francisco de Osuna, *The Third Spiritual Alphabet*, 561. See n. 94 below for full reference.

54. For a summary, see López Santidrián, who also notes that some authors also use fourfold schemas ("Receuillement II," 259–63, esp. 265).

55. Andrés Martín in his *Los recogidos* constructs his account according to the contributions made by members of different religious orders.

56. For a description of the *Libro de la caballeria Cristiana*, see DiSalvo, *Spiritual Literature of Recollection*, 81–86.

57. See the analysis in DiSalvo, *Spiritual Literature of Recollection*, 86–94, where the text on *recogimiento* can be found on 93.

58. For an account, see Andrés Martín, *Los recogidos*, 176–92. There are brief summaries in English in Short, "From Contemplation to Inquisition," 452–53; and DiSalvo, *Spiritual Literature of Recollection*, 76–77. I have not seen the modern edition of Bernabé's work: Teodoro H. Martín, ed., *Via Spiritus de Bernabé de Palma; Subida de Monte Sión de Bernardino de Laredo*, Colección Clásicos de Espiritualidad (Madrid: Biblioteca de Autores Cristianos, 1998).

59. Andrés Martín devotes a chapter to Bernardino (*Los recogidos*, chap. 9, 193–232). E. Allison Peers translated the third book of Laredo's major text, Bernardino de Laredo, *The Ascent of Mount Sion* (New York: Harper & Bros., 1950). This includes a long "Introduction" (11–58), which appears also in Peers, *Studies*, vol. 2. Monographs include Father Fidèle de Ros, *Un inspirateur de sainte Thérèse: Le frère Bernardin de Laredo*, Études de théologie et d'histoire de la spiritualité 11 (Paris: Vrin, 1948); and Jessica A. Boon, *The Mystical Science of the Soul: Medieval Cognition in Bernardino de Laredo's Recollection Method* (Toronto: University of Toronto Press, 2012). There is an edition of the *Ascent of Mount Sion* by Gomis in *Místicos franciscanos españoles*, 2:28–442, but this has errors, so the preferred edition is that of Alegría Alonso González et al., eds., *Bernardino de Laredo, Subida del Monte Sión*, Colección "Espirituales españoles" (Madrid: Fundación Universitaria Española, 2000), which will be used in what follows.

60. See Fidèle de Ros, *Un inspirateur*, chap. 7 (120–35) for a comparison of the two editions. The *Ascent of Mount Sion* was reprinted twice in the sixteenth century and once in the seventeenth.

61. *Ascent of Mount Sion* III.1 (ed. Alonso González, 435; trans. Peers, 63).

62. On Laredo's sources, see Fidèle de Ros, *Un inspirateur*, chap. 8 (136–55); and Peers, "Introduction," 43–48.

63. At the end of chap. 27 (ed., 524–25; trans., 174), Laredo gives a list of some major authorities of "this hidden science of mystical theology."

64. Fidèle de Ros, *Un inspirateur*, 154.

65. For an analysis of the two parts, see Fidèle de Ros, *Un inspirateur*, chap. 6 (105–19).

66. A brief outline of part I is given in Peers, "Introduction," 18–22. After ten introductory chapters, there are six chapters dedicated to seventeen steps leading to God. Then follow three series of seven meditations for the week (chaps. 17–36).

67. Boon, *Mystical Science of the Soul*, 81 (see also 3–7, 15, 25, etc.). Boon describes Laredo's method of passion meditation and its roots in more detail in chap. 5, "Optics, Pain, and Transformation into God" (136–62). Although Boon is correct to stress the "cognitive continuum" between body and soul in Laredo's mysticism (e.g., 15–16, 25, 77, 167, etc.), and therefore the need for a continuing role for the passion in all stages of the mystical path, I am not convinced by her claim that passion meditation is "the central stage of the unitive message" (80; cf. 161–62). This leaves one wondering why Laredo bothered to write and revise part III of the *Ascent* and prompts Boon to make the puzzling claim that Laredo constructed "an intentionally inaccurate presentation of his tripartite way in his preface" (81).

68. Peers, "Introduction," 23.

69. *Ascent of Mount Sion*, III, Prol. (ed., 434; trans. Peers, 60–61). For more on the relation of the three parts of the *Ascent*, see chap. 8 (ed., 462; trans., 96).

70. *Ascent of Mount Sion* III.1 (ed., 435; trans., 63).

71. *Ascent of Mount Sion* III.26 (ed., 517; trans., 166–67). On this division, see Andrés Martín, *Los recogidos*, 216–18. Another fourfold pattern appears late in part III, where chap. 41 dealing with rapture speaks of four movements of the soul: to arrive at the self; to enter into the self; to rise above the self; and to go out of the self in loving ecstasy (ed., 594–95; trans., 256–57).

72. For Laredo, true *recogimiento* always involves the stilling of the faculties and passive reception of God's grace; see, e.g., chaps. 19–20 and 23 (ed., 490–96, 507–9; trans., 134–41, 155). On passivity to the action of grace, see chap. 29 (ed., 532–33; trans., 184).

73. *Ascent of Mount Sion* III.22 (ed., 503–4; trans., 150–51). Laredo says that *reflexión* means "returning to a place which one had left and withdrawing into it"; he cites Gregory the Great's *Homilies on Ezekiel* 2.9.15 and 20 in support.

74. *Ascent of Mount Sion* III.9 (ed., 465; trans., 90–91). Bernardino distinguishes "scholastic contemplation," which we perform with our natural skill and God's aid, from "mystical contemplation," in which God alone is at work (chap. 23; ed., 507–8, trans., 154–55).

75. There are references to mystical theology in chaps. 4, 6, 8 and 9 (both mentioning Dionysius), 11, 14 (citing Dionysius), 17, 19, 20, 22, 23, 24, 27 (using Dionysius), 30, 31, 36, 40 (citing Dionysius), and 41.

76. *Ascent of Mount Sion* III.9 (ed., 465; trans., 100). This teaching occurs often; e.g., III.20.

77. On infused grace, see *Ascent of Mount Sion* III.9, and esp. 25 (ed., 466, 513; trans., 101, 161–62).

78. *Ascent of Mount Sion* III.12 (ed., 473; trans., 111). See also v. 24 in chap. 40 (ed., 590; trans., 251).

79. *Ascent of Mount Sion* III.10 (ed., 467–69; trans., 103–5). The wound of love is also found in III.30.

80. *Ascent of Mount Sion* III.40 (ed., 568–93; trans., 226–55).

81. *Ascent of Mount Sion* III.28 (ed., 526; trans., 175). See also III.29, 31, and 33 (ed., 531, 541, 551; trans., 182, 194, 206–7).

82. *Ascent of Mount Sion* III.4 (ed., 452; trans., 84–85): "De manera que hemos entendido aquí que el amor en perfeción no está en la meditación de la sagrada humanidad, antes consiste en la quieta y perficionada contemplación de la inaccessible divinidad."

83. *Ascent of Mount Sion* III.13 (ed., 476; trans., 115).

84. *Ascent of Mount Sion* III.31 (ed., 545; trans., 199).

85. *Ascent of Mount Sion* III.27 (ed., 523; trans., 172–73): "Así que, si la perfeción de todo contemplativo consiste en el amor de nuestro Christo Jesús, en el qual los pensamientos impiden, necessario es que sintamos que entendió lo que dezía el que dixo que es major en quieta contemplación no pensar nada." The title of this chapter is "Qué cosa es no pensar nada en contemplación perfecta y de la autoridad e utilidad de Mística Theología."

86. *Ascent of Mount Sion* III.41 (ed., 597; trans., 260). In this passage Laredo rejects the medical explanation that a learned colleague heard at Paris for the

wisdom of the unlearned woman. The whole of this chapter on rapture is a key source for Laredo's apophaticism.

87. For some other passages, see *Ascent of Mount Sion* III.2, 11, and 15 (ed., 442–43, 470, 480; trans., 72–73, 108, 120).

88. *Ascent of Mount Sion* III.41 (ed., 594–602; trans., 256–66).

89. *Ascent of Mount Sion* III.41 (ed., 594; trans., 256–57).

90. *Ascent of Mount Sion* III.41 (ed., 598; trans., 262): ". . . no podrá ser otra cosa que, perdido el sentido y movimiento, quede del todo agenada, quede puesta en éxtasis, quede en excesso de la mente o diga que está arrobada."

91. *Ascent of Mount Sion* III.41 (ed., 599; trans., 263).

92. Particularly important for his traditional notion of union as a uniting of the divine and human wills (see 1 Cor. 6:17) are the metaphors for union in III.26 (drop of water, iron in fire, mirror) and the descriptions of sacred inebriation and union of wills in III.30. For a summary of Laredo's teaching on union, see Fidèle de Ros, *Un inspirateur*, chap. 16, "L'union par le seul amour" (273–93).

93. *Epistola XI*. I have adopted the translation of Peers, *Ascent of Mount Sion*, "Introduction," 37.

94. On Osuna, see Andrés Martín, *Los recogidos*, chap. 6 (107–67); and especially Saturnino López Santidrián, "Introducción," in *Tercer abecedario espiritual de Francisco de Osuna*, Místicos franciscanos españoles II (Madrid: Biblioteca Autores Cristianos, 1998), 5–82. Also useful are Fidèle de Ros, *Un maître de sainte Thérèse: Le père François d'Osuna. Sa vie, son oeuvre, sa doctrine spirituelle* (Paris: Beauchesne, 1936); Peers, "Francisco de Osuna," in *Studies,* 2:63–106; and Laura Calvert, *Francisco de Osuna and the Spirit of the Letter,* North Carolina Studies in the Romance Languages and Literatures 133 (Chapel Hill: University of North Carolina Department of Romance Languages, 1973).

95. In numerical order, the *First Spiritual Alphabet* (1528) deals with the passion, the *Second Spiritual Alphabet* (1530) with spiritual exercises, and the *Third Spiritual Alphabet* (1527) with mystical *recogimiento.* The *Fourth Spiritual Alphabet*, also called the *Ley de Amor Santo*, published in 1530, is not alphabetical and lays out fifty-one rules of love. (The Spanish text can be found in *Místicos franciscanos españoles,* 1:221–700.) The final two alphabets were published posthumously: the *Fifth Spiritual Alphabet* (1542), also not alphabetical, contains 112 chapters of consolation for the poor and 73 chapters of advice to the rich, while the *Sixth Spiritual Alphabet* (1554) returns to the passion motif with a series of meditations on Christ's wounds.

96. The best edition is that of S. López Santidrián, *Tercer abecedario espiritual.* Unless otherwise noted, I will use the English version of Mary E. Giles, *Francisco de Osuna, The Third Spiritual Alphabet,* Classics of Western Spirituality (New York: Paulist Press, 1981), although it was made from an earlier edition.

97. For a summary of Osuna's teaching of *recogimiento*, see López Santidrián, "Introducción," 37–75.

98. Osuna uses the term *theología mística* here in Tr. 6.2 (ed., 199), as well as in his *Prólogo* (ed., 87), and in Tr. 12.7 (ed., 354).

99. *Third Spiritual Alphabet*, Tr. 6.2 (ed., 199–203; trans., 161–65).

100. *Third Spiritual Alphabet*, Tr. 6.3 (ed., 203–8; trans., 165–70). The passage cited is on 207.

101. *Third Spiritual Alphabet*, Tr. 6.3 (ed., 208; trans., 170): ". . . has de notar

que este ejercicio se llama recogimiento; lo primero, porque recoge los hombres que lo usan haciéndolos de un corazón y amor, quitando de ellos toda disensión y discordia; con lo cual aún no se contenta; mas sobre todas los otros ejercicios tiene esta maravillosa y sensible o conocida propriedad, que cuando alguno de los que siguen este recogimiento ve a otro que también lo sigue, se mueve en gran manera a devoción. . . ."

102. The breakdown of the Treatises is as follows. Part I contains Tr. 1 on Constant Vigilance; Tr. 2 on Thanksgiving; Tr. 3 on Being Blind, Deaf, and Dumb; Tr. 4 on Safeguarding and Emptying the Heart; Tr. 5 on the Need for Prudence and Experience; Tr. 6 on Practicing *recogimiento* (a central treatise); Tr. 7 on Casting out Evil Thoughts (purgation of thought); Tr. 8 on Teaching and Learning the Life of *recogimiento*; Tr. 9 on Control of Speech (purgation of speech and action); Tr. 10 on the Tears of *recogimiento*; Tr. 11 on Good and Bad Remembering (purgation of memory); and Tr. 12 on Spiritual Pleasure (purgation of will and understanding). Part II contains Tr. 13 on the Stages of Prayer; Tr. 14 on Correcting the Soul; Tr. 15 on Obstacles to *recogimiento*; Tr. 16 on Love; Tr. 17 on Following Christ in Body and Soul; Tr. 18 on Seeking God in Silence and Hope; Tr. 19 on Humility; Tr. 20 on Temptations; Tr. 21 on the Repose of *recogimiento* (also important); Tr. 22 on Solicitude and Zeal; and Tr. 23, a brief chapter on Perseverance.

103. Andrés Martín, *Los recogidos*, 138–42.

104. Ibid., 163–66.

105. This is evident throughout the *Third Spiritual Alphabet*, esp. in Tr. 11–12, and 21. For a summary, see López Santidrián, "Introducción," 55–56.

106. *Third Spiritual Alphabet*, Tr. 21.1 (ed., 543–45; trans., 547–59).

107. As he puts it in Tr. 9.6 (ed., 292; trans., 264): "The less spiritual experiences are tied to physical motion, the more perfect they are."

108. *Third Spiritual Alphabet*, Tr. 6.2 (ed., 201; trans., 162–63).

109. *Third Spiritual Alphabet*, Tr. 8.6–7 (ed., 261–66; trans., 229–35). Similar passages occur in 8.4–5, and 9.

110. *Third Spiritual Alphabet* Tr. 5.3 (ed., 187; trans., 147). This chapter (trans. López Santidrián, 147–52) is entitled "How You Are to Learn from Experience." A reference to the book of experience is also found in Tr. 10.4 (trans. Giles, 280).

111. *Third Spiritual Alphabet* Tr. 18.3 (ed., 490; trans., 485).

112. *Third Spiritual Alphabet*, Tr. 17.6 (ed., 474; trans., 468).

113. A partial list of passages on experience would include Tr. 2.2, 3.3, 4.5, 5.2, 6.3, 6.5, 7.3, most of Tr. 8, 9.6, 10.2, 11.3, 11.5–6, 12.2–3, 12.6, 13.3, 14.3, 14.5–7, 15.1, 15.4, 16.8–9, 17.7, 18.3, 19.2, 20.3–4, 20.10, 21.4–7 passim, and 22.4.

114. Here is a list of the major treatments of *recogimiento*, with the most important in italics: *Third Spiritual Alphabet*, Tr. 1.5, 4.5, *6.1–5*, 7.2, 7.8, 8.2, *8.4*, 9.2–4, *9.6–7*, *10.2*, 11.3, 13.3, *14.7*, *15.1–2*, *16.9*, 18.2, *18.3*, 19.1, 20.3–4, 20.6, 21.1, *21.5*, *21.7*, and 23.1.

115. *Third Spiritual Alphabet*, Tr. 15.2 (ed., 399–400; trans., 386–88).

116. *Third Spiritual Alphabet*, Tr. 3.2 (ed., 147; trans., 103).

117. *Third Spiritual Alphabet*, Tr. 11.5 (ed., 331–32; trans., 308–9).

118. *Third Spiritual Alphabet*, Tr. 11.5 (ed., 333; trans., 311).

119. *Third Spiritual Alphabet*, Tr. 4.5 (ed., 172–73; trans., 131–32). Later in this same chapter Osuna says that the Blessed Virgin is the foremost model of this inner and outer emptying.

120. E.g., *Third Spiritual Alphabet* 19.3 (ed., 507; trans., 504).

121. *Third Spiritual Alphabet*, Tr. 19.4 (ed., 509; trans., 506-7).

122. *Third Spiritual Alphabet*, Tr. 7.8 (ed., 238; trans., 204). See also Tr. 21.5 (trans. Giles, 565).

123. *Third Spiritual Alphabet*. Tr. 9.2 (ed., 274; trans., 244).

124. *Third Spiritual Alphabet*, Tr. 9.7 (ed., 294; trans., 266).

125. *Third Spiritual Alphabet*, Tr. 3.3 (ed., 149; trans., 105). See also Tr. 13.3 (trans. Giles, 348).

126. *Third Spiritual Alphabet*, Tr. 21.4 (ed., 554-57; trans., 559-61).

127. *Third Spiritual Alphabet*, Tr. 8.1 (ed., 241; trans., 207-8).

128. Meditation on the passion appears in a number of other places in the *Third Spiritual Alphabet*; e.g., Tr. 2.7, 13.4, 15.1, 17.3-4, 17.6, and 20.4.

129. *Third Spiritual Alphabet*, Tr. 13.4 (ed., 366; trans., 349).

130. The issue is compounded by Osuna's rather opaque remarks about the role of Christ's humanity in the path of *recogimiento* in his *Prólogo* (ed., 87-92; trans., 38-43), in which he first says that consideration of Christ's humanity does not hinder the soul's *recogimiento* in God and then cites a number of spiritual authorities (Bernard, Cyprian, Gregory, Augustine, Gerson) who seem to suggest otherwise, especially in their interpretation of Christ's leaving the apostles in a physical way at the Ascension so that they could come to know him spiritually (a traditional topos). Osuna's solution is that it was the imperfection of the apostles' love that necessitated Christ's withdrawal of his humanity, but he seems to argue that this will also be necessary for the "recollected" in their path to the higher stages.

131. *Third Spiritual Alphabet*, Tr. 13.4 (ed., 367; trans., 350, slightly altered): "Lo que más puede hacer Dios con su amigo es dares a él, y lo que más puede hacer el hombre es dares a Dios; . . . Empero, han de notar que este darce el hombre a Dios y Dios al hombre es una dádiva tan perfectamente dada que, cuando se da, parece que Dios está en el hombre todo y enteramente. . . . [Y] por el mucho acordarse y darse a Dios están de sí tan olvidados como si no fuesen." On friendship with God, see also Tr. 1.1 (trans. Giles, 48).

132. See, e.g., *Third Spiritual Alphabet*, Tr. 5.1, 8.2, 13.1, 14.7, 16.6, 16.8, and 21.6.

133. *Third Spiritual Alphabet*, Tr. 18.1-4 (ed., 481-97; trans., 479-93).

134. *Third Spiritual Alphabet* 10.5 (ed., 308-9; trans., 282).

135. In his Prologue (trans. Giles, 40) Osuna notes that it is not necessary to enjoy rapture in order to get to heaven

136. Along with the passages cited below, there are discussions of contemplation in Tr. 2.7, 3.1, 4.5, 5.4, 8.1, 15.5, 16.4-5, 16.8, and 20.1.

137. *Third Spiritual Alphabet* 3.2 (ed., 145; trans., 102).

138. *Third Spiritual Alphabet* 3.2 (ed., 146-47; trans., 102-4). Osuna here takes the opportunity to attack "the cursed error of those who claimed to know the essence of God and to see it naked in this mortal life without regard for the mirror of creatures in which he shines." This appears to be a reference to the *Alumbrados*. One of Osuna's colleagues, Fra Francisco Ortiz, was accused of being an *Alumbrado*. On Osuna's relation to the *Alumbrados*, see Santidrián, "Introducción," 16-19.

139. *Third Spiritual Alphabet*, Tr. 12.1 (ed., 338; trans., 315-16).

140. *Third Spiritual Alphabet*, Tr. 21.3 (ed., 551; trans., 556–57).

141. *Third Spiritual Alphabet* 10.2 (ed., 300; trans., 273). Tr. 12.2 notes that God's secret way of inner teaching can involve new understanding of scripture.

142. *Third Spiritual Alphabet*, Tr. 23.1 (ed., 590; trans., 600).

143. *Third Spiritual Alphabet* 12.3 (ed., 343; trans., 323).

144. *Third Spiritual Alphabet*, Tr. 6.2 (ed., 201–2; trans., 163). For some other references to rapture, see Tr. 11.4, 18.4, 19.2, and 21.7.

145. For Osuna's teaching on union, Andrés Martín, *Les recogidos*, 157–61; and Fidèle de Ros, *Un maître de sante Thérèse*, 533.

146. *Third Spiritual Alphabet*. Tr. 6.3 (ed., 207; trans., 169).

147. *Third Spiritual Alphabet*, Tr. 6.4 (ed., 211; trans., 173).

148. *Third Spiritual Alphabet*, Tr. 21.3 (ed., 553; trans., 558–59).

149. *Third Spiritual Alphabet*, Tr. 22.5 (ed., 585–86; trans., 593–95). For other treatments of union, see, e.g., Tr. 11.6, 12.5, 14.3, 19.4, and 21.6 (quoting Dionysius and Gerson).

150. *Third Spiritual Alphabet*, Tr. 16.10 (ed., 453; trans., 445).

151. *Third Spiritual Alphabet*, Tr. 12.2 (ed., 342–43; trans., 322).

152. For an overview, see Bernard McGinn, "'Evil-Sounding, Rash, and Suspect of Heresy': Tensions between Mysticism and Magisterium in the History of the Church," *Catholic Historical Review* 90 (2004): 193–212.

153. In English, *Alumbradismo* has been studied especially by Alastair Hamilton, *Heresy and Mysticism in Sixteenth-Century Spain: The Alumbrados* (Toronto: University of Toronto Press, 1992); and "The *Alumbrados*: *Dejamiento* and Its Practitioners," in Kallendorf, *New Companion to Hispanic Mysticism*, 103–24. In Spanish, see Antonio Márquez, *Los alumbrados: Orígenes y filosofía (1525–1559)*, 2nd ed. (Madrid: Taurus, 1980). The four volumes of Alvaro Huerga, *Historia de los Alumbrados* (Madrid: Fundación Universitaria Española, 1978–88), contain much documentation about later aspects of the movement. See also Stefania Pastore, *Un'eresia spagnola: Spiritualità conversa, alumbradismo e Inquisizione (1449–1559)* (Florence: Olschki, 2004).

154. We do not have writings from the *Alumbrados* themselves, though there are some important trial documents, not all of which have been published.

155. See M. Andrés Martín, "Alumbrados, Erasmians, 'Lutherans,' and Mystics: The Risk of a More 'Intimate' Spirituality," in Alcalá, *Spanish Inquisition and the Inquisitorial Mind*, 457–94, who discusses the *Alumbrados* on 466–69.

156. I thank Gillian T. W. Ahlgren for her suggestions regarding the importance of this aspect of the situation.

157. I largely follow the account in Hamilton, "The Piety of the *Alumbrados* of Toledo," chap. 2 in *Heresy and Mysticism in Sixteenth-Century Spain*, 25–42.

158. The forty-eight propositions of the *Edicto de los Alumbrados de Toledo* are available in Márquez, *Los alumbrados*, Apéndice I (273–83). Number 12 (p. 276) reads: "Que estando en el dexamiento *no avian de obrar* porque no pusieseen obstaculo a los que dios quisiesse obrar y que se desocupassen de todas las cosas criadas e que aun pensar en la humanidad de Xristo estorvaba el dexamiento en Dios e que desechassen todos los pensamientos que se les ofreciessen aunque fuesen buenos porque a solo dios debian buscar e que era merito el trabaxo que en desechar los tales pensamientos se tenia y que estando en aquella quietud por no distraerse tenia por tentación acordarse de dios. esta Proposicion es falssa y

herronea, y escandalosa y heretica." I have slightly adapted the translation given by Hamilton in "*Alumbrados*: *Dejamiento* and Its Practitioners," 104.

159. See Hamilton, "*Alumbrados*: *Dejamiento* and Its Practitioners," 107, citing from the unedited *Proceso de Alcaraz*.

160. See Angel Alcalá, "María de Cazalla: The Grievous Price of Victory," in Giles, *Women of the Inquisition*, 98–118; also Ortega Costa, "Spanish Women in the Reformation," 94–96.

161. Andrés Martín (*Los recogidos*, 363–67) has a helpful list laying out parallels between the 1525 list and passages from Osuna and Laredo.

162. Edicto, No. 10 (ed. Márquez, 276): ". . . el que esta en el dicho dexamiento no a menester oración ni recogimiento, ni lugar determinado ni otra cosa alguna."

163. Edicto, No. 9 (ed. Márquez, 276): "Que el amor de dios en el hombre es dios y que se dexassen a este amor de dios que ordena las personas de tal manera que no pueden peccar mortal ni venialmente."

164. Hamilton addresses the issue, deciding that the *Alumbrados* should be treated as mystics (*Heresy and Mysticism in Sixteenth-Century Spain*, 32, 42); see also his "*Alumbrados*: *Dejamiento* and Its Practitioners," 123–24.

CHAPTER 2

A Mysticism of Apostolic Service: Ignatius Loyola

THE HISTORICAL IMAGE of Ignatius of Loyola (1491–1556)[1] has changed dramatically over the past seven decades.[2] For almost four centuries Ignatius was viewed as the prime soldier of the Counter Reformation, the stern ascetic, the iron-willed founder of the Society of Jesus, and the creator of the rigid Ignatian method of prayer. Access to new materials about him, as well as more penetrating studies of his person and writings fostered by the dramatic changes that overtook the Catholic Church before and after Vatican Council II, brought about what amounts to a "new Ignatius."[3] The Basque priest was a "reformer" of sorts, but he was less concerned with reforming church institutions than with reforming believers through personal conversion, service to the poor, and education of the young.[4] He was appalled by the inroads of the heretics in Germany and northern Europe and organized his followers to combat them. He also approved of the early stages of the Council of Trent and sent some members of the order to participate in its deliberations. Nonetheless, Ignatius was dead before the conclusion of the council and the process of polemical confessionalization later called the Counter Reformation took hold in Roman Catholicism. Ignatius's personality was strong, at times even authoritarian;

I wish to thank Harvey D. Egan, S.J., of the Department of Theology of Boston College for an incisive reading of this chapter and for making many helpful suggestions.

but he was also a master of discernment who sought to win over others through careful cultivation of their natural inclinations.[5] He was a man who had deep affective bonds with many people and to whom his followers were devoted.

Renewed study of Ignatius's *Spiritual Exercises*, as well as the reflections about his life down to 1538 that he dictated to one of his followers between 1553 and 1555, the *Acts* (*Acta*), have helped shift the modern view of Ignatius firmly in the direction of his mysticism.[6] As the Jesuit historian John W. O'Malley puts it, Ignatius and the first Jesuits above all "sought to be mediators of an immediate experience of God that would lead to an inner change of heart."[7] The remaining fragments of Ignatius's *Spiritual Diary*, not critically edited until 1934, have given the modern student access to one of the most fascinating documents in the history of Christian mysticism. Finally, the new picture of the founder of the Jesuits shows him to be a man of great inner strength, but by no means always stern and unyielding. Ignatius had a keen appreciation that God calls people by different ways and that there can never be *one* method of prayer suitable for all.[8] As he once put it to his follower da Câmara: "[H]e said that he thought no greater error was possible in spiritual matters than to seek to direct others according to one's own way."[9]

The fascination of Ignatius's life and the story of the formation of the Jesuit order have produced a large literature that cannot be surveyed here. One chapter cannot exhaust what would need to be said to get a full picture of Ignatius and his early followers, as reflected to us not only in his own writings but in the *Constitutions* he and they drew up for the papal approval of the order in 1540 and which continued to grow in his lifetime and beyond. The evidence of his many letters (over seven thousand survive!), as well as accounts of Ignatius by some early followers, will be touched on only briefly in what follows.[10] My concentration will be on Ignatius the mystic, and specifically on what we can call his mysticism of apostolic service.[11] Speaking of the example Ignatius gave to later Jesuits, Hugo Rahner expresses this apostolic mysticism by saying that "there is in him not so much a mystical running away from the world as a mystical joy in running toward the world in order to win it back again for his divine Leader, Christ."[12]

Many terms have been used to characterize Ignatius's mysticism—trinitarian, christological, eucharistic/sacramental, ecclesial, Marian, as well as a mysticism of discernment, the mysticism of finding God in all things, or the mysticism of joy in the world. All of these elements are present, but they can be brought into focus through the lens of apostolic service, that is, the intent of Ignatius and his immediate followers to bring believers to a deeper sense of God's presence in their lives and to work to convert unbelievers to the true faith. As the first chapter of the *Constitutions of the Society of Jesus* puts it, "The end of this Society is to devote itself with God's grace to the salvation and perfection of the members' own souls, but also with that same grace to labor strenuously in giving aid toward the salvation and perfection of the souls of their neighbors."[13]

Introduction to Ignatius's Life and Writings[14]

Born into a noble family in the Basque region of northeastern Spain at Loyola probably in 1491, Iñigo was raised in a devout but proud and violent society. His mother died when he was young; his father was a powerful nobleman.[15] As a young courtier, Iñigo was brave, vain, and ambitious. Later he freely testified to his sinful early days (violence, sexual escapades, etc.). In service to the duke of Navarre, he was among the soldiers resisting the invading French forces at the siege of Pamplona in 1521. He unwisely convinced his troops to continue to fight the overwhelming French forces, and he paid the price. On May 17 a French cannonball shattered one of his legs and gravely injured the other.[16] The young courtier-soldier was carried back to Loyola to endure several excruciating operations and to come near death.[17] The tough Basque survived, however, and, in the absence of the courtly romances that had thus far been his reading fare, he turned to the only books available—Spanish translations of the fourteenth-century Carthusian Ludolph of Saxony's *Life of Christ*, and a version of the ever-popular *Lives of the Saints* composed by the Dominican James of Voragine at the end of the thirteenth century. These books helped to effect a conversion in the convalescing young man.[18] The *Acts* say, "As he read them over many times, he became rather fond of what he found written there,"[19] even to the extent of dreaming of matching the heroic efforts of saints like Francis and Dominic. Noting that when he thought of the things of the world he was delighted at first, but afterwards "dry and dissatisfied," while thoughts of going to Jerusalem barefoot and performing the rigorous asceticism he saw in the saints had the opposite effect, Iñigo had made the first breakthrough of his developing spirituality: the importance of discerning spirits. There came a "time when his eyes were opened a little, and he began to marvel at the difference and to reflect upon it. . . . Little by little, he came to recognize the difference between the spirits that were stirring, one from the devil, the other from God."[20]

By the time Ignatius was strong enough to leave his ancestral castle at Loyola in February of 1522, his life had changed. He now had become "the pilgrim," as he is so frequently called in the rest of the *Acts*, a man dedicated to God and to a life of severe asceticism, including a desire to go to Jerusalem.[21] Iñigo, however, was still much in search of himself and whatever mission God had in store for him. Given his devotion to Mary, it is no surprise that the pilgrim set out for the great Marian shrine of Montserrat in Catalonia. Here he made a three-day general confession and spent an all-night vigil before the altar, pilgrim staff in hand (*Acts* 17–18). He apparently planned to go on to Barcelona to find a ship sailing for Jerusalem, but instead he decided to stay at the nearby town of Manresa, living as a beggar and discerning God's will in his regard. Iñigo spent almost a year at Manresa (March 25, 1522, to February 18, 1523). His account of the mystical gifts, or consolations, he received there, as well as his trials and temptations (see *Acts* 19–34), is a key to his mysticism and will be taken up later.

Increasingly aware of the vainglory and exaggerated penances of the early days of his converted life, the pilgrim went on to Barcelona for a brief time. In mid-March 1523, he took ship for Italy, making his way to Venice as a beggar to sail to Jerusalem. During this time he continued to receive the visions of Jesus that had begun at Manresa (*Acts* 41, 44). Finally arriving in the holy land, the pilgrim felt "great consolation" as he viewed the sites of the life of Jesus. At this point in the narrative a new dimension enters into the pilgrim's life, one that was to be decisive for the future. In his own words: "His firm intention was to remain in Jerusalem, continually visiting the holy places; and in addition to this devotion, he also planned to help souls." He told the local authorities of the first part of his intent, "but not the second part, about wanting to help souls, because he had not told this to anyone."[22] Here Ignatius the apostolic mystic (as I shall call him hereafter) begins to come into view. Nevertheless, the Franciscan Guardian of the holy places, the papal representative, refused to let him stay, so the pilgrim set sail again (October 23, 1523), eventually reaching Venice in February 1524 after a difficult winter voyage. Ignatius's obedience to the papal representative shows that his process of discernment, even at this early stage, already had a papal dimension.[23]

On his return to Spain, Ignatius began formal studies in grammar and continued a practice he had started at Manresa of engaging in discussions with seekers of a deeper spiritual life. During this time he was also developing the practices of prayer and discernment that eventually formed the *Spiritual Exercises*, but it is hard to know how far advanced the text was. After two years of study at Barcelona (1524–26), he proceeded to the university at Alcalá, where he studied logic, physics, and theology for a year and a half. The spiritual dimension of his vocation was now becoming clearer—"While at Alcalá, he was engaged in giving spiritual exercises and teaching Christian doctrine, and this bore fruit for the glory of God" (*Acts* 57).[24] Another central theme of Ignatius's career enters here: everything should be done for the greater glory of God (*ad majorem Dei gloriam*, subsequently the motto of the Jesuits).

Ignatius now began to encounter the opposition he faced throughout his life and that the Jesuit order would endure for centuries. He was beginning his career as teacher and spiritual guide without any authorization, either priesthood or a university degree. Furthermore, the access to God that his exercises and teaching promised might well be open to the accusations made against the contemporary "Enlightened Ones" (*Alumbrados*), heretics who claimed special access to God and divine illumination (see chap. 1 above). So the pilgrim was accused at Alcalá (*Acts* 58–63), at Salamanca (*Acts* 64–72), as well as later in Paris (*Acts* 86), of being a heretic. After imprisonment and investigation he was acquitted both times in Spain, and was not even arrested in Paris.[25] Many today think of these accusations as made from spite, but ill will need not have been the only motive. What Ignatius was trying to do was to work out a new form of apostolic spirituality, one at variance with traditional ideas, especially as represented by hyper-conservative Spanish Dominicans, such as Melchior Cano (ca. 1509–1560), who remained a lifelong opponent.[26] The "newness" was unacceptable for many, especially those who had not reflected on the passage from Matthew about bringing forth things both new and old from the treasury of faith (Matt. 13:52).

The attacks that Ignatius underwent and the restrictions on his doctrinal preaching convinced him that he needed to become a theologian, despite his advanced age and mediocre academic talents. He therefore went off to study theology at Paris for seven years (February 1528 to April 1535). The account given of these years in *Acts* 73–86 is noteworthy for several reasons. Negatively, Ignatius testifies that the numerous divine visitations and consolations he had enjoyed during his days at Manresa largely vanished while at Paris, incompatible with the many hours he spent in hard study. One gets the sense, however, that his own inner mystical delight was becoming less important than what he thought necessary for his mission. Positively, Ignatius's continuing giving of the exercises and discussion with spiritual seekers, especially at the university, began to bear fruit in the formation of a group of companions, the nucleus of the Jesuit order and a vital factor in the order's development and later success. These companions included men of great accomplishment, such as the theologian Francis Xavier, later apostle to India, Japan, and the Far East, who was canonized together with Ignatius in 1622.[27] On August 15, 1534, the group took private vows of poverty and chastity, also vowing to make a pilgrimage to the holy land, still the goal of Ignatius's aspirations. Significantly, however, they added a qualifier—"and if they were not given permission to remain in Jerusalem, then return to Rome and present themselves to the Vicar of Christ, so that he could make use of them wherever he thought it would be more to the glory of God and the good of souls" (*Acts* 85). So, the root of the special relationship between the new apostolic group and the papacy (later the source of the fourth vow the Jesuits took along with the traditional triad of poverty, chastity, and obedience) was already strong in Paris.

In 1535 Ignatius had to return to Spain for some months for health reasons, but he went on to Italy toward the end of the year to meet with his companions in 1537 in hopes of getting a ship to the holy land. While back in Venice and during a stay in Vicenza (January 1536 to November 1537), he continued to give the exercises (*Acts* 92) and to receive the "visions, consolation . . . , and supernatural experiences" he had experienced at Manresa (*Acts* 95–96). At this time, Ignatius and his friends were ordained priests. Turkish advances in the Mediterranean made a voyage to the holy land impossible, so in late 1537 Ignatius and his friends decided to go to Rome. "On this journey," we are told, "he was visited very especially by God" (*Acts* 96). One of these experiences was decisive for this new stage of the life that the pilgrim was to take up in his last eighteen years in Rome—Ignatius the Founder.

The account of this special visit in the *Acts* is brief: "One day, a few miles before reaching Rome, he was at prayer in a church and experienced such a change in his soul and saw so clearly that God the Father placed him with Christ his Son that he would not dare doubt it—that God the Father had placed him with his Son."[28] In the little church at La Storta about six miles north of Rome, God the Father, the source of all authority and the frequent goal, or *terminus*, of Ignatius's devotion, had "placed" the pilgrim with his Son, that is, given him a share in his saving mission. Diego Laínez (1512–1565), one of Ignatius's first companions who was with him at the time, enriches da Câmara's account by reporting that Ignatius told him that he heard the Father speaking within his heart, saying, "I shall be propitious to you [plural] in Rome," and then saying to Jesus, "I want you, my Son, to take this man as your servant." Christ then spoke to Ignatius, "I want you [singular] to serve us."[29] Thus, the experience at La Storta with its trinitarian, christological, and ecclesial dimensions, marks a turning point for Ignatius and for his brothers in their decision to concentrate their energies on an apostolic mission under obedience to the pope, Christ's vicar on earth. One Jesuit commentator goes so far as to claim that, from the time of this vision, obedience became the characteristic virtue of the Society of Jesus.[30]

Ignatius and his group were once again confronted with suspicions and attacks during their first year in Rome (1538), as da Câmara recounts in *Acts* 98. Alas, the *Acts* end there with remarks that Ignatius made to da Câmara on October 20, 1555, as he was departing for Portugal. This passage, however, is of great significance, not only for Ignatius's comments on how he had composed the *Spiritual Exercises* over many years but also for his mystical life. Ignatius said that "[e]very time, any hour, that he wished to find God, he found him. And even now he often had visions, especially those mentioned above in which he saw Christ as the sun. This often happened while he was engaged in important matters, and that gave him confirmation."[31] Furthermore, Ignatius also told da Câmara that he had had many visions at Mass while he was drawing up the *Constitutions*: "He can now affirm this more easily because every day he wrote down what went on in his soul and he had it now in writing. He then showed me a rather large bundle of writings, of which he read me a good bit. Most were visions."[32] The Portuguese Jesuit asked to look at the bundle, but Ignatius refused. He later destroyed these papers, except for the two fragments discovered in his effects after his death—what we call the *Spiritual Diary*.

Although we lack Ignatius's reminiscences for the final eighteen years of his life, the evidence of his thousands of letters and official documents, as well as the accounts and stories of those who lived with him, give us good knowledge of his activities and the advance of the Society of Jesus. In conformity with the vow they had taken at Paris in 1534, the companions offered themselves to the discretion of Pope

Paul III at an audience he granted them in November of 1538. Since they still expressed a desire to go to Jerusalem, the pope is reported to have asked them: "Why do you want so eagerly to go to Jerusalem? Italy is a good and true Jerusalem, if what you desire is to bring forth fruit in God's Church."[33] The first order of business was to work out a juridical structure for the brotherhood, so from March to June 1539, the group deliberated, following the procedures of the *Spiritual Exercises*, to reach one mind on the issues involved. Meanwhile, they had already begun pastoral ministry in Rome, such as catechizing, working with the poor and homeless, and providing shelter for prostitutes. Ignatius drew up a document of five chapters detailing the fruit of their deliberations. This "First Sketch of the Institute of the Society of Jesus" was presented to Paul III by Cardinal Gasparo Contarini and, after examination by the papal curia, was approved in the bull "Regimini militantis Ecclesiae" on September 27, 1540. The first chapter provides a clear statement of the intent of the founder and his companions:

> Whoever wishes to serve as a soldier of God beneath the banner of the cross in our Society . . . is a member of a community founded chiefly to strive for the progress of souls in Christian life and doctrine, and for the propagation of the faith by means of the ministry of the word, the Spiritual Exercises, and works of charity, and specifically by the instruction of children and unlettered persons in Christianity.[34]

Despite his initial refusal, Ignatius was elected the first general of the order on April 6, 1541, and the Society began to grow. The Jesuits spread rapidly outside Rome, including the establishment of missions in India and Japan by Francis Xavier. By the time of Ignatius's death in 1556, it has been calculated that there were about a thousand Jesuits divided into twelve provinces and living in about a hundred houses or teaching colleges. Quite soon, education became a key part of the Jesuit mission. In 1548 the first Jesuit college opened at Messina, and in 1551 what Ignatius intended to be the crown jewel of Jesuit educational system was established in Rome, the Collegio Romano, today known as the Gregorian University after Pope Gregory XVI, a later supporter. When Ignatius died, there were thirty-nine Jesuit colleges in Europe and abroad. The Society was engaged in a wide variety of other ministries as well.[35] Ignatius's formidable skills as organizer, administrator, inspiring leader, letter writer, and much more put his decisive stamp on the Society.

Ignatius's most pressing task in the early years at Rome was to draw up a set of *Constitutions* for the order, something he labored at, with much assistance from others, over more than ten years, all the while continuing his pastoral work in Rome. It is worth recalling that Ignatius was not really so much an author as he was the inspirer, dictator, and collaborator of the body of writings that constitute the community of the early Jesuits.[36] The complex history of the development of the Spanish and Latin texts of the four parts of the *Constitutions* cannot delay us here.[37] While the document is juridical, it contains important texts concerning the spiritual lives of the members of the Society—"ours," as the Jesuits began to term themselves. Ignatius was accustomed to employing the decision-making techniques he worked out in the *Spiritual Exercises* to search out God's will in making difficult choices. Perhaps the most important of these was the decision about whether the Jesuits should accept fixed revenues to pursue their apostolic work, or should rather practice the apostolic poverty of Christ and the apostles and eschew all fixed revenues. In early February 1544, Ignatius composed a brief "Deliberation on Poverty," setting out the pros and cons of the two options.[38] The actual election, or decision, proved difficult to make, taking forty days. During the election process Ignatius kept a journal, the *Spiritual Diary*, the first part of which contains his record of the consolations and setbacks he received between February 2 and March 12 of 1544 as he struggled with the issue before reaching a decision in favor of apostolic poverty.[39] This record of divine graces offers special insight into the mature mystical life of Ignatius and will be taken up below. A second copy book was also found in Ignatius's papers after his death. This covers a longer period of time (March 13, 1544, to February 27, 1545) but, after some longer entries at the beginning (Nos. 154–234), is merely a series of shorthand notes for the period covered (Nos. 235–490).

Ignatius's health, never strong after the ascetic rigors of his early days, declined in the 1550s. His letters and the accounts of those who lived with him give us considerable information about his day-to-day actions and concerns, and even occasional insights into his inner life. It was only late in life on several occasions (August–September of 1553; March, September, and October of 1555) that he yielded to the requests of his followers, apparently with considerable hesitation, to give the interviews that Gonçalves da Câmara recorded in the *Acts*. By 1556 Ignatius's activities had become quite restricted, and he died on July 31, 1556.

The Foundations of Ignatius's Spiritual Teaching:
The Spiritual Exercises and the Constitutions
of the Jesuit Order

Ignatius's *Spiritual Exercises* is one of the most significant works in the history of Christian spirituality.[40] Spiritual exercises in the broad sense were nothing new, going back to the exercises of the ancient philosophers and transported into a Christian register by the early monks and their medieval successors.[41] Ignatius's *Exercises* is a manual of practical directions, not a book for picking up and reading.[42] Further, it is not an instruction manual like one written for someone learning to play tennis. It is a series of guidelines for a person (the director) about how to work with one or more others (exercitants) to help them to greater self-knowledge, especially of their good and bad intentions, with the eventual goal of making a fundamental religious decision to direct their lives to their salvation and the greater glory of God. Merely reading the *Exercises* has its limitations; they are meant to be experienced in order to be fully appreciated.[43]

The history of the *Exercises* can be briefly summarized. Ignatius began to write down some of the reflections and points that made their way into the book as early as 1521–22. He was already "giving the exercises" to others in the mid-1520s, and they existed in some written form by about 1526–27. By 1540 the book was complete. A manuscript of the Spanish version exists with marginal corrections in Ignatius's hand, and the rather crude first Latin translation, possibly by Ignatius himself (*Versio Prima*), is found in a copy of 1541. A better Latin version (*Versio Vulgata*) was made by the Jesuit Latinist André des Freux under Ignatius's direction in 1546–47. The two Latin versions were approved by Paul III on July 31, 1548, and des Freux's version was first printed in September. The Latin "Vulgate," then, was the form in which the exercises were given for centuries. It was not until the nineteenth and twentieth centuries that the early forms were made available and new translations appeared.

The style of the *Exercises* is brief, often laconic, leaving many issues in need of further development. The *Exercises* were also given in many ways: to individuals (Ignatius's original model) and to groups; sometimes longer (Ignatius says "four weeks"), sometimes shorter. Philip Endean notes that the text has served many functions "because its interactive character encourages a variety of possible responses."[44] The need for further explanation gave rise to a series of *Directories*

(*Directoria*) to provide further explanations for those who gave the *Exercises*. Some of these date back to Ignatius and his immediate followers, and the genre proliferated down to 1599 when the Jesuit general Claudio Acquaviva tried to overcome the differences among the interpretations by publishing the "official" *Directory*. Outsiders may have the impression that there is general agreement about Ignatius's teaching in the *Exercises*, but this is far from true. Even on such a central aspect as discerning God's will, Jules Toner observes that "[t]he most diverse and most sharply opposed interpretations are found regarding the three Ignatian times for, and modes of, seeking God's will."[45] In short, the *Spiritual Exercises*, both in theory and in practice, contain many problems and interpretive pitfalls.

The *Exercises* is not a mystical text in the sense of a writing that either recounts the author's own experience of God (Ignatius says nothing about himself), or that contains traditional teaching about the stages of contemplation, or finding God within the ground of the soul (to mention two late medieval models). Modern interpretations of the *Spiritual Exercises*, starting a century ago, are often divided between the "Electionists," who insist that Ignatius's aim was to move those who engaged in his spiritual program to make a fundamental choice for a converted life, and the "Perfectionists," who contend that he wanted the exercitants to commit to perfect their lives and come to live from a direct consciousness of God's presence. It is obvious that these views need not be exclusive.[46] If Loyola's concentration is on the practices needed to make a fundamental option, or "Election," for God in one's life, by its very nature such a choice should be open to the "consolations without prior cause" that was his language for mystical gifts. The *Spiritual Exercises*, however, rarely mention mystical gifts or experiences. Furthermore, Ignatius's descriptions of mystical graces, both proleptically in the *Exercises*, and in more detail in the *Spiritual Diary* and in the *Acts*, are unusual, even idiosyncratic, in relation to past and contemporary mystical traditions—which often makes them difficult to evaluate.[47]

The *Exercises* begin with twenty "Introductory Explanations" (*anotaciones*) to aid both the one who gives and the one who receives the course of spiritual instruction. Ignatius provides a definition:

> By the term Spiritual Exercises we mean every method of examination of conscience, meditation, contemplation, vocal or mental prayer, and other spiritual activities, such as will be mentioned later. . . . So, the name spiritual exercises is given to any means of preparing and

disposing the soul to rid itself of all its disordered attachments [*las afecciones desordenadas*] and then, after their removal, of seeking and finding God's will in the ordering of our life for the salvation of the soul.[48]

Thus, the negative and the positive aspects of the training process are made evident at the start, as well as the goal, the salvation of the soul (the *Exercises* do not say much directly about service to other souls).[49] The remaining nineteen instructions are mostly for the director. Especially important is the stress on the affective dimension over the intellectual—"For what fills and satisfies the soul consists not in knowing much, but in understanding and tasting the realities interiorly."[50] The flexibility of the "four weeks," which can be shortened or lengthened depending on the circumstances (Point 4), is also emphasized, as is how the director should deal differently with those who are experiencing desolation and temptation (Point 7). Above all, the director must allow God to work in the exercitant. Point 15 states, "During these Spiritual Exercises when a person is seeking God's will, it is more appropriate and far better that the Creator and Lord himself should communicate himself to the devout soul, embracing [some manuscripts read "enflaming"] it with love, inciting it to praise him, and disposing it for the way which will most enable the soul to serve him for the future."[51] These preliminary instructions display Ignatius's insistence that the goal in mind is always "only the service, honor, and glory of his Divine Majesty" (Point 16).[52]

The title of the "Presupposition" that begins the text itself (No. 21) reaffirms the basic message. The *Spiritual Exercises* have as their purpose, "To Overcome Oneself, and to Order One's Life, without Reaching a Decision through Some Disordered Attachment." In order to fulfill this goal, the "Principle and Foundation" of the First Week that immediately follows is central.[53] Five points are made: (1) "Humans are created to praise, reverence, and serve God our Lord, and by means of this to save our souls"; (2) all other things in creation were made to help us achieve this goal; (3) we should use things to the extent they help us, and get rid of them if they hinder us; (4) in order to do this, we must make ourselves "indifferent to all created things";[54] and (5) consequently, "I ought to desire and elect only the thing which is more conducive to the end for which I am created."[55] Having set forth his goal, Ignatius proceeds to give instructions regarding the practices (spiritual exercises) that will enable the exercitant to move toward that end. There are basically four: (1) Examination, both Particular (Nos. 24–31) and General (Nos. 32–43);[56] Meditations (or Contemplations), first of all on sin and hell (Week 1), and then on the Mysteries of Christ's Life (Weeks 2–4);[57] (3) Colloquies, or prayerful conversations with God and Christ induced by the Meditations; and finally (4) the Election, or Choice of a Way of Life, which Ignatius says can be made at three times and in two ways (Nos. 169–89). These exercises are forms of affirmative or cataphatic prayer designed to lead a person in a holistic way deeper and deeper into the saving mysteries of Christ's life, death, and resurrection.[58]

Ignatius's "Particular Examination [of Conscience]," made three times a day, is a meticulous noting down of the various sins or faults one wants to work against each day.[59] Perhaps no part of the *Spiritual Exercises* has done more to foster the view of Ignatian spirituality as a mechanical exercise, an example of what Roland Barthes called "the obsessional character of the *Exercises*,"[60] although this form of self-examination has been imitated by non-Catholics, such as Benjamin Franklin. The "General Examination [of Conscience]" is a broader reflection on the nature of human sinfulness in order to prepare for a general confession of one's sins at the end of the First Week. This section begins with a traditional theme regarding the three sources of our thoughts and inclinations: "I assume that there are three kinds of thoughts in myself. That is, one kind is my own, which arises strictly from my own freedom and desire; and the other two come from outside myself, the one from the good spirit and the other from the evil" (No. 32). One of the puzzling things about the *Exercises* is that thoughts that arise from ourselves are generally not treated, at least in any explicit way. For Ignatius, the bad thoughts and attachments we have to fight against come from *outside* ourselves, that is, from demons, as the next section on "Thoughts" shows by beginning, "There are two ways in which I can merit from an evil thought that comes from *outside myself*" (No. 33, my emphasis). Ignatius's agonistic approach to spirituality fitted an age when demonic influence was seen as omnipresent but is in need of adjustment for those who no longer suppose that demonic forces are constantly active in each person's life.[61]

Ignatius then passes on to the Five Exercises of the First Week, which he describes as Meditations (Nos. 45–72). He starts by outlining the procedure to be followed in meditating. Each meditation begins with a preparatory prayer; then follows the "First Prelude," which is "a composition [*composición*] made by imagining the place," that is, a reconstruction in the imagination of the physical setting where the subject of the meditation happened. This imaginative "composition of place" (*compositio loci*), or creation of a virtual space in the mind, is central to Ignatian prayer. Ignatius insists that such a visualizable space is necessary, in terms of representing the historical events of Christ's life (e.g., the road to Bethlehem and the place of Christ's birth) and abstract doctrinal truth, both of which need a concretized location. He says:

> When a contemplation or meditation is about something abstract and invisible, as in the present case about sins, the composition will be in the imagination and to consider my soul as imprisoned in the corruptible body, and my whole compound self as an exile in this valley among the brute animals, I mean my whole self as composed of body and soul.[62]

The picture of the soul as imprisoned in the body had a long and often unfortunate history in Christian spirituality, as well as a biblical proof-text (Wis. 9:15), but joining it with an image of the person living in the valley of exile amid wild animals (perhaps signifying irrational passions) is unusual. Ignatius seems to want the exercitant to call up images that speak of estrangement and sinfulness.

The "Second Prelude" (Nos. 48–49) consists in asking God for what one desires from the meditation/contemplation: for example, fear regarding meditations on hell; joy from those concerning Christ's resurrection. Specifically with regard to these meditations about the first, second, and third sins (i.e., those of the angels, of Adam and Eve, and any sin of someone in hell), Ignatius gives instructions about how the soul's three powers (memory, intellect, and will) are to function to make the exercise effective (Nos. 50–52).[63] Finally, the exercise ends in a Colloquy (Nos. 53–54) in which the exercitant imagines Christ on the cross before him and engages with him "in the way one friend speaks to another," begging forgiveness, telling one's concerns, and asking for advice.[64]

With the formal structure set, Ignatius goes on to describe the Second Exercise, a meditation on one's own sins (Nos. 55–61); then the Third Exercise, which repeats the First and Second (Nos. 62–63); the Fourth Exercise, which resumes the Third (No. 64);[65] and the Fifth Exercise of the First Week, an extended imagination of the horrors of hell (Nos. 65–72), in which the exercitant is advised to make use of five interior or imaginative senses—eyes, ears, smell, taste, touch—in order to get "an interior sense of the pain suffered by the damned" (Nos. 65–70).[66] Ignatius also utilizes the application of the inner senses throughout the later, positive meditations on Christ's life.[67] The directives for the First Week end with an addendum of ten directives (Nos. 73–90), entering into detail about how the exercises are to be conducted (when, where, in what frame of mind, etc.). Once again, the reader is reminded that the *Spiritual Exercises* are not meant to be read, but practiced.

Between Week One and Week Two Ignatius introduced a contemplation on "The Kingdom of Christ" (Nos. 91–100), which is important for the shift of attention away from the largely negative meditations on sin and hell in the First Week toward the positive choice for Christ that is the goal of the whole process.[68] The remaining weeks of the *Spiritual Exercises* are explicitly christological, although always conducted under the guidance of the Holy Spirit.[69] Speaking in the person of Ignatius, a later Jesuit, Karl Rahner, summarized the christological character of Ignatius's thought by saying, "There is no Christianity that can find the incomprehensible God apart from Jesus."[70] Ignatius begins this Contemplation-Meditation by imaging the call of a human ruler to fight against the enemies of Christendom (Nos. 91–94) and then roots this picture in the deeper invitation of Christ the King to believers to fight for him "and thus enter into the glory of my Father" (No. 95).[71] Here, Ignatius appeals to another essential law of his spirituality, that is, the necessity to work against our human desires and loves (*agere contra*) in order to offer everything to God.[72] The centrality of this meditation is confirmed by the powerful prayer included at this point (No. 98).

The Second Week features Ignatius's incorporation of late medieval meditations on the life of Christ (especially as known through Ludolph of Saxony) into his new spirituality. For Ignatius, these meditations are put within the framework of a new process of coordinated "spiritual exercises." The format of the meditations stays largely the same; the topics change to focus on the historical life of Jesus.[73] A new note, already found in the Meditation on the Two Kings, is the goal of seeking to imitate Christ in all things.[74] The First Day (Nos. 101–31) includes five contemplations (the Incarnation, the Nativity, two "re-seekings" of these, and an application of the five senses to the two meditations). The Contemplation on the Incarnation (Nos. 102–9) begins with the picture of the Trinity gazing down on the world and its people and deciding to send the Second Person to take on flesh and save humanity. Although explicit references to the Trinity are rare in the *Exercises* as compared with the *Spiritual Diary*, there is a sense in which the actions of the Three Persons are present throughout the work—the Father's love for humanity, the Son's obedience to the Father in coming to save us, and the Spirit moving and guiding our desire for God. The Second Day (Nos. 132–33) briefly considers the Presentation in the Temple and the Flight into Egypt, while the Third Day deals with Jesus's life at Nazareth (No. 134).[75]

This leads to one of the central sections of the *Exercises*: the Fourth Day of the Second Week and its "Meditation on the Two Standards [*banderas*], the one of Christ, our supreme Captain and Lord, the other of Lucifer, the mortal enemy of our human nature" (Nos. 137–48). Again, the agonistic nature of Ignatius's spiritual vision comes to the fore. The composition of place takes on universal dimensions. We are to imagine Christ seated on a great plain in the region of Jerusalem, while Lucifer is seated on a plain near Babylon. The consideration of each standard has three points. Christ's call to his servants and friends is to go forth into the world inviting everyone to embrace the "highest degree of spiritual poverty," and, if it would please God, "no less a degree of actual poverty," and also to welcome the reproaches and contempt that lead to humility (No. 146). This Meditation stresses key virtues that govern Ignatius's view of the Christian life, especially that of the Jesuits: devotion, obedience, renunciation, humility.[76] The three Colloquies that follow (Nos. 147–48) illustrate Ignatius's view of the mediatorial nature of prayer—the First Colloquy asks the Blessed Virgin for the gift of imitating Christ; the Second asks it from the Son so that "he may obtain it for me from the Father"; and finally, the Third is a direct petition to the Father.

On the same Fourth Day there follows a "Meditation on Three Classes of Persons . . . made as an aid toward embracing what is better" (*para abrazar el major*).[77] Ignatius always thinks in terms of "more" (*magis*). If the fundamental power leading us to God is love, Ignatius thinks of love as a dynamic power always demanding "more and more" from us as we seek the "greater" glory of the infinite God.[78] This is illustrated in the three classes of people considered here. Ignatius asks the exercitant to imagine three kinds of people who want to be saved but who have been given a sum of money that is a burden to salvation (the importance of poverty again). Those in the first class want to give up the attachment to the money, but they do nothing about it (No. 153); those in the second class give up the attachment but not the money itself (No. 154). The third group are those who have attained *indiferencia*. They "desire to get rid of the attachment, but in such a way that they have no inclination either to keep the acquired money or to dispose of it. Instead they desire to keep it or dispose of it solely according to what God our Lord will move their will to choose, and also according to what they themselves will judge to be better [i.e., more] for the service and praise of his Divine Majesty."[79]

Following these Contemplations, Ignatius returns the exercitant to meditations on the mysteries of Christ's life in Days Five through Twelve of the Second Week (Nos. 158–64).[80] The crucial moment of the process now looms—"Making of an Election [*hacer elección*]," which ideally comes at this time. Ignatius says that consideration of the material belonging to the Election should begin on the Fifth Day (No. 163), but before actually beginning the election process it will be good for the exercitant to ponder three ways of being humble (a kind of restatement of the Meditation on the Three Classes of Persons). The first way of being humble is to be obedient to God's law (No. 165); the second is eschewing all sin, even venial, and attaining indifference regarding created things (No. 166). The third (Nos. 167–68) involves "imitating and serving Christ better," that is, choosing poverty, humility, and even contempt out of love for the Savior. With these Christocentric considerations completed, Ignatius thinks that the exercitant should be ready to make an election, that is, to discern God's will and to make a fundamental option for Christ, although he recognizes that different people will not always come to election in the same way.

We are accustomed to making decisions every day, but Ignatius's notion of election is more than just some particular decision; in its essence it is a choice to put God before all else and to live out of this option for the rest of one's life.[81] The *Exercises* were designed to lead a person to such a fundamental choice, or to reinforce it, if it had already been made. For Ignatius, the end determines the means, so if "the eye of our intention" is focused only on praising God and saving my soul (No. 169), then all things in life are to be chosen insofar as they assist one to this goal. Ignatius provides a number of observations about the nature and time of elections here, although there are many disputes about the interpretation of his brief account.[82]

After some preliminary points about the matters concerning which an election should be made (Nos. 170–74), Ignatius describes three times or occasions (*tres tiempos*) suitable for a sound election (Nos. 175–78): (1) a sudden direct divine action on the will (e.g., the conversion of St. Paul); (2) after a discernment of the varying experiences of consolations and desolations;[83] and (3) in a time of tranquillity when a process of reasoning about and desiring the service of God and "the salvation of my soul" will lead to the election of a state of life within the bounds prescribed by the church.[84] One presumes the first "time" will be rare, and hence it looks as if Ignatius expects those making the exercises will usually fall into the second time after having made their meditations and colloquies and brought to bear the rules of discernment.[85] Nevertheless, it is the "third time" he spends the most effort explaining. If an election is not made during the first or second time, Ignatius gives two methods (*dos modos*) to be employed for making an election in the third time (Nos. 179–88). The first method (179–83), explained in six points, can be described as primarily rational and moving from below (i.e., from our self-examination up to a decision for God), whereas the second method (184–88) comes "from above," that is, it begins with a gift of divine love that initiates a reasoning process that eventually leads to an election. He says:

> That love which moves me and brings me to choose the matter in question should descend from above from the love of God [*descienda de arriba del amor de Dios*], in such a way that the person making the election should perceive beforehand that the love, whether greater or lesser, which he has for the matter being chosen is solely for the sake of our Creator and Lord.[86]

In all cases it seems Ignatius presumes that, after the election has been made, the exercitant will go on to pray, offering the election to God and hoping for divine confirmation.

Not a few problems confront interpreters of these passages on election. Presumably, the second and third times (and perhaps even the first) are not necessarily discrete but can overlap. Jules Toner has a detailed discussion of the problems on which interpreters of the *Spiritual Exercises* are deeply divided: (1) Are there really three distinct forms of election? (2) Are these forms autonomous? And (3) Is any form sufficient in itself for an election, or do they have to be combined in some way?[87] In the face of fundamental disagreements among the Jesuit interpreters, all that an outsider can say is that such disagreements did not prevent the *Exercises* from being used for centuries by directors who did (and still do) disagree about what Ignatius intended.

The Third and Fourth Weeks of the *Exercises* might seem less important than the first two weeks, now that the election has ordinarily been made, but this is not the case, because these weeks are crucial for the process of Christomimesis, which leads the exercitant into deeper and deeper participation in Christ, both in his suffering and death, and in his rising from the dead.[88] The seven days of Week Three are devoted to meditations/contemplations on the events of the passion from the Last Supper to Christ's burial. These follow the standard pattern (three preludes, a series of points, the colloquy, and often added notes). Becoming one with Christ in his sacrificial death for Ignatius, as for so many other late medieval and early modern mystics, is an essential part of the path to God. The Fourth Week is devoted to the events of the life of the risen Christ but also includes a series of additions (Nos. 230–370). The Contemplations of this week focus not on the resurrection itself but on Christ's appearances, first to the Blessed Mother (not in scripture), and then through the other manifestations down to the Ascension (Nos. 218–29). The joy that characterizes these exercises (in marked contrast to the fear of the First Week) includes not only rejoicing in the happiness of Christ our Lord but also a joy in the whole of creation "that will help me rejoice in Christ my Creator and Redeemer" (No. 229). At this point Ignatius introduces what has been seen as the culmination of the *Spiritual Exercises*, the "Contemplation to Attain Love" (Nos. 230–37). Early in the *Exercises*, Ignatius had described the exercises of the First Week as pertaining to the traditional purgative way, and those of the Second Week as belonging to the illuminative way (No. 10), but it is significant that he drops this language, so that those who would identify the Fourth Week, and especially the Contemplation to Attain Love, with the unitive way are pushing Ignatius beyond what he explicitly states.[89]

Ignatius defines love as "a mutual communication between two persons" in which the lovers share all that they have with each other (No. 231). The First Prelude in this Contemplation is to imagine oneself standing before God and the angels and saints; the Second is asking for "interior knowledge" (*cognocimiento interno*) of all the good things we have received from God to spur us to love. Four points follow. The First (No. 234) asks the exercitant "to ponder with deep affection" on God's gifts, most especially how he "desires to give me even his very self," that is, to unite himself with the soul. This leads the exercitant to make the well-known prayer called the *Suscipe*, from its opening word in Latin: "Take, Lord, and receive all my liberty, my memory, my understanding, and my will—all that I have and possess. . . . Give me your love and your grace, for that is enough for me." The Third Point (No. 235) asks the exercitant to consider how God dwells in all things, but especially in the human being "created as a likeness and image of his Divine Majesty."[90] God not only dwells in all things, but he also works in them for the good of humans (No. 236). Finally, the Fourth Point (No. 237) reminds the exercitant that "all good things and gifts descend from above" (Jas. 1:17), so our total love is owed to the God who is the source of every blessing. The Contemplation to Attain Love is a key source for one of the essential characteristics of Ignatian mysticism, that is, finding God in all things. But, as Karl Rahner has reminded us, this is not some form of nature mysticism starting from the world; rather, "Ignatius approaches the world from God. Not the other way about."[91]

The *Spiritual Exercises* close with a series of additions that both cast light on the exercises that have been already performed and help the exercitant carry the election that has been made out into the world of ordinary life. The "Three Methods of Praying" (Nos. 238–60) appear to be directed to the post-exercise life. The section on "The Mysteries of the Life of Christ our Lord" (Nos. 261–312) presents fifty-one brief events from Christ's life and the scriptural sources, meditations that the director might use to supplement those already used. The most important of the additions are the two groups of "Rules for the Discernment of Spirits"—fourteen general rules that Ignatius describes are more suitable for the First Week (Nos. 313–27), and the eight "Rules for a More Probing Discernment of Spirits" belonging to the Second Week (Nos. 328–36).

The discernment of spirits was an ancient theme in Christian spirituality and mysticism with a foundation in the New Testament (e.g., 1 Cor. 12:4–11; 2 Cor. 11:14; 1 John 1:4).[92] Ignatius's contributions to this theme were original, especially in the structural coherence of his discussion, as well as in combining discernment with the act of election and emphasizing the christological and pneumatological nature of the process. A considerable literature exists on what Ignatius meant by these rules and how they are meant to function in practice,[93] but my treatment will be brief.

Ignatius's presentation of the fourteen general rules is based on the opposition of the activity of the evil spirit leading a person on from mortal sin to mortal sin, and the good spirit who aids the person seeking to purge sins and come closer to God. The rules are calculated to enable the exercitant to read his or her inner states, intellectual and affective, positive and negative, and thereby to determine which spirit is at work. The evil spirit helps sinners imagine "the delights and pleasures of the senses," while the good spirit stings the sinner's conscience with remorse (No. 314). The opposite happens in the case of the person making progress; that is, the evil spirit causes anxiety and other problems, while the good spirit gives helpful inner motions (No. 315). Rules Three and Four (Nos. 316–17) discuss the differences between "spiritual consolation" (*consolación espiritual*), "which occurs when some interior motion is caused within the soul through which it becomes inflamed with love of its Creator and Lord" (No. 316) and "spiritual desolation."

Consolations include the "gift of tears" (so characteristic of Ignatius), as well as "any increase in faith, hope, and charity, and every interior joy which calls and attracts one to heavenly things and to the salvation of one's soul." Consolation is a broad category in the *Exercises*, including supernatural graces of every kind, up to and including an infused burning sense of interior love. "Spiritual Desolation" is the contrary of such gifts—everything that disturbs and takes one away from God (No. 317). Rules Five to Nine (Nos. 318–22) provide a detailed analysis of desolations.[94] Such experiences can, of course, have value by teaching us humility, how to stand firm in temptation, and the need to remain confident in God; but we should never make a decision in times of desolation, according to Ignatius (Nos. 318–19). Even in consolations we need to remain humble and aware that times of trial may be right around the corner (Nos. 323–24).

The "Rules for the Second Week" address the temptations and traps of the Second Week, the preferred time of the Election, and introduce a temporal element into the process of discernment. They are also further explorations of the opposition between God and his angels, on the one side, and "the enemy," on the other (No. 329).[95] The Second and Eighth Rules focus on an important aspect of the opening to mysticism in the *Exercises*, what Ignatius calls the "consolation without preceding cause" (*consolación sin causa precedente*). He says that only God can give this form of consolation (i.e., it cannot be imitated by the evil spirit), "[f]or it is the prerogative of the Creator alone to enter into the soul, depart from it, and cause a motion in it which draws the person wholly into love of his Divine Majesty" (No. 330). Good and bad angels can cause true and false lesser consolations in the soul, but only on the basis of some preceding cause, that is, some external influence or motion within the soul. God alone can act "without any previous perception or understanding of some object by means of which the consolation . . . might have been stimulated, through the intermediate activity of a person's acts of understanding and willing." For many recent interpreters of the *Exercises* (e.g., H. Rahner, K. Rahner, H. Egan) the "consolation without cause" is a mystical gift that brings the exercitant into a state of loving union with God.[96] After this discussion, Ignatius includes three addenda. The first is a set of "Rules for the Ministry of Distributing Alms" (Nos. 337–44); the second, "Notes for Perceiving and Understanding Scruples" (Nos. 345–51). The *Exercises* close with eighteen "Rules for Thinking, Judging, and Feeling with the Church Militant" (Nos. 352–70), which serve to remind us that Ignatius saw his efforts at reforming Christian life to be in the service the hierarchical Church Militant on Earth, that is, those who followed the Roman pope.

The final of the rules for "Thinking . . . with the Church Miltiant" returns us to the mystical aspect of the *Exercises*. The greatest service that can be given to God, says Ignatius, comes though "pure love" (*por puro amor*), or "filial fear" (*temor filial*). Nevertheless, the lower "servile fear" is useful insofar as it withdraws sinners from their sins. Ignatius ends on a positive note: "once such a person has arisen [from sin], one easily attains to filial fear, which is wholly acceptable and pleasing to God our Lord [i.e., Christ], since it is inseparably united with him in love."[97] Although union language does not play a large role in Ignatius's writings, it is significant to see it here at the end of the *Spiritual Exercises*.

The *Exercises* did not make any substantial contribution to the vocabulary of mysticism. Although the text features a range of language about experiences of God, most of the terms used, with a few exceptions, such as the *consolación sin causa precedente*, are traditional and employed in general ways.[98] Ignatius defines some words that are essential for his practical purposes, but he uses most spiritual terms interchangeably. This is because the *Exercises* are not interested in providing theoretical spiritual-mystical teaching, but rather in creating a program to effect conversion. Nevertheless, the significance of the *Exercises* for the history of spirituality and even mysticism is evident. As Terence O'Reilly suggests, while the *Exercises* are beholden to aspects of late medieval piety, the work also reflects the new emphasis on the interiorization of the Christian life found in Ignatius's time. They also address, he notes, "popular anxiety about the nature and process of justification, one of the most pressing problems confronting the early sixteenth-century Church." In doing so, Ignatius did not abandon popular piety but renewed it.[99] This new form of popular piety, as Moshe Sluhovsky put it, "increased dramatically the potential for a sacralization of all believers by means of enhancing their experience of the divine presence within themselves."[100] The Jesuits themselves, by breaking with traditional monastic stability, enclosure, and choral prayer (a break already partially begun by the Mendicant orders), were ready to serve in the world in a new way—not only in Europe but all over the globe. Much of this apostolic service came through the *Spiritual Exercises*, a practical handbook that continues to attract spiritual seekers, as well as to defy easy summary and facile interpretation.

Taking the *Spiritual Exercises* was a necessary part of becoming a Jesuit (see *Constitutions* 63), but this course in personal conversion was meant for the profit of all sincere Catholics. The *Constitutions* that Ignatius and his team worked on for a decade and more after the completion of the *Exercises* were intended to inspire and govern the lives of the members of the Society of Jesus.[101] As juridical documents, they are not instruments for mystical teaching, but they do tell us something about the development of the Founder's views concerning apostolic service, and therefore his mysticism. As Peter Schineller has shown, the *Constitutions* shift the focus away from one's personal salvation, as found in the *Exercises,* to the perspective of apostolic love and service to all.[102] Rather than emphasizing *my salvation*, the *Constitutions* speak constantly about apostolic activity, or, to use the biblical term, "working in the vineyard of the Lord."[103] The spiritual progress of the neighbor has become central, not one's personal perfection, which flows *from* apostolic commitment, as numerous texts make evident.[104] In the *Constitutions* the goal of working for the "greater glory of God," frequently found in the *Exercises*, becomes omnipresent, as do references to the "common good" of the members of the church.[105] This shift is evident also in other texts from this period, such as the summation of the Jesuit life in the letter to the "Fathers and Scholastics at Coimbra" written in May of 1547.[106]

The union that the *Constitutions* are concerned with is primarily the union among the members of the Society, although they emphasize that the general himself should be united with God and should therefore help others come to such union (No. 723). Toward the end of the *Constitutions* Ignatius considers how the whole body of the Society can be maintained and developed, noting that the pursuit of virtues, especially charity, is more effective for "the preservation and development of the Society but also its spirit, and for the attainment of the objective it seeks, which is to aid souls to reach their ultimate and supernatural end, the means which unite the human instrument with God and so dispose it that it may be wielded dexterously by his divine hand."[107] Ignatius thinks that the union of the members of the Society with each other is the foundation for the union of the individual members with Christ. This is because, as he put it in a letter, "a union such as this cannot be maintained among many without some order, nor order without a due bond of obedience between superiors and inferiors."[108]

A few passages give further information about the interior life of the members of the Society. Part III of the *Constitutions* concerns the preservation and progress of those who are in probation. No. 260 of this section says that these probationaries "should know the means which can be found to overcome [temptations] and to apply themselves to the fruit of good and solid virtues, whether this be with many spiritual visitations or with fewer . . . ,"[109] so Ignatius seems to have expected that the novices would be visited with internal graces. Also important is the advice given in No. 288, which tells the novices that they should keep their intention rightly ordered in all details. Ignatius says:

> In these they should aim at serving and pleasing the Divine Goodness for its own sake and because of the incomparable love and benefits with which God has anticipated us, rather than fear of punishments or hope of rewards, although they ought to draw help also from them. Further, they should often be exhorted to seek God our Lord in all things, stripping off from themselves the love of creatures to the extent that this is possible, in order to turn their love upon the Creator of them, by loving Him in all creatures and all of them in Him, in conformity with His holy and divine will.[110]

This is a good summary of the Contemplation to Attain Love from the *Exercises.*

Ignatius's Mystical Life

If all we had from Ignatius were the *Spiritual Exercises* and the *Constitutions,* we would know little of his interior life. Ignatius as mystic would be a matter of guesswork in dependence on the stories of his hagiographers. Fortunately, the survival of the *Acts* and especially the fragments of his *Spiritual Diary* gives us rich information about Ignatius the mystic, a person who was able to combine contemplation and action (*in actione contemplativus*), as his friend Jerome Nadal put it.[111] Ignatius's own descriptions of God's direct action in his life are not only striking but also unusual in the annals of Christian mysticism.

The *Acta Patris Ignatii* composed by Luis Gonçalves da Câmara has already been used in the first part of this chapter. The *Acta* is often translated as the *Autobiography,* but this is misleading. Da Câmara is the author of the *Acts,* not Ignatius; da Câmara was the one who shaped the material into what Margaret O'Rourke Boyle has described as a work of Renaissance epideictic rhetoric, which uses some of the remembered events from the life of the Founder to lead the reader to admire and imitate Ignatius, especially in his rejection of his natural temptation to vainglory.[112] Furthermore, as John M. McManamon has shown, the apostolic nature of Ignatius's pilgrimage toward Jerusalem (later Rome) is much influenced by the picture of Jesus and the first disciples in the Gospel of Luke.[113] My purpose, however, is not an analysis of the structure and nature of the *Acts* but a closer examination of the accounts of visions and mystical illuminations contained there, especially those from Ignatius's time at Manresa.

Joseph de Guibert spoke of the visual poverty of Ignatius's visions and the richness of their content.[114] Certainly, the pilgrim's visions do not have the colorful detail of the showings given to such mystics as Hildegard of Bingen, Henry Suso, or Julian of Norwich, but they make up for this supposed defect by their originality and a powerful simplicity that affects the reader as much as it did the pilgrim. Ignatius often invokes the language of the spiritual senses, especially that of the "interior eyes" (*ojos interiores*), which are being gradually purified and strengthened by divine pedagogy to provide secure knowledge of God's will.[115] Thus, Ignatius emphasizes the intellectual content of his visions and other experiences—the opening up of divine truths within the image in ways that can be stated but cannot be easily described or explained. For Ignatius, these are "spiritual," or imaginative, visions that are, however, primarily "intellectual" in nature (to use Augustine's categories). This mixture is not unusual in the history of Christian mysticism, as can be seen in the case of Julian of Norwich. Finally, at least one of Ignatius's showings at Manresa, that of the strange "serpent-like form with things that shone like eyes," introduces the Ignatian theme of the importance of discernment of spirits.

Ignatius's account of the initial appearance of the serpent-like form deserves quotation:

> While in this hospice [at Manresa] it often happened that in broad daylight he saw something in the air near him. It gave him great consolation because it was very beautiful—remarkably so. He could not discern very well the kind of thing it was, but in a way it seemed to him to have the form of a serpent with many things that shone like eyes, though they were not. He found great pleasure and consolation in seeing this thing, and the oftener he saw it the more his consolation grew. When it disappeared, he was displeased.[116]

It was during the time of the appearances of this strange object that Ignatius, despite the severe ascetic and pious life that he had undertaken, began to experience doubts about whether he could endure such a life (*Acts* 20), strange changes of mood (*Acts* 21), crippling scruples (*Acts* 22–23), and even temptations to suicide (*Acts* 24). His surrender to divine grace (also *Acts* 24) represents the beginning of a decisive change. God provided him with "some experience of the diversity of spirits," so that he could understand how the temptation to suicide came over him (*Acts* 25), and he continued to discern about the sources of the visions and consolations he was experiencing (*Acts* 26–27). "God," as he says, "treated him at this time just as a schoolmaster treats a child he is teaching."[117]

After describing five divinely given manifestations (*Acts* 28–30), Ignatius finally reached discernment about the serpent-like thing that seemed so beautiful and even consoling but was actually the source of the inner evils with which he had been struggling. After the last of the five visions, the one at the river Cardoner (fall 1522), Ignatius went to kneel at a cross and thank God. "There," continues the account, "the vision that had appeared to him many times but which he had never understood, that is, the thing mentioned above which seemed very beautiful to him, with many eyes, now appeared. But while before the cross [note the christological focus of discernment], he saw clearly with a strong agreement of his will [i.e., an election] that it was the devil."[118] Although the strange form continued to appear to him, even at Paris, thereafter Ignatius always chased it away. This is a paradigmatic illustration of the need for discernment regarding all but the most indubitable spiritual experiences (i.e., consolations without prior cause).

The famous five divine visions at Manresa have often been discussed.[119] Each starts with an image but moves on to deeper spiritual insight. The first vision concerns the Trinity, always of great importance for Ignatius. *Acts* 28 speaks of his daily prayers to the Trinity and says, "One day while saying the Office of Our Lady . . . , his understanding began to be elevated so that he saw the Most Holy Trinity in the form of three musical keys."[120] Musical keys are an unusual image for the Trinity but may be taken to indicate the harmony of the Three Persons in the one God. The effect of this vision was to induce uncontrollable tears and sobbing, as will be so often the case in the *Spiritual Diary*. "As a result, the effect has remained with him throughout his life of experiencing great devotion while praying to the most Holy Trinity." This account says that Ignatius also felt compelled to keep talking about the Trinity, "using many comparisons," but we are not told what these were.

The second vision (*Acts* 29) was of the way in which God created the world. Ignatius saw "something white, from which some rays were coming, and God made light from this." Again, he says he cannot explain what he saw, nor even remember what the "spiritual enlightenments" (*notícias espirituales*) he received were. The third vision was eucharistic. While hearing Mass at the monastery at Manresa, at the elevation of the host, Ignatius saw Christ, "with his interior eyes something like white rays coming from above. Although he cannot explain this well after so long a time, . . . what he saw clearly with his understanding was how Jesus Christ our Lord was there in that Most Holy Sacrament" (*Acts* 29). Note that Ignatius did not see the body of Christ as a form (as did some of the medieval women mystics), but within the white light emanating from above he gained supernatural knowledge beyond the conviction of faith that Christ is truly present in the host. In the fourth vision, however, he does see the humanity of Christ with his interior eyes (*Acts* 29), but in an unusual way. Again, the stress is on luminosity: "The form that appeared to him was like a white body, neither very large, nor very small, but he did not see any distinction of members." Ignatius says that he saw Christ (and sometimes Mary) this way many times, not only at Manresa but later in Jerusalem and Italy. The emphasis in these accounts is on the effect the visions had on him, giving him a conviction of the truths of faith that he would have had even if there were no scriptures to teach them.

The fifth vision was a pure intellectual illumination with no image. Going out from Manresa to a church about a mile away overlooking the river Cardoner, "he sat down for a little while with his face toward the river, which ran below." The account continues: "While he was seated there, the eyes of his understanding began to be opened; not that he saw any vision, but he understood and learnt many things, both spiritual matters and matters of faith and learning, and this with so great an enlightenment that everything seemed new to him."[121] (At this point da Câmara introduces an aside that Ignatius said he felt like another person after this.) Ignatius could not remember the details of enlightenment he experienced in his understanding at this time, but he avowed, "This was such that in the course of his whole life, after completing sixty-two years, even if he gathered up all the various helps he may have had from God and the various things he has known, even adding them all together, he does not think he had got as much as at that one time." This remark has produced some discussion among students of Ignatius. Was this really his culminating mystical illumination, especially in the light of the testimony of some of those with him in Rome during his mature years about the fact that his later experiences were greater than those of Manresa?[122] Ignatius may be testifying to the intensity of the vision at the river Cardoner, more than its extent, which, of course, cannot be put into words. In any case, the "intellectual" nature of the vision—to use Augustine's terminology—is evident. Ignatius recounts a number of other visions in the *Acts*,[123] including the famous vision-locution at La Storta mentioned above, but the Manresa experiences are central for understanding the mystical gifts that were an integral part of his growth to keen discernment and spiritual maturity. Such texts mark Ignatius out as one of the major visionary mystics of the sixteenth century.

There is more to Ignatius the mystic. The *Spiritual Diary* (*Diario Espiritual*) consists of two fragments, as mentioned above.[124] (The title *Diary* is not original and may be misleading; the work is really a series of notebooks on making an election and the mystical experiences accompanying it—one might even think of it as a "Tear-Journal.") The *Diary* did not feature in the traditional picture of the saint; it was only in the twentieth century that these fragments have produced a new view of Ignatius.[125] As Adolf Haas put it, "In the *Diary* . . . Ignatius lays completely bare the mystery of his intimacy with God."[126] Initially, the reader is likely to find the text puzzling, because even when it is more than a series of stenographical notes, its form and purpose are not easy to evaluate. Three mystical themes appear constantly: (1) Ignatius's eucharistic outlook; indeed, almost all his accounts of the special graces he was given occur in relation to celebrating the Mass—before, during, or after; (2) the centrality of experiences of the Trinity; and (3) the overwhelming presence of the gift of tears, far more than most other mystics of both East and West. How are we to understand these characteristics of Ignatius's mysticism as found in the fragments he wrote down (as was his custom) to remind himself of the stages in his election process about the decision as to whether the Society should live in apostolic poverty or not?

A number of previous mystics, such as the Cistercian nuns at Helfta at the end of the thirteenth century, had constructed mystical narratives around the liturgy and the reception of the Eucharist. Ignatius is different; far more personal, even private. As the celebrant of the Mass, he constantly dwelled on what mystical gifts were granted to *him* in relation to the Eucharist. He would by no means have excluded the communal and ecclesial aspects of Christ's sacrifice, but the focus in the *Diary* is on Ignatius and God.

Although the Trinity played a part in the visions at Manresa and was also present (if mostly implicitly) in the *Spiritual Exercises*, the role of experiences of the Trinity—all Three Persons both individually and as one God, as well as experiences of the divine essence in itself—are overwhelming in the *Diary*. Adolf Haas sees the key to Ignatius's trinitarianism in his concept of God as "the ever greater God [*Deus semper major*], whose simplicity, which comprehends everything in its eternal and essential unity, is eternally being 'surpassed' by the equally eternal fruitfulness and plenitude of the Divine Person."[127] Haas argues for this intratrinitarian tension as the source of the extratrinitarian tension by which the Trinity communicates itself to the world through the mystery of the incarnation and draws all things back into God as three and one. This is true, but a similar theological perspective was shared by many mystics, such as Mechthild of Magdeburg, Eckhart, and especially Ruusbroec, who have more developed accounts of the inner life of the Trinity than what we find in Ignatius's often repetitious visions. Modern interpreters, such as Haas, have developed a theology of the Trinity *out* of these visions; but Ignatius was not so much interested in creating a theology of the Trinity as he was in finding guidance and confirmation *from* the Trinity during his election process.

The "gift of tears," like the discernment of spirits, was one of the ancient traditions in Christian spirituality.[128] But had anyone before Ignatius ever cried so much or taken such meticulous care to record his tears?[129] Some of his companions during his Roman days back up the testimony of the *Diary*, noting that Ignatius experienced floods of tears and sobbings six or seven times every day. It has been calculated that over the course of the *Spiritual Diary* Ignatius refers to his tears some 175 times in the course of the first fragment (February 2 to March 12, 1544), that is, about four times a day, while the brief notations of the second part of the *Diary* mention tears so often as to belie counting.[130] Amid these floods of tears, I cite only a few representative texts. For example, the first entry in the *Diary* (February 2, 1544), states, "Abundance of devotion during Mass, with tears, with increased confidence in our Lady, and with greater inclination to have no fixed income, and, then, throughout the day."[131] February 11 continues: "With weeping and sobbing, on my knees, I made an offering to the Father to have no fixed income. So numerous were the tears flowing down my face and the sobs while I made the offering and after it that I could hardly rise." On February 19, he writes, "During the Mass there were many and very peaceful tears, and very many insights into the Trinity. These enlightened my understanding to such a degree that it seemed to me I could not learn so much by hard study." On March 4: "When I had finished Mass and unvested, during my prayer at the altar there was so much sobbing and effusion of tears, all terminating in the love of the Holy Trinity, that I seemed to have no desire to leave."[132]

It is not easy to understand this element in the Jesuit Founder's spiritual physiognomy, even when we note that tears seem to have been shed more often and more profusely by both men and women in the sixteenth century than is usual today. Furthermore, Ignatius's tears became so frequent as to be injurious to his eyesight and his health in general,[133] and he eventually had to cut back after a warning from his doctor. His tears are even more puzzling when we note the comments on tears in several of his letters. In a letter of spiritual advice to Francis Borgia (September 20, 1548), Ignatius distinguished three kinds of tears: those that come from thinking of our own sins or the sins of others; those that happen while contemplating the mysteries of the life of Christ; and the highest form that comes "from a loving consideration of the three Divine Persons" (as we see in the *Diary*).[134] In this letter the three kinds of tears are all good, but Ignatius seems to have subsequently changed his mind. Writing to Fr. Nicholas Gaudano on November 22, 1553, he says that the gift of tears should not be asked for unconditionally, "nor is it, absolutely speaking, good and proper for all without discrimination." Tears are not necessary for a heart that already feels compassion for its neighbors, although "God our Lord, seeing that it would be good for them, allows them to melt into tears." He concludes by telling the priest what he really thinks: "even if it were in my power to allow this gift of tears to some, I would not give it, because it would be no help to their charity, and would harm their heads and their health and consequently stand in the way of every act of charity."[135] In this text Ignatius reminds us of Catherine of Siena, whose severe food deprivations contributed to her death but who counseled other ascetic women not to fast too much.[136] Nonetheless, Michael Plattig has made a strong case that tears as a special gift of the God of consolation is an important element in Ignatius's growing awareness of his inner movements.[137]

Making sense of the structure of the day-by-day notations of the *Spiritual Diary* is a task. Several principles of organization have been proposed: one based on the process of the discernment about poverty that was the apparent reason for Ignatius's preserving this record;[138] others concentrate on the sequence of consolations and visionary experiences that accompanied the discernment process. Haas, for example, discerns four stages in the trinitarian and christological visions found in the work.[139] The First Stage (February 2–22; Nos. 1–64) moves from the Three divine Persons considered individually to their mutual indwelling, or perichoresis, while the Second Stage (February 23–28; Nos. 65–88) is christological and begins by considering Jesus as man to move to Jesus as God. The Third Stage (February 29 to March 6; Nos. 89–125) returns to the Trinity and moves from the unity of Persons to visions of the divine essence. Finally, the Fourth Stage embraces the whole second part of the *Diary* (March 7, 1544, to February 27, 1545) and is based on "reverential love." Following Joseph de Guibert, Haas says, "We can name the mysticism of this final period of the *Diary* as the mysticism of reverential love [*amor reverencial*], or also of the service of God."[140] Following the lead of Ignacio Iparraguirre, George Ganss, however, divides the text into six stages of a mystical journey, each of which is accomplished in from four to ten segments.[141]

A look at the trinitarian, christological, and pneumatological themes of the *Spiritual Diary* will give some idea of the mystological teaching of this unusual document. De Guibert calculated that there are 170 references to the Trinity in the *Spiritual Diary*, no fewer than sixteen marked off with the lines that Ignatius used to indicate especially strong experiences.[142] Haas, as we have seen, arranged these visions and manifestations of the Trinity into a theological pattern of progression from the individual Persons, through experiences of the circumincession of the Persons, to visitations by the entire Trinity, and even, in the second part of the *Diary*, to experiences of the Divine Unity. Whether the progression is actually that neat,[143] it does reflect aspects of the text.

Ignatius's main focus is on the mystery of the Trinity in itself,[144] but all Three Persons also feature as the goal of his prayers and the "termination" of his desires. The most common way he has of describing his devotional desire is to say that he "terminates everything with the Most Holy Trinity" (e.g., *Diary* 116–17). The Father as the source of all divinity plays a large role in the *Diary*, sometimes in his own right,[145] at other times mentioned along with the other Persons. The Second Person denominated as the Son, and the Third Person, the Holy Spirit, are mentioned more rarely.[146] Almost all these appearances come from the first part of the *Diary*. At the beginning of Ignatius's discernment process, Mary and Jesus Christ appear frequently as mediators with the Father, or sometimes with the whole Trinity, but Mary's role fades after February 18.[147]

Early texts in the *Diary* are important for emphasizing the role of the Father. For example, in *Diary* 8 (February 8), wishing to present his deliberations over the poverty issue to the Father with the mediation of the Mother and the Son, Ignatius says, "I felt in myself a motion toward the Father or that I was being lifted up before him. As I advanced the hairs of my head stood up and I experienced an extraordinary warmth [*ardor notabilísimo*] in my whole body."[148] Note that Ignatius tells us nothing about the Father himself, but only the effect that some kind of rapture (real or mental?) had on him, as well as the warmth he experienced, which, after tears, appears to be the most frequent physical effect of his mystical gifts.[149] Another typical visitation of the Father and the Son occurred on February 14, when Ignatius experienced "an abundance of tears, devotion, great sobbings, . . . with many spiritual understandings, having great access to the Father in naming him as he is named in the Mass, . . . sensing that the Son was very ready to intercede."[150] The experiences relating to the Three Persons become ever stronger, however, so that on February 18 Ignatius turns to all Three to confirm, or validate, his growing conviction about the necessity for absolute poverty for the order. He says, "Later while I was preparing the altar and vesting, words came to me: 'Eternal Father, confirm me! Eternal Son, confirm me! Eternal Holy Spirit, confirm me! Holy Trinity, confirm me! My one and only God, confirm me!'"

This outburst of trinitarian devotion, however, was followed by one of the more puzzling passages in the *Diary*. Later in the morning, Ignatius apparently still had not received word from the Trinity confirming his view, so he decided not to say any more Masses, and even says, "I grew indignant with the Most Holy Trinity. I had no desire to confirm anything farther."[151] Although he later ascribes this "indignation" to the action of the evil spirit, as is his wont (No. 57), this is a rather extraordinary statement. Why was Ignatius indignant with the Trinity? Was this the devil's fault?

The Trinity appears to have taken Ignatius's "indignation" without indignation, because the following passages from the *Spiritual Diary* (Nos. 52–55) contain some of the most powerful experiences of the Three Persons and "their operations and processions, more by experiencing with feeling or contemplating than by understanding." Indeed, Ignatius says that these trinitarian illuminations were so strong that everywhere he walked in the city of Rome that day, whenever he saw three of anything, "I saw them as images reminding me of the Holy Trinity" (Nos. 54–55). Soon another breakthrough took place in his understanding of the Trinity. On February 21, Ignatius says, "I seemed somehow drawn partly upward" (No. 60, another reference to some kind of rapture), and during Mass he thought there was "nothing more to be known about this matter of the Holy Trinity" (No. 62, a rather extraordinary statement). Ignatius explains that, in previously seeking the Trinity, he had prayed to the Father and somehow did not find consolation from the whole Trinity. Now, however, he received a new insight, which he puts as follows:

> During this Mass, I was knowing, or experiencing, or contemplating—the Lord knows (2 Cor. 12:2)—that to speak to the Father was to

recognize that he was one person of that Holy Trinity. This brought
me to love that Person's whole self; and that all the more because the
other Two Persons were by their very essence present in that one. I
experienced the same recognition about prayer to the Son, and again
about prayer to the Holy Spirit. I rejoiced that when I received consolations from any one of them I recognized them with joy as coming
from all three.[152]

Ignatius surely had prior theoretical knowledge of the doctrine of
perichoresis, that is, the interpenetration of the Three Persons of the
Trinity, but he has now received an experiential knowledge that he
describes as untying a knot.

At this stage in the *Diary* (February 23) another major shift occurs.
Thus far Ignatius had concentrated his attention on the eternal Son of
God. Now Jesus, the Incarnate Word and true head of the Society of
Jesus, takes over to provide him with clarity about the difficult poverty
election. "While I was preparing the altar," says Ignatius, "the thought
of Jesus came to me and an urge to follow him" (No. 66). But Jesus is
now viewed from a trinitarian perspective, as Ignatius's reference to the
La Storta experience makes clear: "The fact that Jesus showed himself
or made his presence felt seemed to me to be in some way a work of
the Most Holy Trinity; and I remembered the occasion when the Father
placed me in the Son" (No. 67). The Jesus experience grows stronger in
the following days, as Ignatius has his first "audition," or hearing of a
divine voice (No. 69), as well as "continual devotion and confirmation"
at the thought of Jesus (No. 70). By February 22, he notes, "All the devo-
tions and sentiments terminated in Jesus."[153] From here on, daily experiences of Jesus, both at Mass and throughout the day, become a dominant
feature of his account, although the Trinity is not left behind.[154]

Beginning on March 3, another kind of vision commences—manifestations of the divine essence. Ignatius says, "Entering thus in the
chapel I was overwhelmed with great devotion to the Most Holy Trinity. I felt very increased love and intense tears, though I did not see the
Persons distinctly, as in the past days, but perceived in one luminous
clarity a single essence. It drew me entirely into its love."[155] A similar
vision occurs on March 4 (No. 110). Then, on Thursday, March 6, there
is a succession of five or more similar visions of the divine essence and
the Trinity of Persons throughout the day. The first happens at Mass at
the beginning of the Canon Prayer (*Te igitur*):

It was at the *Te igitur* that I felt and saw, not obscurely, but clearly,
and very clearly, the very divine being or essence [*ser o esencia div-*

ina] under the figure of a sphere, slightly larger than the appearance
of the sun, and from this essence the Father seemed to go forth or
derive [*y de esta esencia parecía ir o deriver el Padre*], in such a way that
saying "*Te*, that is, Father," the divine essence was represented to me
before the Father. In this vision I saw represented the being of the
Most Holy Trinity without distinction or sight of the other Persons.[156]

Unvesting after Mass, Ignatius saw the same luminous sphere of the
divine essence again, but this time with the Three Persons of the Trinity proceeding from it but not "leaving the frame of the vision of the
sphere" (No. 123). Later in the day, when he was in the Basilica of St.
Peter, and then when attending a Mass celebrated by Cardinal Marcello Cervini (later Pope Marcellus II) the same vision was seen again
(No. 124). Finally, Ignatius says that at night after he had written this
down he had several other such manifestations. He continues: "on this
occasion the understanding saw something, though by far the most
part was not so clear, nor so distinct, nor so big; it was like a fairly large
spark; it represented something to the understanding, or was drawing
it to itself, and showed that it was the same."[157] These luminous visions/
manifestations connect the Ignatius at Rome in 1544–45 with the pilgrim at Manresa in 1521–22.

On Friday, March 7, as Ignatius began saying the Mass of the Most
Holy Trinity, he experienced "a new sensation, a fresh and greater
devotion, and a desire to weep" by placing himself in a midpoint
between the Trinity "above" (*arriba*) and the letters on the page of
the missal below him (No. 127).[158] He says that this midway situation increased his devotion and tears, and "I had an increasing affective awe and reverence [*acatamiento y reverencia*] for the visions from
above" (No. 128). The divine visitations that followed terminated now
in the Trinity, now in the Father, now in the Son, now in Our Lady,
and now even in some of the saints (No. 129). From this point on,
Ignatius continued to have visions of the divine essence, usually as
a luminous sphere (Nos. 136, 142, 143).[159] Another important notice
comes from March 9, when he says that his "new devotion and motions
toward weeping" terminate sometimes in the Trinity, sometimes in
Jesus, sometimes in both, but in such a way "that the termination in
Jesus did not diminish devotion to the Holy Trinity and vice versa"
(No. 138). In other words, Ignatius now sees Jesus within the Trinity
and the Trinity within Jesus.

Despite all these manifestations, Ignatius was still not able to make
or confirm his election about poverty, so his troubled mind reacted

even against Jesus. On March 12 he was unable to enjoy his meditations on the Trinity, feeling far away from the Three Persons. He says,
"Instead thoughts came to me sometimes against Jesus, sometimes
against another."[160] Ignatius recognized his own confusion (No. 146),
which seems to have been the final sign of his awareness that it is God,
not Ignatius, who will make the decision, because the election then
rapidly moved to its conclusion (Nos. 146–53). On March 12 he finally
writes the entry "Finished" (*finido*). The long struggle was over.

The unusual aspects of part I of the *Spiritual Diary* are, if anything,
enhanced by a look at part II. Having made his election, Ignatius's
record of the mystical gifts he received from March 13, 1544, to February 27, 1545, switches gears. There is a restricted role for the Persons of the Trinity, as well as Jesus and Mary. Some visions of the
divine essence continue, and they sometimes lead to reflections on the
Three Persons. These notes, extensive only at the start (Nos. 154–240),
emphasize charismatic gifts, above all constant tears. In general, Ignatius's vocabulary for his mystical gifts remains fairly constant through
both parts of the *Spiritual Diary*. Along with the omnipresent *lagrimas*,
we have frequent use of *devoción*, *visiones*, *vistaciones* (often described
as *interna*), *sentimiento* and *inteligencias*. The frequent appeal to *ardor/
calor* has already been mentioned, and there are also references to tasting and sweetness—*gozo espiritual* and *dulzura interior*. There are, however, two forms of language and spiritual experiences largely absent in
part I that come to dominate part II.

The first of these is what Ignatius calls *loquela*, internal or external
words from God, which were also to be important for Teresa of Avila,
although Ignatius, unlike Teresa, never tells us about the content of any
of these mystical communications. Something like a *loquela* appears
only once in part I (No. 69) and is not named as such, but *loquelas*
are frequent in part II.[161] The *loquela* can be both interior sounds and
exterior. On Sunday, May 11, Ignatius writes, "I had tears before Mass
and during Mass too, continuous tears in great abundance." He goes
on, "Along with them was an interior *loquela* of the Mass, which to a
still greater extent seemed to be given by God. On that same day I had
asked for it, because during the entire week I had sometimes found the
exterior *loquela* and sometimes not."[162] Ignatius continues his reflections, noting that the *loquelas* of this Sunday were different from the
ones received during the week, "[f]or they came so slowly, interiorly,
gently, and without noise or great motions that they seemed to arise
so entirely from within that I do not know how to explain the matter."[163] The interior *loquelas*, which bring the soul a great harmony, are

compared with heavenly music (No. 224). *Loquelas* seem to consist of both a musical tone and words, as we are told in the notice for May 22. During Mass that day Ignatius experienced much *loquela* but no tears, which led him to wonder if the *loquela* could be a diabolical temptation. "I thought I might be taking too much pleasure in the tone or sound of the *loquela* and was not paying enough attention to the meaning of the words. Immediately many tears flowed and I thought I was being taught about the procedure I ought to follow."[164]

Reflections on the *loquela* are also found in a letter Ignatius sent to Teresa Rejadell in 1536. Here he says that such inner speaking is irresistible: "He [God] begins by enlightening the soul; that is to say, by speaking interiorly to it without the din of words, lifting it up wholly to his divine love and ourselves to his meaning without any possibility of resistance on our part, even if we should wish to resist." This sounds much like what the *Exercises* call a consolation without prior cause. Nevertheless, after "such consolation or inspiration, when the soul is still abiding in its joy, the enemy tries under the impetus of this joy to make us innocently add something to what we have received from God. . . . His only purpose is to disturb and to confuse us in everything."[165] The devil is always active in trying to undermine the spiritual/mystical life for Ignatius.

A second form of new mystical experience appears in the oft-used formula *acatamiento y reverencia* to describe Ignatius's reaction to the reception of mystical graces.[166] *Acatamiento* appears rarely in part I (only in Nos. 83, 103, 128), but it occurs thirty times or more in part II, often in tandem with *reverencia*. The word has puzzled the translators. George Ganss argues for "affectionate awe" as a translation, while Antonio de Nicolas prefers "respectful surrender."[167] Ignatius says that it is difficult to ascertain if *acatamiento* comes from ourselves or is a pure gift from God, that is, a consolation without cause. On Sunday, March 14, shortly after having made the election for poverty, Ignatius receives tears but no visions. "During all these times, before, during, and after Mass, I had a steady thought which penetrated to the depth of my soul: How great is the *reverencia y acatamiento* with which I ought to pronounce the name of God our Lord, and so on; and further that I ought to seek, not tears, but this *acatamiento y reverencia*" (No. 156). During Mass he fixes his attention on *acatamiento* to the exclusion of other gifts. "I thought that neither I nor anything of mine brought on this *acatamiento* which kept on increasing my devotion and tears. As a result, I became convinced that this was the path which the Lord was seeking to point out to me" (No. 157).[168] The importance of *acatamiento* is enhanced in No. 160, where Ignatius says that he has learned to attend to *acatamiento* first and then tears and visitations will follow, whereas the opposite procedure (i.e., visitations first) is wrong. In other words, spiritual gifts should not be sought before the feeling of absolute surrender or loving awe before God.

Acatamiento is put in the context of other terms representing Ignatius's new spiritual peace of soul after the rigors of the election decision. Particularly revealing is the notation for Sunday, March 30, Passion Sunday. Here Ignatius summarizes his attitude before, during, and after Mass:

> During this period of time I kept on thinking that humility, reverence, and *acatamiento* ought to be not fearful but loving. This thought took root in my mind so deeply that I begged over and over again: "Give me loving humility [*humildad amorosa*], and with it reverence and *acatamiento*." After these words, I received new visitations. Moreover, I repulsed tears in order to attend to this *humildad amorosa*.[169]

Shortly after this passage, Ignatius introduces an important distinction about two forms of *acatamiento*: "When we do not find reverence or *acatamiento amoroso*, we ought to seek *acatamiento temero*, considering our own faults. Our objective is to attain the loving kind."[170] Thus, *acatamiento* serves as a basic attitude in the life of the devout Christian, and, like the gift of compunction (with which it may be compared), it comes in two varieties, what Gregory the Great called the compunction of fear and the higher compunction of love.[171]

Conclusion

This chapter has tried to demonstrate the truth of the remark of Harvey D. Egan that "to miss Ignatius the *mystic* is to miss his heart and soul."[172] The balance sheet of this analysis of the mysticism of Ignatius Loyola, however, leaves us with both some important conclusions and some questions. Ignatius was certainly gifted with unusual forms of direct contact with God, though many of these do not easily fit into the customary mystical categories. To attempt to measure his experience of God by the later systems created on the basis of the Spanish Carmelite mystics (as was often done in the past) makes little sense, because it loses sight of his distinctiveness. Ignatius does not have a developed teaching on contemplation, although later Jesuits were not loath to create one. He was unusual in not using nuptial or erotic themes. He had deep experiences of the Trinity and a powerful identification with

Christ,[173] but he rarely spoke of this in terms of union.[174] His visions are unusual; his constant gift of tears is surprising. His *loquelas* are fascinating, but, in contrast to Teresa of Avila, it is not clear how they functioned in his life. Ignatius is in some senses a troubling mystic—one so distinctive in relation to many traditions of Christian mysticism that he is difficult to place. What is not in question, however, is his major contribution to the history of mysticism, especially as seen in his insistence that deep encounter with God is not an end in itself but should always be a spur to apostolic commitment, service for the good of the church.

Ignatius, of course, was not alone in making such a claim. Many late medieval and early modern mystics broke with the traditional distinction between the active and the contemplative lives to pioneer new ways of living a mysticism of service. Ignatius, however, was special in linking his view of apostolic mysticism to a program of spiritual training (i.e., the *Spiritual Exercises*), to an institution, the Society of Jesus, and to the service of the papacy. This, it can be argued, is the root of the reason that the Jesuits have had such a significant impact on the history of Catholic spirituality and mysticism for centuries. If the inner mystical consciousness that empowered Ignatius to create what he did was sometimes forgotten in later Jesuit disputes about how far the members of the Society were allowed to engage in contemplative prayer, there is no question that Ignatius himself was always a contemplative in action. His inner sense of God's presence in his life was the source for his external life of apostolic witness to the "greater glory of God," as well as to the transformative effect of "ever greater love."

Notes

1. This chapter will concentrate on Ignatius, not on the early Jesuits in general. For a sketch of how Ignatius's spirituality was received and sometimes altered by his contemporaries and followers, see John O'Malley, "Early Jesuit Spirituality: Spain and Italy," in *Christian Spirituality: Post-Reformation and Modern*, ed. Louis Dupré and Don E. Saliers, in collaboration with John Meyendorff, World Spirituality 18 (New York: Crossroad, 1989), 3–27.

2. Ignatius's writings and those of his contemporaries about him have been critically edited in the sections of the vast *Monumenta historica societatis Jesu* devoted to Jesuit sources (1894–). The *Monumenta Ignatiana* (hereafter MI) consist of four subseries: Series I, *S. Ignatii . . . Epistolae et Instructiones*, 12 vols. (Madrid: G. López del Hornoo, 1903–11); Series II, the *Exercitia spiritualia* and the *Directoria exercitiorum spiritualium (1540–1599)*, 2 vols. (Rome: Institutum Historicum Societatis Jesu, 1955–69); Series III, the *Constitutiones et Regulae Societatis Jesu*, 4 vols. (Rome, 1934–48); and Series IV, the *Fontes narrativi de S. Ignatio et de Societatis Jesu*

initiis, 4 vols. (hereafter FN) (Rome, 1943–60). There is a convenient edition of his Spanish writings, not including the letters, in Ignacio Iparraguirre and Cándido de Dalmases, eds., *Obras completas de San Ignacio de Loyola*, 4th ed. (Madrid: Biblioteca de Autores Cristianos, 1982). There are many translations, none complete. In most cases I will use the collection of George E. Ganss et al., *Ignatius of Loyola: The Spiritual Exercises and Selected Works*, Classics of Western Spirituality (New York: Paulist Press, 1991), but I will alert the reader when different versions are being used. I will not cite the Spanish of the critical text except where it seems warranted. Another useful collection is Joseph A. Munitiz and Philip Endean, eds., *Saint Ignatius of Loyola: Personal Writings*, Penguin Classics (London: Penguin, 1996). For the current state of research on Ignatius, see the essays and bibliography in Robert Aleksander Maryks, ed., *A Companion to Ignatius of Loyola: Life, Writings, Spirituality, Influence*, Brill's Companions to the Christian Tradition (Leiden: Brill, 2014).

3. For a summary of the "new Ignatius" and the effect this has had on contemporary Jesuits, see Joseph Veale, "Dominant Orthodoxies," *Milltown Studies* 30 (1992): 43–65. The majority of writings about Ignatius have come from his fellow Jesuits, but others have also taken interest in him; see, e.g., the semiotic analysis of Roland Barthes, *Sade, Fourier, Loyola* (New York: Hill & Wang, 1976).

4. On Ignatius and reform, see John W. O'Malley, "Was Ignatius Loyola a Church Reformer? How to Look at Early Modern Catholicism," *Catholic Historical Review* 77 (1991): 177–93.

5. A good picture of Ignatius's character, including some of his less attractive features, appears in the reminiscences of 1554–55 written down and later expanded on by the Portuguese Jesuit Luís Gonçalves da Câmara, available in English as *Remembering Iñigo: Glimpses of the Life of Saint Ignatius of Loyola. The Memoriale of Luís Gonçalves da Câmara*, trans. Alexander Eaglestone and Joseph A. Munitiz, S.J. (St. Louis: Institute of Jesuit Sources, 2004). Da Câmara notes, "Our Father is accustomed to cooperate very closely with natural inclination, *velut* [as it were] concurring with them, i.e., as far as possible he never deals violently with anyone" (p. 68).

6. The turn toward the mystical Ignatius began in the 1930s, especially after the publication of the full text of the *Spiritual Diary*. There were two Jesuit initiators. The first was Joseph de Guibert, "Mystique Ignatienne: A propos du 'Journal spirituel' de S. Ignace de Loyola," *Revue d'ascétique et de la mystique* 19 (1938): 3–22, 113–40, a study later incorporated in his posthumous *La spiritualité de la Compagnie de Jésus: Esquisse historique*, ed. and trans. George E. Ganss (Rome: Institutum Historicum Societatis Jesu, 1953), chap. 1; translated by William J. Young as *The Jesuits: Their Spiritual Doctrine and Practice. A Historical Study* (Chicago: Institute of Jesuit Sources, 1964), also chap. 1. The second figure was Hugo Rahner (1900–1968), who published "Die Mystik des hl. Ignatius und der Inhalt der Vision von La Storta," *Zeitschrift für Aszese und Mystik* 10 (1935): 202–20. H. Rahner was later to summarize his view of Ignatius the mystic in a number of books, especially *Ignatius the Theologian* (New York: Herder & Herder, 1968), and *The Spirituality of St. Ignatius Loyola: An Account of Its Historical Development* (1953; repr., Chicago: Loyola University Press, 1980). Among the many accounts of Ignatius's mysticism, see Adolf Haas, "The Mysticism of St. Ignatius according to His *Spiritual Diary*," in *Ignatius of Loyola: His Personality and Spiritual Heritage, 1556–1956. Studies on*

the 400th Anniversary of His Death, ed. Friedrich Wulf (St. Louis: Institute of Jesuit Sources, 1977), 164–99; Karl Rahner, "The Logic of Concrete Individual Knowledge in Ignatius of Loyola," in *The Dynamic Element in the Church*, Quaestiones disputatae 12 (New York: Herder & Herder, 1964), 84–170; and "The Ignatian Mysticism of Joy in the World," in *Theological Investigations*, vol. 3 (Baltimore: Helicon, 1967), 277–93; Harvey D. Egan, *Ignatius Loyola the Mystic*, Way of Christian Mystics (Collegeville, MN: Liturgical Press, 1987); and Phylis Zagano, "The Ignatian Mystic," in *The Renewal of Mystical Theology: Essays in Memory of John N. Jones*, ed. Bernard McGinn (New York: Crossroad-Herder, 2017), 109–30. In addition, many papers in the series *Studies in the Spirituality of Jesuits* (St. Louis: Seminar on Jesuit Spirituality, 1969–) are helpful.

7. John W. O'Malley, *The First Jesuits* (Cambridge, MA: Harvard University Press, 1993), 19; see also 83, 373. O'Malley makes a similar point in "Early Jesuit Spirituality," 11: "For Loyola the central issue was right living and loving, based on general spirituality in which certain affectivities were fostered and sustained."

8. The new picture of Ignatius has been somewhat humorously expressed by two Jesuits who wrote addresses to their fellow Jesuits *in persona Ignatii*; see Karl Rahner, *Ignatius of Loyola Speaks* (South Bend, IN: St. Augustine's Press, 2013); and Joseph Veale, "Saint Ignatius Speaks about Ignatian Prayer," *Studies in the Spirituality of Jesuits* 28/2 (March 1996); and "Saint Ignatius Asks: Are You Sure You Know Who I Am?," *Studies in the Spirituality of Jesuits* 33/4 (September 2001).

9. Da Câmara, *Remembering Iñigo . . . The Memoriale*, 149.

10. The earliest published life of Ignatius, by Pedro de Ribadeneira, *Vita Ignatii Loyolae* (1572) is quite hagiographical. The early lives and reminiscences are available in FN 1 and 2.

11. Describing Ignatius's mysticism as a "mysticism of service" or, more precisely, as a "mysticism of apostolic service," is, of course, by no means new. De Guibert used the same terms in his 1938 essay, as well as in his 1942 book. It has also been picked up by many later scholars, e.g., H. Rahner, H. Egan, J. O'Malley, P. Zagano, and others.

12. H. Rahner, *Spirituality of St. Ignatius Loyola*, 44–45.

13. Quotation from Ganss, *Ignatius of Loyola: The Spiritual Exercises and Selected Works*, 283–84. On the importance of the shift to the model of the apostolic laborer in the later writings of Ignatius, see J. Peter Schineller, "The Pilgrim Journey of Ignatius: From Soldier to Laborer in the Lord's Vineyard and Its Implications for Apostolic Lay Spirituality," *Studies in the Spirituality of Jesuits* 31/4 (September 1999).

14. Biographies of Ignatius are many and few are short. One classic is José Ignacio Tellechea Idígoras, *Ignatius of Loyola: The Pilgrim Saint*, ed. and trans. Michael Buckley (Chicago: Loyola University Press, 1994; Spanish original, 1987).

15. We know enough about Iñigo's family and early life (especially through the *Acta*) to tempt psychoanalytic study, such as that found in W. W. Meissner, *Saint Ignatius of Loyola: The Psychology of a Saint* (New Haven: Yale University Press, 1992). Meissner regards his psychoanalytic account of Ignatius's "phallic narcissism" as "reductive but not reductionistic" (p. xxvi), and he insists that his interpretation is only hypothetical.

16. Meissner reflects on this event: "The meeting between Iñigo and the French cannonball was one of those remarkable events in which the course of

history reaches into the lives of men and steers them toward an unseen but determined destiny" (*Ignatius of Loyola*, 37).

17. The details of Ignatius's early life, especially his conversion while recuperating at Loyola, are known to us largely through the *Acta* 1–12 (Ganss, 68–73).

18. Both books had an important impact on Ignatius. As has been pointed out (e.g., Ganss, "Introduction," 19–26), Ignatius's use of meditations on the events of Christ's life in the *Spiritual Exercises* is in many ways based on the imaginative presentations of the life of Christ found in Ludolph's *Vita Christi*. Furthermore, Ignatius's spirituality maintained a strong role for mediatorial figures in approaching God, the saints, and especially Mary, as seen in the *Golden Legend*. Of course, for Ignatius, Jesus Christ is always the ultimate Mediator to the Father. Ignatius also knew and loved *The Imitation of Christ*, which he ascribed to Jean Gerson, but it is unclear when he first read it.

19. *Acta* 6 (Ganss, 70). The critical edition of the *Acta* is *Acta Patris Ignatii scripta a P. Lud. Gonzalez de Camara* in FN 1:354–507.

20. *Acta* 8 (Ganss, 71). More on Ignatius's developing skills at discernment can be found in *Acta* 25–27 and 31. It was at this time that the Basque began his lifelong habit of writing down ideas that came to him from his reading and from his inner observations—the origin of the *Spiritual Exercises*, as well as the later *Spiritual Diary*.

21. The term "the pilgrim" (*el peregrino*) first occurs in *Acta* 15 as Iñigo is on the road to Montserrat and is used some sixty times in the remainder of the text. In contrast "soldier of Christ" occurs only once (*Acta* 21).

22. *Acta* 45. The desire to work to help others becomes a major theme in the rest of the *Acta*; see, e.g., 50, 54, 64, 70–71, and 85.

23. I owe this observation to Harvey D. Egan with thanks.

24. *Acta* 57. *Acta* 67 (Ganss, 97) is important for its information that the *Spiritual Exercises* already existed in a text form of some kind: "The bachelor Frías came to examine each of them separately [in jail at Salamanca], and the pilgrim gave him all his papers, which were the Exercises, to be examined." See also *Acta* 86.

25. Hugo Rahner has a good discussion of the similarities and key differences between the message of Ignatius and that of the *Alumbrados* (*Ignatius the Theologian*, 157–64). His brother, Karl Rahner, goes further when he states: "[I]t will not be misleading not to exclude on principle from the start a certain similarity of outlook between them [i.e., the *Alumbrados*] and Ignatius, that is to say the conviction that there is a real guidance by the Holy Spirit. There is no need to fear an uncontrollable mysticism and Illuminism on that account" ("Individual Knowledge in Ignatius Loyola," 93–94).

26. See Terence O'Reilly, "Melchor Cano and the Spirituality of St. Ignatius Loyola," in O'Reilly, *From Ignatius Loyola to John of the Cross*, essay 4.

27. Besides Francis Xavier, the other companions who joined Ignatius in Paris were Peter Faber, Simon Rodriguez, Diego Laínez, Alfonso Salmerón, and Nicolas Bobadilla.

28. *Acta* 96 (Ganss, 109). This part of the *Acta* was taken down in Italian because da Câmara had no Spanish scribe at hand. The text is as follows: "Et essendo un giorno, alcune miglia prima che arrivasse a Roma, in una chiesa, et facendo oratione, ha sentita tal mutazione nell'anima sua, et ha visto tanto chiara-

mente che Iddio Padre lo metteva con Cristo, suo figliuolo, che non gli basterebbe l'animo di dubitare di questo, senonchè Iddio Padre lo mettava col suo figliuolo" (FN 1:496–98).

29. Laínez's account can be found in FN 2:133 (translated in Ganss, 42). It was at this time that Ignatius decided that the group was to be called the "Society of Jesus" (*Compañia de Jesús/Societas Jesu*). For an analysis of the vision, see H. Rahner (see n. 6 above); and Theodore Baumann, "Die Berichte über die Vision des heiligen Ignatius bei La Storta," *Archivum Historicum Societatis Jesu* 27 (1958): 181–208.

30. F. Charmot, *L'union au Christ dans l'action selon saint Ignace* (Paris: Bonne Presse, 1959), 139.

31. *Acta* 99 (Ganss, 111).

32. *Acta* 100 (Ganss, 111).

33. For this incident and the sources relating to it, see Ganss, "Introduction," 44–45.

34. I use the translation in Ganss, "Introduction," 45.

35. The best account is O'Malley, *First Jesuits*.

36. This point is argued by Pierre-Antoine Fabre, "The Writings of Ignatius of Loyola as Seminal Text," in Maryks, *Companion to Ignatius of Loyola*, 103–22.

37. There is a translation and study by George E. Ganss, *Saint Ignatius of Loyola, The Constitutions of the Society of Jesus* (St. Louis: Institute for Jesuit Sources, 1970).

38. For a study and translation of the "Deliberation on Poverty," see Ganss, *Ignatius of Loyola*, 217–28.

39. The apostolic poverty of the Society of Jesus is treated in part VI, chap. 2 of the *Constitutions* (Ganss, 251–59).

40. The edition I will use is *Ejercicios Espirituales: Comentario pastoral*, ed. Luis González and Ignacio Iparraguirre (Madrid: Biblioteca de Autores Cristianos, 1965). I will generally follow the translation of George Ganss, but I have consulted other English versions (J. Morris, L. Puhl, J. Munitiz-P. Endean) and will occasionally adjust the Ganss versions. There is a huge literature on the *Exercises*. Two helpful introductions are Terence O'Reilly, "The Spiritual Exercises and the Crisis of Medieval Piety," in O'Reilly, *From Ignatius of Loyola to John of the Cross*, essay VI; and Philip Endean, "The Spiritual Exercises," in *The Cambridge Companion to the Jesuits*, ed. Thomas Worchester, Cambridge Companions to Religion (Cambridge: Cambridge University Press, 2008), 52–67. Another classic short account is de Guibert, *The Jesuits: Their Spiritual Doctrine and Practice*, chap. 3 (109–39).

41. Pierre Hadot, *Philosophy as a Way of Life: Spiritual Exercises from Socrates to Foucault* (Oxford: Blackwell, 1995).

42. Reflections on the contemporary giving of the *Exercises* can be found in Philip Sheldrake, ed., *The Way of Ignatius Loyola: Contemporary Approaches to the Spiritual Exercises* (St. Louis: Institute of Jesuit Sources, 1991). See also William Reiser, "The *Spiritual Exercises* in a Religiously Pluralistic World," *Studies in Spirituality* 10 (2010): 135–57.

43. It is worth citing J. de Guibert on this point: "The multiplication of minute directions and precise methods is what generally strikes readers who take up the *Exercises* before they have actually made them. These readers get the impression of a veritable spiritual pillory . . . under which, it seems, a true prayer life could never develop. But one who, on the contrary, had made the *Exercises* in their fullness under an experienced guide generally carries away from them an impres-

sion of a broad and consoling liberty of soul, and often too the feeling of having grasped for the first time what true intimacy with Christ really is" (*Jesuits: Their Spiritual Doctrine*, 132).

44. Endean, "Spiritual Exercises," 65.

45. Jules J. Toner, *Discerning God's Will: Ignatius of Loyola's Teaching on Christian Decision Making* (St. Louis: Institute of Jesuit Sources, 1991), 6. Toner studies some of the divergences in detail on 236–42.

46. On this debate, see de Guibert, *Jesuits: Their Spiritual Doctrine*, 122–28; and Ganss, *Ignatius of Loyola*, 389–90 n. 11.

47. This is a factor in the problems of some earlier writings on the mysticism of Ignatius, which insisted, for example, that his descriptions of consolations were examples of "infused contemplation," such as one finds in Teresa of Avila and John of the Cross. Ignatius knows nothing of this terminology, which does not appear in Teresa, although the language of infusion is found a few times in John.

48. *Spiritual Exercises* 1 (Ganss, 121, adapted).

49. Reiser notes among his five limitations of the outlook of the *Exercises* the fact that "Ignatius tends to focus salvation in terms of the individual alone before God" ("*Spiritual Exercises* in a Religiously Pluralistic World," 148–49).

50. *Exercises* 2 (*Ejercicios*, 5): ". . . porque no el mucho saber harta y satisface al anima, mas el sentir y gustar de las cosas internamente" (Ganss, 121, adapted). See also *Exercises* 3.

51. *Exercises* 15 (Ganss, 125).

52. *Exercises* 16 (Ganss, 126). This is the first entry of the theme of "giving God glory," which was so central to Ignatius. See also *Exercises* 23, 152, 155, 167, 179, 183, 185, 189, 339, 351, 369, etc.

53. On the role of the "Principle and Foundation" and its influence on the *Constitutions*, see Sunny Kokkaravalayil, "The Principle and Foundation of the *Spiritual Exercises* of St. Ignatius of Loyola and the Jesuit Constitution," *Studies in Spirituality* 18 (2008): 229–44.

54. *Indiferencia* is one of the key concepts in Ignatius's spiritual vocabulary. It does not mean "unconcerned" or "uninterested" but rather being free from disordered attachments centered on our own pleasure or self-interest, or being open to letting God act in us. Thus, it is not unlike Eckhart's view of "detachment." For more on *indiferencia*, see *Exercises* 155, 157, 166–67, and 179. See also the remarks of David Marno, "Attention and Indifference in Ignatius's *Spiritual Exercises*," in Maryks, *Companion to Ignatius of Loyola*, 234–36.

55. *Exercises* 23 (Ganss, 130). Stress on the purpose of human life as the goal controlling elections is also found in *Exercises* 46, 169, 177, 178, and 185.

56. Ignatius merely says *Examen particular y cotidiano* and *Examen general*, but the translators invariably add "of conscience." Here Ignatius is tapping into a long spiritual tradition, on which see the multiauthor articles "Examen de conscience," and "Examen particular," DS 4:1789–1849.

57. Ignatius often uses *meditación* and *contemplación* interchangeably (e.g., *Exercises* 2, 49, 74–77, 261, etc.). Some texts (e.g., *Exercises* 91, 101–10, 118, 209, 230, 249) seem to suggest a distinction between a lower discursive *contemplación* that is the equivalent of *meditación*, and a higher *contemplación* that leads to nondiscursive prayer, but Ignatius is not clear on this.

58. See Harvey D. Egan, "Affirmative Way," in *The New Dictionary of Catholic Spirituality*, ed. Michael Downey (Collegeville, MN: Liturgical Press, 1993), 16–17.

59. See George Aschenbrenner, "Consciousness Examen," *Review for Religious* 31 (1972): 13–21.

60. Barthes, *Sade, Fourier, Loyola*, 70–71.

61. Toner notes this problem (*Discerning God's Will*, 155).

62. *Exercises* 47 (Ganss, 136). On this statement, see Walter J. Ong, "St. Ignatius' Prison-Cage and the Existentialist Situation," in Ong, *The Barbarian Within and Other Fugitive Essays and Studies* (New York: Macmillan, 1954), 242–59.

63. Ignatius's use of the traditional triad of powers of the soul (memory–understanding–will) appears throughout the *Exercises* but not in any technical way (e.g., *Exercises* 45, 50–52, 56–60, 246, etc.).

64. It is interesting to reflect that twenty years later Teresa of Avila considered prayer to be nothing other than conversation with Christ as a friend (see *Life* 8).

65. These *repeticiones* (e.g., Nos. 62, 118, 120, etc.) are to be understood not as mere repeating but as "re-seeking," or "deeper investigations" (Endean, "Spiritual Exercises," 56).

66. The process of articulation here has been seen by Barthes as essential to the *Exercises*: "Whoever reads the *Exercises* sees at first glance that the material is subjected to an incessant, painstaking, and almost obsessive separation; or, more exactly, the *Exercises* is this separation itself, to which nothing is pre-existent: everything is immediately divided, subdivided, classified, numbered off in annotations, meditations, Weeks, points, exercises, mysteries, etc." (*Sade, Fourier, Loyola*, 52; see the whole section from 52 to 58).

67. For the use of the imaginative senses in the Meditations on the life of Christ, see, e.g., *Exercises* 121–25, 159, 226, etc. Ignatius's teaching on the application of the senses and its relation to the tradition of the "spiritual senses" has been treated by H. Rahner, *Ignatius the Theologian*, chap. 5 (181–213), who argues for a mystical interpretation of this aspect of the *Exercises*.

68. Louis J. Puhl argues against placing this Meditation in Week Two (*The Spiritual Exercises of St. Ignatius: Based on Studies in the Language of the Autograph* [Chicago: Loyola University Press, 1951], 177–78).

69. On the Christology of the *Exercises*, see esp. H. Rahner, *Ignatius the Theologian*, chap. 3 (53–135); and Egan, *Ignatius Loyola the Mystic*, chap. 4 (86–118). In *The Spirituality of St. Ignatius Loyola* (37–38), H. Rahner argues for a christological influence in the First Week.

70. K. Rahner, *Ignatius of Loyola Speaks*, 25.

71. The military implications of this section are obvious, but military images and language are actually rather rare in the *Exercises* (e.g., *Exercises* 74, 136–48).

72. The need for "acting against the self (i.e., the selfish self)" is a major theme in the *Exercises*; see, e.g., 13, 97, 325, 350–51, etc.

73. In the meditations on the mysteries of Christ's life, the First Prelude becomes a review of the *historia*, that is, the biblical narrative, while the Second Prelude is the "composition of place," and the Third is the accustomed asking for what one seeks.

74. *Exercises* 98; on imitating Christ, see also 109, 139, 147, 167, 248, 344, etc.

75. At this point the *Spiritual Exercises* introduce a "Consideration on States

of Life" (No. 135), a topic that really seems to belong to the later section on the election. It is worth noting, however, that here Ignatius insists that "we can come to perfection in whatsoever state of life God our Lord may grant us to elect" (Ganss, 154).

76. For a summary, see H. Rahner, *Spirituality of St. Ignatius of Loyola*, 40–45.

77. Always desiring and trying "to do what is better" is another key feature of Ignatius's spirituality; see *Exercises* 23, here at 149, as well as 152, 155, 170–89, etc.

78. H. Rahner, *Spirituality of St. Ignatius Loyola*, xii: "love . . . is characterized by a word distinctive of Ignatius's whole nature, the word 'more' (*magis*); love which wants to do ever 'more and more,' which is essentially limitless, always open as it were to promptness in the service of God and willingness to become like to Christ." This theme was taken up in an essay by Hugo's brother Karl, "Being Open to God as Ever Greater," in *Theological Investigations*, vol. 7, *Further Theology of the Spiritual Life* (New York: Herder & Herder, 1971), 25–46.

79. *Exercises* 155 (Ganss, 157).

80. *Exercises* 158–64. The fact that the Second Week has twelve days shows that these exercises are not meant to be taken literally, because "the number of contemplations can be increased or lessened" according to what fits the exercitant (No. 162).

81. To be sure, Ignatius thinks that one can make an election about many decisions, such as whether the Jesuits should adopt apostolic poverty, but these choices are made in relation to the fundamental option that is the purpose of the *Spiritual Exercises*, that is, the decision to live a life of serving and praising God and saving one's soul (No. 169).

82. On the question of making an election, see Egan, *Ignatius Loyola the Mystic*, 149–55; and H. Rahner, *Ignatius the Theologian*, 125–30. K. Rahner's essay "The Logic of Concrete Individual Knowledge in Ignatius Loyola" features a dense analysis of Ignatius's view of election in terms of Rahner's theology of the universal action of grace (89–114 and 156–69). In a shorter and less complex essay ("The Immediate Experience of God in the Spiritual Exercises of Saint Ignatius of Loyola," in *Karl Rahner in Dialogue: Conversations and Interviews, 1965–1982*, ed. Paul Imhof and Hubert Biallowons [New York: Crossroad, 1986], 174–81), Rahner insists that the *Exercises* are designed to provide an immediate mystical experience of God. A detailed study of the disputes regarding the forms of election is found in Toner, *Discerning God's Will*, chap. 13.

83. The language of *consolaciones* and *desolaciones* may be somewhat strange to contemporary readers—*consolaciones* are attractions to God, while *desolaciones* are basically negative feelings, or repulsions, from God and holy things. *Consolación* is a broad term for Ignatius, as can be seen from *Exercises* 316. Once again, for Ignatius, these attractions and repulsions come not from us but from the actions of good and bad spirits on us.

84. Ignatius speaks of the three elections in terms of *tres tiempos* (No. 175), and then discusses *dos modos*, or two ways, "for making an election in this third time" (Nos. 178, 184). Nevertheless, many commentators persist in talking about the "three times" as "three modes," which is often confusing in relation to the "two modes" of the third "time" of election.

85. The general rules for discerning God's will are found in *Spiritual Exercises*

169–89, but Ignatius obviously has in mind also the later specific rules for the discerning of the difference between motions from good and from evil spirits that he sets out in *Exercises* 313–36. This once again points to the fact that the *Exercises* were not meant to be read, but rather to be used by a director who knew the whole process.

86. *Exercises* 184 (Ganss, 164); see also 237, 338. The phrase *de arriba* is an essential aspect of the teaching of Ignatius, as shown by H. Rahner, *Ignatius the Theologian*, 3–10.

87. Toner, *Discerning God's Will* (chap. 13, and appendix A) answers yes to all three questions and thereby takes a stance against many modern interpreters, such as K. Rahner and H. Egan.

88. The growing identification with Christ in the *Exercises* is obviously a form of union, but Ignatius does not talk much about "union" or analyze different kinds. This has not prevented later Jesuit commentators from making union a central category for treating Ignatius and the *Exercises*; see, e.g., Charmot, *L'union au Christ selon saint Ignace*.

89. It was only in the *Directories*, especially the official *Directory* of 1599, that Ignatius's distinctive spiritual path was explained in terms of the usual triple itinerary.

90. God's presence in all things is a constant motif in all Ignatius's writings and also appears in *Exercises* 39 and 229. For other texts, see Ganss, 419 n. 113. For a study, see K. Rahner, "Ignatian Mysticism of Joy in the World," esp. 288–92.

91. K. Rahner, "Ignatian Mysticism of Joy in the World," 290.

92. For general background, see the multiauthor article "Discernement des esprits," DS 4:1222–91; and Mark A. McIntosh, *Discernment and Truth: The Spirituality and Theology of Knowledge* (New York: Crossroad, 2004), who treats Ignatius on 67–73.

93. On Ignatian teaching on the discernment of spirits and its relation to earlier traditions, see H. Rahner, *Ignatius the Theologian*, chap. 4 (136–80). Brief accounts of Ignatian discernment can be found in Egan, *Ignatius Loyola the Mystic*, 146–70; Michael Buckley, "The Structure of the Rules for Discernment," in Sheldrake, *Way of Ignatius Loyola*, 219–37, especially on the structural dynamics of the rules; and Susan E. Schreiner, *Are You Alone Wise? The Search for Certainty in the Early Modern Era*, Oxford Studies in Historical Theology (New York: Oxford University Press, 2011), 270–85. Longer accounts include Jules J. Toner, *A Commentary on Saint Ignatius' Rules for the Discernment of Spirits: A Guide to the Principles and Practice* (St. Louis: Institute of Jesuit Sources, 1982), and *Discerning God's Will*. See also Timothy M. Gallagher, *The Discernment of Spirits: An Ignatian Guide to Everyday Living* (New York: Crossroad, 2005), and *Discerning God's Will: An Ignatian Guide to Decision Making* (New York: Crossroad, 2009). For a Husserlian analysis of Ignatius on discernment, see Joseph T. Papa, *A Phenomenological Analysis of St. Ignatius of Loyola's Rules for the Discernment of Spirits* (Doctoral Dissertation, Pontifical Athenaeum of St. Anselm, 2007).

94. For a discussion of consolations and desolations as affective states of direction, see Buckley, "Structure of the Rules of Discernment," 225–27.

95. The formal opposition is laid down in *Exercises* 329 and expanded upon in 332–35. No. 335 contains the image of the difference between a drop of water

falling on a sponge and on a rock. For those going from good to better, the action of the good angel is like water falling on sponge, while the action of the evil spirit is like water falling on a stone. This is reversed in the case of souls going from bad to worse.

96. See the helpful note in Ganss, 427 n. 142. Ignatius returns to the consolation without cause in *Exercises* 336, emphasizing that while this divine gift cannot be doubted, the exercitant needs to be careful in distinguishing the time of the gift itself from the time immediately after it when one needs to continue to use rational discernment to separate good from bad influences. Although he does not use the term "consolation without prior cause," Ignatius is obviously talking about this mystical gift in the famous letter he wrote to the nun Teresa Rejadell in 1536; see the translation in *Letters of St. Ignatius of Loyola*, selected and translated by William J. Young (Chicago: Loyola University Press, 1959), 18–21, esp. 21–22.

97. *Exercises* 370 (ed. González and Iparraguirre, 127; Ganss, 214): ". . . y salido fácilmente viene al temor filial, que es todo acepto y grato a Dios nuestro Señor, por estar en uno con el amor divino."

98. Among the terms used by Ignatius (not an exhaustive list and giving only a few examples) are *mociones espirituales* (Nos. 5, 182, 313, 316–17); *acatamiento y reverencia* (a combination frequent in the *Spiritual Dairy*; see 39, 114; see further below); *sentimiento espiritual* (62, 193); *conocimiento interno del Señor* (104); *toca* (335); *el sinderese de la razon* (314); *consolación espiritual* (316); *sentido* (352); *internas noticias, consolaciones y divinas inspiraciones* (212); *mociones y gustos espirituales* (227); *gusto y consolación* (252); and, of course, the omnipresent *meditación y contemplación*. Suprisingly little literature has been devoted to Ignatius's spiritual vocabulary. An exception is the study of Henry Pinard de la Boullaye, who shows that, while this range of words signifies affectivity, it is an affectivity under the control of discernment ("Sentir, Sentimiento, Sentido dans le style de Saint Ignace," *Archivum Historicum Societatis Jesu* 25 [1956]: 416–30).

99. O'Reilly, "Spiritual Exercises and the Crisis of Medieval Piety," 110.

100. Moshe Sluhovsky, "Loyola's *Spiritual Exercises* and the Modern Self," in Maryks, *Companion to Ignatius of Loyola*, 230.

101. I will use *Saint Ignatius of Loyola, The Constitutions of the Society of Jesus*, translated with an introduction and a commentary by George E. Ganss (St. Louis: Institute of Jesuit Sources, 1970). The original four parts of the *Constitutions* (General Examen, Declarations on the Examen, Constitutions, Declarations on the Constitutions) are here combined with the "Formula of the Institute of the Society of Jesus" approved by Paul III in 1540, and reapproved by Julius III in 1550. On the rhetorical style of the *Constitutions*, see J. Carlos Copeau, "The Constitutions of the Society of Jesus: The Rhetorical Component," *Studies in Spirituality* 14 (2004): 199–208.

102. Schineller, "Pilgrim Journey of Ignatius."

103. See, e.g., *Constitutions* 2, 5, 144, 243, 308, 338, 573, 603, 622, and 654.

104. On this, see the observations in Zagano, "Ignatian Mystic," 117–18. Also important is Michael Buckley, "Ecclesial Mysticism in the *Exercises*," *Theological Studies* 56 (1995): 441–63.

105. Military images, relatively rare in the *Exercises*, seem to increase in the *Constitutions*; see, e.g., "Formula," 3, 4, and 6; "General Examen," 102; and "Constitutions," 400.

106. Young, *Letters of St. Ignatius of Loyola*, 120–30.

107. *Constitutions* 813 (Ganss, 332).

108. Letter to the Community at Coimbra (January 1548), in Young, *Letters of St. Ignatius of Loyola*, 159.

109. *Constitutions* 260 (Ganss, 158).

110. *Constitutions* 288 (Ganss, 165). Insistence on imitating Christ, so strong in the *Exercises*, also features in the *Constitutions*, e.g., 101–3 (Ganss, 107–9).

111. The expression *in actione contemplativus* was used twice by Nadal in relation to Ignatius in his letters; see *Epistulae et Monumenta Patris H. Nadali*, 6 vols., 4:461 and 5:162. There is a translation of the first passage in Ganss, "Introduction," in *Ignatius of Loyola*, 44. Ignatius reflects the same teaching without using the phrase in one of his letters: "The distracting occupations undertaken for His [God's] greater service in conformity with His divine will can be, not only the equivalent of the union and recollection of uninterrupted contemplation, but even more acceptable, proceeding as they do from a more active and vigorous charity" (MI, Series I, *S. Ignatii Epistolae et Instructiones*, 4:127). This theme has often been written about; a good treatment is Emerich Coreth, "In Actione Contemplativus," *Zeitschrift für katholische Theologie* 76 (1954): 55–82.

112. Marjorie O'Rourke Boyle, *Loyola's Acts: The Rhetoric of the Self*, New Historicism 36 (Berkeley: University of California Press, 1997), xiii, 4–7, 170, etc. While I think Boyle is right about the nature of the text, I do not share many of her particular interpretations.

113. John M. McManamon, *The Text and Contexts of Ignatius Loyola's "Autobiography"* (New York: Fordham University Press, 2013), esp. chap. 4 (99–114).

114. De Guibert, *Jesuits*, 31: "Two things strike us at once [about the visions]: the remarkably great poverty of the imagistic element of these visions, and the contrasting importance and richness of their content."

115. On Ignatius's understanding of the spiritual senses, especially in the *Acta* and *Spiritual Diary*, see Timothy O'Brien, "'Con Ojos Interiores': Ignatius of Loyola and the Spiritual Senses," *Studies in Spirituality* 26 (2016): 263–81.

116. *Acta* 19 (ed. FN 1:390; Ganss, 76).

117. *Acta* 27 (ed. FN 1:400; Ganss, 79).

118. *Acta* 31 (ed. FN 1:406; Ganss, 81).

119. For brief accounts, see Ganss, "Introduction," 28–34; de Guibert, *Jesuits*, 30–32; and, for a psycholanalytic reading of their role in Ignatius's transformation, Meissner, *Ignatius of Loyola*, 80–86.

120. *Acta* 28 (ed. FN 1:402; Ganss, 79–80): "Y estando un día rezando en las gradas del mismo Monasterio las Horas de nuestra Señora, se le empeçó a elevar el entendimiento, como que vía la santísima Trinidad en figura de tres teclas." The Latin version (ed. FN 1:403) expands on the three keys: "quasi Sanctissimam Trinitatem triplicis plectra seu pulsatilis clavicordii tabella specie cerneret." I am not convinced by Boyle's argument (*Loyola's Acts*, 85–93) that the three musical keys (*teclas*) are a mistake for the three sacramental keys (*llaves*) of confession.

121. *Acta* 30 (ed. FN 1:404; Ganss, 80–81, adapted): "Y estando allí sentado se la empeçaron abrir los ojos del entendimiento: y no que viese alguna visión, sino entendiendo y conociendo muchas cosas, tanto de cosas espirituales, como de cosas de la fe y de letras: y esto con una illustración tan grande, que la parecían todas las cosas nuevas." On the illumination at the Cardoner, see Leonardo R.

Silos, "Cardoner in the Life of St. Ignatius," *Archivum Historicum Societatis Jesu* 33 (1964): 3–43. Harvey D. Egan has reminded me of the importance of the note of infused knowledge in this experience.

122. See the *Epistola P. Lainii de P. Ignatio* of June 16, 1547, caput VI.57 in FN 1:140.

123. Other visions and inner illuminations are described in *Acta* 41 (a vision of Christ on the road to Venice), 44 (frequent appearances of Christ as "something round and large, as though it were of gold"), 48 (where he seems to see Christ over him in Jerusalem), 95 (many spiritual visions, consolations, etc.), and 99 (frequent visions of Christ as the sun while in Rome).

124. I will use the edition of Victoriano Larrañaga in *Obras completas de San Ignacio de Loyola* (Madrid: Biblioteca de Autores Cristianos, 1947), 683–792, which has very full notes. Larrañaga, however, uses Ignatius's original, rather confusing numbering system, so I have replaced this with the numbers introduced by most modern editors and translators. There is one full English version, Antonio T. de Nicolás, *Ignatius de Loyola, Powers of Imagining: A Philosophical Hermeneutic of Imagining through the Collected Works of Ignatius de Loyola* (Albany: State University of New York Press, 1986), 189–238, as well as partial translations in Munitiz and Endean, *Saint Ignatius of Loyola: Personal Writings*, 73–109, and Ganss, *Ignatius of Loyola*, 238–70. I will use the Ganss version unless otherwise noted.

125. The first detailed study of the *Spiritual Diary* was J. de Guibert, "Mystique Ignatienne." There is an important essay by Adolf Haas, "The Mysticism of St. Ignatius according to his *Spiritual Diary*," in Wulf, *Ignatius of Loyola: His Personality and Spiritual Heritage, 1556–1996,* 164–99. For summaries, see Ganss, *Ignatius of Loyola*, 229–37; and Egan, *Ignatius Loyola the Mystic*, 67–76 and 87–94.

126. Haas, "Mysticism of St. Ignatius," 165.

127. Ibid., 169.

128. For background, see Pierre Adnès, "Larmes," DS 9:287–303, who considers Ignatius in col. 300. See also Piroska Nagy, *Les don des larmes au Moyen Âge: Un instrument spirituel en quête d'institution (Ve–XIIIe siècle)*, Bibliothèque Albin Michel (Paris: Albin Michel, 2000).

129. For a detailed study of the importance of tears in Ignatius's development, see Michael Plattig, "Vom Trost der Tränen: Ignatius von Loyola und die Gabe der Tränen," *Studies in Spirituality* 2 (1992): 148–99.

130. See the discussion in de Guibert, *Jesuits*, 62–66.

131. *Spiritual Diary* (Ganss, 238).

132. For these passages, see Ganss, 241, 245, 253.

133. In *Spiritual Diary* 107 (ed. Larrañaga, 725–26), Ignatius says he experienced great pain in one eye and thought that he might be in danger of losing his vision due to his tears (see also Nos. 148, 367–69). In Nos. 119 and 136 Ignatius wonders if it might be more pleasing to God if he were deprived of the gift of tears. In subsequent references to *Spiritual Diary*, "ed." refers to the edition of Victoriano Larrañaga (see n. 124 above).

134. This letter can be found in Young, *Letters of St. Ignatius of Loyola*, 179–84 (quotation at 181).

135. This translation is from Young, *Letters of St. Ignatius of Loyola*, 311–12.

136. See McGinn, *Varieties*, 200–201.

137. Plattig, "Vom Trost der Tränen," esp. 181–94.

138. Toner uses the first part of the *Diary* to show how Ignatius combined both the second and third time elections in a four-phase development (Feb. 2–11, Feb. 12–18, Feb. 19–March 11, and March 12) (*Discerning God's Will*, 194–201 and 213–15).

139. Haas, "Mysticism of St. Ignatius," 169–73.

140. Ibid., 172.

141. Ganss, *Ignatius of Loyola*, 232–37. The six stages are (1) considering the pros and cons of the poverty election and offering it to God (Feb. 2–12; Nos. 1–22); (2) repeating the election, offering, and thanksgiving (Feb. 13–18; Nos. 23–44); (3) renewing the offering and giving thanks (Feb. 18–22; Nos. 45–64); (4) gaining clarity through the mediation of Jesus (Feb. 23–March 4; Nos. 65–110); (5) experiencing devotion and making the decision (March 5–12; Nos. 111–53); and finally (6) a record of gratitude for mystical favors (March 13, 1544 to Feb. 27, 1545), which takes up the whole of the second part of the *Diary* (Nos. 154–480).

142. De Guibert, *Jesuits*, 50.

143. Haas seems more interested in having Ignatius's account conform to traditional trinitarian theology than in listening to the nuances of the text.

144. The references to the Trinity are predominantly in the First Part of the *Spiritual Diary* 15–16, 22–23, 39, 42–44, 46, *48*, *50*, 51, *52*, *54–55*, *63*, 64, *67*, 74, 76, *83*, *85*, 87, 88, 89, 93, 94, 98, *101*, 102–9, *110*, 112, *113*, 115, 116, 117, *121–23*, 127, 129, 130, 137, 138, 140, and 153 (the most important texts in italics). In the Second Part, the Trinity is mentioned only in 159, 160, 162, 172, 174, 180, and 183.

145. For the role of the Father, see *Diary* 4, *8*, 19, 24, *27*, 30, 32–35, 38, 63, *72*, 77, 83–84, 102, 113, 115, 140, *142–43*, and 153 (with the most important texts in italics). In part II the Father is found only in 156 and 183.

146. The Son appears in *Diary* 4–5, 27, 33, 72, 123, 129, and 156 in part II. The Holy Spirit is found in *Diary* 14–15, 18, 36, 63, 123, 140, and 169 in part II.

147. On Mary and Christ as mediators, see *Diary* 4, 8, 12, 15, 23–24, 38, and 46. Mary appears also in Nos. 1, 3, 29–30, 31, 35, 47, 120, 140, and 143. The most interesting text on Mary occurs on the Marian Feast of February 15, when Ignatius feels Mary's pleading for him with the Father before, during, and after Mass. He goes on: "During the prayers to the Father and the Son, and at his Consecration, I could not but feel and see her, as though she were part or rather portal of the great grace I could feel in my spirit. (At the Consecration she showed that her own flesh was in that of her Son) with so many understandings [*inteligencias*] that they could not be written" (*Diario* 31 in ed. Larrañaga, 695; trans. Munitiz and Endean, *Saint Ignatius of Loyola: Personal Writings*, 78, adapted).

148. *Spiritual Diary* 8 (Ganss, 240).

149. Warmth/heat is mentioned constantly in the *Diary*; e.g., 8, 11, 22, *39*, 40, 43, 45, 56, 60, 64, 71, 74, 92, 104, 111, 117, 134, 136, 139, 143, 144, and in part II at 197.

150. *Diary* 27 (ed., 694; my trans.).

151. *Spiritual Diary* 50 (ed., 704, with a long note; trans. Ganss, 245): "Después de la Misa, quietándome y midiendo mi mesura con la sapiencia y grandeza divina, andando adelante por algunas horas hasta venire pensamiento de no curarde decir más Misas, indignándome con la Santísima Trinidad."

152. *Spiritual Diary* 63 (ed., 709; Ganss, 247).

153. *Diary* 72 (Ganss, 249). This termination in Jesus as Son of God, however, does not exclude a reference to the Father: "Therefore I could not apply them [these devotions] to the other persons, except, . . . inasmuch as the First Person was the Father of such a Son. In regard to that, spiritual responses came to mind: 'What a Father! And what a Son!'"

154. For these experiences of Jesus, see *Diary* 74–75, 77–78, 80–84, 86–88, 93, 95, 98, 101, 102, 105, 108, 112–15, 137–38, 140. Some of these Jesus visions are reminiscent of what Ignatius saw at Manresa. For example, "At the time of Mass, when saying 'Lord Jesus Christ, Son of the Living God' and so on . . . it seemed to me that in spirit I saw Jesus in the same way I described the first time, as something white, that is, his humanity" (No. 87).

155. *Diary* 99 (ed., 723; trans. de Nicolás, 207)

156. *Diary* 121 (ed., 730–31; trans. de Nicolás, 211, adapted).

157. *Diary* 125 (ed., 732; trans. Munitiz and Endean, *Saint Ignatius of Loyola: Personal Writings*, 94).

158. These three levels (above–between–below) in Ignatius's view of the world (see also *Diary* 135–36, 143), have been analyzed by H. Rahner, *Ignatius the Theologian*, 3–31.

159. These essential visions continue on into part II of *Spiritual Diary*, e.g., 172, 174, 180, 183.

160. *Diary* 145 (Ganss, 257). I am not sure of the meaning of "another." Another Person of the Trinity?

161. For seventeen appearances of the *loquelas*, see *Diary* 221–22, 224–34, 237–40.

162. *Diary* 221 (Ganss, 267).

163. *Diary* 222 (Ganss, 267). On the *loquela*, see Egan, *Ignatius the Mystic*, 193–96.

164. *Diary* 234 (Ganss, 268).

165. Young, *Letters of St. Ignatius of Loyola*, 22–23.

166. On the background and meaning of *acatamiento*, see Joan Nuth, "*Acatamiento*: Living in an Attitude of Affectionate Awe—An Ignatian Reflection on the Unitive Way," *Spiritus* 10 (2010): 173–91. She argues that *acatamiento* expresses "a fundamental contemplative attitude of mind" (175), combining the desire to draw near to God at the same time that one maintains a respectful appreciation of divine transcendence. Nuth further suggests (184) that the same attitude (if not the word) is expressed in the *Suscipe* prayer of *Exercises* 234.

167. Ganss, *Ignatius of Loyola*, 443 n. 56; de Nicolás, *Ignatius de Loyola*, 113. Young, *Saint Ignatius of Loyola: Personal Writings* prefers "submission" (e.g., 103–4).

168. *Diary* 157 (Ganss, 260). That *acatamiento* is a divine gift and not a result of our own efforts seems to be suggested in No. 173 (Ganss, 263), where Ignatius says he cannot make any progress toward finding it by his own efforts.

169. *Diary* 178 (Ganss, 263–64).

170. *Diary* 187 (ed., 762; my trans.): "No hallendo reverencia o acatamiento amoroso, se debe buscar acatamiento temeroso, mirando las propias faltas, para alcanzar el que es amoroso."

171. On Gregory and the two kinds of compunction, see McGinn, *Growth*, 48–50.

172. Egan, *Ignatius Loyola the Mystic*, 16.

173. Robert Ricard ties Ignatius's trinitarian mysticism to the strong tradition of trinitarian devotion in Spain since Visigothic times ("Deux traits de l'expérience mystique de Saint Ignace," *Archivum Historicum Societatis Jesu* 25 [1956]: 431–36).

174. Ignatius speaks of union, as we have seen, in only a few texts. Of course, many of his contemporaries spoke of how he was united with God (e.g., *Memoriale*, 93, 107–8, 117).

Carmelite History and Spirituality

Lo, brought into the wine cellar by the King of Kings, we seek an ordered charity within us. How rightly it is called the wine cellar, for in that cell the Holy Spirit soberly intoxicates the true cell-dwellers with the wondrous wine of devotion and makes them fall asleep on the glorious bed of sweet contemplation.[1]

THE ORIGINS of the Carmelite order are to be found in the western European hermits who came to the holy land in the time of the Crusades, seeking a life of austerity and contemplation on the sites made famous in the Bible.[2] Late twelfth-century accounts speak of individuals or groups of hermits who located on Mount Carmel, the long ridge of hills above Haifa that had associations with the prophet and ascetic Elijah the Tishbite (1 Kings 17–18). In the early years of the thirteenth century a group of hermits living in the Wadi-ain-es-Siah approached the newly elected patriarch of Jerusalem, Albert of Vercelli (patriarch 1206–14), with the request for a "formula of life" (*formula vitae*) that would organize their community practices. Albert was a skilled canonist, and he provided the hermits with a brief document probably around 1207. This "Rule of St. Albert" is the birth certificate of the Carmelites.[3] Although not a papally approved "rule" until later, it remained a touchstone for the later history of the order.[4]

Albert's Rule is typically eremitical, marking a difference

from the coenobitical ideal of Benedict's Rule, as well as the soon-
to-be mendicant rules of the Franciscans and Dominicans with their
emphasis on apostolic activity and preaching in the world. The picture
that emerges is of a community of lay hermits under the leadership of
a prior, living in solitary places with no pastoral ministry. Each hermit had a separate cell in which he was to stay, "pondering the Lord's
law day and night and keeping watch at his prayers unless attending
to some other duty" (Rule 10). The literate brothers read the Psalms
according to the usual monastic office; the illiterate repeat the Our
Father at the canonical hours (Rule 11). All the brothers repair to the
oratory each morning for Mass (Rule 14), thus indicating the presence
of some coenobitical elements within the larger eremitical picture,
not unlike the Carthusians. All property is held in common (Rule 12),
manual labor is enjoined (Rule 20), and there is a strict fast, although
dispensations are allowed for necessary reasons (Rules 16–17). Equally
stringent are the rules for silence (Rule 21). Albert's Rule is short, strict,
and sober, but with a sense of balance and discernment, closing with
the admonition, "See that the bounds of common sense [*discretio*] are
not exceeded, however, for common sense is the guide of the virtues."

As the last remnants of the Crusader states became more and more
threatened by the Muslim resurgence, the hermits living under the
Rule of Albert began returning to western Europe in the 1220s and
1230s, scattering over a number of countries. They did not always seek
out "solitary places," however, but, like the friars, often settled in or
near towns. Popes began granting the Carmelites privileges similar
to those of the mendicants, and in 1247, in response to Carmelite
requests, Pope Innocent IV issued an apostolic letter "Quae honorem
conditoris" that promulgated a revised version of the Rule of Albert.
The changes were not great, but they were significant. The prior and
brothers are no longer restricted to "foundations in solitary places,"
and they now can eat in a common refectory and have common recita-
tion of the Office. Some adjustments were made in poverty, and the
severe fasting and silence were also reduced. In 1252 papal documents
now refer to the Carmelites as an *ordo* in the canonical sense; in 1253
they were given the right to preach and hear confessions. In 1261 lay
people were allowed to worship in their churches. What is evident is
that the Carmelites had quickly become an order of mendicants, the
"Whitefriars" of English tradition, because of their white capes. Along
with the new lifestyle came a clericalization of what was originally a lay
group, as well as an emphasis on preaching and serving as confessors,

which meant that the Carmelites, like the Dominicans and Franciscans, needed advanced theological education.

This transition did not proceed without opposition, the kind of tension between action and contemplation often seen in the history of religious orders. Nicholas of Narbonne, prior general from 1266 to 1271, issued a treatise called *The Fiery Arrow* (*Ignea sagitta*), in which he roundly condemned most of the changes, especially the dangers of living in the city.[5] Nicholas did not reject Gregory the Great's model that the contemplative might at times be called to share the fruits of contemplation in preaching, but he insisted that the desert of the solitary and contemplative life in the cell, as noted above, formed the true center of Carmelite spirituality. Alas, Nicholas was swimming against the tide, although his protest introduced issues characteristic of Carmelite history—the tension between pastoral ministry and solitude, between apostolic mobility and contemplative stability, and between competing views of poverty. As Keith J. Egan put it, "The paradox of a call to solitude and at the same time a call to ministerial community was, during the Middle Ages and thereafter, the critical source of the vitality of Carmelite spirituality."[6]

After a crisis at the Second Council at Lyons in 1274, when it looked like the Carmelites might lose papal approval, the order rebounded in the late thirteenth century, spreading throughout Europe, moving into the world of the universities and gaining more papal support, especially from Boniface VIII, who guaranteed their status in 1298. The organization of the order mimicked that of the other mendicants, as befitted a European-wide organization. While the Carmelites produced some noted Scholastics, such as the English friar John Baconthorpe (d. 1348), what is surprising is how little spiritual, let alone mystical, literature seems to have come from the order in the Middle Ages. An exception to this is the treatise known as the *Book of the Institution of the First Monks* written by the Catalan provincial Philip Ribot by 1391.[7] The book played a key role in the formation of the Carmelite myth, that is, the claim that the order was actually founded by the prophet Elijah himself, who looked forward to the coming of Jesus and to Mary as the future "Mother of the Carmelite Order."[8] These claims, which are partly explainable by the competition among the various orders of mendicants, became central to the identity of the Carmelites down to modern times, although they were contentious from the beginning. Ribot pretended that his book was actually a fifth-century account of the history of the Carmelites written by John, the patriarch of Jerusalem, giving the story of the order from Elijah on, and with later additions bringing it down to the present. The legendary excesses of the book, however, did not prevent it from becoming necessary reading for all Carmelites (including Teresa of Avila, it seems). Furthermore, the *Book of the Institution* was important for its stress on the role of prayer and contemplation as essential to the Carmelite vocation. Speaking of the goal of the Carmelite life in chapter 2, Ribot says:

> The goal of this life is twofold. One part we acquire by our own effort and the exercise of the virtues, assisted by divine grace. . . . The other goal of this life is granted to us as the free gift of God, namely, to taste somewhat in the heart and to experience in the mind the power of the divine presence and the sweetness of heavenly glory, not only after death but in this mortal life. This is to "drink of the torrent" of the pleasure of God. God promised this to Elijah in the words: "And there you shall drink of the torrent" (1 Kgs. 17:4).[9]

Later Carmelite insistence on the distinction between acquired and infused contemplation is already adumbrated here.

The disturbances of the fourteenth century, both in the church and in society at large, had their effect on the Carmelites. Not only were disputes with other orders rife, but internal relaxations from the Rule became widespread, especially with regard to poverty, since many friars now appear to have possessed their own resources. The fifteenth century witnessed attempts at reform, similar to what was going on among the Benedictines and in the other mendicants, but that age also, rather paradoxically, saw recognition by the papacy of the less rigorous form of Carmelite life. In 1452 Eugene IV in his bull "Romani Pontificis" approved a mitigated form of the Rule, which cut down on fasting and allowed more freedom of movement to the friars. At the same time as the order was officially becoming more relaxed, however, a number of reforms began in different provinces, some of which had considerable success. An Italian reform established the Congregation of Mantua recognized by the same Eugene IV in 1442, while John Soreth (ca. 1395–1471), prior general from 1451 until his death, set out reformed statutes that were approved by Callixtus III in 1457 (the "Callixtine Reform"). The Carmelite order seems to have been much disturbed by internal disputes about the best way to live their ideal.

John Soreth's priorate also marked a decisive moment in the evolution of the order—the official acceptance of a female branch.[10] The mendicant way of life had proven attractive to women from the start, and, despite the opposition of some of the leaders of the friars, it proved impossible to keep women out. There are references to some

independent women (*conversae/pinzocchere*) who tried to affiliate themselves with the Carmelites as early as the late thirteenth century, but
these are scattered and often suspect. The Carmelites had little to do
with women before the mid-fifteenth century, when Soreth responded
to a request from a beguinage in a Carmelite parish in the Netherlands
to be incorporated into the order. He welcomed this, providing statutes
for the nascent Carmelite nuns in several places in the Low Countries.
A similar movement in Florence, also encouraged by Soreth, appealed
to Rome and received papal approval from Nicholas V in 1452 for the
creation of houses of "White Ladies." Female Carmelite houses spread
rapidly in the Netherlands, France, and Italy. The growth was slower
in Spain, where some communities of "holy women" (*beatas*) did come
to live according to Carmelite ordinances but without accepting formal claustration, or mandatory enclosure in a convent. The oldest of
such houses in the Kingdom of Castile was the monastery of the Encarnación in Avila established in 1479. This was the community that the
young Teresa de Ahumada joined in 1535.

The order into which Teresa and her friends and followers entered
was both successful and troubled. While not as widespread as the Franciscans and Dominicans, the Carmelites were a major force in early
modern Catholicism as it faced the challenge of the Reformation. The
approved form of life in the order was relatively relaxed, but there was
a tradition of attempts at more rigorous reforms stretching back for
a century. Above all, the original role of solitude and contemplative
prayer, foundational for the Carmelites, was still held up as an ideal by
many. It is also noteworthy that the female branch of the order lacked
any compelling founding figure or impressive leader, such as Clare of
Assisi for the Franciscans, or Catherine of Siena for the Dominicans.
Teresa of Avila was to provide such a model.

Notes

1. Nicholas of Narbonne, *Ignea Sagitta*, cap. IX, in Adrianus Staring, "Nicolai
Prioris Generalis Ordinis Carmelitarum Ignea Sagitta," *Carmelus* 9 (1962): 295:
"Ecce in cellam vinariam a Rege regum introducti ordinatam in nobis consequi-
mur caritatem (Song of Songs 2:4). O quam bene appellatur cella vinaria, nam in
ea Spiritus Sanctus veros cellitas vino devotionis mirifico sobrie inebrians, suavis
contemplationis glorioso lectulo efficit obdormire (Song 1:15)."

2. Andrew Jotischky, *The Perfection of Solitude: Hermits and Monks in the Crusader
States* (University Park: Pennsylvania State University Press, 1995).

3. For the history of the Carmelites, see the multiauthor article, "Carmelitani,"

DIP 2:460–521; and Frances Andrews, *The Other Friars: Carmelite, Augustinian, Sack and Pied Friars in the Middle Ages* (Rochester, NY: Boydell, 2006), part 1. There is a helpful collection of documents in Steven Payne, *The Carmelite Tradition*, Spirituality in History (Collegeville, MN: Liturgical Press, 2011). For a brief sketch of Carmelite spirituality, see Keith J. Egan, "The Spirituality of the Carmelites," in *Christian Spirituality: High Middle Ages and Reformation*, ed. Jill Raitt et al., World Spirituality 17 (New York: Crossroad, 1987), 50–62. See also Wilfrid McGreal, *At the Fountain of Elijah: The Carmelite Tradition* (Maryknoll, NY: Orbis Books, 1999). The best large history is Joachim Smet, *The Carmelites: A History of the Brothers of Our Lady of Mount Carmel*, 4 vols. (Darien, IL: Carmelite Spiritual Center, 1975–85), with vol. 1 dealing with the period up to the Council of Trent.

4. There is a translation of the original version of the Rule of Albert, as well as the modified form that received official recognition from Innocent IV in 1247, in Payne, *Carmelite Tradition*, 5–9.

5. The *Ignea sagitta* is both a polemical and a mystical work in its emphasis on the delights of contemplation. See the edition of A. Staring noted above (*Carmelus* 9 [1962]: 237–307), as well as the translation of Michael Edwards, *Nicholas of Narbonne, The Flaming Arrow (Ignea Sagitta)* (Durham: Teresian Press, 1985).

6. Egan, "Spirituality of the Carmelites," 60.

7. There is unfortunately no modern edition of this work. For a description and a translation of some sections, see Payne, *Carmelite Tradition*, 21–25.

8. For this process of "mythologization," see Jane Ackerman, "Stories of Elijah and Medieval Carmelite Identity," *History of Religions* 35 (1995): 124–47. A more detailed account can be found in Andrew Jotischky, *The Carmelites and Antiquity: Mendicants and Their Pasts in the Middle Ages* (Oxford: Oxford University Press, 2005).

9. *The Book of the Institution of the First Monks*, chap. 2, as translated in Payne, *Carmelite Tradition*, 24–25.

10. There is a general account by Joachim Smet, *Cloistered Carmel* (Rome: Institutum Carmelitanum, 1987), although Smet seems somewhat uncritical about the early development of the female Carmelites.

CHAPTER 3

Teresa of Avila:
The Contemplative in Action

It is necessary that we bear our weakness and not try to
    constrain our nature.
Everything amounts to seeking God, since it is for him that
    we search out every kind of means, and the soul must be
    led gently.

—Teresa, Letter 69, to Teutonio
de Braganza (July 3, 1574)[1]

ANY ARE FAMILIAR with Teresa of Avila (Teresa de
Jesús) as a great contemplative, a teacher whose
mystical treatises have been read for centuries
and whose theological contributions led her to
being declared the first female Doctor of the Church by Pope
Paul VI in 1970. Her two most read works are the *Life of Mother
Teresa de Jesús* (*Libro de la Vida*) and the *Interior Castle* (*Moradas del Castillo Interior*), her recognized masterpiece, written in
1577.[2] Many will also recognize Teresa as the founder of the
Carmelite reform known as the "Discalced," or barefoot Carmelites (they actually used sandals rather than shoes).[3] Fewer,
however, will know just how active the contemplative Teresa
was, especially in her last fifteen years of life (1567–1582).

I wish to express my deep thanks to Prof. Peter Tyler of St. Mary's
College, Twickenham, London, for his helpful reading and suggestions
regarding this chapter.

Although her reform reintroduced long periods of contemplative prayer into the Carmelite life, as well as insisting on strict enclosure of the nuns, Teresa herself became incredibly busy during these years, traveling throughout Castile, engaging in complex personal, institutional, and financial negotiations for spreading the reform, and writing thousands of letters (468 survive) about a multitude of topics to recipients from King Philip II to humble folk, such as a friend's widow whom she had never met (Letter 349).

Although Teresa's personality comes across in all her writings, it is in the Letters that we get the best insight into her native shrewdness, her firm resolve despite many difficulties and much ill health, and her steadiness and prudence as a spiritual advisor.[4] In reading the Letters and the account she wrote of her activity as a reformer and founder, the *Book of the Foundations* (*Libro de las Fundaciones*), we begin to get a sense of just what a dynamo Teresa was. Teresa of Avila presents us with one of the best cases in the history of Christian mysticism of "a contemplative in action," a description first used of her older contemporary, Ignatius of Loyola.[5]

Most of this chapter will concern Teresa's teaching about contemplation and mystical union, but I have chosen the description of the Carmelite as a contemplative in action to try to do justice to both sides of her life, and also to show her place in the history of one of the central themes in the history of Christian mysticism, that is, how to relate the demands of contemplation and action, or love of God and love of neighbor. Teresa not only created one of the most influential theologies of the contemplative life but also left us a rich and developing teaching on how to relate the active and contemplative dimensions.

The scriptural injunction concerning the two great commandments of love of God and love of neighbor (Deut. 6:4–5; Matt. 22:37–39) has had a complex interaction in Christian history with the Greek philosophical theme of the distinction between the "contemplative life" (*bios theōretikos*) and the "practical, or active, life" (*bios praktikos*), since at least the second century. For the Greeks, the contemplative life was that of the philosopher, a person separated from the ordinary demands of society (literally "without a place," *atopos*) in his gaze (*theōria*) toward ultimate Truth. The practical life was that of the citizen engaged in the life of the city (*polis*).[6] Christian use of this paradigm, stretching back to Clement of Alexandria and Origen, and moving through the Fathers of East and West, adopted the two forms of life to help explain the dual commands required of all believers: love of God in contemplative absorption and love of neighbor in active works of charity.[7] Unlike the Greeks, Christians considered both forms of life necessary—love of God and love of neighbor could never be separated. But Christian thinkers found confirmation for the biblical teaching that the love of God is the higher form in Greek philosophical teaching that the contemplative life was superior to the active life. Eventually, three principles were established for relating the two modes of life: (1) both types of life were necessary; (2) the contemplative life was higher and was the proper goal of all Christians; and (3) on earth contemplation had to yield to action when the neighbor's need demanded it. This yielding, however, was seen as a distraction, an unfortunate condescension to humanity's fallen state. Although some authors recognized that loving action in the world could be seen as part of the fruit of contemplation and could even add to its heavenly merit, for most of the Middle Ages we see what can be called an "oscillation model" of the relation of contemplation and action—a person could not be contemplative and active at the same time, and, while action might be more meritorious, it was always in some way a come-down.[8] A biblical basis for this understanding was found in the account in Luke 10:38–42 of Jesus's reception by Martha and Mary. Martha rushing around to serve Jesus was identified with the active life, while Mary, sitting and listening to Jesus, figured the contemplative life, which Jesus says is the "better part" (Luke 10:42).[9]

This understanding of the relation of contemplation and action was challenged in the late Middle Ages. The notion that it might be possible to contemplate God within the business and distractions of everyday life may sound strange, but this is just what some late medieval mystics began to teach. Among the earliest was Meister Eckhart (ca. 1260–1328). Eckhart himself was a busy teacher and administrator, but in a sermon preached on Luke 10 he set forth a new interpretation of action and contemplation that is also adumbrated in other places in his writings.[10] Eckhart reversed the usual interpretation by saying that Mary was indeed "possessed with a longing for her soul's satisfaction," but that Martha "had lived long and well and life gives the finest understanding." Therefore, Martha was so well grounded that she was not "hindered by things," that is, "her activity was no hindrance to her work and activity she turned to her eternal profit." Martha's words to Jesus bidding him to have Mary get up and help her (Luke 10:40) are interpreted as, "I want her [Mary] to learn life and possess it in essence; bid her arise that she may be more perfect." Contemplation, therefore, is like going to school, but life changes contemplative "school learning" into perfecting action.[11]

Eckhart's message about the need to combine action and contemplation to reach perfection was taken up by his follower John Tauler (d. 1361) and by the Flemish mystic Jan van Ruusbroec (d. 1381) with his notion of the "common life" (*ghemeyne leven*). The theory found a practical example in the person of Catherine of Siena (1347–1380), the second woman Doctor of the Church, and someone well known to Teresa.[12] In his *Long Life of Catherine* (*Legenda major*), the Dominican Raymond of Capua portrays the saint's transition from a reclusive contemplative living in a room in her parental home to an active public figure, conducting her ministry first in her native Siena about 1369, and then, beginning about 1374, in the wider arena of Italian and European politics, both ecclesiastical and secular. As Raymond put it, Catherine was "to follow lines far different from those of other women. . . . She was sent out to live in the public eye, working for the honor of God and the salvation of souls."[13] In short, Catherine, like the Mary Magdalene of hagiographical legend, was able to be both contemplative and active. The Magdalene, the great lover of Jesus, was also the *apostola apostolorum* ("apostle of the apostles"), who brought the Twelve news of the resurrection (John 20:18) and who preached the gospel in Gaul. She was thus a model for both Catherine and Teresa, although Teresa, unlike Catherine, does not seem to have self-identified as an apostle.[14]

Teresa's career not only followed a similar pattern to that of Catherine, but she went further than the Sienese mystic in working out a theology that saw the fusion of action and contemplation as the distinctive mark of the highest stage of union with God, that of mystical marriage. Teresa's life and message were of particular relevance for her Carmelite order. The Carmelites, as noted above, originated in the twelfth century among hermits on Mount Carmel dedicated to a life of strict silence and contemplative prayer. The Carmelites won papal approval as a mendicant order, but the tension between the contemplative solitude of the cell and pastoral activity in the world remained an issue in the order during the fourteenth and fifteenth centuries. Teresa was a special case, but her life and teaching show that it was possible for a Carmelite, indeed a female Carmelite, to combine action and contemplation.

Teresa's mystical teaching developed over time in close association with the increasing reformist activity of the last fifteen years of her life. Hence, I will approach Teresa biographically, following her career and studying her writings in relation to the stages of her life.[15] We are fortunate in having a wealth of information about her, not only in the well-known *Life* but also in her surviving letters, the *Book of the Foundations*, and in many accounts of her contemporaries, including the materials from her canonization process.[16]

Teresa the Nun (1515–1555)

Teresa's life was remarkable and often controversial.[17] She encountered opposition on many fronts. As Deirdre Green put it, Teresa "was working within an oppressive, racist, sexist, and fanatically dogmatic system," but, "in spite of her vulnerability as a woman, a *conversa* [i.e., of Jewish background], and a visionary, she managed to escape serious condemnation."[18] Her position as someone of Jewish origin, as a proponent of controversial interior prayer, and as a reformer working against established religious interests and authorities singled her out as suspect for the last twenty-five years of her life. Showing how she managed to avoid censure while making such an outstanding contribution to the story of Christian mysticism is the task of this chapter.

Teresa was born in Avila on March 28, 1515, the daughter of Alonso Sánchez de Cepeda and his second wife, Doña Beatriz de Ahumada. Teresa's silence about her family's purity of blood allowed Carmelite hagiography to cover over the *converso* origins of her family until new documents were discovered in the middle of the last century. At Toledo in 1485, her grandfather, Juan Sánchez, a successful merchant, had been hauled before the Inquisition with his sons to accept a penance and public infamy for sliding back into Jewish practices. The family soon fled to Avila, where they would be less known. Teresa's father, Alonso, whom she always praised for his religious devotion, married twice, his second wife being of an Old Christian family. While Teresa was a child (1519–20), Alonso and his brothers conducted a difficult, but ultimately successful, campaign, mostly through bribery, to have themselves recognized as members of the nobility and thus possessing the requisite purity of blood to take their fitting station in society. Teresa must have known about her family's origins. Her reaction was twofold: first, never to speak about her own purity of blood, because she knew she did not have it; and, second, to reject the whole concept of false human honor in favor of the true honor founded in love of God and neighbor.

Modern recognition of Teresa's Jewish roots and the effect this had on her life has raised the question of how far her mysticism may have been influenced by Jewish and possibly even Islamic mysticism. Despite much well-intentioned ecumenical investigation, the answer is "little or nothing." There is absolutely no hard evidence that indicates the monoglot young woman could have had any direct contact with Hebrew or Arabic mystical texts, which she could not have read anyhow. History will never know if Alonso and his brothers discussed the *Zohar* or other Jewish mystical texts (texts closed to women), but it seems highly unlikely.[19] The similarities that have been pointed out between themes in Teresa's mysticism, such as the seven mansions of the *Interior Castle* and the appearance of seven concentric castles in a number of Sufi texts,[20] remain no more than parallels between related but independent mystical traditions. The claims for Teresa's dependence on Jewish and Islamic mysticism come down to vague assertions of "oral traditions" that cannot be verified and that remain highly dubious.

Teresa's *Life*, like Augustine's *Confessions*, gives us her own perspective on her childhood, adolescence, and early adulthood. The comparison with Augustine is important, because we know that this was one of the books that deeply influenced her. The *Confessions* (up to the beginning of book 11) were published in Spanish in 1554 and were soon read by Teresa. This is how she describes the effect the book had on her:

> As I began to read the *Confessions*, it seemed to me I saw myself in them. I began to commend myself very much to this glorious saint. When I came to the passage where he speaks of his conversion and read how he heard that voice in the garden [*Conf.* 8.12.29], it only seemed to me, according to what I felt in my heart, that it was I the Lord called. I remained for a long time totally dissolved in tears and feeling within myself utter distress and weariness.

Teresa goes on to speak of the difficulty she had in giving up her old false self before coming into full possession of her new self dependent on God. She says, "Dear God, what a soul suffers and what torments it endures when it loses its freedom to be its own master! I am astonished now that I was able to live in such a state of torment!" Nonetheless, from the perspective of the transformed Teresa now writing of her former self, she concludes, like Augustine, with an act of confession (*confessio laudis*—confession of praise): "God be praised, who gave me the life to forsake such utter death!"[21]

Thus Teresa relives Augustine's experience of being turned (*convertere*) to God, although here the divine instrument is the text of Augustine and not the voice of the child in the garden. Like Augustine, Teresa is now telling the story of God's work in her life through a book that interweaves the various forms of confession used by the bishop: confession of praise (*confessio laudis*), confession of sin (*confessio peccati*), and confession of faith/truth (*confessio fidei/veritatis*).[22] Again like Augustine, Teresa's account of God's turning her from sin to grace is the story of a process, with the reading of the *Confessions* as one decisive moment in a series of graced interventions. Making public her account was not her own decision, she says, but is presented as an act of obedience to her confessors. Since she is no longer her old self-willed self but is now a mystical self transformed by God's love, Teresa is obeying God through her confessors. The point is underlined in chapter 23, when she returns to the story of her post-conversion life after some chapters discussing prayer: "This is another, new book from here on—I mean another new life. The life dealt with up to this time was mine; the one I lived from the point where I began to explain these things about prayer is the one God lived in me."[23] At the end of the *Life* she reiterates the point. Addressing her confessor, the Dominican García de Toledo, who had commanded the work to be written, she hopes that the book "may bring someone to praise God, if only once." Hence, she asks García and three other confessors/advisors to pass judgment on it, and, if it is badly done, they can blame her; but "if it is well done, they are good and learned men, and I know they will see where it comes from and praise him [i.e., God] who spoke it through me (*y albarán a quien lo ha dicho por mí*)."[24]

In order to understand Teresa's account of her life and conversion it is necessary to understand what kind of book the *Life* is and the circumstances and audience for which it was written. Like the *Confessions*, the *Life* is often treated as an autobiography.[25] Nevertheless, if we consider autobiography as a self-narrative describing the construction of an autonomous, independent person, the individual as individual, it is hard to think of the *Life* as meeting this definition, however much the book uses aspects of Teresa's story in presenting its message about grace, conversion, prayer, and union. Like Augustine, Teresa subverts modern expectations for autobiography through the theological construction of her narrative. Hence, many recent studies of Teresa have either questioned or denied that the book should be thought of as an autobiography.[26] Teresa is interested in presenting her "old self" and her "new self," not for self-revelation but for helping her readers recognize the role of grace and prayer in their own lives. Her purpose is apologetic (as we will see below) but also didactic and exhortatory in trying to move the reader to praise and thank God, that is, to engage in the speech-act of *confessio*.

The question about the genre of the book leads to another disputed area, that is, the issue of the style and rhetorical strategy of the *Life*. A long-received view of the book, going back to hagiographical accounts about Teresa writing in ecstasy under the direction of the Holy Spirit, holds that the saint's style is a marvel of spontaneity, that she wrote just as she spoke, and that this artlessness explains some of the orthographical, grammatical, and structural peculiarities of the book. Teresa herself speaks of "my rough style" (*mi grosero estilo, Way* 16.6) or "heavy style" (*mi estilo es tan pesado, Foundations* Prol. 3). But we must remember that Teresa loved to read and had devoured courtly tales as a girl and was familiar with a good deal of spiritual literature,[27] although she was not formally educated. In recent years a number of scholars have shown that Teresa was a diligent and careful writer, although one with a distinctive mode of presentation. Teresa seems to have worked hard to provide an illusion of artlessness, because that was the style expected of a woman.[28] The appearance of "plainness" (*llaneza*) gives a sense of the sincerity of the author.

Since the time of Hildegard of Bingen in the twelfth century women mystics had deployed an arsenal of strategies—literary, theological, and political—to get a hearing within the unfriendly confines of the male-dominated church. Teresa used many of these but also refined and added to them, because the situation she faced in sixteenth-century Spain was particularly inimical to women. Alison Weber and others have analyzed such things as Teresa's use of the humility topos, that is, "I'm only a weak woman" (both ironically and nonironically),[29] as well as her techniques of self-deprecation, self-censorship, concessions, alternate narratives, deliberate obscurity, appeals to the authority of God and/or her confessors, and the like.[30] To note just one such strategy, the reader should be on the lookout for how Teresa often qualifies her claims by statements like, "so it seems to me at least,"[31] thus allowing her confessors and/or inquisitors to amend or correct the possible theological errors of "a simple nun." All of this goes to show that Teresa was far from simple as a writer.

In order to get a sense of the audience that Teresa had in mind for the *Life,* it is important to consider the genesis of the text over the course of the decade from 1555 to 1565.[32] The condemnation of the *Alumbrados* in 1525 intensified the link between women ecstatics and visionaries and the dangers of heresy and/or diabolical deception that had been growing in Europe from around 1300. The fact that a number of these women were of Jewish background was also significant. When Teresa began to receive increased mystical favors at the time of her second conversion (ca. 1554), she obviously recognized the dangers of her situation. How could she be sure that these were truly gifts of God, not deceptions of the devil?[33] How could she protect herself against accusations before the Inquisition? Hence, the *Life* began in the context of spiritual direction, as Teresa wrote down short accounts of her gifts for her confessors and other learned spiritual men (*letrados*) from whom she sought advice.[34] It is difficult to know who took the initiative—Teresa or her advisors. Teresa wanted to get her story out; her male advisors wanted to discern the truth of her claims, especially in the context of the times. Teresa's relationship to her confessors and advisors, although rocky at times, appears to have been overall more collaborative than adversarial. Some confessors misjudged her; at other times they misunderstood her or corrected her incorrectly. She candidly speaks about how much harm the bad advice of some of her confessors had done to her.[35] But she praised other confessors highly, and, in the delicate dance of gender politics necessary in sixteenth-century Spain, both the nun and her clerical advisors needed each other. In the end they achieved something remarkable: the writing of a classic of mystical literature, and, after much difficulty, its approval and publication.

Teresa began writing a brief "account of my life and sins" sometime about 1555 for the secular priest, Gaspar Diaz, and for the pious lay-man Francisco de Salcedo. It was not an auspicious beginning, because these holy but unlearned men told her that her experiences were from the devil, as she herself had feared. But Teresa, despite her fears, did not really believe them, so she sought a second opinion by composing "as clear an account of my life as I knew how to give" for her new confessor, the young Jesuit Diego de Cesena, who "explained to me what I was experiencing and greatly encouraged me."[36] Without condemning the good intentions of those who gave her bad advice, Teresa, for all her doubts (real or rhetorical) had already arrived at a fundamental rule of her mystical life: the experienced mystic will know more about spiritual matters than ignorant theologians, though a confessor who is both a man of prayer and of learning will be the best guide.[37]

Teresa was silent for about four or five years after this as her mystical gifts, later described at length in the *Life*, grew stronger and more numerous. In 1560–62 she once again began to record these divine favors in her earliest surviving writings, the first two of her *Spiritual Testimonies* (*Cuentas de conciencia*). These were both directed to her then confessor, the Dominican Pedro Ibáñez. The first is entitled the *Manner of Proceeding in Prayer* (*Su maniera de proceder en la oración*) and dates from late 1560; the second, *Detachment and Other Virtues Flowing from God's Favors*, was probably written in Toledo in 1562. A third *Testimony* entitled the *General account of her state of soul* was written to another new confessor, the Dominican García de Toledo, at St. Joseph's in Avila in 1563.

Teresa wrote these accounts at the command of her confessors, who were friends and supporters. There was, however, another audience looming over her shoulder in a more threatening way—the Inquisition.[38] The condemnation of the *Alumbrados* and, perhaps even more, the 1546 trial of the Franciscan prioress Magdalena de la Cruz, famous for her penances and spiritual gifts, shocked Teresa. At her trial in Córdoba, Magdalena confessed that she had entered into a pact with the devil at the age of twelve and that all her gifts were diabolical in origin. She was condemned to life imprisonment.[39] Although Teresa cautioned against the severe penances practiced by people like Magdalena, her ecstasies, visions, and other mystical graces were exactly the kind of thing to attract the interest of the Inquisitors. But when some people came to Teresa to warn her she was in danger of being delated to the Inquisition, she said, "This amused me and made me laugh, for I never had any fear of such a possibility. If anyone were to see that I went against the slightest ceremony of the church in a matter of faith, I myself knew well that I would die a thousand deaths for the faith or for any truth of sacred scripture."[40] Teresa might have reason for her humor, but she could not disregard the Inquisition. Gillian Ahlgren only exaggerates a little when she says, "Teresa's interaction with the Inquisition—both direct and indirect—was the most significant influence on her career as a writer."[41] Previous mystical women had had their works examined by Inquisitorial authorities; Teresa was the first woman to write with the Inquisition in mind.[42] In order to make her message heard, she, with the aid of her confessors and friendly critics, needed to forestall the Inquisitors. She had to construct a *confessio fidei* that would make it difficult (though scarcely impossible) to declare her a heretic.

Confessors and Inquisitors were not the only audience for what she always called "my book" (*mi libro*).[43] By the time Teresa actually began to write the first draft, probably in late 1561 or early 1562, she already felt that she had to produce an account of her prayer life and mystical gifts for the instruction of her fellow nuns, if not for an even wider audience. A famous text in the *Life* tells us about the genesis of this conviction. In 1559 the Dominican Archbishop of Seville and Inquisitor General, Fernando de Valdés, issued a condemnation of 253 books, ranging from vernacular versions of the Bible through translations of works of Erasmus and the Protestants to a large array of the spiritual and mystical literature that had been encouraged under Cardinal Cisneros.[44] Valdés is (in)famous for his statement condemning writers who were trying to instruct carpenter's wives and other simple women in interior prayer (he seems not to have heard of Mary of Nazareth).[45] This blanket exclusion was a blow to Teresa and her nuns. At this juncture, Jesus came to the rescue. The *Life* records a locution, probably of 1560, in which the Lord assured her that all would be well. "When they forbade the reading of many books in the vernacular," Teresa tells us, "I felt that prohibition very much because reading some of them was an enjoyment for me, and I could no longer do so since only the Latin editions were allowed." She continues, "The Lord said to me: 'Don't be sad, for I shall give you a living book.' I was unable," admits Teresa, "to understand why this was said to me, since I had not yet experienced any visions. Afterward, within only a few days, I understood very clearly, because . . . I had very little or almost no need for books. His Majesty had become the true book in which I saw the truths. Blessed be such a book that leaves what must be read and done so impressed that you cannot forget it."[46] I quote this passage at length, not only because it combines the motif of the inner "book of experience" (*liber experientiae*) with another mystical motif, that of Jesus on the cross as the book revealing God's love for humanity, but also because it explains why Teresa's *libro*, which she began writing a year or so later, was not a document just for clerical and Inquisitorial eyes but also for the nuns who would follow her in reforming Carmel,[47] and even for the many readers over the centuries desirous to learn how interior prayer leads to union with God.

Let us now turn to the *Life* itself and what it has to tell us about the first forty years of Teresa's life as a child, young woman, and an ordinary nun.[48] Teresa's purpose in the first nine chapters of the *Life* is to give us a picture, not unlike Augustine's *Confessions*, of indolent self-reliance as the weight holding the soul back from God, even when it really desires to do God's will. Teresa's childhood pious desires, such as her attempt to go off to Muslim lands to be martyred for Christ (*Life* 1.4) help paint a picture of someone raised in a fervent religious environment, with many good intentions, but unable to follow through. The unspecified sin of her teenage relationship to a cousin (*Life* 2.2, 6–7 [we are not told exactly what this was]) is presented as an offense both against God's law and against the Spanish conception of female honor. In the manner of many saints, Teresa seizes on what may seem like small things (e.g., her vanity, her liking of secular literature, etc.) as evidence of her deep sinfulness. Nevertheless, she was quite pious in the conventional Spanish manner, so it makes perfect sense that, after some hesitation, she entered the Carmelite convent of the Encarnación in Avila in 1535. The Encarnación was a large community and observant in its way, but it did mirror contemporary Spanish society and the rather relaxed life of the unreformed Carmelite houses. As Doña Teresa de Ahumada, Teresa was among the wealthier nuns with a private room and many privileges. She fulfilled her religious duties but also took advantage of her status to receive guests in the convent parlor and to spend long periods outside the walls, especially when ill. Teresa wanted to have it both ways, that is, as she once put it, "to practice prayer and to live for my own pleasure"[49]—the divided will that Augustine portrayed so well in *Confessions* book 8.

Chapters 3–8 of the *Life* feature many descriptions of Teresa's often serious illnesses during these twenty years (1535–55). These include fainting fits, severe fevers and pains, and even a paralysis that brought her near death and from which she did not recover for three years (ca. 1539–42; see *Life* 6.2, 6–8). In the nineteenth century these accounts, as well as her subsequent descriptions of ecstatic raptures and diabolic assaults, led to Teresa being named "the patron saint of hysterics."[50] Hysteria has gone the way of other pseudo-illnesses, but attempts to account for the nun's medical problems and her detailed descriptions of her bodily and spiritual paranormal states continue to attract interest. Was Teresa an epileptic?[51] Do her ecstatic seizures match the perinatal symptoms of regression to the birth experience in order to be reborn as described by Stanislav Grof and his followers?[52] Were her early illnesses, including the long paralysis, psychosomatic reactions to her interior struggles over her dissatisfaction with her fragmented inner life? It is hard to know, especially when so many competing diagnoses have been offered. Despite their troubling nature, there seems to be a growing recognition that Teresa's illnesses, diabolical attacks, and ecstasies were not expressions of some degenerative pathology but were side effects of the transformation of her consciousness from the selfish ego of Doña Teresa de Ahumada to Teresa de Jesús, the new mystical self grounded in God. As she became more and more rooted in contemplation, Teresa was better able to put her bad health in perspective. As she says in *Life* 13.7: "I have seen clearly that on very many occasions, though I am in fact very sickly, it was a temptation from the devil or from my own laziness—for afterward when I wasn't so cared for and pampered, I had much better health."

For two decades Teresa lived as an average nun in the Encarnación, better than many we may suppose, and worse than others, at least in her mind. She participated in the common prayer of the community, observed the rules, and even practiced interior prayer, if half-heartedly. Her devotion to mystical prayer emerged early. In 1538, while staying with her uncle Pedro, she read Francisco Osuna's *Third Spiritual Alphabet*, the bible of the prayer of recollection. Teresa says, "And so I was very happy with this book and resolved to follow that path with all my strength. Since the Lord had already given me the gift of tears and I enjoyed reading, I began to take time out for solitude, to confess frequently, and to follow that path, taking the book as my master."[53] Through reading Osuna, and later Bernardino de Laredo's *Ascent of Mount Sion*, Teresa came in contact with mystical *recogimiento* and its deep rooting in the "Affective Dionysianism" of the late Middle Ages, in which ecstatic love unites the soul to God above all understanding. This was to be a major source of her own later writing.[54] But while Teresa had begun to practice mystical prayer at a fairly early stage, she did so on her own terms, not on God's. Nonetheless, some special graces were given her. For example, in *Life* 4.7 she mentions brief moments of being given the "prayer of quiet" (an ambiguous term across her writings) and even talks about attaining some kind of "union" with God. Christ appeared to her, possibly in 1539, but in a judgmental way, threatening her about a bad friendship that was leading her astray (*Life* 7.6). The devil tempted her to give up mental prayer for some time, but with the advice of the Dominican Vicente Barrón she took it up again (*Life* 7.17). Teresa *wanted* to devote herself wholeheartedly to interior prayer and love of Jesus, but she continued to oscillate and waver. Throughout the chapters dealing with her first twenty years in the convent (*Life* 4–8), she was reliving the dilemma Augustine described in book 8 of the *Confessions*, the agony of the divided soul who knows what is the right thing to do but who cannot really do it wholeheartedly because of its dependence on self, not on divine grace. Conversion comes from God, not from one's own efforts.[55]

From this perspective, chapters 9–10, which close off the first section of the *Life*, take on a central importance. In chapter 9 Teresa recounts the events (probably in Lent of 1554) that have been described as her "second conversion" (i.e., after the first conversion to the religious life). The first event was seeing a statue of Jesus as the familiar medieval "Man of Sorrows" (*Ecce Homo*), an object that the Encarnación had borrowed for Lent (*Life* 9.1–3). Teresa testifies to the emotional reaction she experienced in fully realizing Christ's sufferings for her. Even more important was the effect this had in helping her put her trust in

God and not in herself. She says, "I was very distrustful of myself and placed all my trust in God. I think I said that I would not rise from there until he granted what I was begging him for. I believe certainly this was beneficial for me, *because from that time I began improving* [my italics]."[56] Teresa had come to a new realization of God's love for her. It was around the same time (Teresa's chronology is rarely exact) that the reading of Augustine's *Confessions* recounted above took place (*Life* 9.7–8). Teresa reflects on the decisive change in her in chapter 10, an important transition both in her life and in the text.

The beginning of chapter 10 is noteworthy for how Teresa attempts to locate her experiences of God in the tradition of Christian mysticism.[57] Teresa could not read Latin, but it is obvious that before 1559 she had read fairly widely in the Spanish translations of spiritual classics, such as Augustine, Jerome, and Gregory the Great, as well as in the Franciscan writers on recollection, especially Francesco de Osuna and Bernardino de Laredo. Hence, it is not surprising to find a reference to the key Dionysian term "mystical theology" at this point in the *Life*.[58] In her own words, "It used to happen, when I represented Christ within me in order to place myself within his presence, or even while reading, that a feeling of the presence of God [*un sentimiento de la presencia de Dios*] would come upon me unexpectedly so that I could in no way doubt that he was within me or I was totally immersed in him. This did not occur after the manner of a vision. I believe they call the experience mystical theology [*mística teoloxía*]."[59] Teresa goes on to appeal to another key motif of Western mysticism, this time Augustinian, when she describes this state as one where "[t]he will loves; the memory, it seems to me, is almost lost; the intellect does not work discursively, in my opinion, but is not lost." Granted that this tripartite view of the powers of the soul was a commonplace, Teresa is bold in appealing to such theological categories. As we shall see, especially in her mature writings, Teresa's use of this triple formula became much her own—not so much as an exercise in Scholastic faculty psychology but as a way of analyzing the interior dynamics of the path to union. Teresa was quite correct in saying that "mystical theology" is concerned with life and not study, a knowing given by God, not learned by effort. Nor does it necessarily involve visions. Given that Teresa used the term only in the *Life*, however, it may well be that she later decided to avoid technical theological vocabulary to forestall Inquisitorial scrutiny. This did not preclude later Dionysian echoes in her teaching.

Another major theme surfaces in chapter 10.7–9: Teresa's insistence on the radical change in her life at the second conversion and what this means for her narrative. Once again, she notes that she is writing under obedience to her confessors (10.7), but she also stresses that she is happy that the story of her former "wretched life" should become common property to disabuse readers about her *own* goodness. At this point, as she shifts to recounting God's favors toward her, she says, "I do not give this permission, nor do I desire, if they [her confessors] should show it to someone, that they tell who it is who experienced these things. Or who has written this." Teresa wants to become anonymous, but, of course, she cannot. Concerning anything said after this, however, she insists, "if it is good, it will be his [God's] and not mine," and she goes on instruct her confessor, "What is bad will be from me, and your Reverence will strike it out." Teresa pretends to be a writer who is not really a writer. With the Inquisition constantly in mind, she repeats that whatever she says should be "in conformity with the truths of our holy Catholic faith" (10.8).[60] She closes (10.9) by emphasizing the importance of experience for understanding all that will follow: "These matters of prayer will be really obscure for anyone who has not had experience."

This first section of Teresa's *Life* (chaps. 1–10) displays close links with Augustine's *Confessions*, not only in telling the story of a sinner converted by grace but also in the frequency with which the speech-act of *confessio* appears.[61] Another analogy between the two texts is the way in which they reveal the role of human relations, both good and bad, in the path to God. Augustine's portrayal of the meaning of sin in the pear-tree incident in *Confessions* 2 emphasized both the individual perverted will and the solidarity of sinning in the company of others. Throughout the book he often reflected on how good and bad friendship has a part on the path to God. Teresa has a similar, if not quite as developed, picture in her reflections on how some people she felt attracted to led her away from God, but how important true spiritual friends, such as her father, good confessors, and pious nuns, were in her turning to God.[62] Later in the *Life* she even recounts something like a mutual rapture she and García de Toledo, for whom the book was written, once enjoyed while discussing prayer.[63]

There are, to be sure, major differences between the *Confessions* and the *Life*. Not least is the role that accounts of mystical consciousness play in the two works. Augustine's *Confessions* contain only a few passages about his heightened experiences of God's presence in his life (e.g., *Conf.* 7.10, 23; 9.10; and 10.6, 27, 40). Teresa's narrative of her life between ca. 1554 and 1566 switches to another mode, an account of frequent visions and mystical experiences not unlike those found in some medieval visionary narratives she may have read, such as Angela of Foligno's *Book*, or *Memorial*, and Mechthild of Hackeborn's *Book of Special Grace*. In the whole process of self-revelation leading up to the final composition of the *Life*, as Elena Carrera has shown, Teresa made use of various kinds of written materials, such as sermons, hagiography, and mystical narratives, and especially the practice of sacramental confession that was so much a part of the life of a sixteenth-century nun.[64]

Teresa the Ecstatic Contemplative (ca. 1555–1565)

The story of the writing of the *Life* helps explain the shift in the narrative that now turns to Teresa the ecstatic contemplative.[65] As noted above, Teresa composed two accounts of her spiritual life for her confessors and friends in 1554–55 after her conversion. These do not survive, but the first two of her *Spiritual Testimonies* do. The first, her earliest surviving writing, is entitled "Her spiritual state and manner of prayer" ("Su maniera de proceder en oración") and dates from late 1560. Written for Fr. Pedro Ibáñez (*Life* 33.5–6), it already demonstrates Teresa's interest in analyzing her modes of prayer. Her prayer, she says, is not intellectual in a discursive way (i.e., meditation) but is "a recollection and elevation of spirit that comes upon me so suddenly that I cannot resist."[66] This gift does not involve any vision and is a purely divine initiative. A second type is described by Teresa as "a very intense, consuming impulse for God that I cannot resist," which involves pain and frenzy, as well as "a certain rapture (*algún arrobamiento*) in which everything is made peaceful" (1.3). A third kind of mystical grace is apostolic: "At other times, some desires to serve God come upon me with impulses so strong I don't know how to exaggerate them." Paradoxically, this gift makes her desire to do great things for God but also binds her and prevents her from acting (1.4). Other graces make her want to do penance (1.5), move her to seek solitude (1.6), and inspire her to perform all her actions for God (1.7). She summarizes: "All these desires and those, too, for virtue were given me by our Lord after he gave me this prayer of quiet with these raptures [*esta oración quieta con estos arrobamientos*]; and I found I was so improved that it seems to me I previously was a total loss."[67]

Teresa then talks about the effect of these experiences on her life

(1.9–10). After beginning to give an account of her various kinds of visions,[68] she proceeds with further, rather scattered remarks on the nature of her raptures (1.11–29). She also notes that sometimes the experiences last for three to five days, but then they are taken away so that she cannot even remember them or know what good she received from them (1.22). Suddenly, however, on the occasion of a short prayer or the reception of communion, "my soul and body will become very quiet and my intellect very sound and clear." At such moments she says that feelings of well-being come to her from raptures that can last up to three hours (1.23). Teresa insists that the virtues these experiences have given her convince her that they are favors from God, not deceptions of the devil (1.24–26). When some people (i.e., her first spiritual advisors) tried to tell her that the devil was the cause, she said, "At the first locution, or experience of recollection, or vision, all they told me was blotted out; I couldn't do anything but believe God was the cause."[69] She frequently appeals to the test of experience to determine what may be from God and what from the devil—"Between the different effects, the person who has experience will not be deceived, in my view."[70]

This first of the *Spiritual Testimonies* is worth studying because it functions as a kind of trial run for the *Life*, both in its concern to explain Teresa's spiritual experiences for her confessors (and possible Inquisitors) and for her desire to describe her mystical gifts. The *Second Spiritual Testimony*, also written for Pedro Ibáñez probably in 1562, is much the same but briefer. "The visions and revelations have not ceased," she tells him, "but they are much more sublime,"[71] featuring new modes of prayer God taught her and more raptures. Once again, Teresa stresses how these experiences have increased her virtues, such as love of poverty, desire for solitude, and commitment to detachment. The third of the *Spiritual Testimonies*, the "General account of her state of soul" ("Su estado de conciencia"), was written for García de Toledo in 1563 shortly after the first version of the *Life* was finished. Teresa again appeals to her experience, but with an important caveat that was a constant throughout her life. Personal experience is important for grasping high mystical matters, but experiences are valid only if they conform to scripture and the teaching of the church. At the end of this *Testimony* she appends an account of her mystical gifts that she gave to Fr. Domingo Bañez, who went over it along with another Dominican theologian, Fr. Mancio de Corpus Christi. Teresa goes on to say, "They found that none of my experiences was lacking in conformity with sacred scripture. This puts me very much at peace."[72]

These early writings reveal the centrality of the appeal to experience from the outset of Teresa's writing career. To attempt to calculate how often she speaks of the need for experience in the *Life*, as well as in later works like the *Way of Perfection* and *Interior Castle*, would be an exhausting task. As she summarized in *Life* 22.3, "Afterward I understood that if the Lord didn't show me, I was able to learn little from books, because there was nothing I understood until his Majesty gave me the understanding through experience."[73] Appeals to experience were scarcely new for mystical authors, who had been speaking of the need for *experiencia* for more than four centuries. But what is "experience" for Teresa? Many modern readers have read Teresa and other mystics as saying that one must have *felt* something new to appreciate what she (and they) are saying, but "to have experience" (*tener experiencia*) is not the same as "to feel" (*sentir*), a word that Teresa also used frequently. For Teresa, "experience" is coming to *know* something in a vital and holistic way, a gift that does not exclude some kind of external or internal perception, but that necessarily goes beyond mere feeling to knowing and loving. "Experiencing" is not having a sensation *of* something ("I experienced pain when I touched the hot iron"), but becoming experienced *in* something by having been engaged with it ("He was an experienced wine taster").[74] Experience is a dynamic and relational term. Throughout her works, Teresa will say that she *knows* whereof she speaks, because God has given her experiential knowledge of his special gifts. Those who have not received such gifts may know *that* they exist, but they have not known *them* as realities for contemplating, loving, and acting. Cardinal Newman's distinction between *notional* and *real* knowledge may help to illustrate this important difference.

During 1561–62 Teresa was writing the first version of the *Life*, finishing it in June 1562 (see *Epilogue* 4). She addressed the book to her new spiritual director and confessor, García de Toledo, but since he had only become her confessor earlier that year (*Life* 34.6–7), the initial stimulus probably came from other of her confessors and advisors, such as Pedro Ibáñez or Domingo Bañez. Toledo returned the first version to her, perhaps in 1564, with corrections and requests for expansion. In the same year she showed the first version to her friend, the Inquisitor Francisco de Soto y Salazar, who suggested she send it to the well-known theologian and preacher Juan de Avila (1499–1569), the author of the spiritual classic *Audi filia* (*Listen, O Daughter*).[75] Teresa finished the revised version of the text in 1565 and sent it back to Toledo. She also had a copy sent to Juan de Avila. For the next quarter century the *Life* had what Alison Weber calls "a *samizdat* life, characterized by the semi-clandestine copying and circulation of manuscripts."[76]

The first version of the *Life* does not survive, but we know that it did not include the Treatise on Prayer (chaps. 11–22), the more didactic part of the final text, and probably not chapters 33–40, the account of the foundation of St. Joseph and the appended chapters on various mystical gifts. Thus, in this early version Teresa moved from her conversion account (chaps. 9–10) to the narration of her mystical gifts of ca. 1554–62 (chaps. 23–31). The coherence of the first structure was altered not only by adding the Treatise on Prayer but also by the addition of chapters 32–36, recounting the foundation of St. Joseph and the beginning of the reform (an addition that makes some sense), and then tacking on the rather anomalous chapters 37–40, containing a succession of repetitive descriptions of further visions and mystical gifts, something Teresa may have done at the behest of her confessors (see *Epilogue* 2).

Teresa uses many terms for her mystical gifts (*mercedes*) throughout the *Life*—consolations or delights (*gustos*), feelings of devotion (*devociones*), favors (*regalos*), delights (*deleites*), joys (*gozos*), as well as visions (*visiones*), locutions (*palabras*), and states of union (*unión*).[77] These terms begin in the early chapters and are richly developed in chapters 23–31, and she often appeals to her own experiences to illustrate points in the prayer treatise. It is possible to date some of these gifts, but Teresa was not interested in careful chronology, so many of them can be located only approximately. Many of the experiences conform to what can be found in the lives of late medieval saints, especially women,[78] but there are also new notes, especially in the precision of observation and descriptive amplitude Teresa achieved in presenting her experiences. Teresa revels in telling us how often and in what manner Jesus spoke to her, how he appeared, and how she felt about this. She also goes into detail about the psychosomatic effects that both divine and diabolical experiences had on her. Teresa's meticulous descriptions of her inner states have been seen as marking a new era of the "pyschologization" of mysticism, one in which interior experience and its analysis became the basis for establishing the new "science of mysticism" (*la mystique*).[79] But things were not so simple. Analyses of the "book of experience" had been growing since the twelfth century, though few, if any, mystics were quite as introspectively penetrating as Teresa. Attempts to discern which visions and other experiences might be from God, and which might be from the devil disguised as the "Angel of Light" (2 Cor. 11:14), had tortured mystics long before Teresa, as the case of Catherine of

Bologna (d. 1463) shows.[80] Teresa's *Life* represents an intensification of a long trajectory, more than a decisive shift. Thus, we need not be surprised that the devil puts in an appearance in almost every chapter of the *Life*, as well as in many of her letters.[81] Teresa's use of her own experiences, however, always had a didactic, indeed a theological, purpose.[82] As Gillian Ahlgren put it, "One of her unique gifts as a theologian rests in her ability to create and shape a narrative interpretation of personal experience that reveals to readers the reality of a God who is active in human affairs and engages us to see the presence of God in our own life journeys."[83]

With regard to experiences of delight, visions, locutions, raptures, forms of mystical prayer, and states of union, Teresa fits within, but also extends, important traditions in the history of Christian mysticism. As noted above, she had been practicing the prayer of recollection learned from reading Osuna's *Third Spiritual Alphabet* for a number of years, so we need not be surprised that shortly after her second conversion Teresa tells us that she began enjoying the higher states she refers to as the prayer of quiet and the prayer of union (*Life* 23.2, 9). In describing the "third water," or degree of prayer, in *Life* 16.2, she says that "five or even six years ago [ca. 1557–58] the Lord often gave me this prayer in abundance." Such prayer was not a "complete union of all the faculties" with God, but it did leave her in a state of loving inebriation in which "the faculties are almost totally united to God but not so absorbed as not to function." At the time, Teresa could not understand what was going on. "I am extremely pleased that I now understand it," she says.[84] The Treatise on Prayer was inserted to provide a structured explanation of the various stages of prayer and growing union with God she enjoyed over about a dozen years. It was to be her first, but not her last, such exposition.

During these same early years (ca. 1555–60) Teresa had been receiving a range of mystical favors—locutions, visions, and raptures—that she presents in chapters 23–32. Christianity has always been a religion of visions and locutions.[85] Both the Old and the New Testaments contain accounts of visions of heavenly beings and of hearing the voice of angels and/or God. In the New Testament, the Second Person, the Son of God, takes on human nature and is therefore made visible to human eyes, both during his time on earth and potentially in his now glorified flesh. Early Christian literature contains many references to visions and locutions. Augustine of Hippo brought order into the plethora of vision narratives of the Bible and later Christianity. In the twelfth book of his *Literal Commentary on Genesis* he sought to clarify biblical visions by placing them within a theory of three forms of seeing: corporeal seeing with physical eyes; spiritual seeing of images in the mind; and intellectual seeing, the sudden appearance of truth in the mind. These three forms can be realized naturally but also by divine intervention when God causes objects to appear to the eye, creates forms in the imagination (e.g., the visions of the John of the Apocalypse), or instantly reveals supernal truths without any form or image.[86] Although some medieval theologians created new theories of visions—and not all visionary manifestations conveniently fit into the Augustinian categories—the bishop's tripartite division was the dominant way that medieval and early modern mystics, like Teresa, understood and presented their visions. Teresa had access to this theoretical paradigm through several channels and was doubtless familiar with some of the many visionary narratives of late medieval and sixteenth-century Spain.[87]

Teresa's visions began early.[88] As noted above, she recalls a frightening vision of Christ warning her about her wayward life at an early date (*Life* 7.6). She presumably began receiving more positive visions shortly after her second conversion, but it is hard to provide precise dates. *Life* 27.2–5 contains a narrative of an intellectual vision of Christ probably on June 29, 1559, the Feast of St. Peter. This experience started with a locution. She says, "I saw, or to put it better, I felt Christ beside me; I saw nothing with my bodily eyes or with my soul, but it seemed to me that Christ was at my side—I saw that it was he, in my opinion, who was speaking to me." The vision troubled Teresa, because it was not an imaginative vision, which seems to imply that thus far she had been receiving only this kind of seeing. Teresa gives a careful and theologically correct analysis of the experience: "In this vision there is nothing of this [sensory experience], nor do you see darkness; but the vision is represented through knowledge given to the soul that is clearer than sunlight." She also distinguishes it from what takes place in the prayer of union or quiet.[89]

The first imaginative (i.e., spiritual) visions described by Teresa that we can more or less date, come from 1559–60, but she must have received some before this. The first of these accounts of imagistic visions was not a direct appearance of Christ. Teresa's "Transverberation," that is, the vision of an angel piercing her heart, was an erotic experience involving both severe pain and supreme delight (*Life* 29.13). She does not date it, but 1559 seems likely. This piercing of her heart is among the most famous visions in the history of Christianity, not only because it was so memorably transformed into marble in G. L.

Bernini's theatrical portrayal of "Teresa in Ecstasy" in the Church of Santa Maria della Vittoria in Rome (1647–51), but also because it appears to be the only vision that was ever accorded its own feast day.[90] After a discussion of how God's sending of a "wound of love" induces both pain and delight (29.7–12), Teresa describes a vision that she says she sees "sometimes." The portrayal is highly imaginative, the picture of an angel plunging a fiery dart into her heart. Teresa was confused about the angel, whom she calls a cherub, but since she identifies the angel with divine love, it is more likely a seraph, the angelic order traditionally identified with supreme love of God. Here is her account:

> It seemed to me that this angel plunged the dart several times into my heart and that it reached deep within me. When he drew it out, I thought he was carrying off with him the deepest part of me, and he left me all on fire with great love of God. The pain was so great that it made me moan, and the sweetness this greatest pain caused me was so superabundant that there was no desire capable of taking it away; nor is the soul content with less than God. The pain is not bodily but spiritual, although the body does not fail to share in some of it, and even a great deal.[91]

Teresa's embodied experience fits into the tradition of the "wound of love" dating back to patristic interpretations of Song of Songs 2:5 ("He has wounded me with charity"), one extended by medieval mystics, especially women, in physically erotic terms.[92] No one, however, had given this theme as detailed a description and as direct an erotic tone, especially in its evocation of both inner (spiritually erotic) and outer (orgasmic) effects. Teresa's mysticism, for all that it attempts to fit within traditional "spiritualized" categories, remains deeply embodied in nature—inner pleasure-pain overflows into the physical senses.[93] Bernini's rendering may be the most powerful portrayal of sexual-spiritual ecstasy in Western art.[94]

The second imaginative vision that Teresa describes is a vision of Christ. *Life* 28.1–4 recounts the gradual showing of Christ's beautiful hands and face that seemingly prepares her for seeing the full glorious body of the resurrected Christ on the Feast of St. Paul, probably January 25, 1560 (some think 1561). She says, "[T]his most sacred humanity in its risen form was represented to me completely, as it is in paintings, with wonderful beauty and majesty. . . . And writing about it was very difficult for me to do because one cannot describe this vision without ruining it."[95] Teresa insists this was an imaginative vision, not one seen with corporeal eyes (Teresa never received any purely corporeal visions). She tries to describe it at length using comparisons about how the inner vision of Christ's glorious body differs from what we see here on earth—its splendor does not dazzle, and its brightness is supreme, so that "the sun's brightness that we see appears tarnished in comparison with that brightness." It is like the difference between clear water flowing over crystal and muddy water flowing over dirt. Sunlight seems artificial, she says, while the vision alone appears natural. "In sum," Teresa concludes, "it is of such a kind that a person couldn't imagine what it is like in all the days of his life no matter how powerful an intellect he might have."[96] These passages provide a sense of the detail of Teresa's descriptions of her mystical experiences and how she makes use of analogies she says were sometimes revealed to her by God, and at other times were her own attempts to describe the indescribable.[97] At the beginning of chapter 29 she recounts a whole series of other forms of imaginative showing of Christ.[98]

In her narrations of mystical gifts in *Life* 23–29, Teresa was also concerned to describe and analyze when and how God spoke to her.[99] Hearing God's voice is a motif rooted in the Bible, and there had been considerable interest since the fourteenth century in the discernment needed to distinguish the divine voice from one's own inner voice (what we might call the subconscious), or the misleading voice of the devil. Many mystics, especially women, had given accounts of God's speaking to them, but few analyzed the nature of such locutions as carefully as Teresa. Although she was well aware of the possibility of deception regarding locutions, modern readers of Teresa's works can still be permitted some skepticism about how far her own inner need to be convinced of divine support for her actions may have been involved in the messages she said she received from God in so many difficult situations.[100]

Teresa notes that she was quite surprised when Christ first began to speak in her mind, probably about 1557. While praying the Psalms, she began to meditate on how many favors she had received from God in comparison with his other servants. Christ suddenly spoke up to correct her: "You answered me, Lord: 'Serve me, and don't bother about such things.' This is the first locution I heard you speak to me, and so I was very frightened."[101] Teresa soon got over her fright and for the remainder of her life (1557–82) divine locutions were a constant feature. In the midst of her greatest difficulties and challenges, Christ seemed always ready to give her verbal advice or to assure her that all would turn out right.[102] Teresa incorporated these locutions into her life story both as contemplative and as active reformer in order to strengthen the sense that God was guiding her on a day-to-day basis.

Chapters 25–27 of the *Life* give Teresa's first extended analysis of God's manner of speaking to her. "It seems to me that it would be good to explain how this locution [*este hablar*] the Lord grants takes place and what the soul feels [*siente*], so that your Reverence may understand it."[103] Teresa says such words are explicit and clear, but not heard with bodily ears. They are also irresistible in the sense that we cannot not hear them. Discernment is important in order to tell whether the inner speaking comes from a good spirit, a bad spirit, or from one's own spirit (25.2: a traditional motif).[104] The marks of clarity, irresistibility, and effectiveness enable us to tell what is from us and what from God (25.2–4), and Teresa goes into considerable detail as she discusses how to distinguish locutions that originate in our minds from those that come from God (25.6–9). Fears of locutions from the devil were widespread in the late Middle Ages and early modern Europe, so Teresa also spends much time analyzing how to determine if an inner voice might be diabolical in origin (25.10–16), with a primary test being the conformity of the locution with the "truth that the church holds" (25.12–13). The last part of this chapter (25.17–22), as well as the first part of the next (26.2), provides examples of some of the divine locutions given her and the great difficulty she had in convincing her early spiritual advisors that these voices were, indeed, from God.[105] The deepest positive criterion for a divine origin is experience: "I firmly believe that whoever has had the experience will understand and see that I succeeded in saying something; whoever has not had the experience—I wouldn't be surprised if it all seems to be nonsense to such a one."[106] Chapter 27, while primarily dealing with intellectual visions, also touches on the kinds of locutions that often accompany them. It was after two years of repeated locutions of the kind analyzed in chapter 25 that Teresa received her first intellectual vision (27.2). After describing this vision and her confessor's reaction, she introduces a different manner of speaking, one in which "[t]he Lord puts what he wants the soul to know without image or explicit words very deeply within it, and there he makes this known without image and explicit words, but in the manner of this vision we mentioned."[107] In other words, there is an intellectual form of locution, a heavenly understanding without any speaking, that is parallel to intellectual visions, one that Teresa contrasts with the more usual heard locutions (27.7–10).

Not all of Teresa's mystical gifts were pleasurable. Drawing near to God often involves distress and suffering as the soul realizes its sinfulness and its need to undergo purgation. Sometimes God plunges souls seeking him into states of alienation, dereliction, and interior torture as part of the purgative process. Teresa suffered much from the assaults of the devil, but her most intense inner sufferings came from God. This, again, was not new. The mysticism of dereliction had biblical prototypes in the sufferings of Job and of Christ in the Garden of Gethsemane and on the cross. The theme appears as early as Gregory the Great and is found in a number of late medieval mystics, both men, such as John Tauler, and women, like Angela of Foligno.[108] Three passages in the *Life* place Teresa in this tradition. The first is in chapter 20.9–16 (1565?) and is described as a painful experience (*pena*) coming "much later than all the visions and revelations I shall write of" (20.9). Teresa distinguishes this from the corporeal pleasure-pain that accompanies the experience of the wounding of the soul (e.g., 29.8–14). It is an extreme desolation like being placed in a desert bereft of all creatures. Paradoxically, "when it seems to me that God is then exceedingly far away, he communicates his grandeurs in the most strange manner thinkable," a way that Teresa cannot describe.[109] In this manner of prayer, the soul receives no consolation from anything, so that it seems like it is crucified. Its desire for heaven increases to an intensity that takes away sensory consciousness, though in a manner different from the usual raptures (20.10–11). Teresa testifies to García de Toledo that other nuns will vouch for the rigidity that overtook her body when she was having this kind of experience (20.12). Despite Teresa's many comparisons (20.13–16), she has trouble explaining such a form of solitude, desolation, and suffering, something that sounds much like what her friend John of the Cross would later analyze as the passive night of the spirit.[110] God tells her not to fear this pain but "to esteem this gift more than all the others" because of the way it purifies the soul (20.16).

Life 30.11–14 recounts a trial that God permitted the devil to inflict on Teresa on the day before the Vigil of Corpus Christi, but which she says she also experienced during Holy Week. Here the devil distracts and upsets the soul so that she walks in the dark and cannot find any relief (30.11). The soul can find no satisfaction in any spiritual practice, but only anguish. "In my opinion," she says, "the experience is a kind of copy of hell, . . . for the soul burns within itself without knowing who started the fire or where it comes from or how to flee from it or what to put it out with."[111] Teresa recounts the difficulties she had discussing this kind of suffering with her confessors, and she also mentions the locutions she received from God encouraging her to persist through these purgative trials, which were ultimately of great benefit for the soul (30.14).

The most terrible of these events seems to have happened about 1560. "While I was in prayer one day," Teresa says, "I suddenly found, without knowing how, I had seemingly been put in hell."[112] Although the vision was brief, Teresa says she can never forget it, as her vivid description of her infernal sufferings demonstrates. She expands on her trials, both the fire she felt in the soul and the "constriction, suffocation, and affliction" that made it feel like the soul was tearing itself to pieces (32.2). Teresa says she was placed in a "kind of hole made in the wall" where she was enveloped in darkness and experienced a sense of suffocation (32.3). She declares that she never imagined that such a fearful vision was possible, but she recognizes "that this experience was one of the greatest favors the Lord granted me because it helped me very much to lose fear of the tribulations and contradictions of life, as well as grow strong enough to suffer them and give thanks to the Lord who freed me . . . from such everlasting and terrible evils."[113] Teresa ends by saying that the vision inspired her apostolic desire to save all souls (especially Lutherans!) from hell (32.6). These experiences of suffering and dereliction show that Teresa's path included moments of terrible pain, along with the more familiar locutions and visions.[114]

Although Teresa's account of her mystical gifts in the *Life* is not chronological or very well structured, it is possible to discern a kind of itinerary. Right from the time of her second conversion (probably 1554) she had begun to experience deep prayer states, what she calls the prayer of quiet and the prayer of union (16.2; 23.2, 9). These constitute the state of spiritual betrothal. Locutions and visions began after this (25.11), with the locutions starting about 1557 (19.9). Teresa's first intellectual vision took place on the Feast of Sts. Peter and Paul, most likely in 1559, but she had been receiving spiritual (i.e., imaginative) visions for several years before this. Although she distinguishes the two theoretically, according to the Augustinian pattern, in practice the two forms of vision were closely related. As she says in chapter 28.9: "These two kinds of vision almost always come together. This is the way they occur: with the eyes of the soul we see the excellence, beauty, and glory of the most holy humanity; and through intellectual vision . . . we are given an understanding of how God is powerful."[115] Teresa's first rapture occurred while chanting the hymn "Veni Creator Spiritus," probably around 1558 (24.5–7). Although she says that no visions or locutions can be experienced during rapture (25.5), locutions can come shortly after such experiences (24.5; 32.12). In conclusion, Teresa's phenomenology of divine gifts and forms of mystical consciousness as presented in these chapters of the *Life* is rich, if not always clear.

The Four Waters of Prayer (Chapters 11–22)[116]

It was apparently to remedy this imprecision that Teresa, in consultation with García de Toledo, expanded the first version of the *Life* with the Treatise on Prayer that takes up chapters 11–22. This section provides a kind of road map for her nuns in their own prayer lives. Itineraries of the mystical path were many; Teresa's is unusual both for its fourfold structure and its basic metaphor of water.[117] The notion of the soul as a garden (*hortus conclusus*) is rooted in the Song of Songs 4:12, and the "garden of the soul" has a rich history, especially in the late Middle Ages.[118] Teresa was much taken with it (see *Life* 14.9). Her use of the comparison of different ways of watering the garden speaks to the experience of her nuns cultivating their convent gardens in arid Castile (11.7), as well as to the usefulness of the metaphor in distinguishing between the stages of prayer where the nuns can work with God (later called acquired contemplation), and the higher states that depend solely on divine operative grace (later called infused contemplation). This section is also the first place where Teresa tries to explain the role of the faculties of memory, intellect, and will in the progress of prayer.

Interior prayer was central to Teresa's reform, so the most important lesson to be learned from the *Life* is how to pray. Teresa's definition of prayer is simple, "Mental prayer in my opinion is nothing else than an intimate sharing between friends."[119] But just as friendship is meant to keep growing, prayer should be a developing reality in the life of the nun. The first stage of the watering of prayer (chaps. 11–13) is compared to the laborious work of drawing water from a well, and Teresa says, "the greatest labor is in the beginning because it is the beginner who works while the Lord gives the increase" (11.5). Beginners must recollect their senses in the discursive work of the intellect and get used to silence and solitude (11.9). Such labor can go on for years, as Teresa notes regarding her own life (11.11). This laboriousness also teaches us our own worthlessness, that is, the foundational virtue of humility, which returns again and again in her account.[120] She gives shrewd insights into the aridity of prayer that frequently marks this first stage (11.13–17), and she also emphasizes that everything is in God's hands, criticizing learned men who complain that God does not give them devotion, which she says, "I believe is a fault" (11.14). She concludes, "Experience is a great help in all, for it teaches us what is suitable for us; and God can be served in everything."[121]

Chapter 12 continues this practical vein, emphasizing that the effort of trying to keep Christ present in our minds is more important than feeling consolation or devotion. It is not we who are able to raise ourselves up to a higher stage; this is God's work (12.6–7). In this first stage temptations from the devil often occur, and Teresa spends chapter 13 discussing these in some detail. Chapter 13 also mentions another central motif in her teaching, the necessity for total commitment to prayer without worrying about the body and worldly matters. If we split our intention between prayer and our own pleasure, as Teresa did for so many years, we will never reach "the freedom of spirit" that characterizes true prayer.[122]

The second degree of prayer (*Life* 14–15) is compared to watering the garden by a water wheel and aqueducts, a less laborious exercise because divine grace is gradually taking over, although the human faculties are still operative. Teresa uses Augustinian language, noting how the powers of memory, intellect, and will start to be gathered together as the will (always central for her) begins to become captive to God (14.2–3). Teresa's notion of the will, however, is not so much a capacity to act, as it is the general disposition or attitude of the soul, which is here becoming more docile to divine action.[123] Along with the change in the will, the involvement of the intellect in meditating slows down, and the virtues grow more quickly, as God's action is slowly mastering the soul (14.4–6). As Teresa puts it, the effects in the soul are now becoming "supernatural," that is, caused only by God (14.8). In this "prayer of quiet" (*oración de quietud*) the will is being united with God, although the faculties of memory and intellect are still distracted, despite being drawn into recollection by the will (15.1). This prayer is "a little spark of God's true love" (15.4), one that demands careful cultivation (15.5–14), especially because diabolical deceptions are still frequent at this stage. For Teresa, this mode of prayer is "the beginning of all blessings" (15.15).[124]

The final two stages of prayer are fully passive states in which the soul receives progressively more exalted favors from God. These are more fully explored than the first two kinds of "waters." The third stage (chaps. 16–17) is compared to water from a spring or river flowing through a garden. Teresa says, "The Lord so desires to help the gardener that he himself becomes practically the gardener and the one who does everything."[125] This stage is identified as the "sleep of the faculties" (*sueño de las potencias*), where the powers of the soul do not totally die but do not advert to their own functioning.[126] Teresa illustrates this kind of prayer from her own experience (16.2), saying that she finds it hard to describe the differences between the various kinds of union with God, although she has now come to understand that in this stage "the faculties are almost totally united with God but not so absorbed as not to function."[127] Teresa tries to explain this by noting that here the faculties only have the ability to be occupied with God, and that the intellect is "worth nothing" (presumably in its discursive activity). She calls the state "delicate" because it is pleasing, and "heavy" because it is often difficult to bear, although we do not want to be freed from it (16.5).

Chapter 17 turns to a discussion of the effects of the third state of prayer. Teresa says that the soul must totally abandon itself to God—"If he wants to bring the soul to heaven, it goes; if to hell, it feels no grief since it goes with its God."[128] In the discussion that follows (17.3–8) Teresa attempts to distinguish, not always with complete clarity as she admits, three kinds of union that come from the "spring." The highest form is the one she has described in chapter 16, as she says in 17.5. In this chapter, however, she is talking about two other forms. The lower (17.1–4) is described as "a very apparent union of the whole soul with God, but seemingly his Majesty desires to give leeway to the faculties so that they may understand and rejoice in the many things he is accomplishing here."[129] In this kind of union the will is in deep quiet, but the intellect and memory can engage in works of charity, so that the soul rejoices both in the idleness of Mary and the active life of Martha (Luke 10:38–42) "in such a way that it is as though engaged in both the active and the contemplative life together."[130] Higher than this is "another kind of union" set out in 17.5–7. In speaking of this union Teresa distinguishes three kinds of grace. "For it is one grace," she says, "to receive the Lord's favor; another, to understand which favor and which grace it is; and a third, to know how to describe and explain it" (17.5). She says that she often receives this kind of union in which God takes the will and even the intellect to himself, but the memory and the imagination remain free and "carry on such a war that the soul is left powerless" (17.6). Teresa says she was troubled for years by the annoying distractions of memory-imagination (she often yokes the two) until she finally learned to pay no more attention to them than one would to a "madman" (17.7). Teresa closes her account of the third water by once again emphasizing the difference between experiencing these states and understanding what they are (17.8).

The longest treatment of the *Life* is given to the fourth and highest degree of prayer, which Teresa compares to heavy rain soaking the ground (chaps. 18–22). Here "the soul isn't in possession of its sense, but it rejoices without understanding what it is rejoicing in." Because this prayer features "the union of all the faculties" (*union de todas las potencias,* 18.1), it is even more difficult to expound. Teresa says these things are explained in mystical theology, whose vocabulary she does not know (18.2). "What I'm attempting to explain," she says, "is what the soul feels when it is in this divine union."[131] She also notes that she will speak of the graces and effects that this water leaves in the soul and whether the soul can do anything on its own to attain it (18.6). It is important to distinguish between the union itself and the "elevation of spirit" (*levantamiento de espíritu*) that accompanies it, which, although it seems very similar, is marked by a greater increase in "detachment from creatures" (*desasir de la criaturas*). Those who have experience of raptures understand the difference (18.7). Teresa notes that the fourth water, since it is a purely divine gift, can come at any time, but it usually occurs after a long period of mental prayer (18.9). Experientially, it is a "swoon" (*desmayo*) in which all the faculties fail and the senses become oblivious to what is around them (18.10). It cannot last very long, certainly not longer than a half hour (18.12). Once again, she insists that it is the will that holds on to the union when the intellect and memory-imagination return to themselves in at least a partial way (18.13). In trying to communicate what the soul does during this experience of rapture, Teresa once received a locution after communion in which the Lord told her: "It detaches itself from everything, daughter, so as to abide more in me. It is no longer the soul that lives but I [Gal. 2:20]. Since it cannot comprehend what it understands, there is an understanding by not understanding."[132] This language of unknowing links Teresa's thought to aspects of the Affective Dionysianism of the late Middle Ages.

Chapter 18 sets out the general characteristics of the fourth water, while chapter 19 begins to discuss its effects in the soul. Joyous tears, consolations, and deeper humility are marks of the fourth water (19.1–2), but the major theme of this chapter is Teresa's insistence on the fact that, despite the assaults of the devil, no soul who has reached this level should abandon mental prayer, the way she did for about a year and a half early in her career (19.4, 10–15). The long chapter 20 returns to the difference between union and rapture, a key to the fourth water. Teresa insists that rapture is higher than union: "The advantage rapture has over union is great. The rapture produces much stronger effects and causes many other phenomena. Union seems the same at the beginning, in the middle, and at the end; and it takes place in the interior of the soul. But since these other phenomena are of a higher degree, they produce their effect both interiorly and exteriorly."[133] Teresa uses the term *unión* in so many different ways in these chapters that it is difficult to be sure precisely what she means in each case.[134] Later, in the *Interior Castle*, she will try to sort out the different forms of union more clearly and will also reject the naïve understanding of the deepest form of union as being characterized by psychosomatic abstraction, sense immobility, and rapture. One can say that at this stage in her life (and under the dubious guidance of some of her confessors), this was all she could speak to.

Teresa engages in her usual method of trying to find natural comparisons for understanding these raptures (20.2–4). She notes that she fought against them, though at other times it was impossible for her to resist, so that the ravishment carried off her soul, her head, and "sometimes the whole body until it was raised from the ground."[135] By this stage in the narrative, Teresa has distanced herself from a teaching voice in the third person to feature first-person accounts of her mystical gifts, whether in response to the requests of her confessor, or because of her inner impulse to tell her story. It is here, for example, that she introduces the long account (20.9–16) of the painful experience already discussed above. Finally, she recalls that she is supposed to be talking about raptures (20.17), so she returns to discussing levitation (20.18), the temporal duration of raptures (20.19), and the way that even intellect and memory are temporally suspended in such states (20.20). Teresa has been accused of a lack of order in her presentation of the progress of prayer in the *Life*. Chapter 20, especially in its meandering conclusion (20.21–29), shows there is some truth to this critique.

The final two chapters of the fourth water conclude the Treatise on Prayer and underline an important aspect to Teresa's mysticism not always evident from what has been presented thus far in the *Life*, namely, the christological center of her teaching.[136] Chapter 21 continues her account of the effects of the fourth water, concentrating on how at this stage God gives the soul strong desires not only but also "the strength to put these desires into practice" (21.5). She has a long address to the Lord asking him for the strength to serve him better (21.5–6), like Paul and Mary Magdalene. Raptures make the soul grow in the virtues, as well as in perfection and detachment, as she knows from her own experience (21.8–12). "Here in this ecstasy [*en este éstasi*]," she concludes, "are received the true revelations and the great favors and visions—and all serves to humiliate and strengthen the soul, to lessen its esteem for the things of this life, and to make it know more clearly the grandeurs of the reward the Lord has prepared for those who serve him."[137] Chapter 22 follows this up with an exposition of the christological nature of her prayer life.

Teresa begins by noting that some books say that the necessary work of the soul to prepare itself for the gift of union/rapture is to get rid of all corporeal images, even that of the humanity of Christ (22.1). She goes on: "This is good, it seems to me, sometimes; but to withdraw completely from Christ or that this divine body be counted in a balance with our own miseries or with all creation, I cannot endure."[138] Teresa is careful not to condemn "the learned and spiritual men" who teach this, and she herself tried to follow this practice for a time. But now she is certain that "if I had kept to that practice, I believe I would never have arrived at where I am now because in my opinion the practice is a mistaken one" (22.2). Teresa recounts how she tried to rid her prayer of the image of Jesus, but she could not. She even laments, "Is it possible, my Lord, that it entered my mind for even an hour that you would be an impediment to my greater good?" (22.4). This emptying practice, she says, is why many souls do not advance beyond the prayer of union (i.e., stage 3). She analyzes two reasons for failure to progress to the highest states of prayer. The first is a lack of humility (22.5), which she later describes as "wanting to raise the soul up before the Lord raises it, in not being content to meditate on something so valuable [i.e., Christ's humanity], and in wanting to be Mary before having worked with Martha."[139] The second reason is that "we are not angels but we have a body. The desire to be angels while we are on earth— and as much on earth as I was—is foolishness."[140] Teresa's earthy good sense and her conviction that she needs the support of Christ, her true friend, throughout her mystical path made the way of complete abstraction a burden and a danger (22.6–7). Turning aside from corporeal things is certainly good, but only for the very advanced. Until then, God must be sought through creatures. Above all, she insists: "What I wanted to explain was that the most sacred humanity of Christ must not be counted in a balance with other corporeal things" (22.8). In other words, Christ's humanity is not just one *thing* among other things—it is the reason for the existence of all things.[141] It is true that when God suspends our faculties, the intellectual sense of his presence is taken away from the subject's consciousness. "Then let it be so, gladly; blessed such a loss that enables us to enjoy more that which seems to be lost."[142] In such rapture the soul completely loves the One whom it no longer understands. What Teresa is dead set against is that we should try to lose the sense of the presence of Christ's humanity *before* God gives us the gift of rapture.[143] Rapture is God's gift, not our work.

In the remainder of chapter 22, Teresa draws out the message of the need for humility, not seeking consolation, and placing ourselves totally at God's command in the path of prayer. If we become like little donkeys faithfully turning the water wheel, we will obtain more of the water of grace than the most industrious gardener (22.12). She then addresses García de Toledo, asking him why, when the soul has begun to receive the higher graces she has been describing, it seems to progress so much faster and more surely than before (22.15). The comparison she comes up with is that of food: a little is always tasty, but the person who eats more receives more and more nourishment (22.16). Teresa ends the treatise on prayer with a fitting address to her Divine Lover: "O Lord of my soul, if only one had words to explain what you give to those who trust in you, and what is lost by those who reach this state yet keep themselves to themselves! It is not your will, Lord, that they should, for you do more than this when you come to a dwelling as mean as mine."[144]

Teresa the Active Contemplative (1566–1582)

The years 1566–67 marked a watershed in Teresa's life: the full transition to a life of a "contemplative in action." As Edward Howells has suggested, the uniting of inner contemplation and exterior reforming action is the key to Teresa's life, and the combination of the inner and the outer dimensions is evident in her view of the new reformed communities. "Thus," as Howells puts it, "she [Teresa] moves from a reactive and interior conception of religious life to a kind of social reform, intended as a corrective to Spanish society and the church, making concrete the mystical insight that God is with the soul in an equal union of love."[145] This shift away from pure inwardness was already under way during her first five years at St. Joseph. The first chapter of the *Book of Foundations* paints an idyllic picture of these years as "the most restful of my life."[146] Yet Teresa was already at work on plans to spread the reform, and she was continuing her writing to teach her nuns about interior prayer and the path to union with God. St. Joseph was officially opened on August 24, 1562, but, owing to complications, Teresa had to return to the Encarnación for a few months before she could move to the new foundation, whereupon she changed her name to Teresa de Jesús. She became the prioress of the house in early 1563. Among her first tasks was to compose a set of *Constitutions* for the reform.

Teresa was not the first female founder to write a rule of life for her followers. That privilege belongs to Clare of Assisi. Nevertheless, Teresa's achievement was notable and the *Constitutions* (*Constituciones*), which she began writing in 1563, tell us much about her view of religious life and the best way to cultivate prayer. In early 1567, when the Carmelite prior general visited Avila, Teresa was able to show him the *Constitutions*, which he approved. This first version does not survive. What we have at present are three early copies that already show evidence of a process of expansion and modification, especially with regard to the long penal code (chaps. 10–15) at the end, which was not written by Teresa but was probably taken over from the Rule at the Encarnación.[147] Furthermore, from the time of the establishment of Apostolic Visitors for the reformed houses in 1569, new regulations (not always favored by Teresa) were added in haphazard fashion. Finally, in 1581, the longer and official Constitutions of Alcalá for the Reformed Congregation were published by Jerónimo Gracián, Teresa's friend and the provincial. They were put under his name and that of the prior general (Teresa's role was concealed). This document, however, still represented her vision, but it was to be rejected in 1592 by the new provincial, Nicolás Doria. The irony is clear: the woman who engineered the reform was rejected by the male leaders as soon as convenient.

Fortunately, Teresa's *Constitutions* do exist and provide us with a sense of what she had in mind.[148] She was concerned to form small, tightly knit, poor, humble communities of women dedicated to mental prayer. In the manner of many rules, Teresa begins by laying down regulations for the saying of the office (chap. 1), and the reception of communion (chap. 2). Spiritual reading is important, however, in a "cell or hermitage" where the sister can be devoted to "recollection" (*recogimiento*), the heritage of the ancient Carmelite tradition and recent Spanish mysticism.[149] It was probably only in 1562 that Teresa had learned from María de Jesús about the practice of poverty in the primitive Carmelite Rule (*Life* 35.1–6), but she embraced it heartily, as is evident both in the *Life* (e.g., 33.13; 35.2–6) and here in the *Constitutions*: "Let them always live on alms and without any income, but insofar as is possible let there be no begging."[150] Teresa wants her nuns to be engaged in useful, but not distracting, labor, such as spinning and sewing, so their minds can be open for meditation and contemplation. Fasting and other forms of penance are moderate (chap. 4), but the rules for enclosure are strict (chap. 5), both in criticism of what Teresa had experienced at the Encarnación and in line with what the just-concluded Council of Trent was legislating for female religious. Teresa's egalitarian program is evident when she insists that worthy applicants are not to be turned away because they cannot provide alms to the house (chap. 6.21). Above all, one gets the sense that Teresa wanted to form a loving community of dedicated religious women, which is why she insists that the prioress should be first in line for the duty of sweeping (chap. 7.22). She also encourages time for community conversation at the prioress's discretion (chap. 8.26 and 28). Teresa's strong opposition to importing the rigid hierarchical structures of contemporary Spain into her new houses is evident: "Never should the prioress or any of the sisters use the title Doña [i.e., My Lady]." Rather, her model is that the prioress "should strive to be loved so that she may be obeyed" (chap. 10.34).

The written record of Teresa's concern for the spread of the reform as found in the *Constitutions* is only one aspect of her activity as founder and director. St. Joseph and the other reformed houses were also seedbeds for nourishing and spreading a new form of religious life by personal contact, instruction both individual and communal, and the discipline of convent life. Teresa's letters, which really do not become frequent until the 1570s, give us much evidence for this process, which surely began, however, a decade earlier.

The Way of Perfection

The last of Teresa's years of "peace and quiet" at St. Joseph (1565–67) were of great importance to her mystical writings. She appears to have sent off the revised version of the *Life* in 1565 and was later chagrined not to have a copy for herself as various other eyes, critical or friendly, perused the book. Despite this annoyance, she resolved to continue writing, and 1566 seems to have been a banner year in which she produced two texts, the *Way of Perfection* (*Camino de perfección*),[151] and the first version of the *Meditations on the Song of Songs* (*Meditaciones sobre los Cantares*). Although these works are less well known than the *Life* and the *Interior Castle*, had these been all of the Carmelite's writings that survived, she would still rank high among early modern Catholic mystics.

Teresa's *Way of Perfection*, a kind of "how-to-do-it" book concerning prayer, has also been called "the programmatic writing of her reform."[152] The book is related to the *Life*, as she herself tells us. Her confessor, Domingo Bañez, had read the *Life* and approved of its contents, but he forbade Teresa from circulating it (she had, however, sent some copies to clerical censors). The community at St. Joseph had been asking Teresa for some time to write them reflections about prayer (see *Way*, Prol. B.1; chaps. 15.1; 16.3–5; 32.9; and 42.6), and Teresa received Bañez's permission to go ahead with this. As the conclusion tells us (chap. 42.6–7), Teresa hoped that both books would soon be made available to her nuns, but this was not to be in her lifetime. In the *Way*, Teresa expresses greater confidence in her teaching role than she had dared in the *Life*: "I can even say 'teach you,' because as a Mother, having the office of prioress, I'm allowed to teach."[153] She apparently wrote quickly, finishing off the first version of seventy-two chapters (the Escorial text), which she sent to García de Toledo for correction probably early in 1566. García sent back about fifty corrections and Teresa dutifully incorporated them and other changes in a second version of forty-two chapters (the Vallidolid text). This version, which also seems to have been finished in 1566, underwent further corrections (Toledo version). The changes often tone down some of Teresa's more direct and critical statements, nowhere more than in what she wrote in defense of women in chapter 3. I quote this passage at length with the excised texts from Version 1 in brackets. Teresa says, addressing Christ and speaking of her nuns:

> I think you will not fail to do what they beg of you. Nor did you, Lord, when you walked the world, despise women; rather, with great compassion, you always helped them. [And you found as much love and more faith in them than you did in men. . . . Is it not enough, O Lord, that the world has intimidated us . . . so that we may not do anything worthwhile for you in public or dare speak some truths that we lament over in secret, without your failing to hear so just a petition? I do not believe, Lord, that this could be true of your goodness and justice, for you are a just judge and not like those of the world. Since the world's judges are all sons of Adam and all of them men, there is no virtue in women that they do not hold suspect.][154]

Teresa seems less concerned about the danger of Inquisitorial investigation in this book, possibly because she was writing with the explicit permission of Bañez, although she still submitted her reflections to "the learned men [*letrados*] who will see this work to look it over carefully and to correct any mistake there may be as to what the church holds, as well as any other mistakes in other matters."[155] The content, at least with regard to the stages of prayer, mostly mirrors what is found in the *Life*, but the presentation is more direct and practical and there are some differences. Once again, the appeal to experience is to the fore, mentioned over forty times. The message begins right with the Prologue, where the nun says, "I shall say nothing about what I have not experienced myself or seen in others [or received understanding of from our Lord in prayer]."[156] Speaking of the kind of clear knowledge of celestial things sometimes given by God about the difference between loving a creature and loving God, Teresa avers "this is seen through experience [*por espiriencia*], which is entirely different from merely thinking about it or believing it."[157] Apologizing for not writing much about her own contemplation in chapter 23.4, Teresa says, "Those of you who . . . experience supernatural prayer may obtain that account [i.e., the *Life*] after my death; those of you who do not, need not worry about it." Commenting on the phrase from the Our Father, "Who art in heaven," she says that it is vital not only to believe the truths in the prayer, but "to strive to understand them through experience" (28.1). Over and over, Teresa turns to the test of experience, that is, real knowing, as opposed to abstract speculation, and even faith, as the criterion for her teaching.

The reverse side of the experience of God-given knowing and loving is the possibility of deception by the devil, who, as in the *Life*, plays a large role.[158] The devil is the general opponent of the whole reform movement (a job he also has in many of Teresa's letters), but he is primarily the great deceiver, always ready to lead the sisters away from the path to union, either by discouraging good practices, or encouraging things that seem helpful but that are in reality dangerous. Sometimes the devil frightens nuns by insinuating that acts of penance will harm their health (10.6–8); at other times he discourages people from the life of prayer through various subterfuges (21.7–9). Above all, the devil tries to undermine the determination necessary to begin the life of prayer in people who have not yet experienced God's goodness (23.4–5). The devil also tempts us to pride, convincing us we possess virtues that are not really ours (38.2–5), and gives us a false self-assurance that we are making good progress and will not slip back into our former bad ways (39.1–4). The sure cure for diabolical deception, for Teresa, involves something always fundamental to her teaching—humility.

The structure of the *Way of Perfection* is fairly clear, although Teresa continues the meandering style and frequent digressions seen in the *Life*. The first three chapters introduce the nature of the reform, while chapters 4–15 contain a treatment of the three foundations of a sound prayer life: love of neighbor (chaps. 4, 6–7); detachment (chaps. 8–11,

13.7); and humility (chaps. 12–15). Love is the whole purpose of the Christian life, especially the life of the sisters in the communities of the reform, where "all must be friends, all must be loved, all must be held dear, all must be helped."[159] Following Augustine, Teresa is anxious to show that all true love and friendship are based on the priority of loving God, so that experiencing the difference between loving the Creator and loving the creature is essential for the nuns (6.3–7). Such perfect love imitates the love of "the Commander-in-Chief of love, Jesus, our good" (6.9; 7.4). Humility is also vital: "Let each one see what humility she has, and she will see what progress has been made" (12.6). And, of course, there is also need for detachment, which, Teresa says, "if practiced with perfection, includes everything" (8.1). These chapters on the foundations for an effective contemplative community show the practical character of the *Way*. They also serve to introduce some of the other fundamental values of the Carmelite reform: poverty of spirit (2.5–11); the need for silence and solitude (4.9; 11.4); discretion to unmask the devil's wiles (7.7; 10.6; 15.3), and the goal of attaining freedom of spirit (8.3–4; 9.4; 10.1; 15.7).

Humility, which also frequently appears in later chapters,[160] assumes great importance because it is the enemy of what Teresa considered the ultimate danger threatening the reform—allowing the Spanish concept of social honor and privilege into the cloister to destroy the harmonious life of the community.[161] As noted above, Teresa broke with contemporary Spanish culture by insisting on the fundamental difference between the false honor of lineage and wealth and the true honor given by love and friendship with God. Perfect souls can be detached and humble anywhere and have no need for the honor that counts for so much in the world. "God deliver us," she says, "from persons who are concerned about honor while trying to serve him. Consider it an evil gain, and, as I said, honor is itself lost by desiring it, especially in matters of rank. For there is no toxin in the world that kills perfection as do these things."[162] She returns to this attack often, especially in chapter 36, where a mini-treatise on the topic contains the adage, "the soul's profit and what the world calls honor can never go together." The devil even invades the religious life, establishing hierarchies that foster pride and a preoccupation with one's standing, or honor. At this point Teresa bursts out, "One doesn't know whether to laugh or cry; the latter would be more fitting."[163]

Chapters 4–15 complement chapters 1–3 in providing a picture of the kind of reformed house that Teresa had in mind. She was concerned with the crises facing the Catholic Church, especially the spread of the

"Lutheran" heretics (she thought that all those who broke with Rome were "Lutherans"). Women, of course, could not preach against the heretics, but they could pray that all may return to the true faith (chap. 1), and Teresa sees the devotion of her nuns to Christ in the Eucharist as a way to atone for Lutheran attacks on the sacrament (chap. 35). The insistence that the new Carmels be poor and small in 2.9–10 echoes what was found in the *Constitutions.* Teresa is also eager to remind her nuns of the rigors of the eremitical life of the first Carmelites as a model (4.9; 11.4; 13.6). Appealing to an ancient theme in the history of religious life, Teresa sees her community of St. Joseph as heaven on earth: "This house is a heaven, if one can be had on this earth. Here we have a very happy life if one is pleased only with pleasing God and pays no attention to her own satisfaction."[164]

Teresa's method of prayer is the major focus of chapters 16–42 of the *Way of Perfection.* She begins this section with three chapters introducing contemplative prayer, because, as Rowan Williams put it, Teresa's purpose in the work was "to de-mystify mental prayer."[165] The differences between mental prayer and contemplation are discussed in chapter 16. Meditation is necessary for all Christians as a way to attain virtue (16.3), but not all are called to contemplation. Only God can make a contemplative, but we can prepare ourselves so that God can lead us along this path.[166] It is not necessary to be a contemplative to be saved (17.2), and those called to contemplation always need to resist pride, because even simple nuns with a deep devotion to vocal prayer can reach union with God (17.3). The prioress's shrewd sense of people is evident in a frequently repeated adage: "As I have said, it is important to understand that God doesn't lead all by one path, and perhaps the one who thinks she is walking along a very lowly path is in fact higher in the eyes of the Lord."[167] Contemplation is a higher but also more difficult life. Teresa insists that "the trials God gives to contemplatives are intolerable" (18.1; see also 36.8), a statement that reflects the accounts of her inner trials in the *Life.* She also echoes the teaching of many mystics that the test for true prayer is not in consolations, delights, and raptures, which will come and go; but rather in "deeds done for your own spiritual growth and for the good of others" (18.7).

Teresa's formal teaching on prayer is divided into two parts: chapters 19–26 on prayer in general; and chapters 27–32, which form a commentary on the Our Father, the prayer par excellence. She begins by noting that there are many good books on prayer (19.1), but that does not prevent her from adding this account for her nuns. In the *Life* she had used the metaphor of four ways of watering the garden of the soul to describe progress in prayer. Throughout the *Way* she also utilizes water, specifically the desire of thirsty souls to press ahead through difficulties eventually to slake their thirst at the living waters, of which the Savior said, "Whoever drinks of it will never thirst" (John 4:4). Chapter 19.3–10 features an account of the three properties of water that are applicable to true prayer—it refreshes; it cleans; it satisfies. The water motif returns often in the succeeding chapters.[168] Reading chapters 19 and 20, the reader is struck by the practical insights from her own prayer life that Teresa uses in her teaching. Searching for a guiding structure for her account, in chapter 21 she says, "So it seems to me now that I should proceed by setting down some points here about the beginning, the middle, and the end of prayer." Since no one will be able to take away "the books" of the Our Father and the Hail Mary from the nuns (a dig at the Inquisition), she proposes to explain the progress of prayer according to these familiar orations, although she says she is not claiming the right to compose a commentary, but only to "mention some thoughts on the words of the Our Father" (21.3).[169]

Teresa prefaces the commentary with several more introductory chapters to clarify essential terms. The first is "mental prayer" (*oración mental*), which is attending to God within whether we are speaking prayers out loud or silently (22.1). Thus, mental prayer and vocal prayer should always be joined (22.3), so that we should never be thinking of other things when praying to God. She returns to this in chapters 24 and 25. By "centering the mind upon the one to whom the words are addressed" (24.6), we can be given contemplation in the midst of vocal prayer. "I tell you that it is very possible," claims Teresa, "that while you are reciting the Our Father or some other vocal prayer, the Lord may raise you up to perfect contemplation" (25.1). This raising up, however, means the cessation of both inner and outer activity. "The soul understands that without the noise of words this divine Master is teaching it by suspending its faculties."[170] As in the *Life*, the suspension of faculties means that such souls enjoy, but without understanding how they are enjoying; they are enkindled with love, without understanding how; nor can the will grasp what is happening. In regular vocal and mental prayer we can perform some work of our own with God's help, but the contemplation involving the suspension of the faculties is a pure supernatural divine work (25.3). Teresa says that because she treated contemplation at length in the *Life*, in this work it will be merely touched on from time to time (25.4).

Chapter 26 rounds off the preliminary part of the Our Father treatise by discussing how "to recollect the mind" (*recoger el pensamiento*).

Recollection, which for Teresa is especially important for beginners, is the simple exercise of turning the eyes of the soul toward God (26.3). In other words, it is a form of meditation not unlike the exercises of Ignatius of Loyola. Teresa gives some practical advice about this activity, including the use of holy images and books (26.9–10).[171] Chapter 26 is also of importance for highlighting the rule of Christ as the Divine Spouse in Teresa's understanding of the path to perfection. She often speaks in this work of the sisters as spouses of Christ,[172] although generally without employing erotic images. A few chapters, such as 13.2–3; 22.7–8; and especially here 26.2–8, are more detailed. All the sisters, even those not gifted for higher prayer, should practice representing Christ beside them as they begin any kind of prayer (26.1). Teresa is not asking them to make "long and subtle reflections with the intellect," but only to look at Jesus (26.3). Christ never takes his eyes off his spouses, no matter how often they fall. "Behold, he is not waiting for anything else, as he says to his bride (Song 2:14), than that we look at him. In the measure you desire him, you will find him."[173] Teresa's advice to the sisters about picturing the events of Christ's life, especially his passion (26.4–8), include examples of fervent prayer to the Divine Lover: "O Lord of the world, my true Spouse! (You can say this to him if he has moved your heart to pity at seeing him thus, for not only will you desire to look at him, but you will also delight in speaking to him, and not with ready-made prayers, but with those that come from the sorrow of your own heart, for he esteems them highly.)"[174] As in the *Life*, Teresa's prayer is deeply Christocentric. Jesus prays in and with us when we pray with attention.

The final part of the *Way of Perfection* (chaps. 27–42) contains the Carmelite's commentary on the Our Father.[175] Explanations of the Lord's Prayer began in the third century with Tertullian and Origen and had proliferated for centuries; but few, if any, had been written by women. In 37.1 Teresa praises the "sublime perfection of this evangelical prayer," saying, "I marvel to see that in so few words everything about contemplation and perfection is included; it seems we need to study no other book than this one."[176] Teresa uses the phrases of the Lord's Prayer as a template for expounding her model of how God draws us to himself in three stages of prayerful ascent: recollection, or mental prayer, in which we cooperate with God (see chaps. 28–29, 37.1); the prayer of quiet, which is the first stage of supernatural prayer (29.4; 30–31; 37.1); and the final prayer of union, which she identifies with contemplation (31.6; 36.11; 37.1). This threefold pattern is more or less conformable with what was laid out in the *Treatise on Prayer* in the *Life*, but Teresa's presentation is, once again, more direct, and also somewhat different at the end. Only a few aspects of the treatise can be considered here. In her expositions, Teresa intersperses acts of adoration to God and invocations to her community with explanations of the stages of progress in prayer.

The first phrase ("Our Father who art in heaven"), treated in chapters 27–29, contains teaching on the nature of recollection. Teresa's *Life* also viewed meditative recollection as preparing the soul for the gift of the "prayer of quiet" (28.4), an ambiguous term across her writings. What it seems to mean here is that assiduous practice of recollecting the senses in meditation can prepare the soul for the higher transfusions of divine grace. Once again, Teresa underlines that "this recollection is not something supernatural, but that it is something we can desire and achieve with the help of God. . . . It is not a silence of the faculties, but it is an enclosure of the faculties in the soul."[177] The next phrase of the Prayer moves on to the second stage, where God begins to give the soul favors it can never gain on its own. "Hallowed be thy name; thy kingdom come" applies to the prayer of quiet, which, Teresa says, "is something supernatural, something we cannot procure through our own efforts. In it the soul enters into peace or, better, the Lord puts it at peace in his presence" (31.2). The "kingdom of God" is the presence of the Trinity within the soul (27.7), so this state as an "interior and exterior swoon" (32.2) is analyzed in terms of how it affects the three powers of the soul (memory/intellect/will), as we have seen in the *Life*. In this section (31.3–8) Teresa seems to be trying to simplify things she set out at greater length in the former book, and the prayer of quiet is more closely tied to the stages of preparation and less of a sudden irruption of God's action into our prayer life.[178]

Chapter 33 treats the third phrase of the Lord's Prayer, "Thy will be done," which Teresa equates with the highest stage of prayer, total surrender of the will to God in which he draws us into contemplation and full union. This stage is also termed rapture:

> O my Sisters, what strength lies in this gift. It does nothing less, when accompanied by the necessary determination, than draw the Almighty so that he becomes one with our lowliness, transforms himself into us, and effects a union of the Creator with the creature. . . . Not content with having made the soul one with himself, he begins to find his delight in it, reveal his secrets, and rejoice that it knows what it has gained and something of what he will give it. He makes it lose these exterior senses so that nothing will occupy it. This is rapture [*esto es arrobamiento*].[179]

Several things are noteworthy here. Although Teresa says she will not say much about the higher state of contemplation/union in the *Way*, she does insert some descriptions based on what she had said in the *Life*. Second, her accounts in the *Way* of union and of the difference between union and rapture are generic and not detailed, though this is scarcely surprising given the genre and purpose of the book.[180]

In the remaining chapters, Teresa moves on to the later verses of the Lord's Prayer. The phrase "Give us this day, our daily bread," naturally suggests the Eucharist, on which she spends three chapters (chaps. 33–35). In receiving Christ in communion the sacred event is happening now, so communicating is superior to reflecting on the saving events of the past (34.7–8). The presence of Christ in the Eucharist was always central to Teresa's spiritual life.[181] The whole purpose of prayer is to make Christ present and available to us, and there is no greater availability of the Savior-Spouse than that found in the sacrament of the altar. Teresa's *Spiritual Testimonies* make it clear that many of her deepest experiences of Jesus, especially after 1570, took place at or immediately after receiving communion, not unlike what we find in Ignatius of Loyola's *Diaries*.

Chapter 36 turns to the phrase "Forgive us our debts, as we forgive our debtors." Teresa uses this passage to mount an attack on false conceptions of honor and to insist that the soul that has been granted "the prayer of perfect contemplation," that is, "the prayer of union," automatically will have a "resolute desire" to pardon any injury it may receive (36.8 and 11). Another of the effects of the highest form of prayer is treated in chapter 38 under the phrase "And lead us not into temptation, but deliver us from evil." Contemplative souls do not wish to be freed from trials and troubles, Teresa says, but rather want to continue to struggle for the Lord, both against the devils and the public enemies of the church (38.1–2). Chapter 39 distinguishes between the true humility that always brings "peace, delight, and calm," and the false humility sent by the devil, which causes disquiet concerning the gravity of our sins (39.1–2). The devil always lies in wait for contemplatives to mislead them, even in the case of consolation. So, argues Teresa, "Strive, without hiding, to discuss these favors and consolations with someone who will enlighten you. And take care about this: however sublime the contemplation, let your prayer always begin and end with self-knowledge."[182]

Chapters 40–41 advance this practical vein by treating of the love and fear of God as the essential guides to keep contemplatives on the right track in the midst of so many temptations from the devil. Love is the distinguishing mark of all contemplatives, like Paul and Mary Magdalene (40.3–4), but fear of God and humility are equally necessary. "Once the soul has reached contemplation," says Teresa, "the fear of God also, as with love, becomes very manifest. . . . Despite the fact you may watch these persons very carefully, you will not see them become careless."[183] Teresa concludes: "With these two virtues—love and fear of God—you can advance on this road calmly and quietly, but not carelessly, since fear must always take the lead" (41.9). Finally, chapter 42 of the *Way of Perfection* meditates on what it means "to be freed from all evil. Amen." As long as we are in this life, we will never be free of *all* evil, but we need to continue to make this prayer, confidently awaiting our ultimate deliverance in death. "Even though our desire may not be perfect," Teresa says, "let us force ourselves to make the request" (chap. 42.4). Teresa closes her *Way of Perfection* with reflections on how, even when spiritual books have been removed from the sisters, they have been left all they need in the profundity of the Our Father. "Certainly," she says, "it never entered my mind that this prayer contained so many deep secrets; for now you have seen the entire spiritual way contained in it, from the beginning stages until God engulfs the soul and gives it to drink abundantly from the fount of living waters, which he said was to be found at the end of the way."[184] Teresa's commentary on the Our Father takes a worthy place in the tradition of exegesis of the Prayer in which we become one with Christ praying to his Father.

Meditations on the Song of Songs

It was unusual for a woman to produce a commentary on the Lord's Prayer; it was shocking for one to write an exposition on the Song of Songs, especially in the Catholic lands of the sixteenth century, where women were barred from direct contact with scripture. It was not that women mystics of the past four centuries had not used the erotic poems of the Song to help express their love for their Divine Spouse. Hildegard of Bingen, for example, cites exactly half the verses of the Song in her writings. She and other female mystics, however, stopped short of writing anything like a commentary on this central mystical text of the Bible.[185] Teresa knew it was dangerous for a woman to comment on the Song of Songs in the manner of the verse-by-verse expositions of the male masters of biblical studies, so she carefully qualified her work as merely reflections on a few verses.

The Valdés Index had banned vernacular versions of the Bible, so Teresa had no access to these.[186] What she knew of the Song of Songs came to her from Spanish citations in the *Book of Hours of the Blessed Virgin*, which the nuns recited once a week (see *Meditations* 6.8), as well as from Latin texts both of the breviary and Marian feasts. She says, "For a number of years now the Lord has given me great delight each time I hear or read some words from Solomon's Song of Songs. The delight is so great that without understanding the vernacular meaning of the Latin my soul is stirred and recollected more than by devotional books written in the language I understand."[187] As with the *Way of Perfection*, Teresa felt a call to communicate the understanding that the Lord had given her, in this case of the meaning of the Song. "I think these words will bring consolation to the sisters Our Lord leads by this path and also to me. For at times the Lord gives understanding of so much that I find myself hoping I won't forget, but I didn't dare put anything in writing."[188] In 1566, having consulted with her confessors (and under their command, she insists), she decided to begin to put her thoughts on paper. Teresa does not appear to have been fully satisfied with this first version. Sometime between 1572 and 1575 she wrote an expansion of it, one that received the approbation of Fr. Bañez on June 10, 1575. But the story does not end there. In 1580 her new confessor, Diego de Yanguas, O.P., learned of the existence of the book and insisted that she destroy it, "because he thought it unfitting that a woman should write on the Song."[189] Teresa dutifully obeyed and burned her copy, but doubtless with the knowledge that the text would survive in copies already sent to other Carmels. Her friend Jerónimo Gracián first published it in 1611. There is some variety in the four surviving manuscripts and the first printed version, so the evolution of the text is not easy to determine. The history of the first female commentary on the Song witnesses both to the fears of male authorities and to the ingenuity of women, like Teresa, in making their voices heard.

This quasi-commentary raises the question of the role the Bible plays in Teresa's mysticism.[190] Given the strictures of early modern Spain, she could not even pretend to the use of the Bible found in many late medieval women. Nevertheless, Teresa's resourcefulness allowed her to hint at the important role scripture had for her, although she had to disguise this fact from the Inquisitors, who would have taken extensive knowledge of the Bible in a woman as tantamount to heresy. Teresa's most important use of the Bible is general, that is, her insistence that everything she says should be measured against the witness of the Bible, and (what for her was the same) "the faith of the church." She often, of course, cited individual scriptural texts in her writings. (Sometimes her interpretations provoked the attacks of clerical critics who knew what the passages "really" meant.[191]) Teresa's understanding of the Bible adheres to the patristic and medieval view of the paramount position of the "spiritual" meaning of the text—the Bible is meant to nourish the inner life of prayer.[192] Her exegesis depends on several principles designed to undercut the objections that her male readers might use against her. The first, as we shall see below in the *Meditations*, is the appeal to humility as the fundamental attitude for understanding God's word. The biblical text is beyond human comprehension, so unless we begin with the kind of humility displayed by the Virgin Mary, how can we ever pretend to understand what God is saying? Along with humility comes the need for experience, at least in interpreting a text like the Song of Songs with its deeply personal language. Teresa never denied the importance of the learning necessary for uncovering the doctrinal meaning of scripture, but learning without spiritual experience had its limits, both in confessors and in exegetes.

Teresa was well aware of the male critics who cited Pauline verses against women preaching, teaching, or making other unruly noises in the church (e.g., 1 Cor. 14:34–35; 1 Tim. 2:11–12). Her response is the claim that scripture must be taken as a whole, so one must appeal to the entire Bible to understand God's teaching, rather than citing a single verse out of context. She puts this well in a passage in the *Spiritual Testimonies* 15 (dated 1571), a text that comes with divine approbation. One day as she was thinking about whether it was right for her to go about founding monasteries rather than being constantly engaged in prayer, God said to her, "While one is alive, progress doesn't come from trying to enjoy me more, but by trying to do my will." She continues:

> I thought that their recommendation [i.e., her male advisors] would be God's will, because of what St. Paul had said about the enclosure of women, of which I was recently told and had even heard before. The Lord said to me: "Tell them they shouldn't follow just one part of Scripture but that they should look at the other parts, and ask them if they can by chance tie my hands."[193]

The thirteenth-century Beguine, Mechthild of Magdeburg, had seen God defend her book by daring anyone to tear it out of his hand. In the sixteenth century, Teresa hears God defending her right to do apostolic work by appealing to the whole of the Bible in which "there is neither Jew nor Greek, male nor female" (Gal. 3:28). God's voice dares her critics to try to limit his power in using Teresa for his purposes.

Teresa's *Meditations on the Song of Songs* could not set itself out as a formal commentary but rather features a series of considerations of key verses and images from the Song.[194] Teresa equates these images, such as "the kiss of the kiss of the mouth" (Song 1:1) and the "breasts better than wine" (Song 1:2) with fundamental themes of the mystical teaching she had been developing over the past decade, such as the prayer of quiet, the prayer of union, and the suspension of the faculties. As several recent studies have suggested,[195] the *Meditations* represent a transitional work in which the prioress was distancing herself from some of the views found in the *Life*, such as the supreme status of rapture, toward the more mature positions of the *Interior Castle*, especially with regard to the embodied character of mystical union and the need to combine Mary with Martha, that is, to fuse inner delight and outward active service.

The seven chapters of the *Meditations* comment on only five verses of the Song of Songs (Song 1:1 in chaps. 1–3; Song 1:1–2a in chap. 4; Song 2:3b in chap. 5; Song 2:4 in chap. 6; and Song 2:5 in chap. 7), but six other verses are treated along the way (Song 2:6; 6:2; 4:9; 4:7; 6:9; and 8:4). The first chapter is largely an *apologia* for Teresa and her sisters as readers/speakers of the Song. The prioress subtly undermines the objection that a book so deep in mysteries, so multiple in meanings, and so shocking in style is beyond simple women. "Many things are not meant for women to understand," she admits, adding, "nor even for men" (chap. 1.1). Teresa advises her nuns not to tire themselves out with trying to grasp the mysteries of the book by subtle acts of the intellect, but to wait humbly for God's aid for an understanding of the words that will be helpful for their meditations (1.2).[196] What the difficult text and its surprising style reveal about God is the depth of the mystery of the divine nature, and also the surprising love he bears toward us. "Being what we are," she says, "the love that he had and has for us surprises and bewilders me more; for knowing that he has such love I already understand that there is no exaggeration in the words by which he reveals it to us" (1.7). What the Song showed Teresa during her years of fear about whether she was being misled by the devil was that her favors were indeed from God, not from the foe: "she [i.e., Teresa] understood that it was possible for a soul in love with its Spouse to experience all these favors, swoons, death, afflictions, delights, and joys in relation to him."[197] In other words, the somatic nature of Teresa's mystical gifts was a guarantee of their divine source in the case of someone who had totally abandoned the world's joys, not just in words but also in deeds (1.6).

Yes, the Song of Songs is difficult, admits Teresa. Again, slyly poking fun at her critics, she says that in trying to understand these "great things and mysteries," she consulted "learned men" (*letrados*) about what they meant, only to be told that "the doctors wrote many commentaries and yet never finished explaining the words fully" (1.8). Teresa says it is humility, not pride, that moves her; she writes not thinking she can get to the bottom of the Song, but to console her sisters: "Just as I delight in what the Lord gives me understanding of when I hear some passage from the Song of Songs, you will perhaps find consolation in it, as I do, if I tell you" (1.8). As long as we do not depart from the faith of the church and do not engage in idle curiosity, "I hold it as certain that we do not offend him when we find delight and consolation in his words and works" (1.8).

After this defense, Teresa turns to the famous first verse, "Let him kiss me with the kiss of his mouth" (Song 1:1a), noting that she has heard many explanations she does not remember, but that she is only interested in what will be beneficial for those engaged in prayer (1.9). What is the bride asking for? Isn't the language here too bold for a human to address to God? Teresa can think of several explanations for the request, but the one that is most profitable for the contemplative is seeing the kiss as "the sign of great peace and friendship among two persons." (Remember in *Life* 8.5 Teresa had defined prayer as conversation between friends.) As for the boldness of the language, Teresa says that taking these words literally would certainly be shocking, "But the one whom your love, Lord, has drawn out of himself, you will truly pardon if he says them and also others, even though to say them is daring."[198] The Song of Songs is written in the key of ecstasy.

Teresa gets down to the actual exposition of Song 1:1 in chapters 2 and 3. The long chapter 2 begins by warning the sisters against nine kinds of false peace presented by the world, the flesh, and the devil (2.1–15), before taking up divine peace and the reason for the strange phrasing "with the kiss of the mouth" (2.16). The goal that Teresa has in mind for her nuns is to help them "prepare rooms within our souls for our Spouse and reach the stage in which we can ask him to give us the kiss of the mouth." She goes on, "What a great state of life we are in, for no one but we ourselves can keep us from saying these words to our Spouse since we took him for our Spouse when we made our professions."[199] Nevertheless, the religious life itself is not the peace and friendship the bride asks for, but only a preparation for it (2.30). Chapter 2.16–30 consists of a mini-treatise on the forms of friendship with God that are not evil in themselves, but that are not the ultimate peace and friendship that the bride is asking for when she demands the kiss. Teresa analyzes a number of kinds of imperfect friendship: the friendship content with minor faults (2.17–19); the friendship of those careless about venial sins (2.20–21); the friendship of those who don't want to give up their comforts (2.22–25); the friendship of holy people who are still attached to their honor (2.26–27); and the friendship of the pusillanimous who never dare enough for God (2.28–29).

Chapter 3 returns to the fundamental theme of the first verse—what is the true kiss of peace? This is nothing other than union with the will of God, that is, "such a union that there is no division between him and the soul, but one and the same will."[200] Without citing the biblical prooftext of becoming "one spirit with God" (1 Cor. 6:17), Teresa here joins the tradition of Western monastic mysticism about union as the loving uniting of the divine and human wills. This is the "kiss of the kiss of the mouth," which can be judged by its good effects on the soul (3.2). In conformity with her earlier works, Teresa characterizes this union as supra-intellectual, even saying that "the soul tramples the intellect underfoot" (3.3). She expands on examples of the "strong love of God" that motivates those who have arrived at this level of friendship and who have received the gift of union (3.3–14). As in the *Way of Perfection*, Teresa is concerned to give practical examples and encouragement to her nuns to strive, despite the weakness of the flesh (3.10), for the highest state of union with the Divine Spouse, where the soul may be able to speak the second phrase of the Song, "Your breasts are better and more delightful than wine" (Song 1:1b).

This second phrase, as well as verse 2a: "They [the breasts] give forth the most sweet fragrance," are taken up in chapter 4, whose title announces it will deal with "the prayer of quiet and the prayer of union," presumably the two breasts under discussion. Teresa begins, once again, with an appeal to experience: "Oh, my daughters, what deep secrets there are in these words! May the Lord give us experience of them, for they are very difficult to explain."[201] She notes that she has already said much about the "prayer of quiet" in her earlier books (e.g., *Life* 14–15; *Way* 30–31), so she does not intend to do more than touch on the matter here. Nonetheless, she goes into some detail about the inner and outer comforts of the prayer of quiet (4.2), linking it to the sweetness and fragrance of the Song text about the Bridegroom's breasts. The prayer of quiet communicates heavenly truths to the soul in "a kind of divine intoxication." At this point Teresa introduces a threefold analysis of the soul's progress tied to the understanding of how the soul can make the statement "Your breasts are better than wine." The first stage is that of wine—"a kind of divine intoxication so that the soul doesn't know what it wants or what it says or what it asks for. In sum, it doesn't know itself; but it isn't outside itself [*no sabe de sí*] to the extent that it fails to understand something of what is going on."[202] So, this state is not the suspension of the faculties but their gathering together and pacification in the prayer of quiet. The next stage comes when "the Bridegroom desires to enrich and favor the soul more," changing it into himself to such a degree that the soul "swoons" from pleasure and happiness and "is left suspended in those divine arms [see Song 2:6], leaning on that sacred side and those divine breasts." Here the soul can only rejoice, "sustained by the divine milk with which its Spouse is nourishing it."[203] This is the ecstatic prayer of union and the suspension of the faculties. The third stage is when the soul awakens from that sleep and intoxication yet "remains as though stupefied and dazed and with a holy madness. It seems to me it can say these words: 'Your breasts are better than wine'" (4.4). In the wine, or intoxication, stage the soul thought it could go no higher; but its experience of the swoon of union allows it to reflect in the post-swoon stage that the milk of the divine breasts ("the greatest pleasure that can be tasted in life") is better than wine. This is a totally passive state beyond the operation of the intellect, which Teresa compares to an infant unconsciously nourished by its mother (4.5–6). She prays that her sisters may be given some understanding—or better, "taste"—of this highest gift (4.7). In trying to describe what this union involves Teresa turns to texts from the Song of Songs expressing the complete mutuality of the lovers: "I look at my Beloved and my Beloved at me" (*que mire yo a mi Amado y mi Amado a mí,* Song 6:2).[204] She also cites a noted passage from Augustine's *Confessions* where he prays for God's continued grace: "Give me what you command and command what you will."[205]

Chapter 5 deals further with the prayer of union by way of comments on Song of Songs 2:3b: "I sat down under the shadow of him whom I desired and his fruit is sweet to my taste." Teresa meditates on Song 2:3b, the bride sitting under the shadow of the "apple tree" (Song 2:3a), as well as the following verse 2:4, "The king brought me into the wine cellar and set charity in order in me." Souls that practice prayer will realize how many different kinds of food God gives, including the manna of Wisdom 16:20, which conforms its taste to each who receives it. Along with the Blessed Virgin (Luke 1:35), they also are delighted to sit under the shadow of the Most High. This sitting emphasizes their total dependence on God (5.3), as well as the stilling of the faculties necessary for the soul to be given the taste of the divine fruit. All this happens in the "shadow," that is, the obscurity of the divine nature.

Teresa says, "I know that anyone who has undergone this experience will understand how truly this meaning can be given to these words spoken by the bride."[206] In the second part of this chapter, the trinitarian and christological dimensions of the prayer of union come to the fore. The Holy Spirit is the mediator between the soul and God, and Christ waters "the divine apple tree" with his precious blood to enrich its fruit (5.5). Teresa emphasizes that the nourishment of milk from the breasts is for beginning contemplatives, while the nourishment with apples is for the advanced soul, which "he [Christ] wants to understand how it is obliged to serve and suffer" (5.5). Thus, ecstatic enjoyment and rapture are not the height of the mystical path, as suggested in the *Life*.

Suffering and serving become important in the final two chapters of the *Meditations*, both of which treat the prayer life of the bride-nun as an ongoing process. Chapter 6 continues the account of the prayer of union with an exposition of Song 2:4—"The king brought me into the wine cellar and set charity in order within me"—one of the most frequently discussed verses of the Song. Teresa analyzes the verse and enriches her treatment by citing or referencing four other verses from the text (Song 4:9; 4:7; 6:9; and 2:5). The soul who has enjoyed resting under the divine apple tree may think she has made it to the end of her journey, but Teresa says that "the Lord is never content with giving us as little as we desire" (6.1). He will increase our capacity both for suffering and for enjoyment more than we imagine. Picking up on a frequent theme in her writings, viz., the variety of God's gifts, she says that being brought into the wine cellar and having charity set in order indicate that God gives souls different amounts of wine of differing strengths (6.3). The soul needs to have the courage to drink as deeply as possible, even to the extent of dying "in this paradise of delights," the "mystical death" (*mors mystica*) that brings true life. The soul that attains "happy inebriation" and the "suspension of the faculties" in the union with "the very Lord of love" will find its love sent forth from the will with irresistible force so that "it truly must wound his Majesty" (an implicit reference to Song 4:9), another major motif of the erotic mysticism of the Song of Songs.

The wisdom that God gives the soul in such high states of prayer comes only after the surrender of the intellect. Teresa criticizes "some learned men" who think they can come to know the grandeurs of God by their own efforts, refusing to follow the example of the Blessed Virgin, who surrendered to the Holy Spirit in humility (Luke 1:34–35). In line with traditional Marian interpretations of the Song of Songs,

Teresa sees Mary as the perfect model for all that is said about the bride in the Song (6.8). Such souls are praised by the Bridegroom with the words, "You are all beautiful, my love" (Song 4:7). God cannot fail to give himself to these golden souls, embellishing their own gold with rich designs and gems and thus setting charity in order in them (6.9–10). In this brief union (6.11) there is no understanding on the intellect's part, but afterward the intellect beholds the soul's new glory (Song 6:9 is cited), and the virtues and favors it received are evident. Teresa closes this chapter with a traditional picture of the ordering of the various forms of charity that she may have learned from her discussions with the *letrados* who would have read commentators like Bernard of Clairvaux.[207]

At this point the soul-bride's desire is so strong that she is willing to suffer much for God and neighbor, and even to die, so chapter 7 takes up Song 2:5: "Sustain me with flowers and surround me with apples, for I am languishing with love" (Latin: *quia amore langueo*; Spanish: *porque desfallezco del mal des amores*). Teresa puzzles over this verse. She says she herself has known ecstatic delight so strong it made her want to die,[208] but the bride's request is for flowers in order to be *sustained* and therefore indicates "the desire to serve in some way the one to whom she sees she owes so much" (7.1). Mystical death is a well-known theme in the history of mysticism,[209] one to which Teresa refers in other places.[210] She now knows, however, there is more to God's plan than immediate death, because the bride of the Song of Songs "begs him for another good so as to escape from the one that is so extraordinary, and thus it says: 'Sustain me with flowers'" (7.3). Teresa says by these words "the soul is asked to perform great works in the service of Our Lord and of its neighbor. For this purpose it is happy to lose that delight and satisfaction." She goes on: "Martha and Mary never fail to work almost together when the soul is in this state. For in the active and seemingly exterior work the soul is working interiorly. And when the active works rise from this interior root, they become lovely and very fragrant flowers."[211] To be sure, there are many kinds of good works that are performed with mixed motivation, partly for God and partly for our own benefit (7.4–5), but what Teresa is talking about is the activity of advanced souls who "look only at serving and pleasing the Lord, . . . and forget themselves for their neighbor's sake" (7.5). Her scriptural example is another woman, the Samaritan in John 4, who gave up conversing with Jesus to spread the good news to her village.

Teresa has now arrived at the insight that combining contemplation and action is the highest form of life—the one in which good works (*obras*) are performed most effectively. She might be even describing herself when she goes on to say:

> So I say that much good is done by those who, after speaking with his Majesty for several years, when receiving his gifts and delights, want to serve in laborious ways even though these delights and consolations are thereby hindered. I say that the fragrance of these flowers and works produced and flowing from the tree of such fervent love lasts much longer.[212]

From these flowers comes the fruit of the apples, which Teresa identifies with trials and persecutions. Having attained this breakthrough, Teresa once again invokes Christ. Citing Song 8:4 ("Under the apple tree I raised you up"), she identifies the apple tree with the cross. Hence, the soul that is surrounded by crosses and persecutions has a powerful remedy against too-frequent delight in contemplation. Its suffering through action does not debilitate it as do the frequent suspensions of the faculties. The soul has thus come to realize that "it must not be always enjoying without serving and working in something" (7.8). Teresa cautions that such a joining of the contemplative and active dimensions of life is not for beginners, who need nourishment on the milk of the Bridegroom's breasts until they are weaned (7.9). But the message is clear: the prioress hopes that her reflections will have some effect, once again turning to the appeal to experience in closing. "Beseech his Majesty that I may understand through experience what has been said. Any sister who thinks she has some experience of these delights should praise Our Lord and make the request just mentioned so that the gain will not be just for herself."[213] Nourishing the life of the community is Teresa's reason for sharing her thoughts on the Song of Songs.

Teresa and the Spread of the Reform

The year 1567 marked another turning point in the life of the prioress of St. Joseph, since it was then that Teresa began to spread the Carmelite reform outside the small house in Avila. The story of the last fifteen years of Teresa's life is set out in considerable detail in her letters and in the chapters of the *Foundations*. This material is important for understanding Teresa and her plans, though we should always remember she was writing with an agenda in mind.

Teresa's apostolic ardor was whetted in mid-1566 when the Franciscan Alonso Maldonado, recently returned from Mexico, visited St.

Joseph's and told her of the many souls being lost for Christ because there were not enough missionaries. She wept bitterly at hearing this and went about in great affliction until one night the Lord appeared to her and comforted her with the message: "Wait a little, daughter, and you will see great things."[214] Teresa realized that there were many forms of apostolic activity, and while she and her nuns could not go off to preach and teach, they could pray for conversions. The more prayers, the more powerful the message. One can suppose, therefore, that Teresa was already thinking about expanding the reform, although she presents the events that made this possible as a surprise.

In 1564 the Carmelite General Chapter had elected the Italian John Baptist Rossi (1507–1578, called Rubeo in Spain) as the new prior general. In 1567 he came to Spain for the first visitation of a general to the Spanish Carmelites. Following the initiative of a number of fifteenth-century Carmelite leaders, Rubeo was a reformer, so he welcomed Teresa's initiative when he met her in Avila in February of 1567. He provided her with letters allowing her to found more houses in Castile, even without approval of the provincial authorities. He even allowed her to begin to spread the reform to male houses. In August of 1567, Teresa inaugurated her second Carmel at Medina del Campo. She also met the young friar Juan de Yepes, soon to change his name to John of the Cross, and recruited him for the reform. In 1568 Teresa set up two further Carmels at Malagón and Valladolid, where she instructed John of the Cross about her understanding of the Carmelite life. On November 28 John and Antonio Heredía established the first male house at Duruelo.[215] The reform was well under way.

In 1569 and 1570, with the reform spreading, Teresa received further encouragement from the Lord. According to the Augustinian Fray Luis de León, who produced the first edition of the saint's works, it was in 1569 that Teresa composed the seventeen "Soliloquies," or fervent prayers to God that she composed after receiving communion.[216] These prayers resemble the popular genre of *meditationes* pseudonymously ascribed to Augustine, Anselm, and Bernard and widely disseminated in the late Middle Ages, although some influence from the prayers of Catherine of Siena, translated into Spanish in 1512, cannot be excluded. Even more important was the imaginative vision of February 9, 1570, recounted in the Sixth of the *Spiritual Testimonies*. Again after communion, Teresa says she had a vision of Christ's passion in which her grief over the Lord's sufferings led him to command her "to hurry to establish these houses" in precisely the way she had been doing. He also told her that she should write about the foundations of the houses.[217] Although Teresa was not to begin writing the *Book of Foundations* until 1573, the divine command once again provided her with the highest backing, not only for her efforts as a reformer but also for recording and publicizing this activity.

Teresa's career as a letter writer took off at the same time. Only twenty-three of her surviving 468 letters date from 1546 to 1569, with all but five coming from 1568–69. Her production was still modest for the next few years, with 1570–71 seeing fifteen letters, and 1572–73 eighteen. As the efforts of the reform gained steam, however, Teresa came to rely more and more on letters to advance her plans (twenty letters in 1574, twenty-one in 1575, and seventy in 1576). Unlike Catherine of Siena, Teresa did not generally use her letters to communicate her mystical teaching.[218] Her missives, however, give us an insight into her struggles to advance the reform, as well as the problems she had with many people, both admirers and detractors, and the personal bonds that nourished her, especially with her dearest "soul-friend," the friar Jerónimo Gracián (1545–1614).

Gracián played such a large role in Teresa's life and writings that some notice must be taken of the relation between him and the saint.[219] Though Teresa is most often linked with John of the Cross in the popular mind, and there can be no doubt about their connection and mutual respect,[220] it was Gracián who was her closest ally and dearest friend, as countless letters show. Fray Jerónimo came from a well-connected, if poor, family and was trained at the University of Alcalá before being ordained and joining the Reformed Carmelites in 1572, where he was soon promoted to official positions because of his talents and connections. Teresa did not meet him until the spring of 1575, but she was immediately attracted to him, identifying him as just the kind of young, energetic, and spiritually gifted leader needed to spread the reform. He was her "Paul," as she affectionately described him in the code language used in many of their epistolary exchanges. Teresa took the unusual step of taking a vow of obedience to him at Pentecost of 1575 (*Spiritual Testimonies* 35–36), and he in turn elected to consult with her on all matters relating to the reform. Teresa viewed her vow to Gracián as a kind of spiritual marriage engineered by Christ as matchmaker, as she says in a letter to him from January 1577. She says she wants "to kiss his hands repeatedly and to tell you to be at ease, for the Matchmaker was so qualified and made the knot so tight that it will be taken away only when life ends. And after death the knot will be even tighter."[221] Gracián's efforts for the reform between 1575 and Teresa's death in 1582 were significant, especially after his election as the first provincial of the new Reformed Carmelite Province on March 2, 1581. He and Teresa did not always agree, but a survey of her letters to him indicate that she had a bond with him that was different from her relation to any other man.

Gracián's later career was tumultuous. In 1585 he promoted Nicolás Doria to be the new provincial, but Doria soon turned against him and by 1592 Gracián was thrown out of the Carmelite order. While traveling to Rome to appeal his case, he was captured by Turkish pirates and spent two years as a galley slave. Gracián was finally freed and received papal absolution in 1596, but the Spanish Reformed Carmelites would not take him back, so he remained in Italy, where he continued to work on editing Teresa's writings. After preaching in Morocco and a brief time back in Spain, he went to the Spanish Netherlands in 1607, where he continued to promote the publication of Teresa's writings. He lived long enough to learn of Teresa's beatification in April of 1614.

The spread of the reform between 1570 and 1576 cannot be taken up here. In terms of Teresa's mystical writings, many of her *Spiritual Testimonies* date from this period and give us a sense of her ongoing reception of mystical favors during these busy years. Many of the experiences recounted in the *Testimonies* took place in connection with the reception of Christ in the Eucharist. They also feature a more prominent role for the Trinity than what was found in the *Life* or the *Way*. For example, *Testimonies* 13 and 14 recount related intellectual visions of the Trinity that took place at Avila on May 29 and June 30, 1571. In the first of these Teresa says that on the Tuesday after Ascension Thursday, while praying after communion, "it seemed to me I knew clearly in an intellectual vision that the entire Blessed Trinity was present. In this state my soul understood by a kind of representation . . . how God is three and one." At this time each of the Three Persons spoke to her and promised her a particular gift.[222] In *Spiritual Testimonies* 14 of June 30, she notes that the Trinity had been habitually present in her soul for the past month. "Since I was accustomed to experience only the presence of Jesus," she continues, "it always seemed to me that there was some obstacle to my seeing the Three Persons, although I understand there is only one God." The Lord then tells her that spiritual things are very different from corporeal things, but Teresa still has to use a material example. She describes herself as a sponge filled with the Trinity and "in a certain way rejoicing within itself and possessing the three Persons." Again, God corrects her: "Don't try to hold me within yourself, but try to hold yourself within me." As a result, Teresa seems to see the Three Persons within herself, but "communicating themselves to all creation without fail."[223] Teresa's sense of the inner life of the Three Persons and their immanence in creation is a new aspect of her teaching.

Spiritual Testimonies 22, which probably took place at Avila in March of 1572, contains a new kind of eucharistic experience. Teresa says that she remained in such a deep suspension of the faculties after receiving the host that she could not swallow it. Holding it in her mouth, after she returned to herself, she says, "it truly seemed to me that my entire mouth was filled with blood. I felt that my face and all the rest of me was also covered with this blood, as though the Lord had just finished shedding it. It seemed to me warm and the sweetness I then experienced was extraordinary."[224] This form of blood experience, reminiscent of Catherine of Siena, is unusual in Teresa. Among the most noted accounts in the *Spiritual Testimonies* is No. 31, describing the spiritual marriage with Christ she received on November 18, 1572, while serving as prioress of the Encarnación. Again, the context is eucharistic. Teresa had just received communion from John of the Cross and wondered if she had displeased him in some way. Christ then appeared to her in an imaginative form and gave her his right hand, saying, "Behold this nail; it is a sign you will be my bride from today on. Until now you have not merited this; from now on not only will you look after my honor as being the honor of your Creator, King, and God, but you will look after it as my true bride. My honor is yours, and yours mine." Teresa speaks of how she remained entranced for the whole day, although "[a]fterward I felt great pain, and greater confusion and affliction at seeing I don't render any service in exchange for such amazing favors."[225] Several later *Testimonies* talk about this spiritual marriage and the effect it had on her.[226]

Three of the late *Spiritual Testimonies* are important for understanding Teresa's contemplative life in her final years. No. 58 is an account of her spiritual pilgrimage over the past forty years, written in 1576 for Fr. Rodrigo Alvarez, S.J., the Inquisitor of Seville, who became her spiritual director while was she was founding a house there. This third-person narrative is a good summary of her reflections on her life, mystical gifts, and writings up to that point.[227] Also apparently written for Fr. Alvarez around the same time, but in his capacity as her director, was a mini-treatise entitled "On the Grades of Prayer" (*Los grados de la oración*).[228] This bears comparison with her other maps of prayer, but it need not delay us here, since the prioress was to give her final thoughts on these issues a year later in the *Interior Castle*. Finally, at Palencia in May of 1581, Teresa wrote an account of the present state of her spiritual life for her former confessor, now bishop of Osma, Alonso Velázquez. Here she summarized a number of spiritual themes, such as the importance of inner peace and quiet, intellectual visions of the Trinity and of the humanity of Christ, and the continuous presence of the Trinity in her soul.[229]

Over the course of the years of apostolic activity found in the *Foundations* (ca. 1573 and 1582), the text provides us with much information about Teresa and her activities and thoughts. This account of her career, written at the request of both Jesus and Fr. Gracián, although primarily historical, is not without interest in providing insight into her teaching about contemplation. The reflections she offers in chapters 4–8 are central. Chapter 4 treats of some of the mystical favors found in the nuns of the monasteries of the reform, noting that many of these women were so advanced in contemplation that they had reached rapture (4.8). In chapter 5 Teresa meditates on the relation of knowing and loving in matters of prayer and revelations. Without trying to settle this complicated issue (which in some ways remained fluid throughout her writings), she says, "I am only anxious to explain that the soul is not thought [*pensamiento*], nor is the will controlled by thought—it would be a great misfortune if it were. The soul's profit consists not in thinking much, but in loving much."[230] The superiority of the will to rational thinking is evident throughout her works, but exactly how this is understood is not always clear. (We will see more of this in the *Interior Castle*.) What is important to note is that, as ever, Teresa insists that it is not in raptures, visions, or in interior delights that true perfection is found, but only in conformity with God's will (5.10). Therefore, as she puts it, "I consider one day of humble self-knowledge a greater favor from the Lord . . . than many days of prayer."[231]

Various spiritual gifts are treated in *Foundations* 6, such as those already discussed in *Life* 20. Suspensions, raptures, the prayer of quiet, delight, and other gifts are brought up (6.2–4). Teresa is anxious to provide some guidelines for distinguishing between true and false paranormal experiences, especially the kinds of pseudo-contemplation that comes from bodily weakness or from mental melancholy, which is probably best thought of in present-day terms as depression. She gives a good deal of practical advice gleaned from her years as prioress, but we cannot go into that here. She continues in the same vein in chapter 7, which is devoted to the unfortunate nuns "who have that bodily humor called melancholy." Teresa is clear about the need for the superiors to be both strict and kind to the women who suffer from this illness and who can cause real harm in the community if they are allowed to get their own way. Finally, chapter 8 gives some counsels about what to do with nuns who claim to have received revelations and visions.

Two other brief documents from these years give us an intriguing insight into Teresa and the reform. The first is a kind of game, or spiritual tournament, that dates from late 1572, when Teresa had been called back to serve as prioress at the Encarnación and enlisted John of the Cross to serve as confessor for the nuns. "The knights and daughters of the Virgin" at Pastrana (i.e., the discalced friars and nuns there) issued a challenge to the Avila community, apparently containing remarks about forms of penance and spiritual practice (the document does not survive). Twenty-four members of the community at Avila responded to the challenge, including John of the Cross and Teresa.[232] The responses take the form of counter-challenges to the "knights and daughters of the Virgin" to perform good works and the promise to repay them if they accomplish these. For example, "Sister Ana Sánchez says that for any knight or daughter of the Virgin who daily asks the Lord to give her his love she will recite daily three Hail Marys in honor of the purity of our Lady." Teresa's response is humorous, promising that to any knight of the Virgin who is willing to suffer everyday from "a superior who is very wicked, vicious, gluttonous, and badly disposed to him," she will give each day half of what she merits, although that "will be very little."[233]

The second document is somewhat later. Teresa had once heard Christ say, "Seek yourself in me." She sent an account of this to her brother, Lorenzo de Cepeda, who puzzled over the locution and decided to consult his spiritual friends. At Christmas in 1576, some of them met at St. Joseph's in Avila for a discussion. Along with Lorenzo, there were Francisco de Salcedo, Julián of Avila, and John of the Cross. Teresa was in Toledo, so they wrote out their reflections and sent them to her so she could judge which was best. She took this challenge humorously, writing out a satirical reply to their thoughts in which she asks for the grace "not to say anything that might merit my being denounced to the Inquisition." She also writes, "I have no intention of saying anything good about what the contestants have written."[234] Her humorous remarks about their reflections include a playful jab at John of the Cross. "In his answer," she says, "he presents a very good doctrine for anyone who might want to follow the exercises they make in the Society of Jesus, but not for what we have in mind. Seeking God would be very costly if we could not do so until we were dead to the world." She goes on: "God deliver me from people so spiritual that they want to turn everything into contemplation, no matter what. Nevertheless, we are grateful to him for having explained so well what we did not ask."

The Interior Castle (Moradas del Castillo Interior)

It was in 1577 that Teresa produced her most mature mystical work, the *Interior Castle*.[235] The new book came at the initiative of Gracián, then serving as the Carmelite provincial. In May 1577, Teresa was complaining to him about not having access to the *Life*, still in the hands of the Inquisition, in order to explain a point about prayer. Gracián answered, "Since we cannot have it, recall what you can and other things and write another book, but put down the doctrine in a general way without naming the one to whom the things you mentioned there happened."[236] Teresa took this as a welcome order. Conceiving of the work according to seven "dwelling places" (*moradas*) divided into chapters, she wrote I.1 to V.2 at Toledo between early June and mid-July. She then had to return to Avila, where much business awaited, so that it was not until November that she was able to get back to the longer section of V.3 to VII.4, which she wrote rapidly. An observation of Rowan Williams is apt regarding the rapidity of the composition: "the speed, fluency and confidence also confirm what a more careful reading will reveal: that she is writing out of an unprecedentedly coherent and synoptic vision of the growth of the spirit towards union."[237] Throughout the book, as well as in some of her letters, Teresa testifies to the new and deeper understanding she had gained about many issues since writing the *Life*.[238] She also says in several places that it is God, not she, who is really responsible for the book.[239] In a letter to Gracián of 1580, Teresa, still trying to get a copy of the *Life*, says, "In my opinion the one I wrote afterward [i.e., the *Castle*] is superior, even though Fray Domingo Báñez says it's not good; at least I had more experience at the time I wrote it."[240] In the "Epilogue" she also expressed her satisfaction with the book, saying, "[N]ow that I am finished I admit the work has brought me much happiness, and I consider the labor, though small, well spent. . . . I think it will be a consolation for you to delight in this interior castle since without permission from the prioress you can enter and take a walk through it at any time."[241]

Many of the characteristic themes of Teresa's earlier works are present in the *Interior Castle*, though some are muted, altered, and developed. For example, she expresses obedience to the church and its teachings and says that anything erroneous in the work should be corrected by the "learned" (e.g., Prol. 3; Epil. 4), but she seems less concerned about the Inquisition. She pays lip-service to the weakness of women (e.g., I.2.6; IV.3.11; V.3.10; VI.4.2), but one is permitted to wonder if this has become mostly a rhetorical trope by this stage in her life. The devil has a significant part to play in the advice she gives to her nuns, but one senses that she is more concerned about self-deception after serving as a religious superior for so many years.[242] Teresa continues to worry about the harm done to the nuns, especially those advanced in the contemplative life, by unskilled confessors, mostly in Dwelling Place VI.[243] Her standard counsel in this regard is now clear: (1) the nuns should search out confessors who are learned *and* spiritual; (2) they should not heed those who do not know what they are talking about; and (3) the prioresses must give the nuns freedom to find good confessors.

Despite her insistence that the higher stages of the mystical life are a pure gift of God, Teresa does not neglect the necessity for one's own preparation ("doing what is in one," in the medieval phrase).[244] With regard to the use of the Bible, the *Interior Castle* displays an easy familiarity with scripture, despite the strictures of contemporaneous Catholicism, though a full survey of the role of the Bible in Teresa's writings remains to be done.[245] As we might expect, the need for experience to understand what she is saying is more insistent than ever in the *Interior Castle*. Relatively muted in Dwellings I–III,[246] it becomes frequent in IV–VI, especially in Dwelling VI, which describes special mystical gifts.[247] For example, discussing the need to continue to meditate on the mysteries of the sacred humanity of Christ, she notes the contrary advice she received from some of her confessors, but goes on: "I myself see that the devil tried to deceive me in this matter, and thus I have so learned my lesson from experience that I think, although I've spoken on this topic at other times, I will speak of it again here so that you will proceed very carefully in this matter."[248] A rich treatment comes in VI.11.1–4 in the discussion of the various kinds of "impulses" (*impulsos/impetus*) from God, including the wound of love, where the language of experiencing and feeling the divine blows and arrows is strongly emphasized.[249] Appeals to experience are slightly more muted in Dwelling VII (possibly because Teresa thinks few will arrive at this height), but the need for experience remains a major theme of Teresa's teaching.

For whom was the *Interior Castle* written? There is no doubt that Gracián asked Teresa to write the book for the communities of the reformed nuns. Whether she had a wider audience in mind is a question, though several passages and the subsequent history of this classic work allow us to conclude that Teresa hoped her message would have an effect outside the houses of the Carmelite order. In *Castle* III.1.5 Teresa says, "I believe that there are many of these souls in the world [i.e., who have entered this stage of progress]." She goes on to claim, "In my opinion, there is no reason why entrance even into the final dwelling place should be denied these souls, nor will the Lord deny them this entrance if they desire it, for such a desire is an excellent way to prepare oneself so that every favor may be granted."[250] Teresa may have been writing primarily for her nuns, but her insistence that it is not visions, consolations, special gifts, or the like that mark real union with God, but only holiness as found in loving union of wills shows that she was sure that the heights of mystical union were open to all believers.[251] God does not need our works (let alone our *own* enjoyment); he wants our determination to serve him (III.1.7).

The *Interior Castle* is Teresa's most finished work, especially in the way it addresses what has now become an essential question for her, that is, in Edward Howells's formulation, "How the extraordinary life of mystical union can be combined in a single soul with ordinary knowing and action."[252] Thus, the *Castle* is a practical work, intended as a book of spiritual exercises based on a profound grasp of mystical theology.[253] The *Interior Castle* is also the best structured of Teresa's writings, largely due to its dominant symbolism of the soul as a crystal castle containing many rooms, or dwelling places.[254] The castle "has many dwelling places: some up above, others down below, others to the sides; and in the center and middle is the main dwelling place where the very secret exchanges between God and the soul take place" (I.1.3). This central dwelling is the source of the soul's "magnificent beauty and marvelous capacity" (I.1.1), which Teresa compares to the shining sun (I.2.3, 8), the "tree of life planted in the very living waters of life" (I.2.1, citing Ps. 1:3), and the fountain of life that is the source of all the waters of grace that flow through the soul (I.2.2–3).

Although Teresa does not say so in explicit fashion, it is obvious that this center is the soul conceived of as created in God's image and likeness (I.1.1, citing Gen. 1:26). Rather surprisingly, she had not used this key biblical text in her earlier works, but she employs it four times in the *Castle*.[255] It may well be that she found the connection between the center of the soul and the image of God in her friend Peter of Alcántara's *Treatise on Prayer and Meditation*, a work she read and praised.[256] Particularly revealing is a passage in VII.2.8. After discussing the soul's heavenly union with the Uncreated Spirit and citing Christ's prayer that all may be one with him in the Father (John 17:21) and that he may be in them (John 17:20, 23), Teresa marvels at these words and our frequent failure to understand them and put them into practice. She continues: "But since we fail by not disposing ourselves and turning away from all that can hinder this light, we do not see ourselves in this mirror that we contemplate, where our image is engraved."[257] The mirror (*espejo*), then, is the union of Christ and the soul in which the soul's image-nature is brought to full fruition when it reaches its "center," as we shall see below. Thus, the "center of the soul" (*centro del alma*),[258] as well as the soul as "image and likeness of God," are different ways of expressing the heart of Teresa's mature understanding of human nature.[259] Mary Frohlich speaks of the center of the soul as the "ground of consciousness" from the viewpoint of philosophical interiority analysis;[260] theologically speaking, it is realization of the *imago Dei*.

The castle symbol is rich and multidimensional, and considerable literature has been devoted to its possible sources.[261] Architectural symbolism, of course, has a long history in Christian mysticism, but there is no direct predecessor for Teresa's architectonic use of the multivalent castle. Teresa says that the image suddenly came into her mind as she was thinking about carrying out Gracián's orders (I.1.1), but we have seen that she already had used the image in the *Way of Perfection*. As noted earlier, seven-sectioned castles had appeared in some Sufi mystical works, but it is doubtful Teresa could have had knowledge of these, and her development of the image is quite her own. A hint for the symbol is found in a work she did know, Osuna's *Third Spiritual Alphabet*, where chapter 3 of the Fourth Treatise is entitled "How You Are to Guard Your Heart like a Castle."[262] Osuna, however, uses the castle of the heart as one symbol among many; it does not structure his text. Another suggestive image occurs in the second book of Bernardino de Laredo's *Ascent of Mount Sion*, which has an extended treatment of the Celestial City, whose crystal walls and angelic and human inhabitants are illuminated by the light of the great paschal candle at the center representing Christ.[263] Nevertheless, Laredo's heavenly city has many differences from Teresa's castle of the soul. The prioress's literary skill is evident in the flexible way she develops this master symbol.

At the beginning (I.1–2), Teresa comments on the castle image in some detail to set up a journey within the self that expresses the dynamic character of the symbol. The journey is an entering into the self (I.1.5–6; IV.3.2), what she sometimes calls "the spiritual path" (*el camino spiritual*, II.1.8). Although Teresa does not use the language of itinerary in as explicit a fashion as some other sevenfold mystical texts, such as Bonaventure's *Mind's Journey into God*, the notion of moving ever inward is implied throughout. A crucial implication of this fact, one found in many mystics, is the insistence that not to continue to progress is actually to regress. As she puts it in IV.1.3: "For when a soul is in one continual state, I don't consider it safe, nor do I think it possible for the spirit of the Lord to be in one fixed state during this exile" (see I.2.8; VII.4.9). Nevertheless, a careful reading shows that Teresa's castle both employs and subverts the notion of itinerary. As Frohlich observes, "This foundational image is profoundly non-linear. . . . It is more like an account of a series of finer and finer refractions of one's awareness of the light from a single divine 'place' that encompasses the whole world."[264]

There are a variety of ways in which one can be within the castle, that is, different modes of consciousness of the self and its relation to God (I.1.5). Those in the outer courtyards are people in serious sin, who do not want to enter into the castle itself but are content with living with the "insects and vermin" in the castle walls, that is, amid their sins and bad habits (I.1.5–6). The "gate of entry to this castle," says Teresa, "is prayer and reflection" (I.1.7), because even vocal prayer demands reflective attention to the one we are speaking to. Those who begin to devote themselves to prayer, therefore, enter the first, or lowest, rooms of the castle, although they drag in many reptiles with them (I.1.9). The castle has a multitude of rooms, or dwelling places, and they do not follow in any sequential way but are like the leaves of the palmetto surrounding the heart or center in concentric circles (I.2.8). In the Epilogue to the *Castle* she once again reminds her readers of the variety in the castle of the soul: "Although no more than seven dwelling places were discussed, in each of these there are many others, below and above and to the sides, with lovely gardens and fountains and labyrinths."[265] This observation fits with Teresa's constant claim that there are many ways to God; she is just treating the path she has taken. Teresa does not advert to the master symbol in every chapter, although it occurs three times in Dwelling VII. The sevenfold structure of the rooms gives unity to the work, despite the varying length of the treatment of each dwelling place.[266]

The journey through the rooms is a process of deepening self-knowledge and growing humility, as we are told in *Castle* I.2. These related themes play a decisive role in all Teresa's writings. An important text discussing the variety of rooms in I.2.8 says that the soul should never stay in any one room too long, except for the one that will accompany it throughout the whole journey—"the room of self knowledge" (*el proprio conocimiento*). Self-knowledge is necessary at the beginning of the itinerary when the soul is still plagued with vermin, but it grows in importance, because "that which applies to what is less applies so much more to what is greater, as they say."[267] Humility is the reverse side of self-knowledge.[268] "While we are on this earth," Teresa says, "nothing is more important to us than humility. So, I repeat that it is good, indeed very good, to try to enter first into the room where self-knowledge is dealt with rather than to fly off to other rooms." This self-knowledge is not a kind of solipsistic exercise, or species of "navel-gazing." No, says Teresa, "let's strive to make more progress in self-knowledge, for in my opinion we shall never completely know ourselves if we don't strive to know God." By gazing at God's grandeur we see our own lowliness, and by pondering the humility of the God-man we see how far we are from being really humble.[269] Thus, as in the *Life*, the humility that comes from knowledge of our own sinfulness and need for God's grace is the only true form of self-knowledge.[270] In that sense the *Interior Castle* is an attack on false interiority in the name of truly humble self-knowledge.[271]

The castle symbol provides the basic structure of the book, but what is impressive about Teresa's masterpiece is the way she interweaves many other symbols and symbolic motifs into the *Castle*.[272] Prominent among these are light and water. At the very center of the castle is the illumination of the soul as God's image and likeness, where the soul "is as capable of enjoying his Majesty as a crystal is capable of reflecting the sun's brilliance" (I.2.1). The sinners outside the castle have become total darkness and their works are equally dark (I.2.2). This darkness extends into the lower dwelling places (e.g., II.2.14). The whole of the *Interior Castle* is diffused with gradually increasing light as we approach the final dwelling place where union with the Trinity is described as "an enkindling in the spirit in the manner of a cloud of magnificent splendor" (VII.1.6), a relatively rare use of Dionysian language in Teresa.[273] Closely related to the symbolism of light are the appearances of fire and warmth to indicate God's action on the soul.

Water as the source of life is a frequent symbol in Teresa's mysticism. The four waters of *Life* 11–22 are among her most noted uses, but the "living water" of John 4:10–11 played an important role in the *Meditations on the Song of Songs*, as we have seen. In the *Castle*, Teresa makes considerable use of water without, however, giving it the central role it enjoyed in the *Life*. For Teresa, water is the divine life, that is, the grace that enables the soul to undertake the journey to the center. It appears in a number of contexts. First, throughout her writings Teresa often referred to her tears, an ancient theme in Christian mysticism.[274] By the time of the *Interior Castle* she was able to present a clear distinction between the tears related to the *contentos* of human effort, which might be helpful or harmful, and those flowing from divine gifts, or *gustos* (see IV.16; VI.6.1, 7–9). Second, in *Castle* IV (2.2–4, 9–10; 3.8-9; see also VI.5.3) Teresa employs water in a way reminiscent of the four waters in the *Life* to symbolize the difference between the aqueducts of the prayer we can attain on our own (i.e., acquired gifts of prayer) and the overflowing spring of the prayer that God pours into the soul. A third appearance of water is in the final stages of unitive prayer, which uses the image found in *Life* 18–22 of steady rain flooding the soul as a helpful description of the Seventh Dwelling Place (VII.2.4–6, 9; VII.3.13). Finally, Teresa does not forget the notion of "living water" that had been important in the *Meditations on the Song of Songs*. In the midst of the severe spiritual trials found in the Sixth Dwelling Place, where the soul feels it is like a "person hanging in the air" with no support, Teresa boldly claims, "Nor does the soul desire that the thirst be taken away save by that water of which the Lord spoke to the Samaritan woman (John 4:7–14). Yet no one gives such water to the soul." Only the water of spiritual marriage will slake this thirst.[275]

Another form of symbolism used by Teresa in her previous works also appears in the *Interior Castle*: spiritual warfare. Teresa lived in a combative era. Several of her brothers fought in the New World, and as a girl she loved reading knightly romances. Teresa employs images of struggle, warfare, and overcoming our enemy the devil throughout her writings, not least in the *Interior Castle*.[276] More important for the structure of the *Castle* is a form of symbolic discourse also found in earlier works: the mystical marriage. Teresa explored marital mysticism in her *Meditations on the Song of Songs*, but she now takes marital symbolics to a new level. The prioress's audience was composed of nuns who had vowed their lives to Jesus as their Divine Bridegroom, so Teresa introduces marital symbolism early in the work. In the Second Dwelling Place, she says, "Embrace the cross your Spouse has carried and understand that this must be your task."[277] Marriage involves sharing all things, but mutual carrying of the cross is more important than participating in the delights of the embrace of love. It is not until the final three dwelling places, however, that the marital motif comes to the fore. In Dwelling V Teresa begins to increase her use of the Song of Songs,[278] and in V.4.3–11 she explicitly explains the meaning of spiritual espousal and marriage: "You've already heard that God espouses souls spiritually. . . . This spiritual espousal is different in kind from marriage."[279] The prayer of union that is the main subject of Dwelling

V is not yet spiritual betrothal but is compared to two people becoming engaged (V.4.4). Here Teresa is making use of the contemporary Spanish practice of marriage, involving (1) acts leading to engagement (meeting, falling in love, exchange of gifts), which are treated in *Castle* V; (2) followed by spiritual betrothal in *Castle* VI (especially VI.1.1; 2.1; 4.1; 7.9; 11.1 and 6); and finally, the (3) spiritual marriage described in *Castle* VII.1–4.

There is, however, a new form of symbolism, one not previously employed by Teresa, that becomes important in the *Interior Castle*: the mystical transformation figured in the silkworm's change into a butterfly. Teresa says she has not actually seen a silkworm, but on the basis of reports she introduces this motif early in the Fifth Dwelling Place (V.2.2–3). Nourished by the sun, little seeds become fat silkworms, which spin the silk, make a cocoon, and die. Then, "a little white butterfly, which is very pretty, comes forth from the cocoon." Teresa asks her sisters to marvel at God's natural wonders and to see in this process an image of what the Carmelite life calls them to do. "Let's be quick to do this work and weave this little cocoon by taking away our self-love and self-will, our attachment to any earthly thing, and by performing deeds of penance, prayer, mortification, obedience, and of all the other things you know." She continues by once again invoking the notion of mystical death (*mors mystica*). "Let it die; let this silkworm die, as it does in completing what it was created to do."[280] This is what happens in the prayer of union that marks the Fifth Dwelling Place. The brief contact with God in which the soul dies to the world effects a transformation in the soul. "How transformed the soul is," says Teresa, "when it comes out of this prayer after having been placed within the greatness of God and so closely joined with him for a little while. . . . Truly, I tell you the soul doesn't recognize itself."[281] The soul now is ready to die a thousand deaths for the Lord and is strong to undergo all manner of trials. It has learned through experience that no creature can give it true rest (V.2.8).

Teresa returns to the silkworm–butterfly transformation several times in the course of her analysis of the Fifth Dwelling Place (V.3, 1, 5; V.4.2), sometimes calling the butterfly a dove (see Song 2:10). She continues to identify the soul with the butterfly in the two highest Dwelling Places. The butterfly appears several times in the raptures of the stage of spiritual betrothal (VI.4.1; VI.6.1, 4; VI.11.1) and is also cited in her treatment of spiritual marriage (VII.2.5; VII.3.1, 12). In Dwelling VII the butterfly is once again used as a symbol for death to the world and new life in Christ. Teresa opens VII.3 with this address: "Now, then, we are saying that this little butterfly has already died with supreme happiness for having found repose and that Christ lives in it. Let us see what life it lives, or how this life differs from the life it was living."[282]

The general structure of the treatise with its seven dwelling places echoes the main division of the four waters of the *Life*, insofar as it distinguishes between the rooms, or modes of prayer, that are attainable by our own efforts in cooperation with grace (Dwelling Places I–III), and those rooms that are strictly divine gifts (Dwelling Places IV–VII). Teresa does not say a great deal about the first three active rooms, or Dwelling Places, probably because her immediate audience was contemplative nuns who for the most part were already receiving some of the higher graces of prayer (Prol. 4). The two chapters of the First Dwelling Place, as we have seen, set up the basic model by insisting that the beginning of the path to God is turning to prayer and that the whole journey must be accompanied by humility and self-knowledge. Souls enter here in many ways (Teresa says there are a million rooms; I.2.12), and the devil will be active to mislead them (I.2.12–18). He especially tries to cool the love and charity the sisters should have for each other, so it is vital to remember that perfection consists in love of God *and* love of neighbor.

Teresa devotes only one chapter to the Second Dwelling Place, which is where the soul has abandoned mortal sin and has made some progress in prayer so that it is able to begin to hear the Lord's callings (II.1.2). Above all, perseverance is necessary at this stage to keep one on the path (II.1.3). Here Teresa introduces her first discussion of the three powers of the soul—reason, memory, and will. On this low level, the three function as faculties of ordinary life (II.1.4). Later on, in the levels of infused prayer, Teresa will use the transformed activity of intellect, memory-imagination, and will to understand the new interiority given the soul through mystical gifts. In this Second Dwelling Place the soul should not expect consolations but should labor to carry the cross with the Divine Spouse and conform the will to God's will (II.1.7–8).

In the Third Dwelling Place, with two chapters, further progress has been made. Souls on this level guard themselves from even venial sin and they begin to practice recollection (III.1.5). As we have seen, recollection (*recogimiento*) was a key spiritual practice for Teresa, as well as for other Spanish spiritual authors. Teresa does not define it here, but it is clear from IV.3.1–3 that she conceived of recollection in two ways. The first is the active form referred to here in which the person retreats into a darkened room or some similar situation, closes her eyes, and strives to put her powers to rest and concentrate on prayer. The second kind is infused recollection, a strictly supernatural gift (IV.3.1). Teresa claims that there are many souls in the world who reach the Third Dwelling Place and who aspire to go higher. What is crucial is to have determination and humility (III.1.7–9).[283] In the second chapter of Dwelling III she gives some good advice about how to deal with dryness in prayer. Dwelling III.2.9-10 introduces a distinction that will become important as the *Interior Castle* proceeds—the difference between "consolations" (*contentos*) and "spiritual delights, or tastes" (*gustos*),[284] although she postpones her discussion until the Fourth Dwelling.

The beginning of the Fourth Dwelling Place represents a shift away from human activity and understanding. Teresa asks for the assistance of the Holy Spirit to explain the difficult "supernatural things" (*cosas sobrenaturales*) that begin here (IV.1.1). The three chapters in this section deal with major, and sometimes rather confusing, topics. The first is the issue of consolations and spiritual delights. Teresa makes a clear distinction: "The term consolations . . . can be given to those experiences we acquire through our own meditations and petitions to the Lord, those that proceed from our own nature."[285] Consolations can be both about worldly things (e.g., inheriting a fortune) and about the things of God, but the main point is that they begin in us. To the contrary, "[t]he spiritual delights begin in God, but human nature feels and enjoys them as much as it does those I mentioned [the consolations]— and much more."[286] Teresa turns to the Bible here, using Psalm 118:32 (Vg.)—"When you expanded my heart" (*Cum dilatasti cor meum*)—to suggest how the divine *gustos* both expand the heart and yet also constrain it. In other words, God himself provides the capability of receiving a gift that goes beyond our nature. Teresa says that this issue is difficult to explain, but anyone who has had the experience will understand what she means (IV.1.5-6). When such experiences come, including the gift of tears, she says it is better to abandon discursive meditation. In order to ascend to the higher dwelling places: "the important thing is not to think much but to love much, and so do that which most stirs you to love."[287] *Gustos*, or spiritual delights, are important for Teresa but are not to be thought of as more than a preliminary stage of higher mystical graces.

At this point Teresa introduces an important introspective analysis (IV.1.8-14) of a problem that had long troubled her, that is, the issue of distractions during prayer that happen at all levels prior to the final Dwelling Place VII.[288] In this treatment she says that a "learned man" (possibly John of the Cross) had helped her understand the problem better. "A little more than four years ago I came to understand through experience that [wandering] thought [*pensamiento*], or imagination to put it more clearly, is not intellect [*entendimiento*]. . . . For, because intellect is one of the faculties of the soul, I found it very hard to see why at times it was so irresolute, and ordinarily thought flies so quickly that only God can control it when he holds it to himself in such a way that it seems to be loosed from this body."[289] As the discussion proceeds, what Teresa is wrestling with is her frequent experience that the faculties, especially intellect (*entendimiento*) and will, can be recollected in God while wandering or imaginative thought, which she here calls *pensamiento* (sometimes associated with memory) can be "on the outskirts of the castle suffering from a thousand wild and poisonous beasts, and meriting by this suffering" (IV.1.9). These often painful distractions are part of the divine plan—we are meant to endure them patiently and gain merit. Teresa says they cease only when God suspends the faculties (IV.1.11), or when the soul reaches the last Dwelling Place (IV.1.12). She hopes her advice will help others, but, once again, experience is the best teacher. She concludes with the consoling message, "But it is necessary and is his Majesty's will that we take proper measures and understand ourselves and not blame the soul for what a weak imagination, [fallen] nature, and the devil cause."[290]

In IV.2–3 Teresa tries to sort out two terms she had used as early as the *Life*, which remained a focus of discussion in all her writings. Teresa was not a trained theologian, or a systematic thinker, so what she ultimately meant by the "prayer of quiet" (IV.2.2–7; IV.3.9–13) and its relation to the "prayer of recollection" (IV.3.1–8) seems to have undergone a development that she does not advert to and that has led to some confusion among her readers. Here in the *Interior Castle* she treats them in reverse order, beginning with "the prayer of quiet" (*oración de quietud*), which she says is the same as the *gustos*, or spiritual delights (IV.2.2). Their strictly supernatural origin leads her to compare them to filling a trough with water from a nearby welling spring, whereas the *contentos*, as the product of human effort, are like bringing water to a trough from far away by many aqueducts (IV.2.3). Teresa's analysis of the *gustos* (IV.2.4–7) makes it clear that, although the gifts are received "in the very interior part of ourselves" (2.4), "the body shares in them" (2.6), in other words, there is an "overflow" of pleasure into the senses. As embodied gifts, they must be experienced to be truly understood; they cannot be imagined. Recollection unites the faculties, but here "the faculties are absorbed and looking as though in wonder at what they see" (2.6).

Chapter 3 turns to "the prayer of recollection," specifically infused and not acquired recollection, that is, the stilling and drawing together of the senses and faculties that occur through the action of grace (IV.3.1). (Acquired recollection is not properly the "prayer of recollection.") The senses and faculties are often distracted, but if the will to serve God is present, he takes pity on them. "Like a good shepherd," says Teresa, "with a whistle so gentle that even they themselves almost fail to hear it, he makes them recognize his voice and stops them from going so far astray and brings them back to their dwelling place."[291] We cannot attain this on our own, but we can desire it, and, Teresa says, "if we desire to make room for his Majesty, he will give not only this but more, and give it to those whom he begins to call to advance further."[292] Here Teresa disputes those spiritual authors who claim that human effort to still the faculties and empty the mind is needed. No, says Teresa, only God can bring this about—"If his Majesty has not begun to absorb us, I cannot understand how wandering thought [*pensamiento*] can be stopped."[293] The last of the four arguments Teresa gives here introduces an important distinction between two kinds of knowing:

> When his Majesty wishes the work of the ordinary understanding [*entendimiento*] to cease, he employs it in another manner, and gives a light in the recognition [*una luz en el conocimiento*] to so much higher a degree than we can attain that he leads it into a state of absorption, in which, without knowing how, it is much better instructed than it could ever be as a result of its own efforts, which would only spoil everything.[294]

This, and other passages of the *Interior Castle*, show that Teresa had worked out a nonsystematic but subtle phenomenological understanding of the operations of the soul's powers (*potencias*) in the path to union. The fundamental distinction, echoed by many mystics, is between the "center of the soul" and its higher powers. She adopted a basically Augustinian tripartite distinction of the powers as memory (*memoria*), understanding (*entendimiento*), and will (*voluntad*), with the priority being given to the last. But her analysis of her inner states led her to add three other categories. Closely related to *memoria* was *imaginación*. Teresa does not say so explicitly, but *memoria* seems to feed *imaginación* various images and forms. *Entendimiento*, or general understanding, is the discursive power of reason, and Teresa always held it was essential, especially for meditation. In the higher stages of prayer, however, as the soul moves from active to passive recollection, *entendimiento* begins to operate as what she called *pensamiento*, which is something like "wandering thinking," which causes the distractions that Teresa had to learn to deal with over many years. As several passages show, however, God could, in a supernatural way, give the soul a higher, we might say intuitive, way of knowing, one she often called *conocimiento*, a recognition that implies a personal contact with God.

If God gives the gift of recollection to the will (IV.3.7), one in which the intellect is often briefly suspended, we should not try to understand what is happening but rather "surrender oneself into the arms of love" (IV.3.8). After this treatment of the prayer of recollection, Teresa returns to a matter left hanging in her discussion of the prayer of quiet, that is, its effects (IV.3.9–13). Exactly why she chose to present the two forms of prayer in this somewhat disjointed way is not clear, but this section contains some shrewd practical advice, especially regarding women who think they are experiencing the prayer of quiet, or even the higher "spiritual sleep" (*un sueño que llaman espiritual*), or rapture, but who are actually only enjoying interior consolation (*contento interior*) and giving in to weakness of the body. Rather than a "rapture" (*arrobamiento*), says Teresa, "I call it foolishness [*abobamiento*], because it amounts to nothing more than wasting time and wearing down one's health."[295] The true prayer of quiet does not cause languor in the soul, but joy in being near God; it is always short, not like the lengthy languor of phony self-absorption (IV.3.12).

The Fifth Dwelling Place takes up four chapters, as Teresa lengthens her account of the higher stages of prayer and begins to analyze the various states of union. "Union" is an analogical category in the *Interior Castle*. At the risk of simplification, we can say that Dwelling V deals with what we can call (Teresa does not) Union I, that is, the prayer of union, while Dwelling VI will deal with Union II, the union of spiritual betrothal that takes place in the higher powers of the soul; Dwelling VII will treat Union III, the union of spiritual marriage that takes place in the center of the soul. These are intensifying degrees of the fundamental uniting of wills between God and the human that is always central to Christian mysticism (e.g., V.1.11; VI.8.10; VI.9.15; VII.4). Once again, Teresa begins her treatment of Dwelling V by asking for divine help in explaining matters that cannot really be understood about the "remaining rooms" (V.1.1). Addressing her audience of nuns, she says that many of them will enter this Fifth Dwelling Place, but not all will experience all the things she will describe (V.1.2).

In the account that follows, Teresa seems to introduce all the higher forms of union ("the remaining rooms") by way of emphasizing the continuity of the three highest Dwelling Places. This is a significant point because all the later forms or, better, mediations of union are founded on what she calls "true union" (*unión verdadera*, V.3.3), that is, loving union with the divine will. Without such union, which is manifested primarily in love of neighbor, any claims to rapture and other special mystical gifts will be false. (She already hinted at the differentiation between the true and the false union in her analysis of the spiritual sleep mentioned at the end of Dwelling IV.) Anxious to show that this form of prayer is not the "dreamy state" of those pretending to special divine gifts, she says there is no need to use any technique to still our wandering thinking (*el pensamiento*), because in spiritual sleep God's grace has already taken over so that the soul has neither sensation nor the power of understanding—in loving, the soul does not understand how or what it loves. This is death to the world in order to live more completely in God, "a delectable death" (*una muerte sabrosa*, V.1.4). In the prayer of quiet in the Fourth Dwelling Place, the soul could still be doubtful about whether the experience was given by God or was a product of the devil, but such doubts do not obtrude in the Fifth Dwelling Place, "for there is neither imagination, nor memory, nor intellect that can impede this good" (V.1.4). There are many forms of union, but this union is "above all earthly joys, above all delights, above all consolations. . . . The feeling is very different, as you will have experienced" (. . . *que es muy diferente su sentir, como lo ternéis espirimentado*, V.1.).

The infallible test of such an experience of union, according to Teresa, is the lasting certitude it brings so that "the soul can neither forget nor doubt that it was in God and God was in it" (V.1.8). In what follows (V.1.9–12) Teresa so emphasizes the certainty of the experience that she slips into talking about the highest form of union to be treated more fully in Dwelling VII. She says that whoever does not have this absolute certitude of union may have experienced a uniting of one or the other faculties with God, but not the union of the whole soul (V.1.10). What is more, appealing to the bride of the Song of Songs (Song 2:4), such a soul is brought into the King's wine cellar. "His Majesty must place us there and enter himself into the center of our soul"—it is God's work, not ours. Teresa realizes she has gotten ahead of herself and says, "Further on you will see in the last Dwelling Place how his Majesty desires that the soul enjoy him in its own center even much more than here."[296]

The second chapter of the Fifth Dwelling Place returns to the prayer of union and its effects. Union is God's work, but we are able to dispose ourselves for his gift, which is why Teresa turns to the silkworm–

butterfly exemplum to illustrate how our efforts, like the worm's spinning silk, prepares for God's action (V.2.2–9). Teresa daringly says that in "this prayer of union [God] becomes the dwelling place we build for ourselves" (2.4), not that we are really capable of this work, but that he unites us with him in our activities and he himself becomes the reward of the work. What is needed on our part is to perform the tasks assigned to us and to die to ourselves and to the world, so that God can transform our lowly worm into a beautiful butterfly (2.6–9). Teresa notes that even the butterfly that has experienced such divine favors will not be free of trials, because, "in one way or another there must be a cross while we live" (2.9). The pain and grief that come from considering the many offenses committed against God and the souls that will be lost are troubling, but they are not like worldly grief (V.2.10–11). When God brings the bride into the wine cellar (Song 2:4) he "ordered charity in her," that is, she surrenders herself to God so that she "neither knows nor wants anything more than what he wants with her" (V.2.12). This leads Teresa to a christological reflection on how much more the Lord Jesus Christ suffered in his desire to save sinners than anything she or others can imagine (V.2.13–14).

Chapters 3 and 4 of Dwelling V take up two kinds of union. At the outset Teresa makes it clear that it is not necessary for salvation to experience "the delightful union" (*unión regalada*) she has been speaking about thus far; what is essential for anyone to be saved (mystic or not) is attaining "the union that comes from resigning our will in God's will" (*la unión de estar resignada nuestra voluntad en la de Dios*, i.e., *unión verdada*).[297] According to Teresa, "In the delightful union, the experience of seeing oneself in so new a life greatly helps one to die; in the other union, it's necessary that while living in this life, we ourselves put the silkworm to death."[298] So there is a double mystical death. The "delightful union" marks an important mediation of what is essential (i.e., the "true union"), helping the soul to progress to higher and more fruitful realizations of being one with God. Still, as Teresa insists, "[t]he union with God's will is the union I have desired all my life; it is the union I ask the Lord for always and the one that is clearest and safest."[299] Teresa counsels her nuns that their main concern should always be with the union of wills with God shown in love of God and love of neighbor, and that the only way we can recognize if we really love God is by the strength of our love of neighbor (V.3.7–8). Works of love are what the Lord wants, says Teresa, not empty imagining about our states of prayer, which often come from the devil (V.3.10–11). "If we fail in love of neighbor, we are lost" (V.3.12). Teresa completes this important discussion in the brief chapter 4, where the marital analogy comes to the fore. This chapter actually marks the division between the first period of writing the *Castle* and the second, begun in November of 1577. She starts this part by saying that the prayer of union does not reach the level of spiritual betrothal to which she will soon turn (V.3.2–4). It is more like a meeting between the two lovers (V.3.5). She then warns that at this stage backsliding is still a possibility, especially through the wiles of the devil (V.3.7–10).

Dwelling Place VI has eleven chapters and constitutes over a third of the *Interior Castle*. One may ask whether this length creates a certain imbalance in the book. A possible reason for the excessive attention given to this Dwelling rests in the fact that Gracián asked Teresa to recall what she had written in the *Life* and that her first book had concentrated on special mystical gifts. Another possibility is that these gifts emphasize the transformation of consciousness that the mystical journey involves, though this development will be realized by different persons in diverse ways.[300] Many mystical favors are reprised in Dwelling Place VI, though they are now ordered under the general heading of spiritual betrothal. What is new is that Teresa has come to realize that these expressions of betrothal, while important, are not the final stage of the path to God. Nevertheless, the concentration on this sometimes exotic material (e.g., inner trials, impulses, locutions, raptures, visions, both imaginative and intellectual, suspensions, and the wound of love) suggests that this part of the *Interior Castle* may have had some unfortunate effects in the history of Christian mysticism, because it has led some investigators to think of mysticism as basically constituted by the special charisms given to only a few and an object of wonder to other believers, who may themselves be trying to realize their own deeper union of wills between God and the human in the absence of such gifts. Recognizing that these extraordinary experiences are not the essence of union but only mediations of it,[301] however, does not address the question of how far they may be considered to be *useful* mediations. Given the overlap with much of what is found in the *Life*, it will not be necessary to give an extended description of all these chapters here, but only to touch on some salient points.[302]

Throughout her writings Teresa had insisted on the necessity of inner and outer trials in the journey to the center of the soul.[303] Until one attains the permanent union of the Seventh Dwelling and the fortitude that comes with it, suffering and disturbance are necessary to the soul seeking God. "O God help me," Teresa exclaims, "what interior and exterior trials the soul suffers before entering the Seventh

Dwelling Place!"[304] In the remainder of chapter 1 (VI.1.3–15) Teresa gives consolation to her readers by recounting a number of her trials, beginning with the smallest (gossip and envy) and proceeding through illness, bad confessors, and diabolical attacks (1.9–13). She concludes by insisting once again that severe suffering is necessary to reach Dwelling Place VII (VI.1.15).

The second chapter of Dwelling Place VI concerns some of the ways that the Lord awakens the soul to prepare for spiritual betrothal. Teresa introduces a new kind of spiritual gift here, what she calls "impulses" (*impulsos*). These are "delicate means" (*medios delicatos*) that "proceed from very deep within the interior part of the soul," and are described as "far different from all that we can acquire of ourselves here below and even from the spiritual delights."[305] Again, the nun says that it is very hard to describe this spiritual gift to those who have not experienced it. Impulses include the wound of love that is both painful and delightful (VI.2.2, 4), as well as "a whisper so penetrating that the soul cannot help but hear it" (2.3), and a "fragrance" that spreads through all the senses and moves the soul to intense acts of love (2.8). One cannot doubt the divine source of these impulses because "all the senses remain free of any absorption, wondering what this could be, without hindering anything, or being able, in my opinion, to increase or take away that delightful pain."[306] The devil is not able to mimic a spiritual gift like this (2.6), nor can the soul counterfeit it (2.7).

Chapter 3 takes up the related topic of locutions, already discussed in the *Life*, noting that there are many kinds: "Some seem to come from outside oneself; others, from deep within the interior part of the soul; others, from the superior part; and some are so exterior that they come through the sense of hearing."[307] Teresa warns that the claims of locutions made by persons suffering from melancholy (i.e., depression or other mental illness) or with sick imaginations should be dismissed. As in the *Life*, Teresa says that locutions can come from three sources: God, the devil, or one's imagination (VI.3.4). She then provides a list of the signs by which one can determine whether God is the source of either external or internal locutions (3.5–9).[308] None of these signs is present when the locutions come from the imagination, although Teresa says sometimes people engaged in deep recollection imagine they hear words spoken to them that are actually the products of their "weak constitution and imagination" (3.10). More dangerous are the locutions that come from the devil, where the advice of a good confessor will be helpful (3.11). At this point Teresa typically moves to a related topic, how God sometimes speaks to souls in the context of an intellectual vision. These locutions come from deep within the soul and Teresa gives another list of five tests the soul can use to determine their authenticity (3.12–16), noting that she will speak of intellectual visions later (see chaps. 8 and 10). She closes by recalling how she herself ("a certain person" in the text) had had to wrestle painfully to determine whether her locutions came from the devil or from God (see *Life* 25.14–19).

Teresa had treated suspension, ecstasy, and rapture in chapter 20 of the *Life*. She returns to the topic in chapters 4–6 of Dwelling Place VI.[309] The reason that God gives the soul raptures that draw it out of its senses is because at this stage of spiritual development the soul might die if its powers were still functioning as it approaches the Divine Majesty (VI.4.2). Teresa begins her discussion by saying, "I want to put down some kinds of raptures [*arrobamientos*] that I've come to understand because I've discussed them with so many spiritual persons."[310] She speaks from her own experience, though she admits she often finds it hard to convey the nature of these divine gifts. The first kind of rapture occurs when the soul, even when not in prayer, hears some word about God that enkindles the spark of love within and gives it a "deep enlightenment and knowledge of his Majesty" (4.3–4). This kind of rapture does not involve total loss of all the senses. Teresa notes that what she will be speaking about pertains to both the Sixth and the Seventh Dwelling Places, because "there is no closed door between the one and the other" (4.4). In this kind of suspension the Lord shows the soul heavenly secrets, sometimes by way of imaginative visions, which can be partially described, but other times by intellectual visions that the soul cannot speak of (4.5).

At this point Teresa introduces a discussion of mystical ineffability—How can one speak about sublime favors that cannot be remembered? Her answer (4.6–9) is ambiguous. Admitting that she does not really know, she says that she is sure that "some truths about the grandeur of God remain so fixed in this soul" that even if faith did not teach her who God is, "she would adore him as God, as Jacob did when he saw the ladder" (Genesis 28).[311] Although she says that the kind of vision she is talking about is intellectual, not imaginative, the example she gives is imaginative: just as a person brought into a rich treasure chamber filled with rare objects will have an impression of splendor without remembering everything there, so too the soul will have a remembrance of God's grandeur without being able to give a detailed description (4.8–9).[312] The remainder of chapter 4 (13–17) talks about the brief raptures characterized by what Teresa calls "extreme suspension" (4.13).

Teresa continues the topic in chapter 5 with an account of "another kind of rapture—I call it flight of the spirit [*vuelo del espíritu*]—that, though substantially the same as other raptures, is experienced very differently."[313] The suddenness and strength of this type of experience make it seem like both soul and body are being carried aloft (the feeling of levitation). Much courage is needed on such occasions, she says. As a comparison for this experience, Teresa turns once again to water (5.3). The soul is like a little boat suddenly lifted up beyond its control by powerful waves. In this sudden rapture the spirit seems to go out of the body, but the person does not really die (5.7). For Teresa, the experience is marked by infused knowledge, both in terms of what is revealed in imaginative visions during the flight (5.7), and especially what is conveyed in intellectual vision. Her explanation is noteworthy:

> Without seeing anything with the eyes of the body or the soul, through an admirable intuition [*conocimiento admirable*] I will not be able to explain, there is represented what I'm saying and many other things not to be spoken of. Anyone who experiences them and has more ability than I will perhaps know how to explain them, although doing so seems to me very difficult indeed.[314]

In order to try to understand the experience, Teresa turns to an introspective analysis (5.9). Just as the sun and its rays can be distinguished but are really one, so the soul and the spirit are one, but the spirit can be raptured far away from the soul and shown divine mysteries.[315] When it returns to itself, remarkable benefits remain—knowledge of the grandeur of God; great self-knowledge and humility; and esteem for earthly things only insofar as they can be used in the service of God (5.10).

Chapter 6 continues the exploration of raptures and their effects, which, says Teresa, "are very common in this Dwelling Place and there is no means to avoid them even if they take place in public."[316] Reflecting on her own previous experience, Teresa says that the "poor little butterfly" has inner confidence that it is on the right path, despite the exterior distress it suffers as it is told by so many spiritual advisors that it is mistaken and even a victim of diabolical deception (6.2). These suspensions and ecstasies leave the soul with an intense desire to praise God and to suffer for his sake, as well as the realization that all its power is given by God. Making a rare use of the language of annihilation, she says, "This truth is seen with a clarity that leaves the soul annihilated within itself and with deeper knowledge of God's mercy and grandeur."[317] Teresa is aware that such intense desires for God can be mimicked by the devil, who tempts some people with weak constitutions to think that they should weep over everything, because they have heard that tears are good (6.6–7). Tears should never be encouraged or induced, says the prioress, "Let the tears come when God sends them" (6.9). Finally, Teresa takes up one more aspect of the experiences that are both painful and delightful—"jubilations and a strange prayer it does not understand" (*júbilos y oración estraña que no sabe entender*, 6.10). In her view, this charism takes place in a deep union of the faculties in which the soul and the senses remain free to enjoy God in such a way that they wish others to share in this joy, and hence the person wants to cry out, shout, and sing as a herald of God (6.10–11). What Teresa is referring to here is close to the wordless singing (*jubilus*) characteristic of many medieval Beguine mystics. She did not know of these women, but she cites the examples of Francis of Assisi and her departed friend, Friar Peter of Alcántara.

At this point in the Sixth Dwelling Place, Teresa feels compelled, as she did in *Life* 22, to take up the question of meditation on the humanity of Christ in the highest stages of mystical prayer. There are two issues concerning advanced souls she wishes to clear up. The first is the question of sorrow for sin (VI.7.1–4), which Teresa says does not cease in the higher stages but, on the contrary, "increases the more one receives from our God" (7.1). Second, she says it may seem to some in her audience that they should be engaged entirely in acts of pure love and forgo meditating "on the mysteries of the most sacred humanity of our Lord Jesus Christ" (7.5). Noting that she had already discussed this in the *Life*, she summarizes her teaching again (7.5–6), showing how harmful this distancing from Christ's humanity can be. Teresa admits that some souls who are brought to perfect contemplation (*contemplación perfecta*) in loving acts of the will find discursive meditation about the mysteries of the passion and Christ's life, which utilize the intellect, difficult (7.7); but as long as we are in this life, Teresa argues, both intellect and will are necessary. Even in the highest stages in which the will is most active there are times when the fire of love dies down and the work of the intellect in seeking God's presence is needed, just as the bride in the Song of Songs went out to seek her Lover (Song 3:1–3). "Such a person," says Teresa, "walks continually in an admirable way with Christ our Lord, in whom the divine and human are joined and who is always that person's companion."[318] In other words, to reject meditation on Christ's humanity is to sunder the two natures of the God-man.

Knowledge of Christ, however, can come in various ways as Teresa shows in VI.7.10–11. Meditation is discursive reflection with the intellect (*entendimiento*) in which we think about God's gift of his Son to us and go on to consider all the mysteries of the Savior's life. It is true that persons in the state of perfect contemplation will not be able to practice this, but, says Teresa, "a person will not be right if he says that he does not dwell on these mysteries or often have them in mind, especially when the Catholic Church celebrates them" (7.11). This is because they can be known in *another* way. Here Teresa invokes the dynamic interaction of the three faculties in the higher mystical knowing, or intuition/recognition (elsewhere called *conocimiento*) where "these mysteries are known in a more perfect way." In this way of knowing, the intellect represents the mysteries in a new mode and impresses them on the memory so that the mere sight, say, of Christ in agony in the garden, contents the intellect "not only for an hour but for many days, while it looks *with a simple gaze* [my emphasis] at who he is and how ungrateful we have been for so much suffering." Discursiveness is at an end; pure simple regard enflames the will "with the desire to serve somehow for such a great favor and to suffer something for the one who suffered so much."[319] Such a simple regard of Christ's mysteries will not impede the most sublime prayer, and even if the Lord suspends all action of the intellect, "this procedure is not a hindrance but a very great help toward every good" (7.12). When they reach the prayer of quiet, some people think that they should try to remain continually in that state (7.13). Teresa says this is impossible; we need to continue to look at Christ as our model. She says she would be suspicious of anyone who claims that their delight is continual; such folk should be given some demanding task lest counterfeit absorption harm their brains. Teresa speaks from experience, because she says she herself had suffered from this error early in her prayer life (7.14–15).

Chapters 8 and 9 of Dwelling Place VI take up another form of spiritual favor found mostly on the level of betrothal to Christ—visions, both intellectual and imaginative. Much of what is said here can also be found in the *Life*. Chapter 8 deals with intellectual visions, which Teresa opens by referring to the unexpected intellectual vision she had of Christ recounted in *Life* 27.2–5 (VI.8.2–7). Teresa repeats her analysis of this manifestation to instruct her nuns about how they should treat such experiences, especially by consulting with their confessors (8.8–10). God also communicates through imaginative visions, and

Teresa is aware that these are more open to diabolical meddling, so she provides more extensive guidelines for understanding them (VI.9.1). These appearances of the sacred humanity of Christ, especially in his earthly or resurrected state (9.3), are seen "in the inner eye" like an infused light, usually in rapture (9.4).

This brief reference to the inner eye raises the question of Teresa's understanding of the difference between our outer physical senses and the inner spiritual senses, which she mentions from time to time but lays out in more detail in *Spiritual Testimonies* 59. The notion of "spiritual senses," a parallel set of inner modes of perception, goes deep into the Christian mystical tradition, often invoked as a way to utilize the highly somatic language of the Old Testament, especially the Song of Songs, for spiritual teaching.[320] According to Edward Howells, Teresa does make a distinction between two sets of senses: one by which the soul feels natural things; the other by which it senses the *impulsos* in its interior.[321] As she says, "It appears that just as the soul has exterior senses, it also has other senses through which it seems to want to withdraw within itself, away from exterior noise."[322] Nevertheless, on the basis of her distinction between imaginative visions and purely intellectual visions, Teresa seems to suggest, at least in some places, that the inner senses that grasp imaginative visions are completed by some kind of inner "sensing" attuned to intellectual visions, but what this "sensation" that has no form or created content might be is not clear.

Teresa says that these imaginative visions can be easily confused with likenesses fashioned by our own imaginations (9.8–9), so she provides some tests to distinguish the true from the false, notably the certitude and happy peace that result from a real imaginative vision (9.10). A confessor with learning, especially one who also has experience, will be able to discern whether such visions come from God, the imagination, or the devil (9.11). Almost obsessively, Teresa returns to her own story and recounts, once again, the trials she endured from those who doubted her early visions and locutions (9.12–18). She ends this long chapter with some observations about the ultimate irrelevance of all such special gifts in comparison with the real test of love of God: "So there are many holy persons who have never received one of these favors; and others who receive them but are not holy."[323]

The last two chapters of the Sixth Dwelling Place recapitulate things already treated, though with some nuances. Chapter 10.2 talks about suspensions in which an intellectual vision provides an understanding of how all things are seen in God and how he contains them all in himself, a type of experience also mentioned in *Life* 40.9. Such a showing should teach us how terrible it is to sin because we are, in a sense, bringing evil into God (10.2–4). At other times God reveals another kind of truth within himself, namely, that he is the real and only Truth, so that we always need to walk in humility knowing that "of ourselves we have nothing good but only misery and nothingness" (10.7). These are the kinds of gifts the Lord gives to his betrothed. The final chapter of Dwelling Place VI deals with desires God gives the beloved soul that are so strong they place it in danger of death. As we have seen, the notion of *mors mystica* is fairly frequent in Teresa's works, not least in the *Castle*.[324] The little butterfly of the soul, despite all the favors she has received, moans and aspires to more love for God. As desire increases, the soul suddenly experiences "a blow, or as one might say a fiery arrow [*un golpe, u como si viniese una saeta de fuego*]."[325] This is another description of the "wound of love," but here Teresa insists that the wound is in the deep and intimate part of the soul and not at all in the body (11.3), so that she is convinced that feelings in the soul are much deeper than in the body, as will be the case in purgatory. We are, nevertheless, left with uncertainty about how the two wounds may be related. This is heightened by the fact that this inner experience brings peril of death as the body weakens and the heart is in danger of stopping (11.4).

One can understand that Teresa's detailed, sometimes confusing accounts of her spiritual-somatic states provoked a large, and not always helpful, literature that tried to sort out things that may not be capable of logical ordering. Teresa plunges ahead in further attempts to describe the indescribable (11.4–11), with constant appeals to her own experience. Echoing language found in mystics such as Angela of Foligno (11.5) and Catherine of Genoa (11.6), she talks about the intense sufferings of the soul in this penultimate state, even down to calculating the temporal duration of such trials (11.8). She concludes by saying that she is going into all this detail to help her nuns who may also have to deal with such experiences in which "the soul dies with the desire to die" (11.9). But, she insists, when the Lord takes away such pain, either through a rapture or a vision, the benefits it has for the soul are great. Dangers rest on both sides of the spectrum: "Two experiences . . . that lie on this spiritual path put a person in danger of death. The one is of this pain, for it is truly a danger, and not a small one; the other is overwhelming joy and delight, which reaches so extraordinary a peak that the soul, I think, swoons to the point that it is hardly kept from leaving the body."[326] On this note Teresa concludes her most intensive exploration of ecstatic gifts.

Dwelling Place VI leaves the reader very much where the *Life* did with its detailed, at times obsessive, attention to ecstatic states and their effects. What is new with the mature Teresa comes in Dwelling Place VII, where she says that God's grace can take the soul beyond ecstasy to a state where the bride can be truly married to the Bridegroom and enjoy a life in which contemplation is fused with action, where Mary and Martha will no longer be in tension or opposition. As I have been suggesting throughout this chapter, Teresa's life both as a contemplative and as an active founder of religious houses gradually led her to this realization. In the *Interior Castle* she tried to put into words what God had taught her in life. Her account is brief, at least in comparison with Dwelling Place VI, but is of great importance. One issue she does not address, because she is speaking out of her own life experience, is whether someone whom God has given the gift of being able to combine action and contemplation needs to have experienced the ecstatic gifts of Dwelling Place VI, though one senses she would have insisted that such a person would have to undergo inner and outer suffering to reach the goal. Teresa did, however, say that there were many dwelling places and that God had different plans for different people.

The first chapter of Dwelling Place VII sets the tone for the whole final section, reemphasizing Teresa's purpose in writing: "Thus you will understand how important it is for you not to impede your Spouse's celebration of this spiritual marriage with your souls, since this marriage brings so many blessings, as you will see."[327] The Lord takes pity on his betrothed who has suffered so much for him and finally brings her into the Seventh Dwelling Place where "the spiritual marriage is consummated" (VII.1.3). Teresa goes on to say, "He desires that the favor [i.e., the marriage] be different from what it was at the other times when he gave the soul raptures."[328] Raptures and the prayer of union unite the soul to God, *but not in the center of the soul, only in the superior part* (1.5). The notion of the "center of the soul" (*centro del alma*) thus has a decisive role in Teresa's new view of the highest stage of mystical consciousness. The center serves as something like the metaphor of the "ground of the soul" in Meister Eckhart and the northern European mystics of the Late Middle Ages, but there are significant differences. Unlike Eckhart and his followers, Teresa does not engage in detailed speculative analysis of the term.[329]

In the union of rapture, such as Paul experienced at his conversion (Acts 9:8), the soul is made blind and deaf as the faculties are suspended, but in this union, "[o]ur good God now desires to remove the scales from the soul's eyes and let it see and understand, although in a strange way, something of the favor he grants it."[330] This is a form of trinitarian consciousness. Teresa describes it as follows:

> When the soul is brought into that Dwelling Place, the Most Blessed Trinity, all three persons, through an intellectual vision is revealed to it through a certain representation of the truth. First there comes an enkindling of the spirit in the manner of a cloud of magnificent splendor; and these persons are distinct, and through an admirable knowledge [*notitia admirable*] the soul understands as a most profound truth that all three persons are one substance and one power and one knowledge and one God.[331]

Teresa does not try to unpack what this "admirable knowledge" is, because it cannot be put into the categories of dogmatic theology. It is a permanent, intersubjective, or connatural, and more intense awareness *that* God is one and three. It is not some better (and misleading) way to try to say *how* God is one and three. Teresa says that the soul now knows by sight what it formerly held by faith, but that this seeing is not with bodily eyes, nor with the eyes of the soul—it is an intellectual, not imaginative, vision. The visions of the Trinity that Teresa had recounted in the *Spiritual Testimonies* (e.g., No. 13) have now been incorporated into her general account of mysticism. Teresa's mystical thought may not be constitutively trinitarian throughout, as is that of John of the Cross, but it can certainly be said that Teresa's mysticism is *decisively* trinitarian.

The presence of the Trinity within the soul is continuous, says Teresa: "Each day this soul becomes more amazed, for these persons never seem to leave it any more, but it clearly beholds . . . that they are within it; in the extreme interior, in some place very deep within itself."[332] Even more, this unitive presence is not absorptive. Teresa says that the soul is not outside itself in ecstasy: "On the contrary, the soul is much more occupied than before with everything pertaining to the service of God." To be sure, the presence is not always adverted to in the same way. The first time the soul is given this trinitarian presence, it is like a clear light in which one sees other persons in a well-lit room. After that, the presence of the Trinity is like being in a dark room where we sense others are with us. Nevertheless, "the soul finds itself in this company every time it takes notice" (1.9), and God will from time to time allow "the window of the intellect [*la ventana del entendimiento*] to be opened" for the full awareness of the Trinity to return. Teresa says that "the essential part of her soul never moved from that room," although she does, indeed, sometimes feel a division in the soul in which the busy Martha complains to the Mary sitting in inner quietude (1.10). She explains this rest by referring, once again, to the difference between the soul (i.e., Martha) and the spirit (i.e., Mary) who are both one but who function differently and receive different savors from the Lord (1.11).

The Second Chapter of Dwelling Place VII explains the spiritual marriage more fully, emphasizing the christological dimensions of this ultimate blessing. According to Teresa, the first time the favor was granted to her, after she had received communion, his Majesty showed himself at her right side through an imaginative vision of his resurrected sacred humanity, though she recognizes that "with other persons the favor will be received in another form."[333] Teresa had seen such visions of Christ before, but this one, which appears to have been subsequent to the vision of the Trinity, was different in several ways, not least because it took place in the "interior of her soul" (i.e., the center). Teresa spells out how the visions received in the spiritual marriage are different from all previous showings, even those of spiritual betrothal. This secret union takes place "in the very interior center of the soul," where God himself is always found (VII.2.3). Previous visions, including those of Christ's humanity, took place by means of the interior senses and faculties of the soul, but the vision in the soul's center is intellectual and more delicate than others. "What God communicates here to the soul in an instant," according to Teresa, "is a secret so great and a favor so sublime—and the delight the soul experiences so extreme—that I don't know what to compare it to."[334] After the union of spiritual betrothal, God and the soul can separate. Not so in the case of spiritual marriage—"The soul always remains with God in the center" (2.4). Teresa provides a number of comparisons for this, and even cites Paul's famous text on union: "He that is joined or united to God becomes one spirit with him" (1 Cor. 6:17), as well as Philippians 1:21, "For me to live is Christ and to die is gain." The christological core of Teresa's mysticism is aptly summarized by her succinct comment in VII.2.5: "her life is now Christ" (*su vida es ya Cristo*).[335]

She then turns to two of her favorite images—water and light—to illustrate how the delight the soul experiences at the center flows out to the other people in the castle, that is, to the senses and faculties. Streams of milk bring comfort to all the people in the castle, like a full-flowing river. "Someone in the interior depths . . . shoots these arrows and gives life to this life, and there is a Sun in the interior of the soul from which a brilliant light proceeds and is sent to the faculties."[336] The notion of the "overflow" from the union realized in the center of the soul out to the faculties and down into the senses and exterior charitable action is an essential part of Teresa's mature mystical theory.[337]

Teresa does not explicitly relate the vision of the Trinity in Dwelling Place VII.1.6 and the intellectual vision of Christ's humanity in VII.2.3–4, but it is obvious from the whole development of the *Interior Castle* that the two are fully integrated. Teresa's notion of the ultimate form of our consciousness of union is both trinitarian and christological—or, better put, it is trinitarian *because* it is christological. Because we come to participate more and more deeply in Jesus Christ, as both God and man, we are brought into the mutual inner life of the Three Persons, in accordance with Jesus's prayer in John 17, "That all may be one, as you, Father, in me, and I in you," through the loving bond of the Holy Spirit.

Teresa explains that when the Lord puts the soul in its very center, which is his own dwelling place, the soul no longer undergoes the disturbing movements of the imagination and faculties she had once experienced (VII.2.9). This does not mean that the soul is assured of her salvation, which still depends totally on God. Hence, the soul actually goes about in great fear of offending God and with pain at seeing how little good she really does. Nevertheless, in its center the soul remains in peace, although the faculties, senses, and passions may suffer disturbance (2.10). This is hard to understand, so Teresa uses the example of a king who is at rest in his palace even though wars may be raging in his realm.

Chapter 3 of the Seventh Dwelling Place deals with the effects of the prayer of spiritual marriage. Teresa lists seven, interspersing her explanations with further comments on major aspects of the marriage.[338] Several of these are worthy of comment. The desire to serve God has now overcome the desire to die and be with the Lord, because the soul wishes to be active and to help the crucified Christ (VII.3.6). She can always turn within and "look within herself and at how continually she enjoys his presence, and with that she is content and offers his Majesty the desire to live as the most costly offering she can give him."[339] The soul continues to experience the "impulses" (*impulsos/impetus*) mentioned in VI.2, but in the most gentle way, "so that one experiences here that this interior movement proceeds from the center of the soul and awakens the faculties" (3.8). Teresa uses a new vocabulary when she speaks of these interior movements as "touches of his love" (*estos toques de su amor*, 3.9).[340] We should always respond, at least interiorly, to these touches, even when engaged in exterior activity. As Teresa says, "this touch, which is so delicate, almost always disposes the soul to be able to do what was said [by God] with a resolute will."[341] Teresa continues to explore the role of the faculties in this state. God and the soul dwell in "deepest silence" in the center, so the intellect does not need to seek anything. "In my opinion," she says, "the faculties are not lost here [as they are in rapture]; they do not work, but remain as though in amazement."[342] Rapture ceases; peace descends; the bride has received the kiss of the mouth she requested.[343]

The final chapter of the *Interior Castle* explores God's purpose in granting such a great favor to the soul and emphasizes, once again, the union of the active Martha and the contemplative Mary in this state. The reason the Lord gives such great favors to us is not for our own pleasure but to draw us closer to Christ, so that "we may be able to imitate him in his great sufferings" (VII.4.4), as well as in all the good works he did for the human race. Again, Teresa emphasizes how much all the Lord's closest friends mentioned in the Bible suffered for him (4.5). Echoing an ancient theme in Christian mysticism, she says, "This is the reason for prayer, my daughters, the purpose of this spiritual marriage: the birth always of good works, good works."[344] In other words, the only test of the reality of mystical graces is the effect they have in increasing love of God and love of neighbor. The model for this is, as always, Christ: "Fix your eyes on the Crucified and everything will become small for you. If his Majesty showed us his love by means of such works and frightful torments, how is it that you want to please him only with words?"[345] Teresa reminds her sisters that even those who reach the heights cannot neglect the virtues, especially humility. Rather, the overflow from the center into the outer senses and powers will give them the fortitude the saints showed in suffering and dying (4.10–11). She turns to Martha and Mary once more to illustrate this: "Believe me, Martha and Mary must join together to show hospitality to the Lord and to have him always present. . . . How would Mary, always seated at his feet, provide him with food [i.e., bring souls to him] if her sister did not help out?"[346] Teresa has thus worked out a satisfactory theological grounding for the embodied nature of her mystical teaching.

Teresa recognizes that some may question her unusual interpretation of Martha and Mary.[347] Didn't Christ say Mary had chosen the "better part" (Luke 10:32)? Her answer to this objection (4.13) is that Mary had already showed her active love for Christ in washing his feet (Luke 7:37–38), and she would do so in the future through her apostolic ministry known to Teresa through hagiographical accounts of the story of the two sisters. The second objection comes from nuns who ask how it is possible for them as enclosed religious to provide an active ministry for the church. Nonsense, says Teresa, your prayers can help everyone, and you "must concentrate on those who are in your company, and thus your deeds will be greater since you are more obligated to them" (4.14).

Teresa never says it is easy to combine action and contemplation. Her account shows that, even in the highest stages of prayer, trials, imperfections, and difficulties remain. But these no longer disturb the center, where union with the Bridegroom is permanent, though it will be adverted to in different ways. A clue to her understanding of how this is possible is found in *Spiritual Testimonies* 59.5, where she identifies Mary with the transformed will in the essence of the soul and Martha with the other faculties of memory and intellect. Thus, even when there seems to be a division in the soul in which the harried Martha complains to Mary about her not helping out, "it [the will] was always there enjoying that quietude in its own pleasure while leaving her in the midst of so many trials and occupations that she could not keep it company."[348] Let us also remember that the fortitude that Martha needs to carry on her labors comes down to her from the center of the soul where Mary and Christ are in marital union.

What is essential is to recognize that, for the mature Teresa, action and contemplation are not opposed modes of life that can be realized only by a kind of oscillation between one and the other. They are interdependent, united, and equally valuable. Like Meister Eckhart, Tauler, Catherine of Siena, and Ignatius of Loyola, Teresa sees the two sides of the Christian life as conjoined ways of showing our love for God and neighbor—equally necessary and nourishing. As Peter Tyler puts it, "What she is proposing is *union with God through action in the world*—essentially the thesis developed in the previous decade as she drafted *The Way* and the *Foundations*."[349] As she puts it at the end of this last chapter in the *Castle* with some irony about constructing castles, "In sum, my sisters, what I conclude is that we should not build castles in the air. The Lord does not look so much at the greatness of our works as at the love with which they are done. And if we do what we can, his Majesty will enable us each day to do more and more."[350]

The differences between the *Life* and the *Interior Castle*, for all their overlap, are evident, especially with regard to the goal of mystical union. In the *Life* union is temporary, ecstatic, and marginal to the body's senses and faculties, which are in absorption. In the *Interior Castle* the union of spiritual marriage is permanent in the center of the soul (though apprehended in different ways). The body and its apostolic activity partake of this union and receive strength to act from the union enjoyed in the center of the soul. The graces Teresa had received over the past decade and more led her to this breakthrough, which is set forth with subtlety in the *Interior Castle* but had appeared already in the *Meditations on the Song of Songs*. Many readers, both those contemporary with Teresa and later students, have read the *Castle* as a psychological portrait of ecstatic mystical gifts. Teresa, as I have suggested, lays herself open to this interpretation, especially given the length of Dwelling Place VI. Nonetheless, a careful study of the book shows that it is fundamentally not a record of ecstatic gifts but a journey with Jesus Christ, God and man, to the center where he brings his followers into the inner life of the Trinity.

Conclusion

This chapter is long, but Teresa of Avila is among the most significant mystics in Christian history. Her influence in Spain and on later Spanish mysticism was immense. The *Way of Perfection* was first published in 1583, and in 1588 Luis de León brought out the first edition of her collected works (though missing the *Foundations* and the *Meditations on the Song of Songs*). Thirteen later editions appeared by 1636, and no fewer than eleven biographies were published in Spain between 1590 and 1677. Her *Life* became the model for the many convent "autobiographies" of Golden Age Spain, and many of the women mystics or would-be mystics claimed that Teresa had appeared to them.[351] Of course, it was not only in Spain that the saint of Avila had a large impact, but throughout Europe, and then the world.

The era is past when Teresa and John of the Cross were held up as the supreme Catholic mystics against whom all others were measured. Nor is it correct to think of Teresa and John as a kind of team presenting the same teaching. For all the links between them, there are significant differences, which cannot be explored here. Teresa needs to be seen on her own terms and evaluated for her own contribution. Perhaps it is best to close on an official note, namely, the words Pope Paul VI used in declaring Teresa the first woman Doctor of the Church: "We do not doubt that We should proclaim her a Doctor of the Church, the first among women, especially due to her understanding and teaching of divine things. In fact, we are sure and have confidence that Teresa of Jesus, being declared by solemn decree a master of the Christian life, strongly moves even people of our age to nourish above all what favors the soul's love for contemplation and the search for the things of heaven."[352]

Notes

1. For Teresa's letters I use the translation of Kieran Kavanaugh, *The Collected Letters of St. Teresa of Avila*, 2 vols. (Washington, DC: ICS Publications, 2001), 1:172.

2. There are a number of editions of Teresa's writings. I will use Efrén de la Madre de Dios and Otger Steggink, eds., *Obras Completas de Santa Teresa de Jesús: Edición Manual* (Madrid: Biblioteca de Autores Cristianos, 1986). Unless noted, I will use the translation of Kieran Kavanaugh and Otilio Rodriguez, *The Collected Works of St. Teresa of Avila*, 3 vols. (Washington, DC: ICS Publications, 1976–85), although its numbering of sections in chapters sometimes differs from the Madre de Dios-Steggink edition. Unless otherwise noted, subsequent references to "*Obras Completas*" refer to the Madre de Dios and Steggink edition, and "trans." refers to the translation of Kavanaugh and Rodriguez.

3. For a history of the Discalced branches, both female and male, of the Carmelite order, see V. Macca, "Carmelitane Scalze" and "Carmelitani Scalzi," DIP 2:423–54 and 523–602.

4. On Teresa as a letter writer, see Bárbara Mujica, *Teresa de Ávila: Lettered Woman* (Nashville: Vanderbilt University Press, 2009).

5. The phrase *in actione contemplativus* is found in a letter of Jerome Nadal regarding Ignatius. For a translation, see Ganss et al., *Ignatius of Loyola: The Spiritual Exercises and Selected Works*, 44.

6. For a history of this theme, see Nikolaus Lobkowicz, *Theory and Practice: History of a Concept from Aristotle to Marx*, International Studies of the Committee on International Relations (Notre Dame, IN: University of Notre Dame Press, 1967).

7. On the Christian adoption, see P. T. Camelot, "Action et contemplation dans la tradition chrétienne," *La vie spirituelle* 78 (1958): 272–302; Aimé Solignac, "Vie active, vie contemplative, vie mixte," DS 16:592–623; and Hans Urs von Balthasar, "Action and Contemplation," in Balthasar, *Explorations in Theology*, vol. 1, *The Word Made Flesh* (San Francisco: Ignatius Press, 1989), 227–40.

8. This common teaching is summarized by Thomas Aquinas in his STh IIaI-Iae, qq. 180–83.

9. For an overview, see Aimé Solignac and Lin Donnet, "Marthe et Marie," DS 10:664–73. For a more detailed study, see Giles Constable, "The Interpretation of Mary and Martha," in Constable, *Three Studies in Medieval Religious and Social Thought* (Cambridge: Cambridge University Press, 1995), 3–141.

10. Eckhart, Pr. 86 in *Meister Eckhart: Die deutschen und lateinischen Werke* (Stuttgart: Kohlhammer, 1936–) in two series: *Die deutschen Werke* (DW) and *Die lateinischen Werke* (LW). Pr. 86 is in DW 3:481–92. I use the translation in Bernard McGinn, *The Essential Writings of Christian Mysticism* (New York: Random House, 2006), 530–34.

11. On the significance of this shift, see Dietmar Mieth, *Die Einheit von Vita Activa und Vita Contemplativa in den deutschen Predigten und Traktaten Meister Eckharts und bei Johannes Tauler: Untersuchungen zur Struktur des christlichen Lebens*, Studien zur Geschichte der katholischen Moral-theologie 15 (Regensburg: Pustet, 1969).

12. Teresa mentions Catherine as one of the great contemplatives (*Life* 22.7). In addition, she recounts a story from Catherine's life in Letter 294.7, indicating she knew Raymond of Capua's *Legenda major S. Catharinae*, which had been translated into Spanish in 1511. On the role of Catherine of Siena in female Spanish mysticism, see Gillian T. W. Ahlgren, "Ecstasy, Prophecy, and Reform: Catherine of Siena as a Model for Holy Women of Sixteenth-Century Spain," in *The Mystical Gesture: Essays on Medieval and Early Modern Spiritual Culture in Honor of Mary E. Giles*, ed. Robert Boenig (Burlington, VT: Ashgate, 2000), 53–65.

13. Raymond of Capua, *Legenda major* I.12.116 (trans. Conleath Kearns, *The Life of Catherine of Siena by Raymond of Capua* [Washington, DC: Dominica Publications, 1980], 108).

14. Teresa mentions Mary Magdalene in many places, notably *Life* 9.2; 21.7; 22.12, 15; *Way of Perfection* 16.7; 17.5; 26.8; 34.7; and 40.3; *Interior Castle* I.1.3; VI.7.7; VI.11.12; VII.4.12–13. On Mary Magdalene as an apostolic model for Catherine, see Bernard McGinn, "Catherine of Siena: Apostle of the Blood of Christ," *Theology Today* 48 (2001): 329–42.

15. Teresa's major writings in chronological order are (1) *Libro de la vida*, abbreviated here as *Life*; (2) *Camino de perfección* (*Way*); (3) *Meditaciones sobre los Cantares* (*Meditations*); (4) *Moradas del Castillo Interior* (*Interior Castle*); (5) *Cuentas de conciencia* (*Spiritual Testimonies*); (6) *Libro de las fundaciones* (*Foundations*). In addition, there are a number of shorter prose works: *Exclamaciones* (*Soliloquies*); *Constituciones* (*Constitutions*); *Visita de descalzas* (*On Making the Visitation*), as well as her *Epistolario* (*Letters*) and *Poesías* (*Poems*).

16. There are a number of lives of Teresa available in English, but no up-to-date full biography. Still useful for her story and that of the reform is E. Allison Peers, *Handbook to the Life and Times of St. Teresa and St. John of the Cross* (Westminster, MD: Newman Press, 1954). There are helpful chronologies of Teresa's life in *Obras Completas*, 19–29; and Kavanaugh, *Collected Works*, 3:83–91. Much information about Teresa's family, historical context, life, and writings can be found in Tomás Alvarez, *St. Teresa of Avila: 100 Themes on Her Life and Work* (Washington, DC: ICS Publications, 2011).

17. Given how much has been written about Teresa, I will mention only a few helpful works here. For a brief introduction, see Teófanes Egido, "The Historical Setting of St. Teresa's Life," in John Sullivan, *Spiritual Direction*, Carmelite Studies 1 (Washington, DC: ICS Publications, 1980), 122–82. Among the shorter books on Teresa, see Rowan Williams, *Teresa of Avila*, Outstanding Christian Thinkers (London: Geoffrey Chapman, 1991), chap. 1; and Peter Tyler, *Teresa of Avila: Doctor of the Soul* (London: Bloomsbury, 2013). For her urban context, see Jodi Bilinkoff, *The Avila of Saint Teresa: Religious Reform in a Sixteenth-Century City* (Ithaca, NY: Cornell University Press, 1989).

18. Deirdre Green, *Gold in the Crucible: Teresa of Avila and the Western Mystical Tradition* (Shaftesbury: Element Books, 1989), 145–46.

19. For arguments about Teresa's dependence on Jewish mysticism, see Catherine Swietlicki, *Spanish Christian Cabala: The Works of Luis de León, Santa Teresa de Jesús, and San Juan de la Cruz* (Columbia: University of Missouri Press, 1986), chap. 3; and Green, *Gold in the Crucible*, chap. 3, who claims that Teresa's use of Jewish mystical symbolism may be either "fully thought-out and conscious,

or the result of some inspiration coming . . . spontaneously from semi-conscious inner depths" (p. 85).

20. Luce López-Baralt, "Teresa of Jesus and Islam: The Simile of the Seven Concentric Castles of the Soul," in Kallendorf, *New Companion to Hispanic Mysticism*, 175–99.

21. *Life* 9.7–8 (*Obras Completas*, 65; trans. 1:72–73). I have emended the second part of the translation. In the interests of space, I will generally not provide the Spanish texts, unless the vocabulary is especially important.

22. For more on the comparison of Augustine and Teresa, see Bernard McGinn, "True Confessions: Augustine and Teresa of Avila on the Mystical Self," in *Teresa of Avila: Mystical Theology and Spirituality in the Carmelite Tradition*, ed. Peter Tyler and Edward Howells (London: Routledge, 2017), 9–29. Teresa also refers to *Confessions* explicitly in *Life* 13.3 and 40.6.

23. *Life* 23.1 (*Obras Completas*, 126; trans., 1:152). Teresa insists on her new self in other places, e.g., *Life* 15.7; 16.6; 25.19; and 27.1.

24. *Life* 40.24 (*Obras Completas*, 229; trans., 1:284). The other three are probably Domingo Báñez, Baltasar Alvarez, and Gaspar de Salazar.

25. An example is Karl Joachim Weintraub, *The Value of the Individual: Self and Circumstance in Autobiography* (Chicago: University of Chicago Press, 1978), who treats Teresa's *Life* in chap. 9. Fernando Dúran López considers Teresa the primary source for what he calls "feminine conventual autobiographies" ("Religious Autobiographies," in Kallendorf, *New Companion to Hispanic Mysticism*, 15–38, here 18–20). Jane Tylus deals more with the *Interior Castle* but also considers the *Life*, both as examples of "mystical autobiography" ("Between Two Fathers: Teresa of Avila and Mystical Autobiography," in Tylus, *Writing and Vulnerability in the Late Renaissance* [Stanford: Stanford University Press, 1993], 54–79). See also Elena Carrera, *Teresa of Avila's Autobiography: Authority, Power and the Self in Mid-Sixteenth-Century Spain* (London: Legenda, 2005).

26. Denials that the *Life* is an autobiography can be found in Kavanaugh, "The Book of Her Life: Introduction," in *Collected Works*, 1:19–20; Carole Slade, *St. Teresa of Avila: Author of a Heroic Life* (Berkeley: University of California Press, 1995), chap. 1; and Elisabeth Rhodes, "What's in a Name: On Teresa of Avila's Book," in Boenig, *Mystical Gesture*, 79–106, esp. 80–82.

27. For example, in *Life* 6.4 (*Obras Completas*, 50; trans., 1:52) she says, "I liked to read good books very much."

28. Among those who have questioned the spontaneity of Teresa's style, see Slade, *St. Teresa of Avila*, 23–30; Alison Weber, *Teresa of Avila and the Rhetoric of Femininity* (Princeton: Princeton University Press, 1990), 5–16; and Gillian T. W. Ahlgren, *Teresa of Avila and the Politics of Sanctity* (Ithaca, NY: Cornell University Press, 1996), 77–80. On Teresa's unique style, see also Tyler, *Teresa of Avila*, part 1, chap. 1. There is also a large literature in Spanish.

29. Teresa refers to herself as a "weak woman" quite often, e.g., *Life* 9.9; 10.8; 11.6, 13; 12.7; 18.4; 28.18; and 33.11.

30. Weber, *Teresa and the Rhetoric of Femininity*, introduction and chaps 1–2. See also Slade, *St. Teresa of Avila*, chaps. 1 and 3; Ahlgren, *Teresa of Avila and the Politics of Sanctity*, chap. 3; and Peter Tyler, *The Return of the Mystical: Ludwig Wittgenstein, Teresa of Avila, and the Christian Mystical Tradition* (London: Continuum, 2011), chap. 6.

31. See, e.g., *Life* 10.1 and 6. The key passage on this strategy comes in *Castle* V.1.6, where Teresa says, "In difficult matters, . . . I always use this expression 'It seems to me.' For if I am mistaken, I'm very much prepared to believe what those who have a great deal of learning have to say."

32. For an account of the evolution and early reception of the *Life*, see Alison Weber, "The Three Lives of the *Vida*: The Uses of Convent Autobiography," in *Women, Texts, and Authority in the Early Modern Spanish World*, ed. Marta V. Vicente and Luis R. Corteguera, Women and Gender in the Early Modern World (Aldershot: Ashgate, 2003), 107–25.

33. This theme has been analyzed by Sluhovsky, *Believe Not Every Spirit*, who errs, however, in supposing that the complex of ideas he studies begins in the fifteenth and sixteenth centuries, rather than at the end of the thirteenth (see 6–7, 29, 98–100, 113, etc.).

34. Weber thus distinguishes three stages in the evolution of the *Life*: a life written in obedience to spiritual directors; a *samizdat* life of circulation of manuscripts; and a life in print. She provides a handy chart of the dating of the versions ("Three Lives of the *Vida*," 109).

35. Teresa's reflections on her confessors are scattered throughout the *Life*. For comments on bad confessors and the difference between good and bad confessors, see, e.g., 4.7; 13.14–20; 34.11; 37.5; and 40.8.

36. Neither of these texts, which are discussed in the *Life* 23.14–18, survives.

37. Sluhovsky discusses Teresa's notion of discernment of spirits (*Believe Not Every Spirit*, 210–15). See also Schreiner, *Are You Alone Wise?*, 304–20.

38. For a general account, see Kamen, *Inquisition and Society in Spain*.

39. On Magdalena, of whom Teresa is reported to have said, "I never remember her without trembling," see Ahlgren, *Teresa and the Politics of Sanctity*, 21–22, 29, and 46–47.

40. *Life* 33.5 (*Obras Completas*, 179; trans., 1:222).

41. Ahlgren, *Teresa of Avila and the Politics of Sanctity*, 33. Ahlgren shows that Teresa was investigated at least six times by the Inquisition (1570, 1575, 1576, 1578–79, 1579–80). After her death, her writings were examined from 1589 to 1593.

42. On Teresa's relation to the Inquisition, see Enrique Martínez Llamas, *Santa Teresa de Jesús y la Inquisición española* (Madrid: Editorial de Espiritualidad, 1972).

43. On the correct title as *mi libro*, or once as *libro de las misericordias de Dios*, see Rhodes, "What's in a Name," 85–87. Teresa often mentions the book in her letters; see 5.1–2; 7.3; 9.2; 10.2; 14.2; 73.4; 88.9–11; 115.7; 178.19; 182.5; 219.8; 324.9; 415.1–3 (especially important); and 419.1.

44. For a discussion, see Ahlgren, *Teresa of Avila and the Politics of Sanctity*, 15–21.

45. The Valdés Index, a typical expression of Spain's Inquisitorial culture, was followed by the even more repressive Quiroga Index of 1583–84.

46. *Life* 26.5 (*Obras Completas*, 142; trans. 1:172–73).

47. A number of passages in the *Life* explicitly mention nuns and general readers as her audience, e.g., Prol. 1; 7.9; 18.8; and 21.12.

48. Helpful for this period is Williams, *Teresa of Avila*, chap. 2.

49. *Life* 13.6; see also 7.17.

50. As mentioned by Evelyn Underhill, *Mysticism* (3rd ed., 1911; repr., New York: E. P. Dutton, 1961), 58.

51. Marcella Biro Barton argues that Teresa's symptomatic descriptions are compatible with the psychomotor seizures of temporal-lobe epilepsy ("Saint Teresa of Avila: Did She Have Epilepsy?," *Catholic Historical Review* 68 [1982]: 581–98).

52. Christopher M. Bache, "A Reappraisal of Teresa of Avila's Supposed Hysteria," *Journal of Religion and Health* 24 (1985): 300–315.

53. *Life* 4.7 (*Obras Completas*, 42; trans. 1:43). Teresa's *Life* often notes the effect that reading spiritual literature had on her. We have already looked at the importance of the *Confessions*; see also her comments on Jerome's *Letters* (3.7), Gregory the Great's *Moralia* (5.8), Alonso de Madrid's *Art of Serving God* (12.2), Bernardino de Laredo's *Ascent of Mount Sion* (23.12), Peter de Alcántara's *Treatise on Prayer and Meditation* (30.2), and Ludolph of Saxony's *Vita Christi* (38.9).

54. The connection with Affective Dionysianism is stressed by Tyler, *Return to the Mystical*, part 2; and *Teresa of Avila*, part 1, chap. 2.

55. Williams puts this well: "If chapters 1 to 10 [of the *Life*] describe God's victory over Teresa's weakness, 23 to 40 set out God's victory *through* Teresa's weakness over the skepticism and hostility of the religious establishment, and how this victory in turn overcomes Teresa's own doubts and scruples" (*Teresa of Avila*, 72).

56. *Life* 9.3 (*Obras Completas*, 64; trans., 1:71).

57. The question of Teresa's sources, direct and indirect, has not been exhausted. Still useful is Gaston Etchegoyen, *L'amour divin: Essai sur les sources de sainte Thérèse*, Bibliothèque de l'École des hautes études hispaniques 4 (Paris: De Boccard, 1923), esp. 33–49. On the possibility of Teresa's contact with northern European mysticism, see Silvia Bara Bancel, "La Escuela Mística Renana y *Las Moradas* de Santa Teresa," in *Las Moradas del Castillo Interior de Santa Teresa de Jesús: Actas del IV Congreso Internacional Teresiano en Avila, 2–9 Septembre 2013*, ed. Francisco Javier Sancho Fermín and Rómolo Cuartas Londoño (Burgos: Monte Carmelo, 2014), 179–219 (I thank the author for bringing this article to my attention).

58. On Teresa's indirect but significant contact with Dionysianism, see Luis M. Girón-Negrón, "Dionysian Thought in Sixteenth-Century Spanish Mystical Theology," *Modern Theology* 24 (2008): 693–707.

59. *Life* 10.1 (*Obras Completas,* 66; trans., 1:74). Teresa employs the phrase three other times in the *Life* (11.5; 12.5; and 18.2) but, interestingly, never again in her writings. See the entry "místico," in Juan Luis Astigarraga, *Concordancias de los escritos de Santa Teresa de Jesús*, 2 vols. (Rome: Editoriales O.C.D., 2000), 2:1657. Teresa may have seen the term in Osuna's *Third Spiritual Alphabet*, Tr. 6, chap. 2; but it is more likely that she encountered it in book 3 of Bernardino de Laredo's *Ascent of Mount Sion*, where it is used about seventeen times. In his *Ascent*, chap. 41, Bernardino even uses the phrase *la experiencia de mística teología*, which conforms to Theresa's use (*Místicos franciscanos españoles*, 2:435). On Teresa's relation to the broad tradition of *theologia mystica*, see Tyler, *Return to the Mystical*, 141–44.

60. The importance of the conformity of her account to scripture and the faith of the church is a constant motif of the *Life*, e.g., 13.16, 18; 25.13; 32.17; 33.5; and 40.1–2. It is also prominent in later works, such as the *Castle*, Prol. 3

and Epil. 4. The emphasis on both experience and the faith of the church shows that, for Teresa, there was no opposition between mysticism and theology; see Otger Steggink, "Esperienza e teologia nella storia della mistica Cristiana: Teresa di Gesù, donna e mistica, di fronte alla teologia e ai teologi," in *Sentieri illuminati dallo Spirito: Atti del Congresso internazionale di mistica* (Rome: Edizioni O.C.D, 2006), 243–68.

61. Understanding *confessio* broadly as speech-act addressed to God that expresses belief in him, praises him for his goodness and mercy, and admits one's own sinfulness, I count about twenty-six passages in the *Life* that can be described as confession with ten coming in the first ten chapters. Another eight occur in the treatise on prayer (chaps. 11–22). Carrera has reflections on the relation between the *Life* and the *Confessions* (*Teresa of Avila's Autobiography*, chap. 7, "Writing the Self [1562–1565]," 163–90), although I do not share her description of these works as "autobiographies."

62. *Life* 7.20–22. There is also an important reflection on the assistance given by spiritual friends in the *Way of Perfection* 7, esp. 7.4.

63. *Life* 34.15–16. This appears to have taken place sometime between 1562 and 1564 and is reminiscent of the famous shared "Ostia rapture" of Augustine and Monica in *Confessions* 9.10.

64. Carrera, *Teresa of Avila's Autobiography*, chaps. 1–3 on the various kinds of written materials that influenced Teresa, and chaps. 4–6 on the role of confession.

65. Helpful here is Weber, "Three Lives of the *Vida*."

66. *Spiritual Testimonies* 1.2 (*Obras Completas,* 588; trans., 1: 311): ". . . darme tan presto este recogimiento y levantamiento de espíritu, que no me pucdo valer."

67. *Spiritual Testimonies* 1.8 (*Obras Completas* at 1.12, p. 589; trans., 1:312–13).

68. *Spiritual Testimonies* 1.10 (*Obras Completas* at 1.17, p. 589; trans., 1:313): "From almost all the visions I've experienced, I've received some benefit, except in those cases where there is deception from the devil. In this I submit to my confessors."

69. *Spiritual Testimonies* 1.26 (*Obras Completas* at 1.35, p. 592; trans., 1:317).

70. *Spiritual Testimonies* 1.27 (*Obras Completas* at 1.36, p. 592; trans., 1:317): ". . . mas trai diferentes efectos, y a quien tiene espiriencia no le engañará, a mi parecer" (my trans.). The first *Spiritual Testimony* refers to experience about thirteen times.

71. *Spiritual Testimonies* 2.2, entitled "Detachment and the other virtues flowing from God's favors" ("Examen de sus mercedes y virtudes"), in *Obras Completas*, 593 (trans., 1:318).

72. *Spiritual Testimonies* 3.13.

73. *Life* 22.3 (*Obras Completas,* 121; trans., 1:145): ". . . y despúes entendí que, si el Señor no me mostrara, yo pudiera poco con los libros deprender, porque no era nada lo que entendía hasta que Su Majestad por espiriencia mo lo dava a entender."

74. See Tyler, *Return to the Mystical*, 178–80; and Edward Howells, *John of the Cross and Teresa of Avila: Mystical Knowing and Selfhood* (New York: Crossroad, 2002), 94–95.

75. Joan Frances Gormley, ed. and trans., *John of Avila: Audi, filia–Listen, O Daughter*, Classics of Western Spirituality (New York: Paulist Press, 2006). Juan

also was of *converso* background and had been imprisoned by the Inquisition for a year (1532–33).

76. Weber, "Three Lives of the *Vida*," 108.

77. On the meaning and difficulty of translating terms like *gusto, regalo, deleite, gozo,* and the like, see Tyler, *Teresa of Avila,* 77–84.

78. In *Life* 40.8 Teresa notes, partly on the testimony of Peter of Alcántara, "There are many more women than men to whom the Lord gives these favors" (*Obras Completas,* 225; trans., 1:280).

79. This is part of the argument of Michel de Certeau's *The Mystic Fable,* vol. 1, *The Sixteenth and Seventeenth Centuries,* Religion and Postmodernism (Chicago: University of Chicago Press, 1992), though there is much more in this remarkable book.

80. On the role of diabolical temptation in Catherine of Bologna's *Seven Spiritual Weapons,* see McGinn, *Varieties,* 294–303.

81. Sluhovsky is primarily concerned with possession and exorcism but also deals with the discernment of spirits in Spain, including Teresa (*Believe Not Every Spirit,* 180–92, 210–15). See also Marcel Lépée, "St. Teresa of Jesus and the Devil," in *Satan,* ed. Bruno de Jésus Marie, O.C.D. (New York: Sheed & Ward, 1952), 97–102.

82. For an analysis of Teresa's notion of mystical experience, see Macario Ofilada Mina, "The True Truth (Book of Life 21.9): Teresian Comprehension of Mystical Experience," *Studies in Spirituality* 25 (2015): 223–46. Mina notes, "Teresa . . . was not interested in the experience itself, but in the truth, even to the point of the trueness of this truth which was guaranteed by God" (244).

83. Gillian T. W. Ahlgren, *Entering Teresa of Avila's "Interior Castle": A Reader's Companion* (New York: Paulist Press, 2005), 9.

84. *Life* 16.2 (*Obras Completas,* 93; trans., 1:109).

85. For an overview, see Pierre Adnès, "Visions," DS 16:949–1002, who discusses Teresa on 981–83. See also Bernard McGinn, "Visions and Visualizations in the Here and Hereafter," *Harvard Theological Review* 98 (2005): 227–46; and "*Visio dei*: Seeing God in Medieval Theology and Mysticism," in *Envisaging Heaven in the Middle Ages,* ed. Carolyn Muessig and Ad Putter, Routledge Studies in Medieval Religion and Culture 6 (London: Routledge, 2007), 15–33.

86. On Augustine's theory of visions, see *De Genesi ad litteram* 12, esp. 12.6–7 and 24.

87. See William A. Christian Jr., *Apparitions in Late Medieval and Renaissance Spain* (Princeton: Princeton University Press, 1981).

88. For more on Teresa's visions, see Fortunato de Jesús Sacramentado, "Images et contemplation, IV: Dans l'école Carmélitaine," DS 7:1491–93.

89. See the account in *Life* 23.2–5 (*Obras Completas,* 126–27; trans., 1:174–75). After a brief discussion of locutions (27.6–10), Teresa returns to further analysis of the nature of intellectual visions in 27.10–12.

90. The Feast of Teresa's Transverberation, set for August 27, was established by Pope Benedict XIII for the Discalced Carmelites in 1726 and extended to all Spain by Clement XII in 1733.

91. *Life* 29.13 (*Obras Completas,* 158; trans., 1:194).

92. On the "wound of love" (*vulnus amoris*), see A. Cabassut, "Blessure d'amour," DS 1:1724–29.

93. A number of studies explore the embodied character of Teresa's mysticism; see, e.g., Beverly J. Lanzetta, "Wound of Love: Feminine Theosis and Embodied Mysticism in Teresa of Avila," in *The Participatory Turn: Spirituality, Mysticism, Religious Studies*, ed. Jorge N. Ferrer and Jacob H. Sherman (Albany: State University of New York Press, 2008), 225–44.

94. On Bernini's portrayal, see Irving Lavin, *Bernini and the Unity of the Visual Arts*, 2 vols., Franklin Jasper Walls Lectures 1975 (New York: Oxford University Press, 1980), vol. 1, part 2.

95. Teresa's comparing this vision to a painting, as well as the issues involved in visual perceptions of paintings and divinely given imaginative visions, have been studied by Luis R. Corteguera, "Visions and the Ascent of the Soul in Spanish Mysticism," in *Looking Beyond: Visions, Dreams, and Insights in Medieval Art & History*, ed. Colum Hourihane, Index of Christian Art: Occasional Papers 11 (Princeton: Index of Christian Art, 2010), 255–63.

96. *Life* 28.3–5 (*Obras Completas*, 149–50; trans., 1:182–83). Chapter 28.6–13 provides an extended treatment of the nature of imaginative visions and how to tell true visions given by God from false visions coming from the devil or our own imagination.

97. In *Life* 16.2; 18.8, 14; and 20.1, Teresa speaks about being given comparisons to help her explain her states by God. At other times (e.g., 17.2) she says that she is making her own comparisons.

98. *Life* 29.1–4 (*Obras Completas*, 154–55; trans., 1:188–90).

99. For an introduction to Teresa's treatment of these "locutions" (*hablas*), see André Derville, "Paroles intérieures," DS 12:252–53.

100. For some reflections on the problem of Teresa's locutions, see Williams, *Teresa of Avila*, 73–74.

101. *Life* 19.9 (*Obras Completas*, 106; trans., 1:126).

102. The accounts of locutions increase in the chapters devoted to the foundation of St. Joseph (*Life* 32.11–12, 14, 18; 33.3, 8, 12, 16; 34.10–11, 18–19; 35.6, 8; 36.16, 20). They are also found in the tacked-on final chapters (38.3, 16; 39.3, 23–24; 40.1, 16, 19, 20–21).

103. *Life* 25.1 (*Obras Completas*, 134; trans., 1:161–62).

104. "Discernment of spirits" (*conocer espíritu*), as well as "discretion" (*discreción*) in the general sense of spiritual insight, are frequent themes in the *Life*; see, e.g., 11.16; 13.1, 3, 8; 16.6; 19.14; 21.9; 22.18; 27.15; 29.9; 33.10; 34.11; 39.10; etc. See Colin Thompson, "Dangerous Visions: The Experience of Teresa of Avila and the Teaching of John of the Cross," in *Angels of Light? Sanctity and the Discernment of Spirits in the Early Modern Period*, ed. Clare Copeland and Jan Machielsen, Studies in Medieval and Reformation Traditions 164 (Leiden: Brill, 2013), 53–73.

105. Teresa often returns to the pain and suffering that the disbelief of her five earliest spiritual advisors in her mystical gifts had on her; see, e.g., *Life* 25.14–15; 28.17–18; 29.4–5, and 30.6.

106. *Life* 26.6 (*Obras Completas*, 142; trans., 1:173).

107. *Life* 27.6 (*Obras Completas*, 144; trans., 1:176).

108. Bernard McGinn, "Three Forms of Negativity in Christian Mysticism," in *Knowing the Unknowable: Science and Religions on God and the Universe*, ed. John Bowker, Library of Modern Religion 2 (London: I. B. Tauris, 2009), 99–121.

109. *Life* 20.9 (*Obras Completas*, 110; trans., 1:132). Like many mystics, Teresa

often appeals to the motif of inexpressibility in her narrative; see, e.g., 16.1; 18.8, 14; 38.2; 39.22; etc.

110. *Life* 20.15 says that in this prayer the body shares only in the pain, while the soul both suffers and rejoices.

111. *Life* 30.12 (*Obras Completas*, 162; trans., 1:199).

112. *Life* 32.1 (*Obras Completas*, 173; trans., 1:213).

113. *Life* 32.4 (*Obras Completas*, 174; trans., 1:214–15).

114. Teresa recounts two later negative visions in *Life* 39.17–20. There are also later accounts of experiences of intense pain, such as the "transpiercing of the soul," similar to what the Blessed Virgin had endured at the cross, as described in *Spiritual Testimonies* 12 at Salamanca in April 1571 (*Obras Completas*, No. 13, at 598–99; trans., 1:325–26).

115. *Life* 28.9 (*Obras Completas*, 151; trans., 1:185). P. Adnès notes: "En réalité, ses propres visions sont rebelles à toute classification rigide. Chez elle [Teresa], les phénomènes fusionnent. . . . La vision imaginative ne se sépare guère de la vision intellectuelle" ("Visions," DS 16:981).

116. There are a number of analyses of Teresa's treatise on the four waters of prayer. In English, see E. W. Trueman Dicken, *The Crucible of Love: A Study of the Mysticism of St. Teresa of Jesus and St. John of the Cross* (New York: Sheed & Ward, 1963), 178–87; Williams, *Teresa of Avila*, 54–75; and Tyler, *Teresa of Avila*, 90–101.

117. Teresa may have been inspired in part by Osuna's *Third Spiritual Alphabet*, where Treatise 3, discussing "Safeguarding the Heart," once refers to the heart as "the garden of King Assuerus where he plants by hand a variety of virtues" (Tr. 3, chap. 5; trans. Giles [see chap. 1, n. 96 above], 135). Later in Treatise 18, chap. 1 (trans. Giles, 479), Osuna uses the metaphor of water to describe the three ranks of the devout: "the beginners have a cistern; the proficients, a flowing well; and the perfect enjoy streams supplying others."

118. See Émile Bertaud, "Hortus, Hortulus, Jardin spiritual," DS 7:766–84, which treats Teresa on 775. On the use of gardens in Teresa's writings, see Maryrica Ortiz Lottman, "The Gardens of Teresa of Avila," in Kallendorf, *New Companion to Hispanic Mysticism*, 323–42.

119. *Life* 8.5 (*Obras Completas*, 61; trans., 1:67): "oración mental, a mi parecer, sino tratar de amistad." On the importance of friendship in Teresa's thought, see Williams, *Teresa of Avila*, 102–6.

120. Growth in prayer is also a growth in the virtues (see *Life* 17.8; 19.2–3), especially humility, so it is no surprise that humility is mentioned under each of the four waters, that is, here in *Life* 11.11, and subsequently in 13.3–4; 14.10; 17.3; 19.4; 21.8, 11; and esp. 22.5, 9, 11–12.

121. *Life* 11.16 (*Obras Completas*, 74; trans., 1:85).

122. *Life* 13.5 (*Obras Completas*, 79; trans., 1:90). The notion of "freedom of spirit" (*libertad de espíritu*), based on Paul (2 Cor. 3:17) is a traditional mystical theme that Teresa mentions often (see 16.8; 20.23; 21.6; 22.5, 12; 24.8; 31.14; etc.).

123. For some remarks on Teresa's notion of the will, see Williams, *Teresa of Avila*, 94.

124. On the ambiguities of this description of the "second water," see Williams, *Teresa of Avila*, 61–63.

125. *Life* 16.1 (*Obras Completas*, 93; trans., 1:108).

126. The "sleep of the faculties" was discussed in one of the works we know

Teresa read, Bernardino de Laredo's *Ascent of Mount Sion* III.19–20 (trans. Peers [see chap. 1, n. 59 above], 134–42).

127. *Life* 16.2 (*Obras Completas*, 93; trans., 1:109).

128. *Life* 17.2 (*Obras Completas*, 96; trans., 1:112). This theme of the willingness to be consigned to hell, if it be God's will (*resignatio ad infernum*), often invoked by mystics, is based on Romans 9:3.

129. *Life* 17.3 (*Obras Completas*, 96–97; trans., 1:113).

130. *Life* 17.4 (*Obras Completas*, 97; trans., 1:113).

131. *Life* 18.3 (*Obras Completas*, 99; trans., 1:117): "Lo que yo pretendo declarer es qué siente el alma cuando está en esta divina unión."

132. *Life* 18.14 (*Obras Completas*, 102; trans., 1:121): "Deshácese toda, hija, para ponerse más en Mí; ya no es ella la que vive, sino Yo. Como no puede comprehender lo que entiende, es no entender entendiendo." The notion of understanding by not understanding due to the suspension of the faculties occurs elsewhere in the *Life* (e.g., 12.5). The phrase is originally Dionysian (e.g., MT 1) but was taken up by later authors in various ways. It is frequently discussed by Bernardino de Laredo (e.g., *Ascent of Mount Sion* III.2; III.11; III.15; III.41; and esp. III.27). Peers argues that Teresa took it over from the Franciscan ("Introduction," in Bernardino de Laredo, *Ascent of Mount Sion*, 48–53).

133. *Life* 20.1 (*Obras Completas*, 108; trans., 1:129). Teresa discusses rapture often later in the *Life*, as she recounts her own experiences; see 24.5–7; 33.14–15; 34.2, 17; 35.6; 38.1, 5, 10–11, 17–18; and 40.7, 9. On rapture–ecstasy–suspension in Teresa, see Tomás de la Cruz, "L'Extase chez Saint Thérèse d'Avila," DS 4:2151–60; and Fr. Theophilus, "Mystical Ecstasy according to St. Teresa," in *St. Teresa of Avila: Studies in Her Life, Doctrine and Times*, ed. Father Thomas and Father Gabriel (London: Burns & Oates, 1963), 139–53. These terms are often treated as synonymous, but perhaps incorrectly, as argued by Donald Blais, "Contextualizing Teresa, Vida 20.1: Are the Phenomena Identical?," *Studies in Spirituality* 12 (2002): 141–46.

134. Williams notes "the pervasive problem of the *Life*: it is brilliant and clear as individual phenomenology; strained and muddled as a structural map of Christian growth" (*Teresa of Avila*, 69, discussing *Life* 20.1). But perhaps Teresa was not really trying to present a structural map.

135. *Life* 20.4, with an extended discussion in 20.5–8 (*Obras Completas*, 109–10; trans., 1:130–31). This text shows that hagiographical claims for Teresa's levitation have a foundation in her text. Did Teresa really levitate, or did she "feel" like she needed to levitate, because since the late thirteenth century levitation had become a mark of mystical piety?

136. For an overview, see Eamon R. Carroll, "The Saving Role of the Human Christ for St. Teresa," in *Centenary of St. Teresa*, Carmelite Studies 3 (Washington, DC: ICS Publications, 1984), 133–51; also Tomás de la Cruz (Alvarez), "Humanité du Christ, IV: L'École Carmélitaine," DS 7:1097–1100.

137. *Life* 21.12 (*Obras Completas*, 119; trans., 1:144).

138. *Life* 22.1 (*Obras Completas*, 120; trans., 1:144). What books did Teresa have in mind? Teresa may have been thinking of the "Prologue" to Osuna's *Third Spiritual Alphabet* (trans. Giles, 39–43), where the Franciscan sets forth a rather confusing account about abandoning consideration of Christ's humanity, at first adopting a view not unlike Teresa's, according to which "the most blessed Human-

ity of Christ our Lord and God in itself neither impedes nor hampers recollection, no matter how refined and lofty it is"; and subsequently, on the basis of the authority of Cyprian, Bernard, Gregory, Augustine, and Gerson, says that the imperfection of the apostles at the time of Christ's Ascension while awaiting the coming of the Holy Spirit indicates that ceasing to contemplate Christ's humanity "also seems appropriate for all who desire to rise to a higher state." E. Allison Peers hints that a book Teresa had studied recently, Laredo's *Ascent of Mount Sion* (e.g., III.4 and III.13), may have been what she had in mind (see Peers, "Introduction," in Bernardino de Laredo, *Ascent of Mount Sion,* 41). Tomás de la Cruz ("L'Humanité du Christ, IV: L'École Carmélitaine," 1099) thinks that Teresa may have read this view in the *Via spiritus* of Bernabé de Palma, published in 1541. What is clear is that Teresa found this teaching in some of the Franciscan *recogimiento* authors, but rejected it.

139. *Life* 22.9 (*Obras Completas*, 123; trans., 1:148).

140. *Life* 22.10 (*Obras Completas*, 123; trans., 1:148).

141. Teresa does not have a speculative Christology. Nevertheless, her insistence on the unique character of Christ's sacred humanity is conformable with the Pan-Christic ontology of many mystical authors of both East and West.

142. *Life* 22.9 (*Obras Completas*, 123; trans., 1:147).

143. *Life* 22.10 summarizes: "He will absent himself when he sees such absence is fitting and when he desires to draw the soul out of itself."

144. *Life* 22.17 (*Obras Completas*, 125; my trans.).

145. Edward Howells, "Early Modern Reformations," in *The Cambridge Companion to Christian Mysticism*, ed. Amy Hollywood and Patricia Z. Beckman, Cambridge Companions to Religion (Cambridge: Cambridge University Press, 2012), 123–24.

146. *Foundations* 1.1 (*Obras Completas*, 676; trans., 3:99).

147. This summary is based on Kavanaugh, "The Constitutions—Introduction," in *Collected Works,* 3:311–18. Kavanaugh translates the core first nine chapters (3:319–33) and relegates the penal chapters to his notes (447–55). The full fifteen chapters are available in *Obras Completas*, 819–40.

148. For a useful analysis of the *Constitutions*, see Alison Weber, "Spiritual Administration: Gender and Discernment in the Carmelite Reform," *Sixteenth-Century Journal* 31 (2000): 123–46.

149. *Constitutions* 2.8 (*Obras Completas*, at 1.13, p. 821; trans., 3:321). See also 8.32.

150. *Constitutions* 3.9 (*Obras Completas*, at 2.1, p. 822; trans., 3:321).

151. On the *Way of Perfection*, see Williams, *Teresa of Avila*, chap. 3; and Tyler, *Teresa of Avila*, part 2, chap. 5. Tyler is helpful for describing the three differing versions of the text.

152. Egido, "Historical Setting of St. Teresa's Life," 158. Williams summarizes: "In essence, [the *Way*] is an exploration of how Christ, the incarnate Christ, is to be communicated to the world in the lives of Christians in general and Carmelites in particular" (*Teresa of Avila*, 102).

153. *Way* 24.2 (*Obras Completas*, 336; trans., 2:128).

154. *Way* 3.7 (*Obras Completas*, where this is 4.1, p. 249; trans., 2:50–51). For other passages on women, including the use of the "weak woman" topos, see Prol. B.3, chaps. 1.2; 7.8; 21.2; and 28.10.

155. *Way*, Prol. A.1 (*Obras Completas*, 236; trans., 2:38). The *letrados* also appear in 3.5–6 and in 5.2.

156. *Way*, Prol. B.3 (*Obras Completas*, 238; trans., 2:40).

157. *Way* 6.3 (*Obras Completas*, 263; trans., 2:62).

158. The devil appears in twenty of the forty-two chapters of the *Way*.

159. *Way* 4.7 (*Obras Completas*, 254; trans., 2:55).

160. Among the other mentions of the need for humility, see, e.g., *Way* 10.3; 16.2; 17.1, 3–7; 18.4–6; 32.13; 33.5; 38.4–5; 39.1; and 40.4.

161. On Teresa's break with the Spanish conception of honor, see Williams, *Teresa of Avila*, 18–26.

162. *Way* 12.7 (*Obras Completas*, 286; trans., 2:84); she is referring back to 7.10.

163. *Way* 36.3–5 (*Obras Completas*, 393–94; trans., 2:178–79). Other passages attacking false honor can be found in 2.6; 16.11; 22.5; 27.6; and 36.10.

164. *Way* 13.7 (*Obras Completas*, 290; trans., 2:87–88).

165. Williams, *Teresa of Avila*, 88.

166. *Way* 17.4. Teresa appeals several other times to the need for our own efforts, echoing the familiar theological axiom of "doing what is in one" (e.g., 19.4; 34.14), as a necessary but never sufficient part of the path to union.

167. *Way* 17.2 (*Obras Completas*, 303; trans. 2:99). For other appearances of this adage, see 5.5; 20.1; and 24.1. It is found in all Teresa's writings, e.g., *Life* 13.13; 22.2; *Foundations* 5.1; *Interior Castle* VI.7.12.

168. For some appearances of water, see *Way* 20.2; 21.2, 6; 23.5; 28.5; 32.9; 42.5–6; etc. Another favorite motif of Teresa, touched on by some commentators but not pursued here, is the combat motif, that is, viewing the Christian life as a constant battle against the devil, evil in the world, and in ourselves; see, e.g., *Way* 3.4; 10.3; 16.7; 18.3–6; 23.5; 26.2; 38.1–2; etc. Chapter 28.6 and 9 also use the metaphor of the soul as a castle with God within that will serve as the organizing symbol for the *Interior Castle*.

169. *Way* 21.3 (*Obras Completas*, under 21.4, p. 324; trans., 2:118). Teresa intended to get to the Hail Mary but did not have the time (see 24.2; 42.4).

170. *Way* 25.1 (*Obras Completas*, 338–39; trans., 2:131).

171. Besides *Way* 26, Teresa also discusses recollection in 28.1–12; 29.4–5 and 7.

172. On the nuns as spouses of Christ, see 2.1; 7.8, 10; 9.4; 18.4; 23.2; 26.10; 28.3; 29.4; 33.4; and 34.3–4.

173. *Way* 26.3 (*Obras Completas*, 341; trans., 2:134).

174. *Way* 26.6 (*Obras Completas*, 342; trans., 2:135).

175. On Teresa's commentary on the Lord's Prayer, see Williams, *Teresa of Avila*, 88–102.

176. *Way* 37.1 (*Obras Completas*, 396; trans., 2:183).

177. *Way* 29.4 (*Obras Completas*, 356; trans., 2:147).

178. As argued by Williams, *Teresa of Avila*, 93–94.

179. *Way* 32.12 (*Obras Completas*, 374–75; trans., 2:164).

180. Union with God is mentioned in the *Way* but is not a separate major topic; see, e.g., *Way* 16.6; 19.6; 30.7; 31.1, 4–5, 10; 32.11–12; and 37.1.

181. See Rowan Williams, "Teresa, the Eucharist, and the Reformation," in Tyler and Howells, *Teresa of Avila: Mystical Theology and Spirituality in the Carmelite Tradition*, 67–76.

182. *Way* 39.5 (*Obras Completas,* under 39.7, p. 404; trans., 2:190).

183. *Way* 41.1 (*Obras Completas,* 410–11; trans., 2:196).

184. *Way* 42.5 (*Obras Completas,* 418; trans., 2:203).

185. For background on women and the Song of Songs, see Bernard McGinn, "Women Reading the Song of Songs in the Christian Tradition," in *Scriptural Exegesis: The Shapes of Culture and the Religious Imagination. Essays in Honour of Michael Fishbane,* ed. Deborah A. Green and Laura S. Lieber (Oxford: Oxford University Press, 2009), 281–95, which discusses Hildegard on 284–90.

186. Partial translations of the Bible into Castilian had existed in the fifteenth century, but these became suspect and were banned in the first half of the sixteenth century.

187. *Meditations,* Prol. 1 (*Obras Completas,* 423; trans., 2:215).

188. *Meditations,* Prol. 2 (*Obras Completas,* 423; trans., 2:215).

189. This statement is from Doña María Enríquez de Toledo y Colona, duchess of Alba, for the 1610 canonization proceedings, as cited by E. Allison Peers, *Complete Works of St. Teresa,* 3 vols. (London and New York: Sheed & Ward, 1957), 2:354.

190. On the role of the Bible in early modern Catholic mysticism, see Max Huot de Longchamp, "Les mystiques catholiques et la Bible," in *Le temps des Réformes et la Bible,* ed. Guy Bedouelle and Bernard Roussel, Bible de tous les temps 5 (Paris: Beauchesne, 1989), 587–612, who mentions Teresa on 598–99, 608–9. No in-depth study of Teresa's use of the Bible exists, to my knowledge; but see Pietro della Madre di Dio, "La Sacra Scrittura nelle Opere di Teresa di Gesu," *Rivista di Vita Spirituale* 18 (1964): 41–102; and Slade, *St. Teresa of Avila,* chap. 2, "Teresa's Feminist Figural Reading of Scripture," which I find problematic.

191. An example can be seen in *Way* 19.4, where the clerical censor disagrees with Teresa's reading of Ps. 81:7.

192. As with other spiritual exegetes, Teresa insists that passages in the Bible often contain many meanings—"one word of his will contain within itself a thousand mysteries" (*Meditations* 1.2; cf. 1.10).

193. *Spiritual Testimonies* 15 (*Obras Completas,* under No. 16, p. 601; trans., 1:328).

194. On the *Meditations,* see Etchegoyen, *L'amour divin,* 297–315; Carole Slade, "Saint Teresa's *Meditaciones sobre los Cantares*: The Hermeneutics of Humility and Enjoyment," *Religion and Literature* 18 (1986): 27–43; Kevin Culligan, "Mary and Martha Working Together: Teresa of Avila's *Meditations on the Song of Songs,*" in *Seeing the Seeker: Explorations in the Discipline of Spirituality. Festschrift for Kees Waaijman on the Occasion of His 65th Birthday,* ed. Hein Blommestijn et al., Studies in Spirituality Supplement 19 (Leuven: Peeters, 2008), 315–29; Peter Tyler, "Teresa of Avila's Transformative Strategies on Embodiment in *Meditations on the Song of Songs,*" in *Sources of Transformation. Revitalising Christian Spirituality,* ed. Edward Howells and Peter Tyler (London: Continuum, 2010), 135–45; and Bernard McGinn, "'One Word Will Contain within Itself a Thousand Mysteries': Teresa of Avila, the First Woman Commentator on the Song of Songs," *Spiritus* 16 (2016): 21–40.

195. See Howells, *John of the Cross and Teresa of Avila,* 83–88; Tyler, "Teresa of Avila's Transformative Strategies," 136–39, 143; and McGinn, "'One Word Will Contain within Itself a Thousand Mysteries,'" 33–35.

196. Slade stresses what she calls Teresa's "hermeneutics of humility," that is,

the superior position that God gives humble nuns over the learned in interpreting the mysteries of the Song ("Saint Teresa's *Meditaciones*," 31–32).

197. *Meditations* 1.6 (*Obras Completas*, 425; trans., 2:218): ". . . conocío que es possible pasar el alma enamorada por su Esposo todos esos regalos y desmayos y muertes y aflicciones y deleites y gozos con El." I cite the Spanish here because it is a good summary of many of Teresa's terms for spiritual gifts.

198. *Meditations* 1.12 (*Obras Completas*, 428; trans., 2:221): ". . . mas a quien vuestro amor, Señor, ha sacado de sí, bien perdonaréis diga eso y más, aunque sea atrevimiento."

199. *Meditations* 2.5 (*Obras Completas*, 431; trans., 2:224).

200. *Meditations* 3.1 (*Obras Completas*, 445; trans., 2:236).

201. *Meditations* 4.1 (*Obras Completas*, 449; trans., 2:242).

202. *Meditations* 4.3 (*Obras Completas*, 451; trans., 2.244).

203. *Meditations* 4.4 (*Obras Completas*, 451; trans., 2:244).

204. *Meditations* 4.8 (*Obras Completas* at 4.6, p. 453; trans., 2:246). One of Teresa's mystical poems is based on this verse from the Song; see "Mi Amado para Mí" (also known as "Sobre Aquellas Palabras 'Dilectus Meus Mihi'") in Kavanaugh and Rodriguez, *Collected Works*, 3:379–80 (ed., 654). Teresa left some thirty to thirty-five poems, including ten mystical lyrics, whose poetic value has been variously judged. Teresa reflects on her need to write poetry in *Life* 16.4.

205. This passage is from *Confessions* 10.29. The text of chap. 4 in *Obras Completas* ends here. Kavanaugh's translation, using the text of Fr. Alvarez, adds several more paragraphs (2:246–47).

206. *Meditations* 5.4 (*Obras Completas* at 5.5, p. 456; trans., 2:249). The "cloud" and "shadow" language (*sombra de la divinidad*) here hints at a Dionysian influence, although Teresa uses biblical rather than Dionysian terms (see Girón-Negrón, "Dionysian Thought in Sixteenth-Century Spanish Mystical Theology," 699).

207. *Meditations* 6.13 (*Obras Completas* at 6.14, p. 463; trans., 2:255). Five loves are set in order: (1) love for the world is taken away; (2) love for self is turned to disregard; (3) relatives are loved only for God; (4) neighbors and even enemies are loved with great strength; and (5) love for God is boundless.

208. *Meditations* 7.2 (*Obras Completas*, 464; trans., 2:256) contains a personal reference to an occasion in Salamanca in 1571 when Teresa was in ecstasy and heard someone singing so beautifully she believed that her soul would have left her body had not the singing stopped. The incident is found in *Testimonies* 12.1 (*Obras Completas* at 13.1, p. 598; trans., 1:325). Thus, this part of chap. 7 was written after 1571.

209. See Alois M. Haas, "Mors Mystica: Ein mystologisches Motiv," in Haas, *Sermo mysticus: Studien zu Theologie und Sprache der deutschen Mystik*, Dokimion 4 (Freiburg, Schweiz: Universitätsverlag, 1979), 392–480, who mentions Teresa on 424.

210. Two of Teresa's poems are devoted to this theme: "Vivo Sin Viver En Mí" ("I Live without Living in Myself"), and "Ayes del Destierro" ("Sighs in Exile") (*Obras Completas*, Poesías Nos. 2 and 6, 654–55, 656–57; trans., 3:375–76, 382–84).

211. *Meditations* 7.3 (*Obras Completas*, 465; trans., 2:257). On the importance of this theme, see Culligan, "Mary and Martha Working Together."

212. *Meditations* 7.7 (*Obras Completas*, at 7.8, p. 467; trans., 2:259).

213. *Meditations* 7.10 (*Obras Completas* at 7.12, p. 468; trans., 2:260, adapted).

214. See *Foundations* 1.7 for the story of Fray Alonso, and 1.8 for the locution (*Obras Completas* 678; trans., 3:101–2).

215. On this foundation, see Alvarez, *St. Teresa of Avila*, 149–52.

216. For an edition of these "Exclamaciones," see *Obras Completas*, 635–49 (trans., 3:373–93).

217. *Spiritual Testimonies* 6 (*Obras Completas*, Testimony 5, 596; trans., 1:323).

218. The major exception are the letters she wrote to her brother, Lorenzo de Cepeda, to guide him in his prayer life; see, e.g., Letters 177 (January 17, 1577) and 182 (February 10, 1577) in Kavanaugh, *Collected Letters*, 1:473–79 and 493–99. In Letter 297, written to Gracián on June 10, 1579, she says, "I could speak of many things that bring me joy, but I fear putting them in letters, especially in matters of the soul" (trans. Kavanaugh, 2:195).

219. On Teresa and Gracián, see Mary Luta, "A Marriage Well Arranged: Teresa of Avila and Fray Jerónimo Gracián," *Studia Mystica* 10 (1989): 32–46; Mujica, *Teresa de Avila: Lettered Woman*, 103–16; and "Paul the Enchanter: Saint Teresa's Vow of Obedience to Gracián," in *The Heirs of St. Teresa of Avila*, ed. Christopher Chadwick Wilson, Carmelite Studies (Washington, DC: ICS Publications, 2006), 21–44.

220. Teresa always praised John as a skilled confessor, spiritual guide, and deep contemplative. She strove valiantly to get him released from unjust imprisonment. In her letters she has nothing but respect for him. Alas, he destroyed the letters he received from her, so it is difficult to uncover the details of their bond. For Teresa's comments on John, see Letters 13.2, 5; 45.4; 48.2; 51.1; 89.4; 171.1; 177.2; 215.6; 218.6; 221.7; 226.10; 232.3; 233.3; 238.6, 14; 247.4; 256.4; 251.1; 258.6; 260.1, 3; 261.3; 267.1; 270.2; 271.8; 272.4; 274.8; 277.1, 2; 323.1; 333.1; 340.5; 384.4; 421.2; 451.13, 18; and 465.16. (Many of these were pleas for John's release from jail.)

221. Letter 174 of January 9, 1577 (*Obras Completas, No. 173, 1073; trans., 1:464).

222. *Testimonies* 13.1 (*Obras Completas*, No. 14.1, at 599–600; trans., 1:326–27).

223. *Testimonies* 14 (*Obras Completas*, No. 15.1–4, at 600–601; trans., 1:327–28). A number of later *Testimonies* also deal with infused knowledge of the Trinity and the difference between imaginative and intellectual visions of the Three Persons. See *Testimonies* 29 (*Obras Completas*, No. 28, at 604–5; trans., 1:334); *Testimonies* 42 (*Obras Completas*, No. 40, at 612; trans., 1:343); *Testimonies* 51 (*Obras Completas*, No. 46, at 613–14; trans. 1:345–46); *Testimonies* 59.21–23 (*Obras Completas*, No. 58, at 629; trans., 1:360); and *Testimonies* 65.3 and 9 (*Obras Completas*, 65.3 and 10, at 631, 633.; trans., 1:364–65).

224. *Testimonies* 22.1 (trans., 1:330–31). This *Testimony* is not found in manuscripts used by Frs. Madre de Dios and Steggink in *Obras Completas*.

225. *Testimonies* 31 (*Obras Completas*, No. 29, at 605–6; trans., 1:336).

226. *Testimonies* 34 and 46 (*Obras Completas*, No. 32, at 607, and No. 46, at 613–14; trans., 1:337–38, and 344).

227. *Testimonies* 58 (*Obras Completas*, No. 57, at 617–24; trans., 1:349–54).

228. *Testimonies* 59 (*Obras Completas*, No. 58, at 625–29; trans., 1:355–61).

229. *Testimonies* 65 (*Obras Completas*, 631–33; trans., 1:363–65).

230. *Foundations* 5.2 (*Obras Completas*, 688; trans. Peers, *Complete Works*, 3:19–20, which I find superior here to Kavanaugh, 3:117).

231. *Foundations* 5.16 (*Obras Completas,* 692; trans., 3:123).

232. Kavanaugh translates this text as *A Response to a Spiritual Challenge,* while the Spanish is *Desafío Espiritual* (*Obras Completas,* 1427–30; trans., 1:365–69).

233. These two responses are in Kavanaugh, *Collected Works,* 1:367–69.

234. Kavanaugh calls this brief work *A Satirical Critique,* but the Spanish title (possibly not by Teresa) is *Vejamen.* It can be found in *Obras Completas,* 1431–33; and Kavanaugh and Rodriguez, *Complete Works,* 3:359–62. See Alvarez, *St. Teresa of Avila,* 383–86.

235. The *Castle* is found in *Obras Completas,* 470–583. I will use the translation of Kavanaugh and Rodriguez, but as it appears in Teresa of Avila, *The Interior Castle,* Classics of Western Spirituality (New York: Paulist Press, 1979). There are many popular introductions to the *Castle,* such as Ahlgren's *Entering Teresa of Avila's "Interior Castle": A Reader's Companion.* For analyses, see Williams, *Teresa of Avila,* chap. 4; Mary Frohlich, *The Intersubjectivity of the Mystic: A Study of Teresa of Avila's "Interior Castle,"* American Academy of Religion Academy Series 83 (Atlanta: Scholars Press, 1993), chaps. 6–7; Howells, *John of the Cross and Teresa of Avila,* chaps. 5–6; and Tyler, *Teresa of Avila,* part 2, chap. 6.

236. This passage is cited in Kavanaugh, "Introduction," in *Teresa of Avila: The Interior Castle,* 15–16.

237. Williams, *Teresa of Avila,* 139.

238. See, e.g., *Castle* I.2.7; IV.1.1; IV.2.7; IV.3.3.

239. *Castle,* Prol. 4; IV.1.1; V.4.11; VI.4.9.

240. Letter 324.9 (*Obras Completas* No. 312.12, pp. 1253–54; trans. Kavanaugh, *Collected Letters,* 2:257). Other letters that refer to the *Castle* include 412.18 and 426.8.

241. *Castle,* Epilogue 1 (*Obras Completas,* 582–83; trans., 195).

242. The "Index" to the Paulist Press translation shows how often the devil makes an appearance. Among the important discussions are I.2.12–18; V.4.6–10; VI.8.7; and VI.9.10.

243. On inexperienced confessors and the harm they can do, see V.1.7–9; VI.3.8; VI.6.1–2; VI.8.9; VI.9.10 and 13.

244. See, e.g., V.2.1.5–6, 12; V.3.3.

245. My count of direct or implied biblical citations in the *Castle* comes to a bit over a hundred, with the majority taken from the Gospels (Matthew 14x; Luke 15x; John 23x). In the Old Testament the Song of Songs is cited nine times, and Psalms twelve times.

246. See *Castle* I.1.4; I.1.9; I.2.12; II.1.10; III.2.11.

247. Without giving a listing of specific texts, I count 14 references to experience in Dwelling IV; 11 in Dwelling V; 45 in Dwelling VI; and 13 in Dwelling VII.

248. *Castle* VI.7.5 (*Obras Completas,* 548–49; trans. 145).

249. *Castle* VI.11.1–4 (*Obras Completas,* 562–64; trans. 166–68).

250. *Castle* III.1.5 (*Obras Completas,* 488; trans. 57). Teresa says much the same in III.2.4.

251. On holiness as love of God and neighbor, see, e.g., *Castle* I.2.17; III.1.7; IV.1.7; V.3.1, 7–9, 11; VI.8.10; VII.9.16–18; and VII.4.6.

252. Howells, *John of the Cross and Teresa of Avila,* 93.

253. Tyler, *Teresa of Avila,* 130, 142–43.

254. Teresa equates the crystal palace of the soul with paradise and its many

dwelling places, alluding to John 14:2: "In domo Patris mei mansiones multae sunt."

255. The soul as made to God's image and likeness appears in I.1.1; VII.1.1; VII.2.8; and Epilogue 3. The importance of the theme of the soul as image and likeness of God in the *Castle* is treated in Howells, *John of the Cross and Teresa of Avila*, 95–101, and 115.

256. See Peter of Alcántara, *Treatise on Prayer and Meditation*, trans. Dominic Devas (Westminster, MD: Newman Press, 1949), part I.12, counsel 8 (p. 115).

257. *Castle* VII.2.8 (*Obras Completas* at 2.10, p. 573; trans., 181): ". . . mas como faltamos en no disponernos y desviarnos de todo lo que puede embarazar esta luz, no nos vemos en este espejo que contemplamos, adonde nuestra imagen está esculpida."

258. The *centro del alma* appears for the first time in another reference to the soul as mirror, the vision of the mirror-soul with Christ seated in its center in *Life* 40.5 (*Obras Completas*, 224; trans., 1:278), but center language does not feature again in her writings until the *Castle*, where the term occurs seventeen times (see Astigarraga, *Concordancias* 1:453). It is first found here at I.2.3 and is cited twice in Dwelling IV (1.9 and 2.5), three times in Dwelling V.1.11, and occurs nine times in Dwelling VII.

259. Howells expresses their relation as follows: "The difference between the image and the center is that the image is a reflection of God's likeness in the soul which is present from creation, whereas the center is the *goal* of this likeness when it is restored from the damage of sin *and* raised above the level of nature, specifically in mystical union" (*John of the Cross and Teresa of Avila*, 96).

260. Frohlich, *Intersubjectivity of the Mystic*, 224, and elsewhere.

261. For a discussion of views on the sources of the image and the genre of the *Interior Castle*, see Frohlich, *Intersubjectivity of the Mystic*, appendix B, "Literary Sources and Influence on the Text" (369–82).

262. Francisco de Osuna, *Third Spiritual Alphabet*, 121–27.

263. Bernardino de Laredo, *Subida del Monte Sión* II.46–53 (BAC ed., 270–96). For an analysis, see Jessica A. Boon, *The Mystical Science of the Soul*, 125–31, who argues for an influence on Teresa on 174–75.

264. Frohlich, *Intersubjectivity of the Mystic*, 191–92. See also Mary Coelho, "St. Teresa of Avila's Transformation of the Symbol of the Interior Castle," *Ephemerides Carmelitanae* 38 (1987): 109–25.

265. *Castle*, Epil. 3 (*Obras Completas*, 22, p. 583; trans., 196).

266. After *Castle* II there is little direct advertence to the symbol until VII, where it is noted in VII.2.6; and VII.4.1, 10–11.

267. *Castle* I.2.8 (*Obras Completas*, 477; trans., 42–43).

268. We have already seen how important humility is in Teresa's earlier writings. Its importance, if anything, increases in the *Castle*. Some of the most significant of the more than thirty treatments can be found in I.2.11; III.2.8–10; VI.9.15; VI.107; and VII.4.8, 14. Teresa describes humility using several suggestive analogies, such as "the mirror of humility" (I.2.5) and the "bee" who is always at work making honey (I.2.9).

269. *Castle* I.2.9 (*Obras Completas*, 478; trans., 43).

270. For more on self-knowledge, see I.1.2; I.2.11–12; II.1.11; IV.1.9; VI.5.10; and VI.9.15.

271. See the reflections in Williams, *Teresa of Avila*, 114–17.

272. An up-to-date survey of Teresa's symbolism is needed, but there is a still useful survey in Etchegoyen, *L'amour divin*, 225–307.

273. In Dwelling VII Teresa also refers to the clarity of the divine light as strongly given at the beginning but then removed so the soul can continue to act in the world (VII.1.9).

274. For a survey and analysis of Teresa's references to tears, see Elizabeth Knuth, "The Gift of Tears in Teresa of Avila," *Mystics Quarterly* 20 (1994): 131–42.

275. *Castle* VI.11.5 (*Obras Completas*, 564; trans., 168). The story of the Samaritan woman was a favorite of Teresa; see *Life* 30.19; and *Meditations* 7.6.

276. For some uses of warfare imagery in the *Castle*, see II.1.3, 5, 9; III.1.1–2; IV.1.12; IV.3.10; VI.1.9–10; VII.2.10–11; and VII.4.10.

277. *Castle* II.1.7 (*Obras Completas*, 484; trans., 52).

278. In V.1 she cites Song 2:4 and 3:2, while in V.2 she again uses Song 2:4.

279. *Castle* V.4.3 (*Obras Completas*, 520; trans., 103).

280. *Castle* V.2.6 (*Obras Completas*, 513; trans., 93).

281. *Castle* V.2.7 (*Obras Completas*, 513; trans., 93).

282. *Castle* VII.3.1 (*Obras Completas*, 574; trans., 182).

283. It is interesting to note that in III.1.8 (*Obras Completas*, 489; trans., 2:308) Teresa makes her sole reference to the suspect term *dejamiento*, or abandonment.

284. *Contento/contentos* and *gusto/gustos* are frequent terms in Teresa's writings; see Astigarraga, *Concordancias*, 575–81 and 1251–53.

285. *Castle* IV.1.4 (*Obras Completas*, 495; trans., 68).

286. *Castle* IV.1.4 (*Obras Completas* at 1.5, p. 496; trans., 69).

287. *Castle* IV.1.7 (*Obras Completas*, 497; trans., 70). Teresa notes that she had discussed the difference elsewhere, referring probably to *Way* 16–20.

288. Teresa had treated the problem of distractions in *Life* 17.7 and *Way* 31.8.

289. *Castle* IV.1.8 (*Obras Completas*, 497; my trans.): ". . . y havrá poco más de cuatro años que vine a entender por espiriencia que el pensamiento o imaginativa, por que major se entienda, no es el entendimiento. . . . Porque como el entendimiento es una de las potencias del alma, hacíaseme recia cosa estar tan tortolito a veces, y lo ordinario vuela el pensamiento de presto, que solo Dios puede atarle cuando nos ata a Sí de manera que parece estamos en alguna manera desatados de este cuerpo." My version is close to that of Peers, *Complete Works,* 2:233. Teresa does not have a developed theory of the faculties, but she does display great skill in analyzing the inner dynamics of their relationship, and hence Frohlich correctly speaks of Teresa's contemplative interiority analysis (*Intersubjectivity of the Mystic*, 190ff., esp. 231–34). Howells notes Teresa's view of "the *dynamic relations* between the faculties and their objects of knowledge" (*John of the Cross and Teresa of Avila*, 121; his italics).

290. *Castle* IV.1.14 (*Obras Completas*, 499; my trans., close to Peers, *Complete Works,* 2:236): ". . . mas es menester y quiere Su Majestad que tomemos medios y nos entendamos y lo que hace la flaca imaginación y el natural y demonio; no pongamus la culpa a el alma." I translate *el natural* by "fallen nature," because that is what Teresa argues in IV.1.11.

291. *Castle* IV.3.2 (*Obras Completas*, 502; trans., 78).

292. *Castle* IV.3.3 (*Obras Completas*, 503; trans., 79). Teresa explicitly mentions married people in this connection.

293. *Castle* IV.3.4 (*Obras Completas*, 503; trans. adapted, 79). Teresa goes on (3.5–7) to give four arguments for her position.

294. *Castle* IV.3.8 (*Obras Completas*, 504, adapting the translation of Peers, *Complete Works*, 2:243); "Cuando Su Majestad quiere que el entendimiento cese, ocúpale por otra manera, y da una luz en el conocimiento tan sobre la que podemos alcanzar, que le hace quedar absorto; y entonces, sin saber cómo, queda muy major enseñando, que no con todas nuestras diligencias para echarle más a perder." The Kavanaugh translation misses the key distinction between *entendimiento* and *conocimiento*. This term is the last in Teresa's list of modes of interior activity. *Conocimiento* is used forty-seven times in Teresa's writings (Astigarraga, *Concordancias*, 1:459), often in the sense of pure self-knowledge but also with regard to the special knowing that God implants in the soul.

295. *Castle* IV.3.11 (*Obras Completas*, 506; trans., 83). Bernardino de Laredo, *Ascent of Mount Sion* III.41 (trans. Peers, 262–65) also discusses the difference between true and false raptures.

296. *Castle* V.1.11 (*Obras Completas*, 511; trans., 90). The "center of the soul" (*el centro del alma*), briefly mentioned in I.2.3; IV.1.9; and IV.2.5, appears three times in V.1.11.

297. *Castle* V.3.3 (*Obras Completas*, 517; trans. adapted, 98).

298. *Castle* V.3.3 (*Obras Completas*, 517; trans. 98).

299. *Castle* V.3.5 (*Obras Completas*, 517; trans. 99).

300. I owe this suggestion with thanks to Fr. Gregory Burke, OCD.

301. A point made by Frohlich, *Intersubjectivity of the Mystic*, 216.

302. It will be helpful to give an outline of the eleven chapters of Dwelling Place VI. Chapter 1 concerns the trials of the soul, while chap. 2 deals with "divine impulses," especially the wound of love (*Life* 29). Chapter 3 concerns locutions (*Life* 26), and chaps. 4–6 treat raptures (*Life* 20). The need to maintain attention to the sacred humanity of Christ takes up chap. 7, as it does in *Life* 22. Intellectual visions are treated in chap. 8 (*Life* 27), and imaginative visions in chap. 9 (*Life* 28). Finally, chaps. 10–11 deal with a variety of other divine favors, such as suspension and the wound of love (*Life* 29).

303. Interior and exterior trials feature prominently in Dwelling VI (e.g., 1.1–15; 4.7; 9.15; and 11.1–9) but are also discussed in V.2.9–11; V.3.4; and VII.2.9.

304. *Castle* VI.1.1 (*Obras Completas*, at 1.2, p. 524; trans., 108).

305. *Castle* VI.2.1–2 (*Obras Completas*, 528-29; trans., 115). We have, then, a hierarchy of *contentos–gustos–impulsos*. The *impulsos* are treated in VI.2.1–8; VI.8.4; VI.11.2–4; and VII.3.8.

306. *Castle* VI.2.5 (*Obras Completas*, 530; trans., 117). The wound of love is mentioned in VI.1.1 and is treated again in VI.11.2–4.

307. *Castle* VI.3.1 (*Obras Completas*, 531; trans., 119).

308. There are three fundamental signs for determining if locutions are from God: (1) "the authority they bear, for locutions from God effect what they say" (VI.3.5); (2) "the great quiet left in the soul" (3.6); and (3) that "the words remain in the memory for a very long time" (3.7).

309. Discussions of rapture are also found in several other places in Dwelling VI, notably 9.5; 10.2; and 11.2–3, 9–11.

310. *Castle* VI.4.2 (*Obras Completas*, 536; trans., 127).

311. *Castle* VI.4.6 (*Obras Completas*, 537; trans., 128). Teresa has several discussions of the problem of ineffability later in Dwelling VI (e.g., 10.6; 11.3).

312. *Castle* VI.4.8–9. Teresa may have taken this analogy from Bernardino de Laredo, *Ascent of Mount Sion* III.41 (trans. Peers, 261–62).

313. *Castle* VI.5.1 (*Obras Completas*, 540; trans., 133). The difference between raptures and the flight of the spirit is also treated in *Life* 18.8 and 20.1. See also *Testimonies* 59.9–10.

314. *Castle* VI.5.8 (*Obras Completas*, 542; trans., 136). Note once again the importance of *conocimiento*.

315. Teresa discusses the relation of soul and spirit in a number of places, e.g., VII.1.11; *Life* 20.14; *Testimonies* 59.11 and 25.

316. *Castle* VI.6.1 (*Obras Completas*, 544; trans., 138).

317. *Castle* VI.6.5 (*Obras Completas*, 545; trans., 139). Teresa also talks about the soul being "annihilated for the greater honor of God" (*aniquilada para la mayor honra de Dios*) in VI.9.20. Teresa's use of annihilation language is metaphorical, not part of a speculative teaching about the need to negate the created self. She uses *aniquilado* only four times in her writings (Astigarraga, *Concordancias*, 1:176).

318. *Castle* VI.7.9 (*Obras Completas*, 550; trans., 147).

319. *Castle* VI.7.11 (*Obras Completas*, 550; trans., 148): ". . . aquello le basta para no solo una hora, sino muchos días, mirando con una sencilla vista quién es y cuán ingratos hemos sido a tan gran pena, luego acude la voluntad . . . a desear server en algo tan gran mercced y a desear padecer algo por quien tanto padecío."

320. There is an extensive literature, especially Paul L. Gavrilyuk and Sarah Coakley, eds., *The Spiritual Senses: Perceiving God in Western Christianity* (Cambridge: Cambridge University Press, 2012). The volume does not have essays on either Teresa or John of the Cross.

321. Howells, *John of the Cross and Teresa of Avila*, 74–78.

322. *Testimonies* 59.3 (*Obras Completas*, 58.3, at p. 625; trans., 1:355).

323. *Castle* VI.9.16 (*Obras Completas*, at 9.17, p. 560; trans., 162).

324. Mystical death is referred to in *Castle* in V.1.3; V.2.6–7, 14; V.3.5; VI.6.1; VI.7.3; and esp. here in VI.11.4, 9, 9–11. It will also occur in VII.2.5 and VII.3.1, 6.

325. This convoluted passage in VI.11.2 (*Obras Completas*, 563), seems better rendered in Peers, *Complete Works*, 2:324 than in Kavanaugh, 166.

326. *Castle* VI.11.11 (*Obras Completas*, 566; trans., 170).

327. *Castle* VII.1.2 (*Obras Completas*, 567; trans., 173).

328. *Castle* VII.1.5 (*Obras Completas*, at 1.6, p. 568; trans., 174).

329. See Howells, *John of the Cross and Teresa of Avila*, 114–18, who describes the center as "the attainment of the dynamic structure of the Trinity, in the mutual exchange between God and the soul of the spiritual marriage. Furthermore, it is the conforming of the rest of the soul to this Trinitarian structure, enabling the whole soul to work together in performing good works in accordance with the divine will" (93).

330. *Castle* VII.1.6 (*Obras Completas*, at 1.7, p. 568; trans., 175).

331. *Castle* VII.1.6 (*Obras Completas*, at 1.7, pp. 568–69; trans., 175).

332. *Castle* VII.1.7 (*Obras Completas*, at 1.8, p. 569; trans., 175).

333. *Castle* VII.2.1 (*Obras Completas*, 570; trans., 177). The reference here is to the experience recounted in *Spiritual Testimonies* 31 mentioned above.

334. *Castle* VII.2.3 (*Obras Completas*, at 2.4, p. 571; trans., 178).

335. *Obras Completas,* VII.2.6 (572). The christological core of the *Castle,* while not obtrusive, is evident in Teresa's constant use of the notion of *imitatio Christi,* especially in his passion; e.g., I.2.11; II.1.7; V.2.4; V.3.12; VI.1.7; VI.5.6; and VI.7.13.

336. *Castle* VII.2.6 (*Obras Completas,* at 2.8, p. 572; trans., 180); see also VII.4.10.

337. See *Castle* VII.3.9 and VII.4.10–11. On the importance of the overflow effect in Teresa, see Howells, *John of the Cross and Teresa of Avila,* 78, 120, 123–25.

338. The seven effects are (1) forgetfulness of self, (2) desire to suffer, (3) interior joy when persecuted, (4) increasing desire to serve God, (5) detachment from everything, (6) lack of *interior* disturbance and fear of the devil's action, and (7) an end to raptures.

339. *Castle* VII.3.7 (*Obras Completas,* at 3.4, p. 575; trans., 184).

340. The metaphor of "touch" used to describe the immediacy of mystical consciousness was widespread in Christian mysticism. For an overview, see Pierre Adnès, "Toucher, Touches," DS 15:1073–98, who discusses Teresa on 1082. Among the books read by Teresa, both Francisco de Osuna and Bernardino de Laredo mention such "touches."

341. *Castle* VII.3.9 (*Obras Completas,* 576; trans., 185).

342. *Castle* VII.3.11 (*Obras Completas,* 576; trans., 186).

343. *Castle* VII.3.13 contains a rich series of biblical images for this final state of union.

344. *Castle* VII.4.6 (*Obras Completas,* 579; trans., 190).

345. *Castle* VII.4.8 (*Obras Completas,* at 4.9, p. 580; trans., 190).

346. *Castle* VII.4.12 (*Obras Completas,* at 4.14, p. 581; trans., 192).

347. Teresa's developing views on the relation of Martha and Mary as symbols of action and contemplation are treated in Howells, *John of the Cross and Teresa of Avila,* 83–88.

348. *Spiritual Testimonies* 59.5 (*Obras Completas,* 58.5, p. 625; trans. Kavanaugh, 1:356).

349. Tyler, *Teresa of Avila,* 153.

350. *Castle* VII.4.15 (*Obras Completas,* at 4.19, p. 582; trans., 194).

351. For these and more details on Teresa's impact on later Spanish mysticism, see Haliczer, *Between Exaltation and Infamy,* 60–62, 232–34.

352. My translation from the Apostolic Letter "Multiformis Sapientia Dei," as available online at http://www.vatican.va/holy_father/paul_vi/apost_letters/documents/hf_p-vi_apl.

CHAPTER **4**

John of the Cross: Night, Flame, and Union

T HE EXPLANATORY TITLE that John of the Cross (1542–1591) gave to his longest work, the double treatise *The Ascent of Mount Carmel (Subida del Monte Carmelo)* and *The Dark Night (Noche Oscura)*, is an admirable statement of his agenda: "This treatise explains how to reach divine union quickly. It presents instruction and doctrine valuable for beginners and proficients alike that they may learn to unburden themselves of all earthly things, avoid spiritual obstacles, and live in that complete nakedness and freedom of spirit necessary for divine union."[1] The essentials of John's program are conveyed here.

John of the Cross blazes as a star of the first magnitude in the constellation of Christian mysticism. Although much has been written about him, significant questions about the nature and import of his writings remain. Different approaches have been taken to presenting the essentials of his teaching, often centering on his notion of the "dark night" (*noche oscura*), which is certainly among his most important contributions. As my title suggests, however, in order to do justice to John's teaching I think that the night motif needs to be joined to its necessary fulfillment, the "flame of love," that is, mystical transformation conceived of as sharing God's nature and freedom of spirit (2 Cor. 3:17). What follows in this chapter cannot settle all the

I wish to thank Professor Edward Howells of Heythrop College, London, for his kindness in reading this chapter and making a number of valuable suggestions.

questions about John and his teaching. What I will attempt to do is to present the Carmelite's message and to provide evidence for why his place in the story of mysticism is incontestable.[2]

Life and Reception[3]

Born Juan de Yepes in the little Castilian town of Fontiveros sometime in 1542, John was the son of Gonzolo de Yepes and Catalina Alvarez.[4] Catalina was a poor weaver probably of Moorish background, and Gonzolo's family of wealthy silk merchants, originally of Jewish (*converso*) stock, disowned him when he married her. The family (there were three sons of whom Juan was the youngest) was extremely poor, a poverty enhanced by Gonzolo's death when Juan was two. Catalina struggled to support the family and had to move to Medina del Campo to continue work as a weaver. There Juan was educated at a school for poor children. When he was a teenager, the administrator of the local hospital, Don Alonso Alvarez, found the young Juan an able nurse for ministering to the sick. Don Alonso also enrolled him in the local Jesuit school, where he received a first-rate primary education.

Rather than enter the Jesuits, in 1563 Juan elected to join the Carmelite order, which had recently established a house in Medina. Taking the name of John of St. Matthias, he spent a year of novitiate studying the Carmelite Rule before being sent off to the university at Salamanca to pursue philosophy and theology. He was enrolled in the Arts Faculty there for three years, and then in theology for 1567–68. We do not know exactly what courses he took, but Friar John received a good education. He was certainly familiar with Aristotle and other philosophers; he knew Thomas Aquinas, whose *Summa theologiae* by this time was a major textbook in the universities, but there were a number of theological traditions taught in Salamanca. As a Carmelite, he would have become familiar with the thought of John Baconthorpe (d. 1348), who was the official Carmelite theologian. John was not a professional theologian, but he was well trained.

Friar John was an able student and might have been expected to pursue a university career after his ordination in 1567, but he was clearly more devoted to contemplative prayer than the classroom. For a time he considered leaving the Carmelites for the more austere contemplative life of the Carthusians. Then came the first major turning point in his life—his meeting with Teresa of Avila. In early 1567, the Carmelite general John Baptist Rossi (Rubeo) approved Teresa's incipient reform of the order. Probably in September of the same year Teresa met John at Medina del Campo and convinced him to join the reform because of its stress on contemplative prayer. At this time, Friar John also took the new name by which he is known to history—John of the Cross (Juan de la Cruz). When he finished his theological studies in 1568, he spent several months with Teresa to learn how to live the reformed style of Carmelite life.[5] On November 28, John and another friar established the first male house of the reform at Duruelo, thus making John the founder of the male branch of the Reformed (Discalced) Carmelites.

John took a leading role in the spread of the reform, both as founder of houses, as spiritual director of the reformed nuns, and as rector of the new college for the Discalced at Alcalá de Henares in 1571. In May of 1572 Teresa asked John to help her as confessor at the convent of the Encarnación in Avila (an unreformed house) to which she had been recalled as prioress. Thus, for some years (1572–77) the two worked together and doubtless had much discussion on the nature of mystical prayer and union. Teresa, although not above poking fun at the serious John from time to time, consistently testified to his sanctity and spiritual wisdom. In a letter to Mother Ana de Jesús, who was having doubts about John's capacities, dated November 1578, she says:

> I was amused, daughter, of how groundless is your complaining, for you have in your very midst, *mi padre*, John of the Cross, a heavenly and divine man. I tell you daughter, from the time he left and went down there I have not found anyone in Castile like him, or anyone who communicates so much fervor in walking along the way of heaven. . . . I declare to you that I would be most happy to have my Fray John of the Cross here, who truly is the father of my soul and from whom it benefited most in its conversations with him.[6]

For Teresa, John had become a pillar of the reform and a skilled spiritual director.

All was not well, however, with the Spanish Carmelites. The tensions between the reformed and the unreformed camps of the order were growing and the internal dynamics of the order and its relation to the general in Rome were dysfunctional. The reforming camp went beyond their official mandate in some instances, and the unreformed group (originally favorable or indifferent) soon reacted in a strongly negative way—another sad chapter in the history of internal squabbles in religious orders. In January 1576, John was arrested by the unreformed (Observant) Carmelites but was soon released. On

December 2, 1577, however, he was abducted by the Observants in Avila and brought to Toledo, where he was imprisoned in the monastery jail for nine months. This was a crisis for the reform movement, especially because the secrecy of his arrest left his friends in the dark about his whereabouts and health. Teresa of Avila penned a series of letters of complaint and petition, doing all in her power to free her friend.[7] Challenging as it was, the imprisonment marked the second great turning point in the life of John the mystic.

The idea of monastic prisons seems strange today, but they were a part of medieval religious life for the correction of wayward priests and nuns who had chosen a consecrated life, who had betrayed it in some way, and whom the church would not allow to return to a secular state. John's Observant Carmelite captors were convinced that he was a dangerous renegade and therefore used the opportunity to treat him savagely. It was during these nine months of torture by supposed brothers that John learned the real cost of discipleship. The details of John's mistreatment are well known—imprisonment in a small cell with little light; wretched food; no change of clothes; constant harassment, especially about the failure of the reform; suffering from both cold and heat; savage beatings by the whole community once a week. In short, his treatment was totally inhuman. John testifies to the difficulty of the ordeal in the first of his surviving letters (1581), where he says to the nun Catalina de Jesús, "Be consoled with the thought that you are not as abandoned and alone as I am down here [at Baeza]. For after that whale swallowed me up and vomited me out on this alien port (Jonah 2:1–2), I have never merited to see her again [referring to Teresa of Avila] or the saints up there." John's reference to Jonah's three days in the belly of the whale (a type of Christ's death and resurrection) was an evocation of the transformation he experienced during his imprisonment, as the letter makes clear in what follows: "God has done well, for, after all, abandonment is a steel file and the endurance of darkness leads to great light. May it please God that we do not walk in darkness."[8]

The testimonies collected from the Carmelite nuns and priests who knew John during the process for his canonization are filled with accounts of his sufferings in prison and his dramatic escape.[9] What we might not expect is the witness they bear to the divine consolations he experienced in the midst of such trying circumstances. A letter of María de Jesús testifies that John told her "that our Lord showed him many favors during this period by communicating Himself to him with great consolations." Another nun, María del Encarnación, reports that "he would say that his soul had never been more contented, nor had he ever rejoiced in the sweetness and light of Our Lord as during that long period while he was in prison."[10] It was in the belly of the whale that Friar John began to write, composing some of the most moving poetry—religious or secular—in any language.

Most of John's prison poems are either doctrinal (the nine "Romances"), or lyrics about the love between God and the soul, such as the first version of the "Spiritual Canticle" ("Canciones entre el alma y el esposo") and the "The Song of the Soul that is Glad to Know God by Faith"). One remarkable poem, however, is a testimony to the interior suffering he endured. Psalm 136 (Vg.: *Super fluminis Babylonis*) is a lament of the children of Israel in exile in Babylon—"Upon the rivers of Babylon, there we sat and wept when we remembered Sion." John composed a paraphrase of the Psalm in prison, beginning, "Over the streams of running water / Which by Babylon are crowned, / There I sat, with bitter teardrops / Watering the alien ground."[11] Several stanzas of lament for the lost Sion of the reform give way to a remarkable turn not found in the psalm—John's testimony to the fact that he saw this experience as a trial sent by Divine Love to purify him. "There did love so sorely wound me / And my heart from me withdrew. / I entreated him to kill me / Since he wounded me so sore. / And I leaped into his fire / Knowing it would burn the more."[12] But this fiery immolation brought new life: "In myself for you I perished / Yet through you revive once more, / Whose remembrance gives me life / Which it took from me before." The new life did not take away John's pain and the sad memory of Sion, as the following stanzas show; but the end of the poem reveals another transposition of the biblical prototype. The conclusion of Psalm 136 (vv. 7–8) is a curse on the daughters of Babylon and the vengeful hope that her children might be killed by dashing their heads against a rock (Christian exegetes had long struggled over what to make of this). John says that God will give the daughters of Babylon their just reward, but he emphasizes the theme of salvation by interpreting the rock as Christ (1 Cor. 10:4): "He [God] will join me with his children / Because to you [Sion] my tears were due, / And bring me to the Rock of Jesus / By which I have escaped from you."[13] Christ the rock is not a rock of condemnation, but of salvation.

By the summer of 1578, John was convinced he was dying and resolved to try to escape. Later accounts emphasize miraculous aspects of the story, especially the aid of the Blessed Virgin;[14] but the event is remarkable enough in itself. On the night of August 15–16, John pried open his cell door, ripped up his sheets to serve as a rope and descended into an enclosed garden, having entrusted himself to a dangerous leap (a leap of faith!) to complete his descent. Eventually he got over the garden wall to reach safety. Near death with exhaustion, he showed up at the convent of reformed Carmelite nuns in Toledo, who hid him from his Observant pursuers until a friendly cleric spirited him out of the city to the protection of his brethren. Soon after his release, John began sharing his prison poetry with the reformed nuns and friars and explaining its meaning. A major mystical voice had been born. One of the most remarkable things about John's imprisonment is that being locked up seems to have unlocked his creativity. Although known as an excellent spiritual director during the first decade of his life in the reform (1567–77), he wrote little, save perhaps for a few letters that have not survived. Subsequent to his release he spent the next seven years producing more poems, a series of aphorisms, and four important prose commentaries.

John's spiritual counsel had been valued before his imprisonment, as we can see from the testimony of Teresa. Nevertheless, the interest the nuns and friars took in his poetry, his explanations of it, and his spiritual direction grew greatly in the following years. The nuns and friars who submitted testimonies about his sanctity dwell on the effect of his conversation. For example, the report of Fray Lucas de San José given in 1604, says that with both religious and laity, "He would at once lead the conversation to the things of Our Lord, and for this he had a most singular ability; he spoke of Our Lord better than I have ever heard anyone else speak of Him." Fray Juan Evangelista, who lived with John for eleven years and was his confessor, leaves particularly powerful testimony. "In speaking of God," says Fray Juan, "and in expounding Scripture, he had a marvelous gift; he was never asked about any passage that he could not expound in full detail."[15]

The years following John's 1578 escape were busy. The reform movement of the Discalced was officially recognized by Gregory XIII in June of 1580. During the next decade John was elected to a number of leadership posts and was quite active, despite his lifelong commitment to solitude and silence. For the understanding of his mystical teaching it is important to consider the development of his writings during this time. As noted, John began sharing his prison poems with his brothers and sisters, especially the nuns of the convent of Beas, where he served as confessor and spiritual director in 1578 and 1579. It was in response to the questions of the nuns about the meaning of these poems that he first began writing commentaries, specifically what became the *Ascent of Mount Carmel*, dedicated to explaining the poem "En una noche oscura" ("On a dark night"), as well as the *Spiritual Canticle*, which commented on the "Canciones," the long poem beginning, "A donde te escondiste?" ("Where have you hidden . . . ?"). John's prose works were an outgrowth of his vocation as a spiritual director. We also possess other, briefer witnesses to John's spiritual counsel, such as the four groups of *Sayings of Light and Love*, consisting of 175 aphorisms taken down by those he was advising.[16]

Fray Juan Evangelista provides testimony about John's writing habits: "I saw him write these books and I never saw him open a book in order to write them. He relied upon his communion with God, and it can be clearly seen that they are all the result of experience and practice and that he had personal experience of the subject of his writings."[17] Both during his time as rector at the College at Baeza (1579–82) and after his transfer as prior to the convent at Granada (1582–85) John continued to work on the commentaries, revising and expanding both the base poem "A donde te escondiste?" by adding new stanzas and working on the prose explanation. In 1582 John met the pious widow Doña Ana del Mercado y Peñalosa, who soon became his penitent and friend. It was for her that he wrote the last of his mystical poems, "O llama de amor viva" ("O living flame of love"). At her request, he also wrote a commentary on the poem, probably at Granada in 1585. Juan Evangelista testifies that he composed it in two weeks. A second, slightly revised version of this commentary was his last work, produced in the final months of 1591.

The relation between John's three surviving prose works (counting the *Ascent/Night* as a single work) is complicated. Hans Urs von Balthasar, following Jean Baruzi, notes that each treatise "in its own way contains the whole on different levels that are not logically commensurable."[18] Thus, it is hard to decide how and in what order to read the corpus. The *Ascent of Mount Carmel* is the longest and most detailed work, but it deals primarily with the initial stages of the mystical path and John abandoned the book as its endless subdivisions became unworkable. The *Dark Night* is shorter and more coherent, but it too abandons commentary on the poem after a few stanzas and was not meant to be an account of the whole spiritual life. The *Spiritual Canticle*, which sticks closely to the forty stanzas of the final version of the "Canciones," tries to give a more complete analysis of the traditional three stages of spiritual progress from beginners, through proficients, on to the perfect. Finally, the late and short *Living Flame of Love*, dealing primarily with the goal of mystical union and transformation, has often been seen as John's masterpiece, although it describes mystical states that even the author admitted may seem incomprehensible to most people.[19] This chapter will first consider the *Ascent/Dark Night*, and follow with treatments of the *Canticle* and the *Living Flame*.

During these years of writing, John was busy furthering the reform. In 1585 he was elected vicar provincial for Andalusia, which meant that he had to travel extensively, founding seven new convents. In 1588 he was chosen as the first advisor for the new government of the Reformed Carmelites (called the *Consulta*) and therefore took up residence at Segovia. In June of 1590, however, the provincial Nicolás Doria (1539–1594) summoned a special chapter at Madrid in order to attack his foe, Jerónimo Gracián (1545–1614), the great friend of Teresa. John did not agree with Doria's action or with his attempts to change the rules regarding the nuns, and so he was relieved of his office in 1591. More disturbing was the effort of some of his enemies in the order to expel him from the Discalced. To someone who had suffered so much for his commitment to Teresa's vision this must have been a hard cross. Nonetheless, John took these events in stride, welcoming the solitude he found in the small convent of La Peñuela and planning to go to Mexico as a missionary. It was not to be. In September he became ill with a foot infection and was transferred to Ubeda. Once again, John was badly treated by his brethren (this time reformed Carmelites). During these final months he experienced a second intense sharing in Christ's passion, both through his illness and painful medical treatments and through rejection by his fellow friars. According to the accounts we have, he remained patient and serene, preparing for death. On the night of December 13, John received the last rites. Fray Juan Evangelista reports, "On the night of his death he kept asking very anxiously what hour it was. When they told him it was eleven o'clock he said: 'Ah! At midnight we shall go and sing Matins in Heaven.'"[20] And so it was.

Although John was attacked by Doria and his party, his friends among the reformed nuns and friars did not abandon his memory but rallied around his cause. In the first decade of the seventeenth century, materials began to be collected in view of starting a canonization process, and the task of getting his writings into print was begun. The differing versions of his prose works made this a difficult endeavor. The first edition published at Alcalá in 1618 lacked the *Spiritual Canticle* and contained many errors. Nevertheless, this edition was of importance because of the "Notes and Remarks" (*Apuntamientos y advertencies*) by John's confrere Diego de Jesús (1570–1621) designed to "facilitate the understanding of the mystic phrases [i.e., ways of speaking] and doctrine of Saint John."[21] The *Spiritual Canticle* first appeared in the French translation of René Gaultier in 1622,[22] and the Spanish original was included in the first edition of the complete works published in Madrid in 1630.

Not unlike Fray Juan himself, his writings had to endure their trials. In 1622 a group of *Alumbrados* at Seville appealed to John's *Dark Night* treatise in support of their views, and a copy of the 1618 edition was sent to the Inquisition at Madrid for examination.[23] In 1623 the Dominican friar Domingo Farfán accused John's works of containing the errors of the *Alumbrados*. In the course of this debate, on July 11, 1622, the Augustinian Basilio Ponce de León, professor of theology at Salamanca and nephew of the mystic Luis de León, published a spirited defense of John's orthodoxy, responding to thirty-seven propositions from his writings that some members of the Inquisition deemed erroneous or heretical.[24] Fray Basilio pointed out that even passages from scripture taken out of context could seem heretical and that the points found in the thirty-seven articles were in accord with the teaching of Teresa (by now a canonical figure), as well as other masters of the contemplative life. Basilio praised John's teaching, especially on interior abnegation and the avoidance of error regarding revelations. On the use of John made by the *Alumbrados,* he says, "In these things we must not consider the evil use made of them by a few, but the advantage of all. And the advantages of these writings, if prayer does not make it clear, can be demonstrated by experience, which is a faithful witness to them."[25]

This defense, the reputation John enjoyed for sanctity, and especially the inherent value of his writings turned the day in his favor. Nevertheless, John's progress toward official acceptance was slower than that of Teresa. He was beatified in 1675 and canonized in 1726. In later centuries John's prose writings continued to be read, but mainly by Carmelites; his poetry was largely forgotten. Although never as popular as Teresa, John became better known in the nineteenth century, but it was not until the twentieth century that John of the Cross emerged as one of the premier mystics of the Christian tradition, a status cemented by Pius XI in his declaration on August 24, 1926, of John as a Doctor of the Church. John's poetry, long neglected, also returned to favor, not only among those interested in contemplative prayer but also with literary scholars who hailed him as one of the greatest lyricists of Spanish and, indeed, of world literature.[26]

Poetry and Prose in John of the Cross

The issue of the relation between prose and poetry in mystical discourse reaches a high point in John of the Cross. A number of mystics wrote poetry, and a smaller number contributed both poems and prose works, such as Simeon the New Theologian in the Orthodox East, and the Anglican Thomas Traherne in the West.[27] No Christian mystic before John, however, provides us with a better example of superb mystical poetry combined with long and intricate commentary composed by the author of the poems.[28] What are we to make of this? For many centuries, as pointed out, John's poetry did not feature in investigations of his mysticism. The twentieth-century recognition of the stature of John as poet has produced a situation that might be described as "John of the Cross: Mystical Poet and/or Mystical Theologian?," in the sense that some Sanjuanist scholars have found John's poems more important than his sometimes-tedious prose expositions. This view is put forth by literary scholars such as Willis Barnstone, who judges that John's poems are primarily erotic, that is, descriptions of sexual love, rather than mystical, and that therefore the commentaries are misleading.[29] Some theologians seem to agree, at least in part. Hans Urs von Balthasar, for example, on the basis of his analysis of "The Paradox of Mystical Poetry," made the claim that "we must see that it is as a poet rather than as prose writer that he [John] is a Doctor of the Church."[30] Others have echoed Balthasar.[31] Alternate views, arguing that *both* the poetry *and* the prose are necessary for a full picture of John as mystic, have also had defenders, as can be seen in the writings of Michel de Certeau and Colin Thompson, to name but two.[32] My own position is that it is unnecessary to choose between John the poet and John the commentator, though admittedly the prose expositions often lack the immediacy and the evocative power of the poems. The two sides of John's literary production are complementary. To cite Michel de Certeau, "These two discourses, like the two halves of the hermaphrodite described in Plato's *Symposium*, reflect one another: they seek, call out to, mutually change, and embrace one another. The separation that distinguishes them establishes strange links between them."[33]

We should not separate John's poetry and prose because no human form of expression, poetry or prose, is adequate to express the depth of the Divine Word in its encounter with the human spirit. It is true that the mystical graces John received, especially during his time of trial "in the belly of the whale," found their first expression in poetry, but John never hesitated at a later stage to seek to give some explanation of the poems in his prose commentaries. When asked by Madre Magdalena de Espíritu Santo whether the words of his poems had been given him by God, John responded, "Daughter, sometimes God gave them to me and at other times I sought them."[34] Thus, John was both divinely inspired and a conscious literary artist. This message is also found in the "Prologue" to the B Version of the *Spiritual Canticle*, an important text for understanding the two sides of John's production.

John began teaching and explaining his poems not long after his release, and his oral reflections soon grew into lengthy commentaries.[35] Although the style of the commentaries is sometimes convoluted and hard to follow, they contain passages of great beauty and deep mystical teaching. As the hermeneutical theory he sets out in the B Prologue makes clear, John recognized that all prose explanation of his poetry must be partial and open-ended. Addressing his friend Madre Ana de Jesús, he says:

> It would be foolish to think that these expressions of love arising from mystical understanding [*inteligencia mística*], like these stanzas, are fully explainable. The Spirit of the Lord, who abides in us and aids our weakness, as St. Paul says [Rom. 8:26], pleads for us with unspeakable groanings in order to manifest what we can neither fully understand nor comprehend. Who can describe in writing the understanding he gives to loving souls in whom he dwells? And who can express with words the experience he imparts to them? Who, finally, can explain the desires he gives them? . . . Not even they who receive these communications.[36]

Those who receive these gifts "let their experience overflow in figures, comparisons, and similitudes" (*figuras, comparaciones, y semejanzas*) to pour out divine "secrets and mysteries" (*secretos y misterios*) in poetic form rather than "rational explanations" (*razones*). Rational explanation, while called for in the work of spiritual teaching and direction, is a necessary but impossible task, "since the abundant meanings of the Holy Spirit cannot be caught in words." Thus, John shows that he has no intention of trying to give a final exposition of the poems that flowed from the "abundant mystical understanding" he had received. His is *one* explanation; not the final one.[37] There always remains a surplus of meaning in the poems, one that will continue to inspire new readings. However—and this is central—*both* poetry and prose are secondary, epiphenomenal, fallible instruments for the inexpressible communication of love. "For mystical wisdom [*la sabiduría mística*]," says John, "which comes through love and is the subject of these stanzas, need not be understood distinctly in order to cause love and affection in the soul, for it is given according to the mode of faith through which we love God without understanding him."[38] Hence, it is in the interaction, or conversation, between poetry and prose within the wider horizon of the inexpressibility of mystical wisdom where John's teaching comes to its true expression.

What is the chronological relation between the poems and the commentaries John wrote on them? According to the testimony of Madre Magdalena de Espíritu Santo:

> When the holy father left his prison, he took with him a little book in which he had written, while there, some verses based on the Gospel *In principio erat Verbum* [these are the "Romances"], and some verses which begin "Que bien sé yo la fonte que mana y corre, Aunque es noche" ["How well I know the fountains rushing flow, although by night"] and the stanzas or *liras* that begin "A donde te escondiste?" ["Where have you hidden?"] as far as the stanzas beginning "O ninfas de Judea."[39]

Sister Magdalena goes on to say that the rest of the poems were written during the time John was rector at the College at Baeza, while the expositions were composed in response to the questions of the nuns at Beas and Granada. These and other comments by John's friends have allowed modern scholars to establish a relative chronology for his works. Scholars have also come to general agreement that, despite early doubts raised by some,[40] the second, or B versions, of the two full commentaries (*Canticle* and *Flame*) are authentic reworkings of the first, or A forms. It may be helpful to provide a chart of John's poems and prose works, based on the findings of Kieran Kavanaugh, but with a few adjustments.[41]

The Prison Works (1578)
Poems: "The Spiritual Canticle" (CO, original version of 31 stanzas)
    "The Song of the Soul that is Glad to Know God by Faith" (12 stanzas)
    "The Romances" (9 theological poems on the Gospel text, *In principio erat Verbum* [John 1:1])
    The poetic paraphrase of Psalm 136, *Super flumina Babylonis* (14 stanzas)

Calvario-Beas-Baeza (1578–81)
    "The Dark Night" poem (8 stanzas, probably 1578)
    "The Spiritual Canticle" (CA, first reworked version of 39 stanzas)

Other poems difficult to date

The Sketch of the Ascent of Mount Carmel (an annotated drawing)

The Sayings of Light and Love (175 aphorisms based on his spiritual
    direction)

The Precautions (17 short pieces of advice for religious)

Counsels to a Religious (9 pieces of advice) and *Degrees of Perfection* (17
    short pieces of advice)

The Ascent of Mount Carmel (treatise on the first stanzas of "The Dark
    Night," begun in 1581, probably not complete until 1584)

Granada (1582–88)

The Spiritual Canticle A (first redaction of the treatise on the 39-stanza
    poem; probably 1584–85)

The Dark Night (further commentary on "The Dark Night" poem,
    1584–85)

Poem "The Living Flame of Love" (4 stanzas, probably 1585)

The Living Flame of Love A (first version of the commentary on the
    poem, 1585–86)

The Spiritual Canticle B (commentary on the 40-stanza poem [CB,
    second revision], probably 1585–86)

Other poems difficult to date

Letters (John of the Cross's 33 surviving letters date from 1581 to
    1591)

La Peñuela (1591)

The Living Flame of Love B

The complexity of this corpus with its interactions and different versions suggests why some scholars contend that we still do not have an adequate critical edition of John's writings.

Sources/Resources

John's poetic and prose works make use of a range of sources from the Bible and Christian tradition. The Carmelite, however, does not often cite passages directly, except from the Bible, so that David Perrin suggests that it might be better to speak of his "resources," that is, his wide reading and transmuting of tradition, rather than specifically cited "authorities."[42] John's primary resource was the Bible, which Jean Vilnet says he quotes 924 times explicitly in his major prose works, about two-thirds of these passages from the Old Testament.[43] The christological and mystical interpretation of the Old Testament, especially the Psalms and the Song of Songs (his favorite texts) was traditional among Christian mystics, so we should not be surprised by John's frequent references to these books, as well as to the Old Testament wisdom literature, and especially to John and Paul in the New Testament. John of the Cross had a profound knowledge of the whole Bible, as the canonization materials make clear. Fray Juan Evangelista says, "He was very fond of reading from the Scriptures, and I never saw him read any other books than the Bible (almost all of which he knew by heart), Saint Augustine *Contra Haereses*, and the *Flos Sanctorum* [a hagiographical collection]."[44] Like Teresa, John makes it clear that everything he says on the basis of his own experience is subject to the authority of the Bible as interpreted by the church. As he puts it in the Prologue to the *Ascent*:

> In discussing this dark night, therefore, I will not rely on experience or science, for these can fail and deceive us. Although I will not neglect whatever possible use I can make of them, my help in all that with God's favor I shall say will be Sacred Scripture. . . . Taking Scripture as our guide we do not err, since the Holy Spirit speaks to us through it. Should I misunderstand or be mistaken on some point, whether I deduce it from Scripture or not, I will not be intending to deviate from the true meaning of the Sacred Scripture or from the doctrine of our Holy Mother the Catholic Church. Should there be some mistake, I entirely submit to the Church.[45]

Thus, Henri Sanson is correct in saying that, of the three interrelated sources for John's teaching (science, experience, and the Bible), it is the Bible that is given the controlling role.[46] As Keith J. Egan put it, for John "the bible was a vivid record of God's presence in human life, a loving presence that he perceived in his own life and that of others."[47]

John's teaching is integrally biblical, and, in line with the mystical tradition, he emphasizes the spiritual sense of the biblical text, especially passages from the Old Testament. A typical example of a spiritual-allegorical reading is found at the beginning of the *Ascent*, where he gives a biblical basis for the three reasons why the journey to union with God should be called "night" by appealing to the three nights that the young Tobias had to wait before he could unite with his bride (Tob. 6:18–22).[48] Another good example of an extended mystical-allegorical interpretation is found in *Night* 2, 17, 8, where the Carmelite uses verses 17–18 of Psalm 76 (Vg.) to give a detailed account of the nature of mystical knowing.[49] These kinds of readings are omnipresent in John's writings. To be sure, the spiritual sense never cancels out its basis in the literal and historical sense. From this perspective, it is worth noting one of the longer treatments of biblical texts in the discussion in *Ascent* 2, 17–22 of why even visions and locutions sent from God are not to be taken at face value.[50] In these chapters John cites multiple passages from the Old Testament where divine messages or predictions did not come to pass, at least from the human perspective, either because: (1) human understanding of the divine message was defective (God's words are not our words); or (2) God's words are always true but not always certain due to their relation to changeable human actions. Chapter 22 concludes the discussion as to why divine messages are not to be sought after Christ's coming by insisting that the Incarnate Word is God's final message, using a range of New Testament texts to prove the point. Most of John's interpretations in these chapters deal with what actually did or did not happen historically. John points out that the mistakes made by Old Testament figures about God's promises mostly came from the fact that they read the promises literally and not spiritually. Hence, in the midst of his expositions, he warns, "Anyone bound to the letter, locution, form, or figure apprehensible in the vision cannot avoid serious error." After citing 2 Corinthians 3:6 ("The letter kills and the spirit gives life"), he concludes, "The soul should renounce, then, the literal sense in these cases and live in the darkness of faith, for faith is the spirit that is incomprehensible to the senses."[51] Above all, John's understanding of the meaning of the Bible is christological—the Holy Spirit who speaks in the Bible is the Spirit of Christ who reveals that Jesus is the only way to union with God.

Jean Vilnet's book on John of the Cross's use of the Bible provides a good foundation for studying this fundamental aspect of his teaching. With regard to John's other sources/resources there is less agreement and fewer aids. What was John's relation to nonbiblical authors, theological and mystical?[52] The Carmelite rarely mentions names, but he was certainly familiar with many of the mystics of the Western church, such as Augustine, Cassian, Pseudo-Dionysius, Gregory the Great, the Cistercians and Victorines, and possibly the Franciscans (though he never cites Bonaventure), as well as late medieval figures like Jan van Ruusbroec, Jean Gerson, and Hendrik Herp. He also knew earlier Spanish mystical writers, like Bernardino de Laredo, who would have provided him with access to some authors he never cites. Some of these resources will be discussed below when appropriate.

One contentious issue concerns John's relation to Thomas Aquinas, with whom he certainly was familiar from his days at Salamanca.

John refers to Thomas only a few times in his writings.[53] Early twentieth-century Sanjuanist scholarship, written in the days of the dominance of neo-Thomism, tended to make John out to be far more of a Thomist than he actually was.[54] Many aspects of John's thought, not least his anthropology and notion of union with God, are not Thomist, and most recent scholars have found in Thomas only a quite partial resource for the Carmelite. A second disputed area concerns John's relation to the northern European mysticism of the Late Middle Ages, whose major initiatior was Meister Eckhart, and which was carried on by mystics like John Tauler, Henry Suso, Ruusbroec, and Herp (Harphius). How much contact might John have had with these figures, especially because some of their writings had been made available in Latin in the translations of the Carthusian Laurentius Surius and were known to have circulated in Spain? It is not possible to decide this question here. Some scholars have argued for a significant influence of the northern mystics on John,[55] but other Sanjuanists have resisted this claim. In reading John of the Cross I have noticed a number of parallels between his thinking and that of Eckhart and his followers (some of these will be mentioned in what follows), but the extent to which these may be due to literary dependence, or are only the result of shared engagement with key issues in the Christian mystical tradition, cannot be taken up in detail here. Above all, I would insist that John is too original a thinker to be reduced to the study of his sources and resources.

The Doctrinal Foundations of the Teaching of John of the Cross[56]

It would be an exaggeration to say that there is a Sanjuanist system, although John has a coherent theological viewpoint. As mentioned above, the Carmelite doctor wrote primarily as a spiritual director to guide those he was advising about the path to union. Complex as his commentaries are, he was capable of succinct summaries of his message, as in the brief poem "Suma de la perfection"—"Olivido de lo criado / memoria de Criador, / atención a la interior / y estarse amando al Amado" ("Forgetting the created, / remembering the Creator, / attending to the interior, / and staying in love with the Beloved").[57] In what follows, I will try to present a brief account of the major doctrinal bases of John's thought before moving on to his properly mystical teaching.

John's commentaries are not doctrinal treatises. Often overlooked, the "Nine Romances," poems he composed while in prison in imitation of contemporary popular ballads, are perhaps the best source for the doctrine that underlies his teaching.[58] These poems, the product of his meditations on the Prologue to John's Gospel, may not be his most inspired, but they allow us to see how deeply rooted his mysticism is in the fundamental doctrines of Trinity, creation, incarnation, and theological anthropology. One may wonder why during his time "in the belly of the whale" John worked on this cycle of doctrinal poems. He does not tell us, but I think the answer lies in love—the dominant theme of the Romances is the love of the Three Persons of the Trinity, which manifests itself in the creation of the universe as the fitting home for humanity, the creature destined to be united with God through the incarnation of the Word and the gift of eternal life. These Romances, in conjunction with sections of John's later prose works, provide a sketch of the fundamentals of his theology.

God as Three and One

The first two Romances deal with the Trinity, beginning with No. 1 under the title, "Romance on the Gospel *In principio erat Verbum* relating to the Most Holy Trinity," and continuing with the poem "On the communication of the Three Persons." The first Romance is a succinct presentation of the relations of the Three Persons, emphasizing the love at the heart of the trinitarian mystery.[59] Speaking of the bond between the Father and the Son, John says, "As the loved-one in the lover / Each in the other's heart resided; / And the love that makes them one / into one of them divided . . . ." John then broadens the picture to embrace all Three Persons: "There is one love in all three Persons: / One lover in all Three provides; / And the beloved is the lover / Which in each of them presides." This perichoretic love is the unfathomable being of God: "This very Being is Each One, / And it alone, in its own way, / Has bound them in that wondrous knot / Whose mystery no man can say." The "infinite love" (*infinito el amor*) that binds the three into one is the more unified the more it is love and vice versa ("que el amor cuanto más uno / tanto más amor hacía").[60] The second Romance continues the theme of the love between the Father and the Son: "Out of the love immense and bright / That from the two had thus begun, / Words of ineffable delight [*palabras de gran regalo*] / The Father spoke unto the Son." Despite the impossibility of grasping the inner communication of the two Persons, John hints at it through a constructed dialogue between the Father and the beloved Son. Already, however, the Father expresses the openness of his love to sharing with others *insofar as* they participate in the life and love of the Son. The Father says, "The man who loves You, O my Son, / To him Myself I will belong. / The love that in Yourself I won / I'll plant in him and root it strong, / Because he loved the very one / I loved so deeply and so long."[61]

God is radically unknowable—the Father and Son are one "in an ineffable bond that cannot be spoken" (En un ineffable nudo / Que decir no se sabía, Romance I). Or, as the *Spiritual Canticle* put it, "What God communicates to the soul in this intimate union is totally beyond words [*totalmente es indecible*]. One can say nothing about it, just as one can say nothing about God that resembles him."[62] For John, as for Pseudo-Dionysius and the other masters of negative theology, God is a dark, hidden, inexpressible mystery.[63] Nevertheless, God has revealed himself in the Word Incarnate and, in scripture, has given us language about the hidden mystery, however partial and inadequate it may be. This message uncovers, at least in some way, the mystery of trinitarian love. In his prose commentaries John maintains the trinitarian perspective of the first two Romances, although he also says more about other attributes shared by the three divine Persons, as we shall see regarding stanza 3 of the *Living Flame of Love*, where he analyzes the meaning of the "lamps of fire."[64]

The Trinity often appears in John's commentaries, especially in the later versions of both the *Spiritual Canticle* and the *Living Flame of Love*.[65] The Trinity also features in another of John's prison poems, "The Song of the Soul that is Glad to Know God by Faith," which begins, "For I know well the spring that flows and runs, / although it is night" (*aunque es de noche*). [66] This deeply apophatic poem is a meditation on and re-presentation of basic themes from John's Gospel, employing the symbols of light and darkness, water and bread, in a rich, often paradoxical, manner. The spring, of course, is the divine nature, the source of all things, which can never be known because it is without origin, without bottom, and of a surpassing brightness that blinds creatures (stanzas 2–5). The night is our night, especially that of John in his dark cell. The spring gives rise to a "stream [*corriente*] . . . mighty in compass and power," namely, the Son (stanza 7), and there is a third stream "proceeding from these two," the Holy Spirit (stanza 8). The poem concludes with three stanzas rejoicing in the presence of the "eternal spring" (*eterna fonte*) in the bread of life of the Eucharist.

The Carmelite's trinitarian theology developed and deepened during his brief writing career. Although the Holy Spirit is present in the

Romances, there is little there of the rich theology of the Spirit as "the warm south wind that breathes through the soul," or the "inner torrent," or the "divine unctions" that are so important in the late works for expressing how our union with God takes place through coming to share (or better, to *be*) the inbreathing of Father and Son that is the Holy Spirit.[67] Like William of Saint-Thierry, John of the Cross's mysticism can be described as "Spirit-centered."

Along with love, we can say that perhaps the most important divine attribute for John is beauty (*hermosura*). As is well known, John composed the new concluding stanzas 36–40 of the B version of the *Canticle* as a result of being inspired by a conversation with Sor Francisca de Madre di Dios about God's beauty.[68] Despite his often negative language about created reality in comparison with God (something to be taken up below), John had a refined aesthetic sense, as is evident in his poetry. He insisted, however, that the beauty of created things is misleading and dangerous unless we see it not in itself but as the manifestation of God's infinite beauty. Speaking of John's aesthetic spirituality, Balthasar noted, "For this spirituality, *hermosura* signifies the supreme affirmation about God. 'Beauty' for John is an obsession; it is not only the end, it is also the means. He may have rediscovered the beauty of the world through the beauty of God, but he could never have done this had he not known about beauty from the beginning."[69]

Creation as the Overflow of Divine Love

Selective readings of John of the Cross, especially of the *Dark Night*, have made it easy for some to accuse him of unrestrained negativity about the world and human nature. An example can be found in Dean Inge, who once complained, "The world simply does not exist for St. Juan; nothing exists save God and human souls. The great human society has no interest for him; he would have us cut ourselves completely adrift from the aims and aspirations of civilized humanity."[70] Nonetheless, the second and third of the Romances treat of creation and show us that both the making of humanity as the bride of the Word and the formation of the universe as the fitting dwelling for humans were part of the divine plan from all eternity. An integral reading of John's works indicates that he had a profound and profoundly positive doctrine of creation.[71] Romances III and IV stress how deeply the creation of the universe was rooted in the inner conversation of the Trinity (*consilium Trinitatis*). Romance III discusses how the Father wishes to give the Son a lovely bride who will share everything with him, something to which the Son responds in erotic terms, demonstrating that John, like Dionysius, rooted human love for God in God's own *eros* for humans. The Son tells the Father, "I'll hold her in My arm reclining / And with your love will burn her so / That with an endless joy and wonder / Your loving kindness she may know."[72] The long Romance IV details how the universe forms "the palace for the bride" (*palacio para la esposa*), with its two main components, the heavens that are the abode of the angels, and the earth, the place for humans. The Father's desire is that eventually the inhabitants of both realms will be united in "the love of the one sole Bridegroom." In order for this to happen, however, it is necessary for the Bridegroom to take on human nature: "And so the God would be the Man / And the Man would be the God: and then / He would roam amongst them freely / And eat and drink with other men."[73] (It is interesting to note that in this review of the necessity of the incarnation John says nothing about the Fall and original sin—the Father intends the Son's incarnation as the goal and purpose of his creative love.) The union of the Word with created humanity is not simply taking on human nature but is taking on a specifically marital human nature, that is, becoming the Bridegroom of humans. In Romance IV John expresses this in the kind of erotic terms that will later feature in the *Canticle*. The goal of the incarnation, as John insists, is both God becoming man *and* man becoming God.

The Christocentric view of creation evident in Romances III and IV shows that John does not disparage the created world. This position is evident throughout his works, such as in *Canticle*, stanza 14/15, where he discourses on how all aspects of the natural world reveal the beauty and love of their Creator.[74] Commenting on St. Francis's prayer, "My God and all things," John explains, "Since God is all things to the soul and the good that is in all things, the communication of this superabundance is explained through the likeness that the goodness of the things mentioned in these stanzas has to it."[75] Hence, the natural beauty of mountains, lonely wooded valleys, strange islands, resounding rivers, and love-stirring breezes, all reveal aspects of God's relation to the purified soul. Later in his comments on stanza 36, John notes the difference between the "morning knowledge" of all things, that is, the essential knowledge of creation in the Divine Word, and the "evening knowledge," which is "God's wisdom in his creatures, works, and wondrous decrees." Although the former is higher, the soul asks the Divine Lover for both kinds of knowledge.[76] John is uncompromising in his insistence that the true beauty and meaning of God's creation can be understood only by those who have rejected the beauty of creatures taken *in themselves*, and who therefore can appreciate their beauty as manifestations of God (e.g., *Canticle* 6, 2; *Ascent* 2, 5, 4; 2, 8, 3). This "all or nothing" attitude of John of the Cross is both a strength and perhaps also a problem that some have seized on to characterize him, mistakenly, as a world-denying opponent of the goodness of the created universe. For John there is no middle ground: creation is indeed beautiful *when seen from God's perspective.*

Christology

The goal of the incarnation, as noted, is not just God becoming man, but man becoming God. In Romance IV John emphasizes the corporate dimension of this deification, that is, the role of Christ's Mystical Body: "To her beauty all the members / Of the just He will enlace / To form the body of the Bride / When taken into His embrace." The poem ends with the promise of eternal joy of the Body of Christ: "Each one living in the other; / Samely loved, clothed, fed, and shod. / She, absorbed in Him forever, / She will live the life of God."[77] John has been criticized for lacking an ecclesiology. While it is true that mention of the role of the church is sparse in the prose works,[78] the mystagogical genre of the commentaries helps explain this, and the evidence of the Romances shows that the corporate dimension of salvation history was important for him. In Romance V, for example, John stresses the universality of the hopes and cries for the coming of the God-man. Romance VI concentrates this universal yearning on the figure of "The aged Simeon, taking fire / With inward love . . ." (Luke 2:25–35) to whom the Holy Spirit made the promise that he would not die until he had seen the Messiah, and so Simeon "Folded his arms about him fondly / And held Him closely to his breast."[79]

Romance VII (beginning, "Ya que el tiempo era llegado") returns to the divine perspective of the plan for salvation, once again using the device of a conversation between Father and Son to reveal the depths of God's saving love. The Father addresses the Son, "You see how Your beloved bride / After Your image has been made [Gen. 1:26]. / In what she most resembles You / Her loveliness I have arrayed." Although the bride differs from the Word by being only in human flesh, in order to make the bond between the God and humanity even stronger the Word will take on this flesh to be as like to the bride as possible. The Son responds by fully agreeing with the Father's plan and proclaiming that the incarnation will be the definitive revelation of the Father's

power, justice, wisdom, beauty, sweetness, and sovereignty. He concludes:

> I will go now and seek My bride,
> And take upon My shoulders strong
> The cares, the weariness, and labours
> Which she has suffered for so long.
> And that she may win new life
> I myself for her will die,
> Rescue her from the burning lake,
> And bear her back to You on high.[80]

The two final Romances are relatively brief reprisals of the beginnings
of the drama of salvation, with Romance VIII devoted to the annun-
ciation, and Romance IX to the nativity. Romance VIII notes how it
was only through Mary's consent that the mystery of the work of the
Three Persons in clothing the Word with flesh was possible. Romance
IX speaks of the joy of men and angels over the wondrous marriage in
which God and man exchange what seemed so strange and alien—the
joy of God coming to humans and the tears of humans being taken up
by the Holy Infant.

The Romances provide a basis for the role that Christ plays in John's
prose writings. Although John did not compose any works dealing
explicitly with Christology, Christ the Divine Bridegroom is everywhere in his writings and Christ the Savior of humanity dying on the
cross and providing the source and model for the purgation needed to
attain union appears frequently in the commentaries. The Carmelite is
not interested in speculation about the nature of the hypostatic union
between God and man, nor in dwelling on the physical events of his life
on earth, even the bloody details of his suffering and death (so popular
in the Late Middle Ages and in contemporaneous Spain). Rather, he
wishes to emphasize the message that Jesus is the source, model, and
goal of the path to union. It is only through the person of the God-man
that we can come to share in the inner life of the Trinity.

Romances II and III, as we have seen, make it clear that the incarnation was intended by God from all eternity, irrespective of sin. The
universe was created as the palace for the humanity intended to be wed
to the Word made flesh. This does not mean that John did not recognize that the incarnation was also a remedy for original sin, though he
speaks of this only rarely.[81] The incarnation is the greatest work of all
the divine outpourings (*Canticle* 5, 1–3) and therefore has a pan-cosmic

dimension. Just as all things were created as "very good" (Gen. 1:31) in the Son as the image of the Father's substance (Heb. 1:3), so too creatures were given more glory when the Son took on human nature and elevated it into God's own beauty. "And in this elevation of all things through the Incarnation of his Son and through the glory of his resurrection according to the flesh, not only did the Father beautify creatures partially, but, we can say, he clothed them entirely in beauty and dignity."[82] The soul is given initial knowledge of the incarnation and the other divine mysteries through the "sore wound" of faith that cuts into it to cause a more intense love than can be given by the knowledge of God available through creation. It is thereby impelled to seek deeper and deeper knowing of the Incarnate Word until it reaches face-to-face vision in heaven.[83]

The important christological text in *Ascent* 2, 22 underlines the centrality and finality of the Word's coming in the flesh as the Father's ultimate message to humanity. Since the incarnation, John says, we should not seek any new messages, visions, or revelations from God but fix our eyes on Christ as "brother, companion, master, ransom, and reward" (*Ascent* 2, 22, 5). Because Christ redeemed the soul solely for his own sake, she now owes him a total response of love (*Canticle* 1, 1). As John insists in another key christological chapter (*Ascent* 2, 7), the path leading to eternal life is narrow. Although the path is a constricted one (Matt. 7:14), Jesus told us how it may be traversed when he preached the necessity of taking up one's cross and following him (citing Mark 8:34–35 and many other texts). If we walk the road in nakedness and detachment, we will discover that "[t]he cross is a supporting staff and greatly lightens and eases the journey" (*Ascent* 2, 7, 7). John insists, "A person makes progress only by imitating Christ, who is the Way, the Truth, and the Life" (*Ascent* 2, 7, 8, citing John 14:6). This imitation must extend even to annihilation, because the journey of following Christ, "does not consist in consolations, delights, and spiritual feelings, but in the living death of the cross, sensory and spiritual, exterior and interior."[84] Although John sometimes talks about a general imitation of Christ in one's life,[85] his fundamental concern is imitating Christ in bearing the cross. Truly devout people "seek the living image of Christ crucified within themselves, and thereby they are pleased rather to have something taken away from them and to be left with nothing."[86] The necessity of taking up the cross is a frequent theme in John's writings.[87] As he succinctly put it in a fragmentary letter to Padre Luis de San Angelo, "Do not seek Christ without the cross."[88]

Theological Anthropology

John of the Cross's mystical message is practical and mystagogical, a teaching about the transformation of the human person through union with God. Hence, it is also anthropological through and through. In this context I will not analyze the process of the mystical transformation of the person (this will be taken up below) but only provide a schematic outline of John's understanding of human nature, the abstract picture at the basis of his dynamic account of the path to God.[89]

Although he does not cite the text often, John agreed with Genesis 1:26 that the fundamental essence of human nature is its creation in God's image and likeness.[90] Flowing from this, an important theme in the Sanjuanist writings is the distinction between three forms of likeness, presence, or uniting with God. The first is the presence or similarity of essence by which God is found in all things, giving them life and being. The second similarity is "his presence by grace, in which he abides in the soul, pleased and satisfied with it." "The third is his presence by spiritual affection [*afección espiritual*], for God usually grants his spiritual presence to devout souls in many ways by which he refreshes, delights, and gladdens them."[91] This motif will be important for his description of the soul's transformation.

From time to time John of the Cross repeats the hoary language about the soul being a "prisoner in the body" (e.g., *Ascent* 1, 3, 3; 1, 15, 1; 2, 8, 4), and there is no doubt that he establishes a strong contrast between what he calls the lower, or sensory, part of human nature (*parte sensitiva*) and the higher part, or spirit (*parte espiritual*).[92] Nonetheless, a careful reading of his writings shows that John has a holistic view of the union of the soul and body as a single suppositum, or concrete subject.[93] John often speaks of the *alma*, or soul, when he refers to purification and transformation, but this is synecdoche for the whole human person. It is important to remember that both the sense part of the person and the higher part, the spirit, need to be purified in order to attain God, and that annihilation of the spirit is the far more difficult task. Sense and spirit must both work to overcome the false self and to realize their true unity in one supposit. We should also keep in mind that John was not writing technical treatises on philosophical or theological anthropology, so there are imprecisions and loose ends in some of his presentations, as well as possible developments.

Stanzas 20–21 of the *Spiritual Canticle* are an address by the Bridegroom to the bride picturing the world of nature and inviting her to be soothed and be at rest. In his commentary John allegorizes this natural description in terms of how spiritual transformation integrates and harmonizes the powers of sense and spirit. "In these two stanzas," he says, "the Bridegroom, the Son of God, gives the bride-soul possession of peace and tranquility by conforming the lower part to the higher, cleansing it of all its imperfections, bringing under rational control the natural faculties and motives, and quieting all the other appetites."[94] The passage provides a handy starting point for a look at the Carmelite's view of human nature.

Stanza 20 of the poem speaks of "Swift-winged birds, / lions, stags, and leaping roes, / mountains, lowlands, and river banks, / waters, winds and ardors, / watching fears of night."[95] John interprets these images as the disordered faculties and activities of the soul that must be cleansed and made tranquil by the Bridegroom. The sensory part of the human consists of the body and its five exterior senses (not explicitly treated here),[96] as well as the "swift-winged birds," which he identifies with the interior senses of fantasy and imagination. Although some texts differentiate between these two interior senses,[97] John often treats them together, as he does here: "He calls the wanderings of the imagination 'swift-winged birds,' for these digressions are quick and restless in flying from one place to another." The soul also contains two inclinations, or appetites (*apetitos*)—the irascible appetite, or inclination to avoid or resist what is opposed to the soul, which is figured in the "lions," and the concupiscible appetite, the inclination to seek what is good and flee what is evil (the "stags, and leaping roes").[98] Although much of what John has to say about the sensory part and its appetites is negative, especially in the *Ascent* and the *Dark Night*, a comprehensive study of his corpus demonstrates a more integrated view of human nature than many passages, at least at first glance, seem to suggest. From this perspective we should note that John distinguishes between the "natural appetites" (*apetitos naturales*), which are of little or no hindrance to the soul's progress, and the "voluntary appetites" (*apetitos voluntarios*), which in fallen humans almost always involve some selfishness or overattachment to created things (*Ascent* 1, 11, 1–4). Although John does not always explicitly invoke the distinction, a number of passages show that his negative attitude toward the *apetitos* is directed toward the inordinate voluntary attractions that the soul has for created things.[99] The Carmelite's program for purifying and even annihilating inordinate appetites, or cravings, is more systematic, severe, and perhaps even ruthless, than many other spiritual writers; but his goal with regard to both the sensitive and spiritual appetites was one that Steven Payne aptly characterizes as "complete psycho-physical integration."[100] This is why in speaking of the union of love in the *Dark Night* he says, "God gathers together all the strength, faculties, and appetites of the soul, spiritual and sensory alike, so the energy and power of this whole harmonious composite may be employed in this love."[101]

The higher, spiritual part of the soul John traditionally describes as threefold—the three faculties of intellect (*entendimiento*), memory (*memoria*), and will (*voluntad*). In stanza 20, John says that the "mountains, lowlands, and river banks" figure the vicious and inordinate actions of these three powers—mountains are too high by "inordinate excess," lowlands are acts that are low and defective, and even the river-banks are not totally level and thus signify some imperfection of intellect, memory, or will (20/21, 8). Finally, John reads the "waters, winds, and ardors, watching fears of night" as the four natural passions, or emotions. "The waters denote the emotions of sorrow . . ."; and "The winds allude to the emotions of hope. . . ." "The ardors refer to the emotions of the passion of joy that enflame the heart like fire . . ."; and "By the watching fears of night are understood the emotions of fear" (20/21, 9).

The threefold distinction of spiritual powers as memory, intellect, and will goes back to Augustine[102] and was a commonplace in Scholastic and mystical discourse, although not with Thomas Aquinas and his followers, who followed Aristotle in distinguishing only intellect and will.[103] The three powers, or faculties, are of great importance for John in his analysis of how the theological virtues of faith, hope, and charity purify and prepare the soul for union with God. John was also aware that Augustine found an image of the Trinity in the three higher powers, although he himself does not explicitly relate the three powers to the Three Persons.[104]

The intellect has priority for John of the Cross in the sense that the other two spiritual powers depend on it—the memory helps recall what has been understood by the intellect, and the will is drawn to what the intellect presents to it.[105] John seems to have adhered to an epistemology based on abstraction not unlike what we find in Thomas Aquinas: the intellect abstracts or forms "intelligible species," that is, acts of understanding (*inteligencias*), from the images and phantasms that the interior senses have created from sense impressions.[106] Thus, the intellect has both an active aspect or function—the agent intellect that abstracts the intelligible species—and a receptive, that is, possible or passive intellect, which is the soul's capacity for knowledge.[107] Like many mystics, such as Eckhart and his followers, John insists that mystical knowledge is not *actively* gained by the intellect but is a pure gift infused into the passive intellect. Given the mystagogical purpose of his writings, John is less interested in pursuing expositions of the ordinary natural forms of knowing than he is in describing the supernatural activity of the spirit.[108] What is, indeed, central to his teaching is the fact that the intellect has *two ways* of knowing, the natural and the supernatural. As he says in *Ascent* 2, 10, 2,

> It is noteworthy that the intellect can get ideas and concepts in two ways, naturally and supernaturally. Natural knowledge includes everything the intellect can understand by way of the bodily senses or through reflection. Supernatural knowledge comprises everything imparted to the intellect in a way transcending the intellect's natural ability and capacity.[109]

Supernatural knowledge can be either corporeal (i.e., supernatural infusions into the exterior and interior bodily senses), or spiritual. The latter comes in two forms: the distinct knowledge given in visions, revelations, locutions, and spiritual feelings, and the "dark and general knowledge" (*inteligencia oscura y general*), that is, the contemplation given in faith (*Ascent* 2, 10, 3–4). (We will see more about supernatural knowing when we speak about faith below.) Nonetheless, John so emphasizes the difference between natural and supernatural knowing (as well as the activity of the memory and the will under supernatural impetus) that he seems at times to threaten the unity of the human subject. Given the fact that the soul possesses two ways of knowing and loving that seem, at least initially, to be opposed to each other, how can we say that the person who attains union with God is one and the same as the person who began the journey?[110] John's account of the dynamic path to union will show that union not only transforms the one subject but also unifies all the powers and levels of consciousness.

The status of the faculty of memory is one of the more contentious issues in Sanjuanist studies. Following the lead of André Bord, most scholars now agree that John's view of memory is not really Augustinian,[111] especially because he does not think of memory as a receptacle of images and forms to be called upon,[112] but rather as what might be called a faculty of attention or relation—an attention of recall to the past images and concepts that reside in the fantasy or in the soul itself in natural knowing (see, e.g., *Ascent* 3, 7, 1), or an attentive hope directed to the mystery of God in supernatural knowing (see *Ascent* 2, 6, 3; 3, 7, 2). Like the will, the memory operates in close dependence on the intellect; and, like the intellect, it needs to be purged of its natural mode of operation in relation to particular created things by the action of the supernatural virtue of hope (*Ascent* 3, 2–15).[113] On the natural level, memory is the ability to remember, forget, or set aside objects of thought, which may happen either voluntarily or involuntarily, and which can be aroused either by ourselves, or by God, or even the devil. Supernaturally, the activity and direction of memory is reversed. The purgative power of hope helps the memory strip itself of attention to "all forms that are not God." John is quite insistent on this, affirming that "[t]here is no way to union with God without annihilating the memory as to all forms" (*Ascent* 3, 2, 4). As the memory gradually empties itself of creatures, hope directs it to God (*Flame* 3, 21), the God who cannot be understood and therefore is not a new "form" in the mind but the supreme source of hope for final blessedness.

On the natural level, the will has a reciprocal relation to the intellect. Nothing can be loved unless it is in some way known, so that the will is a "rational appetite." On the other hand, John also affirms that "the intellect and the other faculties cannot admit or deny anything without the intervention of the will" (*Ascent* 3, 34, 1) to direct attention to the object under consideration. Although the will is the spiritual faculty of appetite and affectivity, it employs and coordinates all the "appetites" (*apetitos*), as well as the "affections" (*afecciones*), "longings" (*ansias*), "pleasures" (*gustos*), "emotions" (*pasiones*), and "desires" (*deseos*) found on both the sensory and the spiritual levels. The precise differences among these terms (John is rarely interested in defining or discriminating among them) need not delay us. What is crucial is to recognize that desire and longing are key elements both in John's affective vocabulary and in the dynamics of the path to union. The Carmelite analyzes the active purgation of the sensory appetites in book 1 of the *Ascent*, and he presents an account of the active purging of the memory's natural and supernatural apprehensions (*Ascent* 3, 1–15), as well as an unfinished analysis of the purification of the will's emotions of joy, hope, sorrow, and fear in *Ascent* 3, 16–42. Once again, his attention is on how we must empty ourselves of all *voluntary* appetites, desires, and emotions insofar as they are directed to creatures, if we are to be open to receiving the supernatural grace of charity, the "dark and obscure love" (*Flame* 3, 49) paralleling the "dark knowledge" of faith that gives access to the infinite God and, along with him, true love for created things. This is memorably expressed in Letter 14 sent to an anonymous Carmelite probably in 1589. Here John says:

> It is worth knowing, then, that the appetite is the mouth of the will.
> It is opened wide when it is not encumbered or occupied with any

mouthful of pleasure. When the appetite is centered on something, it becomes narrow by this very fact, since outside God everything is narrow. That the soul have success in journeying to God and being joined to him, it must have the mouth of its will opened only to God himself, empty and dispossessed of every morsel of appetite, so that God may fill it with his love and sweetness; and it must remain with this hunger and thirst for God alone, without desiring to be satisfied by any other thing, since here below it cannot enjoy God as he is in himself.[114]

John's teaching on the mystical path, then, is both noetic and affective. Transformation takes place by giving up the possession of created things, which can never fulfill the infinite dynamism of the soul's higher powers anyhow, and by realizing that it is only in relation to the infinite goodness that personal integration is possible.

The triadic nature of the spirit is a given in much of the literature about John of the Cross and is evident across his works. Recently, however, Dominic Doyle has suggested that in his later texts, especially those dealing with union in *Canticle B* and *Flame B*, John seems to move toward describing the higher powers in a dyadic way, emphasizing the transformation of the powers of intellect and will and gradually identifying memory with the soul's substance or self rather than with a distinct faculty.[115] For example, toward the end of stanza 3 of the *Living Flame* John notes how the gift of union calls forth the soul's reciprocal supernatural giving back to God:

> Corresponding to the exquisite quality with which the *intellect* receives divine wisdom, being made one with God's intellect, is the quality with which the soul gives this wisdom, for it cannot give it save according to the mode in which it was given. And corresponding to the exquisite quality by which the *will* is united to goodness is the quality by which the soul gives in God the same goodness to God. . . . And, no more no less, according to the exquisite quality by which it knows the grandeur of God, being united to it, the *soul* shines and diffuses the warmth of love.[116]

One can see here that the memory has dropped out and it is now the entire substance of the soul that reflects a particular form of knowing God's grandeur. While John never repudiated the triad of intellect, memory, and will, it does appear that there developed a kind of tension between the triadic and the dyadic picture of the soul in his later works, especially with regard to union. Doyle concludes that John's works show "a clear trajectory towards the recognition that the memory is not a parallel faculty alongside the intellect and will, but instead is a way of talking about the temporal unfolding of an individual's knowing and loving."[117]

The dyadic picture of the soul casts further light on the final feature of John's anthropology to be discussed here, his notion of the "substance of the soul" (*sustancia del alma*), or its "ground/depth" (*fondo*), or "center" (*centro del alma*).[118] John's teaching about the substance of the soul is difficult, and in this context I do not pretend to solve all the issues concerning it, its relation to the soul's three spiritual faculties, especially in their quality as deep caverns of feeling, and its role in mystical transformation. We do need to note, however, that John's view of the soul's *sustancia* is not one of conceptual essence as conceived in academic theology, but is rather a dynamic actuality at the basis of the soul's powers of knowing, remembering, and loving.[119] Presumably, this core of the soul's reality is given in the divine likeness humans have from creation, but John seems to consider it largely hidden in natural activity and only gradually accessible through the supernatural actuation of grace. There is thus a relation of reciprocity between the substance of the soul and the three powers of the spirit. As Edward Howells puts it, "[T]he substance of the soul is intended always to work in an equal partnership with memory, intellect, and will in their spiritual operation." Howells goes on to suggest an analogous relation between the three powers and the substance of the soul and the relational identity of the Three Persons of the Trinity to the divine essence, although John never says this explicitly.[120] There are, however, some remaining distinctions. The substance of the soul, according to John, is the place of permanent union with God at the height of the mystical path, while the faculties enjoy intermittent experiences of union. Speaking of the drink of union that "deifies, elevates, and immerses" the soul, he says,

> For even though the soul is always in this sublime state of spiritual marriage once God has placed her in it, the faculties are not always in actual union although the substance is. Yet in this substantial union [*unión sustancial*] the faculties are frequently united too; and they drink in this inner wine cellar, the intellect understanding, the will loving, and so on.[121]

In supernatural knowing and loving, the bodily senses cannot play any direct role, because they are not proportioned to the divine nature. Hence, John creates an original teaching about the new function of intellect, memory, and will acting spiritually in the substance, or depth, of the soul as "the profound caverns of feeling" (*las profundas cavernas del sentido*), the infinite capacity of the soul to receive the divine "substantial touches and wounds" that give direct access to God in a way analogous to how natural knowing begins in the senses. Stanza 3 of the *Living Flame of Love* describes the soul's contact with God in the following terms: "O lamps of fire! / in whose splendors / the deep caverns of feeling, / once obscure and blind, / now give forth. So rarely, so exquisitely, / both warmth and light to their Beloved."[122] These caverns of feeling are analyzed in detail in John's commentary on stanza 3 (*Flame* 3, 18–23, 26–29, 68–71, 76–77, and 80) and will be discussed below. Here I wish to note only that, when the caverns are purged and emptied of all created things, their quasi-infinite nature becomes more evident, first as an overwhelming and painful thirst for God and, then, when God sends his touches and wounds into these depths, as the most profound satisfaction and delight (*Flame* 3, 19–23). There is thus an epektetic, or constantly growing, fusion of desire and satisfaction in the soul: "Thus it seems that the more the soul desires God the more it possesses him, and the possession of God delights and satisfies it. . . . Since there is no disgust, they are always desiring; and they do not suffer, for they have possession."[123] Picking up on a Psalm text used by previous mystics, John sees the relation between the infinite God and the infinite caverns of feeling as the "abyss calling out to the abyss" (Ps. 41:8 Vg.).[124] The remains, or "memories," of the substantial touches, according to John, are stored in what he calls "the feeling of the soul" (analogous to the interior common sense in natural knowing) where they can be drawn on to increase the loving knowledge that characterizes growing union with God.[125] This takes place in what John in the *Living Flame*, stanza 4, 3, refers to as *el centro y fondo de mi alma, que es la pura e íntima sustancia de ella.*[126]

The language of *centro del alma* does not emerge until this last work of the Carmelite as a way to express the deepest possible union with God in this life. John says that the soul has many centers, that is, levels of union with God, although one is the deepest. In *Living Flame* 1, 9–14, he has an extended discussion of these centers of the soul. The "wound of love" mentioned in the first stanza of the poem ("O living flame of love / that tenderly wounds my soul / in its deepest center!") takes place "in the substance of the soul where neither the center of the senses nor the devil can reach." He continues, "By saying that the flame wounds in its deepest center the soul indicates that it has other, less profound centers, so we ought to explain what is meant by these words" (1, 9). Although the language of high and low in relation to spiritual realities is only metaphorical, John insists that "[t]he deepest center of an object we take to signify the farthest point attainable by that object's being and power and force of operation and movement" (1, 11). Thus, the deepest center of the soul is the point of attraction and power (John appeals to the examples of both rock and fire), which draws and eventually integrates all the powers of the human supposit, both the sensory and the spiritual. Yet more, John daringly proclaims, "The soul's center is God" (1, 12). While we are in this life, the soul is capable of going deeper and deeper through growing love into various centers until it reaches this deepest center. "Once it has attained the final degree," says John, "God's love has arrived at wounding the soul in its ultimate and deepest center, which is to illuminate it and transform it in its whole being, power, and strength, and according to its capacity, until it appears to be God [*hasta ponerla que parezca Dios*]."[127] While this union is not as great as the union to be enjoyed in heaven, it is still worthy to be called *el último centro y más profundo de el alma*.[128]

Negation and Purgation in
John of the Cross: The Nights

John's mystical teaching is found primarily in his commentaries on three mystical poems. The three books of the *Ascent of Mount Carmel* and the two books of the *Dark Night* form the two parts of a single treatise on the four "Nights" as revealed in the poem "En una noche oscura." This constitutes the largest part of John's prose works and is the most read part of the corpus. This fact has some disadvantages. The long *Ascent*, despite its importance, progresses at times in confusing fashion until John finally abandons it. The two books of the *Night*, dealing with the passive Night of the Spirit, are more cohesive and are central to John's view of purgation, but their primarily negative perspective can give a limited view of the whole of his teaching. Hence the importance of the two other commentaries. The *Spiritual Canticle*, which exists in two versions, provides a more comprehensive view of John's teaching about all the stages of the soul's progress to loving union. Many Sanjuanist scholars, however, consider John's last and shortest treatise, *The Living Flame of Love* (also found in two versions), as his most finished work. Before turning to a presentation of these commentaries, it will be helpful to consider by way of "Prolegomena" some general mystical themes that the Carmelite doctor inherited from tradition and incorporated into his thought.

Prolegomena

For centuries Christian mystics had employed threefold itineraries to give an overview of the path to union. The most common was the distinction of the purgative–illuminative–unitive ways, which was also seen as representing three groups of persons: the beginners of the purgative way, the proficient of the illuminative, and the perfect of the unitive. John of the Cross uses this schema often. In the Prologue to the *Ascent* he notes that his message here is limited to the first two groups (*Ascent* Prol. 4; see also 1, 1, 3), while at the start of the *Night* he summarizes all three:

> Souls begin to enter this dark night when God, gradually drawing them out of the state of beginners [*estado de principiantes*], that is, those who practice meditation on the spiritual road, begins to place them in the state of the proficients [*los aprovechantes*], that is, those who are already contemplatives, so that by passing through this state they might reach the state of the perfect [*estado de los perfectos*], which is the divine union of the soul with God.[129]

This passage is also important for introducing the distinction between the discursive *meditation* (*meditación*) of beginners and the intuitive and deepening *contemplation* (*contemplación*) of the two higher stages. Both types of prayer were of ancient provenance and wide use among mystics, but John was to give them his own distinctive spin, as we will see below. Another significant inherited term John used was "mystical theology" (*teología mística*), which he mentions fairly often and which will also be discussed below. Those we call mystics today were referred to in earlier ages as "contemplatives," or "spiritual persons."[130] John speaks of "truly spiritual persons" most often in book 2 of the *Ascent* where he deals with the active purgation of the spirit (e.g., *Ascent* 2, 1, 3; 2, 7, 1 and 8; 2, 11, 7; 2, 17, 9), but he does not use the term "spirituality" (*espiritualidad*).[131]

Since at least the twelfth century, when Bernard of Clairvaux spoke of "reading in the book of experience," the appeal to experience as a source of a special type of knowledge among mystical authors had been common. Not all these appeals were the same, however, and we must avoid the temptation to think that what we might mean by "experience" today is the same as what authors centuries removed from us meant. Especially misleading are modern empiricist views of mystical experience as some kind of extraordinary inner or outer perception separated from the normal beliefs and practices of the mystic's life. As

John J. Murphy puts it, "The mystic's life of faith is not something separate from the mystical experience. Rather, the spiritual practices of the
mystic's life are part of the setting for the concept-formation of mystical experience."[132] Above all, we must remember that experience was
not a norm or rule for these mystics, but rather a confirmation of what
was taught by scripture and the church. In using the word *experiencia*
John sometimes refers to his skill and knowledge as a confessor and
guide of souls (e.g., *Night* 1, 13, 3; 1, 14, 6; *Flame* 3, 30). He sometimes
(but rarely) employs *experiencia* in discussing his inner states or those
of others, as, for example, when he says that forgetfulness when one
is absorbed in God "is noted every day through experience."[133] Most
often, however, he does not use the word "experience" itself (despite its
omnipresence in most English translations) but talks about "having,"
"feeling," or "tasting" divine sweetness, spiritual delights, etc.[134] John
of the Cross, like Teresa of Avila and other mystics, does claim that
what he is saying will not be understandable to those who have not
had experience of what he is talking about. For example, in discussing
the freeing of the soul from its "house of sensuality" in *Night* 3, 14, 3,
he says, "This good fortune, in my opinion, can only be understood
by the ones who have tasted it."[135] Nonetheless, as noted above, in the
Prologue to the *Ascent*, despite saying that the book will be talking
about the many things that happen to people on the road to God (e.g.,
"joys and afflictions and hopes and griefs," Prol. 7), John insists, "I will
not rely on experience or science, for these can fail and deceive us" (*no
fiaré ní de experiencia ní de sciencia, porque lo uno y lo otro puede faltar y
engañar*, Prol. 2).

While it may be true that Teresa and John speak of states of inner
experience in greater detail and with more psychological penetration
than their predecessors and thus shine a spotlight on the subject of
divine graces, it is not correct to accuse them of basically altering the
relation between experience and doctrine, or of being primarily concerned with some form of mystical experientialism.[136] As Alois M. Haas
puts it, "The hidden character of mystical experience is also that it is
an experience of not-experience."[137] The same view has been advanced
by many other Sanjuanist scholars.[138]

Here there arises a related issue about John's experience and the
path to union. Hans Urs von Balthasar was not alone in claiming that
John seems to present his teaching about negation and transformation as *the* path to God—a kind of norm or pattern for all who want
to reach the final union possible in this life. He summarizes, "the
internal coherence of the entire corpus is so great that, despite all the

open-ended freedom it imparts, it appears as *the* way to God."[139] Still, Balthasar thinks that John's doctrine can be considered normative for the church, but only analogically, not normatively, the way John himself seemed to wish it to be. As what Balthasar calls "a guiding star" for contemplatives, John must still leave freedom for other Christians to follow other ways. There are, indeed, a few texts in which the Carmelite explicitly says this. For example, in *Ascent* 2, 5, 10, he notes that the degree of union souls attain will be proportional to their capacity and to the grace God wishes to give them; and in *Canticle* we read, "To some souls he gives more and to others less, to some in one way and to others in another, although all alike may be in the same state of spiritual betrothal."[140] His strongest statement comes in the *Flame*, stanza 3, 59: "God leads each one along different paths [*por diferentos caminos*] so that hardly one spirit will be found like another in even half its methods of procedure."[141] Despite these texts, John's general tone seems to presuppose that the essential structure of his account is still *the* way to God, even if it will be realized in different ways by different people. Given the variety of forms of mysticism in the history of Christianity, one is permitted to wonder if this is really the case.

A third area in which John of the Cross may be usefully compared with the broader mystical tradition is in his use of symbols and images.[142] A full study of John's symbols is not possible here, but it is worth noting that one of the major paradoxes in reading John of the Cross is the contrast between his rigorous program of stripping away every created image from the soul while at the same time creating a dense and compelling world of images and symbols—natural and artificial, erotic and evocative—first of all in his poetry, but also in his commentaries. However much the prose works seek to provide a detailed speculative analysis of the path to God, they cannot be detached from John's concrete symbols, which capture our attention while both revealing and concealing the mystery beyond corporeal reality and images.

Among John's traditional mystical images is that of the journey, both the journey along a horizontal path and the ascent, or journey above, as his first work, the *Ascent of Mount Carmel* with its famous diagram, shows. Ascensional symbolism is omnipresent in Christian mysticism, and John would have known many examples, such as Bernardino de Laredo's *Ascent of Mount Sion*, and probably Bonaventure's *Mind's Journey into God*. Nonetheless, as Balthasar noted, John's "criticism of all acts and habits places him far beyond these ways of ascent."[143] It is the leap of faith when all is abandoned that is essential for finding God. Indeed, a reading of the *Ascent* and the *Dark Night* shows that

John's references to ascending and climbing are less than we might expect (e.g., *Ascent* 2, 11, 9–10; 2, 18, 2; *Night* 2, 18, 1–2; 2, 19–20). Still, ascending and descending are important metaphors, as we see from the general principle announced in *Night* 2, 18, 3 (ed., 602; trans., 439): "The soul never remains in one state, but everything is ascent and descent [*sino todo es subir y bajar*]." Perhaps the most striking of John's presentations of the soul's ascent is found in the short poem transposing a popular love song into a spiritual picture of the pursuit of God ("Otras del mismo a lo divino").[144] Here the poet imagines himself as a hawk inspired by love hunting its unnamed prey (God) and compelled to fly ever higher and higher: "I went out seeking love, / and with unfaltering hope / I flew so high, so high, / that I overtook the prey." The flight takes place in darkness (stanza 2), and also, as is typical with the pursuit of God, it paradoxically involves lowering or abasing the self in order to fly higher (stanza 3). Stanza 4 concludes by saying that one such flight based on hope for heaven will surpass a thousand others and gain the divine prey. Nonetheless, the journey motif in John is not just ascensional. As earlier mystics insisted, "To go above is to go within,"[145] and one may say that, with John as with other mystics, the introvertive road into the depths of the soul cannot be separated from the path ascending toward God.[146]

Many other biblical and general symbols appear throughout John's writings. Some of these are taken from the world of human relations, such as his treatment of God as a loving mother,[147] and, of course, as ardent Bridegroom.[148] Other symbols come from the world of nature and were used by earlier mystics, such as the cloud (*Night* 2, 8, 1) and the desert.[149] Some of John's most frequent symbols are universal in human experience, for example, fire and water,[150] and especially light and darkness, as the title *The Dark Night* demonstrates.[151] John compares the whole process of mystical transformation to the passage from dusk, through deep midnight, to the light of the rising dawn (*Ascent* 1, 2, 5; 2, 2, 1–2; *Canticle* 14/15, 21–23).[152] He often uses particular light images, such as sunlight passing through a window,[153] or the supreme brightness of divine light encompassing but not extinguishing our created light (*Canticle* 26, 16). Fire images were particularly favored by the Carmelite. The *Living Flame of Love* shows that John found no more potent symbol for transformation into God than the fire of love, often illustrated with the example of the inert dark log of wood being gradually transformed by the power of fire until it too becomes a flame.[154] This mystical metaphor is found as early as Hugh of St. Victor, but Jean Orcibal has shown that John most likely adapted it from its more developed use in a sermon of John Tauler, which would have been available to him in Surius's Latin version of the *Opera Tauleri*.[155]

What is especially impressive about John of the Cross, however, is not just his use of individual mystical symbols and metaphors, but especially the way in which he builds up an entire world of images in his poems, adopting and subtly altering them for his purposes and then making them the subject of his prose analyses of mystical states. Speaking of the *Spiritual Canticle*, Colin Thompson summarizes:

> Images from nature and human art; images from biblical, classical, and Renaissance traditions; images of wide landscapes, of mountains, woods and rivers, plants and animals; images, many of which recur across the text, some of which point to the locus of the poem, others of which express the lovers' fear of disruptive elements and delight in each other's presence and beauty: all contribute to the creation of a world constituted of elements from the familiar world but arranged so that unexpected connections are made between them. In one sense, the fabric of the world is dismantled into its constituent parts, then rebuilt into new shapes.[156]

Given John of the Cross's reputation as a champion of negation, it is worth looking at one more traditional theme in the history of mysticism that John made his own—the category of the ineffable, that which cannot be understood or expressed. It may be helpful to distinguish between the objectively ineffable (i.e., the divine mystery in itself) and the subjectively ineffable (i.e., a person's attempt to describe her or his consciousness of God), though the two are obviously inseparable. John inherited many aspects of Dionysian objective apophatic theology, but he spends more time talking about the subjective inability of humans to convey consciousness of union with God. For example, in the Prologue to the *Spiritual Canticle* addressed to Mother Ana de Jesús, referred to above, John asks, "Who can describe in writing the understanding he gives to loving souls in whom he dwells? Who can express with words what he has given them to feel [*lo que las hace sentir*]? Who finally, can express the desires he imparts to them?"[157] In the *Dark Night* 2, 17, 3–4, he provides a more extended discussion of subjective ineffability. Identifying "dark and secret contemplation" with Dionysian "mystical theology," he says that such contemplation is secret not only because of our inability to understand it but also because of the effects it produces in the soul, that is, the person is both reluctant to talk about it and also unable to find a way to express it because it can be spoken of only in similes that hide its secret. He concludes, "The language of God has this trait: Since it is very spiritual and intimate to the soul, transcending everything sensory, it immediately silences the entire ability and harmonious composite of the exterior and interior senses."[158]

John experimented a good deal with the necessary but impossible task of saying the unsayable. One typical strategy he shares with other mystics is the creation of oxymora (e.g., "sweet burnings," "silent music," "dark light") in order to skew ordinary speech and suggest a new realm of knowing and loving.[159] Another procedure is creating neologisms that mark the place of God but do not have identifiable content. One of John's markers for ineffable communion with God is to speak of the "I-don't-know-what" behind the stammerings of those who have experienced God's presence (*un no sé qué que quedan balbuciendo*, "Canciones," stanza 7).[160] John so liked the expression *un no sé qué* that he made it the refrain for another of his short poems, the "Glosa a lo divino," that begins *"Por toda la hermosura."* The first stanza announces the motif explored throughout the poem of giving up the taste of everything created for the inexpressible delight of the divine "I-don't-know-what": "Not for all of beauty / will I ever lose myself, / but for I-don't-know-what / which is so gladly gained."[161] This apophatic formula, both poetic and speculative, once again testifies to the Carmelite's verbal creativity. It also highlights the paradox already mentioned regarding John: What goes beyond the senses and the intellect can be best, if inadequately, revealed in the concrete and sensual language of poetry.[162] Nonetheless, both poetry and prose remain suggestions, not declarations or final statements. Although John of the Cross was not a theorist of ineffable language, his was an insistent voice proclaiming our need for embracing "nothing"—*nada*—to which we now turn.

The Dialectic of Todo–Nada: Negation in John of the Cross

In the popular mind, John of the Cross is most frequently associated with negation—the dark night, annihilation of self, the insistence on *nada*. Few Christian mystics have a more developed doctrine of negativity than John, one that embraces negative language about God but that especially stresses the negation of desires and even the negativity of dereliction.[163] Nevertheless, it is in the dialectical relationship of *todo–nada*, everything and nothing, that the fullness of the Carmelite doctor's teaching emerges.[164] Letter 17 to the nun Magdalena del Espíritu Santo puts it in a nutshell: "To possess God in all, you should possess nothing in all. For how can a heart that belongs to one belong completely to the other?"[165] Better known are the formulations that John gives in *Ascent* 1, 13, 6–12 for entering into the dark nights, both active and passive. After providing nine counsels stressing the need always to choose not the easiest path but the most difficult (1, 13, 6), John says that to overcome both the sensory and the spiritual barriers to union with God illustrated in his diagram of the ascent of Mount Carmel it is necessary to realize that:

> To reach satisfaction in all (*todo*) / desire satisfaction in nothing (*nada*).
> To come to possess all / desire the possession of nothing.
> To arrive at being all / desire to be nothing.
> To come to the knowledge of all / desire the knowledge of nothing.

He then adds:

> To come to taste what you have not / you must go by a way where you taste not.
> To come to the knowledge you have not / you must go by the way you know not.
> To come to the possession you have not / you must go by the way you possess not.
> To come to be what you are not / you must go by the way in which you are not.

John concludes with the following summary of the dialectic of *todo/ nada*:

> When you delay over something [i. e., anything created] / you cease to rush towards the all [*al todo*]. To go from the all to the all / you must deny yourself of all in all [*del todo al todo*]. And when you come to the possession of the all / you must possess it without wanting anything, / because if you desire to have anything in having all, / you do not hold your treasure purely in God.[166]

These pregnant lines encapsulate John's dialectical message about the relation of the divine "All" and the created "nothing." The investigation of the *Ascent* and the *Dark Night* will help us better understand what the Carmelite had in mind with these challenging mystical aphorisms.

John, as said above, was an absolutist thinker—it is always all or nothing for him, or perhaps more accurately all *and* nothing. On a deep level, truly realizing and living *nada*, that is, the negation of our desire for creatures, is the only way to attain the *todo*, God as the goal of human life. The uncompromising mentality of an opposition that also seeks to effect a conjunction is both a great insight of the Spanish mystic and also the reason why some who have misunderstood the dialectic of his thought have dismissed him as hopelessly negative. Such absolutism seems to have been a part of John's temperament, but he found a good philosophical grounding for it in the law of contraries frequently cited in his works.[167] Aristotle had said that two contraries cannot exist in the same subject,[168] an axiom that John repeats often and that helps him ground his view of the need for total negation of the desire for created things. For example, in arguing for the necessity of passing through the dark night to attain union, he says, "The reason, as we learn in philosophy, is that two contraries cannot exist in the same subject. Darkness, an attachment to creatures, and light, which is God, are contraries and bear no likeness to each other."[169] He further explains in *Ascent* 1, 6, 1: "Since attachment to God and an attachment to creatures [*una afición de criatura*] are contraries, there cannot exist in the same will a voluntary attachment to creatures [*una voluntad afición de criatura*] and an attachment to God."[170] Because God is infinite and the creature finite there can be no proportion between the two (*Ascent* 2, 12, 4; 2, 24, 8; 3, 12, 1). Hence, hanging on to the least bit of what is created will mean that the Uncreated cannot take possession of the soul. John interpreted the law of contraries to mean that affection for God and affection for creatures were so opposed that any appetite or attraction to creatures had to be expunged, even annihilated, if true love of God was to find its place in the soul.[171] Nevertheless, contraries are not contradictories. As noted above, John distinguished between our natural appetites, good creations of God, and our voluntary appetites, toward which he was unrelentingly negative. Hence, perfect love for God, having driven out its contrary, can include a love for creatures, but it must be without "attachment."[172] Thus, there seem to be two ways to read John's persistent negative statements in the *Ascent* and the *Dark Night*—either as directed only to our selfish appetites or as aimed at a wider dissatisfaction with the whole human condition, with a view toward a transformation that he admits can only be attained by very few.[173]

The Four Nights

On the basis of the contrast between *todo y nada* rooted in the law of opposed contraries, John constructed his schema of the four nights.[174] The nights form a single multifaceted process of the purgation necessary to attain God, an ongoing battle between the contraries in the soul as the love of God progressively casts out selfish attachment.[175] As George Tavard puts it, "The principle of the mutual exclusion of contraries takes on a function that may be described as agonistic: it explains the sufferings of the night of the spirit as resulting by the struggle of two contraries."[176] As terrible as the nights are, especially the night of the spirit, we must remember that the process of intense mortification and inner suffering they involve is not suffering for the sake of suffering, but suffering necessary to attain the *todo* that is God and the proper relation to God's good creation.[177] In this sense, Balthasar suggests that it is perhaps better to speak of John of the Cross's "reduction" rather than "negation." He says, "Throughout all of John's works there runs a massive *negation*, or more precisely reduction. No created thing is God, and because every created thing has form, all forms must be surmounted and abandoned if the vision of God is to be possible."[178] It is also important to remember that God is not in reality absent in the midst of the dark nights; rather, he is present in the action of faith, hope, and charity, but present as hidden and burning away the false affection of the soul—the "refiner's fire" (Mal. 3:2–3).[179] To cite John J. Murphy, "God's presence is only realized with the recognition of God's absence. In this way, the concept of an infinite God is mediated in and through the limitations of a finite world."[180]

John introduces the nights in commenting on the opening stanza of "En una noche oscura." In order to depart from its "inordinate sensory appetites and imperfections," he says, "a soul must ordinarily pass through two principal kinds of night . . . in order to reach the state of perfection." He goes on, "Here we will term these purgations nights because in both of them the soul journeys in darkness as though by night." He then summarizes:

> The first night or purgation to which the stanza refers and which will be discussed in the first section of this book concerns the sensory part of the soul [the active night of the senses in *Ascent*, book 1]. The second night to which the second stanza refers concerns the spiritual part. We will deal with this second, insofar as it is active, in the second and third sections of the book [the active night of the spirit in *Ascent*, books 2 and 3]. In the fourth section we will discuss the night insofar as it is passive [passive night of the spirit in *Dark Night*, books 1–2].[181]

These nights form the subject matter of the double treatise *Ascent of Mount Carmel–Dark Night of the Soul.*

Iain Matthew points out that John conceives of the nights as the process of growth in prayer that involves three components: first, "an inflow of God," that is, God's entering into the soul; second, "darkness—that is, the suffering, with the accent on bewildered suffering"; and, third, "a creative response—faith, acceptance."[182] As the nights proceed from the active night in which the soul cooperates with divine grace to the passive night, these three components become more and more the work of God's operative grace alone: God flows in ever more powerfully; we passively receive ("suffer") this influx; and faith, which is God's work in us, grows darker and stronger.

There are a number of practices that John considers essential on the path of the nights and the progressive growth of union. Mortification, both internal and external, is a given for John, especially prominent in the active night of the senses. Active mortification, however, is far less important than humble submission to the internal mortification sent from God in the passive nights of sense and spirit. John was no fan of extreme works of penance: "The ignorance of some is extremely lamentable; they burden themselves with extraordinary penances and many other exercises, thinking that these are sufficient to attain union with divine Wisdom."[183] What is really needed is renunciation of desire, a message that is similar to that of Eckhart.

Among the exercises or practices that are essential for John is devotion to silence and, so far as possible, solitude. The importance of silence is rooted in the very nature of God. No. 100 of the *Sayings of Light and Love* says, "The Father spoke one Word, which was his Son, and this Word he speaks always in eternal silence, and in silence must it be heard by the soul."[184] In Letter 8 to the Carmelite nuns at Beas, he insists, "There is no better remedy than to suffer, to do, and to be silent, and to close the senses through the inclination toward and practice of solitude and forgetfulness of all creatures. . . . It is impossible to advance without doing and suffering virtuously, all enveloped in silence." He concludes with the aphorism, "Our greatest need is to be silent before this great God with the appetite and the tongue, for the only language he hears is the silent language of love."[185] It would be easy to collect many other passages throughout the commentaries that echo this teaching on the necessity of silence and solitude for all spiritual progress.[186]

Silence and solitude are often linked with another fundamental spiritual practice—recollection (*recogimiento*). Commenting on the third stanza of the "Flame" poem, John is at pains to advise his readers about the devil's distractions. "He consequently distracts it [the soul] very easily and draws it out of that solitude and recollection in which, as we have said, the Holy Spirit is bringing about those secret marvels."[187] John had read Bernardino de Laredo and other mystics who made *recogimiento* central to the mystical path. While he does not present a formal teaching on the nature and characteristics of recollection, the need for recollection is for him another way of expressing the importance of silence and solitude. For example, in *Ascent* 3, 40, 2, warning against the harm that comes from sensible gratification in the use of devotional objects and places, he says, "Should a soul become bound to the delight of sensory devotion, it will never succeed in passing on to the strength of spiritual delight, which is discovered through interior recollection in spiritual nakedness [*en la desnudez espiritual mediante el recogimiento interior*]."[188] Recollection begins in the active night of the spirit as the three faculties of intellect, memory, and will are gradually stilled, and it advances during the passive night to find its perfection in "the hiding place of interior recollection with the Bridegroom" (*Canticle* 40, 3). Recollection is always necessary for the advanced soul. In *Flame,* stanza 3, in the midst of his attack on the bad spiritual advisers who hinder advanced souls by insisting they go back to meditation, John says, "Once individuals . . . have reached the quiet recollection that every spiritual person pursues, in which the functioning of these faculties ceases, it would not merely be useless for them to repeat the acts of these same faculties in order to reach this recollection, but it would be harmful."[189]

John wrote mystical commentaries, not moral treatises, so throughout his works he presupposes the practice of the virtues, rather than discussing them in detail. Like many mystics, however, John often pointed out that the practice of humility, following the example of the humble Christ, was the bedrock of any progress toward union with God. John was especially worried about the spiritual pride and presumption that beginners might take in the gifts they receive, as is evident in book 2 of the *Ascent* (see chaps. 22–32) and in other places (e.g., *Ascent* 3, 9; *Night* 1, 2; 1, 12). As he summarized in the *Sayings of Light and Love,* "The humble are those who hide in their own nothingness and know how to abandon themselves to God."[190] Here humility becomes the focus of the whole Sanjuanist teaching.

John begins the *Ascent* by explaining why the journey toward God is called a "night." First, he says, night is the point of departure, that is, the depriving of ourselves of all our appetites is like a night for the senses; second, the road is the road of faith, "and for the intellect faith is also like a dark night." Third, the point of arrival, that is, God, "is also a dark night to the soul in this life."[191] Night and darkness are fundamental categories for John that capture, as best we can, the process of moving ever deeper into the divine mystery. As Edward Howells puts it, "Darkness is not any single experience but the ongoing experience of the one whose reality is infinitely deeper than one's experience, being open, especially in the inability to understand oneself fully, to what is wholly other."[192]

The remainder of book 1 deals with the first reason, that is, night as the mortification of the disordered sense appetites. The reasons for mortifying the appetites are multiple: from philosophy and theology (chap. 4), from the Bible (chap. 5), and from the various harms caused by the appetites (chaps. 6–12). It is not until chapter 11 that John makes the important distinction between the neutral *natural appetites* and the disordered *voluntary appetites* that qualifies some of the negative expressions of these sections of book 1. Then in chapter 13 John lays out the "Counsels on the manner and method for entering the dark night," that is, the dialectic of the all and nothing referred to above. At the end of book 1 (chaps. 14–15) the Carmelite provides a brief sketch of what he intends to cover in book 2, which will deal with the active night of the soul's spiritual part, that is, a treatise on faith as the dark way of progress to God.

The active night of the senses, while necessary, is only preparatory to the real work of purification, that is, the passive purging of the three powers of the spirit—intellect, memory, and will—by the supernatural gifts of faith, hope, and charity.[193] The "secret ladder" of the second stanza of "En una noche oscura" represents faith, because, as John claims, "All that is required for complete pacification of the spiritual house is the negation through pure faith of all the spiritual faculties and gratifications and appetites"[194] The goal is distant at this stage, since it will involve not only the soul's active cooperation with the divine influx of faith, hope, and charity (*Ascent*, books 2–3) but also the far more difficult passive purgation of the spiritual powers detailed in the *Dark Night*, books 1–2.

John of the Cross's theology of faith has attracted much attention and may even offer some comparison with that of his older contemporary, Martin Luther.[195] Both theologians put faith, conceived of as more than just an intellectual adherence to the formulas of belief, at the center of their thought. It would be a mistake to think that John's notion of faith as the purgation of the intellect is the same as Luther's notion of fiduciary faith as the anchor of salvation, but it cannot be denied that both thinkers rejected the narrow conceptualist version of faith as adherence to formulae of belief often present in late medieval theology.[196] What then is faith?[197] John begins book 2 (*Ascent* 2, 3, 1) with a reference to "School Theology," saying, "The theologians say that faith is a secure and obscure habit of soul ["*La fey dicen los teólogos que es un hábito del alma cierto y oscuro*"], [one that] brings us to believe divinely revealed truths that transcend every natural light and infinitely exceed all human understanding."[198] Thus, John agrees with Scholastics like Thomas Aquinas in holding that faith is a supernatural habit in the intellect (i.e., a perfection of the faculty in the order of operation), one that is directed to God. The Carmelite's interest, however, is not so much in the content of the habit, as in its certainty (*cierto*) and, above all, in its obscurity (*oscuro*). His attention focuses on the effect on the recipient, that is, on how the light of faith darkens all natural knowledge and replaces it with obscure knowing—"The light of faith in its abundance suppresses and overwhelms that of the intellect. For the intellect, by its own power, extends only to natural knowledge, though it has the potency to be raised to a supernatural act whenever our Lord wishes" (*Ascent* 2, 3, 1). John's view of faith is existential, not propositional.[199]

Once again, John thinks in terms of contraries and oppositions. Natural knowledge that comes through the senses is never proportioned to the supernatural faith that comes through hearing alone (*Ascent* 2, 3, 3). Hence, "[f]aith nullifies the light of the intellect," although paradoxically the darkness of faith is in reality the bright light of God, which the soul is too weak to behold in this life (2, 3, 4–5). "This knowledge is night to souls because they do not yet possess the clear beatific wisdom, and because faith blinds them as to their own natural light." John is consistent in his insistence on "leaning on dark faith" alone (2, 4, 2). All natural knowledge, and even supernatural communications that are not of the essence of faith, need to be rejected, because nothing we can know or taste of God, however great, is *really* like God (2, 4, 3 and 6). Naked belief in God's existence alone can lead to union (2, 4, 4)—faith is the necessary "means to union." John says that those who reach the state of absolute reliance on faith no longer have any "modes or methods" (*no tiene modos ni maneras*) of understanding, or tasting, or feeling, because they have passed beyond the natural world into the supernatural realm which possesses all modes and methods (2, 4, 5). A more extensive survey of what John has to say about faith in book 2 would demonstrate that faith is, indeed, a form of knowledge, but a new kind of knowledge for the soul, one that is passive and infused, obscure (in relation to us), loving, absorptive, and ineffable.

John of the Cross uses the following chapters of book 2 to draw out the implications of dark faith as the means, or path, to union. Chapter 5 features his first discussion of union,[200] which he delineates into total, transitory, and permanent union (2, 5, 1). At this stage he treats only total and permanent union, in both the substance and faculties of the soul, that is, what he calls "the obscure habit of union" (*hábito oscuro de unión*, 2, 5,2). There is a natural substantial union by which God dwells in every creature, but the object of John's attention is the supernatural union of loving likeness to God that is effected by stripping ourselves of all that is not God. "The person who has reached complete conformity and likeness of will," says John, "has attained total supernatural union and transformation into God" (2, 5, 4). John does not hesitate to use strong language about such union. God communicates his being to the soul so that "it will appear to be God himself and will possess what God himself possesses" (*que parece el mismo Dios y tiene lo que tiene el mismo Dios*). The Carmelite qualifies this by appealing to the example of sunlight (i.e., God's communication of himself) passing through a perfectly clear window (i.e., the soul):

> When God grants this supernatural favor to the soul, so great a union is caused that all the things of both God and the soul become one in participant transformation [*en transformación participante*], and the soul appears to be God more than the soul. Indeed, it is God by participation. Yet truly its being (even though transformed) is naturally as distinct from God's as it was before, just as the window, although illuminated by the ray, has being distinct from the ray's.[201]

The soul, then, *appears* to be God; it is God, *but by participation*. Its substance remains its own. This was John's constant teaching, however strong his union language was at times.

Chapter 6 summarizes the structure of books 2 and 3 of the *Ascent* as comprising the purgation of the three powers of the spirit—"We shall explain how in order to journey to God the intellect must be perfected in the darkness of faith, the memory in the emptiness of hope, and the will in the nakedness and absence of every affection."[202] Chapter 7 emphasizes that "this supreme nakedness and emptiness of spirit" are essentially christological. Citing a range of Gospel texts, John says that true following of Christ demands total purification and annihilation. Those who have a "spiritual sweet tooth" will bask in enjoyment in God, but that was not Christ's way of abnegation and the cross. He makes an original distinction here: "Seeking oneself in God is the same as looking for the caresses and consolations of God. Seeking God in oneself entails not only the desire to do without these consolations for God's sake, but also the inclination to choose for the love of Christ all that is most distasteful whether in God or in the world; and this is what loving God means."[203] Finally, chapters 8–9 flesh out why supernatural faith alone, not any creature or natural knowledge, is proportionate to God and therefore the way to union.[204] Paradoxically, the intellect advances by unknowing rather than knowing,[205] by remaining in blindness and darkness rather than opening its eyes (2, 8, 5). Citing Dionysius on the ray of divine darkness (MT 1, 1), he says, "Contemplation by which the intellect has a higher knowledge of God is called mystical theology, meaning the secret wisdom of God."[206]

These introductory chapters to *Ascent* 2 provide a key to John's thought. What follows in chapters 10–32 is an example of the thoroughgoing approach of the Carmelite. It is interesting for a detailed study of his mysticism, though sometimes tedious to the modern reader. John considers the relation between the forms of intellectual apprehensions (natural and supernatural) and the way of dark faith, beginning with the distinction of intellectual apprehensions into natural and supernatural (chap. 10). It is obvious from what John said in the earlier chapters that no natural apprehensions are useful in moving toward God, but what is perhaps surprising about these chapters is his resistance to so many forms of supernatural communication—be they sense apparitions (chap. 11), imaginative visions or locutions (chaps. 16–22), or even intellectual apprehensions (chaps. 23–32), which he believes can lead us away from the path of dark faith.[207] "The eyes of the soul," says John, "should ever be withdrawn from distinct, visible, and intelligible apprehensions" (2, 16, 12). Later in book 3 he sums up his suspicions of most special mystical experiences: "All heavenly visions, revelations, and feelings [even presumably the licit ones]—or whatever else one may desire to think on—are not worth as much as the least act of humility."[208] Books 2 and 3 of the *Ascent* are among the most detailed treatments of mystical gifts in the history of Christian mysticism, but what is striking is John's rejection of any form of communication, whether truly from God or from the devil masquerading as "the angel of light," which would impinge on the dark way of faith. What John presents here casts doubt on large aspects of earlier Christian mystical traditions (including Teresa's) with their emphasis on visionary and other unusual manifestations of God.[209]

For the Carmelite doctor, it is vitally important to recognize the signs for when the soul is meant to move from meditation, with its discursive and imaginative emphasis, to the obscure loving knowledge of God that is contemplation. Chapter 14 discusses three signs for this development. The first is that a person has already gained all the spiritual good found in meditation (*Ascent* 2, 14, 1), and the second is that meditation with the knowledge and love of God it grants has become habitual in the soul. This growing familiarity with God allows the transition from the particular and distinct ideas of God found in meditation to the third sign, the beginning of "knowledge or general awareness of God that is loving" (*la noticia o advertencia general en Dios y amorosa*, 2, 14, 6). John says that this happens "[t]he moment the soul recollects itself in the presence of God and enters into an act of general, loving, peaceful, and tranquil knowledge, drinking wisdom and delight and love."[210] While the proficients who are in the second stage of the journey to God will continue to make use of both meditation and contemplation (2, 15, 1–5), John thinks that perfect souls will no longer require discursive meditation.

Book 3 of the *Ascent* deals with the active purgation of the memory through the virtue of hope and of the will by charity. John distinguishes three objects of memory—natural, imaginative, and spiritual—and hence three kinds of knowing (3, 1, 2). The purging of the natural apprehensions of memory is treated in chapters 2–6, and the purging of the supernatural imaginative apprehensions in chapters 7–13. Chapters 14–15 concern the memory of the spiritual apprehensions of the intellect. As pointed out in the discussion of memory above, John did not consider memory a depository of past images and apprehensions, but rather the faculty to direct attention to the various images found in the interior sense, the fantasy.

Ascent 3, 2 offers John the opportunity for a defense of his program of stripping and annihilating the faculties against the objections of an anonymous critic. In response to someone who might say that the destruction of the natural operations of the faculties begun in his treatment of faith is a tearing down of what is naturally good, John responds that he is writing for contemplatives, not for everybody (3, 2, 2). He also insists that for those who wish to attain union "the soul must journey by knowing God through what he is not rather than through what he is; it must journey, insofar as possible, by way of denial and rejection of the natural and supernatural apprehensions." John now applies this negative way to the memory, which he says must withdraw its attention from all the particular forms and images stored in the fantasy and direct itself to "supreme hope in the incomprehensible God."[211] Since God cannot be encompassed by any form or distinct knowledge, the memory must forget *all* forms—both natural and supernatural imaginative forms (i.e., the images given supernaturally in visions, revelation, locutions, etc.). According to John, the soul must be prepared to enter into a state of oblivion so great that at times "the whole head swoons and consciousness and sensibility are lost and it has to struggle to remember anything" (3, 2, 5). (This sounds like a personal witness.) John proceeds with an important discussion of this oblivion in relation to his teaching on union. These states of suspension, and even insensibility, particularly when caused by what John terms "touches of union," affect souls at the beginning of the unitive stage (3, 2, 6), not at its conclusion: "Yet once the habit of union—which is a supreme good—is attained, one no longer experiences these lapses of memory concerning the moral and natural life. Rather, such persons will possess greater perfection in actions that are fitting and necessary" (3, 2, 8). Just as he taught with regard to union in *Ascent* 2, 5, 4–7, John says that, when habitual union has been attained, the operations of the memory become divine and are not different from those of God— "they are transformed into divine being" (*pues están transformadas en ser divino*, 3, 2, 9). While God alone can bring this state about in the passive night of the spirit, the contemplative must do what is in him or her to prepare for the higher grace—"In the measure that they enter into this negation and emptiness of form through their own efforts, they will receive from God the possession of union."[212]

Most of the discussion in chapters 3–13 of book 3 concerns the various harms that come to the soul from not giving up memories of natural apprehensions, as well as supernatural imaginative ones. The souls must rather enter "the abyss of faith [and hope], where all else is absorbed" (3, 8, 2). The case is different with regard to the apprehensions of spiritual knowledge, which are given directly by God without any form or image (*Ascent* 2, 26). These apprehensions do not reside in the sensory fantasy but are remembered through a form imprinted on the soul or by its effect (3, 14, 1). When these pertain to God himself, the soul remembers them through recalling the effects of "touches and feelings of union," such as light, love, and spiritual renewal (3, 14, 2). Finally, in *Ascent* 3, 15, John gives his paradoxical summary of the action of hope. "Our aim," he says, "is union with God in the memory through hope; the object of hope is something unpossessed; the less other objects are possessed, the more capacity and ability there is to hope for this one object, and consequently the more hope." In this life we can never fully possess God, but "in the measure that individuals dispossess their memory of forms and objects, which are not God, they will fix it on God and preserve it empty, so as to hope for the fullness of their memory from him."[213]

John then turns to charity and its action on the will (*Ascent* 3, 16–42). All three supernatural virtues unite the soul with God, but charity's purgation of the will from its disordered emotions and false affections culminates the unifying process. The four emotions of the will (*afecciones de la voluntad*) are the traditional natural passions/emotions—joy, hope, sorrow, and fear. John once again insists that these all must go: "The entire matter of reaching union with God consists in purging the will of its appetites and emotions [*sus afecciones y apetitos*] so that from a human and lowly will it may be changed into the divine will, made identical with God."[214] The principle is clear; the actual exploration of how to purge the *afecciones* is long, often meandering, and finally abandoned. Fortunately, the positive role of charity in bringing the soul to union with God was to be amply developed later in the *Canticle* and the *Flame*.

John plunges into a long treatment of how the soul must rid itself of the five active sources of the first emotion, that is, the *joy* received from creatures (chaps. 17–33).[215] He then turns to the sixth source of joy, the passive joys found in spiritual goods, that is, the graces directly related to God (chaps. 33–44). Here (*Ascent* 3, 33, 3–5) John makes a distinction between (1) *delightful spiritual goods*, which can be either *clear* or *obscure,* and (2) *painful spiritual goods,* again both of a *clear* and of an *obscure* nature. The painful spiritual goods will be discussed under the passive night of the spirit (*Night* 2), while the clear and distinct spiritual goods are to be treated at this point.[216] Chapter 35, 1 distinguishes four kinds of clear and delightful spiritual goods (motivating, provocative, directive, and perfective). John begins a discussion of the motivating spiritual goods, which he identifies with the "statues, paintings of saints, oratories, and ceremonies" designed to inspire devotion to and reverence for the saints. The chapters devoted to this topic (chaps. 36–44) concern the proper use of sacred images in the context of John's radical denial of the use of all forms, external and internal, on the path to God. This section represents John's somewhat tortured attempt to deal with images in a mysticism where they would seem to have little place.[217] Some critics have surmised that these chapters contain a number of later interpolations designed to bring the Carmelite closer to the Post-Tridentine affirmation of the importance of religious images and iconography.[218] In any case, John abruptly gave up the writing of the *Ascent of Mount Carmel* after a brief chapter (3, 45) introducing the "provocative" spiritual gift of preaching.

In theory, John's double treatise carefully divides the active night of the *Ascent* from the passive night of the *Dark Night*; in practice there is much overlap between the two parts. The *Night* is shorter, tighter, and more challenging, because the passive night, in which the soul surrenders itself totally to God's action, is more terrible than the active purgations where *we* cooperate with God. Here, everything is in God's hands, and the soul will often feel that God is a divine torturer, extracting pain and suffering from the human subject. Mystical negation as the experience of desolation and dereliction was not invented by John of the Cross but was a tradition with deep biblical roots (Job, and Jesus in the passion). Mystics since Gregory the Great had spoken of it, and it was found among many late medieval mystics, both women and men. Still, John's *Dark Night* remains the best known treatment of mystical dereliction in Christian history.

Because the Carmelite focuses so much on the inner experience of the mystic, there have been comparisons made between his accounts of the passive dark night, especially in book 2 of the *Night*, and contemporary discussions of the disintegration of the self, such as in psychological depression.[219] Was John a depressive? The Carmelite certainly testifies to the wrenching pains of the destruction of his pre-union identity in the crucible of the passive night of the spirit, but he was at pains to distinguish what God does in the dark night from the "melancholia" that was the sixteenth-century equivalent of much modern mental illness, including depression (see *Ascent*, Prol. 4–6; 2, 13, 6; *Night* 1, 4, 3). John thought intense mental and even physical suffering was an aspect of the purgative process necessary to produce the new "mystical self." One thing seems clear: John of the Cross was scarcely a depressed and ineffective person for the last fifteen years of his life, whatever form of depression he might have undergone in his experience of imprisonment.

The key difference between the active and the passive nights of the spirit is not so much in the supernatural gifts of faith, hope, and charity, already at work in the active night, as in the fact that the soul loses its sense of *cooperating* with God in the emptying process and is placed in a situation where it has no control or activity, where its efforts mean nothing, and where God does with the soul what he wills, even seemingly sending it to hell. *Night* 2, 3, 3 encapsulates this grim message: "He leaves the intellect in darkness, the will in aridity, the memory in emptiness, and the affections in supreme affliction, bitterness, and anguish by depriving the soul of the feeling and satisfaction it had previously obtained from spiritual blessings" (ed., 570; trans., 399). The last phrase is significant: in the passive night there is no joy in spiritual things, only pain and suffering. "Whatever is received is received according to the mode of the receiver," a Scholastic adage that John quoted,[220] meant for him that any spiritual gift we receive, however exalted, will be proportional to our limited being; so, for example, divine brilliance will be perceived as darkness. It is only in such "pure and dark contemplation" (*Night* 2, 3, 3), however, that we are given real contact with God. This contact is not clear but obscure; it is now limited but potentially infinite; it is not intellectually cognitive but provides the loving unknowing in which we can find the hidden God (Isa. 45:15).

Book 1 of the *Dark Night*, dealing with the passive night of the senses, prefaces a treatment (chaps. 1–7) of the imperfections found in beginners from the action of the seven deadly spiritual sins (pride, avarice, lust, anger, gluttony, sloth, and envy).[221] The second part of the book (chaps. 8–14) begins the exposition of what is meant by the *noche oscura* of the first line of the poem. In chapter 8, 1, John says, "The sensory night is common and happens to many. . . . The spiritual night is the lot of very few, those who have been tried and are proficient." The passive night of the senses treated in *Night* 1, 8–14 is the realm of the proficient souls and therefore overlaps with the active night of the spirit discussed in books 2–3 of the *Ascent* (they are two sides of the same process). Book 2 of the *Night* will treat the perfect in their progress through the passive night of the spirit.

When the soul enters into aridity and no longer feels any satisfaction in spiritual practices, the cause may be either the beginner's continuing imperfections, or it may be a sign of God's interior action moving the soul to the level of the proficient. John gives three signs for determining if it is God who is at work. The first (*Night* 1, 9, 2) is that the soul gets no consolation either from the things of God or from creatures. "The second sign . . . ," he says, "is that the memory ordinarily turns to God solicitously and with painful care, and the soul thinks that it is not serving God but turning back, because it is aware of this distaste for the things of God" (1, 9, 3). John goes on at some length about how the sensory part of the soul is much weakened as God transfers his gifts to the spiritual part, which, however, is not yet sufficiently purged to taste them. The food that God is giving the soul "is the beginning of a contemplation that is dark and dry to the senses. Ordinarily this contemplation is hidden from the very one who receives it" (1, 9, 6).

The third sign (1, 9, 8) is the inability to meditate and to use the imagination, which John says will be continuous. (These three signs parallel the three marks for discontinuing the practice of meditation in *Ascent* 2, 13, 2–4.) Souls who have entered into the passive night of the senses in which the spirit is also still being *actively* cleansed by faith, hope, and charity need patience and perseverance in prayer, and, above all, freedom from "ideas and thoughts," "thinking and meditating" (*Night* 1, 10, 4). John sees this stage as the beginning of what he calls for the first time "infused contemplation" (*contemplación infusa*), which he memorably defines: "Contemplation is nothing else than a secret and powerful and loving inflow of God, which, if not hampered, fires the soul in the spirit of love."[222]

At this stage John returns to the exegesis of the poem "En una noche oscura" as a guide, explaining the first three verses of stanza 1 in chapter 11, tying them to what he has already expounded. The benefits of this sensory dark night are dual: knowledge of oneself and one's own misery, and the corresponding knowledge of God's grandeur and majesty (chap. 12). Other benefits of the passive night of the senses include the cleansing of the imperfections of the seven spiritual sins and the freedom of spirit to begin to acquire the twelve fruits of the Holy Spirit (chap. 13), although John notes that there are also particular forms of temptation that can assail the soul in this stage (chap. 14). Therefore, the passive night of the senses is a kind of analogue to the active purgation of the spirit described in books 2–3 of the *Ascent*.

What follows in book 2 of the *Dark Night* is original, as John already noted. He begins by observing that, after spending many years in the state of proficients with "much more freedom and satisfaction of spirit" (*Night* 2, 1, 1),[223] God may decide to lead some souls on to the ultimate purgation, "the coming night of the spirit." Here both the habitual and the actual imperfections of even the proficients must be purged in order to attain union with God (2, 2, 1). This "complete purification" affects the two parts of the soul (the whole human supposit). God purifies all the soul's powers, inner and outer, sensory and spiritual. According to John, "He leaves the intellect in darkness, the will in aridity, the memory in emptiness, and the affections in supreme affliction, bitterness, and anguish by depriving the soul of the feeling and satisfaction it had previously obtained from spiritual blessings."[224] There are many terms to describe this process, ones that John uses frequently throughout his writings. He employs some of them here, calling the complete purification a "contemplative purgation or nakedness and poverty of spirit" (*purgación contemplativa o desnudez y pobreza de espíritu, Night* 2, 4, 1).[225] He also refers to "the annihilation and calming of the powers, passions, appetites and affections of my soul" (*de aniquilarse y sosegarse las potencias, pasiones, apetitos y afecciones de mi alma*, 2, 4, 2). John often spoke of the annihilation of the soul and its powers.[226] Christ on the cross at the moment of his death crying out, "My God, my God, why have you forsaken me?" (Matt. 27:46), is the model of John's view of annihilation. Christ had been abandoned by all—his human nature was "annihilated" in death, and, what is more, "he was forsaken by his Father at that time, annihilated and reduced to nothing [*así anihilado y resuelto así como en nada*], so as to pay the debt [of sin] fully and bring people to God."[227] Only the person who is prepared to undergo a similar annihilation through the experience of being abandoned by God in the dark night of the spirit can gain the loving union that is a proleptic sharing in Christ's resurrection. Annihilation is not the destruction of the soul as a created reality but rather a total emptying of the interior content of the soul in order to let God in. Stanza 26 of the *Canticle* puts it well: "[T]his inflaming of the heart is a change of the soul according to her operations and appetites into God, into a new kind of life in which she is undone and annihilated [*deshecha y aniquilada*] before all the old things she formerly made use of. . . . Not only is all her old knowing annihilated, seeming to her to be nothing, but her old life and imperfections are annihilated, and she is renewed in the new self [Col. 3:10]."[228]

The Carmelite next turns to an analysis of the afflictions that the three higher powers of intellect, will, and memory undergo in this final purgation (*Night* 2, 5–8). "This dark night is an inflow of God into the soul . . . which contemplatives call infused contemplation or mystical theology" (2, 5, 1). It both purges and illuminates the soul, darkening it because divine wisdom exceeds the soul's powers and causing affliction and torment in the soul because of its remaining impurities (2, 5, 2). John is deadly serious about the soul's torment—"persons feel so unclean and wretched that it seems that God is against them and they are against God" (2, 5, 5); and "they suffer so much in their weakness that they almost die" (2, 5, 6). In line with some late medieval mystics, John says that the conviction that God has abandoned them is a "heavy affliction" for the soul (2, 6, 2). "Sometimes this experience is so vivid," he continues, "that it seems to the soul that it sees hell and perdition open before it." This purgation on earth is similar to what takes place in hell.[229] Similar afflictions beset both the will (2, 7) and the memory (2, 8). Although souls in this state continue to love God, "they are unable to believe that God loves them" (2, 7, 7). The greater the light, the deeper the darkness and suffering: "The more simply and purely the divine light strikes the soul, the more it darkens and empties and annihilates it in its particular apprehensions and affections concerning both earthly and heavenly things" (2, 8, 2). Nonetheless, darkness and suffering are not the goal, but only the necessary means to attain the "general freedom of spirit" of the children of God (2, 9, 1).[230] After the purging and annihilation of the intellect, memory, and will through what John calls "substantial darkness [*tinieblas sustanciales*], since it is felt in the substance of the soul" (9, 3), the soul will become pure, simple, purged, "and ready to feel [*sentir*] the sublime and marvelous touches of divine love" (9, 3).

In chapter 10, John invokes his favorite analogy for the spiritual purgative process, the fire that transforms a log into itself, noting seven points to be learned from the example (2, 10, 2–9). This reminds him to return to the poem, so the concluding chapters of book 2 (11–25) offer a digressive commentary on the remaining verses of stanza 1 and the whole of stanza 2 of "En una noche oscura." Verse 2 ("Fired with love's urgent longings") refers to the enkindling of the dark fire of love in the spiritual part of the soul (2, 11, 1). This fire bestows "the wound of love," an important theme in the history of mysticism and also for John. The wounding or touch of love is a gradual process. When it is first felt, the soul is still in darkness and doubt (2, 11, 5), but in the midst of these doubts and fears, divine love is enflaming it with the loving wound and providing it with "a certain companionship and an interior strength" (2, 11, 7). Although the night resembles purgatory (2, 12, 1), in this purgation contemplation infuses love into the will and wisdom into the intellect, uniting them by "a certain touch of divinity and already the beginning of the perfection of the union of love for which the soul hopes" (2, 12, 6). In chapter 13, John has an interesting discussion of the relation of will and intellect in the ongoing purification of the soul (note that memory is not discussed). Sometimes mystical knowledge is given to the intellect, while the will remains in dryness (2, 13, 1), and sometimes contemplation acts on both faculties equally (13, 2). More often, the burning in the will is felt rather than the touch in the intellect. This is because burning love is more a passion (i.e., a reception from God) than an act of the will itself, and this reception can be assisted by the human passions themselves in the feeling of "impassioned love" (*amor impasionado*).[231]

Exegeting the last three lines of stanza 1 ("Ah the sheer grace! / I went out unseen, / my house being now stilled") allows John to emphasize the need for silence and solitude in undergoing the action of the dark night (2, 14), before turning to stanza 2, which reprises the darkness theme. "In darkness, and secure" (v. 1) refers to the total darkening and sleep of all the sensory and spiritual appetites and faculties, as John explains in the long chapter 16. Chapter 17 says, "The secret ladder, disguised" (v. 2) refers to the ladder of contemplation, or mystical theology, which hides the soul within it and cannot be communicated. John has a section here (2, 17, 6) on the "secret abyss," "deep and vast wilderness," and "unbounded desert" of such mystical wisdom. This secret wisdom is also a ladder by which we ascend to the high knowledge of God, while at the same time we descend in growing humility (2, 18, 1–3).[232] The "disguised" character of the soul in this night is read as the three garments that cover the soul and hide her from her three enemies—the devil, the world, and the flesh. While she is being purified, the white inner tunic of faith blinds the intellect (2, 21, 4–5); the green coat of mail signifying hope gives the soul courage and valor (21, 6–9); and the precious red toga of charity elevates the soul near God (21, 10–12).

The last chapters of Book 2 of the *Dark Night* take up the final verses of stanza 2 and give a brief explanation of stanza 3. "In darkness and concealment" again speaks to the soul's concealment from the activity of the devil (chap. 23).[233] Concealment, however, also refers to the hiddenness of the soul necessary for receiving the highest spiritual gifts. The secret and intimate communications between God and the soul are described as "all substantial touches of divine union between God and the soul."[234] "In one of these touches," continues John, "since this is the highest degree of prayer, the soul receives greater good than all else" (2, 23, 11). Next (2, 23, 12) John turns to the Song of Songs and the bride's bold request, "Let him kiss me with the kiss of the mouth" (Song 1:1) to illustrate the substantial touches the soul receives when it has attained true freedom of spirit. These touches take place in the higher spiritual part of the soul, which, at this stage, is so withdrawn from the sensory part that there is no communication between them (23, 14). (John does not say so here, but we can presume that this is the state of spiritual betrothal.) Finally, "My house being now all stilled" refers to the perfect reformation, pacification, and reordering of both the spiritual and sensory parts of the soul (2, 24, 1–2). This is the stage of spiritual marriage (where the spiritual and sensory parts will be reunited). John does not explain this here, leaving it to the *Spiritual Canticle* and the *Living Flame of Love*.[235]

Transformation and Loving Union: The Flame

The fact that John of the Cross ended the *Dark Night* with a nod to the marriage of the soul with God indicates that his other two commentaries are necessary to give a full account of his mystical teaching. Although the interconnections of the prose works mean that much of what John had to say about the higher stages of union were at least adumbrated in the *Ascent-Night*, many important issues still remained to be analyzed. The *Spiritual Canticle* and the *Living Flame* are more truly commentaries than the earlier works—John explains his poems image by image, albeit with many digressions. Both in the *Canticle*, with its dialogue of Divine Lover and bride, and in the *Flame*, with its ecstatic love-language, John seems to have found a more apt way of presenting his message about union than through the sometimes scholastic "arborizations" (i.e., constant subdivisions) of the *Ascent* and even the *Night*.

Spiritual Canticle

The *Spiritual Canticle* is a meta-commentary on a poem (properly called the "Canciones entre el Alma y el Esposo"), which is itself both a commentary on and a re-creation of what was traditionally a founding narrative of Christian mysticism, the biblical Song of Songs.[236] The fact that John of the Cross chose to write his own Song of Songs, although in constant dialogue with the biblical original, is one of the marks of his boldness and originality. Like the Song, the "Canciones" is elusive and open-ended, featuring shifting voices and often dreamlike scenes and images.[237] Both poems invite multiple readings and interpretations, none of which can be final. In the "Prologue" to his interpretation in the *Canticle* John himself admits this—"Though we give some explanation of these stanzas, there is no reason to be bound to this explanation." While I cannot give a full analysis of the interrelation of the Song of Songs and the "Canciones," I hope to reflect on how John uses some of the Song's images, transforming them for his own purposes.[238] John does not explicitly reflect on how he transposed the Song, but one can surmise that he was convinced (as were mystics like Eckhart) that the person to whom God had given access to the divine source of holy writ was free to refashion it in a new context without altering its basic message.

The poem underwent an evolution in tandem with the two versions of the commentary.[239] The "Canciones" developed in three stages. The first (CO) consisted of the thirty-one stanzas John wrote in prison, which he reworked between 1579 and 1584 by adding eight new stanzas (CA). The first, or A, version of his *Spiritual Canticle* treatise was a commentary on this poem. Between 1584 and 1586 John added one more stanza but also changed the order of the stanzas to produce the full forty-stanza poem (CB), which was the subject of the longer B version of the *Spiritual Canticle*. Like the Song of Songs, the "Canciones" can be described in Origen's words as "an epithalamium, that is to say, a marriage-song."[240] The dramatic structure features an interplay of voices, with the bride speaking in thirty-two stanzas, the Bridegroom in seven (stanzas. 13, 20–23, 34–35), and the voice of the creatures only in stanza 5. The speeches are also directed to other audiences, some silent. The bride mostly speaks to the Bridegroom (stanzas 1, 6–11, 14–16, 19, 24–33, 36–40), but also to the shepherds (stanzas 2–3), the creatures of nature (stanzas 4, 17), the crystalline fount (stanza 12), and the nymphs of Judea (stanza 18). The poem presents an ongoing dynamic of desire and eager searching leading to encounter and union, one that captures the elusive presence and absence of the Divine Lover. It is one of the premier examples of what is often called "bridal mysticism."

In the "Theme" introducing the *Canticle* treatise, John says that the poem refers to the three states or ways of spiritual exercise, the initial stanzas dealing with the state of beginners, the subsequent ones with the illuminative way of the proficients and spiritual betrothal, then the unitive way of the perfect, and finally some stanzas dealing with the beatific vision.[241] This enables the Carmelite to connect his poem to a traditional account of mystical progress, but one can wonder if such a straitjacket does full justice to the subtlety and suggestiveness of the individual stanzas and the way they deal with the ever-shifting game of love.

Stanza 1 provides a good example. The bride calls out to her absent lover: "Where can your hiding be, / Beloved, that you left me thus to moan / While like the stag you flee / Leaving the wound with me? / I followed calling loud, but you had flown."[242] The bride yearns for the absent lover, but she has already been wounded by him, thus indicating previous reception of high mystical graces. John says that the bride suffers from the love that has caused her to go out from all creatures and herself (another advanced mystical state), and this will always be the case until she enjoys "the manifest presence and vision of his divine essence . . . in the next life."[243] Thus, there seems to be a circular character to the pursuit of the Bridegroom, which is what the game of love portrayed in the Song of Songs indicates. The first three stanzas reprise many themes found in the *Ascent–Dark Night* about finding the hidden God in dark faith (e.g., 1, 11–12) and the divine touches and wound of love (1, 15–22), as well as the role of intellect, memory, and will in God's absence (2, 6–7). The "shepherds" addressed in stanza 2 are both the desires and affections that draw the soul to God and the angels who serve as messengers between the divine and human realms.

If the first three stanzas deal with the soul's self-knowledge as an impetus for seeking God, as John says (4, 1), stanzas 4–6 turn to seeking God in creation. The bride addresses the woods and thickets, the green meadow and its flowers, asking, "Tell me, has he passed you by?" She asks both earth and heaven to reveal where her Beloved has gone. While these creatures can disclose traces of God's grandeur and excellence, their revelatory power cannot equal "the greater works, . . . the Incarnation of the Word and the mysteries of the Christian faith" (*Canticle* 5, 3). Nevertheless, the soul must continue seeking, because these inferior communications are mere messengers, not the Beloved himself. So, she boldly asks in stanza 6, "Ah, who has the power to heal me? / now wholly surrender yourself! / Do not send me / any more messengers. . . ."[244]

The narrative then shifts in the following four stanzas (Nos. 7–10) to verses about the wound of love and the necessity of knowing God by not knowing. Once again, these mystical themes go beyond what would be experienced by beginners. The soul is wounded by the knowledge she receives both from irrational creatures and from rational creatures, none of whom really discloses God, leaving the soul dying of "An I-don't-know-what behind their stammering" (*Un no sé que quedan balbuciendo*, "Canciones" 7, line 5). This phrase, as we have seen, points to the ineffable divine reality hinted at by the created universe, but infinitely beyond it. In commenting on stanza 7, John distinguishes three forms of "wounding" based on three ways of knowing the Beloved (*Canticle* 7, 2–4): (1) the simple wound arising from the knowledge the soul receives from creatures; (2) the sore wound of faith produced by the knowledge of the incarnation and the other mysteries of belief; and, finally, (3) the "festered wound" (*llaga afistolada*) in which the soul lives by dying after receiving "a touch of the supreme knowledge of the divinity," that is, the "I-don't-know-what." Again, we are not on the level of beginners, as the further comments on the wound of love in the expositions of stanzas 8–10 indicate. These stanzas are rich with the personal appeals of the wounded soul asking the Divine Lover for healing (*Canticle* 9–10), though the wounds are both painful and sweet.

The wound of love was an ancient topos in Christian mysticism, but John of the Cross expands on it in ways not found previously.[245]

The final stanzas of what is supposedly describing the state of beginners (*Canticle* 11–12) are also concerned with those to whom advanced spiritual gifts have already been given but who now burn with desire for more. The bride-soul asks the Bridegroom to "reveal his presence" and slay her with love, because love's sickness cannot be cured in any other way (11, 2). The comment on this stanza is another analysis of God's presence by spiritual affection even when the soul is suffering from "the sickness of love." This sickness is both presence and absence: "In this spiritual sense of his presence he revealed some deep glimpses of his divinity and beauty by which he greatly increased her fervor and desire to see him."[246] The desire for further experience of the divine beauty is highlighted in the second line of "Canciones," stanza 11: "And may the vision of your beauty be my death" (*Y máteme tu vista y hermosura*). John comments, "She knows that the instant she sees this beauty she will be carried away by it, and absorbed in this very beauty, and transformed in this beauty, and made beautiful like this beauty itself, and enriched and provided for like this beauty."[247] Citing an adage from Bernard of Clairvaux that the soul lives more where it loves than where it gives life,[248] John says the soul's true life and health are not here on earth but in heaven with the Bridegroom. "The love of God is the soul's health, and the soul does not have full health until love is complete [i.e., in heaven]" (11, 11). The Carmelite concludes this long commentary by noting that "love never reaches perfection until the lovers are so alike that one is transfigured in the other" (11, 12).

Stanza 12 returns to the theme of faith, comparing enlightened faith with a "crystalline fount" (*cristalina fuente*), which provides a reflection of the Beloved but not the full vision: "If only on your silvered-over faces, / you would suddenly form / the eyes I have desired, / which I bear sketched deep within my heart."[249] Faith is like a spring of water nourishing the soul (John 4:14 and 7:39 are cited) and also a crystal because its truths are clear and certain. The propositions and articles of faith are "silvered-over faces" concealing the gold of divinity (12, 3–4). In this life the "eyes" of the divine truths are sketched out by obscure faith and love deep within the intellect and will (12, 6). The sketch drawn by love is so intimate and vivid in the will "that it is true to say that the Beloved lives in the lover and the lover in the Beloved." John goes on, "The reason is that in the union and transformation of love each gives possession of the self to the other and each leaves and exchanges the self for the other, . . . and both are one in the transformation of love."[250] John concludes this account of union by citing Paul's text, "I live now not I, but Christ lives in me" (Gal. 2:20), noting that even the highest form of transformation of love found in this life, that is, the "spiritual marriage" (*matrimonio espiritual*), is still but a foretaste of the full painting that will come in heaven (12, 8).

Stanzas 13–19 of the "Canciones" deal with the second stage in the spiritual life, the illuminative way of the proficient, but they also circle back to considerations of the purificatory suffering discussed in book 2 of the *Dark Night*. The illuminative stage features intense purification and the beginnings of mystical gifts, such as rapture, which are characteristic of spiritual betrothal (*desposorio espiritual*).[251] Introducing stanza 13 John says, "The reason the soul suffers so intensely for God at this time is that she is drawing nearer to him; so she has greater experience within herself of the void of God (*el vacío de Dios*), of the very heavy darkness, and of the spiritual fire that dries up and purges her so that thus purified she may be united to him."[252] The language of "the void of God" is not to be taken as an apophatic marker, as if John were speaking about God as a void, or "nothing" (*nihil*); rather, the void is that of the soul empty and waiting for God to fill it.[253] The paradox is that the greater the void and absence of God—and the suffering it brings—the more God sends "some of his divine rays with such strong love and glory that he stirred her [the soul] completely and caused her to go out of her senses" (*Canticle* 13, Intro. 1). John interprets stanza 13 of the "Canciones" as a plea from the bride that the Beloved withdraw the grace of rapture he has granted because it is too great for her body to bear (lines 1–2), followed by the Bridegroom's response in lines 3–6: "Return, dove / the wounded stag / is in sight on the hill, / cooled by the breeze of your flight." Christ himself is the stag who has been wounded by the love and asks the dove (i.e., the soul) to return to him for further mystical graces, but this time given to the spirit, which is capable of enjoying them, not to the body, which would be overwhelmed.[254] Stanza 13 thus represents a turning point in the soul's journey. Whereas the earlier stanzas had emphasized the longing and woundedness of the bride, the stag representing the Bridegroom is now also revealed as wounded in his reciprocal love for the human bride. "Among lovers," says John, "the wound of one is a wound for both, and the two have but one feeling."[255]

Stanzas 14 and 15 of the "Canciones," which are treated jointly, begin by interpreting the dove's spiritual flight as "a high state and union of love, . . . called spiritual betrothal with the Word, the Son of God" (14/15, Intro. 2). John says that these and the following stanzas speak more of the peaceful love between the bride and her Lover, although at the illuminative stage purification is not complete. John does, however, launch into a rich description of the delights the soul now enjoys (14/15, 4), which includes her ability to echo St. Francis's prayer, "My God and all things" (14/15, 5). This means that descriptions of the beauties of nature found in "Canciones" stanza 14 can be read as natural analogues for how God pacifies and delights the soul's faculties and passions (14/15, 6–15). "The whistling of love-stirring breezes" (the last line of stanza 15) indicates spiritual touching and hearing received in the substance of the soul and communicated to the passive intellect.[256] This hearing of the soul is the vision of the intellect (14/15, 15). It is still not clear but is rather the "ray of darkness" spoken of by Dionysius. This reminds John of another noted biblical text on dark contemplation, the night vision of Eliphaz the Temanite (Job 4:12–16), a passage he exegetes at length, just as Gregory the Great had before him.[257]

Stanza 15 ("The tranquil night / at the time of the rising dawn, / silent music, / sounding solitude, / the supper that refreshes and deepens love") John reads as pertaining to the "quietude and tranquillity" that come after the dark night of midnight with the rising dawn of the stage of perfect union now in sight (14/15, 22–23). Here the contemplative is portrayed as the "solitary sparrow" of Psalm 102:7 (14/15, 24), another traditional biblical image. John now invokes two paradoxical images: the "silent music," which is the peaceful way in which the Creator is seen in all creation; and the closely related "sounding solitude" of his presence in the spiritual faculties that have been emptied of all noisy natural forms (14/15, 25–27). Finally, the Carmelite takes up the "supper that refreshes and deepens love," which is nothing else but the Bridegroom himself as the food of the soul. "These words," says John, "declare the effect of the divine union of the soul with God, in which God's very own goods are graciously and bounteously shared in common with his bride, the soul. He himself is for her the supper that refreshes and deepens love."[258]

After the fervid description of the betrothal, "Canciones" 16–18 return to a more didactic, if still not exactly prosaic, mode, as John interprets the images in these stanzas to indicate the three opponents of the high stage the soul has attained. The first enemy is the "little foxes" (Song of Songs 2:15), which are the images the devil stirs in the imagination in order to disturb the quiet rest of the spiritual part (*Canticle* 16, 2–5). The second opponent, figured in the "deadening north wind" of stanza 17, is the spiritual dryness that hampers interior satisfaction (*Canticle* 17, 2–3). To counter this, the soul asks the "south wind," that is, the Holy Spirit (Song 4:16 is cited), to awaken love in her by breathing through her garden-soul so that the Beloved will come and feed among her flowers, that is, the virtues. The third obstacle is "the nymphs of Judea" (*ninfas de Judea*; see Song 2:7; 5:8; 8:4), whom the bride commands to stay away from her garden—"Do not so much as seek to touch our thresholds." These girls are "the imaginations, fantasies, movements, and affections of the lower part of the soul," which should not even touch the threshold of the upper part to disturb its rest in the Beloved (*Canticle* 18, 3–4, 8). John's allegorizations of each image in these stanzas is part of his overall hermeneutical model. If the individual applications sometimes seem forced, the way he develops each description is itself often quite poetic.

Stanza 19 of the "Canciones" closes off the account of the proficient souls who have attained, at least for a time, spiritual betrothal, and prepares the way for the unitive stage of the perfect described in stanzas 20–35. Here the bride asks for four gifts from her Beloved: (1) that he communicate himself inwardly in the superior part of the soul, not in the body; (2) that he inform her faculties with the glory of his divinity; (3) that the communication be indescribable, as Paul's was (2 Cor. 12:2); and (4) that he continue to love the virtues he has granted her (19, 2). Daringly, John says that the soul no longer wants a vision of "God's back" as Moses saw (Exod. 33:23) but desires the vision of his face (Exod. 33:13), that is, "the essential communication of the divinity to the soul." This communication employs no medium or means of any kind and is neither sensory nor accidental; rather, "it is a touch of naked substances, that is, of the soul and divinity" (*toque de sustancias desnudas, es a saber, de el alma y Divinidad*, 19, 4).

The account of the two highest stages of the mystical path, that is, spiritual betrothal and spiritual marriage, as found in *Canticle*, stanzas 13–34, and *Flame*, stanzas 1–4, are nearly equivalent in length. One reason that John of the Cross became a premier figure for the study of mysticism in the twentieth century is that few other mystics give more attention to these ultimate realizations of the path to God, or describe them in more detail. The fact that John's treatments of the earlier stages of the soul's progress, both the levels of beginners and those in the second stage prior to betrothal, so often jump ahead to talk about the higher stages means that some of the main features of union have already been touched on. Nonetheless, nuances and enrichments continue to appear in the later part of the *Canticle* and the whole of the *Flame*, and more emphasis is put on how the Bible, especially the Song of Songs and the Psalms, reveals the characteristics of John's view of union and the transformation and freedom it gives to the purified soul.

The long treatment of the unitive stage starts out with stanzas 20/21 and 22, which provide a foundation for what follows. Stanzas 20/21 summarize the meaning of spiritual marriage. In this state the Divine Bridegroom finally unifies the lower and higher dimensions of the soul (the sense and spirit) that the bride had so long pleaded for. As noted above in our treatment of John's anthropology, he interprets the images evoked in stanza 20 as the divine pacification and harmonization of the sense and spiritual powers during the process of transforming union (20/21, 4–11). John now is describing deep union, as can be seen from his claim that "the substantial spiritual communication" means that the soul no longer rejoices in exterior things but only in what she has within her (20/21, 12). This is a "habitual embrace" (*ordinario embrazo*), which is ineffable (20/21, 14–15), just as the soul had previously requested. Stanza 22 advances this general discussion with a summary account of the spiritual marriage as comprising *union* with God, *deification*, that is, *participation* in the divine nature, as well as *transformation* into God—four related aspects of the deep merging and communion between God and the soul. John reprises the three stages leading to the final earthly union: first, exercises in mortification and meditation; second, entering the contemplative way, which culminates in spiritual betrothal; and now advancing to the unitive way and the visits of the Bridegroom in spiritual marriage. He says, "The spiritual marriage is incomparably greater than the spiritual betrothal, for it is a total transformation (*una trasformación total*) in the Beloved, in which each surrenders the entire possession of the self to the other with a certain consummation of the power of love."[259] This transforming union "between the two natures and the communication of the divine to the human is such that even though neither changes its being, both appear to be God" (22, 4). Always mindful of the Song of Songs, John incorporates into stanzas 21 and 22 a series of texts from the biblical song of love to illustrate the nature of spiritual marriage (Song 3:5; 5:1; 6:1–2).

The next five stanzas (23–27) John reads as describing the gifts that the soul receives in the spiritual marriage. The tender mutuality and total sharing of the marriage shower graces on the soul that has reached union. These explanations also appeal to the images of the Song of Songs, either by direct reference, or by hint. For example, stanza 23 takes as its theme the divine secrets that the Bridegroom communicates to the bride, using the image of the apple tree (Song 8:5)—"Beneath the apple tree: / there I took you for my own, / there I offered you my hand." Just as Eve was corrupted under the apple tree in the Garden, so Christ has redeemed us on the tree of the cross and gradually communicates the mysteries of the incarnation and redemption to the bride. If these communications seem more a matter of faith than of loving union in stanza 23, the picture changes in stanza 24, where John takes up the image of the "little flowery bed" of Song of Songs 1:15. This represents the Bridegroom himself on which the soul reposes in peace, enjoying the gifts he bestows—the delight of union (24, 2-3), her perfect virtues (24, 4-6), and the greatest gift of all, charity (24, 7), as well as the perfect peace of soul that casts out fear (24, 8).

The conversation with the Song of Songs continues in stanza 25, where the soul becomes mindful not only of the favors she receives from the Divine Lover but also of those he bestows on other souls (25, 1-4). She singles out three particular favors: the touch of a spark; spiced wine; and flowings from the balsam of God. "The touch of the spark," which John connects with Song of Songs 5:4 ("My Beloved put his hand through the opening and my heart trembled at his touch"), is the subtle touch that the Beloved produces in the soul to inflame her with the fire of love (25, 5-6). "The spiced wine" (Song 8:2) leads to a lengthy treatment (25, 7-11) of the theme of mystical inebriation,[260] that is, the intoxication the soul experiences in the love of the Holy Spirit, which lasts much longer than the transient spark—as long as a day or two or longer, says John (27, 8). John cites a number of biblical passages in this connection (Ps. 39:3; Ecclus. 9:10, 14). Although the Song is not explicitly quoted, he probably also has in mind the inebriating cellar of Song of Songs 2:4. Finally, the "flowings from the balsam of God" are the acts that the balsam of divine love produces in the soul (recalling the *unguentum optimum* of Song 1:2).

Mystical inebriation is important for John, so he spends the whole of the long treatment of stanza 26 expounding it further. The opening lines of "Canciones" 26 echo Song of Songs 2:4—"In the inner wine cellar / I drank of my Beloved. . . ." Embraced by the Bridegroom (Song 2:6) and inebriated with the plenty of God's house, the bride drinks of the "torrent of your delight" (Ps. 36:8-9), that is, the Holy Spirit, who is the "river of living water" (Rev. 22:1). This initial part of John's commentary (26, 1) is a good illustration of his use of a rich net of biblical texts to bring out different aspects of the delights of union. In order to explain the symbol of the wine cellar, John calls on the Holy Spirit to inspire him, because "[t]he wine cellar is the last and most intimate degree of love in which the soul can be placed in this life."[261] John says there are seven degrees or wine cellars corresponding to the seven gifts of the Holy Spirit, and the comment on stanza 26 proceeds with a description of the nature of the cellars, or at least the initial four (26, 5–9). The first three cellars are illustrated by texts from the Song of Songs—drinking divine delight substantially (Song 5:6); drinking divine wisdom in the intellect (Song 8:2); and drinking love in the will (Song 2:4). John makes an important point here. When the will drinks the Divine Love that "sets charity in order in her" (Song 2:4), she seems to contradict the natural working of the faculties, because something must be known before it can be loved. This is true naturally, says John, "but supernaturally God can infuse and increase love without the infusion or increase of particular knowledge." This," he goes on to say, "is the experience of many spiritual persons."[262] In the fourth cellar, the memory drinks the Beloved so that it is illumined to remember the goods the soul possesses in union.

"Canciones" 26 then says that after drinking in the wine cellars the soul "went abroad." John reads this as the cessation of union in the soul's higher faculties, because, although substantial union is permanent once God has introduced the soul to the state of marriage, union in the faculties is not (26, 11). The soul wanders in the world, but she knows nothing of it, because the supernatural knowledge she retains makes all natural forms of knowing superfluous (26, 13). Rather than pursue the three highest wine cellars at this stage, John returns in the remainder of stanza 26 to further comments on the union of the three higher faculties. The elevation of the mind in God when absorbed in love does not allow attention to or knowledge of any earthly thing, even evil (26, 14). The Carmelite probes the nature of this unknowing. Such unknowing does not mean the loss of acquired habits of knowledge; the soul still utilizes these, but as absorbed within the ambit of the light of divine wisdom (26, 16). What is lost is particular knowledge of forms, acts, and other apprehensions, because the annihilated soul is aware only of God, who has no form. The absorption in love wipes the soul's slate clean (26, 17). Despite the height of this wonderful state, however, there always remain imperfections in intellect, will, and memory as long as we are in this life (26, 18–19).

Stanza 27 concludes the treatment of the gifts the Bridegroom bestows on the soul, again on the basis of passages from the Song of Songs and the Psalms: "There he gave me his breast; / there he taught me a sweet and loving knowledge; / and I gave myself to him." So deep is the union that the bride has gained with the Divine Lover that John daringly says that God as both Father and Mother "himself becomes subject to her for her exaltation, as though he were her servant and she his lord."[263] The exchange of breasts indicates the mutuality of the spiritual marriage: God gives his breast to the soul (citing Isa. 66:12), and the soul gives her breasts to the Beloved, that is, puts the delights of her will in God's love (Song 7:10–12). The giving of breasts indicates the perfect communication between the two partners (27, 4). This produces the "sweet and loving knowledge" that is mystical theology, or contemplation, a loving knowledge that delights both the intellect and the will (27, 5). Such a soul is "as it were divine and deified" (*porque está como divina, endiosada*, 27, 7) and knows nothing else but love.

The last section of this treatise on spiritual marriage (*Canticle* 28–34) elucidates further characteristics and effects of loving union. Treating spiritual marriage as a gem or crystal, John turns the subject around, studying new aspects in the changing light, once again, of images often taken from the Song of Songs. Sometimes it is not clear how these facets fit together, or even if they are in tension.[264] Stanza 28 speaks of the perfect love and equality between the bride and the Bridegroom—"For the property of love is to make the lover equal to the object loved" (28, 1). John interprets the stanza's first verses ("Now I occupy my soul / and all my energy in his service") to mean that the three higher powers of intellect, memory, and will are now fully occupied in God, while the energy of the sensory part of the soul, including the body, the exterior and interior senses, as well as the four passions, incline toward God and work for him (28, 3–5). This is a happy life and state, which John illustrates by texts from the Psalms (Ps. 59:10) and the Song of Songs (Song 7:13).

Stanza 29 is unusual in having a long introduction (29, 1–4), as well as a commentary (29, 5–11). The theme is the relation of contemplation and action, and the introduction and commentary seem at odds. In the introduction John adheres closely to the traditional pattern of relating the two aspects of life: the necessity of the Martha of active love to yield to the Mary of contemplative love (Luke 10:39–41) in the higher stages of the mystical life (29, 1). John says, "It should not be doubted that until the soul reaches this state of the union of love, she should practice love in both the active and the contemplative life. *Yet once she arrives* she should not become involved in other works and exterior exercises that might be of the slightest hindrance to the attentiveness of love for God, even though the work be of great service to God."[265] This view is found in many mystics but is clearly at odds with Teresa of Avila (as well as some other teachers), who argued for the union of action and contemplation, Martha and Mary, in the state of spiritual marriage (see *Interior Castle* 7.1 and 10–11). The commentary, however, appears to agree with Teresa, because John here affirms, "Those who love are not abashed before the world because of the works they perform for God, nor even if everybody condemns these works do they hide them in shame" (29, 7). He goes on to say that a soul possessed of the spirit of love glories "in beholding that she has achieved this work in praise of her Beloved and lost all things of the world" (ibid.). John admits that very few people will reach the stage of being lost to themselves in their own works, but we can ask, "Should those in the state of spiritual marriage still perform works or not?" A subsequent passage (*Canticle* 36, 4) seems to claim that they do, but that leaves *Canticle* 29, 1–4, as rather an anomaly.[266]

Stanza 30 returns to the theme of the communication of goods between the lovers, especially the virtues and gifts they bestow on each other in the communion of love (30, 2). It adds little that is new to what we found in stanzas 23–27, save in one particular, by bringing in an ecclesiological dimension. John says that the verse "We shall weave garlands / flowering in your love" refers most appropriately to the church and Christ. The garlands indicate all the holy souls engendered by Christ in the church—the white flowers of the virgins, the resplendent flowers of the doctors, and the crimson carnations of the martyrs. These are all are bound with one hair of the bride, that is, her love for the Beloved.[267] Stanza 31 returns to the themes of union and divinization, illustrating these by potent poetic images: the Bridegroom's gazing at one hair fluttering on the bride's neck, and the bride's wounding of the Bridegroom with "one of her eyes" (images from Song 4:9). Again John commences by stressing the love bond as divinizing: "So great is this union that though they differ in substance, in glory and appearance the soul seems to be God and God seems to be the soul."[268] Although the Beloved is the active party throughout, there is a mutuality of love, because the bride attracts the Lover's attention by the single strand of hair on her neck and wounds him with one of her eyes. The hair that attracts the Bridegroom is the fortitude of her love that alone binds all the virtues together (31, 4–8), while the eye that wounds him is faith. The images are interpreted as signifying the amorous knowledge or sapiential love that is the essence of union: "The soul accordingly mentions in this stanza the eye and the hair, for through them she denotes her union with God in the intellect and in the will. . . . She is then united with God in the intellect through faith, and in the will through love."[269]

Lest the reader think, on the basis of the last stanza, that the soul is taking credit herself for the marital union, in stanza 32 John carefully explains that divine grace is the total operative source. The stanza begins with the bride saying, "When you looked at me / your eyes imprinted your grace in me." For God to look upon the soul is the same as God's loving the soul (32, 3), so the love that is figured in her hair and the faith that is figured in her eye are both nothing but gifts from the Bridegroom (32, 5). God loves nothing outside himself. John continues, "He loves all things for himself; thus love becomes the purpose for which he loves. He therefore does not love things because of what they are in themselves. With God, to love the soul is to put her somehow in himself and to make her his equal."[270] This is why the soul is worthy to perform the works of God; when she is united to him in marriage, these works are God's works (32, 6–8).

The two following stanzas turn to other images from the Song of Songs to further illustrate aspects of the soul in the state of spiritual marriage. In Song 1:4–5 the bride had described herself as "black but beautiful" and therefore as worthy of being led into the king's inner chamber. John says that the soul was first dark with the ugliness of sin, but God's gaze has wiped away her sin and exalted her through grace (*Canticle* 33, 1–2). Now, she begs God to look on her again so that her grace and beauty may continue to grow (33, 3–6). God's continued gifts enable him to love the soul now both for himself and for herself, and he becomes more and more captivated with her beauty and thus leads her into the inner chamber of love (31, 7). Stanza 34 expresses the mutuality of the lovers from the Bridegroom's perspective as he praises the bride not as black with sin but as the "white dove" of Song of Songs 1:14 and 2:14. She is both the "small white dove" because of her purity, simplicity, and loving contemplation (34, 3) and the "turtledove," the faithful bird that looks only for its one mate (34, 4–5). John of the Cross has now finished his long exposition of spiritual marriage, but he adds a coda or appendix in stanza 35 on the solitude and detachment that are essential for the soul to come to enjoy the grace of union and true liberty of spirit (35, 2) and to experience the mutual wound of love (35, 7).[271]

The final five stanzas of the *Spiritual Canticle* deal primarily with the goal of union, the enjoyment of God in the endless bliss of heaven. Nevertheless, since the delights of final and perfect union are begun in this life, John has much to say on what we might call the eschatological direction of spiritual betrothal and spiritual marriage as found in this life. Stanza 36 is a kind of summary of the mutual love of the bride and the Bridegroom in the spiritual marriage, as the bride says, "Let us rejoice, Beloved, / and let us go forth to behold ourselves in your beauty." Once the soul has reached "the peak of perfection and free-dom of spirit," she rejoices in the communication of love and desires that the sweetness she enjoys in "habitual union" may overflow in the will and then into affective acts, or even "exteriorly in works" (36, 4). In a noted passage, the soul asks to be so transformed in God's beauty that she sees herself in this beauty and he sees himself in hers—"my beauty will be your beauty and your beauty my beauty."[272] The soul cannot see herself in God's beauty unless she is also transformed into God's wisdom (36, 8–9). Desiring to have a clear and pure understand-ing of God's truths, however, also implies a corresponding wish to enter "deep into the thicket," which John interprets both as the thicket of the incomprehensible judgments of God (36, 10–11) and as a multi-tude of trials and tribulations (36, 12–13). This is what true love for the Divine Lover, crucified for our sakes, means. John summarizes:

> Oh! If we could but now fully understand how a soul cannot reach the thicket and wisdom of the riches of God, which are of many kinds, without entering the thicket of many kinds of suffering, finding in this her delight and consolation. . . . The gate entering into these riches of his wisdom [Eph. 3:13, 17–19 is cited] is the cross, which is narrow, and few desire to enter by it, but many desire the delights obtained from entering there.[273]

Stanzas 37 and 38 turn to heaven, describing its rewards with the use of scriptural texts and images. John first analyzes the soul's desire for further knowledge of the mysteries of God, especially of the incar-nation, which he sees illustrated in the desire that we shall enter into the "high caverns of the rock" (37, 2–5), citing a number of biblical texts on rocks, such as 1 Corinthians 10:4, Exodus 33:21–23, and Song of Songs 2:14. The plural "we" of "Canciones" 37, line 1, indicates that the bride wants to enter into the knowledge of the mysteries together with the Bridegroom to be transformed by him through her love of God's judgments (37, 6). The image of tasting the juice of the pome-granates, which John appropriates from Song of Songs 8:2, also is given a spiritual reading, that is, "the fruition and delight of the love of God overflowing from the knowledge of his attributes" (37, 8). Both forms of knowledge are begun in this life, but John emphasizes their fulfillment in heaven. The heavenly perspective is more explicitly to the fore in stanza 38, which deals with the soul's desire to reach the most perfect form of equality with God in loving. John insists, as ever, that this is not possible in this life, but that in "the clear transforma-tion in glory" the soul will attain a state in which she knows as she is known (1 Cor. 13:12), that is to say, "her intellect will be the intellect of God, her will then will be God's will, and thus her love will be God's love." Once again, John's formulations regarding union are daring, but qualified by immediately noting that "the soul's will is not destroyed." As he explains in what follows, it is the operations of the soul that can be described as divine, not its nature (38, 3). This is John's constant teaching, even when he does not explicitly mention such qualifications. Given the practical, nonspeculative nature of John's mystagogy, we should not expect more, though important metaphysical and theological questions might be posed. For example, how does John understand participation? And what is the relation of the ongoing *created* soul to its now divine activity?[274]

John does not take up these issues here. He continues by citing the Pseudo-Thomas treatise *On Happiness* (*De beatitudine*) in confirmation of his view on attaining equality of love in heaven (38, 4), and then by reflecting on the relation of loving and knowing in the state of glory: "[I]t is impossible to reach the perfect love of God without the perfect vision of God. With love the soul pays God what she owed him; with the intellect, on the contrary, she receives from him."[275] Stanza 38 concludes with a short treatment of "what you gave me the other day," that is, the reward that God predestined for her in the day of eternity (38, 6–9). This "what" is nothing else but the vision of God, the sight that cannot be described (1 Cor. 2:9 and Isa. 64:4 are cited). Indescribable as it is, John goes on to try to say something about it by citing a number of texts from Revelation 2–3 in reference to heaven, as well as Psalm passages.

Stanza 39 continues with the impossible task of saying something about the "what" of the vision of God in heaven, because the soul in the state of spiritual marriage has already begun to feel within herself something of this "what." The poem gives five images suggesting something of the perfect fruition to come. The "what" will first involve "the breathing of the air," which John says indicates an entering into the very life of the Trinity through the breath of the Holy Spirit as the "spiration of love that the Father breathes in the Son and the Son in the Father." This transformation "is so sublime, delicate, and deep a delight" continues John, "that a mortal tongue finds it indescribable, nor can the human intellect . . . in any way grasp it."[276] Even the share given in this life is unspeakable, that is, when "the soul united and transformed in God breathes out in God to God the very divine spiration that God—she being transformed in him—breathes out in himself to her."[277] This trinitarian, Spirit-centered absorption in God's inner life, which will also be seen in the *Living Flame of Love*, marks an important new dimension in the Carmelite's presentation of spiritual marriage.[278]

The second characteristic is "the song of the sweet nightingale," which John reads as the sweet voice of the Beloved calling to her (39, 7–9). She responds in delightful jubilation, and both voices come together in the nightingale's song, indicating her feeling of "a new spring in spiritual freedom and breadth and gladness" (Song 2:10–14). The third image for heaven's joy is "the grove and its living beauty" (37, 10–11). The "grove" is God, who nourishes the beauty of all creation within himself. John demonstrates his great love and appreciation for the beauty of creation in what follows: "She [the soul] intends to beg for the grace, wisdom, and beauty that every earthly and heavenly creature not only has from God but also manifests in its wise, well ordered, gracious, and harmonious relation to other creatures. . . . The knowledge of this harmony fascinates and delights the soul."[279]

The fourth gift given in this life and aimed at the reward of heaven is "the serene night," which John understands as the night of contemplation, or mystical theology, now dark and obscure in which we "know by unknowing" through the reception of substantial knowledge in the passive intellect (39, 12). Although this night grows in sublimity during this life in those who have reached the spiritual marriage, it must wait until heaven before it will be changed into "day and light for my intellect" (39, 13). The fifth and final image is "a flame that is consuming and painless." This is the flame of perfect love, which, according to John, must have two properties: "It must consummate and transform the soul in God; and the inflammation and transformation engendered by this flame must give no pain to the soul, which cannot be true except in the beatific vision where this flame is delightful love."[280] God is a consuming fire (Deut. 4:24), and his power will always cause some pain; but in the next life he is both "consummator and restorer." In the next life God will "consummate the intellect with his wisdom and the will with his love" (39, 14).

The final stanza of the "Canciones," one of the most poetically elusive, was added later, and it is hard not to think that these mysterious lines were constructed with their theological interpretation in mind (i.e., the theology shaped the poetry). The stanza says, "No one looked at her, / nor did Aminadab appear; / the siege was still; / and the cavalry, / at the sight of the waters, descended."[281] These lines are interpreted as signifying five blessings that come to the soul when it is deep in "interior recollection" (the phrase appears three times). "No one looked at her" means that the soul is now so detached and withdrawn from things that creatures do not move her (*Canticle* 40, 2). "Nor did Aminadab appear" (see Song 6:11) signifies the inability of the devil (i.e., Aminadab) to trouble her (40, 3). "The siege was still" because the passions and appetites are conquered and calmed (40, 4). Finally, "The cavalry, / At the sight of the waters, descended." John reads these images as the "cavalry" of the bodily senses, when the spiritual marriage has been attained, now being able "to share in and enjoy in their own fashion the spiritual grandeurs [i.e., the waters] that God is communicating in the inwardness of the spirit" (40, 5). The sensory part of the soul cannot taste these waters. "It can, though, through a certain spiritual overflow [*por cierto redundancia del espíritu*] receive refreshment and delight from them."[282] This teaching about the "overflow" from the spirit to the senses is of importance for John's view of the ultimate harmony of the whole person through the action of Divine Love.

Living Flame of Love

The *Living Flame of Love*, the last and shortest of John's prose works, deals primarily with the state of spiritual marriage, though from time to time it returns to some of the themes of the earlier works, such as the transition from meditation to contemplation and the role of purgation in the transformation of the soul. Along with image of the "night," the multivalent "flame," present in all John's commentaries, comes to the fore here as a master metaphor. The fact that John wrote this work for a laywoman, his friend and penitent Doña Ana de Peñalosa, shows that he did not think that the heights of mystical union were restricted to enclosed men and women. He was concerned, however, that Doña Ana get good spiritual advice, as the long digression on spiritual direction indicates (*Flame* 3, 30–46).

John begins the work by insisting on the need for deep recollection and proclaiming his fidelity to the teaching of the church and scripture (Prol. 1). As he deals with the deepest levels of mystical transformation, John says his verses will treat of the soul who is not only united in the habitual state of transformation but also actively producing flames of love (Prol. 2–3). Flaming and wounding are the brunt of stanza 1, which begins, "O living flame of love / That tenderly wounds my soul / In its deepest center!" In this stanza John goes back over a number of issues already discussed in the *Canticle* (e.g., the wound of love, the kinds of union, the purification of the dark night), but he also expounds on further dimensions of the soul's transformation, such as the three centers of the soul (a new term), and the veils that impede union with God.

The "living flame of love" (*llama de amor viva*) is the Holy Spirit, who has transformed the soul both in terms of giving it the habit of charity and in producing acts of love. Again, John turns to his analogy of the burning log: "The same difference lying between a habit and an act lies between the transformation of love and the flame of love. It is the difference between the wood on fire and the flame leaping up from it."[283] In this state, according to John, the soul makes no acts of its own; they are all divine as proceeding from the Holy Spirit (*Flame* 1, 4). The flame is "living" because it makes the soul live in God, and it is a "flame" because "it wounds the soul with the tenderness of God's love . . . in its deepest center" (1, 7–8). The notion of the center of the soul, as we have seen above in our discussion of John's anthropology, is a new way of talking about the soul's substance. In the discussion that follows, John explains that there are actually many centers of the soul (1, 9–14). He speaks of the "center of the senses," as well as many centers corresponding to the degree of love of God the soul has gained (citing the "many mansions" of John 14:2). "But once it has attained the final degree, God's love has arrived at wounding the soul in its ultimate and deepest center (*el último centro y más profundo de el alma*), which is to illuminate and transform its whole being, power, and strength, according to its capacity, until it appears to be God."[284] This center is the furthest attainable in this life, though still not equal to what will come in glory (1, 14).

The Holy Trinity inhabits such a soul and enflames it in two ways—through the habitual union of love like glowing embers, and through the union of active burning love like flames shooting from embers (1, 16). This love completely purges the substance and the faculties of the soul and is so gentle that its action is no longer oppressive or painful as it was in the state of spiritual purgation.[285] At this point, John says that he feels he must digress for the sake of Doña Ana and go back over material on purgation that he had already treated in the *Dark Night*.[286] After this aside, the Carmelite returns to explaining the final images of stanza 1. The line "Now consummate! If it be your will" speaks of the soul's intense desire for the consummation of love in heaven, partly revealed here below by "the sudden flashes of glory and love that appear vaguely in these touches at the door of entry into the soul" (1, 28). The final line of stanza 1, begging the living flame to "Tear through the veil of this sweet encounter" provokes a discussion of the three veils and the soul's desire for glory (*Flame* 1, 28–35) that in some ways parallels material treated in *Canticle* 36–40 but adds some new particulars. Here John identifies three veils that hinder union with God (1, 29). The first is the temporal veil of creatures; the second is the natural veil of our own inclinations and operations, while the third is the sensitive veil of the union of body and soul. The first two veils must be removed in order to attain union with God in this life. In order to gain heaven the third veil must also go; only then will the soul fully enjoy the "sweet encounter." Nonetheless, even in this life the purified soul can already begin to experience the "encounters by which he ever penetrates and deifies the substance of the soul, absorbing it above all being into his own being" (1, 35). The purified soul sometimes feels almost at the point of rending this last and thinnest veil, since it desires to die and be with Christ (Phil. 1:23),[287] having reached the point where "[a]ll things are nothing to it, and it is nothing in its own eyes; God alone is its all."[288]

The second stanza of the *Living Flame* addresses the wound of love in greater detail: "O sweet cautery, / O delightful wound! / O gentle hand! O delicate touch / That tastes of eternal life / And pays every debt! / In killing you changed death to life." John uses the images of cautery/wound, hand, and touch to expand on the role of the Three Persons of the Trinity in loving union. He says:

> Thus the hand, the cautery, and the touch are in substance the same. The soul applies these terms to the Persons of the Trinity because of the effect each Person produces. . . . The first is the delightful wound. This it attributes to the Holy Spirit, and hence it calls him a sweet cautery. The second is the taste of eternal life. This it attributes to the Son, and thus calls him a delicate touch. The third is transformation, a gift by which all debts are fully paid. This it attributes to the Father, and hence calls him a gentle hand.[289]

The cautery of the Holy Spirit burns the soul more or less greatly according to the soul's desire. It is of infinite power but still is experienced as "sweet" because it enlarges and delights the soul and does not destroy it (*Flame* 2, 2–5). John extends his discussion by a treatment of the delightful wound that is the result of the cautery (2, 6–14). In contrast to a material cautery, which can be healed only by other medicines, the spiritual cautery has the paradoxical nature of both wounding and healing—"for the very cautery that causes it, cures it, and by curing it, causes it." This is the constant dialectic of the divine wound: "As often as the cautery of love touches the wound of love, it causes a deeper wound of love, and thus the more it wounds, the more it cures and heals. . . . [t]o such an extent that the entire soul is dissolved into a wound of love."[290]

John praises the "happy wound" in ecstatic terms, noting that its delight is because "the cautery touched the intimate center of the substance of the soul," which it could do because "this cautery is a touch only of divinity in the soul, without any intellectual or imaginative form or figure" (2, 8). This distinguishes it from the cautery through an intellectual form, that is, when the soul inflamed with love feels that a seraph is assailing it with the fiery arrow of love—an obvious reference to Teresa of Avila's Transverberation.[291] He goes on to say that such high spiritual gifts have been given especially to the founders of religious orders. Although the wound is in the spiritual part of the soul, "God sometimes permits an effect to extend to the bodily senses in the fashion in which it existed interiorly, the wound and the sore appear outwardly, as happened when the seraph wounded St. Francis" (2, 13). The Carmelite insists on the priority of the spiritual wound over the bodily. Bodily activity can never attain the level of the spirit, but it is different when the spirit overflows into the senses, which is what happened with St. Paul when he said he bore Christ's wounds in his body (Gal. 6:17).

The "gentle hand and delicate touch" are the merciful and omnipotent Father and his action through the Son (2, 16). The Father's hand is powerful enough to have created the world but also gentle and healing in its dealings with the soul. Since Father, Son, and Holy Spirit are one in substance, John can say, "Your only-begotten Son, O merciful hand of the Father, is the delicate touch by which you touched me with the force of your cautery and wounded me" (2, 16). The world has never experienced the gentle touch of the Son, but those who withdraw from the world will enable themselves "to feel and enjoy you" (*te puede sentir y gozar*). John continues: "The more you dwell permanently within them, the more gently you touch them, so the substance of their soul is now refined, cleansed, and purified. . . . As a result, you hide them in the secret of your face, which is your Word."[292] The touch of God is a substantial touch, a direct contact between the divine substance and the substance of the soul. It is indescribable and best honored by silence (2, 20–21). Although it is given to the soul, once again John speaks of how the Holy Spirit's unction can overflow into the body and the senses with great delight and glory, even down to the hands and feet! (2, 22).

Having been so eloquent about the supreme pleasure of unity with the Holy Trinity, John digresses again to remind Doña Ana and his other readers that such an exalted state cannot be attained without many tribulations and trials from the world, the senses, and also from the spirit (2, 25). We must be prepared to carry the cross, be placed on it, and drink gall and vinegar as Christ did in order to be worthy of so great a reward (2, 28–30). Finally, he completes the exegesis of stanza 2 with a brief treatment of the new spiritual life of union with God (2, 32–36). All the soul's operations are now in God, because the soul has changed its animal life for a spiritual life. The intellect has become divine because it is informed not by natural knowing but by the supernatural divine light. The will loves "in a lofty way with divine affection." "And the memory, which by itself perceived only the figures and phantasms of creatures, is changed through this union so as to have in its mind the eternal years mentioned by David" (Ps. 77:5).[293] What is more, even the natural appetite tastes and savors the divine, and the "movements, operations, and inclinations" of the soul are changed into divine movements. Although the soul "cannot undergo a substantial conversion into God, it has become God through participation in God, being united to and absorbed in him, as it is in this state" (2, 34). In closing his remarks on stanza 2, John turns to the language of scripture, using both the Song of Songs (1:4–5; 2:16) and a number of other texts.

The commentary on stanza 3 of the *Living Flame* is twice as long as that on stanza 2, but about half of it (3, 28–67) is a digression in four parts on the transition from meditation to contemplation, a topic already considered in both the *Ascent* and the *Night*. This does not mean that stanza 3 is all repetition; as a matter of fact, John adds important new dimensions to his treatment of union in his discussions of the "lamps of fire" (*lámparas de fuego*; see Song 8:6) and the "deep caverns of feeling" (*las profundas cavernas del sentido*; see Song 2:14). The Carmelite indicates the importance of this stanza by beginning with a prayer for help in explaining the meaning of the stanza, as well as a warning that those who have no experience of such high states will not be able to make much of what is to come (*Flame* 3, 1). Lamps, says John, have two properties: they transmit light and give off warmth. These lamps signify the essential attributes of God, and, since God now dwells in the soul, the soul, like God, can give off the light and heat of the divine attributes (3, 2). All God's attributes are identical with the divine essence, so the soul experiences the attributes both as many and yet as one. God is the lamp of omnipotence, the lamp of wisdom, the lamp of goodness, and so forth. "Immensely absorbed in delicate flames, subtly wounded with love through each of them, and more wounded by all of them together, more alive in the love of the life of God, the soul perceives clearly that this love is proper to eternal life."²⁹⁴

The great figures of the Old Testament (Moses, Abraham, David, and others) all had knowledge of these divine lamps, which can also with poetic license be described as "waters of the spirit" (citing Song 4:15; Ps. 46:4; Acts 2:3; Ezek. 36:25–27; etc.). The splendors of these lamps of fire (line 2 of stanza 3) are the "loving acts of knowledge" (*las noticias amarosas*) that God's attributes send into the soul so that the soul becomes like air within the flame, that is, "enkindled air" (*aire inflamado*, 3, 9). John uses this material analogy to suggest how both the soul and God cooperate in these motions: "The movements of these divine flames . . . are not produced by the soul alone . . . nor does the Holy Spirit produce them alone, but they are the work of both the soul and him since he moves it in the manner that fire moves enkindled air."²⁹⁵ Properly speaking, since God does not move, these motions are more the motions of the soul striving toward the same perfect stability that God enjoys (3, 11). They can also be called "overshadowings" (see Luke 1:35) in the sense that they are expressions like shadows on the soul from God's perfect attributes (3, 12–15). Through a kind of knowing by way of eminence we come to understand something of God's beauty in the shadow of the beauty he casts over the soul, and the same is true for the other attributes. John ends this section with an impassioned hymn of praise to the divine attributes, especially Divine Wisdom, the "deposit of the Father's treasures" (3, 17).

John then turns his attention to the deep caverns of feeling.²⁹⁶ In creating the category of the deep caverns of feeling in the *Flame*, John seems to be responding to one of the problematic aspects of his thought, that is, the relation between nature and grace. Those who strove to make John a kind of Thomist often tied themselves in knots by claiming that John, like Thomas Aquinas, thought that grace builds on nature (*gratia supponit naturam*). Despite a few references that might pay lip service to this principle, John seemed to believe that grace must cancel out or, perhaps better, *suspend* nature, if it is to have the ability eventually to restore the harmony of the human supposit.²⁹⁷ In other words, some kind of annihilation of the current state of the created soul is the only way to guarantee its restoration through the grace of spiritual marriage. With regard to the soul's higher faculties (intellect/memory/will), the purgation of the dark night must negate them, at least to the level where they cease to operate, if only because all their knowing, remembering, and willing are based on created things. How then can the soul who has attained union know, remember, or will anything, since it no longer has access to the natural process of under-standing and knowing based on sense experience? John's answer was "the caverns of deep feeling," potential (almost infinite) depths within its *created nature* which God is capable of infusing with spiritual "quasi-sensations" to provide the starting point for supernatural acts of know-ing and loving. John's solution was brilliant, an original contribution to the problem of the special nature of mystical knowing in relation to ordinary knowing.[298] The problem of how to evaluate this claim remains, however, especially because John tells us at the start of stanza 3 that those who have not had the experience cannot understand what he is saying.

John does set forth his view of the meaning of the caverns, for all his appeal to what will be unknown and incomprehensible to many of his readers. The power of the image of the "deep caverns of feeling" is evocative but puzzling. Reframed, his argument seems to go like this: because the soul is created in the image and likeness of God, it must possess within itself an image of divine infinity, that is, potential (not naturally active) depths in the core of the faculties of intellect, mem-ory, and will, depths that are open to divine action, that is, what he calls "divine touches." These supernatural touches serve as the start-ing place for the new epistemology of supernatural knowing and lov-ing. In perfected souls this supernatural knowing and loving can reach the stage, under divine grace, where it overflows back to the senses (and presumably also natural knowing and loving), thus harmonizing the whole human supposit. John's goal is a unified human person, but apparently only very few (as he says) will receive the grace to achieve this end.

The profound caverns are introduced in stanza 3 as voids waiting for God, "since anything less than the infinite fails to fill them" (3, 18). Created things can enter into the ordinary caverns of the faculties, but the caverns do not reveal their true capacity in such activity, that is, the profundity that can be satisfied with nothing less than God. One must therefore empty the caverns of everything created to be ready to receive God. The first cavern is the intellect, "its void is a thirst for God"; the second is the will, whose void is an intense yearning for God. The third void is the cavern of the memory, "a yearning and melting away of the soul for the possession of God" (3, 19–21). Since God is infinite, the caverns must "in a certain fashion" also be infinite, and thus they partake of the peculiar characteristic of unending desire for God, what Gregory of Nyssa called *epektasis*, although it is Gregory the Great whom John cites here—"The more that God possesses the soul,

the more it desires him, and the possession of God delights and satisfies it. . . . As a result it seems the greater the soul's desire, the greater
will be its satisfaction and delight rather than its suffering and pain."[299]
John then applies this teaching about the caverns of the soul to the
difference between betrothal and marriage. As exalted as the state of
betrothal is, it involves the Bridegroom visiting the soul with his gifts,
ones that leave the caverns somewhat anxious despite the "delicate unctions" they are receiving to prepare them for spiritual marriage (3, 27).
It is at this point that John felt compelled to launch into a long digressive section about how souls should act in the space between betrothal
and marriage. I shall make a few comments on this below, but it seems
more useful to finish off his commentary on the caverns as anointings
of the Holy Spirit found in *Flame* 3, 68–77.

The suffering in the caverns is intense, says John, as God disposes
the person for full union (3, 68). As ever with John, the more hunger,
thirst, and suffering the soul endures in this state due to its lack of
fulfillment, the greater will be the "fruition of its feeling" (*fruición de
su sentido*) when marriage has been attained. When God sends supernatural quasi-sense experiences into the soul's caverns, John explains
how these work by introducing a rather mysterious entity, what he calls
the "feeling of the soul" (*este sentido de el alma*), which he describes as
"the power and strength the substance of the soul has for feeling and
enjoying the objects of the spiritual faculties; through these faculties a
person tastes the wisdom and love and communication of God."[300] The
divine touches sent into the caverns of the faculties "administer" these
gifts to the spiritual feeling of the soul in a way similar to how the "common sense of the fantasy" in Scholastic psychology receives the forms
derived from natural sensation (see *Ascent* 2, 12, 3). Thus, the "feeling
of the soul" is described as "the receptacle and archive of these forms."
These spiritual touches residing in the common feeling of the soul can
then be called upon as the basis for the unknowing knowing and the
obscure love that are the proper acts of the faculties in union. John's
solution to the problem of mystical knowing and loving is ingenious,
but we need to investigate what he means by the "feeling of the soul."

This is where the question of John's relation to the mystical tradition
of the "spiritual senses" comes in. Beginning with Origen, many mystics had taught that the soul possesses spiritual senses analogous to the
external physical senses, new forms of experiencing the things of the
spirit that can be activated from sinful dormancy to vivid life through
the action of grace.[301] John does not appear to have developed a full
teaching on the spiritual senses, although he does mention them from

time to time. The Carmelite distinguishes two modalities of the external physical senses, the natural and the supernatural (see *Ascent* 2, 11,
1-6), but he is ambivalent about even the supernatural sense experiences sent from God, as we have seen.[302] In other places, such as *Ascent*
2, 23, 2-3, he speaks of "the spiritual eye of the soul" and the "spiritual
feelings" (*sentimientos espirituales*) that enable the soul to receive visions,
revelations, locutions, and feelings." "Spiritual feelings" appear in a
number of places in his writings,[303] and his constant appeal to the language of "touch" (*toque*) to describe God's direct action on the soul's
substance indicates the importance of the analogy of spiritual "sensation" for his teaching. This is what the Carmelite seems to intend
by the *sentido de el alma* in this passage. Nonetheless, further work is
needed to see how far John may be said to have a proper doctrine of
spiritual senses, and not just physical senses supernaturally moved.[304]

John illustrates this mystical knowing by the example of spiritual
sight, so that he can bring the deep caverns of feeling and the splendors of the lamps of fire together. The deep caverns of feeling were
"once obscure and blind." God is the light and object of the soul (3,
70). Obscurity comes about when God does not illumine the caverns;
blindness results from the attachment to sin even when God may be
shining on the soul. Obscurity is of two kinds: natural obscurity when
we lack knowledge of natural things; and supernatural obscurity when
we do not have light about supernatural things. Until God said "Let
there be light" (Gen. 1:3) darkness was over the face of "the abyss of
the caverns of the soul's feeling" (Gen. 1:2). But God's shining fills the
abyss of the caverns so that "one abyss calls out to the other abyss" (Ps.
42:7), that is, "The light of grace that God had previously accorded
this soul (by which he had illumined the eye of the abyss of its spirit,
opened its eye to the divine light and made it pleasing to himself)
called to another abyss of grace, which is the divine transformation
of this soul in God."[305] The result is that the soul's natural light is so
united with the supernatural light that only the supernatural light is
seen as shining.

Sin and natural appetites blind the spiritual eye from seeing God
and the things of God (3, 72-74), so "the appetites and satisfactions
must be totally rejected." To someone who objects that therefore all
natural desire for God will lack merit, John responds that this is really
true, whether one likes it or not (3, 75). Only supernatural desire for
God and for God alone is meritorious. When we become attached to
spiritual things and their savor, we are exercising our natural appetites,
thus blinding ourselves and becoming animal, not spiritual. If we have

any doubt about this, John says, read it again and hope to understand. Finally, John says that, when the caverns of the faculties are illumined by the splendors of the burning lamps of God's attributes, "they give forth to God in God with loving glory . . . these very splendors they have received" (3, 77).

Before taking up John's summary on the transforming union of love (*Flame* 3, 78–85), we can return to give a brief account of the digression that split the analysis of the deep caverns of feeling into two parts. John apparently felt he needed to provide Doña Ana with practical advice regarding the transition from meditation to contemplation and the role of spiritual direction in this process. This treatise (*Flame* 3, 28–67) falls into four parts. In the first (3, 28–29) he insists that God is the principal agent of this transition, and he warns against three blind guides who will work to derail the process. The second part deals with the first blind guide, bad spiritual directors (3, 30–62). This long section is important for giving John's views of spiritual direction, both the qualities of good directors (3, 30–42), and the mistakes made by bad ones (3, 43–46, 53–58).[306] The third part of the digression deals with the devil as the second of the blind guides (3, 63–65), while the last part deals with the third blind guide, the soul that "by not understanding itself, disturbs and harms itself" (3, 66–67).

The last chapters (3, 68–85) of the commentary on the third stanza of the *Living Flame* are a profound summary of the transforming union of love. Commenting on the line "so rarely, so exquisitely," John talks about the exquisite ways in which the soul receives the divine gifts of wisdom, goodness, grandeur, and the like, and equally exquisitely gives them back to God. The perfect mutuality of giving by which the soul has become God through participation prompts John to dynamic formulations: "Being the shadow of God through this substantial transformation, it [the soul] performs in this measure in God and through God what he through himself does in it. . . . Since God gives himself with a free and gracious will, so too the soul . . . gives to God, God himself in God; and this is the true and complete gift of the soul to God."[307] In this gift the soul is offering God the Holy Spirit, thus giving back to God the infinite Gift he had bestowed on her. The reciprocal love between God and the soul means that they have all things in common, just as the Son told the Father, "All my goods are yours and yours are mine" (John 17:10). The communication of all Three Persons of the Trinity to the soul shows that the soul itself now possesses the warmth and light of the *lamparas de fuego* (3, 80). John ends the commentary

(3, 82–85) by enumerating a series of triads that are the exquisite qualities of love, of fruition, of praise, and of gratitude.[308]

In the short chapters devoted to stanza 4 of the *Living Flame*, John's prose reaches an almost incantatory level as he praises the awakening of God in the soul and God's breathing within his transformed bride. "How gently and lovingly / You wake in my heart, / Where in secret you dwell alone; / And in your sweet breathing, / Filled with good and glory, / How tenderly you swell my heart with love." The Bridegroom awakens "in the center and depth of my soul, which is its pure and intimate substance" (*Flame* 4, 3). Although there are many kinds of awakening, this awakening is the movement of the Word in the soul's substance, which John compares to the movement of the earth in the new Copernican astronomy (4, 4). The soul now knows creatures through God rather than God through creatures. After some reflections on how God may be said to move in the soul and in all things (4, 6–7), John returns to the theme of awakening. Because we are now joined with God, "our awakening is an awakening of God" (4, 9), which is beyond words as a "communication of God's excellence to the substance of the soul" (4, 10).

To those who doubt that the weakness of the flesh could endure such a powerful divine communication, John answers that it is possible because, first, the fully purged lower part of a soul in such a high state does not feel the pain the unpurged souls do, and, second, God shows himself gently to the soul, as the poem says (4, 11–12). The soul is now a brother to the King of Heaven, and also a queen who has been transformed in the attributes of the Heavenly King (4, 13). The final paragraphs (4, 14–17) deal with the experience of the secret divine indwelling in the center of the soul. God dwells secretly in every soul in its substance, but in differing ways. The rule is "he dwells more in secret, the more he dwells alone." Therefore, to the soul emptied of all other appetites, forms, and images, "the Beloved dwells secretly with an embrace so much closer, more intimate and interior, the purer and more alone the soul is to everything other than God."[309] This presence is not a secret to the soul, who can feel these awakenings when God stirs to communicate knowledge and love to her. Therefore, God both rests and reposes in the substance of the soul, and at times awakens— the difference between habitual union and actual union. At last John turns to the "sweet breathing," which he identifies with the breathing of the Holy Spirit. He says, "I do not desire to speak of this spiration, filled for the soul with good and glory and delicate love for God, for I am aware of being incapable of doing so; and were I to try it would seem less than it is."[310] John ends by paraphrasing the last lines of the poem, leaving the rest to the silence and inner life of his audience.

Conclusion

At the end of this consideration of the intricacies and profundity of John of the Cross's writings, both the poems and the extensive (sometimes opaque) commentaries, it is vital to recall that John conceived of his message as a simple one. Rather than turning to the ever-elusive poems or to the long commentaries, I will end with a passage from the *Sayings of Light and Love*, those mystical aphorisms consisting of few but deep words in which the Carmelite tried to express the inner meaning of what had been given him by God. Number 60 of the *Sayings* is among the most simple and moving: "When evening comes, you will be examined in love. Learn to love as God desires to be loved and abandon your own ways of acting."[311]

Notes

1. In citing John I will generally use *The Collected Works of Saint John of the Cross*, trans. Kieran Kavanaugh and Otilio Rodriguez, rev. ed. (Washington, DC: ICS Publications, 1991), where this passage is on 113. The Spanish edition I have consulted is that of Crisógono de Jesús, Matias del Niño Jesús, and Lucinio del SS. Sacramento, eds., *Vida y Obras de San Juan de la Cruz*, 5th ed. (Madrid: Biblioteca de Autores Cristianos, 1964). John's four major prose works are *The Ascent of Mount Carmel* (*Subida del Monte Carmelo*), which will be referred to in what follows as *Ascent*; *The Dark Night* (*Noche Oscura*), abbreviated as *Night*; *The Spiritual Canticle* (*Cantico espiritual*), referred to as *Canticle*; and *The Living Flame of Love* (*Llama de amor viva*), referred to as *Flame*. The *Canticle* and the *Flame* exist in two versions: an earlier (A) and a later (B). I will cite from the B versions unless otherwise noted. Appropriate divisions of the text and references to the translation and edition, where needed, will appear in what follows. Both versions of the *Canticle* and *Flame* were also translated by E. Allison Peers in his omnibus volume, *The Complete Works of Saint John of the Cross, Doctor of the Church* (Westminster, MD: Newman Press, 1964; originally published in three volumes). For John's poetry, I will sometimes use the rhyming versions of Roy Campbell, *Poems of St. John of the Cross* (New York: Pantheon Books, 1956), and sometimes the prose translations of Kavanaugh. A valuable resource for the study of John is Juan Luis Astigarraga et al., eds., *Concordancias de los escritos de San Juan de la Cruz* (Rome: Teresianum, 1990).

2. There is a large secondary literature on John in Spanish, only some of which will be cited here. Twentieth-century French treatment of John was also extensive, but I will concentrate on literature in English, given the audience of this volume.

3. We know a good deal about John's life from the materials collected with a view to his canonization, as well as a number of early lives. Nonetheless, these sources are interested in hagiography, and so a number of the details remain in question. I thank Edward Howells for this reminder.

4. There are many lives of John of the Cross. Two long accounts are Fr. Bruno, *St. John of the Cross* (New York: Sheed & Ward, 1932); and Crisógono de Jesús, *The Life of St. John of the Cross* (London: Longmans, 1958). For a brief life, see Richard P. Hardy, *John of the Cross: Man and Mystic* (Washington, DC: ICS Publications, 2015).

5. From the start, Teresa recognized how fit John would be for the reform and what assets he would bring. In a letter to Don Francisco de Salcedo of September 1568, she says, "Would you speak to this padre [John], I beg you, and help him in this matter, for although he is small, I know that he is very great in the eyes of God. Certainly we will miss him very much here, for he is wise, and just right for our way of life. I believe our Lord has called him for this task" (Letter 13.2 in Kavanaugh, *Collected Letters of St. Teresa of Avila*, 1:60.

6. Letter 278.1–2, in Kavanaugh, *Collected Letters of St. Teresa of Avila*, 2:145–46.

7. For Teresa's concern about John's imprisonment, see Letters 218.6; 221.7; 226.10; 232.3; 233.3; 238.6, 14; 247.5; 256.4; 251.1; and 258.6. For her relief after learning of John's escape, see Letters 260.1, 3; 267.1; 270.2; 272.4; and 274.8.

8. John of the Cross, Letter 1, in Kavanaugh and Rodriguez, *Collected Works*, 736.

9. These testimonies, collected in the early seventeenth century, have been translated by E. Allison Peers in his "Appendices to the Works of Saint John of the Cross," at the end of the final volume of *The Complete Works of Saint John of the Cross, Doctor of the Church*, ed. and trans. E. Allison Peers, 3 vols. (London: Burns & Oates, 1935), 3:296–404. For accounts of the imprisonment and escape, see "Appendix A," 296–98, 316, 318–19, 320–22, 325, and 332.

10. "Appendix A" in Peers, *Complete Works*, 3:321.

11. Poem "Otro de el mismo que va por 'Super flumina Babylonis,'" beginning, Encimade las Corrientes / que en Babilonia hallaba, / allí me senté llorando, allí le tierra regaba . . . (ed., 939–41; trans. Campbell, [79]). On this poem, see Colin P. Thompson, *St. John of the Cross: Songs in the Night* (Washington, DC: Catholic University of America Press, 2003), 66–67; George H. Tavard, *Poetry and Contemplation in St. John of the Cross* (Athens: Ohio University Press, 1988), chap. 1; and Kees Waaijman, "Allí me Hirió: Estudio sobre la poesía 'Super Flumina Babilonis' de Juan de la Cruz," *Studies in Spirituality* 3 (1993): 200–212.

12. "Otro de el mismo . . .": Allí me hirió el amor, / Y el corazón me sacaba. / Díjele que me matase, / Pues de tal suerte llagaba: / Yo me metía en su fuego, / Sabiendo que me abrasaba (ed., 940; trans. Campbell, [79]).

13. These two passages are from "Otro de el mismo." (1) En mí por ti me moría, / Y por ti resucitaba, / Que le memoria de ti / Daba yida y la quitaba. (2) Y juntará sus pequeños, / Y a mí, porque en ti lloraba, / A piedra que era Cristo, / Por el cual yo te dejaba (ed., 940–41; trans. Campbell, [79–81]).

14. "Appendix A" in Peers, *Complete Works*, 3:321–22, 325, 331.

15. Ibid., 314, 350.

16. The *Dichos de luz y amor* are in Crisógono de Jesús et al., *Vida y obras completas*, 956–70, and are translated in Kavanaugh, *Collected Works*, 83–97. For an

interpretation, see Michel de Certeau, *The Mystic Fable: The Sixteenth and Seventeenth Centuries*, 2 vols., Religion and Postmodernism (Chicago: University of Chicago Press, 1992, 2015), vol. 2, chap. 3, "Shards of Speech" (88–97).

17. "Appendix A," in Peers, *Complete Works*, 3:336. Later testimony by Fray Juan specifically mentions each of the books; see "Appendix A," 3:350, 352–53.

18. Hans Urs von Balthasar, "St. John of the Cross," in *The Glory of the Lord: A Theological Aesthetics*, vol. 3, *Studies in Theological Style: Lay Styles* (San Francisco: Ignatius Press, 1986), 105–71, here 169.

19. For an account of the progress of John's teaching over the course of his writings, see Eulogio Pacho, "El 'Gemido Pacifico de la Esperanza': Síntesis definitiva del pensamiento sanjuanista," *Studies in Spirituality* 6 (1996): 152–67.

20. "Appendix A," in Peers, *Complete Works*, 3:340; see also the same story in the testimony of María del Sacramento (ibid., 3:334).

21. On Diego and his annotations (often reprinted), see Certeau, *Mystic Fable*, 1:129–44, as well as the treatment in chap. 5 below (370–71).

22. For the early French reception of John of the Cross, especially by the Jesuit mystic Jean-Joseph Surin, see Certeau, "Uses of Tradition," in *Mystic Fable*, 2:98–119. See also André Rayez, "Gaultier (René)," DS 6:144–47, as well as André Bord, *Jean de la Croix en France*, Beauchesne Religions 21 (Paris: Beauchesne, 1993), part 1.

23. For an account of the *Alumbrados* of Seville and their connection with John, see Hamilton, *Heresy and Mysticism in Sixteenth-Century Spain*, 123–25.

24. This document ("Reply of R. P. M. Fray Basilio Ponce de León, . . . to the Notes and Objections which were Made concerning Certain Propositions from the Book of our Father Fray John of the Cross") is translated by Peers as "Appendix B" in *Complete Works*, 3:355–404.

25. Basilio Ponce de León, "Reply" (Peers, *Complete Works*, 3:404).

26. On the study and evaluation of John's poetry, see Thompson, *St. John of the Cross*, "Introduction." There is a sketch of the modern growth of interest in John, concentrating on America, by Steven Payne, "The Influence of John of the Cross in the United States: A Preliminary Survey," in *John of the Cross: Conferences and Essays by Members of the Institute of Carmelite Studies and Others*, Carmelite Studies 6 (Washington, DC: ICS Publications, 1992), 167–95.

27. On Traherne, see McGinn, *Reformation*, 249–62.

28. There are many analyses of John's poetry; see especially Thompson, *St. John of the Cross*, chaps. 3, 4, and 10. Among earlier treatments I have found helpful are Gerald Brenan, *St. John of the Cross: His Life and Poetry* (Cambridge: Cambridge University Press, 1973), and Tavard, *Poetry and Contemplation in St. John of the Cross*. Translations of John's slim production of twenty-two poems are many.

29. Willis Barnstone, *The Poetics of Ecstasy: Varieties of ekstasis from Sappho to Borges* (New York: Holmes & Meier, 1983), 182–88.

30. Balthasar, "St. John of the Cross," 171 (see also 120).

31. For example, David Tracy, *The Analogical Imagination: Christian Theology and the Culture of Pluralism* (New York: Crossroad, 1981), 174; and (in a nuanced way) David Brian Perrin, *Canciones entre el Alma y el Esposo of Juan de la Cruz: A Hermeneutical Interpretation* (San Francisco: Catholic Scholars Press, 1996), xxi–xxiii.

32. Certeau, *Mystic Fable*, vol. 2, chap. 2, "The Poem and Its Prose" (71–87); Thompson, *St. John of the Cross*, esp. 276–81.

33. Certeau, *Mystic Fable*, 2:71; see also 86, 110.

34. "Appendix A," in Peers, *Complete Works*, 3:298.

35. Thompson provides the following helpful description of John's commentaries: "They are part poetic gloss, part biblical commentary, part ascetic and moral treatise, part devotional text, with numerous digressions; but the balance between these elements is a shifting one" (*St. John of the Cross*, 142).

36. *Canticle*, Prol. 1 (ed., 626; trans., 469). In this chapter I have chosen not to give the Spanish text for all translations but only for those important for John's mystical vocabulary. On the relation of the Prologues to the commentaries, see "Silent Music," chap. 9 in Thompson, *St. John of the Cross* (226–42), as well as Certeau, *Mystic Fable*, 2:80–87.

37. Perrin puts this well (*Canciones*, 373): "The commentary is not a description of the meaning of the *Cántico* itself but is a particular reception of the poem. However, it is not the only possible reception. There are other ways of receiving the poem. . . . The commentary may be viewed as a secondary form of discourse which helps us to understand the poem but does not eclipse the poem's metaphorical referential function."

38. *Canticle*, Prol. 2 (ed., 626–27; trans., 470).

39. "Appendix A," in Peers, *Complete Works*, 3:298. We know from other testimonies that John also wrote the paraphrase of Psalm 136 beginning "Encina de las corrientes" ["Over the streams of running water"] while in prison.

40. The most noted proponent of the case against the B versions was Jean Baruzi, *Saint Jean de la Croix et le problème de l'expérience mystique*, 2 vols. (Paris: Félix Alcan, 1924).

41. Kavanaugh and Rodriguez, *Collected Works*, 34–35. A study of the evolution of John's writings in the context of his life is Eulogio Pacho, *San Juan de la Cruz y sus escritos* (Madrid: Ediciones Cristiandad, 1969).

42. Perrin treats "Juan de la Cruz and the Western Mystical Tradition" (*Canciones*, 121–44).

43. Jean Vilnet, *Bible et mystique chez saint Jean de la Croix*, Études carmélitaines (Bruges: Desclée de Brouwer, 1949), 35. Of course, John has many implicit citations, so others have counted the total number of uses of the Bible at about fifteen hundred. "Note B" in Vilnet (240–48) provides a useful list of explicit citations of biblical verses.

44. "Appendix A," in Peers, *Complete Works*, 3:336.

45. *Ascent*, Prol. 2 (ed., 364; trans., 115). See also *Ascent* 2, 3, 5 and 2, 22, 7. The same point is made in *Canticle*, Prol. 4; and *Flame*, Prol. 1.

46. Henri Sanson, *L'esprit humain selon Saint Jean de la Croix*, Publications de la Faculté des lettres d'Alger 2/22 (Paris: Presses universitaires de France, 1953), 24–26, 43, and esp. 147–95. As Sanson summarizes, "L'expérience que contient l'Ecriture deviant la mesure de l'expérience de l'ame" (171).

47. Keith J. Egan, "The Biblical Imagination of John of the Cross in *The Living Flame of Love*," in *Juan de la Cruz, Espíritu de Llama: Estudios con ocasión del cuarto centenario de su muerte (1591–1991)*, ed. Otger Steggink, Vacare Deo 10; Studies in Spirituality Supplement 1 (Kampen: Kok Pharos, 1991), 507–21, here 516.

48. *Ascent* 1, 2, 2-4 (ed., 368–69; trans., 120–21).

49. *Night* 2, 17, 8 (ed., 601; trans., 438).

50. *Ascent* 2, 17-22 (ed., 427–56; trans., 199–238). In these six chapters John

cites the Bible eighty-one times, with the majority of the citations coming in chap. 19 (19x), chap. 20 (15x), chap. 21 (17x), and chap. 22 (24x).

51. *Ascent* 2, 19, 5 (ed., 438–39; trans., 215). Similarly in 2, 19, 8, John says, "These prophecies about Christ should have been understood in their spiritual sense, in which they were most true."

52. Old but still useful is "A Benedictine of Stanbrook Abbey" [author], *Mediaeval Mystical Tradition and Saint John of the Cross* (London: Burns & Oates, 1954).

53. *Ascent* 2, 24, 1 explicitly mentions Thomas's *Quodlibet* 1.1, and there are other references to Thomas in *Ascent* 2, 3, 1 and 3, 2, 7, as well as in *Night* 1, 4, 2. A special case is the influence of two spiritual treatises (*De beatitudine* and *De dilectione Dei et proximi*) that John cited as written by Thomas Aquinas, although today we know they were the products of a German Dominican Helwic of Germar around 1300 C.E. (see Gilles Meersemann, "A propos de deux écrits de spiritualité attribués à saint Thomas," *Revue Thomiste* 35 [1930]: 560–70). The *De beatitudine* is cited explicitly in *Canticle* 38, 4 (ed., 731; trans., 619); and implicitly in *Flame* 3, 78 and 82–85 (ed., 913–16; trans., 705–8). The *De dilectione Dei et proximi* contains a section *De decem gradibus amoris secundum Bernardum* that is the basis for John's ten degrees of love in *Night* 2, 19–20 (ed., 603–7; trans., 440–45). On this text and its use by John, see P. de Surgy, "La source de l'échelle d'amour chez saint Jean de la Croix," *Revue d'ascétique et de mystique* 27 (1951): 18–40, 237–59, and 327–46.

54. An important work for the Thomist view of John is Jacques Maritain, *Distinguish to Unite: Or, The Degrees of Knowledge* (New York: Charles Scribner's Sons, 1959). Maritain considers Thomas Aquinas the master of the metaphysical and doctrinal knowledge of God capable of being communicated (speculativo-practical knowing), while John of the Cross (chaps. 8 and 9) is the master of incommunicable mystical knowing (practico-practical knowing; see 310–19). Another classic of the Thomist view of John is Réginald Garrigou-Lagrange, *Christian Perfection and Contemplation according to St. Thomas Aquinas and St. John of the Cross* (St. Louis: B. Herder, 1951).

55. The most notable argument for considerable influence is that of Jean Orcibal, *Saint Jean de la Croix et les mystiques Rhéno-flamands*, Présence du Carmel 6 (n.p.: Desclée de Brouwer, 1966). Largely agreeing with Orcibal is Louis Cognet, *La spiritualité moderne*, vol. 1, *L'essor 1500–1650*, Histoire de la spiritualité chrétienne 3.2 (Paris: Aubier, 1966), part 1. See also Helmut Hatzfeld, "The Influence of Ramon Lull and Jan van Ruysbroeck on the Spanish Mystics," *Traditio* 4 (1946): 337–94.

56. The short introductions in English that I have found most helpful for John of the Cross include Balthasar, "St. John of the Cross"; Ross Collings, *John of the Cross*, Way of the Christian Mystics 10 (Collegeville, MN: Liturgical Press, 1990); Iain Matthew, *The Impact of God: Soundings from St. John of the Cross* (London: Hodder & Stoughton, 2010); Hein Blommestijn, Jos Huls, and Kees Waaijman, *The Footprints of Love: John of the Cross as a Guide in the Wilderness*, Fiery Arrow Collection 3 (Leuven: Peeters, 2000); and Peter Tyler, *St. John of the Cross* (London: Continuum, 2014). Among longer studies, see Dicken, *Crucible of Love*; Steven Payne, *John of the Cross and the Cognitive Value of Mysticism: An Analysis of Sanjuanist Teaching and Its Philosophical Implications for Contemporary Discussions of Mystical Experience*, New Synthese Historical Library 37 (Dordrecht: Kluwer, 1990); Howells, *John of the Cross and Teresa of Avila*; and Thompson, *St. John of the Cross*. Special

note may be made of two books on John by important twentieth-century religious figures: Edith Stein, *The Science of the Cross: A Study of St. John of the Cross* (Chicago: Regnery, 1960; German original, 1940–41); and Karol Wojtyla (Pope John Paul II), *Faith according to St. John of the Cross* (San Francisco: Ignatius Press, 1981; Latin original, 1948). Other literature, including some important non-English works, will be cited below as relevant.

57. The poem is found in ed., 947 (my trans.).

58. For introductions to the Romances, see Thompson, *St. John of the Cross*, 56–61; and Tavard, *Prayer and Contemplation*, 20–27.

59. On the place of the "Romances" in what he calls John's "trinitarian theology of negation," see Rowan Williams, "The Deflections of Desire: Negative Theology in Trinitarian Disclosure," in *Silence and the Word: Negative Theology and Incarnation*, ed. Oliver Davies and Denys Turner (Cambridge: Cambridge University Press, 2002), 115–35, esp. 117–20.

60. "Romance sobre el Evangelio" (ed., 932–33). I use Campbell, *Poems of St. John of the Cross*, [48–51] (with Spanish text).

61. "De la communicación de las tres Personas" (ed., 933; trans. Campbell, [52–55]).

62. *Canticle* 26, 4 (ed., 700; trans. Kavanaugh, 575).

63. Balthasar ("St. John of the Cross," 114–17) collects a number of John's key texts on the divine mystery.

64. *Flame* 3, 2–17 (ed., 871–80; trans., 673–80). For more on the divine attributes, see, e.g., *Canticle* 14, 5–15.

65. Important texts on the Trinity in these works include *Canticle* 1, 6–7; 13, 11; 20/21, 2; 39, 3–6; and *Flame* 1, 6 and 15; 2, 1–24; and 3, 79–80.

66. The poem can be found in ed., 930–31, and has been translated by both Campbell (*Poems of St. John of the Cross*, [44–47]) and Kavanaugh (*Collected Works*, 58–60). For commentaries, see Tavard, *Poetry and Contemplation*, 15–19, and esp. Thompson, *St. John of the Cross*, 70–80, who concludes that "the mystery of the Trinity is perhaps more tellingly grasped by the audience San Juan had in mind through his symbolism of the fountain flowing in the darkness than ever it could be through the formal language of scholastic theology" (80).

67. See *Canticle B* 39, 3 (ed., 733): ". . . con aquella su aspiración divina muy subidamente levanta el alma y la informa y habilita para que ella aspire en Dios la misma aspiración de amor que el Padre aspira en Hijo y el Hijo en el Padre, que es el mismo Espíritu Santo." See also *Canticle A* 38, 3–4; *Flame* 3, 79 and 4, 16–17.

68. Along with the passages on God's beauty in *Canticle*, stanzas 36–40, see also such texts as 11, 10; 12, 1; and *Ascent* 1, 4, 4.

69. Balthasar, "St. John of the Cross," 151–52.

70. William Ralph Inge, *Christian Mysticism: Considered in Eight Lectures Delivered before the University of Oxford* (London: Methuen, 1899), 229.

71. The good treatment of John's view of creation is Collings, "Creation 'By the Hand of the Beloved,'" chap. 2 in *John of the Cross* (26–60). Collings's conclusion is worth citing: "A theology of Creation provides the proper foundation for understanding and reconciling two most fundamental features of St. John of the Cross's spiritual life—his uncompromising demand for renunciation and his manifest overflowing joy in created goodness and beauty."

72. Romance III, "Una esposa que te ame" (ed., 934; trans. Campbell, [56–57]).

73. Romance IV, "Hágase, pues, dijo el Padre" (ed., 935; trans. Campbell, [60–61]).

74. *Canticle* 14/15, 5–15 (ed., 661–68; trans., 526–32). See also 5, 1–4 and 39, 10–11.

75. *Canticle* 14/15, 5 (ed., 661; trans., 526).

76. *Canticle* 36, 6–7 (ed., 726; trans., 612).

77. Romance IV (ed., 935–36; trans. Campbell, [62–63]).

78. For some texts on the role of the church in John's commentaries, see *Ascent* 2, 22, 7 and 11; 2, 3, 5; 2, 27, 4; 3, 44, 3; *Canticle*, Prol. 4; 30, 7; 33, 8; and *Flame*, Prol. 1.

79. Romance VI (ed., 937; trans. Campbell, [69]).

80. Romance VII (ed., 937–38; trans. Campbell, [72–73]).

81. On original sin, see *Ascent* 1, 15, 1 (ed., 392; trans., 152); and the address of the Bridegroom to the soul in stanza 23 of the *Canticle*, where Christ says, "For human nature, your mother, was corrupted in your first parents under the tree, and you too under the tree of the cross were restored" (*Canticle* 23, 5 [ed., 691; trans., 564]).

82. *Canticle* 5, 4 (ed., 644; trans., 497).

83. *Canticle* 7, 1–5 (ed., 645–46; trans., 499–501). For more detail, see 37, 1–5.

84. *Ascent* 2, 7, 11 (ed., 408; trans., 172). On the importance of *Ascent* 2, 7 and 2, 22, see Matthew, *Impact of God*, 123–32. The centrality of taking up the cross in imitation of Christ demonstrates the aptness of Edith Stein's title for her book on John—*The Science of the Cross*—by which she meant not the ordinary sense of science but "a known truth, a theology of the Cross, . . . living, actual and active truth" (1).

85. On general imitation of Christ, see *Ascent* 1, 13, 3–4 and 2, 22, 7.

86. *Ascent* 3, 35, 5 (ed., 525; trans., 332).

87. On carrying the cross, see, e.g., *Ascent* 1, 5, 8; *Canticle* 3, 5; 36, 13; and *Flame* 2, 28.

88. *Letter* 24 (ed. No. 23, p. 991; trans., 759).

89. A good short overview of John's anthropology is Payne, *John of the Cross and the Cognitive Value of Mysticism*, chap. 2. Also useful are Howells, *John of the Cross and Teresa of Avila*, chap. 2; and Dominic Doyle, "From Triadic to Dyadic Soul: A Genetic Study of John of the Cross on the Anthropological Basis of Hope," *Studies in Spirituality* 21 (2011): 219–41. In French, see Sanson, *L'esprit humain selon Saint Jean de la Croix*; André Bord, *Mémoire et espérance chez Jean de la Croix*, Bibliothèque de spiritualité 8 (Paris: Beauchesne, 1971); and Max Huot de Longchamp, *Lectures de Jean de la Croix: Essai d'anthropologie mystique*, Théologie historique 62 (Paris: Beauchesne, 1981).

90. Genesis 1:26 is noted in Romance VII and in *Canticle* 39, 4. On the importance of this motif in John, see Hein Blommestijn and Kees Waaijman, "L'homme spirituel à l'Image de Dieu selon Saint Jean de la Croix," in Steggink, *Juan de la Cruz: Espiritu de Llama*, 623–56. The authors conclude, "Quoique Jean de la Croix le mentionne rarement de façon explicite, l'homme créé à l'Image de Dieu apparaît néanmoins comme leitmotive de son développement du processus mystique" (655).

91. *Canticle* 11, 3 (ed., 653; trans., 511). See also *Ascent* 2, 5, 2–3 and *Flame* 4, 4. On this aspect of John's thought, see Blommestijn et al., *Footprints of Love*, chap. 13.

92. See Howells, "The Dichotomy of 'Sense' and 'Spirit,'" in *John of the Cross and Teresa of Avila*, 18–21.

93. John insists on the unity of the human suppositum in *Night* 1, 4, 2; 2, 1, 1; and 2, 3, 1.

94. *Canticle* 20/21, 4 (ed., 683; trans., 552).

95. "Canciones" 20, using the literal translation of Kavanaugh (552).

96. John agrees with the Scholastic axiom that there is nothing in the intellect that is not first in the senses (e.g., *Ascent* 1, 3, 3), so in this sense his epistemology is more like that of Aquinas than that of the Platonists.

97. For further accounts, see *Ascent* 2, 12, 3–4; 2, 16, 2; 2, 24, 5; 3, 13, 7; and *Flame* 3, 69. The fantasy collects the impressions of objects received from the external senses, while the imagination uses these images to construct new and more complex images. Both of these powers work in close collaboration with the memory. At times John speaks of a "common sense" (*sentido común*), which seems to embrace both interior senses. See the summary in Payne, *John of the Cross and the Cognitive Value of Mysticism*, 20–23.

98. *Canticle* 20/21, 6–7. For another brief reference, see *Ascent* 3, 29, 2. John speaks of both sensory and spiritual appetites; e.g., *Night* 2, 16, 1: ". . . los apetitos y potencias sensitivas, interiores y espirituales" (ed., 595). A large part of book 1 of the *Ascent* deals with the mortification of the disordered voluntary appetites (1, 3–12).

99. See, e.g., *Ascent* 1, 9, 2–4; 1, 11, 2–3; and 1, 12, 3–6.

100. Payne, *John of the Cross and the Cognitive Value of Mysticism*, 19; see also 37, 54, etc. The same point is emphasized by many Sanjuanist scholars, e.g., David Brian Perrin, *For Love of the World: The Old and New Self of John of the Cross* (San Francisco: Catholic Scholars Press, 1997); Matthew, *Impact of God*, 46–50; Howells, *John of the Cross and Teresa of Avila*, 34–39, 125–28; Collings, *John of the Cross*, 157–61; and Thompson, *St. John of the Cross*, 276–80.

101. *Night* 2, 11, 4 (ed., 587; trans., 420): ". . . donde Dios tiene recogidas todas las fuerzas, potencias y apetitos del alma, así espirituales como sensitivas, para que toda esta harmonía emplee sus fuerzas y virtud en este amor."

102. The primary source for the threefold distinction in Augustine is *De Trinitate*, esp. books 9–15.

103. The threefold distinction of powers is present throughout John's works. For some important texts, see *Ascent* 1, 8, 2–3; 1, 9, 6; 2, 5, 1; 2, 6; 2, 8, 5; 3, 1, 1–2; *Night* 1, 9, 7; 2, 3, 3; 2, 4, 1–2; 2, 8, 2; 2, 16, 1; 2, 21, 4–11; *Canticle* 1, 20; 2, 6–7; 19, 4; 20/21, 4; 26, 5–11, and 18; 28, 3; 35, 5; *Flame* 1, 20; 2, 34; 3, 18–26; and 3, 47–52. Like many medieval and early modern authors, John has a penchant for triads. For a list of the most important, see Doyle, "From Triadic to Dyadic Soul," 221–24.

104. Some have asserted that he does in *Flame* 1, 15, but this passage does not actually link the three powers to the Three Persons, because here John uses a dyadic pattern for the higher powers, noting that the Son illuminates the intellect, the Holy Spirit delights the will, while the Father is described as absorbing the whole soul, not the memory.

105. See *Ascent* 1, 8, 2. The whole of book 2 of the *Ascent* is an account of the intellect and its natural and supernatural apprehensions.

106. See, e.g., *Ascent* 2, 8, 4–5 (ed., 409–10; trans., 175–76). See also 2, 16, 4.

107. *Canticle* 39, 12 (ed., 736; trans., 626): "For this knowledge [mystical the-

ology] is not produced by the intellect the philosophers call the agent intellect [*el entendimiento activo*]; rather it is produced in the possible or passive intellect [*el entendimiento in cuanto posible y pasivo*]." The passive intellect also appears in *Ascent* 2, 32, 4; *Night* 2, 13, 3; and *Canticle* 14/15, 15–16. On the possible intellect in John, see Jean Orcibal, "Le role de l'intellect possible chez Jean de la Croix: Ses sources scolastiques et Nordiques," in *La mystique rhénane: Colloque de Strasbourg, 16–19 mai 1961* (Paris: Presses universitaires de France, 1963), 235–79.

108. In order to contrast the two forms of activity of the spirit, however, John does need to give some attention to the soul's natural activity, on which see the summary in Howells, "The Natural Operation of the Soul," in *John of the Cross and Teresa of Avila*, 21–26.

109. *Ascent* 2, 10, 2 (ed., 412; trans., 178). John does not have a developed theory of the supernatural, presupposing the thought of Aquinas and the other Scholastics. In *Ascent* 2, 4, 2, he contents himself with saying, "the word 'supernatural' indicates that which is above nature."

110. This question is posed directly by Howells, *John of the Cross and Teresa of Avila*, chap. 2 (38–39; cf. 54), who also gives an extended answer in chaps. 3 and 7. Howells provides a handy table of John's two contrasting epistemologies (30).

111. Bord, *Mémoire et espérance*, esp. 74–98, on the relation to Augustine.

112. As Howells (*John of the Cross and Teresa of Avila*, 24–26), following Bord, shows, the storehouse, or receptacle, aspect of the memory has to fall away in John's epistemology in order to allow all remembered images to reside in the interior senses when the total voiding of the memory is effected by supernatural hope.

113. See Dominic Doyle, "Changing Hopes: A Comparative Study of the Theological Virtue of Hope in Thomas Aquinas, John of the Cross, and Karl Rahner," *Irish Theological Quarterly* 77 (2012): 18–36, as well as Edward Howells, "'O guiding night!' Darkness as the Way to God in John of the Cross's Mysticism" (unpublished).

114. Letter 13 (ed. as Letter 12, 982; trans., 748). See also Letter 7 (trans., 740–41). See Alois M. Haas, ". . . ausserhalb Gottes ist alles eng': Johannes' vom Kreuz 'Appetit' nach Gott," in *Aufgang: Jahrbuch für Denken, Dichten, Musik*, vol. 2, *Sehnsucht* (Stuttgart: Kohlhammer, 2005), 121–41.

115. Doyle, "From Triadic to Dyadic Soul," esp. 224–33.

116. *Flame* 3, 78, my italics (ed., 913; trans., 705). For other texts in which the soul or self replaces memory as a faculty, see, e.g., *Canticle* 2, 6–7; 26, 5; 27, 5; and *Flame* 1, 15, and 26. To be sure, there are still texts, such as *Flame* 2, 34, that speak of the transformation of intellect, will, and memory in union, although Doyle sees these as anomalous ("From Triadic to Dyadic Soul," 236–39).

117. Doyle, "From Triadic to Dyadic Soul," 239.

118. On the substance-ground-center of the soul, see Sanson, *L'esprit humain*, 72–82; Payne, *John of the Cross and the Cognitive Value of Mysticism*, 41–44; and Howells, *John of the Cross and Teresa of Avila*, 31–34.

119. For some texts on the *sustancia del alma*, see *Ascent* 2, 24, 4; 2, 28, 2; 2, 32, 2; *Night* 2, 13, 3; *Canticle* 14/15, 12 and 14; 22, 5; 26, 5 and 11; *Flame* 1, 9; 2, 8–9; 2, 17, 21; 3, 69; and 4, 4, 10 and 13–15.

120. Howells, *John of the Cross and Teresa of Avila*, 32–34, here 32. For passages on the relation of the substance of the soul and the three powers as having a

trinitarian dimension, see, e.g., *Canticle* 39, 3 (ed., 733–34; trans., 622–23); and *Flame* 4, 17 (ed., 925–26; trans., 715).

121. *Canticle* 26, 11 (ed., 701; trans., 577). "Substantial union" and "substantial touches" signify those which bring us into full union with God. On the three senses of *sustancial*, see Sanson, *L'esprit humain*, 71. For the many texts on *sustancia/sustancial*, see Astigarraga, *Concordancias*, 1766–70.

122. *Flame* 3, poem (ed., 870; trans. Kavanaugh, 673).

123. *Flame* 3, 23 (ed., 883; trans., 682).

124. *Flame* 3, 71 (ed., 910): "Y así 'un abismo llama a otro abismo,' conviene saber: un abismo de luz llama a otro abismo de luz, y un abismo de tinieblas a otro abismo de tiniebla, llamando cada semejante a su semejante y cominicándosele." In *Canticle* 13, 9, this mutual relationship is expressed in terms of the mutual wounding of the bride and the Bridegroom.

125. On the "feeling of the soul" as analogous to the interior common sense of natural knowing, see *Flame* 1, 36 and 2, 22, as well as the discussion in Howells, *John of the Cross and Teresa of Avilia*, 35–37, and 53. "The caverns of feeling" and the "feeling of the soul" raise the question of John's teaching on the spiritual senses. This will be taken up below.

126. On the importance of the center of the soul, especially as the place where John's two epistemologies overcome their opposition and are united in one subject, see Howells, *John of the Cross and Teresa of Avila*, 55–59; and his essay, "Is Darkness a Psychological or a Theological Category in the Thought of John of the Cross?," in *The Renewal of Mystical Theology: Essays in Memory of John N. Jones (1964–2012)*, ed. Bernard McGinn (New York: Crossroad-Herder, 2016), 156–57, on the relational nature of the soul's center. More will be said on the center as unifying in the next section. See also Léonce Reypens, "Ame (son fond, ses puissances, et sa structure d'après les mystiques)," DS 1:460–63, on Teresa and John. The notion of the center of the soul played a part in Teresa of Avila's *Interior Castle*, as seen in chap. 3 above (202–6). How far Teresa may have influenced John in this matter (or vice versa) is an open question.

127. *Flame* 1, 13 (ed., 835; trans., 645).

128. Ibid. For another text on the center of the soul, see *Flame* 4, 3. John also mentions "the center of the spirit of the perfect life in Christ" (3, 10), and he frequently talks about being centered on God (e.g., *Ascent* 2, 6, 4; 3, 11, 1; 3, 18, 6; *Night* 2, 19, 2; 2, 21, 11; *Canticle* 1, 13; and 8, 3).

129. *Night* 1, 1, 1 (ed., 541; trans., 361 adapted). The three states are also referred to in *Canticle*, theme 1–2; and stanza 22, 3.

130. On the beginnings of the transition from "contemplatives" to "mystics" in early modernity, see Certeau, *Mystic Fable*, 1:94–97.

131. I find it misleading that the Kavanaugh translation often renders *los espirituales, el verdadero espíritu*, or even just *espíritu* as "spirituality." On the uses of *espiritual* as a qualifier in John, see Astigarraga, *Concordancias*, 775–85. Using *espiritual* as a substantive (i.e., a spiritual person) is also frequent, as shown in *Concordancias*, 785–87.

132. John J. Murphy, "St. John of the Cross and the Philosophy of Religion: Love of God and the Conceptual Parameters of a Mystical Experience," *Mystics Quarterly* 22 (1996): 163–86, here 164.

133. *Ascent* 3, 2, 4 (ed., 478): ". . . como tambien por experiencia se ve cada

día." See also *Canticle* 26, 8 (ed., 701), where he says, "Y esto experimentado está de muchos espirituales." For other such texts, see *Flame* 1, 15 (ed., 836); and 3, 1 (ed., 870).

134. The language of having–feeling–tasting is present throughout John. For some examples, see *Ascent* 2, 4, 3; 2, 26, 5; *Night* 1, 1, 2; 1, 8, 3; 1, 9, 4; 2, 7, 4; 2, 9, 1 and 5; 2, 16, 4; *Canticle* 1, 9; 17, 7; 22, 5; *Flame* 1, 6; 1, 27; 2, 17; 4, 12; and 4, 15–16. According to Astigarraga, *experiencia* appears thirty-three times in John (*Concordancias*, 817–18).

135. *Night* 2, 24, 3 (ed., 594; trans., 428): "No se puede bien entender. Si no fuera, a mi ver, el alma que ha gustado dello." See also *Canticle* 7, 10 (ed., 647): "Esto creo no lo acabará bien de entender el que no lo hubiere experimentado."

136. This point is argued in detail by Denys Turner, who says, "It is, in any case, all too easy to read John of the Cross exclusively as an 'early modern' writer, to detach his work from its roots in the medieval tradition, and in no respect is this more likely, or more misleading, than to characterize John's 'modernity' precisely by its 'experientialism'" ("John of the Cross: The Dark Nights and Depression," in *The Darkness of God: Negativity in Christian Mysticism* [Cambridge: Cambridge University Press, 1995], 226–51, here 226).

137. Alois M. Haas, "Die dunkle Nacht der Sinne und des Geistes: Mystische Leiderfahrung nach Johannes vom Kreuz," in *Die Dunkle Nacht der Sinne: Leiderfahrung und christliche Mystik*, ed. Gotthard Fuchs (Düsseldorf: Patmos, 1989), 108–25, here 123: "Der Geheimnischarakter der mystische Erfahrung besteht also darin, dass sie Erfahrung in Nichterfahrung ist."

138. For example, Jean Baruzi, who says of John, "Il nous apporte une logique de la mystique et même une critique de l'Experience mystique. . . . Négation de tout ce qui apparaît. Rien de ce qui m'apparaît n'est Dieu" ("St. Jean de la Croix et le problème de la valeur noétique de l'expérience mystique," *Bulletin de la Société française de Philosophie* 25 [1925]: 30). Tavard says, "But to seek nothing is not to look for something that would be, precisely, no-thing; it means, literally, to seek nothing, that is, not to seek" (*Poetry and Contemplation*, 79). In other words, we must allow God to seek us.

139. Balthasar, "St. John of the Cross," 169; see the whole discussion on 167–71.

140. *Canticle* 14/15, 2 (ed., 664; trans., 526).

141. *Flame* 3, 59 (ed., 902; trans., 697). On God's giving out graces in different ways, see also *Night* 1, 14, 5; *Flame* 1, 24; 2, 2; 3, 25.

142. There are a number of studies of John's symbols; see, e.g., Georges Morel, *Le sens de l'existence selon Saint Jean de la Croix*, 3 vols., Théologie 45–47 (Paris: Aubier, 1961), vol. 3: *Symbolique*; Elizabeth Wilhelmsen, *Knowledge and Symbolization in Saint John of the Cross* (Frankfurt am Main: P. Lang, 1993). See also the same author's *Cognition and Communication in John of the Cross* (Frankfurt am Main: P. Lang, 1985). There is also the long discussion of "Les grands thèmes du symbolisme nuptial," in Fernande Pepin, *Noces de feu: Le symbolisme nuptial du "Cantico espiritual" de Saint Jean de la Croix à la lumière du "Canticum Canticorum,"* Recherches: Theologie 9 (Paris: Desclée, 1972), 139–293.

143. Balthasar, "St. John of the Cross," 116.

144. The poem "Otras de el mismo a lo divino" can be found in edition, 943–44. I use Kavanaugh's version, 56–57. For commentaries, see Thompson, *St. John of the Cross*, 63–64; and Tavard, *Poetry and Contemplation*, 168–73.

145. Bonaventure's *Itinerarium mentis in Deum* is a prime example. The Seraphic Doctor summarized the coinherence of ascension and introversion in *In II Sent.*, d. 2, p. 2, a. 1, q. 2 (*Opera Omnia* [Quaracchi: Ex Typographia Colegii S. Bonaventurae, 1882–1902], 2:226–27).

146. The journey within is also a form of interior recollection. See *Canticle* 1, 6–9, esp. 6, where, citing the Pseudo-Augustinian *Soliloquies* 1.30 (PL 40:888), John says, "Individuals who want to find him [God] should leave all things through affection and will, enter within themselves in deepest recollection [*recogimiento*], and let all things be as though not" (ed., 631; trans., 480). Recollection is a frequent term in John, one that he learned from the Franciscan mystics of early sixteenth-century Spain, on which see chap. 1 above.

147. On God as a loving mother, see *Ascent* 2, 14, 4; 2, 17, 6–7; 3, 28, 7; and *Night* 1, 1, 2; 1, 5, 1; 1, 8, 3; and 1, 12, 1.

148. God the Word lies beyond gender. Basing himself on the biblical language of the Song of Songs, John mostly identifies the Incarnate Word as the Bridegroom of the feminine human soul, beginning with *Ascent* 1, 14, 2. Nevertheless, at the outset of the *Ascent* (1, 2, 3), when he is referring to the account of Tobias's waiting for the third night before the consummation of his marriage (Tob. 6:18–22), it is Divine Wisdom who is the Bride of Tobias. See Tavard, *Poetry and Contemplation*, 145–48, on this gender malleability.

149. *Night* 1, 9, 5 speaks of God leading the soul into "desert solitudes," while 2, 17, 6–7 goes further in comparing the abyss of the secret wisdom of mystical theology with "a remarkably deep and vast wilderness unattainable by any human creature, an unbounded desert" (ed., 578; trans., 437). The desert motif also occurs in *Night* 2, 19, 4 and is implied in the long discussion of solitude in *Canticle* 35, 1–7. According to Astigarraga (*Concordancias*, 545), John refers to the desert (*desierto*) twenty-one times.

150. On water, see esp. *Ascent* 2, 14, 2.

151. There are important reflections on the symbol of the night in John in Stein, *Science of the Cross*, 25–28.

152. Balthasar summarizes this well: "The 'night' is like a great curve. It begins with the asceticism of radical and active renunciation of the world and continues with the passive deprivation of all delight in things and even in God himself. Then it curves round the midnight of pure sightless faith until it reaches the dawn of a new substantial delight in the ways of God, the beginning of a transparent vision" ("St. John of the Cross," 139). On night and dawn in John, see Pepin, *Noches de feu*, 200–206.

153. The image of sunlight and window is traditional and can be found in *Ascent* 2, 5, 6; 2, 14, 9; *Night* 2, 8, 3; 2, 12, 3; *Canticle* 26, 4; etc.

154. The symbol of the log gradually transformed by fire is found in *Ascent* 1, 11, 6; 2, 8, 2; *Night* 2, 11, 1. The most extensive treatments are *Night* 2, 10, 1–9; and *Flame*, Prol. 3–4; and 1, 3–4, 19, 22–23, 25, and 33. See Clément Sclafert, "L'allégorie de la bûche enflammée dans Hugues de Saint-Victor et dans Saint Jean de la Croix," *Revue d'ascétique et de mystique* 33 (1957): 242–63 and 361–86.

155. Hugh of St. Victor uses the burning log image, for example, in his *Commentarium in Caelestem Hierarchiam*, Cap. XV (PL 175:1139B–42C). See Orcibal, *St. Jean de la Croix et les mystiques Rhéno-flamands*, 82–85.

156. Thompson, *St. John of the Cross*, 100. See his list of images on 98–99.

157. *Canticle,* Prol. 1 (ed., 626; trans., 469 adapted).

158. *Night* 2, 17, 3 (ed., 431–32; trans., 436). For more on ineffability, see *Ascent* 2, 26, 3–5; *Canticle* 19, 2; 20/21, 14–15; 22, 4; 26, 4; 30, 1 and 10; 33, 8; 39, 3; *Flame* 2, 20–21; 4, 10 and 17.

159. On the role of the oxymoron in the mystical "dialect" of the sixteenth and seventeenth centuries, see Certeau, *Mystic Fable,* 1:142–44.

160. On the *un no sé qué* of the poem, see the explanation in *Canticle* 7, 9–10.

161. "Glosa a lo divino" (ed., 945–46; trans. Kavanaugh, 71–73), stanza 1: "Por toda la hermosura / nunca yo me perderé, / sino por un no sé qué / que se alcanza per ventura." For studies, see Thompson, *St. John of the Cross,* 65–66; and esp. Tavard, *Poetry and Contemplation,* 163–67.

162. Reasons of space preclude discussion of one of John's most moving poems on negation, the "Stanzas concerning an ecstasy experienced in his contemplation" with its opening lines: "I entered into unknowing, / and there I remained unknowing / transcending all knowledge," and the constant repetition of the last line at the close of each stanza (*toda sciencia trascendiendo*). The text can be found in ed., 941–42; and Kavanaugh trans., 53–54. See Michael McGlynn, "Silence and Ineffability as Cognition in San Juan de la Cruz' *Coplas del Mismo Hechas sobre un Éxtasis de Alta Contemplación,*" *Studies in Spirituality* 21 (2011): 193–217.

163. On these negativities, see McGinn, "Three Forms of Negativity in Christian Mysticism," in Bowker, *Knowing the Unknowable,* 99–121.

164. On the *todo–nada* dialectic, see Tavard, *Poetry and Contemplation,* 62–67, 73, 78–79, 91–92, 95, 145–47, 169, and 171; also Maritain, "Todo y Nada," chap. 9 in *Degrees of Knowledge,* 352–83.

165. Letter 17 (No. 16 in ed., 885; trans., 752): "Y para tener a Dios en todo, conviene no tener en todo nada; porque el corazón, que es de uno, cómo puede ser todo de otro?"

166. *Ascent* 1, 12, 6–13 (ed., 390–91). My translation of these central texts is an amalgam and adaptation of the versions of Kavanaugh (149–51) and Peers (58–60). Similar passages are found elsewhere, e.g., *Ascent* 2, 4, 5 (ed., 399; trans., 163): "As regards this road to union, entering on the road means leaving one's own road; or better, moving on to the goal. And turning from one's own mode implies entry into that which has no mode, that is, God."

167. The importance of the "law of contraries" was emphasized by Tavard, *Poetry and Contemplation,* chap. 5 (75–92).

168. The principle was annunciated by Aristotle in, e.g., *On Sensation* 8, and became a commonplace in Scholastic thought.

169. *Ascent* 1, 4, 2 (ed., 370; trans., 123–24). For other appearances, see, e.g., *Ascent* 1, 6, 1–4; 2, 24, 8; 3, 2, 4; *Night* 2, 5, 4; 2, 6, 1; 2, 9, 2 and 11; 2, 3, 2; *Canticle* 8, 3; 13, 1; *Flame* 1, 22.

170. *Ascent* 1, 6, 1 (ed., 376; my trans.).

171. Strictly speaking, on Thomist grounds known to John (see STh Ia, q. 3, a. 5, which seems to be cited in *Ascent* 3, 12, 1), there can be no contrary to God, because God does not fall under the classifications of genus and species. That is why John speaks of two contrary *aficiones.*

172. Tavard (*Poetry and Contemplation,* 86–88) notes that in some places (e.g., *Night* 2, 6, 1; *Ascent* 2, 16, 7) John speaks of "extremes" rather than "contraries,"

and affirms that extremes can be united if one takes on the likeness of the other, as humans become like God in mystical union.

173. Turner speaks to this problem: "For like Eckhart, John appears to say that *any* desire for anything other than God is a desire *opposed* to God" (*Darkness of God*, 232). I do not think this represents Eckhart's view of detachment, and it may not also be fair to John, but he often seems to say something like this.

174. Almost everyone who has written about John of the Cross discusses the four nights. Two well-known accounts are André Bord, *Les amours chez Jean de la Croix*, Beauchesne Religions 24 (Paris: Beauchesne, 1998), part 2; and Dicken, *Crucible of Love*, chaps. 5–6 and 8–10. Edith Stein's *Science of the Cross*, part 2, nos. 1–3 (22–114) is basically a long series of quotations and paraphrases from John on the nights. More recently, see Collings, *John of the Cross*, chap. 3; and Matthew, *Impact of God*, part 4, "Healing" (51–93). For a brief summary, see Lucien-Marie de Saint-Joseph, "S. Jean de la Croix," DS 8:419–21 and 434–36. There is an insightful view of the nights in Howells, "Is Darkness a Psychological or Theological Category in the Thought of John of the Cross?," in *The Renewal of Mystical Theology: Essays in Honor of John N. Jones (1964–2012)*, ed. Bernard McGinn (New York: Crossroad, 2017), 140–61. Howells identifies three senses of darkness in John (144–45): (1) the darkness of following Christ even to the annihilation of death; (2) the epistemological darkness of denuding the intellect of everything created in order to attain God; and (3) the "dark contemplation" (*oscura contemplación*, *Ascent*, Prol. 4 [ed., 364]) by which even in union God remains unknown.

175. Constance FitzGerald notes, "Transfiguration does not happen at the end of the road; it is in the making now. . . . Dark night is a sign of *life*, of growth, of development in our relationship with God, in our best human relationships, and in our societal life" ("Impasse and Dark Night," in *Living with the Apocalypse*, ed. Tilden Edwards [San Francisco: Harper & Row, 1984], 93–116, here 97; see also 102).

176. Tavard, *Poetry and Contemplation*, 86.

177. See Keith J. Egan, "Contemplation in the 'Spiritual Canticle': The Program of Dark Night. Education for Beauty," in *Carmel and Contemplation: Transforming Human Consciousness*, Carmelite Studies 8 (Washington, DC: ICS Publications, 2000), 241–66, who notes, "The process of mortification and the dark night of contemplation are the road to the restoration of one's ability to love God and to delight in God's beauty as well as to reclaim the ordered love for all creation" (252).

178. Balthasar, "St. John of the Cross," 127.

179. See the discussion in Hein Blommestijn, "The Dark Night in John of the Cross: The Transformational Process," *Studies in Spirituality* 10 (2000): 228–41, esp. 228–30, 240–41. See also Alain Cugno, *Saint John of the Cross: Reflections on Mystical Experience* (New York: Seabury, 1982), 40: "Thus the emptiness of God is a yearning for him. . . . God's absence is his presence."

180. Murphy, "St. John of the Cross and the Philosophy of Religion," 169.

181. *Ascent* 1, 1–2 (ed., 367; trans., 118–19). See also *Ascent* 1, 2, 5 and 1, 13, 1. This clear outline does not preclude many crossovers and repetitions; for example, the *Night* contains much that pertains to the active night of the senses. This makes sense, however, because the nights remain coterminous throughout.

182. Matthew, *Impact of God*, 72ff.

183. *Ascent* 1, 8, 4 (ed., 381; trans., 136). See also the discussion of the imper-fections of beginners caused by the seven deadly spiritual sins (pride, avarice, lust, anger, gluttony, envy, and sloth) in *Night* 1, 1–7, on which see Tyler, *St. John of the Cross*, chap. 4.

184. *Sayings of Light and Love* 100 (ed., No. 99, p. 966; trans., 92). On God's silence in John, see Louis Roy, "Expérience du silence de Dieu chez Jean de la Croix," *Prêtre et Pasteur* 115 (2012): 79–86.

185. Letter 8 (No. 7 in ed., 975–76; trans., 742).

186. On the need for silence and solitude, see, e.g., *Ascent* 1, 11, 5–6; 3, 3, 4; *Night* 2, 14, 1; 2, 2, 4; *Canticle* 14/15, 7; 16, 10; 35, 1–6 (praise of solitude); *Flame* 3, 35–39, 63, and 65.

187. *Flame* 3, 63 (ed., 904; trans., 699). See also 3, 64–66.

188. *Ascent* 3, 40, 2 (ed., 531; trans., 341). For some other texts on *recogimiento*, see *Ascent* 3, 41, 1; *Night* 1, 8, 4; 2, 23, 5; *Canticle* 1, 6 and 8; 13, 5; 20/21, 9; 40, 2–3 and 6.

189. *Flame* 3, 44 (ed., 893; trans., 690). *Recogimiento* occurs often in the *Flame*, for example, Prol. 1; 3, 45, 53, and 63–65.

190. *Sayings of Light and Love*, No. 163 (ed., No. 172, p. 970; trans., 97). No. 156 provides a catalogue of the virtues and practices John taught to his religious charges: "The twelve stars for reaching the highest perfection: love of God, love of neighbor, obedience, chastity, poverty, attendance at choir, penance, humility, mortification, prayer, silence, peace."

191. *Ascent* 1, 2, 1 (ed., 368; trans., 120). Night is one of the fundamental symbols of Christian mysticism. For an introduction, see Michel Dupuy, "Nuit (Ténèbre)," DS 11:519–26, while a more detailed treatment is Michael Plattig, "Die 'Dunkle Nacht' als Gotteserfahrung: Aspekte und Anregungen für gegenwarts-bezogene Spiritualität," *Studies in Spirituality* 4 (1994): 165–205.

192. Howells, "Is Darkness a Psychological or a Theological Category in the Thought of John of the Cross?," 155.

193. For a short survey of the action of the three theological virtues, see Collings, *John of the Cross*, chap. 5.

194. *Ascent* 2, 1, 2 (ed., 395; trans., 155). John cites and explains the second stanza of "En una noche oscura" here but then abandons commentary on the poem for the rest of the treatise.

195. See Catherine Connors-Nelson, "Touched by the God of Grace: The *Anfechtung* of Luther and the Dark Night of John of the Cross," *Studies in Spiritual-ity* 9 (1999): 109–39.

196. This conceptualist version of *fides* is often described as "Thomist," but while it could and did appeal to texts in Thomas Aquinas, it scarcely represents the Dominican's full teaching on faith.

197. Faith is the basic subject of book 2 of the *Ascent* but is discussed in other works, such as *Night* 2, 21, 4–5; *Canticle* 12, 2–7; and *Flame* 3, 48. Despite its neo-Scholastic cast, Wojtyla's *Faith according to Saint John of the Cross*, 33–182, remains a useful guide to the notion of faith in *Ascent* book 2.

198. *Ascent* 2, 3, 1 (ed., 396; trans., 157). Scholars often reference Thomas's STh, IIaIIae, qq. 1–4, here, which is not incorrect, but John is more interested in the obscurity of faith than is Thomas. It is true that the Dominican also speaks of the *informitas fidei* (IIaIIae, q, 6, a. 2), due to the weakness of the human mind; but

what was for Thomas secondary has become primary for John of the Cross. The Carmelite and the Dominican have different, though not contrary, views of faith. John would have agreed with Thomas that the knowledge of God given in faith moves us to seek ever deeper experience of God (*Summa contra Gentiles* 3.40.5).

199. On the obscurity of faith, see Wojtyla, *Faith according to Saint John of the Cross*, 58–86, who also notes the "existential not speculative" nature of John's teaching (e.g., 47, 69).

200. Union occurs so often in John's writings that it would be otiose to try to give a list of passages. It has been treated by many of John's commentators; see esp. Howells, *John of the Cross and Teresa of Avila*, chap. 3.

201. *Ascent* 2, 5, 7 (ed., 402; trans., 165). See also *Canticle* 26, 5–11; *Flame* 1, 3–4; 4, 14–16.

202. *Ascent* 2, 6, 1 (ed., 403; trans., 166); see also 3, 1, 1. The three theological virtues are described as the three necessary garments of the soul in *Night* 2, 21. All three virtues unite us with God (faith in *Ascent* 3, 7, 2; hope in *Ascent* 3, 30, 4; and charity in *Canticle* 11, 11). For an account of the role of faith, hope, and love in the purification process, see Balthasar, "St. John of the Cross," 133–44 and 159–60.

203. *Ascent* 2, 7, 5 (ed., 406; trans., 170).

204. *Ascent* 2, 8–9, is central to Wojtyla's presentation of John's view of faith.

205. Advancing by unknowing (*no sabiendo/no entendiendo/no comprendiendo*) rather than by knowing, is an ancient mystical theme often found in John, especially in the *Ascent*; see, e.g., *Ascent* 1, 4, 5; 1, 13, 11; 2, 8, 5; 2, 14, 11; 3, 2, 3; 3, 5, 3; *Night* 2, 17, 7; *Canticle* 7, 9; and 39, 12. The theme is central to the poem "Stanzas concerning an ecstasy experienced in high contemplation." On unknowing in John, see esp. Tavard, *Poetry and Contemplation*, 68–73. Speaking of "unknowing knowing," he says that the knowing belongs to God, the unknowing to us: "[I]t is on the basis of divine knowing beyond all human capacity that God gives himself to be known without knowledge, in love" (73).

206. *Ascent* 2, 8, 6 (ed., 410; trans., 176): "Y de aquí es que la contemplación por la qual el entendimiento tiene más alta noticia de Dios llaman Teología Mística, que quiere decir sabiduría de Dios secreta." John refers to the Dionysian ray of darkness in several later passages—*Night* 2, 5, 1 and 3; *Canticle* 14/15, 16; *Flame*. 3, 49—and he also uses *teología mística* in *Night* 2, 12, 5 (*mística y amorosa teología*); 2, 17, 2 and 6; 2, 21, 6; *Canticle*, Prol. 3; stanzas 27, 5 and 39, 12. For a study of the relation of Dionysius and John on *theologia mystica*, see Ysabel de Andía, "San Juan de la Cruz y la 'Teología Mística' de 'San Dionisio,'" in *Actas del Congreso Internacional Sanjuanista: Avila, 23–28 de Septiembre de 1991*, 3 vols. (n.p.: Junta de Castilla y León, Consejería de Cultura y Turismo, 1993), 3:97–125. In English, see Stephen Wlusek, "The Foundations of John of the Cross' Spiritual Theology in the Thought and Writings of Pseudo-Dionysius," *Studies in Spirituality* 18 (2008): 195–213. On John's use of *místico* and *teología mística*, consult Astigarraga, *Concordancias*, 1201 and 1787–88 respectively.

207. The threefold distinction of visions into sensible, imaginative, and intellectual goes back to Augustine (e.g., *De Genesi ad litteram* 12). John broadens the triple pattern. In treating the supernatural intellectual apprehensions, which he divides into visions, locutions, revelations, and spiritual feelings (chap. 23), John does make some exceptions for beneficial divine sendings. He notes, for example, that a few persons in the history of salvation, like Moses, Elijah, and Paul, have

been given substantial divine visions but that these are not to be expected today (2, 24, 3–3). Similarly, naked and ineffable truths about God are concomitant with union itself and are therefore good (2, 26, 3–5). These substantial communications John tends to associate with the "spiritual feelings, or touches" (e.g., 2, 24, 4; 2, 26, 6–9), on which he will have more to say in later works. What he calls "substantial locutions" are also approved (2, 28, 2 and 2, 31, 1–2), as are the spiritual feelings, or "touches, that take place in the soul's substance (2, 32, 1–3).

208. *Ascent* 3, 9, 4 (ed., 487; trans., 282). See *Ascent* 2, 22, 19, where he says the same about charity.

209. On John's negative attitude toward visions and other spiritual gifts, see Payne, *John of the Cross and the Cognitive Value of Mysticism*, 67–69; Balthasar, "St. John of the Cross," 130–33.

210. *Ascent* 2, 14, 2 (ed., 421; trans., 192). These three signs for the transition from meditation to contemplation should be compared with the stronger formulation of the three signs for discerning the transition to the passive night of the spirit in *Night* 2, 9, 1–9.

211. *Ascent* 3, 2, 3 (ed., 478; trans., 268).

212. *Ascent* 3, 2, 13 (ed., 480; trans., 272). In this lengthy treatment of habitual union (3, 2, 8–16) John does not offer his usual qualifications concerning the soul being divine, such as the appeal to deification by participation.

213. *Ascent* 3, 15, 1 (ed., 494; trans., 290). For other treatments of hope, see *Night* 2, 4, 2; 2, 9, 1–2; 2, 21, 6–9; *Canticle* 1, 14 and 20/21, 11.

214. *Ascent* 3, 16, 3 (ed., 495; trans., 293).

215. The five sources of active joy are (1) temporal goods (chaps. 18–20); (2) natural goods (chaps. 21–23); (3) sensory goods (chaps. 24–26); (4) moral good, that is, virtues (chaps. 27–29); and supernatural goods, that is, graces related to creatures (chaps. 30–32).

216. Rather confusingly, John says that the obscure delightful goods "will be left for the end," but where exactly he envisaged that end to be is not evident (see also *Ascent* 2, 10, 4 and 2, 14, 14).

217. John expresses his basic principle regarding images as follows: "Where there is devotion and faith any image will be sufficient, but if they are lacking none will suffice" (*Ascent* 3, 36, 3).

218. For example, Balthasar, "St. John of the Cross," 154–57.

219. See Denys Turner, who argues that, while both depression and the dark night are similar experiences of identity loss, "from the standpoint of prognosis they differ in every respect" ("John of the Cross: The Dark Nights and Depression," chap. 10 in *The Darkness of God*, 226–51, here 237). This mode of interpretation has sometimes been invoked as the basis for a strict opposition between psychological and theological accounts of the "Dark Night," which is, of course, something of a category error. The "Dark Night" is an objective theological category, which nonetheless has an effect *in* the consciousness of the subject and is therefore open to psychological investigation.

220. This principle, important to Thomas Aquinas (see, e.g., STh Ia, q. 79, a. 6), is cited by John in *Night* 1, 4, 2; 2, 16, 4; and *Flame* 3, 34.

221. These chapters, containing many shrewd observations about the faults and temptations of spiritual beginners, testify to John's experience as a spiritual guide; see Tyler, *St. John of the Cross*, chap. 4.

222. *Night* 1, 10, 6 (ed., 557; trans., 382): ". . . la contemplación no es otra cosa que infusión secreta, pacífica y amorosa de Dios, que, si la dan lugar, inflama al alma en espíritu de amor." For another definition of infused contemplation, see *Night* 2, 5, 1. John never uses the term "acquired contemplation," which later became contrasted with "infused contemplation," although some have argued that the acquired version is the substance of what he is talking about in *Ascent* 2, 13, 3–4, which is doubtful. For John's teaching on contemplation, see Maritain, *Degrees of Knowledge*, "Mystical Contemplation," 338–51; and Joseph Maréchal, *Études sur la psychologie des mystiques* (Paris: Desclée, 1937), vol. 2, Appendix 5, "Le sommet de la contemplation d'après Saint Jean de la Croix" (325–62).

223. During this period John says that the communication between the now-contemplative spiritual part of the soul and the sensory part will allow it "to experience the delights of the spirit more easily," though the body's weakness will lead to "infirmities, injuries, and weaknesses of the stomach," as well as "raptures, transports, and the dislocation of bones" (*Night* 2, 1, 2–3).

224. *Night* 2, 3, 3 (ed., 570; trans., 399).

225. "Poverty of spirit" (Matt. 5:3) was a frequent theme with Christian mystics, for example, Meister Eckhart. John uses the term in a number of places, such as *Ascent* 2, 15, 4; 2, 24, 8; 3, 35, 7; 3, 40, 1; *Night* 1, 3, 1; 2, 9, 4; *Canticle* 1, 14; *Flame* 1, 23; 3, 46.

226. According to Astigarraga, *Concordancias*, 199–200, John uses *aniquilación* seven times and *aniquilar* no fewer than sixty-one times. For some representative passages, see *Ascent* 2, 5, 4; 2, 7, 7–8 and 11; 2, 24, 8; 3, 2, 1 and 4; 3, 4, 1; 3, 27, 7; *Night* 1, 11, 1; 2, 6, 5; 2, 7, 6; 2, 8, 2 and 5; 2, 9, 2 and 3; 2, 9, 5; 2, 19, 1; 2, 21, 11; *Canticle* 25, 14; 26, 17; *Flame* 3, 34; 3, 47; and 4, 16.

227. *Ascent* 2, 7, 11 (ed., 407; trans., 172).

228. *Canticle* 26, 17 (ed., 703; trans., 579–80).

229. *Night* 2, 6, 6 (ed., 575; trans., 406). The thirteenth-century German Beguine Mechthild of Magdeburg had a similar experience, which she spoke of as "being under Lucifer's tail" (see McGinn, *Flowering*, 242).

230. Freedom of spirit (2 Cor. 3:17), although once suspect in the fourteenth century due to the heresy of the so-called Sect of the Free Spirit, was an important theme in Christian mysticism and was much emphasized by John of the Cross, as we shall see in what follows. It appears in many passages: *Ascent* Title; 1, 4, 6; 1, 11, 6; 2, 19, 11–12; 3, 20, 2–3; 3, 23, 5; 3, 24, 6; *Night* 1, 10, 4–5; 1, 13, 11 and 14; 2, 1, 1–2; 2, 9, 1; 2, 14, 3; 2, 22, 1; 2, 23, 2 and 12; *Canticle* 35, 2 and 17; 36, 1; 38, 8; *Flame* 2, 13; 3, 38; 3, 46; 3, 59; 3, 61; Letter 16; and *Sayings of Light and Love*, No. 25.

231. *Night* 2, 13, 3. In 13, 5 John distinguishes "esteeming love," by which we always love God even in the midst of dereliction, and "impassioned love," in which we burn with passion for the Divine Lover. At the close of the chapter (2, 13, 11) there is another discussion of the divinizing union in which the soul becomes more divine than human.

232. The mention of the ladder leads John to something unusual in his writings, two chapters (*Night* 2, 19–20) where he takes over someone else's text, the ten steps of the mystical ladder of love given in the section *De decem gradibus amoris secundum Bernardum* contained in the Pseudo-Thomas treatise *De dilectione Dei et proximi*. While these ten steps are not without interest, they represent an anomaly in John's presentations of love, because the Carmelite prefers the poetic love lan-

guage of personal encounter, rather than the enumeration of steps. When he does provide his own ladder of love, it usually consists of a brief mention of seven steps; see, e.g., *Ascent* 2, 11, 9; *Canticle* 26, 3; and *Flame* 2, 29.

233. As with many sixteenth-century authors, the devil plays an important role in John of the Cross, especially the demon's wiles misleading souls to think they are more advanced than they actually are. For an overview, see Lucien Marie de Saint-Joseph, "The Devil in the Writings of St. John of the Cross," in Bruno de Jésus Marie, O.C.D., *Satan,* 84–96.

234. We have already seen a number of texts that refer to the "divine touches," an important theme for John; e.g., *Ascent* 2, 24, 4; 2, 26, 5–9; 2, 32, 2–4; 3, 2, 5–6; 3, 14, 2; *Night* 2, 11, 5; 2, 12, 6; 2, 23, 11–12; 2, 24, 3; *Canticle* 1, 17 and 19; 7, 4; 8, 4; 14/15, 12–14; 19, 4; 25, 5–5; *Flame* 1, 17; 1, 28; 1, 35; 2, 8; 2, 16–17; 3, 28. The touch has a long history in Christian mysticism; for an overview, see Pierre Adnès, "Toucher, Touches," DS 15:1073–98, which treats John in cols. 1083–86.

235. *Night* 2, 25 is a brief comment on stanza 3, mentioning three properties of "that glad night." John says nothing about stanzas 4–8.

236. In the extensive literature on the "Canciones," see especially the work of Perrin, *Canciones*; Pepin, *Noces de feu*; Colin P. Thompson, *The Poet and the Mystic: A Study of the Cántico Espiritual of San Juan de la Cruz,* Oxford Modern Languages and Literature Monographs (Oxford: Oxford University Press, 1977); and Eulogio Pacho, *Vértice de la poesía y de la mística: El "Cántico Espiritual" de San Juan de la Cruz,* Estudios Monte Carmelo 4 (Burgos: Editorial Monte Carmelo, 1983).

237. Brenan, *St. John of the Cross,* 116: "And there is at times a penetrating strangeness of tone that recalls, as very little poetry really does, the poignancy of dreams." Nonetheless, Brenan also insists on "the distinctness and precision of the language." For poetic evaluations, see Brenan, 116–23; and Thompson, *St. John of the Cross,* 95–112, as well as his earlier study, *Poet and the Mystic,* chap. 5.

238. On the relation between the Song of Songs and the "Canciones," see Perrin, *Canciones,* 154–59; Thompson, *Poet and the Mystic,* 60–70; and Pepin, *Noces de feu.* I calculate that John cites the Song seventy times in the *Canticle,* with forty citations coming in stanzas 20–35, devoted to the spiritual marriage.

239. For a sketch of the evolution and structure of the poem, see Perrin, *Canciones,* 226–53, building on Tavard, *Poetry and Contemplation,* chaps. 3, 7, and 12.

240. Origen, *The Song of Songs: Commentary and Homilies,* trans. R. P. Lawson, Ancient Christian Writers 26 (Westminster, MD: Newman Press, 1957), Prologue, 21.

241. The usual reading is to see the purgative way as embracing stanzas 1–12, the illuminative way featured in stanzas 13–19, the unitive way stretching from stanzas 20 to 35, and the foretaste of heaven embracing stanzas 36–40. Nonetheless, there are many interactions and overlaps between the stanzas.

242. Using the Campbell translation (ed., 627; trans., [15]).

243. *Canticle* 1, 2–4 (ed., 630–31; trans., 478–79).

244. "Canciones," stanza 6, lines 3–5 (ed., 644; trans. Kavanaugh, 498). Because the Campbell translation uses the CA version of the poem, I will use Kavanaugh's more literal version of CB in what follows.

245. For a brief and rather inadequate survey of the wound theme, see A. Cabassut, "Blessure d'amour," DS 1:1724–29.

246. *Canticle* 11, 1 (ed., 653; trans., 510). This moves John to discuss the three senses of God's presence (11, 3) commented on above.

247. *Canticle* 11, 10 (ed., 655; trans., 514). This passage can be compared with the famous texts on beauty in *Canticle* 36, 5, and 7–8.

248. See also *Canticle* 8, 3. This theme, often said to go back to Augustine, seems to appear first in Bernard, *De praecepto et dispensatione* 20, 60 (*Sancti Bernardi Opera*, ed. Jean Leclercq et al. [Rome: Editiones Cistercienses, 1957–77], 3:292). For a study, see Jean Orcibal, "Une formule de l'amour extatique de Platon à Saint Jean de la Croix et au Cardinal de Bérulle," in *Mélanges offerts à Etienne Gilson, de l'Académie française* (Toronto: Pontifical Institute of Mediaeval Studies, 1959), 447–63.

249. *Canticle* 12, 1 (ed., 656; trans., 515 corrected). Kavanaugh mistranslates *cristalina fuente* as "O spring like crystal." Wojtyla (*Faith according to Saint John of the Cross*, 203–13) comments on this stanza as stanza 11 (in the A version).

250. *Canticle* 12, 7 (ed., 658; trans., 518).

251. John's teaching on the relation between spiritual betrothal and spiritual marriage is comparable, if not in all particulars, to the teaching of Teresa (see *Interior Castle*, Dwelling Places 6 and 7).

252. *Canticle* 13, Introduction 1 (ed., 659; trans., 519).

253. John often speaks of voiding, or emptying, the faculties (e.g., *Ascent* 1, 3, 1; 1, 5, 7; 2, 6, 2–4; *Night* 1, 11, 2; 1, 12, 6; *Flame* 3, 18, as well as Letter 19), both in the active night through our own efforts, and especially through the action of grace in the passive night of the spirit. These texts and others have been studied by Leonard Albert McCann, *The Doctrine of the Void* (Toronto: Basilian Press, 1955), although with a view to showing John's agreement with Thomas Aquinas.

254. *Canticle* 13, 2–8 (ed., 660–62; trans., 520–23) is a mini-treatise on rapture, which in those who have not yet attained the state of the perfect causes the soul to temporarily leave the body. The famous description of Paul in 2 Cor. 12:2 is cited, as well as the teaching of Teresa (see *Interior Castle* 6, 4–5). It is evident from this passage and others (e.g., *Night* 2, 1, 2; *Canticle* 14, 18) that John thought of rapture (*rapto*) as a frequent component of the stage of the proficient, but something that was meant to be surpassed. John refers to Paul's rapture in several other places (e.g., *Night* 2, 24, 3; 2, 26, 4; *Canticle* 14/15, 15 and 18; 19, 1 and 5; and *Flame* 4, 12).

255. *Canticle* 13.9 (ed., 662; trans., 523). I thank Edward Howells for pointing out the importance of this shift.

256. *Canticle* 14/15, 14–16. John cites Elijah having contact with God through the whistling of a gentle breeze (1 Kgs. 19:11–13 Vg.), an important text in Christian mystical tradition, cited, for example, by Gregory the Great in *Moralia in Iob*, 5.36.66.

257. *Canticle* 14/15, 17–21 (ed., 668–70; trans., 532–34). See Gregory, *Moralia in Iob* 5.23.45–36.66. The fact that John uses both of these biblical passages, which also appear in close association in Gregory, argues to a real dependence on the pope here.

258. *Canticle* 14/15, 29 (ed., 672; trans., 537). This double stanza ends (14/15, 30) with a brief account of the difference between spiritual betrothal and spiritual marriage.

259. *Canticle* 22, 3 (ed., 689; trans., 560).

260. Spiritual inebriation appears often in Christian mysticism; for an overview, see Hermann Josef Sieben and Aimé Solignac, "Ivresse spirituelle," DS 7:2312–37, which treats John in cols. 2333–34.

261. *Canticle* 26, 3 (ed., 700; trans., 575).

262. *Canticle* 26, 8 (ed., 701; trans., 576). Altogether *Canticles* 24–26 contain fifteen citations from the Song of Songs.

263. *Canticle* 27, 1 (ed., 704; trans., 581). My thanks to Edward Howells for drawing my attention to this daring passage.

264. For example, John is supposedly treating spiritual marriage, but he also at times speaks of spiritual espousal (*desposorio espiritual*; e.g., 28, 10; 30, 1). Is this just a slip?

265. *Canticle* 29, 2 (ed., 708; trans., 587; emphasis added). In defending this view, John uses both the apocryphal legend of Mary Magdalene (29, 2) and the text of Song of Songs 3:5 about not awakening the bride from her slumber (29, 1 and 3).

266. *Canticle* 3, 1 is often cited as another text where John insists on the soul practicing "the spiritual exercises of both the active and the contemplative life," but here John is talking about the soul searching for God, not the soul who has attained spiritual marriage. This issue is taken up by Howells, *John of the Cross and Teresa of Avila*, 37–38, who argues that the line taken in the commentary reflects John's main teaching on action and contemplation.

267. *Canticle* 30, 7–9. John illustrates this by citing Song of Songs 3:11. This chapter uses a large number of citations from the Song, such as 6:3; 1:4; 7:1; 6:4; and 2:5.

268. *Canticle* 31, 1 (ed., 714–15; trans., 595). In 31, 2 John speaks of how the Bridegroom's "abyssal love" (*abisal amor*) absorbs the soul in himself even more powerfully than a torrent of fire would devour a drop of dew.

269. *Canticle* 31, 10 (ed., 716–17; trans., 598). Note that there is no mention of the memory here.

270. *Canticle* 32, 6 (ed., 718; trans., 600). The phrase "Love becomes the purpose for which he loves" (*y así el amor tiene la razón del fin*) echoes Bernard of Clairvaux's statement *amo ut amem* in *Super Cantica* 83.4 (*Opera Sancti Bernardi* 2:300).

271. In describing union here, John returns to emphasizing its effect on all three of the soul's higher powers: "He elevates her intellect to divine understanding . . . ; he moves her will freely to love of God . . . ; he fills her memory with divine knowledge" (35, 5).

272. *Canticle* 36, 5 (ed., 725–26; trans., 611–12). Kavanaugh notes that the word *hermosura* appears twenty-three times in this passage.

273. *Canticle* 36, 13 (ed., 727; trans., 614).

274. John does provide more light on this issue in his discussion of the movements of the soul as divine in *Flame* 1, 9, where he says, "Although they [the soul's movements] belong to it, they belong to it because God works them in it and with it, for it wills and consents to them" (ed., 833; trans., 644).

275. *Canticle* 38, 5 (ed., 731–32; trans., 620).

276. *Canticle* 39, 3 (ed., 733; trans., 623).

277. *Canticle* 39, 3 (ed., 733–34; my trans.): ". . . porque el alma, unida y transformada en Dios, aspira en Dios a Dios la misma aspiración divina que Dios—estando ella en El transformada—aspira en sí mismo a ella."

278. John continues with a detailed account of this transformation in the Trinity, begun in this life but to be completed in the next (*Canticle* 39, 4–6). "This is transformation in the three Persons in power [i.e., the Father], in wisdom [the Son], and in love [the Holy Spirit], and thus the soul is like God through this transformation. He created her in his image and likeness that she might attain such resemblance" (39, 4). John continues to stress throughout that the transformation is one by participation, not by nature.

279. *Canticle* 39, 11 (ed., 736; trans., 626).

280. *Canticle* 39, 14 (ed., 737; trans., 627).

281. *Canciones* stanza 40 (ed. 737; trans., 628).

282. *Canticle* 40, 6 (ed., 739; trans., 630).

283. *Flame* 1, 3 (ed., 830; trans., 642).

284. *Flame* 1, 13 (ed., 835; trans., 645).

285. The text on the transformation of the substance and powers in *Flame* 1, 17 shows John's oscillation between a dyadic and triadic view of the soul. He first mentions how the intellect, the will, and the *substance* are transformed, but immediately after also refers to the memory.

286. The digression that follows (*Flame* 1, 19–26) explicitly refers to the *Dark Night* in 1, 25.

287. Mystical death (*mors mystica*) is another traditional theme that appears in John in a number of places. It is also featured in his poem "Stanzas of the Soul that Suffers with a Longing to See God ("Coplas del alma que pena por ver a Dios"); see Kavanaugh, 55–56.

288. *Flame* 1, 32 (ed., 847; trans., 655). This passage aptly summarizes the *nada–todo* dialectic. The treatment of the first stanza ends with a summary in 1, 35.

289. *Flame* 2, 1 (ed., 850–51; trans., 658).

290. *Flame* 2, 7 (ed., 853; trans., 660).

291. *Flame* 2, 9. Like Teresa (*Life* 29, 13–14), John dwells on the delight and effects of such a wound of love. In 2, 10–11, John says that the tiny mustard seed (Matt. 13:31–32) that anoints the tip of the arrow diffuses itself through all the soul's veins and enlarges them to make it seem that the whole universe is a sea of love. The mustard seed image is not found in Teresa's own account.

292. *Flame* 2, 17 (ed., 859; trans., 664).

293. *Flame* 2, 34 (ed., 867; trans., 671).

294. *Flame* 3, 5 (ed., 873; trans., 675).

295. *Flame* 3, 10 (ed., 876–77; trans., 677).

296. John's treatment falls into two parts (3, 18–26 and 68–77) due to the long digression in the middle of *Flame* 3. On the deep caverns, see esp. Howells, "Is Darkness a Psychological or Theological Category in the Thought of John of the Cross?," 151–54.

297. John's view is evident especially in his responses to objectors who claim that his views are destroying rather than elevating nature; see *Ascent* 3, 7–8 and *Flame* 3, 75, as well as passages like *Night* 2, 6, 1–6. There is a discussion in Howells, *John of the Cross and Teresa of Avila*, 48–50, who argues that John's teaching, despite its strong language, suspends rather than destroys the natural actions of the faculties.

298. To my mind, the most original attempt to explain properly mystical

knowing before that of John was created by the twelfth-century Cistercian William of Saint-Thierry, especially in his *Golden Letter* (*Epistola aurea*), on which see McGinn, *Growth*, 256–59.

299. *Flame* 3, 23 (ed., 883; trans., 682). In this connection John cites a text from Gregory the Great's *Homilia 30 in Evangelium* (PL 76:1220).

300. *Flame* 3, 69 (ed., 908; trans., 702).

301. For a historical overview, see the essays in Gavrilyuk and Coakley, *Spiritual Senses*; this volume, however, does not, alas, contain anything on the Spanish mystics.

302. In *Ascent* 2, 11, 6, John seems to hedge, saying that a feeling in the senses sent by God "produces its effect in the spirit at the very moment of the perception" (ed., 414; trans., 181), so one does not have to be worried about being misled by the devil.

303. For more on "spiritual feelings," see *Ascent* 32, 1–4; *Night* 2, 11, 7; and *Canticle* 14/15 passim.

304. I have not found much reflection on this issue, although the supernatural activation of the senses is discussed by Morel, *Le sens de l'existence selon Saint Jean de la Croix*, 2:52–55, 97, 123–26.

305. *Flame* 3, 71 (ed., 909; trans., 703). On the dual abyss, see Howells, "Is Darkness a Psychological or Theological Category in the Thought of St. John of the Cross?," 153.

306. In the course of this discussion, John inserts a digression within the digression, a few chapters in which he reprises his teaching on how God works on the intellect (3, 47–48), the will (3, 49–51), and the memory (3, 53) in the act of contemplation. This is a good summary of issues treated at more length in the *Ascent* and the *Night*.

307. *Flame* 3, 78 (ed., 913; trans., 706).

308. On the profound, and profoundly negative, trinitarian theology of these texts and others in John's prose works, see Williams, "Deflections of Desire," esp. 120–26.

309. *Flame* 4, 14 (ed., 924; trans., 713).

310. *Flame* 4, 17 (ed., 925; trans., 715).

311. *Sayings of Light and Love*, 60 (ed., 985; trans., 90).

CHAPTER 5

Other Voices of
Spanish Mysticism

I N WHAT HAS BEEN CALLED the Golden Age of Spanish Mysticism, the names of Ignatius, Teresa, and John of the Cross
stand out, but there were other figures who made important contributions, though most are little known outside
Spain.[1] Something of the extent of the Spanish mystical wave
can be seen in the history of Jose Maria de la Cruz Molinar, who
provides long lists of the Spanish mystics of the period (many
hundreds in total).[2] Of course, one can wonder if all the figures
he lists are properly "mystical" authors who wrote about the
highest forms of union with God, or rather were primarily ascetical and spiritual writers. Nonetheless, these authors (however
many) played a significant part in early modern Catholicism. In
the context of a general history such as this, it is not possible
to consider more than a handful of the later Spanish mystics.[3]
English-language students of mysticism have the added disad-
vantage that there is no adequate account of the whole range of
Spanish mysticism in our language. The best analysis is still the
three volumes of E. Allison Peers's *Studies of the Spanish Mystics*
(originally published between 1927 and 1936, and in a revised
version in 1951); his essays give extensive discussions of many of
the figures treated here.[4]

Of the contemporaries of Teresa and John, the one who argu-
ably has had the greatest impact was the Augustinian friar Luis
de León (1527–1593). I start with him before proceeding to a
survey of some mystics of the other religious orders during the
period ca. 1550–ca. 1650. The religious orders were powerful in

Catholic Spain—and often powerfully opposed to each other. Although Teresa was friendly with Franciscans and had confessors from both the Dominicans and the Jesuits, such cooperation was not always the case. The dark side of Spanish mysticism is colored not only by the suspicion of mysticism found in the Inquisition but also by the bitter conflicts between and even in the midst of the religious orders. Nevertheless, most Spanish mystics were shaped by the spirituality of their orders, and their religious affiliation provides a helpful organizing template. I will also add two appendices to this chapter, one devoted to mysticism of the other country on the Iberian peninsula (i.e., Portuguese, or "Lusophone," mysticism), and the second concerning Spanish mysticism in the New World. The Americas provided fertile ground for Spanish Catholicism and its mysticism, although many of the predominantly female mystics of the Americas come from the late seventeenth and eighteenth centuries and so lie beyond the limits of this book.

An Augustinian Mystic: Luis de León

The Augustinian order produced several spiritual and mystical writers in the sixteenth century, such as Alonso de Orozco (1500–1591), whose *Mountain of Contemplation* was published in Seville in 1544.[5] Luis de León, however, a contemporary of Teresa and John, was the most significant Augustinian mystic.[6] Luis never met Teresa, but at the instigation of her disciple Ana de Jesús, he put out the first edition of the saint's *Vida* and was engaged in writing her biography when he died. Luis was a different mystic from Teresa and John, and also from the earlier Franciscan mystics like Laredo and Osuna. Among the Spanish mystics of the time, Luis is the great representative of the humanist dimension of early modern Catholicism.

Born at Belmonte in Castile in 1527, Luis came from a well-to-do family, but one that at least on his mother's side had *converso* (i.e., Jewish) blood, something that may have contributed to the opposition he encountered. In 1543 he entered the Augustinian order at Salamanca. Luis received an excellent education both at Salamanca and at Alcalá, where he learned Hebrew. He can be said to be a model of the Erasmian humanist, a fluent writer, well trained in Greek and Latin (he translated classical poems into the vernacular), and skilled in Hebrew, as his biblical translations and commentaries show. Luis rendered the Song of Songs from Hebrew into Spanish and wrote two commentaries on it, a shorter one in Spanish and a longer Latin triple commentary, where the *prima explicatio* deals with the literal level, the *secunda explicatio* concerns the spiritual, or mystical, meaning, and the *tertia explicatio* treats the history of the church, the Bride of Christ.[7] This translation, as well as his vernacular versions of some Psalms and parts of Job, was not welcome in Spain, especially after the Council of Trent had reaffirmed the authority (*auctoritas*) of Jerome's Vulgate. Rigid conservatives interpreted this "authority" as complete inerrancy; Luis and more moderate scholars said that the Vulgate was authoritative in doctrinal matters but that the Hebrew text (*Hebraica veritas*) often contained better readings. This was a major source of his difficulties within the repressive Spanish church-state system.

In 1561, Luis gained a theological chair at Salamanca, but his teaching soon provoked strong reactions, especially among the Dominicans, ever the watchdogs of orthodoxy. Luis himself did not suffer fools gladly and made a number of enemies, sometimes unnecessarily. As a result of the actions of the Dominican Bartolomé de Medina and the Hellenist professor León de Castro, who insisted on the superiority of the Septuagint over all other Bibles, Luis was arrested by the Inquisition in March of 1572 and underwent an investigation of almost five years, all the while in close confinement, before being cleared in December of 1576.[8] He appears to have been treated better than John of the Cross, but he was imprisoned for a longer period of time and was under threat of torture. Luis wrote a number of his poems in prison and also began his greatest work, *The Names of Christ* (*Los nombres de Cristo*).[9] As with John of the Cross, Luis's prison ordeal was a turning point in his life. Upon his release, he was welcomed back to Salamanca by crowds of colleagues and students and then (at least according to one story) began his next lecture with words, *Dicebamus hesterna die* ("As we were saying yesterday").

Luis de León was emboldened by his prison experience to continue his biblical research and writing, as well as to compose both prose and poetry. Despite his status as a university professor, he wrote many of his works in the vernacular, including a long commentary on Job.[10] The third book of *The Names of Christ* contains an eloquent defense of writing theology in the vernacular. Luis says, "Spanish can express the loftiest thoughts. We often misuse it out of ignorance, yet this is our fault, not the fault of the Spanish language. . . . Each and every language is capable of expressing the whole range of human knowledge."[11] Like John of the Cross, Luis de León won equal fame as a prose writer and a poet.[12] No less a figure than his contemporary Miguel de Cervantes (1547–1616) said of him in his *Galatea* (1585), "I would like to end my song . . . with the praise for a genius who astounds the world and in his ecstasy might rob us of our senses. All that I have shown till now appears in the figure of Fray Luis de León, whom I revere, adore, and follow."[13]

Luis's ecclesiastical troubles were not ended, because he was investigated by the Inquisition for a second time in 1582–84, although once again he was exonerated. During this period, in 1583 he published the first edition of his treatise *The Perfect Wife* (*La perfecta casada*), a biblical account of the ideal wife, a work that has remained popular in Spanish literature.[14] The same year saw the first edition of his theological and mystical masterpiece, *The Names of Christ*.[15] Luis's controversial career did not prevent the Augustinians from giving him full support, as can be seen from their electing him provincial for Spain a short time before his death in 1591.

Luis's poems use the same *lira* form as John of the Cross but are different in content and tone from the highly charged spiritual eroticism of his Carmelite contemporary. The poet-translator Willis Barnstone makes the following comparison: "Stated simply, perhaps reductively, in the mystical process sound and astronomy are for Fray Luis what light/darkness and erotic love are for John of the Cross. As the sense of vision in Saint John is the vehicle toward union with God, expressed in the allegory of human love, in Fray Luis the sense of hearing is the vehicle toward union expressed in nocturnal celestial concordance."[16] Not all of Luis's twenty-three original poems are mystical, but a number witness to a sense of God's presence in the natural world, especially the heavens, in a manner reminiscent of other cosmic mystical poets, such as the English Thomas Traherne.[17] A good example can be found in the ode he wrote to his friend, the blind musician Francisco de Salinas.

The fundamental theme of this ode, which begins *El aire se serena / Y viste de hermosura y luz non usada* ("The air become serene / and robed in beauty and an unknown light"), is the role of music in lifting the soul to God—earthly music, the music of the heavenly spheres, and finally the divine music of the life to come.[18] The first three stanzas, in good Platonic and Pythagorean fashion, praise Salinas's skill in arousing the soul to retrieve the memory of "its dazzling and primordial origin" (*de su origen primera esclarecida*) and forgetting the false joys of earth. In stanzas 4–6 Luis paints a picture of the soul rising up through the heavens, first by hearing the music of the spheres (stanza 4), and then the music played by God, "the great Master," on his "immense zither" (stanza 5).[19] The sound produces wonderful harmony (stanza 6).

In stanzas 7 and 8 the music raises the poet briefly up to the ecstasy of heaven itself, where he is drowned and ravished in a "sea of sweetness" (*mar de dulzura*). Luis's language strains to express the limits of ecstatic excess found in union with God:

O desmayo dichoso!	O happy deep collapse!
O muerte que das vida!	O death conferring life!
O dulce olvido!	O sweet oblivion!
Durase en tu reposo,	Now let me never lapse
Sin ser restituído	Into the low vile run
Jamás a aqueste bajo y vil sentido!	Of senses! Let my rest in you be won!

In the final two stanzas, the poet returns to this world after his ecstatic experience. In stanza 9 he expresses the hope that his friend Salinas may experience such ecstasy in his own life,[20] and in stanza 10 he praises Salinas, whose superlative music was the origin of his own awakening of the senses "to the divine good" (*al bien divino*).[21]

Several of Luis de León's other poems express a cosmic mysticism, in which, somewhat like Francis of Assisi, the presence of God in the universe, especially the heavens, inspires the soul to ascend toward union with God. The sixteen stanzas of the poem called "Serene Night," or "The Night of Stars," beginning *Cuando contemplo el cielo / de innumerables luces adornando* ("When I behold the sky / With stars innumerable spangled bright"), provides an example.[22] In contemplating the heavens, the poet is brought to reflect on his own sad condition in "the low prison-house" of this life (stanzas 1–5). He is then moved to issue a call to mortals to awake from slumber and gaze up to the sky to learn their true destiny (stanzas 6–8). The poet next takes the reader on a journey through the heavenly spheres, where "In noblest forms are seen / What is and what shall be and what has been" (*do vive mejorada / lo que es, lo que sera, lo que ha pasado*). We pass through the sphere of the moon, of Mars and Jupiter, and of Saturn (stanzas 9–13). The cosmic trip eventually brings the soul to a vision of heaven, though beheld partially and from afar (stanzas 14–16). Stanza 15 is especially rich:

Immensa hermosura	Here beauty infinite
Aquí se muestra toda, y resplandece	Unveils itself, and light, quintessence pure,
Clarísima luz pura,	Transparent gleams: no night
Que jamás anochece:	Its radiance may obscure,
Eterna primavera aquí florece.	Spring's flowered splendor here is ever sure.

Another of the cosmic mystical poems is called the "Dwelling Place of Heaven" (*Morada del Cielo*). It once again testifies to the role of nature, especially the heavens, in triggering Luis de León's sense of contact with God and a vision of heaven.[23] The poem begins with the contrast between heaven, the "Fair realm of radiant light" (*Alma region luciente*) and the earth, where hail and lightning threaten. The focus is christological, since beginning with stanza 2 the poet sees the "Good Shepherd" leading his flock upward into the joys of the life to come.[24] Stanza 4 includes a eucharistic reference, as the Shepherd both feeds the flock and is their food (*Y les da mesa llena, / Pastor y pasto él solo y suerte Buena*). Once again, music comes to the fore as the Shepherd rests with his flock at midday (see Song of Songs 1:7) and plays music for them (stanza 5). The next two stanzas again reach up toward the level of ecstasy:

Toca el rabel sonoro	Immortal ecstasy
Y el immortal dulzor al alma pasa,	The soul drinks as he strikes the sounding lyre
Con que envilece el oro,	Gold is mere mockery
Y ardiendo se traspasa,	In this consuming fire
Y lanza en aquel bien libra de tasa.	Of endless blessings that outrun desire.

One should note the appeal to mystical epektasis, unending desire, in the final line.

In stanza 7, the poet expresses hope that the music of heaven, at least in some faint way, might descend into his own sensation (*En mí sentido*), so that his soul might journey from earth and be totally changed into Divine Love (*Y toda en ti, ó amor, la convirtiese*). Luis also aspires to this foretaste of heaven in stanza 8, but he knows he is still separated from ultimate rest in the beloved "Spouse," another of the names of Christ— "Ah then would I indeed, / Beloved, know thy noontide resting place! . . . Nor ever from thy fold my steps retrace" (*Conocería donde / Sesteas, dulce Esposo, y desatada. . . . Vivirá junta, sin vagar errada*).

With regard to mysticism of Luis's prose works, I will concentrate on *The Names of Christ*. Although it is not a mystical treatise in the sense of a text dedicated primarily to the themes of recollection, meditation /contemplation, ecstatic states, and union with God, such motifs are vital in the work. *The Names* is a biblical theology, a *summa* of Christian teaching about the history of salvation. The genre, or rather mix of genres, Luis chose was novel. His exegesis of the Bible is set within a Platonic dialogue featuring three Augustinian friars, which is in turn located within a pastoral novel where the beauty of the setting reflects the loftiness of the subjects being treated. Even though Fray Marcelo as the older biblical scholar does most of the talking, the interaction between him and Fray Juliano as a commentator and Fray Sabino as a young poet provides liveliness to the text.[25] The focus is christological throughout: Jesus Christ is the center of scriptural revelation and our only way to salvation. Fray Luis argues this point passionately in the Dedication:

> As Christ Our Savior is a source or rather is an ocean which holds in itself all that is sweet and meaningful that belongs to man, in the same way the study of his person, the revelation of the treasure, is the most meaningful and dearest of all knowledge. . . . Wisdom for man is in the knowledge of Christ and in truth it is the highest and most divine of all wisdoms. . . . All these [divine] perfections or a great part of them can be understood if we grasp the force and the significance of the names which the Holy Spirit gives Christ in the Scriptures. These names are abbreviations of God in which he has marvelously enclosed all that human understanding can grasp and is suitable to grasp.[26]

Luis was convinced that both testaments testify to the saving message about the Savior. His incorporation of mystical elements into this humanist biblical theology formed a new chapter in the history of Spanish mysticism.

For all his talents as theologian, poet, translator, and prose stylist, Luis de León was a biblical professor before all. In his Dedication to *The Names of Christ* he asserts that Scholastic disputes are only the beginning of theology, while its growth is in the "doctrine of the saints." He continues: "Its summit, its perfection and its loftiness are the Holy Scriptures. To understand them is indeed the necessary end."[27] Thus, the bulk of his writings are Bible commentaries.[28] He even wrote a short treatise on the senses of scripture (*Tractatus de sensibus sacrae Scripturae*) in 1581.[29] Like Thomas Aquinas (STh Ia, q. 10), Luis argued that the literal sense of the Bible, that is, the meaning of the words in their grammatical setting, including the figures of speech proper to the original languages, is the fundamental basis for determining the teaching of the church. He also followed a number of other expositors in holding that biblical texts can have several literal meanings. Luis by no means excluded an important role for the allegorical sense, including both what was called *allegoria sermonis/dicti*, that is, a deeper meaning hidden in the words themselves, and *allegoria facti*, "when what the words signify truly happened, but the things that happened and are signified through the words signify and stand for other things."[30] Luis contended that the mystical or allegorical sense was primarily found in the Old Testament, which may be why his commentaries concentrate on revealing the christological meaning of the books of that testament.

Luis de León was a biblical scholar, but was he also a mystic? There has been debate about this. For those who use Teresa of Avila and John of the Cross as the touchstones of all mysticism, and/or insist that mystics must testify to their own personal experience of union, it is clear that Luis cannot be a mystic.[31] Fortunately, other Luisian scholars have taken a less restricted view of mysticism and have pointed to strong mystical elements both in some of the Augustinian's poems and in *The Names of Christ*.[32] The scholar of Spanish spirituality Melquiades Andrés Martín had no hesitation in saying that Luis was a mystic.[33] To measure all mystics against one standard is to deny that someone like Fray Luis might have a distinctive contribution to make to the history of Spanish mysticism. Rather, we need to ask *how* Luis's texts are mystical and *what* they have to tell us about the varieties of mysticism in early modern Spain. In order to do this we now turn to *The Names of Christ*.[34]

Naming the Messiah began in the Old Testament (see Isa. 9:6–7), at least according to the Christian interpretation, and is also found in the New Testament. Devotion to the "Name of Jesus" was a part of Christian spirituality almost from the start,[35] and theological concern for studying the biblical names of Christ has had a long history. As pointed out by Henk J. M. Schoot,[36] naming Christ had a central role in the history of Christianity, not least in Spain, beginning in the seventh century with the chapter *De Filio Dei* in Isidore of Seville's *Etymologies*.[37] Furthermore, as Schoot shows, the endeavor to "name" Christ by investigating the names in scripture forms a part of Christian negative theology—Christ, in his divine-human nature, is both *omninominabile* (named with every name) and also *innominabile* (beyond all naming). Thus, Luis de León's endeavor was not new, but he brought to it three special contributions: a theory of the meaning of "name," a broad and nuanced knowledge of the Bible, and a humanist and aesthetic sensibility toward the natural world as a mirror of God. This unusual combination makes his book not only a masterpiece of Spanish literature but also a significant contribution to theology. As Colin Thompson puts it, "Unlike most theological treatises, it was written with deliberate attention to style, so that its readers might not only learn, but also enjoy what it taught through the harmony and sweetness of its language."[38]

The pastoral fiction of *The Names of Christ* begins in the garden of an estate near an Augustinian monastery with Fray Sabino unfolding a paper on which Fray Marcelo has written down the ten main names of Christ recorded in scripture and asking him for an exposition. Marcelo agrees, but says, "We must first define what a name means, what is its function, for what purpose it is introduced, and in what manner it is to be used."[39] The "Introduction" to book I thus forms a treatise on "Names in General" (*De los nombres en general*).[40] The noun, or name, is defined as "a brief word which is substituted for the thing of which it is spoken and is taken to be the thing itself."[41] Luis's theory of names is resolutely realist: "The name is the same as what is being named" (*O nombre es aquello mismo que se nombra*), not in its real being, but in the mind and the mouth. The root of this correspondence is in the Neoplatonic principle that the perfection of things, especially of rational humanity, means that all things exist in the human mind, which has an affinity to God, who pre-contains everything in himself. Coarse material beings cannot exist in each other, but the *idea* of material beings can exist in the mind as the same as the real being, but "by reason of a similarity, although the quality and mode is different." According to Luis, then, there are two kinds of names, or words: the natural words that are true images of exterior things; and the images of art, that is, the spoken words by which we express what is in the mind. For Luis, any biblical name of Christ, even a metaphorical one, is not a literary creation or convention but an expression of the unity and interrelatedness of things in the created universe.[42]

The theological roots of the Augustinian's theory become clear when he goes on to distinguish between the common names that apply to many objects and the proper names, like those of Christ, which "designate a particularity and express something proper in reference to what they are speaking." These words, in their very sound, should be as similar as possible to the thing they substitute for in order to make it present to the mind. In accord with an ancient tradition, Luis holds that this is particularly true with regard to "the first of all languages, Hebrew," as shown by God bringing all the animals before Adam to be named (Gen. 2:19). There are three kinds of such similarity: in figure or form; in sound; and in the origin of the derivation or meaning. Luis illustrates the similarity in sound and derivation by noting a number of names from the Old Testament, as well as that of Peter from the New. He summarizes: "All the names which are bestowed by God's command bear in them the meaning of some particular secret that the thing named contains in itself and in this meaning the name becomes similar to the thing."[43]

When Luis turns to the similarity between name and thing "by the letters with which we write the name, their number and disposition, and what they habitually cause in us when we pronounce them,"[44] he reveals an acquaintance with Jewish speculation about the Hebrew language, especially as found in the Kabbalah. The fact that some of the Augustinian's distant ancestors were Jewish, as well as his knowledge of Hebrew and Aramaic, has led some investigators to make Luis out to be a crypto-Jew of the kind the Inquisitors feared. There is little evidence for this, but there certainly is a good case to be made for his interest in Christian Cabala, that is, the way some Hebraists made apologetic use of Jewish mystical speculation to show that the inner truth of Judaism revealed God as Trinity and Jesus as the Messiah.[45] Although he does not cite them explicitly, Luis knew the writings of such Christian Cabalists as Johannes Reuchlin (1455–1522), the author of *De verbo mirifico* (1494) and *De arte cabalistica* (1516),[46] as well as Petrus Galatinus (ca. 1460–1540), whose *De arcanis catholicae veritatis* was published in 1518. It seems unlikely that Luis had any direct contact with Jewish Kabbalistic texts themselves, such as the *Zohar*, though some of his Latin sources may have had. The Augustinian's use of Cabalistic motifs appears in this part of the introduction, as well as several later places in the book. It is found elsewhere in his writings, such as in the commentary on Genesis, where he mentions Marsilio Ficino and Giovanni Pico della Mirandola, who had pioneered interest in Cabala.

Luis contends that, in the original Hebrew, the divine books contain numerous examples of similarity by sound and etymological origin, and, with regard to form, there are numerous "secrets and mysteries" (*los secretos y los misterios*) revealed by adding and removing letters to change good fortune to bad and vice versa, as well as male to female significations. Other letters modify their forms and "are transposed and disguised with different faces and gestures like the chameleon." Without using the terms, Luis is referring to some of the standard techniques of Jewish Kabbalah also known to the Christian Cabalists (*gematria/notarikon/temurah*). The illustration he gives concerns the ineffable Four-Letter Name of God (the Tetragrammaton), which, according to Luis, perfectly conforms to his principle of mutual interpenetration—each letter is in all of them and all is in each, revealing both God's simplicity and the unity and identity of his perfections. So, Luis concludes,

"It is not only in the nature of the letters, but also in their form and disposition that the name represents him in some way."[47]

At this point, Juliano and Sabino interrupt Marcello to ask how any name or image can be said to stand in for or replace the unknowable God who resides within all things. Marcello responds that God is indeed present everywhere, but in this life his presence never appears to us in a direct fashion. Only when we get to heaven and see God directly will there be no need for names, or, rather, each saint will be given "a white stone on which will be written a secret name" (Rev. 2:17), which will be an immediate communication of the Divine Being itself. So, all names in this life are in a sense more apophatic than cataphatic, concealing more than they reveal in their plethora of dissimilitude. Since Adam's fall, therefore, we must give God many names, not ones of our own making but those revealed in scripture. The names that God reveals to us are certainly *proper* names (i.e., they reveal something), but they are not perfect or equal names. They disclose something of "the eternal and incomprehensible Word that is born and lives in God's womb," the Word destined to become human from the beginning of creation.[48] Because of the poverty of our understanding, the Holy Spirit gives Christ many names in the Bible, though Marcello says he will concentrate on the ten "most substantial names" (*más substanciales*) of Christ as man, not on his divine names.

In presenting the proper names of Christ (originally ten on the mysterious paper of Marcelo, later fourteen),[49] Luis de León follows a standard pattern. Sabino reads the name and selected biblical texts from the paper, and then Marcelo expounds on these and other texts, sometimes with the interjection of questions from Sabino and Juliano. In what follows I will concentrate on the names that have significant mystical aspects (especially Shepherd, Prince of Peace, Husband, Son of God, Beloved, and Jesus). The names seem to follow a general pattern based on salvation history, beginning with "Bud" to indicate Christ's birth, and closing with "Jesus" as the goal of salvation, forming a fitting conclusion to the whole series. *The Names of Christ*, however, has a more rhetorical than systematic structure. In explaining the names, Luis employs thousands of biblical texts, and liberally cites from a number of patristic sources, especially Augustine.[50]

The name "Bud" (*Pimpollo*) touches on "the quality and order of Christ's birth and his new and marvelous generation" (ed., 406; trans., 53-54). Luis includes a discussion of creation here, affirming that God created the world "to communicate himself to himself and to spread his goodness among his creatures" (ed., 412; trans., 58). Creatures can be united with God in three ascending ways: by nature, by grace, and by personal union. Therefore, the goal of creation was the personal hypostatic union of the Word and human nature in Jesus Christ. Under the influence of Duns Scotus and his followers, Luis, like some other mystics, held to what has been called the absolute predestination of Christ, that is, that the Word would have become flesh even if Adam had not sinned.[51]

The second name, "Face of God" (*Faces de Dios*), is based on Psalm 81:14 and other texts. Humanity was created in the image and likeness of God (Gen. 1:26–27), that is, according to God's true face and image, namely, the Word made incarnate in Jesus Christ. Even as human, Christ is God's true face, "because no creature or assemblage of creatures causes the rays of the divine qualities to shine on our eyes more clearly or abundantly than Christ's soul, his body, all his gifts, deeds, and words, and everything that belongs to his mission."[52]

The third name of Christ is the familiar "Way" (*Camino*) of John 14:6. Luis specifies five senses in which Christ can be called "Way." The image of the journey leads to a rare mention of the traditional three stages of the mystical path—beginners, progressives, and perfect—something that does not play a constitutive role in his mysticism.[53]

The fourth name, "Shepherd" (*Pastor*), gives Luis de León the first opportunity to talk in depth about the love between the Good Shepherd and his sheep and to move into more mystical themes. Christ applied the name to himself (John 10:11), and the Song of Songs, read as pastoral idyll, used the love of two shepherds to reveal the deepest mysteries of the divine–human conjunction. Employing a series of texts from the Song, Luis emphasizes the total love of the Christ the Shepherd for his flock (ed., 448–49; trans., 92–93). Such overpowering love leads the Shepherd to unite himself to each and every member of the flock: "He dwells in the breast of each of his sheep, and, as making them feed, consists in uniting them to himself and making them enter into himself. This, as I have said a little while ago, is the final quality of the shepherd, to realize the unity of the flock belongs to him."[54] Our union with Christ, both personal and communal in the church, is clearly an important theme in *The Names of God*, one that Luis will return to in more detail in the later books.

The final two names in book I are "Mountain" (*Monte*) and "Everlasting Father" (*Padre del Siglo Futuro*, Isa. 9:6), a title that might seem to impinge on the personal property of God the Father, until Luis explains it in terms of the mystery of redemption in which Christ, the God-man, becomes our father in bearing us to new life through his death on the cross. The long analysis of "Everlasting Father" is interesting for its laying out of Luis's theological anthropology and doctrine of redemption. Unlike Scholastic theologians and many previous mystics, the Augustinian displays only marginal concern for anthropology, which may indicate a humanist critique of medieval theology. To be sure, Luis says that humanity was created in the image of God, but his major interest is not in the first birth according to Adam but in the rebirth we can enjoy in our new life, as Christ told Nicodemus (John 3:3). In describing the rebirth, Luis engages in a long analysis of the conflict between the image of God given us in nature and the image of the devil we labor under since Adam's fall. Although he condemns the errors of Luther (ed., 487; trans., 130), Luis's own formulations of the extent of the effects of sin on humanity are sometimes rather extreme, as when he says, "As the termite destroys the piece of wood, similarly our nature has in vain adapted itself to this malice or evil spirit; being absorbed in it, it is almost totally destroyed" (ed., 484; trans., 126–27). Other texts in *The Names of Christ* seem to qualify such views from the perspective of Tridentine orthodoxy. In any case, "Everlasting Father" is central to the Augustinian's Christology and his view of our solidarity in Christ. Luis's view of this solidarity is rooted in Paul (Eph. 1:10; 2:6; 2 Cor. 5:14; Rom. 6:6) and leads him to some telling expressions of God's everlasting plan for our new birth. All who are reborn have preexisted in Christ as their principle. He puts it thus:

> Even those who, each in his time, existed by themselves were to be reborn and to live in justice, and those who after the resurrection of the body—just, glorious, and deified throughout [*por todas partes deificados*], distinct in person—will be one spirit as much among themselves as with Christ. We will all be one Christ. We even, not in actual form, but in original virtuality [*virtud original*], have been in him before having been reborn through God's action and will.[55]

Luis continues his discussion of union and rebirth in Christ through his saving death on the cross in the second long half of the discussion of this name, ending with an interpretation of Psalm 104, a hymn to God the Creator, as well as Sabino's poetic rendering of the Psalm into Spanish.

Book II of *The Names of Christ* is shorter, consisting of only four names: "Arm of God" (*Brazo de Dios*), "King of God" (*Rey de Dios*), "Prince of Peace" (*Príncipe de la Paz*), and "Husband" (*Esposo*). The book is situated later in the afternoon of the same day and takes place on an idyllic small island in the river that flows by the estate. The "Dedication" that opens the book bewails the prevalence of sin in human

life, especially that of the Jews who rejected and killed the long-prom-
ised Messiah, something that fills Luis's heart with grief. This sets up
the first name, "Arm of God," which is largely a dispute with Jewish
exegetes about the meaning of certain messianic texts in the Old Testament. Luis's position here is not that of some imaginary apologist
for Jewish Christianity but is basically Pauline; that is, he insists on the
blindness and errors of current Jews but displays a hope that God will
bring back the Jews to belief in the true Messiah at the end of time (see
Rom. 11:25–35).[56] This treatment of redemption sets up a discussion
that might be called Luis's version of the old theological question—
"Why the God-Man?" (*Cur Deus Homo?*). The Augustinian's argument
follows this pattern: (1) God's loving nature means that humanity must
be saved but in a manner that befits the order that regulates the world;
(2) nonetheless, humanity must be punished for sin; and (3) Lucifer's
act in deceiving humanity must also not go unpunished. In light of
these contradictory premises, Luis argues that, on the basis of God's
equanimity and justice, not his absolute power, he decreed that the
Word was to be made flesh and to be allowed to suffer death on the
cross through the devil's wiles. This, Luis concludes, reconciles all the
seeming contradictions in a satisfactory way.

The name "King of God" specifies what kind of a king Christ is (Psalm
2 and Zechariah 14 are the texts cited). Christ is the ideal fulfillment of
the three qualities of kingship: he is personally fit to rule; he rules over
good subjects; and he is able to carry out his task and improve the lives of
his subjects. The section reviews the life and virtues of Christ, especially
his sufferings on the cross, to show how he is the supreme king, both of
his spiritual kingdom on earth and of his coming heavenly kingdom.[57]
The long chapter concludes with a treatment of how Christ rules over his
kingdom by the law of grace during the course of history.

The third name of book II, "Prince of Peace," begins not with a citation of well-known biblical passages but with a typically Luisian invo-
cation of the beauty of the starry vault of heaven as a witness to the
harmony and peace of God's creation. Following Augustine's notion of
peace as the serenity of order, the chapter proceeds by a treatment of
the three ways in which peace can be established: "By respecting God;
by respecting ourselves; by respecting other human beings."[58] The
three modes are interconnected. An important theme that emerges
in this chapter is the notion of God as our friend, something that Luis
finds throughout the Bible and that appears a number of times in
The Names of Christ.[59] In his digressive treatment of the three modes
of achieving peace, Luis includes a discussion of how Christ was able

to establish peace in the world due to his recognition that sin can be overcome not by external rules for conduct, or even by Plato's instruction of the soul, but rather by the healing of the damaged will through the gift of heavenly grace. "We should conclude," he says, "that grace is a likeness to God that, entering into our souls and taking place in the force of its will has, by its own participating in God, the law, inclination, and desire of everything that is just and good."[60] Since grace brings us close to God, we gradually learn to love God, who is like us, and to trust that he loves us in return. The last part of II, 3 is taken up with a discussion of the nature of loving God, which prepares for II, 4, the Name "Husband."

This consideration of loving God begins with a Socratic dialogue among the three participants on the nature of happiness: Who are those who are truly happy and why is this the case? The humanist dialogue on love that follows has its own charm. Happiness implies a love to attain something, says Luis, because no one can live without love. Still, love can be a source of happiness for some and misery for others. Love is identified as any bond between those who love each other that results in the transformation of the lovers into one and the same thing, and yet love also implies the wish and desire for union. Hence, a truer notion of love reveals two modalities: one founded on desire and the second on possession (trans., 235–36). Both kinds of love are based on union—one striving toward it, the other having achieved it. The final issue discussed is what can destroy the bond between two lovers. Here Luis distinguishes between human love, where multiple dangers threaten the union of will between the loves, and the love of Christ, who, because he is essentially good, is the love that will never abandon us (Pss. 102:25–27 and 45:7 are cited).

This eloquent discussion of love sets up the following chapter II, 4, dedicated to the Name *Esposo/Husband*, which is the most mystical section of the work.[61] The Augustianian's treatment of loving union is original and has not received the attention it deserves. Its salient characteristic is its holistic character: Luis insists that our union with Christ involves the body as well as the soul, and that union necessarily presupposes oneness between Christ and all the members of his body primarily as realized in the sacrament of the Eucharist. Luis begins the chapter with a quasi-Scholastic triple division, identifying three significations of Christ as Husband: the union between Christ and the church; the sweetness and pleasure this union brings; and the preparations and circumstances of the wedding.[62] Like Bernard of Clairvaux, he says that the soul's union with her Divine Husband surpasses all other forms of relation to God. Luis makes use of the traditional Pauline text about loving union with Christ in showing the superiority of heavenly conjugation to its earthly counterpart:

> Not only in words but in deeds he is thus our husband. The closest and most loving union between a wedded couple is cold when compared with the union between Christ and our souls. The first union does not fully and completely fuse the two spirits, the two souls, but the union with Christ puts us in touch and makes us one with Christ's spirit. St. Paul says, "But he who cleaves to the Lord is one spirit with him" [1 Cor. 6:17].[63]

From the start, Luis insists that this union involves not just the spirit but the flesh as well, because we become one with Christ's very body, that is, the church. He then enumerates five aspects of the union between Christ and each person.[64] First, the union is one of mutual love; second, Christ imprints his twofold nature on the soul; third, Christ's vigor infuses our whole self, body and soul, to work for him, acting like a tool in his hand. The fourth characteristic is Christ's introduction into the soul of the Holy Spirit, the bond of union between Father and Son in the Trinity (John 14:28 and Rom. 5:5). This is good Augustinian teaching, but to put it into the context of mystical union is reminiscent of William of St. Thierry's "Spirit-centered" view of union. The fifth note underlines union's holistic nature:

> This is, then, the wondrous effect God's presence achieves in our soul, and the divine influence upon our body is not less remarkable. For God became flesh, made himself human in such a way that the union has become an indissoluble marriage, one in which our flesh and the Word have become one, and the nuptial bed where this union took place was, as St. Augustine states, the immaculate womb of Mary.[65]

Luis supports this position with a number of scriptural and patristic texts, particularly those that stress our union with Christ because we are one body with him and are fed by his eucharistic body: "[A]s the holy wafer received in communion becomes part of our flesh and body, this means that we become one and the same with Christ, flesh of his flesh, and not only in spirit, but also in body we are one and the same. Let no one doubt these conclusions."[66]

Luis de León recognizes that there may be debate about this strongly somatic view of union, so Juliano asks Marcelo to elaborate, which he does by arguing that two things can remain distinct, while still at the same time becoming more and more alike, the way that a red hot iron takes on the nature of flame (a traditional mystical topos). He then advances a number of biblical and patristic texts, as well as some original comparisons, to drive home the message that those who receive Christ reverently in the Eucharist become more and more like him. Eating Christ's life-giving food restores what we lost by Adam and Eve's eating of the forbidden fruit.

The Augustinian then explores the nature of this uniting as a love-union (ed., 629–31; trans., 246–48). Our bond with Christ is based on the mutual love of Father and Son in the Trinity (John 17:20–22). Once again, Luis underlines the ecclesial nature of union—our union with the Savior is based on faithfulness and reception of the Eucharist. "We must all be like one in mind and in body, a divine body, and in touch with God's mind and body we shall endure." Luis describes this as a deification (*y aquí se deifica el alma y la carne*, ed., 630), or perhaps better as a "Christification," because it involves soul *and* body. Here Luis introduces a note typical of mystics: an appeal to the ineffability of the experience of the delight of union.[67] He identifies this state with the "hidden manna" and "new name" of Revelation 2:17, as a foretaste of the full union of heaven.

Marcelo goes on to say that this point will be clearer if we have a better conception of what "delight" (*deleite*) is, so there follows a treatise on the nature of delight, one stressing the superiority of spiritual delights over corporeal ones.[68] "Delight," says Luis, "is the feeling and sweet movement that accompanies and terminates all the activities in which we engage our powers and forces in conformity to their natures and desires without hindrance or obstacle."[69] There are three elements in delight: (1) the sensation of delight from the presence or embrace of the thing desired; (2) an activity that brings us closer to the desired goal; and (3) knowledge of the presence of the goal. Luis next turns to the two main kinds of delight: bodily and spiritual. The actions that define us as human beings are the pleasures that come from God—"contemplating him, loving him, and being occupied with him in our thought and desire" (*son el contemplarle y el amarle y el ocupar en él nuestro pensamiento y deseo*—one of the rare mentions of contemplation in the work). The delights of bodily pleasures are tainted and impure, but since God is "an infinite ocean of goodness" (*un océano infinito de bien*), spiritual delights are unending. "Those who love you are rewarded in such a manner that the more they are rewarded the more they love you. . . . [W]hoever drinks from your sweetness, the more he drinks, the thirstier he becomes."[70] The Augustinian continues to emphasize the superiority of God's embrace over mere human marriage, contrasting the immediacy of union with God with the long process of human sexual relations and saying that marriage with God is more powerful and perduring, like a flowing river (citing Ps. 46:4).

At this point Luis de León returns to the Bible, his favorite source. Scripture offers many images and metaphors for this delight—the hidden manna and small stone of Revelation 2:17 (favorite Luisian symbols), as well as a host of images from the Song of Songs: wine, breasts full of milk, dwelling in the heart, a table covered with food, and drunkenness (Song 5:1). The Song of Songs, he claims, depicts all the pleasures God gives; nothing is left unsaid. Nevertheless, he includes two nonscriptural images as he heads toward the conclusion of this section. The first compares the soul to a ship with its sails filled with a breath of pleasure sailing a sea of sweetness.[71] The second recalls John of the Cross, that is, the wooden log gradually penetrated and transformed by the fire of love until it blazes forth on its own. Finally, Marcelo, in the voice of a person totally uplifted on a great wave of love, ends with a hymn: "O light, love, life, highest rest, infinite beauty, immense and sweetest good, let me be dissolved and totally convert me into you, O my Lord." He then ceases, "because there are things that words cannot express."[72]

After a long silence, Marcelo launches into the final part of the name "Husband," a mini-commentary on the Song of Songs. Once again, the holistic nature of the Augustinian's view of union is evident, because the analysis treats the Song as an account of the history of Christ's marriage with his bride the church, the people of God, which is the foundation for the personal union analyzed in the previous section. Luis uses the analogy (perhaps more comprehensible in sixteenth-century Spain) of a mature man marrying a child, who needs to be instructed before full union. The first period of this relationship (Song 1:1–2:9) describes the time of nature when the bride is a child, while the second period under the Law begins with the flight of Israel from Egypt and entry into the promised land (Song 2:10–5:1). The third period of full marriage starts with incarnation and is still proceeding (Song 5:2–8:14). Luis's rather tortured attempts to try to relate verses from the Song of Songs to historical events form a strange coda to what is a major treatment of mystical union.

Book III of *The Names of Christ* commences with the "Dedication" defending writing in Spanish noted above, and an "Introduction," setting the bucolic scene of the dialogue on the second day. At this point Sabino notes that the name "Jesus" seems to have been neglected in what has transpired. Juliano, however, takes on the task of analyzing the first name, "Son of God."[73] This section is primarily doctrinal, but with mystical overtones. The name "Son" is given to Christ in many biblical passages, and the exploration of how Christ is Son reveals five different levels of Sonship, or births. These five births are another innovation of the Spanish Augustinian. In the first place, the Word is born eternally from the Father as his perfect image, while in the second birth he is born from the Virgin Mary in time. The third birth is Christ's resurrection from the dead, and the fourth is his birth in the Eucharist, by which he makes himself available to all believers. The eucharistic connection is important, because it is closely tied to the fifth form of birth, which is the birth of Christ in the soul, a traditional mystical motif, going back as far as Origen, which Luis here makes his own.[74] Juliano notes, "It is indeed true that all the births we have mentioned are part of one single event, and that each time we are born in God, Christ is born in us: holiness, love of justice, and the renewal of our souls are what make these births possible."[75] Luis illustrates how this union in essence happens by appealing to the threefold structure of the higher powers of the soul (*el entendimiento, con la voluntad y memoria*, ed., 697) and also mentions Christ resting in peace in the "center of the soul" (*centro de ella*). This kind of language is reminiscent of Teresa and John of the Cross, but Luis only mentions the soul's powers and center without pursuing any detailed analysis. His interests are different. The Augustinian does provide a distinction between two kinds of union, or birth of Christ in the soul. One presence or union increases our being, giving us the ability as temples of God to act by spreading God's kingdom; the second presence is brief and more pleasant, the experience of moments of enjoying God in prayer.[76] Luis counsels his readers that for this second birth to happen it is necessary to turn within in self-examination and implore God's mercy.

The last part of the name "Son of God" features another exercise in salvation history, but of a slightly different form, as Luis describes the three steps of Christ's presence in us: childhood and adolescence, the time of the Law; the age of mature understanding and action, that is, the period of grace; and finally, the coming period of glory in heaven. Here the Augustinian returns to theological anthropology—not the Carmelite teaching on the three powers but rather Augustine's doctrine of the two parts of the soul: the higher, or divine, part which is immortal and which "desires contemplation and the love of eternal things" (*en la contemplación y en el amor de las cosas eternas*), and the lower part, which looks toward earth and is closer to the body and its passions. These opposed parts are inseparable but often in conflict. The lower part needs to be obedient to the higher.[77] Luis's sketch of salvation history concludes with a study of the relation of the two parts of the soul over the ages as they gradually become reconciled through the action of grace.

The following two names, "Lamb" and "Beloved," are relatively brief.[78] Lamb, the name given Christ by John the Baptist (John 1:29), indicates three qualities of the Redeemer: the meekness and sweetness of his character; the purity and innocence of his behavior; and his readiness for sacrifice.[79] "Beloved" is a name that scripture gives to Christ in many places, such as the Song of Songs, various Psalms, and Isaiah in the Old Testament, plus Matthew and Paul in the New (ed., 713). In what follows, Luis returns to his theme of the various kinds of love we should have for Christ, stressing the love of friendship (e.g., ed., 718–20; trans, 329–30). The treatment of this name features not only a host of biblical citations but also long passages from patristic authors, such as Origen, Macarius, Ignatius of Antioch, Gregory Nazianzus, and Augustine. At the conclusion Marcelo summarizes the message of love in a beautiful passage. All love comes from God and through Christ, whose image has been engrafted into our souls. "His name is Jesus, a name which still needs our description."[80]

"Jesus" forms a fitting conclusion to the book.[81] Once again, Luis's focus is doctrinal, although there are important mystical elements as well. This chapter also displays his form of Christian Cabala. The Augustinian begins by noting that Jesus is Christ's proper name in the deepest sense, since all the other names point to qualities or things he has in common with others, but Jesus is the name reserved to him alone and contains his whole meaning (ed., 735; trans., 343). Christ has two proper names, "Word" insofar as he is eternally born of the Father, and "Jesus" as born in time. This launches him into a treatment of the Hebrew significance of these two names: *Dabar*, and *Iehosuah*.[82] *Dabar* signifies many things, as Luis shows through an analysis of its three root consonents (D, B, R). The two syllables of the word (DA/BAR) are also meaningful, both read forward and yielding "This is the Son," and read backward to mean "an abundance of excellent qualities." As a whole word, Luis teases out another six meanings of *dabar*. Here Luis is imitating Jewish exegesis, particularly of a Kabbalistic nature.

The name Jesus (*Iehosuah*) is more fitting and adequate to the human nature of Christ than any other. Luis says that he will not deal with the number and meaning of each of the letters in the name, as others have done, but he does note that the name *Iehosuah* contains all the letters of

the Tetragammaton and two more. The unpronounceable Tetragrammaton can be considered a sign of God's ineffability, but when the two
letters (actually two "S" sounds) are added to it, the name becomes
pronounceable, just as the incarnation revealed the mysteries of God,
such as the trinitarian meaning of the Tetragrammaton (ed., 741–42;
trans., 349). The essential meaning of the name of Jesus is "salvation or
health," the name the angel gave him (Luke 1:31). Jesus cures our sinful, wounded, and suffering nature, as well as absorbing all other biblical names into one. Here, as elsewhere in *The Names of Christ* III, 4, Luis
turns to texts from Bernard of Clairvaux on the meaning and power of
the name of Jesus. He goes on to show how Jesus, as our health and salvation, brings together the meaning of all the other names discussed
in his book, as well as much else that can be said about the Savior. He
also returns to a number of themes discussed at length in earlier chapters, such as our goal being to become one with Christ (trans., 358,
360, 362), and Jesus as the food of the soul in the Eucharist (trans.,
362–63). At this point Luis adds some new insights, especially in the
section he devotes to the relation between inner and outer religion
and its implied call to reform. True health is the harmony of the inner
and the outer, so the external works of religion, while necessary, are
not final. The goal is rather to be found in "true sanctification of the
soul, . . . born out of a holy inspiration" (trans., 360). Luis summarizes,
"And also therefore Jesus is all salvation; I say, his words are Jesus [i.e.,
salvation], his works are Jesus, his life is Jesus, and his death is Jesus."[83]

The final pages of *The Names of Christ* bring up more biblical themes
and images for understanding Jesus as our salvation. Jesus is compared
to the tree of life in Revelation 22:2, and Luis interprets the description of the Bridegroom in Song of Songs 1:14 ("a cluster of camphire in
the vineyards of En-gedi") as "the forgiving of sins," saying that Jesus is
health and salvation even for heretics and Jews. Returning to the theme
of creation, Marcelo and Sabino hold a dialogue in which the elderly
scholar shows the young friar how Jesus as Word upholds all creation
and prevents it from sinking back into nothingness. He summarizes,
"And so in Jesus Christ, as a fountain, or an immense ocean, there is a
treasure of all being and all beneficent being, the whole substance of
the world."[84] After piling up more biblical symbols in a rhetorical flour-
ish, Marcelo concludes with a prayer of blessing to God for the gift of
Jesus, after which Sabino provides a fitting end by reciting Fray Luis's
version of Psalm 102.

The Names of Christ is among the treasures not only of Spanish mysticism but of the mystical aspect of Renaissance humanist culture. If

Luis de León personally did not wish to include himself in the list of those who had tasted the full fruits of the union with the Divine Lover set out in the Song of Songs, there can be little doubt that his cosmic, salvation-historical, and holistic view of how the church and its members should strive to attain oneness with Christ enriched the mysticism of Spain's Golden Age.

Later Carmelite Mystics

The significance of Teresa and John of the Cross has often led to neglect of the later Carmelite mystics, both men and women, in the period down to ca. 1650.[85] Although these next generations of Spanish Carmelites can be considered "heirs of Teresa and John," this does not preclude the importance and even originality of some of these figures.[86] Today the later Carmelites are little known outside Spain, although some have begun to become available in English in recent years.

Like many reforms, the history of the Carmelite Discalced order was fractious, not only because of conflict between the adherents of the old "mitigated" form of the Rule and the new more rigorous one but also because of quarrels among the reformed.[87] Tensions surfaced soon after the initial papal approval of the reform in 1580 and Teresa's death in 1582. During the period 1582–84, two of her close associates, John of the Cross and Jerónimo Gracián, disagreed on how much apostolic work the reform should engage in, with Gracián supporting missions abroad and John fearing this might compromise the contemplative character of the order. Disputes reached a more serious level between 1585 and 1594. The Genoese banker Nicolás Doria (1539–1594) had come to Spain and joined the Carmelite reform in 1577. Teresa thought highly of him, and he soon ascended to positions of power. Doria's plans for the order and his imperious personality boded ill for future peace, however, and he and Gracián, the first provincial, were temperamentally ill-matched.[88] Upon becoming provincial in 1585, Doria worked to marginalize Gracián, eventually having him dismissed from the order in 1592. Doria restructured the governance of the Discalced by instituting a centralized board called the "Consulta," and proceeded to reassert control over the nuns by introducing changes to Teresa's *Constitutions*, such as reducing the power of the prioresses and decreeing that the nuns could have only Carmelite confessors. The result has been called "the revolt of the nuns." In 1590 some of Teresa's associates appealed to the pope to support the foundress's rules. Among those who resisted Doria were two of Teresa's closest associates, María de San José and Ana de Jesús, but Ana de San Bartolomé, Teresa's amanuensis and companion in her last days, sided with Doria. Sixtus V supported the rebellious nuns, but his successor Gregory XIV annulled this action in 1591. During this year Doria also moved against John of the Cross, dismissing him from his official duties and sending him off into exile, where he soon died. In 1593 Doria was successful in getting the Discalced recognized as a fully independent order subject only to the pope. He himself was about to be elected the new general when he died in May 1594. The election of Elías de San Martín as the first general brought peace to the Discalced, at least for the next six years. Rivalries, factions, and disputes, however, continued on in the seventeenth century, even over the heritage of Teresa and John. As we have seen in the previous chapter, some, even among the Carmelites, continued to consider John's writings dangerous, while the Carmelite nuns often had to wrestle with the dilemma of whether to be faithful to Teresa's vision for the community or to obey the male authorities who sought to blunt and change the saint's *Constitutions*.

Three developments tell us much about the changes in the reformed branch toward the end of the sixteenth century. The first two are negative. In 1587 the Discalced nuns instituted the payment of a dowry from all aspirants, something that Teresa had opposed. Then in 1597 the order overturned her openness to all candidates by introducing rules about "purity of blood," which meant that someone who had Jewish or Muslim background as far back as four generations could not be accepted. Teresa's Jewish roots had by then been well hidden by the Carmelites, but had she applied at this time, she would have been shown the door! Despite these changes and the tumultuous history of these years, the third development was positive—the continued spread of the Discalced reform. The friars established houses in Portugal and Italy and then went on to other places in Europe and even America (Mexico City received a priory in 1586). The spread of the nuns, first throughout Spain and then across Europe, had an important impact on mysticism. By the time of the death of John of the Cross in 1591 there were eighty-one houses, counting both female convents and male priories.

Reformed Catholic circles in France, where Teresa's fame spread rapidly due to the translations of her works in 1601, were anxious to have her nuns come to help their efforts to revitalize Catholicism and turn back the Protestant threat. After considerable negotiations, in 1604 a group of nuns, including Teresa's associates Ana de Jesús (1549–1621) and Ana de San Bartolomé (1549–1626), came to France and established the first French Carmel in Paris.[89] This expansion was engineered by Jean de Bretigny (1556–1634) and the well-connected cleric Pierre Bérulle (1575–1629). The early history of French Carmelite convents was not always edifying. Bérulle brought the nuns to France to advance his own vision of reform and wanted to keep them under his control. Again the nuns divided; some siding with Bérulle, others resisting. One of the resistors was Ana de San Bartolomé, who said of Bérulle: "I hold that because Msgr. Bérulle went back on his promise to the superiors of the order and to the Spanish nuncio, God now permits him to fall into errors and away from the virtuous beginnings. He gets himself caught in so many snares and everybody else along with him."[90] These quarrels, however, did not prevent the spread of the reformed nuns in France and the Low Countries. By 1625 there were no fewer than thirty-seven convents.[91]

Teresa had formed her houses to encourage contemplative prayer, and many of the early Carmelites followed her directive. Some nuns committed their spiritual experiences to posterity, mostly in the form of accounts of visions and revelations, in which they often model themselves on the mother of the order.[92] A good example is Ana de San Agustín (1555–1624), who joined the reform at Malagon in 1575 under Teresa's guidance and enjoyed a long career in leadership roles.[93] Like a number of sixteenth-century women, Ana was a born visionary, beginning with a manifestation of the Baby Jesus she received at the age of eleven. Her loyalty to Teresa was a major factor in her life, at least as we can recover it from the two *Relations* (*Relaciones*) that she tells us she was commanded to write by her confessors in the early 1600s.[94] Her visions of hell are reminiscent of Teresa's hell experiences (see *Life* 31–32), but the foundress was shown hell to move her to repent of her sins, while Ana, in the manner of some medieval visionaries, seems to take more delight in detailed descriptions of the punishments meted out to sinners. Ana's visions are not mystical in the sense of inviting her readers to a deeper sense of God's presence or teaching them about contemplation. The showings were more concerned with emphasizing how the visionary's contact with Teresa gives her and her program for the future of the Carmelite nuns an authority superior to that of male leaders. Teresa's delicate adjudication of inner and outer authority seems to have been lost on this successor.

Some of Teresa's other close associates, such as María de San José (Salazar) (1548–1603) and Ana de San Bartolomé, also left writings.[95]

María de San José was a prolific author. Her reminiscences of the early days of the reform, the *Book for the Hour of Recreation* (1585), has been translated into English.[96] It is important reading for those interested in the life of the early Carmelite nuns, but is not primarily a mystical text. Still, the second and the seventh of the Dialogues of the book show how concerned the early nuns were with their prayer life, especially the nature and way of attaining the "prayer of quiet," as well as the discernment necessary to give a true evaluation of special consolations and ecstatic states, or "suspensions."[97] María shows herself a faithful disciple of Teresa in the balanced way she approaches prayer and contemplation. Ana de San Bartolomé wrote a *Defense of the Teresian Legacy* (*Defensa de la herencia teresiana*) in 1621, as well as an *Autobiography*, some *Conferences, Meditations,* and a number of *Letters*.[98] In the *Autobiography* Ana tells us that her first vision of Jesus occurred when she was just seven. Later, after the death of her parents when she was ten, she was often consoled by visions of the Infant Jesus. Ana's artless but moving account of how Teresa instructed her and enabled her to overcome her doubts and illnesses is a testimony to the remarkable community spirit that Teresa formed among the early nuns of the reform. Ana also recounts numerous visions of Christ and of Teresa after the saint's death in 1582.

It was not until a generation later that we find, among the female Carmelites, a major mystical author in Cecilia del Nacimiento (1570–1646).[99] Cecilia came from a remarkable family, the Sobrinos of Valladolid. Her father, Antonio, was a lawyer and public official, while her mother, Cecilia Morillas (1539–1581), was a learned woman who trained her large family, both boys and girls, in languages and cultural accomplishments like art and music. Many of these siblings entered the church, including Cecilia and her older sister María, who joined the Discalced house at Valladolid in 1588, taking the names of Cecilia del Nacimiento and María di San Alberto. Cecilia was soon made mistress of novices. Both Cecilia and María wrote mystical prose and poetry,[100] and their older brother, the Franciscan Antonio Sobrino (1556–1622), was so noted for his holy life and mystical learning that the Franciscans (with Cecilia's help) began an unsuccessful process for his canonization after his death. Antonio's surviving letters to Cecilia, advising her about mystical matters, prove him to be conversant in mystical theology, and he claims to have enjoyed contemplative experiences himself.[101] The Sobrinos illustrate an unusual chapter in the history of mysticism—a mystical family.

Cecilia's writings reveal a major dynamic in the story of Carmelite mysticism that is found also in other religious orders: the cooperation of male and female members in the production of mystical texts.[102] In part to forestall Inquisitorial investigation, women needed the support, and/or command, of male authorities to write down their mystical experiences and teachings, as Teresa had done with her *Life* and *Interior Castle*. We need not, however, take all the protestations of reluctant obedience used by Teresa and women like Cecilia to conclude that these nuns were just docile instruments of male superiors. As is often the case in the history of mysticism, significant mystical literature was the result of a collaboration between male and female religious. Cecilia del Nacimiento is a good example.

The Carmelite nun was a prolific writer. At some stage in her early years at Valladolid, the provincial Tomás de Jesús (more on him below) became her confessor. Cecilia was apparently already writing mystical poetry, but it was at Tomás's command, she says, that she produced her earliest prose writings—the lost treatise on *The Three States of the Soul*, as well as a short tract entitled *The Union of the Soul in God* (*Tratado de la unión del alma en Dios*) of 1602. Her masterwork, *The Treatise on the Transformation of the Soul in God* (*Tratado de la transformación del alma en Dios*), a commentary on her sixteen-stanza *lira* of that title, was completed in 1603. During this time, however, Tomás de Jesús fell from grace with the Discalced authorities, and his friend Cecilia was sent away to found a new convent at distant Calahorra, where she remained from 1601 to 1612. Eventually, she was recalled to Valladolid, where she spent the remainder of her long life, dying in 1646. Cecilia had a second writing period in the late 1620s and 1630s, again at the behest of male authorities. Her *First Account of God's Favors* (1629) was written at the command of another Carmelite provincial. Later the new Carmelite general (another of her confessors), Esteban de San José, commissioned her to write a *Treatise on the Mysteries of Our Holy Faith* (1632), a *Second Account of God's Favors* (1633), as well as the first of her *Glosses on the Song of Songs* (1634). In 1637 she wrote a second *Gloss on the Song of Songs* for yet another confessor, Nicolás de Jesús María, one of the commentators on John of the Cross. With her poems (over a hundred), treatises, and letters, Cecilia stands out as an accomplished writer and a significant mystic. None of her writings were published in her lifetime, however, and she soon slipped out of historical memory, only to reappear in the past century.

Cecilia stands squarely in the Discalced tradition, praising Teresa often and using themes from her writings.[103] She was, however, more influenced by John of the Cross, and, like John, she expressed her mysticism in both poetry and prose.[104] It was rare in the earlier mystical tradition to write treatises specifically on union, but the genre began to spread in the seventeenth century. Cecilia's treatise on union, one of the earliest, is written in the first person. At the beginning, she apologizes for her lack of theological skill and says that she speaks from her own experience: "In no way will I make a declaration about the essence of this union [of God and the soul], because that task has been given to theologians, but I will only add a few conjectures or sentiments that can be gathered from this experience, whether through feeling or lack of feeling."[105] She provides an abbreviated sketch of her mystical path from the earliest spiritual exercises, through growth in prayer and ways of service, to the culmination in the gift of God's "touch," which she says, "is the greatest way for the soul to feel him in communication with her own self" (*Treatise on Union* 5). The "substantial touch," as we have seen, was important to both Teresa and John of the Cross and is an essential theme of Cecilia's tract. Such an intimate and secret gift in the soul's essence is the key to union, "because once the touch happens, the two substances [God and the soul] immediately become one" (*Treatise on Union* 9). Many of the major themes of Cecilia's mysticism appear already in this early work, such as references to the "center of the soul" (*Treatise* 9 and 21), and the equation of "pure contemplation and divine union" (*Treatise* 10). Cecilia distinguishes different levels of touch and union, from the beginnings of union when the exterior senses are not lost (*Treatise* 11–12), to the higher union in which God communicates his very self in a substantial manner to the soul, thus effecting transformation, deification, and essential union (*Treatise* 14–20). Cecilia uses some bold expressions, as when she says that "the soul's essence can be joined with the essence of God" (*Treatise* 20),[106] but she qualifies these by insisting on the lasting difference between the Creator and created being (*Treatise* 14).

The second half of the *Treatise on Union* (Nos. 21–40) teases out further implications of the meaning of union. Transforming union is perpetual and enduring (*Treatise* 27, 34), but only in the center of the soul, thus allowing the lower soul to continue to exercise its earthly tasks and even to live in the midst of turmoil and serve God in suffering (*Treatise* 25). In the higher states of union, the soul becomes totally lost in God and loses her interior and natural powers, coming to know the divine essence directly and supernaturally in a way that cannot be later remembered or communicated. "And this is the way the soul supernaturally understands him. This is why declaring all this in human words is impossible. Not even a part can be expressed, because it does not depend on natural understanding. And some holy people [e.g., John of the Cross] say that this is an understanding without understanding."[107] In this highest union all the soul's powers are brought into unity in "the immense abyss that is our God" (*Treatise* 35). In describing this state, Cecilia turns to the language of annihilation, nothingness, and darkness, again with strong links to John of the Cross. The soul sees God, but with blindness; she feels him without feeling; she understands him without understanding. Cecilia continues: "And so it is that those who understand the most about this divine understanding call it a ray of darkness, because when this light greatly exceeds our understanding, and this divine force of love greatly exceeds our will, and this omnipotence and greatness greatly exceed our memory, it does not take much for her to lose everything."[108]

Cecilia del Nacimiento's two later *Accounts of God's Favors* are more autobiographical in nature, describing a number of her visionary experiences. In the *First Account*, she says that by God's great gift she has been given an extraordinary peace and firm state of grace, something that has been confirmed by revelations lasting as long as three days (*First Account* 4). She notes that she has often received such manifestations, even in earlier years when she underwent suffering and persecution. Cecilia mentions a Marian vision of 1628 (*First Account* 13), as well as a protracted series of divine gifts and locutions (*First Account* 26–28). In order to underline the authenticity of these mystical experiences, the Carmelite includes a series of excerpts from the letters of her recently deceased brother discussing her spiritual states (*First Account* 29–52). The *Second Account of God's Favors* continues the story of her prayer life and visions but adds a new note, as Cecilia emphasizes the importance of reading scripture for her inner life. "Many times," she says, "with a few words from the Sacred Scripture, my soul feels these celestial sensations: sometimes a certain passage does it, sometimes another, and these words come at such a perfect time that they lift my soul up to God."[109]

The role of scripture in Cecilia's mystical thought is evident also from the fact that, at the command of her confessors, she, like Teresa, undertook a kind of commentary on the Song of Songs, specifically two *Glosses* on particular verses.[110] The first of these (1634) deals with the text from Song of Songs 2:16, *Dilectus meus mihi et ego illi* ("He is my Beloved and I am his"). This passage allows Cecilia the opportunity to explore the mutuality of love between the Divine Bridegroom and the soul. Although God has given everything to the soul, including his infinite and all-powerful love, he gives it all only so that she

can return it to him and thus say, *et ego illi* (*First Gloss on Song of Songs*
2–4). In the rest of this short work Cecilia discusses the trinitarian
dimension of the gift of love (*First Gloss* 5–7), as well as the soul's love
for the Incarnate Word, especially as available in the sacrament of the
Eucharist (*First Gloss* 12–14). During the course of the work Cecilia
discourses on the game of love set forth in the Song of Songs, that
is, the interplay of presence and absence, seeking and finding, pain
and pleasure in the divine–human relation. As she puts it, "For that
special soul whom he loves so deeply and wants to envelop in divine
fire, in his powerful and loving flames, he is the absence that shows
and proves to be much greater than any presence."[111] The *Second Gloss
on the Song of Songs* concerns the mystical sleep of the Bride in the
arms of her divine Lover.[112] The Bridegroom asks the "daughters of
Jerusalem" (that is, other pious souls, or perhaps the nuns of Cecilia's
convent) not to awaken the Bride who is lost in mystical sleep, where
God holds her in his center (*Second Gloss* 2–5). In that sleep he shows
the soul the mysteries of redemption in a clear light, though not so
clearly as in heaven (*Second Gloss* 6). Citing Teresa, Cecilia encourages
souls to persevere on the path to higher contemplation and the reception of the wound of love (*Second Gloss* 10–12). This divine sleep in
which the Bride is awake in God is seen as an inexpressible darkness:
"Sometimes, while in this divine sleep [Song 5:2], the soul enters into
God's depths where she does not sleep except in the earthly sense.
And for God she is so awake that words cannot express it, because
the more the soul enters into this sweet sleep the more she enters into
him and into the clear darkness that human understanding cannot
comprehend."[113]

The *Treatise on the Transformation of the Soul in God*, Cecilia's major
work, is a line-by-line commentary on her sixteen-stanza poem of the
same title. The lyric echoes many of the themes and images from
John's "Noche Oscura" and "Cántico Espiritual," but Cecilia's poem is
in the third person rather than the first and has a more didactic character than John's allusive mixing of images. Still, the poem has its own
beauty, and the commentary deserves careful study.[114] While somewhat
repetitious, the *Treatise on Transformation* is impressive for its teaching and the boldness of its claims. Cecilia does not try to give a full
account of the mystical path, saying little about ascetic preparation,
or even about the traditional three stages. Rather, she concentrates on
the goal—transformation, union, deification, pure contemplation, and,
in dependence on John of the Cross, the relation of light and darkness.
The closer one approaches the divine mystery, the more one enters

into the light that blinds. More than Teresa, Cecilia emphasizes the power of the divine illumination that plunges the soul into the brilliant darkness of God. As she puts it in the Tenth Song:

> We say it is night not because of the shadowy sufferings . . . that befall a soul in the purification of her spirit, but because of that divine darkness in which she enjoys God in the union she has with him. In addition, while in this darkness, the more she enters, the more things darken over with the greater light received from the transformation of the soul in God. This is the point where description is impossible, even if one wanted to say more about it. Here the soul is blinded by divine light, and we call this night.[115]

This appeal to mystical inexpressibility is typical of the Carmelite nun.[116]

I cannot give a full commentary on this, Cecilia's longest work, but a consideration of some major themes will reveal the main lines of the treatise. The commentary on the first two of the Songs introduces the themes of divine darkness and burning love. Song 1 announces:

Aquella niebla oscura	That shadowy cloud,
es una luz divina, fuerte, hermosa,	is a light divine, strong, and beautiful,
inaccessible y pura,	unreachable and pure,
íntima y deleitiosa,	intimate and delicious,
un ver a Dios sin vista de otra cosa.	a gaze at God without sight of anything else.[117]

This is obviously the world of the *noche oscura* of John of the Cross, as the commentary makes clear. The divine light is so "excessive and immense" that it overwhelms created natures; hence, its communication to the soul involves the paradox of reaching it without ever really reaching it.[118] In the commentary, Cecilia introduces many of her central motifs, such as the fact that the blinding light is communicated to the soul in "pure contemplation" (First Song 11), and that this takes place in the "center of the soul," that is, its most interior and divine dimension (First Song 12). Making use of two traditional metaphors for penetrating into divine darkness, Cecilia appeals to the desert motif (i.e., finding God in the solitude of the desert, as did Moses, Elijah, and Hosea), and the fact that the soul, as made in God's image (Gen. 1:26), "has an immensity so deep that it is like a bottomless well or the depths of the ocean."[119] That the ocean of the soul alone is capable of receiving the infinity of the divine ocean is a frequent theme in this Carmelite mystic.[120] Cecilia obviously had a considerable knowledge of mystical literature to be so skilled in her use of this vocabulary.

The Second Song, or stanza, is close to themes already seen in the nun's treatise on union, such as the nature of substantial union and the paradoxes of the uniting of God and the soul. Once again, the message is presented under the sign of negative theology—"There to take her pleasure, / the soul draws near, enflamed with love, / and so bereft of vision / that nothing can be seen, / knowledge is transcended and attained."[121] The transforming union takes place through the power of love, of which Cecilia distinguishes five kinds (burning and wounding love, sickening love, intoxicating love, consuming love, and transforming love [Second Song 4–5]). The blindness that the soul experiences in this state is not only natural (i.e., the failure of reason) but also "supernatural," that is, it is a knowledge of God and his attributes so far beyond us that we cannot describe it except in mystical paradoxes (Second Song 15). Therefore, knowledge is both transcended and yet also in some mysterious way attained. At this stage most of the main themes of Cecilia's teaching have already appeared, but later Songs add some qualifications and additions.

The Fourth and Sixth Songs expound on the transforming union that takes place in darkness in the center of the soul as God "opens up an immense space in her very center" (Sixth Song 1–2). Cecilia uses a simplified version of the anthropology found in John of the Cross in which the human person is composed of body and soul, and the soul has both a lower and an upper part. The upper part, in turn, contains the three spiritual powers (memory, intellect, and will), as well as the most intimate part, or center, in which God becomes present. The nun often makes reference to the soul's center without engaging in any lengthy theoretical exposition of its nature.[122] The Fourth Song expresses her wonder over this quasi-infinite center. Commenting on the lines "She [the soul] rises to the empyrean heaven and in her most secret center lifts the veil" (*sube al empíreo Cielo / y a su secreto centro quita el velo*), Cecilia says, "I wish to speak of something here that is so inexpressible, because if it were not for those who understand it by experience, the immensity contained in this heaven would not be credible. Because when considering a soul dressed in mortal flesh, who could believe that on the inside there is such an immense center, with such immensity of riches and glory? . . . In this divine center we are like him, and nothing calls us or satisfies us there except God himself."[123]

The Sixth Song speaks about two effects of the union and deification in the soul's center. The first (Sixth Song 2–3) is lasting serenity and peace in the center, while the second (Sixth Song 4) is the overflow of this peace into the senses and the body (something also found in John of the Cross). The supreme state also involves a suspension, or alienation, of the higher powers of the soul (as Teresa had discussed), a suspension that is actually a form of deification (Sixth Song 17–18). The Eighth Song qualifies this picture by insisting that the stillness and cessation of inner and outer activity in suspension is meant to lead to a return to serve God more effectively, as we see in the example of St. Teresa (Eighth Song 3–4). In the Eleventh Song love leads the soul into total darkness and growing union, where God reveals his beauty more fully. Cecilia describes this in terms of the reciprocal gaze of the two lovers, God and the soul (Eleventh Song 5–6). The entry of erotic language leads on to the Thirteenth Song and its treatment of spiritual marriage. This stanza is particularly striking as Cecilia breaks forth with praise: "O crystalline night! / you who have joined with your beautiful light / in a divine union / the Bridegroom and the bride, / making of the two a single thing!"[124] It is in this dark yet crystalline night that God, the "ocean of immensity," shines forth and where spousal union takes place, as Cecilia says citing 1 Corinthians 6:17: "For the one who joins with God, God makes one spirit with him."

The image of crystal returns in the comment on the final Sixteenth Song: "The strength is so forceful / of the one with whom she unites / and she such a weak thing, / giving herself to be conquered / she loses her being and is changed into him."[125] Divine love absorbs her like a drop of liquid in an immense ocean, changing "everything of her in him without making her lose her own nature; rather, both remain in their own being, but together" (Sixteenth Song 1). The soul gives herself to be conquered by her invincible Lover, but "in a way she has conquered him too through her love and for having fought with him until the time was right for him to conquer her" (Sixteenth Song 6)—a powerful expression of the mutual love of the Bridegroom and bride. The soul's old sinful being is now converted and changed into God's being, although she does not lose her created nature as such (Sixteenth Song 7). Cecilia illustrates this mysterious change with the image of the soul as a crystalline glass: "And so the soul is in God always and it is as if the interior of her essence were like a crystalline glass through which rays of the sun are emitted, but in this case she is not a material thing, like real glass is, and thus her light irradiates more than this physical example."[126] Employing other striking images, Cecilia expatiates on how God receives the soul's center into himself and acts in it, moving outward into the other powers and empowering them in a new divine way. This teaching is similar to John of the Cross's view of the divine "overflow," considered in the previous chapter—another mark of the affinity between these two Carmelites.

Cecilia wrote at least a hundred more poems.[127] The quality of these poems has been praised by various investigators.[128] A number of her verses are presentations of aspects of her mystical consciousness, especially in its negative and paradoxical forms. For example, the poem entitled "The Definition of Love" (*Definición de amor*) expands on the Sanjuanist theme of God as the *no sé qué* ("I know not what") to explore the mysterious nature of God's contact with the soul. The opening stanza will give an idea of this evocative lyric:

Es amor un no sé qué	Love is an "I know not what"
que viene no sé de dónde	that comes from "I know not whence"
y se entra no sé por dónde	and enters "I know not where"
y mata no sé con qué.	and kills "I know not how."[129]

Poem 59 entitled "In the Midst of Silence without Sound" is an evocation of the silent birth of the Word from the omnipotent Father and his birth from the Blessed Virgin in the silence of the night of the nativity (see Wis. 18:14). Cecilia uses the image to express her admiration for the powerful love God showed in becoming flesh for our salvation—a love that is compared to an "immense and powerful fire" and "an abundant river of water."[130] Also impressive is Poem 61, "Without a Face in My Memory," another Sanjuanist-style verse that presents the dialectic of "all and nothing" (*todo y nada*).[131] A further aspect of mystical consciousness, the erotic dimension utilizing the Song of Songs, also is found in Cecilia's poetry. It is most evident in the pastoral drama that she composed as a "Celebration for a Religious Profession" (*Fiestecilla para una Profesión Religiosa*).[132] Here the Divine Bridegroom, attired as a shepherd with his accomplice Amor (the mythological god of love), courts the bride, that is, the soul portrayed as a shepherdess. The play is filled with images and language from the Song of Songs and builds to a crescendo of erotic release in lines dedicated to the embrace of the spouses.

One of the accomplishments of twentieth-century scholarship on the history of mysticism has been to uncover figures, especially women, whose voices had been stilled over the centuries. Some of these women, such as the Beguine Marguerite Porete executed as a heretic in 1310, were marginalized by the guardians of orthodoxy. The case of Cecilia del Nacimiento is more puzzling. Although she was controversial,

Cecilia gained the support of many of the male Carmelite authorities of the day, and, despite some daring expressions, she was not deleted to the Inquisition. Perhaps it was the overwhelming figure of Teresa of Avila that relegated Cecilia and other of her daughters into the shadows of history before their modern reemergence.

A number of reformed friars of the generations after Teresa and John also wrote on mystical matters. One early example is Teresa's friend and confidant, Jerónimo Gracián (1545–1614).[133] There is no question of the love (some might even say infatuation) that Teresa had for Gracián, although she was also willing to criticize him and question his judgment at times. The nature of the vow of obedience Teresa made to him in 1575 and the spiritual marriage they pledged has provoked much discussion.[134] Gracián brought great gifts and much energy to the work of expanding the reform, but he was also often involved in controversy and conflict, partly due to his own failings. Gracián's adventures after his expulsion from the Discalced down to his death were many and colorful. He continued to work on editing and spreading the fame of Teresa in his later years while living in the Low Countries.

Gracián wrote an autobiographical *Pilgrimage of Anastasius* (*Peregrinación*), as well as a large number of spiritual treatises. Perhaps the best known of these was *The Burning Lamp*, or *Book of Religious Perfection*, which began as a series of talks given to Carmelite nuns in 1586 and went through many later editions and expansions.[135] He also wrote a treatise on Saint Joseph (the *Josefina*), a saint to whom he and Teresa had great devotion. Gracián composed two works summarizing the mystical teachings of others, the *Dilucidario*, or *Lucidario* (1604), based on Teresa's writings, and the *Heavenly Road* of 1601 and 1607, which rather clumsily brought together materials from Bonaventure. Among his late works was the *Life of the Soul* (1609), an attack on "those who set perfection in total annihilation," that is, early exponents of what has sometimes been attacked as a form of "Pre-Quietism."[136]

One thing evident in the later male Carmelites is the turn to formal presentations of what they now often called "mystical theology," a topic frequently set forth by explanations, commentaries, defenses, and *summae* of the writings of John of the Cross and/or Teresa. This "scholastic" development illustrates what Michel de Certeau identified as an important shift in the Western mystical tradition, namely, the creation of "mysticism" as a discrete category of academic discourse. The ramifications of this shift are still with us. Two writers who illustrate the role that expositions of John of the Cross had in the dissemination of his views and the formation of mysticism as a specific "science" are Diego de Jesús (Salablanca) (1570–1621) and Nicolás de Jesús María (Centurioni) (ca. 1590–1655).

Diego was born at Granada and entered the Discalced in 1586, studying at Alcalá under Tomás de Jesús. Despite opposition on the part of some Carmelites toward John of the Cross, Diego produced the first edition of his works, a partial collection appearing at Alcalá in 1618.[137] In this volume he included both a life of John (written by Quiroga, on whom see below) and an appendix under the title, "Notes and Remarks in Three Discourses for the Very Easy Understanding of the Mystical Expressions and Doctrine of the Spiritual Works of Our Father."[138] This work, as pointed out by Certeau, marks an important stage in the creation of the new science of "mystics" (*la mystique*) and is one of the first examples of a genre that was to culminate in Françoise Fénelon's *Maxims of the Saints* (1697)—a defense of the special language used by those now called "the mystics" by illustrating its characteristics and defending it through appeals to the authority of the saints.

Two things are immediately evident in this work: the expanded use of the term *místico*, both as a qualifier[139] and as a substantive (*el místico/ doctores místicos*) to describe the teachers to whom the Carmelite makes appeal.[140] The second is the wide range of authorities used by Fray Diego, which, however, does not include any of the northern European medieval mystics, such as Tauler, Ruusbroec, or Herp, despite their influence on other Spanish writers.[141] After laying out in the introduction three reasons why John's writings need explanation, the work falls into three parts: (1) an exposition of how the "terms and phrases" (*términos y frasis*), or modes of expression, of John and the other mystics are to be understood (ed., 468–83); (2) an explanation of the elevation of the height of union that the soul can attain in this life (ed., 483–94); and (3) a defense of John's writing in the vernacular (ed., 495–502).[142]

The first and longest section has particular interest. Diego begins by insisting that the mystics cannot be held to the ordinary "rules of rhetoric or elegance" but have their own language, so that terms such as "excess" (*demasía*), "pride and fury" (*soberbia y furor*), "stain" (*macula*), and "annihilation" (*aniquilación*) have transferred meanings from the ordinary sense, a point he proves by appealing to scripture and especially the Dionysian writings. This license belongs to *la teología mística* because it is based on the experience of God, not on teaching and ordinary modes of expression. In "matter . . . so high and so spiritual, . . . experience conquers doctrine" (*En materia . . . tan alta y tan espiritual, donde la experiencia vence a la doctrina*, ed., 470), as Bernard of Claivaux,

Bonaventure, and Dionysius all teach. Much of what follows employs Dionysius to defend such forms of *locución mística* as the oxymoronic "cruel and furious quiet" (CH 2), the superiority of dissimilar expressions (CH 2), and "superfect terms" (*terminus sobreperfectos*, MT 1). Diego presents examples of four forms of "mystical ways of speaking," illustrating each by appeals to authorities both mystical and doctrinal (i.e., Thomas Aquinas) and closing each section with examples from the writings of John of the Cross.[143] Diego insists that the essential union taught by John goes beyond all natural and even the ordinary supernatural works of grace and that this position is in full conformity with the thought of Thomas Aquinas and many recognized mystics.[144]

Some years later, Nicolás de Jesús María, born in Italy but educated in Spain, produced a similar work, this time in Latin. His "Explanation of Phrases of Mystical Theology of the Venerable Father John of the Cross" was first published in 1631 in the midst of ongoing controversies about the orthodoxy of John's doctrine. Thereafter the "Explanation" often appeared in later editions of the saint's work, both in Spanish and in Latin translation.[145] Nicolás's work, written at the command of his superiors, is more than five times longer than Diego's, although it follows the earlier author in many particulars. It makes use of an even wider range of authorities, including, in this case, the northern mystics, such as Ruusbroec,[146] Tauler, Gerson, and Blosius. Teresa of Avila, once again, is frequently featured in defense of John's teaching. Written in elegant Latin, the *Phrasium mysticae theologiae . . . elucidatio* is divided into two books: nine chapters of part 1 that defend John of the Cross against general objections;[147] and twenty-one chapters of part 2 that respond to objections against an equal number of passages drawn from John's works.

The early seventeenth-century Spanish Carmelites produced a range of mystical writers, most of whom depend on the teachings of Teresa and John of the Cross. Three figures who stand out are Tomás de Jesús (Davila) (1564–1627), the most important Carmelite mystic of the second generation,[148] and his contemporaries José de Jesús María (Quiroga) (1562–1626), and Juan de Jesús María (Calagurritano) (1564–1615).[149]

Tomás de Jesús sought to bring together the mystical-contemplative and the apostolic-active dimensions of the Carmelite charism—a continuous issue in the history of the order. Tomás entered the Discalced in 1586 and was ordained in 1589, which gave him the opportunity to come to know John of the Cross personally. During the period between 1592 and 1608 he alternated between times spent in the

Carmelite "deserts" (i.e., hermitages) and positions of leadership in the order. Despite his attraction to the strict contemplative life, about 1606 Tomás experienced a conversion to the apostolic ministry, specifically missionary work in Africa. In 1607 he was called to Rome by Pope Paul V in order to pursue work for the missions. In 1610, however, he was sent to Flanders to spread the Carmelite reform and combat Protestantism. During the years 1610–23 Tomás was active in founding new Carmelite houses across northern Europe and in writing numerous works. In ill health, he retired to Rome to work on revising the Carmelite *Constitutions* in the years before his death in 1627.

Tomás de Jesús wrote at least twenty-four works in Spanish, Latin, and French, some published in the seventeenth century but others appearing only during the past century.[150] A number of these were concerned with the missions, but most deal with spirituality and mysticism. The noted scholar of Spanish mysticism E. Allison Peers, considered Friar Tomás to stand out above all the post-Teresan Carmelite mystics, noting that he had "not only . . . thoroughly absorbed the doctrine of the Carmelite Saints, but he was widely read in the Fathers and the mystics of the Middle Ages, and his combined learning and experience enable him to map out a straight road for others to follow."[151] Tomás's first work was a summary of the teaching of Teresa entitled *Summary and Compendium of the Degrees of Prayer* (Rome, 1610). This appeared with a brief *Treatise on Mental Prayer,* possibly written earlier, which the Carmelite structured according to the traditional three stages of beginners, proficients, and perfect (*principiantes, aprovechados, y perfectos*). The triple pattern was to be a major motif of his writings on mysticism.[152] In his treatise called *The Rules for examining and discerning a soul's interior progress* (1620), the Carmelite summarized the three ways as follows:

> The soul exercises itself in the knowledge of God through the purging of its passions by means of the practice of the virtues; it progresses towards this end through imitating the virtues of Christ our Savior, which is what the mystics call the illuminative life; or if it continues to practice the virtues it becomes united with God by means of the affections and acts of love which the mystics call the unitive way.[153]

This text witnesses to the growing use of the term "mystics" to describe those formerly called "contemplatives," and also stresses the affective nature of union.

Tomás's most notable works on mysticism come from his period in Flanders: *On Divine Contemplation: Six Books* (*De contemplatione divina libri sex*) of 1620, and *The Method, Nature, and Stages of Divine Prayer Infused by God* (*Divinae orationis sive a Deo infusae methodus, natura et gradus*) first published in 1623.[154] *On Divine Contemplation* was much influenced by Victorine mysticism with its distinction of hierarchies of the various types of contemplatives. The first book deals with definition and effects of infused prayer in general, while book 2 treats the first, or beginning, level of infused prayer, as well as the "illuminative hierarchy," in which advancing contemplatives turn their attention first to the soul itself and then to God. The treatment of the third or unitive hierarchy, which is equated with "mystical theology," takes up books 3–5 and deals with pure contemplation of God in darkness. Book 6 concerns what Tomás calls "supereminent contemplation," which appears to be a kind of extension of the direct gifts from God pertaining to God's essential presence in the soul in the unitive stage. This language reflects Tomás's knowledge of Flemish mysticism, especially Hendrik Herp (Harphius).

The four books of the *Divinae orationis* repeat much of the material found in the earlier work but in more detail.[155] Once again, the Carmelite begins in book 1 with a general discussion of infused prayer and its stages. The second book treats the purgative stage of infused prayer, a level similar to John of the Cross's dark night of the spirit with its desolations and teaching about avoiding spiritual gifts and sweetness. The illuminative stage of book 3 is already an advanced form of mystical grace in which the soul enters the divine light that brings it into eminent darkness. Tomás distinguishes two forms of divine contact here:

> In the first the mind, with the passions pacified and phantasms as it were put to sleep, beholds God peacefully and purely in the darkness, that is, under a general mark of incomprehensibility. In the second that darkness is felt, the inaccessible divine light by which the mind is illuminated more perfectly than in the first stage, and also, being nearer to the sun-like rays and nourished by them, it serves in a more ardent way. In the first it is gashed by the wound of love; in the second it is bound and made so ill by the greatness of love that nothing can satisfy it save union with the Beloved which it desires so fervently.[156]

In this state the Carmelite says that visions are often given to the raptured soul, though one must still practice discernment in evaluating them.

Book 4 deals with the highest forms of union of perfected souls. Here, too, Tomás introduces two forms—*unio sobria* and *unio ebria et ecstatica*. This book features ecstatic language and employs many of the symbols and themes used by other mystics to describe marital union with God as Tomás analyzes no fewer than ten effects of union. Although there is a role for the "intellectual power" (*intellectiva potentia*) in the ascent to union, Tomás is insistent that intellectual activity is succeeded by "the most burning and incomprehensible love" which liquefies the soul and transforms it into divine love. "Love alone is the means [*medium*] by which the soul is brought into the divine embrace, is joined to it, adheres to it, and as it were united in the divine marriage."[157] The final five chapters of the book deal with the union between Christ and the soul effected in the Eucharist, a point that seems to have emerged as central among a number of Post-Tridentine mystics (e.g., Cecilia del Nacimiento, Juan de los Angeles).

Another important summary work of Tomás is a bit of a mystery. In 1675 a *Traité de la contemplation divine* by Tomás was published at Liège, a French version of a lost Spanish original that appears to have been a version of book 3 of the unedited *Primera Parte del Camino espiritual*. The *Treatise on Divine Contemplation* has now been translated into Italian with a study by Elisabetta Zambruno. It reveals Tomás's knowledge of the mystical tradition, his considerable originality, and his affinity with John of the Cross.[158] Tomás's most frequently cited source in the *Treatise* is Bonaventure, both authentic works like the *Itinerarium mentis in Deum* and the pseudo-Bonaventure *De septem itineraribus aeternitatis* of Rudolph of Biberach. Next in order of citation are Bernard of Clairvaux, Dionysius, Richard of St. Victor, Gregory the Great, Augustine, and Thomas Aquinas. He twice mentions "the incomparable Saint Teresa our mother"[159] and also uses Luis de Granada and Bernardino de Laredo. Tomás employs northern mystics (Ruusbroec, Gerson, Denys the Carthusian), though sparingly. Curiously enough, he does not mention John of the Cross, although significant portions of the work depend on his Carmelite predecessor.

The *Treatise* is divided into two books, with book I containing nine chapters dealing with contemplation in general, while the fifteen chapters of book II feature more detailed investigations, particularly of the transition from meditation to contemplation and the different levels of contemplation. Tomás gives a short definition of contemplation in book I.3: "Christian contemplation . . . is a simple gaze at truth which proceeds from love and charity" (ed. Zambruno, 27). He also insists that contemplation, at least in its lower stages, is open to all (I.2 and II.8). Like John of the Cross (see *Ascent* 2, 10, 4), Tomás distinguishes between clear and affirmative contemplation, on the one hand, and the higher negative, or obscure contemplation, using the authority of

Pseudo-Dionysius, on the other. As he puts it, "It is useful to know that the more a soul draws near to God, the more it is illuminated by his divine lights and the more it is united and transformed into God, the more it knows that he is incomprehensible."[160] Tomás also distinguishes between acquired and infused contemplation throughout the work.[161] A long chapter (I.8; Zambruno, 61–71) is entitled "What Is Mystical Theology and the Different Names the Saints Give It." According to Tomás, the definition comprises three things: "The first is that mystical theology is a secret knowledge of God; the second is that this knowledge is loving and experimental; the third is that it is tasty [*saporosa*] and accompanied by the greatest enjoyments and most delicious satisfactions."[162]

The second book of the *Treatise on Divine Contemplation* begins with chapters on the rules for determining the passage from meditation to contemplation (II.1), advice for choosing the right level of contemplation (II.2), and discussion of the affections that draw the devout soul to the contemplative life (II.3–5). What interests Tomás the most, however, are the signs and the process for moving into the higher levels of negative, or obscure contemplation (*contemplazione oscura e negativa*). In these chapters the influence of John of the Cross becomes evident. Tomás discusses six steps in the advance to the highest stage of negative contemplation in a way that broadly parallels John of the Cross's account of the purgation of the senses and the spirit in the *Ascent-Dark Night* treatise. The first step (II.9) is a purging of the inner and the outer senses, which the Carmelite treats as a "return to the same purity and nudity in which [the soul] was when God drew it out of nothing to give it existence, in order that through this purity and nudity it might be so closely united with the divine essence that it is the same purity and the same nudity."[163] The second step (II.10–11) is the purification of the intellect by faith, so that the soul abandons all clear knowledge of God, whether natural or supernatural in origin.[164] The third step (II.12) is the purging of the memory and will, which leads to true poverty of spirit. Thus, the practice of the three theological virtues of faith, hope, and charity brings about "perfect union and the happy transformation of the soul into God" (*la perfetta unione e la felice trasformazione dell'anima in Dio*, II.13). The Carmelite describes "this loving union as the union that consists in this, that two things become only one, and that nothing is more clear than that if the soul is to be united to God, it must become one thing with him."[165] He illustrates this by the well-known examples of the drop of water in the jug of wine and the log turned into flame by divine love. Tomás introduces an important qualification, however, when he says that, although the soul must lose its being if it wishes to be united to God in love, this "is not its natural being, but its moral being," that is, the natural operations of the reason and intellect.

The fifth stage is the ascent beyond even mystical theology to the highest level of purity and perfection, which Tomás illustrates by discussing five grades of mystical theology, the fifth of which is described as when the soul is so lost in the divine incomprehensibility "that she would want to be annihilated at the end and to lose herself and be so abyssed in God, as to be thus totally penetrated in him" (II.14; ed., 182). He illustrates this level by citing Richard of St. Victor and Ruusbroec and exegeting passages from Song of Songs 3:6 and 8:5. The influence of Ruusbroec is also strong in the final chapter (II.15), where Tomás notes Ruusbroec's attack on the mystical heretics he calls the *oziosi* ("the indolent ones") and insists on the necessity of the continuing practice of the virtues even in the highest stages of contemplation. Both sweet repose in God and fervent dedication to the practice of the virtues are important, though the Carmelite thinks of these as successive moments in the life of advanced souls. He speaks of these two moments in Ruusbroec's terms as "flowing and reflowing" (*flusso e riflusso*).[166] Finally, it should be noted that throughout his summary of contemplation Tomás de Jesús, like his mother Teresa, insists that consideration of the humanity of Christ, our only path to God, must always be practiced.[167]

The distinction between acquired and infused contemplation is central to Tomás de Jesús and the Carmelites of his generation.[168] Tomás once likened infused contemplation to wind filling the sails and powering a boat over the sea. Nonetheless, he did not neglect acquired contemplation, that is, the efforts of the rower to move a boat ahead. Tomás appears to be the first, or one of the first, to give an actual definition of acquired contemplation, to which he devoted an early treatise *On Acquired Contemplation* (*De Contemplatione acquisita*).[169] The Carmelite again notes that such contemplation is open to all Christians and defines it as "the sincere and loving knowledge of the highest Deity and his effects gained by our own effort" (*contemplatio Christiana est summae Deitatis atque effectuum ejus affectuosa et sincera cognitio, nostra industria comparata*). In this, as in much else, Tomás de Jesús was a representative of the new science of mysticism.

Two contemporaries of Tomás, well known in their time but now mostly forgotten, confirm this picture. José de Jesús María (Quiroga) came from a noble family and entered the Carmelite reform in 1595.[170]

Appointed historiographer of the order, Quiroga traveled widely collecting materials, but his honesty led to opposition and the history was not published. Quiroga wrote extensively in history, biography/hagiography, and mystical theology. Some of his works are defenses of the teaching of Teresa and John of the Cross, such as his anonymous life of John, which appeared in the first edition of the saint's writings in 1618, as well as his *Apología mística* (ca. 1625), defending the orthodoxy of the great Carmelite.[171] Quiroga wrote several mystical works, including *The Ascent of the Soul to God that Aspires to Divine Union* (*Subida del alma a Dios que aspira a la divina unión*), whose two parts were published posthumously in 1656 and 1659. The first is devoted to ordinary prayer, while the second treats extraordinary, or mystical, prayer. Another contemporary was Juan de Jesús-María, born in 1564 at Calahorra (hence the sobriquet "the Calagurritan").[172] In 1585 he was sent to Genoa, the site of the first reformed convent in Italy and spent the rest of his life in Italy, where he rose to be the general of the Italian Reformed Congregation. The Calagurritan was the most prolific of all the writers of the reform, with over seventy titles to his credit. Only three of these are of import for mysticism: the Latin *Theologia Mystica* (1605), and two Italian works, *The Art of Loving God* (1607) and *The School of Prayer* (1611). The two Italian works were translated into a number of languages and widely read.

Although it takes us beyond the chronological limits of this volume, it will be useful here to round off the story of Spanish Carmelite mysticism by noting its final phase, that is, the era of the production of lengthy treatises on mystical theology dependent primarily on Teresa and John and highlighting the division of contemplation into acquired and infused, something that became a feature of the narrowing of Catholic mysticism from the late seventeenth through the beginning of the twentieth centuries.[173] These treatises were produced both in the vernacular and in Latin by friars from different provinces in Spain, Portugal, and France. The Portuguese Joseph of the Holy Spirit (1609–1674) wrote a *Catena of Carmelite Mysticism of Discalced Carmelite Authors* (*Cadena mystica carmelitana de los autores carmelitas descalzos*) published in 1678, as well as a Latin *Enucleatio mysticae theologiae S. Dionysii Areopagitae,* which appeared in 1684.[174] More important was a later friar of the same name in religion, Joseph of the Holy Spirit (the Andalusian) (1667–1736). This Spanish Joseph, who died as general of the Discalced, spent decades working on a massive *Cursus theologiae mysticoscholasticae*, first published between 1720 and 1740, and republished in a critical edition in the mid-twentieth century.[175] Another Portuguese friar, Anthony of the Holy Spirit (1618–1674), wrote three Latin *Directoria*, including a *Directorium mysticum*, between 1661 and 1680.[176] The *Directorium mysticism* was based on the lengthy work of another general of the Discalced, the French Philip of the Trinity (1603–1671), whose *Summa Theologiae Mysticae* was published at Lyons in 1656.[177] These attempts to combine Thomistic theology (at least as understood in the eighteenth century) and the teaching of the Carmelite masters of mystical thought are monuments to an enterprise that today will probably provoke more bewilderment than admiration.

Other Mendicant Mystics

Franciscans[178]

The other mendicant orders also played a part in the Golden Age of Spanish mysticism. In chapter 1 we examined the contributions of the Franciscan Observantine mystics Bernardino de Laredo and Francisco de Osuna, at the beginning of the sixteenth century. Other Observant Franciscans followed in their footsteps. Two noteworthy mid-century examples were Pedro de Alcántara (1499–1562), a friend and supporter of Teresa,[179] and Diego de Estella (1524–1578).[180] Pedro's *Treatise on Prayer and Meditation* (*Tratado de la Oración y Meditación*) was written about 1556 and seems to depend in part on the similar treatise published by the Dominican Luis de Granada in 1555.[181] This short book is more of a guide for meditation of an Ignatian type, but it does speak about the intermingling of meditation and contemplation, and briefly of how devotion leads to union with God.[182] Diego de Estella's *Meditations on the Love of God* (*Meditaciónes devotísimas del amor de Dios*) are a series of one hundred fervent prayers illustrating devotion to the passion and the Eucharist. Meditation 76, "Love Transforms the Lover into the Beloved," dwells on mystical transformation using the language of deification.[183]

A more significant mystic was the late sixteenth-century Franciscan Juan de los Angeles (ca. 1536–1609), a contemporary of Teresa and John, who lived on into the seventeenth century.[184] Little is known about Juan's early life, though he may have studied at Alcalá. He entered the Franciscans about 1555 and was ordained in 1565. A well-known preacher, Juan served in a number of leadership roles and participated in the general chapter in Rome in 1600.[185] His first work was the *Triumphs of the Love of God* published in 1589. Among his other works was the long treatise *Diálogos de la Conquista del Reino de Dios* (*Dialogues on the Conquest of the Kingdom of God*) of 1595, which contains many citations from Ruusbroec and from the *Theologia mystica* of the Dutch Franciscan Hendrik Herp, often ascribed to Bonaventure.[186] Juan also wrote mixed Latin and Spanish *Considerationes spirituales super librum Cantici Canticorum* (1606) and the *Manual of the Perfect Life* (*Manual de vida perfecta*) published in 1608.[187] The Franciscan's most important book was a reworking of the *Triumphs of the Love of God* put out in 1600 under the title *The Loving Struggle of the Soul with God* (*Lucha espiritual y amorosa entre Dios y el alma*). This book shows how traditional Franciscan mystical theology spoke to the new world of the mysticism of Spain's Golden Age.[188]

Fray Juan's treatise is learned, packed with references to such a rich range of mystical sources that one may imagine it was written more for preachers and confessors than for nuns and laity.[189] In his dedication, the friar specifically mentions "the books of Dionysius, St. Bonaventure in his *Mystical Theology* [actually Herp], Blosius and Ruusbroec, and other Fathers who have . . . written on these matters."[190] The Franciscan not only utilizes theological and mystical resources but also cites many philosophers, primarily Plato and Aristotle. *The Loving Struggle*, like Luis de León's *Names of Christ*, has a humanist flavor. Often digressive, the book is impressive in its fervent love-language, recalling such Franciscan classics as *The Goad of Love* (*Stimulus Amoris*) ascribed to Bonaventure but actually written by James of Milan. Divided into two parts and thirty-three chapters, *The Loving Struggle* combines a commentary on the Song of Songs with a number of forms of love-mysticism traditional among Franciscans, such as Richard of St. Victor's four degrees of violent charity (*Loving Struggle* II.1–5) and the Affective Dionysianism pioneered by Thomas Gallus and adopted by Bonaventure, Hugh of Balma, Gerson, and Herp.[191] Also in line with traditional Franciscan mysticism, Juan emphasizes Christ's love for humanity as displayed especially in the passion as the dominant reason for the soul's loving pursuit of the Divine Lover (see *Loving Struggle* I.7; II.3). In conformity with Post-Tridentine piety, the Franciscan is also concerned to show how union with Christ in the Eucharist opens the heights of mystical union to fervent believers (II.12–13).

Friar Juan was typically Franciscan but was also deeply read in many other mystical traditions. He often cites Augustine, Gregory the Great, and Bernard in support of his arguments, as well as more recondite sources. He uses mystical writers from northern Europe (e.g., Tauler, Ruusbroec, Denis the Carthusian, Hendrik Herp, and Blosius),[192] and

also cites Teresa of Avila, especially her account of the Transverberation.[193] The digressiveness of the treatise is somewhat ameliorated by
Juan's overarching metaphor of the love between God and the soul
conceived of as a conflict or struggle after the model of the warfare
metaphors in the Song of Songs (e.g., Song 3:7–8; 4:4; 1:8; 7:1; 8:9).[194]
The Loving Struggle is a kind of "omnium-gatherum" of Western love
mysticism—not original but a useful summation.

Juan appeals from time to time to the traditional mystical itinerary
of beginners–proficient–perfect (e.g., introduction, I.13 and II.9), but
his main concern is in exploring the different modalities of love, as is
shown by beginning the treatise with an analysis of six different divisions of love taken from various spiritual authorities (I.1). Citing Gerson's four kinds of love, he says that he will be particularly concerned
with the "living love, fruitful, ecstatic, and seraphic," which "consists
in a felt and experienced taste of an inner delight which stems from
the intercourse between the soul and the ultimate object of love: God
himself."[195] This is nothing other than the "kiss of the mouth" of Song
of Songs 1:1.

After laying out the different types of love in chapter 1 and describing the transforming quality of love and its extension in chapters 2
and 3, chapters 4 through 6 take up the central theme of the book, the
conflict of love in which the soul wounds God and is in turn wounded
by the Divine Lover (Song 4:9). Love alone can triumph in the struggle
with God, and Juan warns his readers to put the book aside if they have
never experienced the unconditional surrender that love demands
(I.6). The soul can, indeed, wound God in his heart, as is shown by the
Father's sending his Only-Begotten Son to redeem humankind from
sin through his passion (I.7). Exegeting Song of Songs 4:9, "You have
wounded my heart, my sister, . . . with one of your eyes and one hair
from your neck," the friar identifies the two eyes of the soul as the
intelligence and the affection. The left eye of intelligence and scholastic theology has an important preparatory role, but it is the right eye
of affectivity and mystical theology that attains God.[196] "If you wish
to uplift yourselves to God anagogically by way of love and mystical
experience" says Juan, "one thing is essential: using your human intellectual capacity for abstraction, you must empty your mind of images,
resemblances, similarities and representations of all created things."[197]
Deep recollection,[198] as well as the stripping of the mind of all images
is, of course, a Dionysian theme, and this prompts Juan to include two
long chapters that are able but not original reprisals of Affective Dionysianism—chapter 10, devoted to the irrational wisdom of mystical

theology (basically a commentary on MT 1), and chapter 11, dealing with the divine darkness in which ecstatic union with God is achieved. The first book of *The Loving Struggle* closes with three chapters (I.15-17) dealing with the contrast between the love of God and its mortal enemy, love of self.

The second book of the treatise turns to God's wounding of the soul. The first six chapters are loosely based on Richard of St. Victor's four degrees of violent charity as marking the ways God pierces the soul with love in four stages leading to union. The first stage (II.2) is that of the wounding arrow, which is where Juan cites Teresa's Transverberation and also refers to the reception of the stigmata by "our Father, St. Francis." The second stage (II.3) is the binding of the soul with the chains of love, while the third is the languishing, or sickness, brought on by love's power over the soul (II.4). Finally, the soul experiences the fourth stage, the insatiability of spiritual love (II.5). Here Juan expounds on the unending attempt to satiate the infinite Lover, what Gregory of Nyssa referred to as epektasis, something found in many mystics under various names and descriptions. He exclaims, "O my Lord, my good Lord, my love and my food, how you regale those who love you, and by loving you they eat, and are still left so hungry! He who has never tasted you does not know what hunger is; for you alone can so delight our souls that in a superabundance of life and satiety, you leave us hungry for more."[199]

The remainder of *The Loving Struggle* (II.6–16) is a treatment of the nature of loving union with God and the trials and delights it entails. Chapter 6 analyzes two kinds of delight in God, the pure delight, in which the soul experiences something like what the blessed attain in heaven, and the mixed delight, in which the soul has a clear conscience but still experiences the absence of God. Juan here speaks of "the union . . . of the intense love of ecstatic contemplation" as midway between the loving conformity with God's will that all believers possess through grace and the union of identity of substance that the Son has with the Father. Like John of the Cross, he even allows that the inner delight of the spirit can flow over into the body and the senses, conforming them to its spiritual nature.[200] The second form of delight, discussed in II.7, is one in which joy at the presence of God is mingled with anguish at his absence. This shows that there is a place in the mysticism of Juan for a dark night dimension, although it is Tauler rather than John of the Cross who is directly cited here.[201] This theme is continued in chapter 8, where Juan argues that God is found in both presence and absence—"Oh, present absence and absent presence of him whom one loses and at the same time possesses" (II.8, trans., 140). The pain of absence is real and bitter, but the fainting of love brought about by this trial is not the end of love but is rather necessary for its growth and perfection. It can lead to the mystical death (*mors mystica*) and the "hanging in God" (Job 7:15-16) in which the perfectly mortified soul becomes ready for union.

Juan de los Angeles expounds on union, mystical death, inebriation, and rapture in the final chapters of *The Loving Struggle*. Chapter 10 is the most detailed exposition of the nature of union, which Juan insists, once again, is not a transformation of the divine essence into a created nature, but is rather "a union that is aptitudinal [i.e., by affinity], habitual, and actual, that is to say, by means of that ecstatic love which transforms the one who loves into that which he loves" (II.10; trans., 149). Juan proceeds to analyze four kinds of union.[202] The first is the *natural union,* by which God exists in creatures as their efficient, formal, and final cause. The second is the *aptitudinal union,* by which soul is the image of God in its spiritual powers of memory, understanding, and will. Third is the *habitual union,* by which the grace of the three theological virtues makes us pleasing to God. Finally, there is *actual union.* Juan says that this is "the perpetual and experiential operation of the three theological virtues . . . " that is, "the experiential and actual perceptions and tastes that, in the present condition [i.e., our life on earth], bring the soul to God" (II.10; trans., 151). Thus, from the natural aptitudinal union and the graced habitual union comes forth the experiential and actual love union the saints have spoken about. The Franciscan says that many names have been used of this union: transformation, perfect prayer, mystical theology, divine wisdom, and deification.[203]

Chapter 11 of book II is a digression on prayer as the most effective mediator between God and the soul, while chapters 12 and 13 turn their attention to the Eucharist, which, as Christ's body and blood, truly (not metaphorically) unite us with him. Rather than our assimilating Christ into ourselves by the reception of Christ in the sacrament, we assimilate ourselves into him as far as we are able. The ultimate triumph of love is the transformation or death of the soul, as Juan describes it in chapter 14, once again invoking the Song of Songs: "Happy indeed, many times felicitous the soul when God, wholly by means of a kiss, brings her to him, and she is transformed and deified, and in this kiss she dies, and in dying to all that is not of God she lives exclusively in him" (II.14; trans., 183). He explains this by distinguishing (1) transfiguration (the transposition of one thing into another with the original form remaining, as with Christ on the mountain of Transfiguration); (2) transubstantiation, the conversion of one substance into another, as in the Eucharist; and finally (3) transformation, which is when the soul, through the power of love, moves into God, and, although keeping her being intact, works wholly within God, "not as herself but through the Beloved." This is the inebriation of love, on which the Franciscan discourses with many citations in chapter 15. Finally, Juan closes *The Loving Struggle* with a chapter on rapture, which he defines as a violent or intense uplifting of the soul's superior faculties over her inferior ones, causing them to be left behind or even separated. Fittingly for a Franciscan, he ends the chapter with stories about that great Franciscan ecstatic Giles of Assisi.[204]

The controversial figure of María de Jesús de Agreda (1602–1665) should also be considered with the Franciscans.[205] María (born María Coronel y Arana) did not choose to be a nun. Her pious mother converted the family home into a convent and María had to join the discalced Franciscan "Conceptionists" (so-called due to their support for the Immaculate Conception of Mary) in 1620. Her first three years in the convent were a time of interior trials but also of the beginning of mystical gifts, especially her controversial bilocations. María became abbess in 1627, a position she occupied for the rest of her life. The visionary María was politically influential in seventeenth-century Spain due to her close relations with Philip IV. She first met Philip in 1643, when her fame led him to visit her convent, and the two exchanged hundreds of letters over the next two decades. Philip consulted María about many issues but appears to have considered her more as a spiritual advisor and an intercessor with God for his many sins, than as a political guru.[206] María was an able administrator and a prolific author. Despite several investigations by the Inquisition (1631, 1635, and 1650), she emerged unscathed.[207] Her most widely read work was a vast biography of Mary, a highly imaginative spiritual novel, called *The Mystical City of God* (*Mística Cuidad de Dios: Vida de la Virgen María*), begun in 1637, once destroyed at the command of her confessor, and then rewritten.[208] It was finally published in 1670 but was put on the Index in 1681, only to be soon removed. Condemned by the doctors of the Sorbonne in 1696, *The Mystical City* remains a bone of contention down to the present—praised by the so-called "Agredists" as a major spiritual document,[209] and dismissed by others as María's imaginative projection of herself onto the legendary accounts of the Virgin that had been accreting for many centuries. María's heavenly interviews with Mary, with their strong defense of the Immaculate Conception and

Mary's role as Co-Redemptrix, represent one of the most thorough presentations of Mariolatry in Catholic history. Although the Immaculate Conception was affirmed as Catholic dogma in 1848, it was contentious in seventeenth-century Spain (supported by the Franciscans but denied by many others, especially Dominicans), and, despite the support of Pope John Paul II, Mary's status as Co-Redemptrix has not been defined.

María also made claims regarding many mystical gifts, not only the ecstasies and encounters with Jesus featured by other women but especially the ability to levitate, and also bilocate, that is, to be in two places at the same time by divine dispensation, which became fairly common at this time, especially among Franciscan women.[210] Her supposed bilocations involved trans-Atlantic flights.[211] In her early years both María and her Franciscan supporters claimed that during her trance states she traveled to New Mexico to help the friars in their work of converting the Indians. In 1630 Fray Alonso de Benavides, the head of these missions, came back to Spain to testify to María's missionary efficacy, as well as to relate the conviction of the local Indians that "the Lady in Blue" had appeared to them. Both he and María wrote letters back to the missionary priests in New Mexico.[212] It is difficult to know how much of the bilocation claims came from the nun and how much from the friar. María's assertions regarding her bilocation grew more tenuous and guarded in her later years. In a report written to the Inquisitor Fray Pedro Manero in 1650, she insisted that she had only received this gift during the years 1620–23, not as she had said earlier up until the 1630s. She also was unclear about the extent to which the experiences were real or imaginary. Even in 1650, however, the Inquisitors cleared her.[213] With the protection of Philip IV, the complicity of the Inquisition is not surprising. María de Agreda died peacefully in 1665.

This Franciscan nun was an ecstatic and a visionary. In contrast to many of her contemporaries, however, there seems to be little erotic content to her mysticism. The Lord does address her as "My wife and turtledove,"[214] and she quotes the Song of Songs; but the images of kisses, embraces, mystical marriage, and the like, are not features of her writings. María, like Teresa of Avila and Thérèse of Lisieux after her, had a strong apostolic dimension: her desire to convert unbelievers is often noted. For example, in the "Report to Father Manero," she tells of how God revealed to her how few of all the souls that exist are believers. Her reaction was, "No sooner had the Most High revealed to me his will in this matter than my intense feeling of love of God and my neighbor were renewed, and I called out from the innermost part of my being on behalf of these souls."[215] María talks about her visions, but in such a general way that it is difficult to determine much about their nature. She often speaks of being taken up to heaven to converse with God and be shown mysteries hidden from others. She also uses phrases like "infused knowing," "mystical knowledge," "illumination through revelation," and "brilliant light." In one text she says that she was accustomed to seeing God every day, save for a period of eighty days when he absented himself to subject her to a purifying trial. Sometimes she talks about "seeing in abstract images," or seeing all images in God. In sum, however, María de Agreda remains a puzzle. Her reputation is largely dependent on a controversial Marian opus. One can admire her apostolic commitment and the forceful personality and intelligence she showed in dealing with the king of Spain and the Inquisition, but María's properly mystical credentials are open to question.[216]

Dominicans

The Dominican friars, especially of the Reformed branch that began in Italy in the fifteenth century, also produced mystical authors, although the Spanish Dominicans were best known for their revival of Thomism and their rigorous pursuit of orthodoxy. One of the premier Spanish Dominican theologians, Melchior Cano (ca. 1509–1560), was resolutely antimystical. A Dominican who did make a contribution to mysticism was a slightly older contemporary of Teresa and John, Luis de Granada (1504–1588), who spent much of his life in Portugal (1555–88).[217] Luis was once widely read, especially for his *Book of Prayer and Meditation* (*Libro de Oración y Meditación*), first published in 1555. After the book was placed on the Valdés Index in 1559, Luis put out a revised version in 1566 that won approval.[218] (It is interesting to note that these were exactly the years in which Teresa experienced her "second conversion," her crisis over the publication of the Valdés Index, and the beginning of her writing career.) Luis was a friend of the secular priest and noted preacher Juan de Avila (1499–1569), who was also often under suspicion by the Inquisition and who wrote a popular moral and ascetical manual, the *Audi, filia* (*Listen, O Daughter*).[219] Luis himself was a prolific author.[220] He was also a translator, putting out a Spanish version of the *Imitation of Christ* in 1536, as well as a translation of John Climacus's *Spiritual Ladder* in 1562. The *Book of Prayer and Meditation* overlapped with a *Guide for Sinners* (*Guia de pecadores*), which also appeared in several versions. Among the Dominican's later writings that touch on mystical themes are the *Memorial of the Christian Life* (1565) and the subsequent *Additions to the Memorial* (1574). In the 1580s Luis was involved in a scandal that says much about the ambiguous status of ecstatic mystical women—both *beata*s and enclosed nuns—during the great age of Spanish mysticism. María de la Visitación (1551–ca. 1603), prioress of a Dominican convent in Lisbon, had circulated accounts of her mystical gifts, especially the stigmata, and had become famous.[221] John of the Cross was suspicious of her, but Fray Luis became a wholehearted supporter, writing a laudatory *Historia de María de la Visitación*.[222] Luis's reputation suffered considerably when an investigation by the Inquisition in 1588 revealed that Sor María's stigmata were fake and sentenced the nun to life imprisonment.[223]

Both E. Allison Peers and Raphael Oechslin argue for Luis de Granada as a mystic,[224] but it must be said that his treatment of mystical themes seems sporadic, although he does not ignore them. Much of the *Book of Prayer and Meditation* deals with meditations on Christ's life. Luis does say that such meditations can lead to contemplative prayer and even to union with God, although much of what he says about union is standard. The Dominican has a holistic conception of progress toward God, in that he sees it as an expression of "devotion," something that is not to be understood as mere feeling or emotion but is rather a total dedication of the will to the service and love of God. Citing Thomas Aquinas, he says that devotion is "a virtue which makes a person prompt and ready for every good and urges him to and makes him apt for every virtuous work."[225] The primary expression of devotion is prayer, which the Dominican defines as the main activity that brings us to God. "Prayer," he says, "is a raising of our heart to God, by means of which we are united with him and become one with him. . . . Prayer is the soul in the presence of God and God in the presence of the soul."[226] Thus, prayer, contemplation, and union are all more or less equivalent for Luis, at least in his early works. What the later *Memorial* and *Additions to the Memorial* add to this picture, according to Peers and Oechslin, is a more developed treatment of the role of divine love in bringing prayer and devotion toward deeper forms of union.[227]

Jesuit Mystics[228]

Ignatius of Loyola, as we saw in chapter 2, was a mystic, but the story of mysticism in the later Jesuits has been an uneven one. In the Jesuit stress on apostolic service it sometimes happened that the role of contemplative prayer was downplayed and even came under suspicion. This was the case under the generalship of Everard Mercurian (1573–80) with results that affected the whole order, not only in Spain. Nevertheless, the Jesuits were noted spiritual directors and also composers of influential handbooks on spirituality and mysticism. The most popular of the Jesuit spiritual handbooks, *The Practice of Perfection and Christian Virtues* (*Ejercicio de perfección y virtudes cristianas*), written by Alonso Rodriguez (1538–1616), was published in 1609 in Spanish and soon translated into Latin, Italian, French, English, and many other languages.[229] An ascetical and practical manual of the devout life, *The Practice of Perfection* treats of the importance of mental prayer, but largely meditative prayer. Regarding higher infused contemplation, the author does everything in his power to discourage his readers from aspiring to it.[230] In a famous passage on descriptions of mystical union, he tells his reader: "Such analogies, such transformations of the soul, such silence, such self-annihilation, such uniting without mediation, such depth [of the soul] of Tauler, what use is there to talk about such things? If you understand them, I neither understand them or intend them; nor do I know how to talk about them."[231]

In the early years of the Jesuits in Spain, several members of the order gained reputations as mystics and mystical teachers. I will briefly look at two: Baltasar Alvarez (1533–1580), one of the confessors of Teresa of Avila, and his disciple, Luis de la Puente (1554–1624).[232] Baltasar Alvarez entered the Jesuits in 1555 and was Teresa's spiritual director from 1559 to 1565, while he was rector of the Jesuit College at Avila.[233] He helped Teresa in the foundation of her second convent at Medina del Campo in 1567 and served in a number of leadership posts for the Jesuits. After his death, Teresa wrote, "[O]ur Saint seemed to be a companion to me even when he was far away."[234] Nevertheless, the reaction against mystical prayer in the order made Alvarez a controversial figure in the period 1574–77, and his teaching was eventually prohibited by Mercurian.

During Mercurian's generalship two controversies about mystical prayer disturbed the Spanish Jesuits and, at least to some extent, other provinces of the order.[235] The first developed in the Province of Toledo, where the respected Antonio Cordeses (ca. 1518–1601) was deleted to Mercurian about 1573 for teaching in his *Treatise on Mental Prayer* (*Tratado de la oración mental*) the superiority of affective prayer to intellectual meditation. Mercurian forbade Cordeses from continuing to teach about such prayer, and, on November 25, 1574, issued a more general letter in which he insisted that the Jesuits, because they were not a contemplative order, should stick to the meditative prayer of Ignatius's *Institutes* and not provide teaching about contemplation, which should be left up to God. This narrow view (Peers calls it "illiberal") was even more on display on the "Alvarez affair."

The controversy over Baltasar Alvarez's teaching on the prayer of silence has been variously judged. For the ex-Jesuit Henri Bremond (1865–1933) it was a major "event" (*événement*) in the history of early modern spirituality, one that announced the agenda of Jesuit opposition to contemplative prayer for centuries.[236] Bremond's contemporary, the Jesuit professor of spirituality Joseph de Guibert (1877–1942), on the other hand, dismissed Bremond's contention that the Alvarez affair was an important event and relegated it to the status of a "simple incident" in his history of Jesuit spirituality.[237] However judged, the case is significant for the ongoing debates over the nature of mystical prayer that culminated a century later in the Quietist controversy.

Alvarez was the author of a number of works. We have access to his thought also through the incorporation of some documents concerning his prayer teaching into the life written about him by his student Luis de la Puente and first published in 1615.[238] In 1575 Alvarez was asked by his superior to write a treatise attacking the false views of the *Alumbrados*, a part of which was incorporated into chapter 33 of Peunte's *Life*. In 1576 the Jesuit authorities in Alvarez's province of Castile became nervous about the teaching on the prayer of silence that he was giving to younger Jesuits and ordered him to write an account of it. This document, or at least a part of it, was sent to Rome. While not formally condemned, it elicited documents about maintaining the teaching of Ignatius concerning the primacy of discursive meditation. In 1577 the Jesuit Visitor to Castile, Diego de Avellaneda, ordered Alvarez to submit another explanation of his teaching. The Visitor forbade Alvarez to continue such instruction and told him to adhere to the teaching of recognized authorities, such as Augustine, Gregory, Thomas, and, of course, Ignatius's *Exercises*. Rather tellingly, Avellaneda also commanded Alvarez "not to spend time on women, especially on Carmelite nuns, whether in visiting them or in writing letters."[239] (Had Teresa been able to see this letter, it would have probably brought a smile to her face.) Avellaneda also sent his document on to Mercurian in Rome, who approved it. Apologists for the Jesuit authorities have argued that the leaders were only condemning Alvarez's view that mystical prayer was open to many and easily obtained, but their arguments seem stretched, because Alvarez himself (if not perhaps all his students) insisted that higher prayer was *not* for everyone. Balance was finally somewhat restored on May 8, 1590, when the new Jesuit general, Claudio Aquaviva (1581–1615), addressed a general letter to the order, approving the use of contemplative prayer while still emphasizing the importance of apostolic service.[240]

The summaries of Alvarez's teaching in the *Life* by Puente, comprising both the 1576 and 1577 documents, are generic, and it is difficult to know how much is from Alvarez and how much from his student and defender, Puente.[241] In the 1576 document Alvarez provides an auto-biographical account of his sixteen years of struggle with lower stages of prayer before, by divine grace, he was given the gift of a deeper sense of the presence of God. This new form of prayer was characterized, above all, by a union with God that provided great joy, something Alvarez insists is the true goal of all spiritual effort.[242] The Jesuit argues that this form of joyful union was the constant teaching of the saints (e.g., Dionysius, Augustine, Gregory, Bernard, Thomas, and others) and is found throughout scripture. Finally, he notes that such prayer is not meant for everyone and that it fully conforms to the views of Ignatius, who later in his life experienced the Dionysian *patiens divina* (i.e., receiving divine things).[243] In the commentary that Puente added to these short texts, he expatiated (sometimes in passages taken from Alvarez's other works) on the nature of the "prayer of presence, repose, recollection, and silence," and its scriptural foundation.[244]

Luis de la Puente (often cited under the French form of his name, Du Pont) was a more substantial author than Baltasar Alvarez, and an extensive analysis of his writings cannot be given here.[245] He studied at the Jesuit College in Valladolid under the young Francisco Suarez and, inspired by his example, entered the Jesuits in 1574. Luis then went to Medina del Campo, where he was a student of Alvarez. Delicate health meant that most of his career was spent teaching in a variety of Jesuit colleges. Luis was a widely read author and most of his books were rapidly translated into Latin, French, and other languages. His first work was the two-volume *Meditations on the Mysteries of Our Holy Faith* (*Meditaciones de los misterios de nuestra santa fe*) published in 1605. Prefaced by a brief treatise on prayer (chaps. 1–11), this was a collection of doctrinal meditations in six parts arranged according to both the traditional three stages of the spiritual life (purgative, illuminative, unitive) and the major mysteries of the faith.[246] It was immensely popular (perhaps four hundred editions) and has been described by Miguel Nicolau as "[t]he most important and . . . the best collection of meditations realized since the beginning of the modern era." Puente's meditations are primarily doctrinal and practical in good Ignatian fashion, but he also uses mystical language (e.g., transformation, deification, unitive love) in the latter parts, though not in an original way.[247] In chapter 1 of part III, devoted to "Union with Almighty God, which is the End of the Unitive Way," Luis discusses three forms of union (union of understanding, union of will, and union of resemblance), as well as the speculative and experiential ways of knowing God.[248] These discussions, however, seem relatively general, even superficial. Luis's emphasis is on meditation as a way to draw near to true contemplation, experimental knowledge of God, and mystical inebriation—not on mystical states themselves (part III, chap. 2).

Luis's mystical teaching was more fully laid out in his long *Spiritual Guide* (*Guia espiritual*), first published at Valladolid in 1609.[249] This work, which the "Introduction" says is "an abbreviated science of all things pertaining to the spiritual life and to its two main parts, called the active life and the contemplative," has four divisions, based in part on the traditional four practices of the spiritual life first found in the Carthusian Guigo II's *Ladder of Monks* (*Scala claustralium*)—reading, meditation, prayer, and contemplation.[250] The first part deals primarily with mental prayer, according to the traditional pattern of the purgative, illuminative, and unitive ways. The second part concerns "holy reading and meditation," while the third and most mystical section is devoted to "perfect contemplation and union with God." The fourth part treats mortification and other effects of the contemplative life, as well as praising the mixed life of contemplation and action, seen as representative of the ideal of the Jesuits. Peers has provided a helpful analysis of section 3's teaching on perfect contemplation and loving union with God, highlighting Luis's use of terms found in Alvarez, such as "inward solitude, silence, idleness and rest," as well as "spiritual quiet after the manner of sleep, death, and burial." In describing the four degrees of contemplation, Luis distinguishes: (1) the way of affirmation ascribing the perfection of creatures to the Creator; (2) the negative way of Dionysius that shows how God is beyond all created things;[251] (3) spiritual perception of the immediate presence of God (a stage that features language similar to Teresa); and finally (4) "the unitive way," which is both habitual for all those in the state of grace and actual, that is, an intermittent experiential knowledge of God. Puente illustrates this stage by a number of chapters on the characteristics of such union, employing traditional metaphors such as the wine cellar, the mutual wound of love, and uniting in love and knowledge.[252] Luis is encyclopedic without being original.

The longest work of this tireless Jesuit was his *Treatise on the Perfection of All the States of the Christian Life* (*Tratado de la perfección en todos los estados de la vida del cristiano*), four volumes published between 1612 and 1616. In Latin, Luis also issued *A Moral and Mystical Exposition of the Song of Songs* in 1622, really a series of sermons containing some mystical material on the need for personal effort to follow Christ and give obedience to the institutional church.[253] Luis de la Puente's treatises on matters moral, ascetical, and mystical were influential, but, in comparison to the works of Teresa and John and Luis de León, they seem to lack personal engagement—a voice from within. This is partly remedied by the Jesuit's *Spiritual Maxims and Sentiments* (*Sentimientos y Avisos espirituales*), which were not published until after his death, first in 1671 and then again in the last century.[254] Here the Jesuit speaks in a more personal way about his own experiences of mystical illumination and "[t]he various ways of the presence of God that I have experienced both in prayer and outside it."[255] Puente's accounts of his mystical gifts would repay further study and comparison with better known mystics, like Ignatius and Teresa.

The Jesuits, unlike other Catholic orders, refused to have female branches. In recent years some attention has been given to the Spanish noblewoman Luisa de Carvajal y Mendoza (1566–1614), who was deeply influenced by her Jesuit confessors, especially Luis de la Puente, and who strove to imitate the apostolic and missionary work of the order, especially by going off to England to participate with the Jesuits in the dangerous work of trying regain Elizabethan England for Catholicism.[256] Luisa's *Spiritual Life Story* (*Historia de su vida espiritual*), as well her vows, poetry, and letters, have little or nothing that might be described as mystical, despite her yearning for martyrdom.[257] The *Spiritual Life Story* testifies to the severe ascetical practices (even for the time) inflicted on her by the uncle she lived with, which may have been a contributing factor to her desire for martyrdom.

Appendix 1. Mysticism in Portugal

For a time during this period (1580–1640) Portugal was united with Spain under the rule of Philip II and his successors but maintained its own language and cultural identity. The same reforming currents in religious orders that were important in Spain were also strong in Portugal. In addition to the mystics and mystical writers of the religious orders, there were also laypersons and groups of high and low estate that achieved some fame for their devout practices and mystical gifts.[258] Among the laity who made a contribution was the nobleman Francisco de Sousa Tavares, who published a *Book of Spiritual Doctrine* (*Livro de doctrina espiritual*) in 1564, a collection of pamphlets on prayer making use of many mystical authorities.[259] Here I wish to look at only one author, a woman who lies slightly outside our chronological frame but who displays some originality as a mystical author.

Joana Freire de Albuquerque was born of a noble family in 1617. In her teens Joana read Teresa's *Life* and was drawn to the religious life.[260] At some unspecified time she joined the Cistercian convent at Lorvão near Coimbra and began correspondence with the abbot of the Cistercian house at Lisbon, Vivardo de Vasconcelas, who was to become general of the order.[261] At his command, she moved to the strict house of Bernardine Recollects at Lisbon in 1659, where, under obedience to her confessor, she began writing her *Life* in 1661, in the course of which she changed her name to Joana de Jesus. After nine years she went back to Lorvão. Joana left the account behind in Lisbon and did not take it up again until 1676 at the command of a new confessor. From that time until her death in 1681, Sor Joana continued to record her visions and encounters with Christ.

Joana's mysticism was influenced by reading Teresa, but it has a special quality due to her development of the traditional mystical teaching on recollection (*recolhimento* in Portuguese), as well as her use of the theme of "loving anxiousness" (*ancias/ancias amorozas*), that is, the subject's physical and intellectual condition in encountering Jesus in a form of yearning that combines desire and disquiet. Recollection, a term that Joana knew from reading Teresa and also probably Luis de Granada, is one of the most frequent words in her vocabulary.[262] For Joana, recollection is a form of interior prayer involving memory and utilizing both love and knowledge.[263] It is closely connected with loving anxiousness. In one place she says, "On the twenty-fifth of May of the year 1664, a great anxiousness [*huma ânsia*], a desire of giving away my soul to the Lord and to be one with him, came upon me. And as the fire was growing, my soul's powers were recollected [*se me recolherão as potências*] with great peace and suavity. It seemed to me that I was making a spiritual communion and with the love growing with this so many things became understandable to me."[264]

Loving anxiousness, a term also found in John of the Cross,[265] is the leitmotif of Sor Joana's mysticism, pervading her encounters with Christ and the Trinity as an operation of Christocentric love.[266] Joana de Serrado's study of Sor Joana specifies three major contexts of this theme as a mode of constructing mystical subjectivity. The first is the encounter with Christ, especially the suffering Christ. For example, once gazing at the cross, Sor Joana says, "And the Lord putting his divine eyes upon the anxiousness with which I pleaded with him this [request], allowed my poor heart also to be pierced with that nail, and it stayed so stuck there that I could not return to myself." Visualizing Christ being scourged, she asks him to give her some solace, "and this," she continues, "caused in me a love so excessive and a tight anxiousness that I felt myself dying." The passage ends with an embrace between the wounded Savior and his human bride.[267] The second context of anxiousness is as an operation of Christocentric love, the "undergoing" of love that Sor Joana learns by accepting her frequent sufferings, both mental and physical, as gifts from God and modes of coming closer to Christ. Numerous passages testify to this important aspect of anxious suffering as purification—a kind of analogue to John of the Cross's dark night.[268] The operation of love involves many forms of erotic contact with Christ, such as kissing him and drinking from his wounded side, as well as feeling the presence of the Trinity within. Finally, the third context of anxiousness is the special knowledge of God (*notícia*) it conveys, a form of infused knowing of divine mysteries.[269] Sor Joana emphasizes the communal aspect of this knowing, because it is shared by the community of saints and is mediated in a special way by the Blessed Virgin. Joana de Jesus forms an interesting chapter in the history of Cistercian mysticism with affinities to many of the ecstatic and suffering women mystics of the late Middle Ages and early modern Spain.

Appendix 2. Mysticism in Spanish America[270]

The Spanish "discovery" of the New World was a major factor in the emergence of the country as a world power and its Golden Age. The centrality of religion in sixteenth-century Spain meant that the whole drama of discovery, colonization, and conversion of the indigenous peoples was shot through with religious language and values. The strength of the mystical impetus in sixteenth- and seventeenth-century Spain, despite the reaction against it by the dogmatic conservation epitomized in the Inquisition, allowed the mystical element to find expression in varying ways in Spanish America. For example, one of the primary Jesuit synthesizers of mysticism, Diego Alvarez de la Paz (1560–1620), went to Peru at an early age and wrote many of his extensive mystical *summae* in the New World.[271]

The earliest mystic of New Spain (i.e., Mexico) was Gregorio López

(1542–1596), who was born in Madrid and came to Mexico in 1562.[272] López's path to holiness and reputation as a mystic was of ancient provenance—the life of a wandering ascetic. Gregorio said little about his early life. He appears not to have been university trained, but he was able to read, even in Latin. He became a hermit while in Spain and continued this life in the New World, mostly in the neighborhood of Mexico City. Gregorio lived a harsh ascetic life but did not practice the intense self-mortifications ascribed to many saints, especially women.[273] Despite his commitment to silence and eremitical separation, he soon acquired fame as a holy man and spiritual guide. His unusual lifestyle, especially the fact that he apparently went for long periods without attending Mass and was not seen to say the rosary, led to suspicions about his orthodoxy, and Gregorio was several times examined by theologians and ecclesiastical authorities. In 1578 the archbishop Moya y Contreras sent Fr. Francisco Losa to question the hermit. Losa was so convinced by López's sanctity and spiritual gifts that he became his spiritual friend and amanuensis, even to the extent of joining his eremitical life in his last location, the little village of Santa Fe near Mexico City between 1589 and 1596.[274] Here Gregorio López died on July 20, 1596.

The hermit had a reputation for learning, being known for reading the Bible (in Latin) for four hours a day to the point of having it down virtually by heart. Losa's *Life* also refers to his appreciation of mystical authors such as Dionysius, Gregory the Great, Tauler, Ruusbroec, Catherine of Siena, and Teresa of Avila. The hermit left writings of his own: *A Book of Medicine* (not published until 1670), and a commentary on the Apocalypse that shows some knowledge of Joachim of Fiore.[275] Losa's *Life of Gregorio Lopez* has two parts: the thirteen chapters of part I tell the story of the hermit's life, death, and posthumous miracles; and the eighteen chapters of part II recount his spiritual life and contain many of his sayings. From the perspective of López as a mystic, the most important section is chapters 12–16 on his prayer life and union with God.[276] Gregorio's mental prayer is described as having three stages: first, "frequent meditations upon the life of our Lord, and in particular on his infancy and childhood" (Doyle, 190–91); second, the prayer of solitude, featuring constant ejaculations expressing resignation to God's will and acts of love; and finally, a mystical prayer of loving union with God. According to Losa, Gregorio once said, "Visions, revelations, ecstasies, raptures, and the like, are not the height of perfection, nor does perfection consist therein. . . . Souls that are perfect and experienced in the act of a pure, simple, and perfect love, need not the suspension of their senses in order that God should communicate with them" (Doyle, 200). Losa speaks of Gregorio's union with God as "immediate," but he distinguishes this immediacy from the passive union of fruition. Gregorio seems to have experienced fruition at times, but he deemed the active exercise of aspiring for more and more love of God to be the way that was most suitable for him. Losa concludes, "This transformation into Christ with which Gregory was favored, consisted of an ardent love, in consequence of which he desired to follow Christ in his life and imitate him in his cross and labors."[277]

The seventeenth-century mystics of the Americas included a number of women, who were mostly cast as hagiographical images of mystical piety, but sometimes the women themselves became writers, either at their own initiative or at the command of their confessors.[278] Ascetic and thaumaturgic mystics, such as Rose (Rosa) of Lima in Peru (1586–1617) and the indigenous Kateri Tekakwitha (ca. 1656–1680) of French North America,[279] are similar in many ways, despite being constructed in differing Catholic environments. Both women became icons for female mystical sanctity of a New World variety: miraculous (other cultures might say magical) mystics who leave us little or no record of their own thoughts, but whose sanctity was conveyed through carefully constructed narratives by their male clerical managers, Spanish Dominicans in the case of Rosa, and French Jesuits in the case of Kateri.[280] This relation was scarcely new. For centuries women's path to miraculous sanctity and sometimes the status of mystical teacher had been stage-managed by men. Of course, there were women authors, some quite renowned, who largely escaped this trap, as can be seen in extensive writings of the Mexican nun, Sor Juana de la Cruz (1648–1695), who composed both poetry and prose. Juana wrote important theological works, but there is little in her extensive corpus that could be described as mystical in the sense of recounting her own inner experience of God.[281]

A number of the colonial women authors hailed as mystics lie beyond the chronological confines of this volume.[282] Here I will take up only the case of Rosa of Lima, the first canonized saint of the New World and a patron of the Americas, who does lie within our chronological framework and who is a good example of clerical construction of a female mystic.[283] "Rosa of Lima," that is, the saint beatified in 1668 and canonized in 1671, is a mystical icon—an image of what was expected of a female mystic with her almost impossible ascetic prowess and the easy access to Jesus her heavenly spouse whose model had been memorably set down by Raymond of Capua in his *Large Life of Catherine of Siena*, a book that the historical Rosa read and absorbed.[284] Rosa was born Isabel Flores de Oliva of a creole family of modest means, but as a child her name was changed under supposedly miraculous conditions to Rosa. According to the hagiographical accounts and the documents of her canonization process, both in Peru and in Rome, she was extremely pious and severely ascetic from her early years.[285] Lima had a number of religious houses for women, as well as many *beatas*, the independent holy women well known in contemporary Spain. Rosa never entered the convent but lived as a *beata* first under the guidance of the Franciscans and then of the Dominicans (ca. 1606–17). Her reputation as ascetic, miracle worker, and bride of Christ grew large in her last years, though she, like most female ecstatics and mystics, had her detractors. The Inquisition was as active in the Spanish colonies as in the home country. In 1614 Rosa, learning that a commission of the Inquisition was investigating her claims to sanctity, requested a hearing and was cleared of suspicion of being an *alumbrada*, or false mystic.[286] Rosa's mysticism, as described in the lives and other documents, features the standard tropes of female erotic mysticism—devotion to the Christ child and to the Eucharist, flames of passion and wounds of love, and even a staged mystical marriage to Christ that took place in the Dominican church in Lima on Easter Sunday 1617.[287] Rosa died not long after and the contest for gaining her official status as a saint began, a struggle in which the Peruvian Dominicans were eventually successful.[288] It is interesting to note that Rosa left a spiritual journal, poetry, and various papers, but this material was confiscated by the Inquisition in 1624 and has not been seen since.[289] Rosa's own voice was effectively stilled. As Kathleen Myers summarizes, "The portrayal of Rose as a writer and laywoman with a religious vocation was downplayed as posthumous representations fixed on an image of her as the Catherine of Siena of the New World. . . . The church that promoted Rosa was at the same time the church that codified and controlled her."[290]

Conclusion

This chapter does not pretend to have treated all the figures who may be described as mystics, or who made contributions to mystical literature, in the Spanish-speaking world of ca. 1550–1650. Many of these were names well known in their time and were often read for centuries but who have mostly slipped from memory today. On the other hand, recent research, especially by scholars interested in the history of women, have recovered figures who were long neglected and who deserve renewed study. What I have hoped to demonstrate is that the Golden Age of Spanish mysticism was far more than just the great names of Ignatius of Loyola, Teresa of Avila, and John of the Cross, for all that their contributions are justly famous.

Notes

1. For an overview of Spanish spirituality of the time, see the multiauthor "Espagne, III: Age d'Or," DS 4:1127–78. Also useful is "Grandeurs et misères de la spiritualité espagnole," chap. 5 in Louis Cognet, *La spiritualité moderne*, vol. 1, *L'essor: 1500–1650*, 146–86.

2. Jose María de la Cruz Molinar, *Historia de la literatura mística en España* (Burgos: "El Monte Carmelo," 1961), Libro 2, "Autores," 7–473, especially the listing by religious orders (177–473).

3. There are several mystics who fit within the chronological confines of this volume but who will be postponed until vol. 7 because of their connection with Quietism, the opening theme of that volume. Predominant among these is Juan de Falconi (1596–1638), a priest of the Mercedarian order.

4. Peers adopted a broad view of Spanish mysticism, which he expressed as follows: "The scope of these *Studies* allows the inclusion of any writers who may be judged to have envisaged clearly the mystic's ideal, and are, either in their personal experience or in their writings, working towards it, as well as some whose apprehension of their aim and conception of the way to it are vague, but of whom it may be said with absolute certainty that they are mystics at heart" (*Studies*, 2:253).

5. On the Augustinian mystics and spiritual authors, see "Escuela Agustiniana," in Molinar, *Historia de la literatura mística en España*, 363–85. For an account of Orozco, see Peers, "Augustinian Mysticism: Alonso de Orazco," chap. 7 in vol. 2 of *Studies* (191–218). Peers treats several other Augustinians: the preacher St. Thomas of Villanova (1488–1555) in chap. 3 of vol. 2 of *Studies*, and two later writers, Pedro Malón de Chaide (ca. 1540–1589) and Cristóbal de Fonseca (1550–1621), both in chap. 9 of vol. 2 of *Studies*. He also has a general chapter on "Augustinian Mystics" in vol. 3 of *Studies* (chap. 3, 145–72).

6. I will use the edition of Felix García, *Obras Completas Castellanas de Fray Luis de León* (2nd ed. corrected and augmented; Madrid: Biblioteca de Autores Cristianos, 1951). In English, see Colin P. Thompson, *The Strife of Tongues: Fray Luis de León and the Golden Age of Spain*, Cambridge Iberian and Latin American Studies: Literature and Literary Theory (Cambridge: Cambridge University Press, 1988). A general sketch can be found in Manuel Durán, *Luis de León* (New York: Twayne, 1971), as well as the essay by Peers, "Luis de León," chap. 6 in vol. 1 of *Studies* (235–79). See also David Gutiérrez, "León (Luis de)," DS 9:634–43; and Cognet, *La spiritualité moderne*, vol. 1, *L'essor*, 163–71. For a treatment of Luis's style, see

David J. Hildner, *Poetry and Truth in the Spanish Works of Fray Luis de León*, Colección Támesis: Monografías 151 (London: Tamesis Books, 1992).

7. *In Canticum Canticorum Triplex Explanatio* went through several editions, with the definitive version appearing in 1589. There is an account in Thompson, *Strife of Tongues*, 104–21. Luis's second, or mystical, exposition demonstrates wide knowledge of the medieval mystical commentators, especially Bernard of Clairvaux. In one passage Luis says that he has not enjoyed the highest form of mystical experience: "Est enim magna res, et plane supra hominis vires, et denique ejusmodi, ut vix posit intelligi, nisi ab iis, qui eam non tam doctoris alicujus voce quam ipsa re, et suavi amoris experimento a Deo didicerunt, de quorum numero non esse me, et fateor et doleo" (I cite from the text as given by Antonio Márquez, "De mística luisiana: ser o no ser," in *Fray Luis de León: Historia, Humanismo y Letras*, ed. Victor García de la Concha and Javier San José Lera [Salamanca: Ediciones Universidad, 1986], 294). On the basis of this and several other passages (e.g., *Names of Christ* II.6) some writers have denied Luis the title of mystic, but two things cast doubt on this. First, such admissions are frequent among mystical authors; and, second, the fact that Luis says he has not attained the *highest* form of mystical consciousness does not exclude him from all forms.

8. On Luis's imprisonment and trial, see Thompson, *Strife of Tongues*, chap. 2 (36–85).

9. The parable about the small bird attacked by two evil crows found at the end of *The Names of Christ* III.1 has been seen as Luis's reflection on his prison experience.

10. The *Exposición del Libro de Job* can be found in *Obras Completas*, 815–1278. For a brief account, see Thompson, *Strife of Tongues*, 121–39.

11. *Los Nombres de Cristo*, book III, Dedicatorio (*Obras Completas*, 656). For English versions of *The Names of Christ*, I will generally follow *Luis de León, The Names of Christ*, trans. Manuel Durán and William Kluback, Classics of Western Spirituality (New York: Paulist Press, 1984), where this text can be found on 266. Because this translation is at times more of a paraphrase, and sometimes even erroneous, I will sometimes adjust the version or make my own translation. The whole Dedication (trans., 265–68) is an *apologia* for the Spanish language as a fitting vehicle for theological writing.

12. Along with his numerous translations from Greek and Latin poetry (Horace, Vergil, Pindar, etc.), Luis wrote some twenty-three Spanish poems that are ranked among the treasures of Spain's Golden Age. I have compared two bilingual versions: *Lyrics of Luis de Leon*, with English renderings by Aubrey F. G. Bell (London: Burns, Oates &Washbourne, 1928); and *The Unknown Light: The Spanish Poems of Fray Luis de León*, introduction and translation by Willis Barnstone (Albany: State University of New York Press, 1979).

13. Cited by Barnstone in his "Introduction," *Unknown Light*, 14.

14. There is an edition of *La perfecta casada* in *Obras Completas*, 233–342.

15. The 1583 text included only two books. The 1585 edition added book III with four names, and the posthumous 1595 edition added an extra name, "Lamb." I will use the edition in *Obras Completas*, 379–780. On the version of Durán and Kluback (*Luis de León, The Names of Christ*), see Colin Thompson's review in *New Blackfriars* 66 (1985): 201–2. Comparison of this translation with the Spanish original shows a number of misleading translations, such as that in book III.1, "Son

of God" (trans., 282–84), where the version consistently refers to the Father as "creating" the Son (the Arian heresy!), whereas the Spanish text (*Obras Completas*, 678–80) correctly uses the verb *engendera* (i.e., begets or engenders).

16. Barnstone, "Introduction," *Unknown Light*, 15.

17. On Luis as a mystical poet, see E. Allison Peers, "Mysticism in the Poetry of Fray Luis de León," in Peers, *St. Teresa of Jesus and Other Essays and Addresses* (London: Faber & Faber, 1953), 153–73. In considering the mystical character of some of Luis's poems I have profited from the unpublished essay of my former student Robert Baird, "When Can I Free Myself and Fly? Luis de León and the Question of Mysticism." My thanks to him for insights from this essay.

18. There are many editions of Luis's *poemario*, but I will use the Spanish text in *Obras Completas*, 1436–38, and also the translations of Bell, 130–33, and Barnstone, 44–47. There are discussions in Terence O'Reilly, "The Ode to Francisco Salinas," in O'Reilly, *From Ignatius of Loyola to John of the Cross,* essay 11, as well as in Barnstone, "Introduction," 21–27. I will use Barnstone's translation here.

19. A number of critics have questioned the authenticity of stanza 5.

20. There is a bit of a textual problem here, because most early manuscripts read *amigos* ("friends"), but later editors have often preferred the singular *amigo* as referring to Salinas.

21. O'Reilly ("Ode to Salinas") notes the importance of friendship in this mystical poem, concluding, "[T]he musician [Salinas] exemplifies the truths that his music helps to reveal. By the way in which he plays Salinas mediates spiritual sight to a dear friend because, although physically blind, he is spiritually wise, a contemplative like Fray Luis himself" (essay 11, 113).

22. This poem can be found in *Obras Completas*, 1451–53 and is translated in Bell, 98–103, whose translation I use here; see also Barnstone, 58–63. The beauty of the starry night as an image of God is also featured in *The Names of God*, book II.3 (trans., 212–14, 224).

23. This poem, beginning *Alma region luciente* ("O sweet region of light"), can be found in *Obras Completas*, 1458–60, and is translated by Bell, 96–99, and Barnstone, 86–89, whose version I cite here. There is an exposition in Thompson, *Strife of Tongues*, 249–61. See also Peers, "Mysticism in the Poetry of Fray Luis de León," 169–72.

24. "Shepherd" is one of the proper names for Christ in *Los nombres de Cristo*, book I.4.

25. Some scholars have identified Marcelo with Luis and have sought to determine who the other figures might be, but other commentators see the three friars as aspects of Luis's personality; see Durán and Kluback, "Introduction," in *Names of Christ*, 17.

26. *Los Nombres de Cristo*, Dedicatoria (ed., 390–91; trans., 39–40). As in the other chapters, I will provide the Spanish text only where it seems necessary.

27. *Los Nombres*, Dedicatoria (ed., 388; trans., 37).

28. Along with the expositions on the Song of Songs and Job, Luis wrote commentaries on Genesis, Obadiah, and the Psalms. In the New Testament he wrote a short work on 2 Thessalonians and a treatise on the time of the death of Jesus and its relation to Passover.

29. For an analysis of the treatise, see Thompson, *Strife of Tongues*, 86–94.

30. Cited in Thompson, *Strife of Tongues*, 89.

31. Those who deny that Luis de León is a mystic include Ángel Custodio Vega (Luis de León, *Poesías*, ed. Custodio Vega [Barcelona: Editorial Planeta, 1970] and Márquez ("De mística luisiana: ser o no ser," 287–98).

32. Examples of those who have argued for Luis as a mystic include Peers, "Luis de León," 268–79; F. García, "Introducción general," in *Obras Completas*, 1–20; Barnstone, "Introduction," *Unknown Light*, 15–27; Alain Guy, "Fray Luis de León et le mysticisme," in *Santa Teresa y la literatura mística Hispanica*, ed. Manuel Criado de Val (Madrid: EDI, 1984), 521–26. Also positive, if somewhat guarded, is Thompson, *Strife of Tongues*, esp. 105–13, 233, 244, 258–60.

33. Melquiades Andrés Martín, "La espiritualidad de fray Luis de León," in García de la Concha and San José Lera, *Fray Luis de León: Historia, Humanismo y Letras*, 224–39, esp. 239: "Fue un místico esencial a lo que creo, en los años de Teresa, Juan de los Angeles, Juan de la Cruz, Juan Bautista de la Concepción, que se expresó en categorías humanistas vividas, desde le esperanza cristiana. . . . En dos pasajes de sus obras dice que no es místico. En muchos más, algunos recogidos en esta ponencia, expone su experiencia inmediata de Dios y los procesos de la misma."

34. Detailed commentaries on *Los Nombres* can be found in F. García, "Introducción," in *Obras Completas*, 345–78; and Thompson, *Strife of Tongues*, chap. 5 (171–231).

35. Irénée Hausherr, *The Name of Jesus*, Cistercian Studies 44 (Kalamazoo: Cistercian Publications, 1978).

36. Henk J. M. Schoot, *Christ the 'Name' of God: Thomas Aquinas on Naming Christ* (Leuven: Peeters, 1993).

37. *Isidori Hispalensis Episcopi Etymologiarum sive Originum Libri XX*, ed. W. M. Lindsay (Oxford: Clarendon, 1911), Liber VII, 2 (no pagination).

38. Thompson, *Strife of Tongues*, 172.

39. *Los Nombres*, Introducción (ed., 395; trans., 42).

40. The treatise on "Names in General" can be found in *Obras Completas*, 395–406 (trans., 42–53). This part of the work has attracted much attention; see Hildner, *Poetry and Truth*, chap. 2, "Fray Luis's Doctrine of Names" (25–40); Robert Ricard, "Fray Luis de León et le problème du nom," in *Études sur sainte Thérèse*, ed. Robert Ricard and Nicole Pélisson, Collection Études hispaniques: Série Littérature 3 (Paris: Centre de Recherches Hispaniques, 1968), 187–94; Thompson, *Strife of Tongues*, 7–13 and 176–78; and esp. Alain Guy, *Le pensée de Fray Luis de León: Contribution à l'étude de la philosophie espagnole au XVIe siècle* (Paris: Vrin, 1943). Several of these works compare Luis and the epistemology of Thomas Aquinas, something I shall not go into here.

41. *Los Nombres*, I, Introducción (ed., 396; my trans.): ". . . es una palabra breve, que se substituye por aquello de quien se dice y se toma por ello mismo."

42. Helpful in this connection is H. J. M. Schoot, "Friars in Negative Theology: Thomas Aquinas and Luis de León," in *The Myriad Christ: Plurality and the Quest for Unity in Contemporary Christology*, ed. T. Merrigan and J. Haers, Bibliotheca Ephemeridum theologicarum Lovaniensium 152 (Leuven: Peeters, 2000), 331–47. According to Schoot, "Fray Luis is closer to understanding names as parts of divine praise, than as potential pieces of information, closer to names as vehicles of the divine, than as sole products of the human intellect, closer to names as part

of divine ineffability, than names as means of leaving the divine mystery behind" (340).

43. *Los Nombres*, I, Introducción (ed., 401; trans., 48).

44. *Los Nombres*, I, Introducción (ed., 401–2; trans., 49).

45. In this volume, as in McGinn, *Reformation,* I distinguish between the branch of Jewish mysticism called Kabbalah and its Christian adaptation, Cabala, although the two are obviously related. The most balanced account of Luis de León's attitude toward Judaism and use of Christian Cabala is Thompson, *Strife of Tongues*, chap. 4, "The Language of Mystery" (140–70). There is much information, but more extreme claims for Luis's Cabalism, in Swietlicki, *Spanish Christian Cabala*, chaps. 4 and 5 (82–154).

46. For the text, translation, and study of the *De arte cabalistica*, see Johann Reuchlin, *On the Art of the Kabbalah/De arte cabalistica*, trans. Martin Goodman and Sarah Goodman (Lincoln: University of Nebraska Press, 1993).

47. *Los Nombres* I, Introducción (ed., 403; trans., 50). Marcelo also reveals the trinitarian significance of the Tetragrammaton by writing it in the sand in the forms of three *yods*, another theme of Christian Cabala (the Durán-Kluback translation mistakenly renders this as "three sevens"). On this section of the introduction, see the discussion of sources in Swietlicki, *Spanish Christian Cabala*, 89–98.

48. *Los Nombres* I, Introducción (ed., 403–5; trans., 50–52).

49. The names are apportioned as follows: book I (Bud, Face of God, Way, Shepherd, Mountain, Everlasting Father); book II (Arm of God, King of God, Prince of Peace, Husband); book III (Son of God, Lamb, Beloved, Jesus Christ).

50. *The Names of Christ* explicitly mentions Augustine some thirteen times. Other authorities cited more than once include Origen, Gregory Nazianzus, Basil, Jerome, Chrysostom, Macarius, Theodoret, Leo the Great, and Bernard of Clairvaux.

51. This teaching (book I, 1, ed., 413–17; trans., 59–62) appears several times in Luis's writings. Adam's sin, of course, did affect the manner of the incarnation and life of Christ, such as the need for his death on the cross. For a discussion of Luis's treatment of this theme and its background, see Thompson, *Strife of Tongues*, 172–76.

52. *Los Nombres* I, 2 (ed., 427; trans., 72).

53. *Los Nombres* I, 3 (ed., 439; trans., 83–84). The three stages are also mentioned in I, 4 (trans., 96), and in a more historical form in III, 1 (trans., 300–305).

54. *Los Nombres* I, 4 (ed., 456–57; trans., 100): "Y porque El uno mismo está en los pechos de cada una de sus ovejes, y porque su pacerlas es auntarlas consigno y entrañarleas en sí, como ahora decía, pore so le conviene también lo pastrero que pertenece al Pastor, que es hacer unidad y rebaño."

55. *Los Nombres* I, 6 (ed., 490–91; trans., 132). This text is one of the relatively rare mentions of deification in *The Names of Christ* (see also II, 2, ed., 599; III, 3, ed., 724).

56. *Los Nombres* asserts belief in the final salvation of the Jews here (II.1, ed., 520; trans., 158), and elsewhere, e.g., I, 2 (trans., 68) and I, 4 (trans., 86–87).

57. In a rather daring section (II, 2, ed., 559–62; trans. 194–97) the Augustinian criticizes contemporary unnamed kings for their evil and rapacious exercise of kingship, although he admits that no king, however good, could measure up to Christ.

58. *Los Nombres* II, 3 (ed., 588; trans., 216).

59. On friendship with God, see *Los Nombres* II, 3 (ed., 592, 604; trans., 219, 227). Friendship with God appears later in the work, e.g., II, 4 and III, 3 (trans., 240 and 329–31).

60. *Los Nombres* II, 3 (ed., 601; my trans.): "Quedo, pues, concluído que la gracia, como es semejanza de Dios, entrando en nuestra alma y prendiendo luego su fuerza en la voluntad de ella, la hace por participacíon, como de suyo es la Dios, ley e inclinacíon y deseo de todo aquello que es justo y que es bueno."

61. "Esposo" is found in *Obras Completas*, 619–51 and trans., 239–62. For analyses of this chapter, see Hildner, *Poetry and Truth*, 46–71; and Thompson, *Strife of Tongues*, 207–11.

62. *Los Nombres* II, 4 (ed., 619; trans., 239).

63. *Los Nombres* II, 4 (ed., 620; trans., 240). Luis consistently insists on the superiority of the "hot" mystical marriage over the "cold" human marriage, but this does not prevent him from using the sexual image of union between man and woman as an analogue to union with Christ.

64. *Los Nombres* II, 4 (ed., 620–24; trans., 240–43) on these five characteristics.

65. *Los Nombres* II, 4 (ed., 622; trans., 242). The reference to St. Augustine seems to be to *Tractatus in Iohannem* 8.

66. *Los Nombres* II, 4 (ed., 624; trans., 243). The Durán-Kluback version is more an abbreviated paraphrase than a full version.

67. *Los Nombres* II, 4 (ed., 631; trans., 247). For a discussion of Luis's argument about ineffability here, see Hildner, *Poetry and Truth*, 47–51.

68. The treatise on delight can be found in ed., 632–40 and trans., 248–53. There is an analysis in Hildner, *Poetry and Truth*, 51–71.

69. *Los Nombres* II, 4 (ed., 632; my trans.): "Porque deleite es un sentimiento y movimiento dulce que acompaña y como remata todas aquellas obras en que nuestras potencias y fuerzos, conforme a sus naturalezas o sus deseos, sin impedimento ni estorbo se emplean."

70. *Los Nombres* II, 4 (ed., 635; trans., 250). This is the mystical theme of epektasis, the endless but also satiating pursuit of God first clearly expressed by Gregory of Nyssa.

71. *Los Nombres* II, 4 (ed., 639; trans., 253).

72. *Los Nombres* II, 4 (ed., 640; my trans.): "!Luz, amor, vida, descanso sumo, belleza infinita, bien inmenso y dulcísimo, dame que me deshaga yo, y que me convierta en Ti toda, Señor! Mas callemos, Juliano, lo que por mucho que hablemos no se puede hablar."

73. *Los Nombres* III, 1, a long chapter (ed., 664–712; trans., 272–311), is a good illustration of Luis's skill in using biblical texts to buttress his theological constructions.

74. The five births are introduced in *Los Nombres* III, 1 (ed., 669–70; trans., 276) and are discussed in detail in the rest of the chapter.

75. *Los Nombres* III, 1 (ed., 696; trans., 298).

76. *Los Nombres* III, 1 (ed., 697–98; trans., 299).

77. *Los Nombres* III, 1 (ed., 699–700; trans., 300–301).

78. These are in a different order in the *Obras Completas*, with "Lamb" found in 772–90 (trans., 311–25) and "Beloved" in 713–34 (trans., 325–43).

79. *Los Nombres* III, 2 (ed., 772; trans., 311).

80. *Los Nombres* III, 3 (ed., 734; trans., 343).

81. *Los Nombres* III, 4 (ed., 735–69; trans., 343–71). For an analysis, see Thompson, *Strife of Tongues*, 161–65, and 223–27.

82. The exegesis of these two Hebrew names is in *Los Nombres* III, 4 (ed., 735–42; trans., 344–54). For the Jewish background, see Swietlicki, *Spanish Christian Cabala*, 120–26.

83. *Los Nombres* III, 4 (ed., 759; my trans.): "Es tambien Jesús porque es salud todo El. Son salus sus palabras; digo, son Jesús sus palabras, son Jesús sus obras, su vida es Jesús, y su muerte es Jesús."

84. *Los Nombres* III, 4 (ed., 762; my trans.): "De manera que en Jesucristo, como fuente o como en océan inmenso, está atesorado todo el ser y todo el buen ser, toda la substanticia del mondo."

85. For a list of Carmelite mystical authors and some description of their teaching, see Molinar, *Historia de la literatura mística en España*, "Escuela Carmelitana," 239–73. The best account in English is Peers, "Carmelite Mystics," chap. 1 in *Studies*, 3:1–80. There is a detailed treatment of the teachings of Teresa, John, and their successors on acquired and infused contemplation and visions and revelations by Gabriel de Sainte-Marie-Madeleine, "Carmes Déchaussés, II: École mystique Théresienne (Carmes Déchaussés)," DS 2:171–209. See also Cognet, *La spiritualité moderne,* vol. 1, *L'essor,* 171–86.

86. Winifred Nevin, *Heirs of St Teresa of Avila* (Milwaukee: Bruce, 1959); and esp. Christopher C. Wilson, ed., *The Heirs of St. Teresa of Avila*, Carmelite Studies 9 (Washington, DC: ICS Publications, 2006).

87. For a short account of the conflicts of 1582–94, see E. Allison Peers, *Handbook to the Life and Times of St. Teresa and St. John of the Cross* (Westminster, MD: Newman Press, 1954), chaps. 5 and 6.

88. Peers describes the antagonism between Gracián and Doria as follows: "It was largely temperamental: there was a basic incompatibility between the attractive, eloquent, suave, high-minded but often weak-willed idealist [Gracián], and the shrewd, hard-headed organizer and man of business [Doria], who always knew what he wanted and let nothing stand in his way of getting it" (*Handbook*, 76).

89. For a short account, see Kieran Kavanaugh, "Blessed Anne of St. Bartholomew," in Wilson, *Heirs of St. Teresa of Avila*, 59–71.

90. Quoted from Kavanaugh, "Blessed Anne," 70. Ana de Jesús and Ana de San Bartolomé split on a number of issues after 1605 and came to represent two different factions among the reformed nuns in France and the Low Countries. See Christopher C. Wilson, "Taking Teresian Authority to the Front Lines: Ana de San Bartolomé and Ana de Jesús in Art of the Spanish Netherlands," in Wilson, *Heirs of St. Teresa of Avila*, 72–106.

91. Teresa's vision of a reformed Carmelite community of nuns has been influential but also contentious, as various communities claiming to follow her way of life have proliferated over the past four centuries. A sense of this variety can be found in the article "Carmelitane, suore," DIP 2:398–459. The main Discalced order is treated by V. Macca on 423–54.

92. Such religious "autobiographies" were an important feature of nuns' writing in early modern Spain in general, not just among the Carmelites. See Durán Lopez, "Religious Autobiography," 15–38; Isabelle Poutrin, *La voile et la plume: Autobiographie et sainteté féminine dans l'Espagne moderne*, Bibliothèque de la Casa de Velázquez 11 (Madrid: Casa de Velázquez, 1995); and Haliczer, *Between Exaltation and Infamy*.

404404   *Mysticism in the Golden Age of Spain*

93. Elizabeth Teresa Howe, "Heeding the 'Madre': Ana de San Agustín and the Voice of Santa Teresa," in Wilson, *Heirs of St. Teresa of Avila*, 45–58.

94. The Spanish texts of the *Relaciones* have been edited and studied by Elizabeth Teresa Howe, *The Visionary Life of Madre Ana de San Agustín* (Woodbridge, Suffolk: Tamesis, 2004). Ana seems to have had some ambivalence about writing her story down, since she tells us that her first two attempts were victims of spontaneous combustion (diabolical?). In any case, the third time took.

95. These two women, along with selections and translations from their writings, are presented by Electa Arenal and Stacey Schlau, *Untold Sisters: Hispanic Nuns in Their Own Works* (Albuquerque: University of New Mexico Press, 1989), chap. 1 (19–129).

96. For an introduction, see Alison Weber, "María de San José (Salazar): Saint Teresa's 'Difficult' Daughter," in Wilson, *Heirs of St. Teresa of Avila*, 1–20. Weber also is responsible for the translation, *María de San José Salazar, Book for the Hour of Recreation* (Chicago: University of Chicago Press, 2002). For an edition, see Simeón de la Sagrada Familia, ed., *Escritos espirituales* (Rome: Postulación General O.C.D., 1979).

97. See *Book for the Hour of Recreation*, 2nd Recreation (trans., 51–52 and 60), and 7th Recreation (trans., 90–98).

98. Her works were edited by Julián Urkiza, *Obras Completas de la Beata Ana de San Bartolomé*, 2 vols. (Rome: Edizioni Teresianum, 1981, 1985). Selections are available in Arenal and Schlau, *Untold Sisters*, 46–79.

99. Cecilia was briefly treated by Peers, "Carmelite Mystics," 64–70, but has lately been given more attention. See Arenal and Schlau, *Untold Sisters,* chap. 2, "Two Sisters among the Sisters" (131–89); Emily Toft, "Cecilia del Nacimiento: Mystic in the Tradition of John of the Cross," in Boenig, *Mystical Gesture*, 169–84, and Toft, "Cecilia del Nacimiento: Second-Generation Mystic of the Carmelite Reform," in Kallendorf, *New Companion to Hispanic Mysticism*, 231–52. See also Barbara Mujica, "Cecilia del Nacimiento: Un alma inflamando del amor," in Barbara Louise Mujica, *Women Writers of Early Modern Spain: Sophia's Daughters* (New Haven: Yale University Press, 2004), 99–115.

100. The fruitful collaboration of the two sisters is the focus of the treatment by Arenal and Schlau in *Untold Sisters*, chap. 2.

101. Some of Antonio's letters to Cecilia are quoted in her *First Account of God's Mercies* (*Primera relación des Mercedes*) written in 1629. There is a translation in Cecilia del Nacimiento, *Journeys of a Mystical Soul in Poetry and Prose*, ed. Kevin Donnelly and Sandra Sider, Other Voices in Early Modern Europe: Toronto Series 18 (Toronto: Centre for Reformation and Renaissance Studies, 2012), 130–52. See esp. the passages from Letter 19 (145–49), which discuss divine darkness making considerable use of Dionysius.

102. Cecilia's writings, neglected for centuries, were edited by José Diaz Cerón, *Obras completas de Cecilia del Nacimiento* (Madrid: Editorial de Espiritualidad, 1970). This edition is not available to me, so I have used the partial Spanish texts and translations found in several works, especially in Donnelly and Sider, *Journeys of a Mystical Soul.*

103. Cecilia has eight poems in praise of Teresa. These are Nos. 21, 27, 63, 64, 65, 80, 85, and 86 in the translations of Donnelly and Sider, *Journeys of a Mystical*

Soul. In contrast, she has five poems dedicated to the Blessed Virgin (Nos. 40, 44, 45, 66, and 79).

104. On the influence of John of the Cross on Cecilia, see Toft, "Cecilia del Nacimiento: Second-Generation Mystic," 238–48. Cecilia cites John directly in her *Second Account of God's Favors*, section 8 (Donnelly and Sider, *Journeys of a Mystical Soul*, 157–58).

105. *Treatise on Union* 2 (Donnelly and Sider, 110).

106. Another dangerous expression comes in *Treatise* 22 (Donnelly and Sider, 120). Cecilia says that God lifts the soul up in order "to make her God with him." She explains, "This happens in such a way that it can truly be said that by this intimate participation, it is not that the soul will be like God, but that she will be God and the Highest Son." She then references Augustine, but it is hard to know what text she has in mind.

107. *Treatise on Union* 29 (Donnelly and Sider, 123).

108. *Treatise on Union* 36 (Donnelly and Sider, 126). The surpassing of the three higher powers of the soul (intellect, will, and memory) by the divine influx is Sanjuanist, and the reference to the "ray of darkness" evokes Dionysius (MT 1).

109. *Second Account of God's Favors* 10 (Donnelly and Sider, 158). See also 17 and 19. Cecilia's love for scripture is also evident in the way in which she, like Luis de León, wrote poems that were paraphrases of the Psalms; see Nos. 38 (Ps. 49), 39 (Ps. 113), 75 (Ps. 18), and 82 (Ps. 71).

110. Teresa and Cecilia were not the only women who wrote interpretations of the Song of Songs, whether on their own or under instructions from their male superiors. Another example is found in the Augustinian Madre Mariana de San José (1568–1638), whose recently edited writings include a *Commentario al "Cantar de los Cantares"* (ca. 1622–27). See Madre Mariana de San José, *Obras Completas*, ed. Jesús Diez Rastrilla (Madrid: Biblioteca de Autores Cristianos, 2014), 415–581.

111. *First Gloss on the Song of Songs* 9 (Donnelly and Sider, 169).

112. The *Second Gloss* (Donnelly and Sider, 177–85), Cecilia's last mystical text is explicitly concerned with Song of Songs 3:5, where the Bridegroom says, "I adjure you, Daughters of Jerusalem, by the gazelles and hinds of the fields, do not awaken my love until she wishes." This plea not to awaken is coupled with Song 5:2, where the Bride says, "I sleep, but my heart is awake."

113. *Second Gloss* 13 (Donnelly and Sider, 182).

114. The full Spanish text of the "Canciones de la unión y transformación del alma en Dios por la niebla divina de pura contemplación," can be found in Mujica, *Women Writers of Early Modern Spain*, 106–8. I will use the English translation of Donnelly and Sider in *Journeys of a Mystical Soul*, 33–107. For a treatment of Cecilia's poem and commentary, see Toft, "Cecilia de Nacimiento: Mystic in the Tradition of John of the Cross," 173–84, who provides a comparison of Cecilia's poem with John's "Noche oscura."

115. Tenth Song 1 (Donnelly and Sider, 84).

116. Cecilia often appeals to the inexpressibility of her experiences. The topos first is found in the introduction addressed to Tomás de Jesús. Speaking of the love songs found in the Bible and those authored by the saints (e.g., John of the Cross), she says, "[T]hose short texts hold the deepest mysteries, and they contain the most of what is humanly possible to express within them, for they speak of divine things that are incapable of being expressed. There is so much immensity

in each of these songs, though, that it is better to feel it than say it" (Donnelly and Sider, 34–35). For other references to inaccessibility and inexpressibility, see, e.g., Donnelly and Sider, 36, 38, 41, 57, 61, and 93. Similar passages are found in her other writings.

117. I cite here from the version in Arenal and Schlau, *Untold Sisters*, 183, with my own literal rendering.

118. *Treatise on the Transformation*, First Song 11 (Donnelly and Sider, 38).

119. *Treatise on Transformation*, First Song 14 (Donnelly and Sider, 40).

120. God as a bottomless sea or ocean occurs a number of times in the *Treatise on the Transformation*; see, e.g., Donnelly and Sider, 42, 87, 89, 92, 94, and 102.

121. Second Song: La cual a gozar llega / el alma que de amor está inflamada, / y viene a quedar ciego / quedando sin ver nada, / la ciencia trascendida y alcanzada. I use the translation of Arenal and Schlau, *Untold Sisters*, 183. The commentary on the Second Song is translated in Donnelly and Sider, 42–50.

122. Important passages on soul's center can be found in the Third Song 10–13; Fourth Song 1–5, 13–15, and 17–20; Sixth Song 2; Seventh Song 4; Eighth Song 6–7; Tenth Song 3; Eleventh Song 8; Twelfth Song 11; Thirteenth Song 1; Fourteenth Song 7–9; Fifteenth Song 8; and Sixteenth Song 9 (Donnelly and Sider, 53–55; 55–57 and 61–64; 68–69; 76; 82–83; 84–85; 89; 93; 94; 97–98; 100; 106).

123. Fourth Song 14 (Donnelly and Sider, 61).

124. Thirteenth Song (Mujica ed., 107): *¡O* noche cristalina / que juntaste con esa luz Hermosa / en una union divina / al Esposo y la esposa, / hacienda de ambos una misma cosa! (my trans.). The commentary is translated in Donnelly and Sider, 94–95.

125. Sixteenth Song (Mujica ed., 108): Como es tan ponderosa / la fuerza de aquel bien con que está unida / y ella tan poca cosa, / con darse por vencida/ pierde su ser y en Él es convertida. The comment can be found in Donnelly and Sider, 102–7, whose translation I have adapted.

126. Sixteenth Song 9 (Donnelly and Sider, 106). There are remarkable similarities between Cecilia's image and the development of the theme of the soul as the crystal throne of God in Jean-Jacques Olier's *L'âme cristal: Des attributes divins en nous*, ed. Mariel Mazzocco (Paris: Seuil, 2008). Olier's treatise was written about 1656, but it is difficult to think that he could have known Cecilia's *Treatise on Transformation*.

127. Among Cecilia's poems we find a lyric based on Luis de León's *The Names of Christ*. No. 60, "Words with the Name of Christ" (*Letras con los nombres de Cristo*) in Donnelly and Sider, 436–45, has verse treatments of twelve of the sixteen names in Luis's treatise.

128. On the literary quality of Cecilia's poems, see Arenal and Schlau, *Untold Sisters*, 143–46.

129. This poem is No. 23 in Donnelly and Sider, 276–77.

130. *En medio de un silencio sin sonido* (Donnelly and Sider, 434–35).

131. *Sin figura en la memoria* (Donnelly and Sider, 446–49). There are remarks on this poem in Arenal and Schlau, *Untold Sisters*, 144–45.

132. The entire little drama can be found in Donnelly and Sider, 366–93. There are excerpts and a discussion in Arenal and Schlau, *Untold Sisters*, 148–51 and 185–89.

133. For a sketch, see E. Allison Peers, "The Teresan Period: Jerónimo

Gracián," chap. 6 in *Studies*, 2:149–89. See also Ildefonso Moriones, "Jérôme de la Mère de Dieu (Gracian)," DS 8:920–28; and Gregory Burke, "Fr. Jerome Gracián: A Heroic Follower of St. Teresa," *Mount Carmel: A Review of the Spiritual Life* 63 (2015): 49–57.

134. See the treatment by Barbara Mujica, "Paul the Enchanter: Saint Teresa's Vow of Obedience to Gracián," in Wilson, *Heirs of St. Teresa of Avila*, 21–44.

135. A 1731 English translation of this work published in Rome is recorded in Peers, *Studies*, 2:426. The work contains a treatment of mental prayer.

136. On this aspect of Gracián's teaching, see Peers, "The Teresan Period: Jerónimo Gracián," 182–88. In 1611, Gracián also wrote *Diez lamentaciones del miserable estado de los ateistas de nuestros tiempos*, attacking errors old and new, including northern mystical authors like Ruusbroec, Tauler, and the *Theologia deutsch*, as well as contemporary Capuchin mystics such as Benet Canfield. See Otger Steggink, "Jerónimo Gracián und die 'Perfectistas': Eine spanische Auseinandersetzung mit der Mystik des Nordens," *Studies in Spirituality* 2 (1992): 200–208.

137. There is a sketch of the history of the early publication of the works of John of the Cross in Cognet, *La spiritualité moderne*, vol. 1, *L'essor*, 176–79, who stresses unduly the attempt to water down what he holds is John's dependence on northern mystics in favor of a new "orthodoxie pseudothomiste."

138. The *Apuntamientos y advertencias en tres discorsos para más facíl inteligencia de las frases místicas y doctrina de los obras espirituales de nuestro Padre* was printed in most editions of John of the Cross down to the twentieth century. I cite from *Obras del Místico Doctor San Juan de la Cruz*, ed. Gerardo de San Juan de la Cruz, 3 vols. (Toledo: Viuda e Hijos de J. Peláez, 1914), 3:465–502. See the discussion by Certeau, *Mystic Fable*, 1:129–44, as well as Louis-Marie, "Diego de Jesús," DS 3:873–74.

139. For example, *anatomia mística . . . en una alma*; *circumcisión mística*; *locución mística*; *materia mística*; *frasis mística*; *espiritualismo místico*; etc.

140. John of the Cross himself is referred to as *este gran místico* (ed., 483); *este Santo místico* (ed., 490); and *este venerable místico* (ed., 490).

141. By my tally Diego uses Hilary of Poitiers (1x), Basil (1x), Ambrose (2x), Jerome (1x), Augustine (2x), Zeno of Verona (1x), Cyril of Alexandria (1x), Denys the Areopagite (8x), Gregory the Great (4x), Bernard of Clairvaux (7x), Hugh of St. Victor (3x), Richard of St. Victor (3x), Gilbert of Hoyland (4x), and Bonaventure (5x). In addition, Diego cites Thomas Aquinas at length in several sections (ed., 475, 479–81, 484, 489, 490–91), as well as Teresa of Avila (ed., 477, 479, 487, and 502). In defending John's teaching on union, the Carmelite combines the argument from experience with a summary of the agreement of the established teachers as follows: "En consecuencia de lo qual, San Dionisio con sus Místicos, y Santo Tomás con sus Teólogos, poene tal perfección y tal union, que de pura y perfecta, apenas la alcanzamos a entender" (ed., 498–99).

142. In this section (ed., 500), Diego cites Luis de León's defense of Teresa's writing in the vernacular from his edition of the saint's writings. He does not seem to know the Augustinian's other defense of vernacular spiritual writing in his *The Names of Christ*.

143. The four examples are: (1) *macula* and the necessity of strong purgation where the witness of Gilbert of Hoyland, Bonaventure (really Rudolph of

Biberach), and Aquinas are used to defend *Ascent* 1, 9; (2) the suspension and passivity of the powers of the soul in the higher stages of prayer, where a variety of biblical texts and authorities are used to defend the distinction between the active and the passive nights of the spirit (ed., 475–78); (3) the hyperbolic language of annihilation and transformation into God, where Bernard, Teresa, and Gilbert are cited as employing the same language; and (4) John's teaching on "substantial touches" (e.g., *Ascent* 2, 12, and *Living Flame*), which is defended primarily by a number of citations from Thomas Aquinas (ed., 479–83).

144. The second *Discorso* further expands on the agreement between John and the other respected mystics and doctors on (1) purgation (ed., 484–85); (2) the perfection of union (ed., 485–86); (3) the trinitarian nature of union (ed., 486–87); (4) mystical marriage (ed., 487–88); (5) "loving transformation and affective annihilation" (ed., 488–90); and three sections (6–8) on perfect contemplation (ed., 490–94).

145. I have consulted the edition of Nicolás's *Phrasium mysticae theologiae V. P. Fr. Joannis a Cruce . . . elucidatio* found in *Opera mystica V. ac Mystici doctoris F. Iohannis a Cruce* (Cologne: Gualtieri, 1639). The first 469 pages of the book are the Latin version of John's works, while the *Elucidatio* comes at the end with a separate pagination of 200 pages. On Nicolás, see Ildefonso Moriones, "Nicolás de Jésus–Marie," DS 11:286–87.

146. Ruusbroec is cited and praised in the Gualtieri edition on 12–13, 89, and 130.

147. Among the general objections against John are that what he says sounds like the heretics *qui Illuminati dicuntur* (chap. 3); that his books are too difficult (chap. 4); that because they are written in the vernacular they can lead the simple astray (chap. 5). Nicolás also explains "the proper and recondite" phrases of mystical theology (chap. 6) and insists that experience is necessary for understanding a mystic like John (chap. 7).

148. For introductions to Tomás de Jesús, see Peers, "Post-Teresan Mysticism: Tomás de Jesús," chap. 10 in *Studies*, 2:279–306; Miguel Angel Diez, "Thomas de Jésus (Díaz Sánchez Dávila)," DS 15:833–44; and Cognet, *La spiritualité moderne*, vol. 1, *L'essor*, 181–83. The most recent monograph is Elisabetta Zambruno, *Tra filosofia e mistica: Tommaso di Gesù*, Collana di testi mistici 16 (Vatican City: Libreria Editrice Vaticana, 2009).

149. The most complete information in English on these figures is by the indefatigable E. Allison Peers, who, besides the chapter devoted to Tomás in vol. 2 of *Studies of the Spanish Mystics*, discusses all three, along with other figures, in "Carmelite Mystics," chap. 1 in *Studies* 3:3–80.

150. The two volumes of Tomás's *Opera Omnia*, first published at Cologne in 1684, contain only twelve of a projected twenty-four treatises. Tomás's treatise *De contemplatione acquisita* was not published until 1922, and there are important unedited works, such the *Primera parte del Camino espiritual de oración y contemplación* and a *Tratado de la Mística Teología* (see Diez, "Thomas de Jésus," 837–38, for a list of writings). The only English translation of something from Tomás known to me is the brief extract from his *Treatise on Mental Prayer* in Kathleen Pond, *The Spirit of the Spanish Mystics: An Anthology of Spanish Religious Prose from the Fifteenth to the Seventeenth Century* (New York: P. J. Kenedy & Sons, 1958), 154–56.

151. Peers, "Carmelite Mystics," 35.

152. See the analysis of the work in Peers, "Tomás de Jesús," 290–93.

153. I cite from the translation in Peers, "Tomás de Jesús," 295.

154. These works both appear in the Cologne *Opera Omnia*, with the *De contemplatione divina, libri sex* in 2:80–195, and the *Divinae orationis sive a Deo infusae methodus* in 2:197–365.

155. See the more extended analysis of this work in Peers, "Tomás de Jesús," 297–303.

156. I cite this passage as quoted by Peers from the *Divinae orationis* III.3 in "Tomás de Jesús," 299 n. 6, to give something of the flavor of the Carmelite's mystical language: "In primo, mens, pacatis passionibus, phantasmatibus quasi consopitis, tranquille ac pure Deum in tenebra, hoc est sub quadam generali incomprehensibilitatis ratione, contuetur. In secundo, vero, sentitur caligo illa, sive inaccessibile Dei lumen, quo non tantum mens illuminator perfectius quam in primo, sed etiam quasi solaribus radiis vicinior ac eidem perculsa servet ardentius. In primo, amoris vulnere sauciatur; in secundo ligatur, et prae amoris magnitudine ita languet, ut nihil posit ei satisfacere praeter unionem cum dilecto, quam concupiscent ardenter."

157. *Divinae orationis* IV.25, as cited by Peers, "Tomás de Jesús," 301 n. 4.

158. Tommaso di Gesù, *Trattato della contemplazione divina*, Introduzione, traduzione e note a cura di Elisabetta Zambruno (Milan: Edizioni Glossa Srl, 2015). There is an up-to-date and helpful "Bibliografia" on XLVII–LII.

159. For the references to Teresa, see *Trattato* (ed. Zambruno, 98, 190). From time to time Tomás refers to Teresa's term *orazione di quiete* (ed. Zambruno, 70, 92, 182, 185, 190).

160. *Trattato* I.7 (ed. Zambruno, 64).

161. *Trattato* I.5 (ed. Zambruno, 37–41) introduces clear and obscure contemplation and the distinction between acquired and infused. I.6 then describes six grades of clear contemplation following Bonaventure's *Itinerarium*, while I.7 uses Dionysius to distinguish three kinds of negative contemplation: of the intellect, of the will, and of silence and sleep (ed. Zambruno, 57–61).

162. *Trattato* I.8 (ed. Zambruno, 62–63).

163. *Trattato* II.9 (ed. Zambruno, 141): ". . . e che ritorni alla stessa purezza e nudità nella quale era quando Dio la trasse dal nulla per darle l'essere, affinché per questa purezza e nudità essa sia così strettamente unita con l'essenza divina, che è la stessa purezza e la stessa nudità." The stress on the return to primordial emptiness goes beyond the usual categories of John of the Cross and seems to reflect the influence of northern mystics, perhaps Ruusbroec or Herp, although Tomás does not cite any authority here.

164. In *Trattato* II.10 (ed. Zambruno, 146–47) Tomás specifies four kinds of supernatural apprehensions (intellectual visions, revelations, locutions, and spiritual feelings) in obvious dependence on John of the Cross, *Ascent* 2, 23–32.

165. *Trattato* II.13 (ed. Zambruno, 179). Tomás discusses union often in the treatise (see, e.g., 31, 51, 88, 139, 140–41, 143, 152, 175, and 194).

166. *Trattato* II.15 (ed. Zambruno, 187): "I dottori mistici chiamano queste due esercizi flusso e riflusso; il flusso è quando l'anima esce da se stessa per unirsi al primo principio che è Dio, e il riflusso è quando essa esce da quest'unione per practicare eroicamente gli atti delle virtù...." Tomás uses a number of terms that reflect the northern mystics, such as *distacco* (detachment), *atti anagogici* (anagogi-

cal acts, or ejaculations), *santa indifferenza* (holy indifference), *fondo del suo intimo* (interior ground), *annentiarsi e inabissiari* (annihilation and inabyssation). He also uses the images of both *abisso* and *oceano* for the divine nature (e.g., Zambruno, 39, 136, 159, 195).

167. On the necessity of ongoing attention to the humanity and life of Christ, see *Trattato* II.10 and II.14 (ed. Zambruno, 152–56, 184–85).

168. While Teresa and John of the Cross recognized the distinction between forms of prayer and contemplation in which human effort cooperates with divine grace and those that are dependent on grace alone, the vocabulary of the distinction between acquired and infused contemplation comes to the fore with the post-Teresan generation. The unproductive neo-Scholastic debates on the extent to which the acquired–infused distinction goes back to Teresa and John are summarized by Peers, "Tomás de Jesús," 303–6.

169. Ven. P. Thomas a Jesu, *De contemplatione acquisita (Opus ineditum) et Via brevis et plana orationis mentalis*, ed. P. Eugenius a Sto. Joseph (Milan: Tipografia S. Lega Eucaristica, 1922).

170. On Quiroga, see Peers, "Carmelite Mystics," 46–54; and Fortunato de Jesús Sacramentado, "Joseph de Jésus-Marie (Quiroga)," DS 8:1354–59.

171. The *Apología mística* has been edited and studied by Fortunato Antolín, *Primeras Biografías y Apologías de San Juan de la Cruz* (Salamanca: Junta de Castilla y León, 1991), 125–322.

172. On the Calagurritan, see Peers, "Carmelite Mystics," 18–28; Giovanni Maria Strina, "Jean de Jésus-Marie (le calagurritain)," DS 8:576–81; and Roberto de S. Teresa di Gesú, "La contemplazione infusa nel ven. P. Giovanni di Gesú Maria (Sampedro)," in *De contemplazione in Schola Teresiana* (Rome: Teresianum, 1962), 650–90.

173. Some of these figures are briefly noted by Peers in "Carmelite Mystics," 72–80. Most are given entries in the DS and are also treated in the article, "Mystique XVIe–XXe siècles," DS 10:1924–30.

174. Simeón de la Sagrada Familia, "Joseph du Saint-Joseph (le portugais)," DS 8:1395–97.

175. Melchior de Sainte-Marie, "Joseph du Saint-Esprit (l'andaluo)," DS 8:1397–1402; and the same author's "Doctrina Josephi a Spiritu Sancto de contemplazione infusa," in *De contemplatione in Schola Teresiana*, 714–57. The modern edition of this work, prepared by Friar Anastasius of St. Paul, the *Cursus Theologiae Mystico-Scholasticae*, 5 vols. (Bruges: C. Beyaert, 1924–34), takes up 3,202 pages.

176. Elisée de la Nativité, "Antoine du Saint-Esprit," DS 1:717–18.

177. Roberto Morietti, "Philippe de la Trinité," DS 12:1325–28; and Bonifatius Honings, "La contemplazione secondo Filippo della SS. Trinità," in *De contemplatione in Schola Teresiana*, 691–713.

178. For a listing of the many Spanish Franciscans claimed as mystics, see Molinar, *Historia de la literatura mística en España*, 289–322.

179. Peers has a chapter on him, "The Teresan Period: St. Peter of Alcántara," chap. 4 in *Studies*, 2:97–120; a more recent account is Mariano Acebal Luján, "Pierre d'Alcántara (saint)," DS 12:1489–95.

180. See Peers, "Franciscan Mysticism: Diego de Estella," chap. 8 in *Studies*, 2:219–50. Diego's *Meditaciones devotísimas del amor de Dios*, first published in 1576,

can be found in *Místicos Franciscanos Españoles*, ed. Juan Bautista Gomis, 3 vols. (Madrid: Biblioteca de Autores Cristianos, 1948–49), 3:59–367. There is a partial English translation (thirteen meditations) by Julia Pember as Diego de Estella, *Meditations on the Love of God* (London: Sheed & Ward, 1940).

181. There is an English version by Dominic Devas, *Treatise on Prayer and Meditation by Saint Peter of Alcantara* (Westminster, MD: Newman Press, 1949).

182. On the mingling of meditation and contemplation, see the eighth of the counsels on meditation (*Treatise on Prayer and Meditation*, 112–18); on the relation of devotion and union (ibid., 124–25). Pedro also recommends recollection (ibid., 126) and is suspicious of visions and ecstasies (ibid., 145–46).

183. Meditación 76, "Cómo el amor transforma al amante en el amado" (ed., 288–91; trans., 41–47).

184. The most complete account of Juan de los Angeles in English is, once again, from Peers, "Juan de los Angeles," chap. 7 in *Studies,* 1:281–328. See also Fidèle de Ros, "La vie et oeuvre de Jean des Anges," in *Mélanges offerts au R. P. Cavallera* (Toulouse: Bibliothèque de l'Institut Catholique, 1948), 405–23; Manuel de Castro, "Jean des Anges," DS 8:259–64; and Cognet, *La spiritualité moderne,* vol. 1, *L'essor,* 172–75.

185. The most complete edition of the works of Juan de los Angeles is that of Jaime Sala and G. Fuentes, *Obras místicas de Juan de los Angeles*, 2 vols. (Madrid: Nueva Biblioteca de Autores Españoles, 1912, 1917).

186. Juan's close dependence on northern European mysticism in this work was shown by Pierre Groult, *Les mystiques des Pays-Bas et la littérature espagnole du seizième siècle* (Louvain: Librairie Universitaire, 1927), 203–45.

187. The *Manual de vida perfecta*, which is described as the second part of the *Conquista*, can be found in Gomis, *Místicos Franciscanos Españoles*, 3:479–681, which also has an "Introducción" on Juan (461–77).

188. The most recent edition of the *Lucha espiritual y amorosa entre Dios y el alma* is in 2 vols. published in Madrid in 1930 (not available to me). I will use the English translation of Eladia Gómez-Posthill, *The Loving Struggle between God and the Soul* (London: Saint Austin Press, 2000). Despite his heavy use of the *Conquests* in his treatment of Juan, Peers says, "The *Triumphs* and the *Strife*—which, to our way of thinking, constitute his greatest work . . .—are naturally more direct and forceful" ("Juan de los Angeles," 327).

189. Peers provides a sketch of Juan's sources ("Juan de los Angeles," 317–23).

190. *Loving Struggle*, Dedication (trans., xxi).

191. Juan cites from the Dionysian corpus some fifteen times (see especially *Loving Struggle* I.10–11). Thomas Gallus is mentioned explicitly three times (*Loving Struggle* I.11, I.13, and II.15 [trans., 64, 70, 195]), and there are many appeals to Bonaventure (twenty times, but often really to Pseudo-Bonaventure) and Gerson (six times).

192. On Juan's use of northern mystics in general, see Groult, *Les mystiques des Pay-Bas*, 186–265.

193. See *Loving Struggle* II.2 (trans., 105–6), quoting *Life* 29.16–17. Juan was familiar with John of the Cross and Luis de León, although he does not mention them explicitly in the *Loving Struggle*.

194. Jacob's struggle with the angel in Genesis 32 is also cited; see *Loving Struggle* I.4 (trans., 16–17).

195. *Loving Struggle* I.1 (trans., 5). Juan returns to the importance of experience in several other places, such as I.6 (trans., 29), and especially II.10 (trans., 152). In II.6 (trans., 127), Juan admits that he has not enjoyed the highest form of ecstatic contemplation: "To understand this union better, one really ought to listen to those who have experienced it and do know what they are saying, not to those like me who just talk about it." He goes on to note that not everyone can reach this exalted state that "has to be tasted to be loved."

196. Juan mentions the importance of man being made in the image and likeness of God a number of times (see esp. II.10 and 14), but he does not develop an explicit anthropology in the manner of John of the Cross or others, at least not in this treatise.

197. *Loving Struggle* I.9 (trans., 49). For more on the relation between love and understanding and mystical and Scholastic theology, see I.13 (trans., 69–74).

198. On the role of the important Franciscan theme of recollection in Juan's mysticism, see Peers, "Juan de los Angeles," 303–7.

199. *Loving Struggle* II.5 (trans., 121–22). This passage is reminiscent of Eckhart's meditation on hungering and eating in his *Sermones et Lectiones super Ecclesiastici c. 24* n. 58.

200. *Loving Struggle* II.6 (trans., 128): "[T]he spirit, assimilated to God and so adapted and disposed towards love by such copiousness of divine virtue, proceeds consequently to adapt and dispose the body to itself, and is able to clothe it now with spiritual faculties and properties, helpless as it was before, of ever attaining them." There is a similar passage in II.15 (trans., 196).

201. On the role of the dark night in Juan and the links with John of the Cross found elsewhere in the Franciscan's writings, see Peers, "Juan de los Angeles," 297–300.

202. For a summary of Juan's teaching on union across his works, see Peers, "Juan de los Angeles," 300–303.

203. Juan speaks of deification about ten times in the *Loving Struggle*.

204. *Loving Struggle* II.16 (trans., 201–5) distinguishes three kinds of rapture: by imagination; by reason; and by *mens*, or mind, which is the kind to be treated here. For a summary of Juan's teaching on rapture, see Peers, "Juan de los Angeles," 308–10.

205. Attention has recently been given to María de Agreda. She is often cited in Haliczer's *Between Exaltation and Infamy* and has been the subject of several studies in English, such as Clark Colahan, *The Visions of Sor María de Agreda: Writing, Knowledge, and Power* (Tucson: University of Arizona Press, 1994); and Marilyn H. Fedewa, *María of Agreda: Mystical Lady in Blue* (Albuquerque: University of New Mexico Press, 2009). For an introduction, see Julio Campos, "Marie de Jésus (d'Agreda)," DS 10:508–13.

206. Some two hundred of the about six hundred letters exchanged between the king and the visionary survive. For María as primarily a spiritual advisor, see Luis R. Corteguera and Sherry Velasco, "Authority in the Margin: Re-Examining the Autograph Letters of Sor Maria de Agreda and Philip IV of Spain," in *Women's Voices and the Politics of the Spanish Empire*, ed. Jennifer L. Eich, Jeanne Gillespie, and Lucia G. Harrison (New Orleans: University Press of the South, 2008), 235–62.

207. María's investigations by the Inquisition are analyzed in Clark Colahan, "María de Jesús Agreda: The Sweetheart of the Inquisition," in *Women in the*

Inquisition: Spain and the New World, ed. Mary E. Giles (Baltimore: Johns Hopkins University Press, 1999), 155–70.

208. For a recent edition, see Celestino Solaguren, ed., *Mística Ciudad de Dios: Vida de la Virgen María* (Madrid: Castalia, 1991). For an English translation, see María de Agreda, *The Mystical City of God*, 4 vols. (Chicago: Theopolitan, 1914; repr., Albuquerque, NM: Corcoran, 1949).

209. For a contemporary "Agredist" position, see Fedewa, *María of Agreda*.

210. The anthology of María's writings found in Colahan, *Vision of Sor María de Agreda*, contains a number of references to her being rapt to heaven or flying through the air (see, e.g., 82, 86, 111, 121–23, and 144), often with the aid of angels.

211. Bilocation/multilocation seems more frequent in late medieval and early modern times than in antiquity, although a story told about Ambrose of Milan provided a patristic warrant. For a brief, and inadequate, survey, see Aimé Solignac, "Multilocation," DS 10:1837–40. For a study of the eight Spanish female examples, see Jane Tar, "Flying through the Empire: The Visionary Journeys of Early Modern Nuns," in Eich et al., *Women's Voices and the Politics of the Spanish Empire*, 263–302, who discusses María on 283, 287–91, and 295–96. Tar observes, "Above all, bilocation accounts suggest the desire of early modern nuns to undertake a more active role in the Church than that sanctioned by its counter-reformational guardians" (292).

212. These documents are analyzed and translated in Colahan, *Visions of Sor María de Agreda*, chap. 4, "Mystical Journey," 93–115.

213. The important "Text of the Report to Father Manero," is available in Colahan, *Visions of Sor María de Agreda*, 115–27.

214. For references to María as "wife and turtledove," see Colahan, *Visions of Sor María de Agreda,* 86, 140, 141.

215. Ibid., 119; see also 69, 110–11, 112, and 126 for further examples.

216. For a negative view of María as mystic, see the judicious comments by Herbert Thurston, "Maria Coronel de Agreda," in *Surprising Mystics* (Chicago: Henry Regnery, 1955), 122–32.

217. There is a chapter on Luis de Granada in Peers, *Studies*, 1:25–62, but the best account in English is R. L. Oechslin, *Louis of Granada* (St. Louis: Herder, 1962). See also Alvaro Huerga, "Louis de Grenade," DS 9:1043–54; and Cognet, *La spiritualité moderne*, vol. 1, *L'essor*, 156–60. A number of the prolific Dominican's works were translated into English in the seventeenth and eighteenth centuries, but nothing in recent times.

218. There is a modern edition: Luis de Granada, *Libro de la oración y meditación* (Madrid: Ediciones Palabra, 1979). This is not available to me.

219. Juan had a reputation as a mystic, but, perhaps out of fear of the Inquisition, did not write about the topic. See Cognet, *La spiritualité moderne*, vol. 1, *L'essor*, 151–56. Juan worked on the *Audi, filia* throughout his life, but it was only posthumously published in 1574. There is an English translation: John of Avila, *Audi, filia–Listen, O Daughter*, trans. Joan Frances Gormley, Classics of Western Spirituality (New York: Paulist Press, 2006).

220. The edition of Alvaro Huerga, *Fray Luis de Granada: Obras completas* (Madrid: Fundación Universitaria Española, 1994–2008) contains forty-four volumes.

221. On the story of the famous "Nun of Lisbon," see Freddy Domínguez,

"From Saint to Sinner: Sixteenth-Century Perceptions of 'La Monja de Lisboa,'" in Kallendorf, *New Companion to Hispanic Mysticism*, 297–320.

222. See the account in Domínguez, "Sixteenth-Century Perceptions," 304–9.

223. In the last months of his life, Luis wrote two explanations apologizing for his support of the false mystic.

224. Peers provides a helpful collection of passages from Luis's writings on union with God and other topics ("Luis de Granada," 34–36 and 44–48). Peers's judgment is typical: "[W]hatever the extent to which Fray Luis appears as a mystic in his writings, he was undoubtedly a mystic at heart" (44). Citing Peers, Oechslin (*Louis of Granada*, 46) declares "Louis of Granada belongs to the spiritual family of the mystics."

225. Quoted from the *Guia de pecadores* X, 204, in Oechslin, *Louis of Granada*, 59 n. 2.

226. Quoted from the *Libro* II, 11, in Oechslin, *Louis of Granada*, 61.

227. Both of these works contain a "Treatise on Love," on which see Peers, "Luis de Granada," 40–41; and Oechslin, *Louis of Granada*, 102–7.

228. On the Spanish Jesuit mystics, see Peers, "Post-Teresan Mysticism: Luis de la Puente," chap. 11 in *Studies*, 2:307–43; and "Mystics of the Society of Jesus," chap. 4 in *Studies*, 3:173–231. See also Joseph de Guibert, *La spiritualité de la Compagnie de Jésus: Esquisse historique*, Bibliotheca Instituti Historici S.I. 4 (Rome: Institutum Historicum S. I., 1953); and Cognet, "Le crise spirituelle de la Compagnie de Jésus," chap. 6 in *La spiritualité moderne*, vol. 1, *L'essor*, 187–219.

229. Manuel Ruiz Jurado, "Rodriguez (Alphonse), jésuite, 1538–1616," DS 13:853–60; de Guibert, *La spiritualité de la Compagnie de Jésus*, 250–53; and Cognet, *La spiritualité moderne*, vol. 1, *L'essor*, 217–19.

230. The treatment of Rodriguez by Peers, "Mystics of the Society of Jesus," 205–10, provides a number of quotations of the Jesuit's negative attitude toward mystical prayer.

231. My translation from an Italian edition, *Esercitio de Perfettione e di Virtù composto dal R. P. Alfonso Rodriguez . . .* (Venice: Andrea Poleti, 1722), Parte Prima, Trattato V, Cap. IV (286).

232. Other Jesuit mystics studied by Peers include Francisco Arias (1533–1605) and Alvarez de la Paz (1560–1620).

233. On Baltasar Alvarez, see Peers, "Mystics of the Society of Jesus," 191–97; and E. Hernandez, "Alvarez (Balthasar)," DS 1:405–6. On Teresa's appreciation of Alvarez, see *Life* 25.14–15, 26.3, 27.3, 28.14–16, 33.3–11, as well as many letters.

234. Teresa, Letter 363.8 (*Obras completas*, 1317).

235. For brief accounts of these controversies, see Peers, "Mystics of the Society of Jesus," 177–83; James Brodrick, *The Progress of the Jesuits (1556–79)* (New York: Longmans, Green, 1947), 293–98; and Cognet, *La spiritualité moderne*, vol. 1, *L'essor*, 192–200. The most detailed treatment is Philip Endean, "'The Strange Style of Prayer': Mercurian, Cordeses, and Alvarez," in *The Mercurian Project: Forming Jesuit Culture 1573–1580*, ed. Thomas M. McCoog (St. Louis: Institute of Jesuit Sources, 2004), 351–97. Endean's revisionist account is largely devoted to the Cordeses affair and shows that Mercurian's opposition to mysticism has been exaggerated and that his actions against the two Spanish Jesuits were largely conditioned by his efforts to strengthen Jesuit identity in the difficult Spanish situation.

236. See Henri Bremond, *Histoire littéraire du sentiment religieux en France depuis la fin des guerres de religion jusqu'à nos jours*, 5 vols. (Grenoble: Jérôme Millon, 2006), 3:415–81. In the original version this was found in vol. 8, 228–69.

237. De Guibert, *La spiritualité de la Compagnie de Jésus*, 211–18.

238. Luis de la Puente, *Vida del P. Baltasar Alvarez* (Madrid, 1615). There is a modern edition by P. Camilo Maria Abad, *Obras escogidas del V. P. Luis de la Puente*, Biblioteca de Autores Españoles 111 (Madrid: Biblioteca de Autores Españoles, 1958), 19–256. Balthasar's three writings on prayer are quoted and summarized in this work in chaps. 13 (71–77), 33 (156–62), and 41 (192–97). This edition contains "Apendices" of "Algunos documentos espirituales del P. Baltasar" (257–92). Puente's versions of the Alvarez texts are conveniently available in French in Balthasar Alvarez, *Sur l'oraison de repos et de silence* (Mesnil-sur-l'Estrée: Éditions Arfuyen, 2010), from which I will cite, because the most recent edition of Alvarez's writings is not available to me: Baltasar Alvarez, *Escritos espirituales*, ed. Camilo M. Abad (Barcelona: Flors, 1961).

239. I cite from Peers, "Mystics of the Society of Jesus," 183, whose account I basically follow.

240. On Aquaviva's letter, see de Guibert, *La spiritualité de la Compagnie de Jésus*, 228–32. There is a study by A. Coemans, "La letter du P. C. Aquaviva sur l'oraison," *Revue d'ascétique et de mystique* 17 (1936): 313–21.

241. On Alvarez's doctrine of prayer, see Lewis Scott, "Balthasar Alvarez and the Prayer of Silence," *Spirituality Today* 41 (1989): 112–42; and P. Dudon, "Les leçons d'oraison de P. Balthasar Alvarez," *Revue d'ascétique et de mystique* 2 (1921): 36–57.

242. Alvarez, *Sur l'oraison de repos et de silence*, 43–45.

243. Ibid., 54–55.

244. Ibid., 61–65.

245. On Luis de la Puente, see Peers, "Luis de la Puente," 309–43; Miguel Nicolau, "La Puente (Louis de), jésuite, 1554–1624," DS 9:265–76, as well as Cognet, *La spiritualité moderne*, vol. 1, *L'essor*, 205–11.

246. Part I deals with the purgative way and contains meditations on sin, while the illuminative way of Parts II–IV consists of meditations on Christ's life. Parts V–VII on the unitive way have meditations on the risen Christ, the coming of the Holy Spirit, and the divine perfections. The *Meditations* were twice rendered into English in the seventeenth century (1610, 1619). The 1619 edition was revised and reprinted in six volumes as *Meditations on the mysteries of our holy faith, together with a treatise on mental prayer* (London, 1852). The "Prefaces" to the six parts were modernized and made available in *A Treatise on Mental Prayer* (London: Burns, Oates & Washbourne, 1929).

247. See the quotations and comments given by Peers, "Luis de la Puente," 314–17.

248. *A Treatise on Mental Prayer*, part III, chap. 1 (115–21).

249. The work was popular for several centuries, but the most recent Spanish edition appears to be from Barcelona in 1877. There is an abridged English version of the first treatise, *Of Familiar Intercourse with God in Prayer . . . (From the "Spiritual Guide"). Treatise I* (London: Burns, Oates & Washbourne, 1932). The Latin version of all four parts takes up fifteen hundred pages.

250. Puente cites the *Scala claustralium* under the name of Bernard in the

"Author's Introduction" (*Of Familiar Intercourse with God*, xxxi–ii). On this influential treatise, see McGinn, *Growth*, 357–59. In the "Author's Introduction," Puente
refers to the content of the work as alternately "mystical theology" and "mystical
science."

251. On Puente's use of Dionysius, see Robert Ricard, "La tradition dionysienne en Espagne après saint Jean de la Croix: Luis de la Puente, s.j.," *Revue
d'ascétique et de mystique* 45 (1969): 409–24.

252. The foregoing summary is based on Peers, "Luis de la Puente," 320–27.

253. Again, I refer the reader to the longer analysis in Peers, "Luis de la
Puente," 327–36.

254. The *Sentimientos y avisos espirituales*, available in the *Obras escogidas*, 293–
332, comprise thirty-five *sentimientos* and twenty-nine *avisos espirituales*.

255. *Sentimientos* VI. Praesentia Dei (ed., 305): "Varios modos de presencia de
Dios experimentado en la oración y fuera ella."

256. See Glyn Redworth, "A New Way of Living? Luisa de Carvajal and the
Limits of Mysticism," in Kallendorf, *New Companion to Hispanic Mysticism*, 273–95.
The "limits of mysticism" in this essay means that Luisa was not a mystic.

257. Luisa's works are available in a bilingual edition by Elizabeth Rhodes,
This Tight Embrace: Luisa de Carvajal y Mendoza (1566–1614), Reformation Texts
with Translation (1350–1650): Women of the Reformation 2 (Milwaukee: Marquette University Press, 2000).

258. See the surveys by José Adriano de Freitas Carvalho, "Traditions,
Life Experiences and Orientations in Portuguese Mysticism (1515–1630)," in
Kallendorf, *New Companion to Hispanic Mysticism*, 39–70; and Freitas and Maria
de Lourdes Belchior Pontes, "Portugal (16e–18e siècles)," DS 12:1958–73. See also
Robert Ricard, "L'influence des 'Mystiques du Nord' sur les spirituels Portugais
du XVIe et XVIIe siècle," in *La mystique rhénane* (Paris: Presses universitaires de
France, 1963), 219–33.

259. On Tavares, see Carvalho, "Portuguese Mysticism," 64–65.

260. I owe my knowledge of Joana de Jesus to Joana de Fátima Gonçalves Pita
do Serrado, who was kind enough to send me a copy of her dissertation, *Ancias/
Anxiousness in Joana de Jesus (1617–1681): Historical and Philosophical Approaches*
(Ph.D. diss., University of Groningen, 2014).

261. There were other Cistercian mystical women in the Iberian peninsula
during our period. An example is María Vela y Cuerto (1561–1617), an educated
noblewoman of Avila who entered the unreformed Bernardine convent there in
1576 and who sought, unsuccessfully, to reform it. Her mystical narrative, influenced by Teresa's *Life*, was discovered and translated by Frances Parkinson Keyes,
*The Third Mystic of Avila: The Self Revelation of Maria Vela, a Sixteenth Century Span-
ish Nun* (New York: Farrar, Straus & Cudahy, 1960), which was followed by an edition of the Spanish original in 1961.

262. Recollection is treated in chap. 2 (83–114) of Joana Serrado's dissertation, who notes that the nun uses the noun form sixty-one times and verbal forms
seventy-four times (83).

263. Joana Serrado (chap. 2), specifies three meanings of recollection: the
prayer practice; recollection as participation in the Catholic reform movement
(e.g., the Cistercian Recollect convents); and, finally, the social and community
networks that supported Sor Joana.

264. I cite this text from Serrado, *Ancias/Anxiousness*, 88. See also the text on Christ as the true book in which she can recollect herself and quiet the faculties of the soul (*Ansias/Anxiousness*, 71). In another passage (138) Joana says how in recollection God represents himself to her "in the center of my soul" (*em o centro de minha alma*).

265. See, e.g., "Noche Obscura," stanza 1: En una noche obscura, / con ansias, en amores inflamada, / oh dichosa ventura!

266. For what follows I depend on Serrado, *Ancias/Anxiousness*, chap. 3 (115–88).

267. *Ansias/Anxiousness*, 128. Sometimes Sor Joana makes use of the language of the Song of Songs to describe these encounters, as in the passage from *Life*, chap. 22, using Song 2:4, quoted in *Ansias/Anxiousness*, 73.

268. I cite only one from Serrado, *Ansias/Anxiousness*, 150–51: "With this resignation that I practiced in the will of my Lord, I became so valorous and daring in him that, thus, all the body's evils as well as the enemy's temptations seemed flowers and daisies to me. And when I was with these labors I was often surrounded by a very spiritual suavity in the presence of my Lord, which made me gain more spirit to patiate [*padecer*]. On other occasions he gave me to understand that he felt compassion for me, but that it was his will that I should suffer."

269. For some texts on this new way of knowing God, see *Ansias/Anxiousness*, 164, 167, 173, and 185.

270. For an overview of spirituality in Spanish America, see François Mateos, "Espagne, V: Pays de langue espagnole: Amerique du sud," DS 4:1192–1203.

271. For a brief treatment of Alvarez de la Paz, see Cognet, *La spiritualité moderne*, vol. 1, *L'essor*, 211–17.

272. The primary resource for what we know of Gregory is the life composed by his companion for the last eighteen years of his life, the secular priest Francisco Losa (ca. 1536–1624). This was written in 1598 and published in 1613 in Mexico City as *La vida que Hizo el Siervo de Dios Gregorio Lopez en algunos lugares de Nueva Espagña*. It was frequently reprinted in Spanish and translated into French, German, and Italian. The French version appears to have been the source of an English translation of 1638, as well as a 1675 version. Rather unsatisfactorily, I will have to cite from the reworking of that version by Canon F. C. Doyle, *The Life of Gregory Lopez* (London: R. Washbourne, 1876). Doyle claims to have taken all the chief facts from Losa's *Life*, but he has apparently repackaged them with some of his own comments. See also Quirino Fernandez, "Lopez (Grégoire), eremite, 1542–1596," DS 9:996–99.

273. In a chapter devoted to "Mortifications and Sufferings" (*Life*, part II, chap. X; Doyle, 168), Losa says that when Gregory took up the solitary life he began to flagellate himself, but that a divine inspiration told him to stop, because he would have sufficient suffering from his ailments and labors.

274. On the spiritual friendship between Losa and Lopez, see Jodi Bilinkoff, "Francisco Losa and Gregorio López: Spiritual Friendship and Identity Formation on the New Spain Frontier," in *Colonial Saints: Discovering the Holy in the Americas*, ed. Allan Greer and Jodi Bilinkoff (New York: Routledge, 2003), 115–28. Bilinkoff sees Losa as performing much the same function for López as male confessors did for many medieval female mystics.

275. This *Explicación*, as it has been called, first published in 1678, has had

a recent edition: Gregorio López, *Declaración del Apocalypsis*, ed. Alvaro Huerga (Madrid: Fundación Universitaria Espagñola, 1999). On the commentary and its relation to Joachim, see Josep-Ignasi Saranyana, "Análisis doctrinal de l'Tratado del Apocalypsi' de Gregorio López (d. 1596 en México), publicado en Madrid in 1678," in *Storia e figure dell'Apocalisse fra '500 e '600*, ed. Roberto Rusconi (Rome: Viella, 1996), 225–40. The occasion of the writing of the commentary is mentioned several times in the *Life* (Doyle, 113, 116, 148–49).

276. *The Life of Gregory Lopez*, part II, chaps. 12–16 (Doyle, 187–217). Part II, chap. 10 (Doyle, 178–80) also describes Gregorio's prayers in the midst of states of inner desolation.

277. *The Life of Gregory Lopez*, chap. 16, "His Abiding Union with God" (Doyle, 211–17, here 213).

278. For some Mexican examples, see Jean Franco, *Plotting Women: Gender and Representation in Mexico* (New York: Columbia University Press, 1989), chap. 1, "Writers in Spite of Themselves: The Mystical Nuns of Seventeenth-Century Mexico," 2–22.

279. For an introduction, see Allan Greer, "Iroquois Virgin: The Story of Catherine Tekakwitha in New France and New Spain," in Greer and Bilinkoff, *Colonial Saints*, 235–50.

280. See K. I. Koppedrayer, "The Making of the First Iroquois Virgin: Early Jesuit Biographies of the Blesssed Kateri Tekakwitha," *Ethnohistory* 40 (1993): 277–306.

281. There is no space here to refer to the large literature on Sor Juana, but for the religious and theological significance of her works, consult Pamela Kirk Rappaport, ed. and trans., *Sor Juana Inés de la Cruz: Selected Writings*, Classics of Western Spirituality (New York: Paulist Press, 2005).

282. I give only two examples: Kathryn Joy McNight, *The Mystic of Tunja: The Writings of Madre Castillo, 1671–1742* (Amherst: University of Massachusetts Press, 1997); and Kathleen A. Myers and Amanda Powell, eds., *A Wild Country out in the Garden: The Spiritual Journals of a Colonial Mexican Nun* (Bloomington: Indiana University Press, 1998). This volume translates the journals of the Augustinian nun Madre María de San José (1656–1719).

283. The most detailed recent English account of Rose of Lima and the construction of her mystical sanctity is Frank Graziano, *Wounds of Love: The Mystical Marriage of St. Rose of Lima* (New York: Oxford University Press, 2004). Graziano's book is richly detailed but marred by a psychological reductionism, well captured in his concluding words, "[M]ysticism attests to the godlike powers of delusion" (231). Also on Rose, see Kathleen Ann Myers, "'Redeemer of America': Rose of Lima (1586–1617), the Dynamics of Identity, and Conversion," in Greer and Bilinkoff, *Colonial Saints*, 251–76.

284. All of Rosa's hagiographers testify to her admiration for Catherine of Siena. In addition, she was familiar with Luis de Granada's *Book of Prayer and Meditation* and knew of Gregorio Lopez.

285. The most important lives were by Pedro Loyaza, *Vida de Santa Rosa de Lima*, published in 1619 (a modern edition was published in Lima in 1965); and Leonardo Hansen, *Vida admirabile de Santa Rosa de Lima*, first published in 1664.

286. Many women, both in the Old World and in the colonies, ran afoul of the Inquisition, as shown in the essays in *Women in the Inquisition*, which does not, however, have an essay on Rosa. On the 1614 hearing, see Myers, "'Redeemer of America,'" 261–63.

287. See the account in Graziano, *Wounds of Love*, 217–22.

288. Graziano discusses the factors behind Rosa's canonization (*Wounds of Love*, 95–130).

289. A personal record of Rosa's spirituality that does survive is the two captioned collages, or emblemata, of the mystical path she constructed, the first, *The Mercies* (*Las Mercedes*), and the second *The Mystical Stairway* (*La Escala Mística*). For pictures and a discussion, see Myers, "'Redeemer of America,'" 264–70. One letter also survives.

290. Myers, "'Redeemer of America,'" 27.

Conclusion

THE MYSTICS TREATED in volume VI, part 2, *The Golden Age of Spanish Mysticism, 1500–1650*, were contemporary with the Protestant mystics considered in volume VI, part 1. At first glance, the opposition between the two groups seems overwhelming. Although the Spanish mystics lacked any clear idea of what Luther and the other Reformers actually taught, they were convinced that they were dangerous heretics and prayed that they might amend their ways and return to the true church. For the Protestants, the Hapsburg rulers and their subjects, whether in Central Europe or in Spain, were the forces of evil trying to crush evangelical faith. For all the real opposition between the Spanish mystics and the Reformation mystics, however, there were some similar inner trajectories at work that merit reflection. Both groups were heirs to the traditions of patristic and medieval mysticism and read many of the same authors, such as Augustine, Gregory the Great, and Bernard of Clairvaux. Luther and the Radical Reformers were also shaped by their encounter with Germanic mysticism of the late Middle Ages, especially that of Tauler and the *Theologia deutsch*. Although some of the northern mystics were known and used in Spain, they were less influential. Quite apart from the issue of the sources the mystics read is the question of the common themes found in the mystical element of Christian faith that both Protestant and Catholics were called on to address. Themes such as the nature of prayer, the relation between Christ and the believer, the possibility of union with God and deification, and the role of the Holy Spirit acting within the soul were all taken up by both Protestants and Catholics.

There is no place here for a full-fledged comparison, but one difficult issue that faced both Protestants and Spanish Catholics deserves
a brief consideration: the question of the authority to be given to inner
experience in relation to the claims of the outer religious authority,
such as the Bible and the teaching of recognized ecclesial leaders.
Tensions between inner charisms and outer normative practices were
not new in the history of Christian mysticism, but they seem to have
grown from the late thirteenth century on and to have taken on a new
urgency in the sixteenth century. Luther's differences with Andreas
Karlstadt and the other Radical Reformers are a primary case in point
on the Reformation side. For the Radicals the inner witness of the
Holy Spirit trumped all outer religious authority—even the words of
scripture, which were naught but dead letters apart from the breath of
the Spirit. Some of Luther's successors, notably, Johann Arndt, struggled to achieve a balance between the inner and outer claims of belief,
though even Arndt met strong opposition from some of the more rigid
proponents of Lutheran orthodoxy. Valentin Weigel had to keep his
true views hidden while he functioned publicly as a Lutheran pastor.

Spanish mysticism was shaped by the strong contrast between an
increasingly rigid ecclesio-political order and a turn, unprecedented
in earlier Catholic Spain, to interior prayer and insistence on the need
for direct inner consciousness of God. Many authorities in Spain, however, were troubled by the turn within, as shown by the use of the Spanish Inquisition as the guarantor of mystical orthodoxy, by the series of
condemnations of religious books, as well as the quarrels within the
religious orders over reform. The Inquisition played a key role in the
story of Spanish mysticism. The decree against the *Alumbrados* in 1525
was a benchmark of what was forbidden regarding interior claims,
but the radical turn within was characteristic of all the great Spanish
mystics, such as Ignatius, Teresa, John of the Cross, and Luis de León.
However much the mystics strove to demonstrate their orthodoxy
and obedience to ecclesiastical authority, the Inquisitors continued to
worry about them. Perhaps the greatest paradox of Spanish mysticism
was the fact that one of the most extensive, impressive, and influential
bodies of writings in the history of Christian mysticism was produced
within a historical context of such great suspicion and even repression
of claims to inner experience of God.

In this connection, we may ask just how powerful the role of Spanish
mysticism has been in the longer story of Western mystical traditions.
During much of the past century it seemed a given that Teresa of Avila
and John of the Cross represented the acme of Catholic mysticism, the

standard against which all others were to be measured. Nonetheless, the same mid-century theological *ressourcement* that began to question whether Thomas Aquinas was *the* final authority in doctrinal theology also began to eat away at the supremacy of these Spanish Carmelites as the standard bearers for Catholic mysticism. Growing recognition of Ignatius of Loyola as not only a founder and organizer of religious life but also an original, even surprising, mystic gave greater depth and complexity to the standard picture of sixteenth-century Spanish mysticism. Pioneering figures, especially the English scholar E. Allison Peers, had already begun to reveal the variety and richness of early modern Spanish mysticism in the first half of the twentieth century, and toward the end of the century feminist scholars and other historians became interested in the story of neglected Spanish female mystics, both those famous as icons of mystical holiness and others whose writings had been neglected for centuries.

Spanish female mysticism has emerged as a particularly strong area of research in the past decades. It is true that the stories of many of Spain's female mystics have a certain sameness, due to the fact that the stories were expected to adhere to an established narrative about women mystics that had been formed in the late Middle Ages, especially by Catherine of Siena, or rather, the picture of Catherine presented by her confessor and spiritual guide, Raymond of Capua, in his *Legenda maior* of the saint. These Spanish women exhibited prodigious acts of self-denial and asceticism (inedia, flagellation, sleep deprivation, and various others forms of a literal *imitatio Christi*), and often were said to have enjoyed the ultimate form of identification with the suffering Christ, the reception of the stigmata, which Francis of Assisi had received visibly and Catherine of Siena invisibly. Most of these women were also the recipients of mystical graces of sometimes extraordinary kinds. They were visionaries whose lives were filled with manifestations of Christ, Mary, and many saints, and sometimes even the Trinity. On the reverse side, the devil was also a constant presence for these women, a malignant force experienced as both the author of assaults, mental and physical, and even more suspect as the disguised "Angel of Light," who sent false spiritual gifts to mislead the faithful. We need to remember, however, that these mystical (or would-be mystical) women were ambiguous, even liminal, figures in the Spain of their time. On the one hand, they were praised and often viewed with awe by clergy and common folk; on the other hand, they were subject to the strict male control of their confessors on an almost daily basis, with the

Inquisition ever looming in the background as the ultimate arbiter of the authenticity of their claims to direct access to God.

Only a few of these Spanish women made original or lasting contributions to mystical literature, perhaps because of the repetition of their model of mystical devotion. Teresa of Avila is the great exception, a teacher whose writings have continued to inspire all interested in striving for deeper contact with God, and a teacher whose theological originality continues to evoke new insights in every age. I have also suggested in chapter 5 that one of Teresa's forgotten daughters, Cecilia del Nacimiento, merits consideration as an important mystical teacher. There are, of course, other inspiring figures among the many female mystics of Spain's Golden Age. How far they may continue to nourish a contemporary search for God is up to the reader to judge.

Spain's Golden Age of mysticism, like the late medieval centuries before it, witnessed frequent collaboration between female and male mystics in their pursuit of a deeper consciousness of God's transforming presence. These mystical conversations had a profound effect not only on how and what the women mystics wrote, as we can see in the cases of Teresa of Avila and Cecilia del Nacimiento, but also often on the writings of the male mystics. John of the Cross is a noteworthy example. While John's writing career began with the profound lyrics he wrote during the dark days of his imprisonment, his use of these poems in instructing the Carmelite nuns after his release and their requests for help in understanding his message led to the production of the four lengthy commentaries on the poems that constitute a body of mystical teaching almost unrivaled in penetration and scope. Despite the challenges of his uncompromising insistence on the need for complete purgation in the path to God by embracing dark faith, hope, and love, John remains an inexhaustible treasure in the history of mysticism.

Once again, however, we need to remember that John of the Cross was just one, if perhaps the greatest, of the male mystics of the Golden Age of Spanish Mysticism. The recovery of the mystical core of the apostolic mission of Ignatius of Loyola was a major achievement of twentieth-century scholarship, and the ongoing adaptations of the Ignatian *Exercises* for spiritual transformation in the contemporary world speak to the vitality of the Jesuit founder's view of finding God in the midst of everyday life. But there were many other fascinating male mystical writers in the Golden Age of Spain, however little read some of them may be today. I have tried to highlight some of the most important, such as the Franciscan *recogimiento* mystics of the early sixteenth century (chap. 1), and I also considered a number of later mystics, both male and female, in the Spain of roughly 1550–1650 (chap. 5). A number of these figures had an impact on mystical traditions in the centuries after their deaths; some even promise to find new readers in the midst of the contemporary revival of mysticism.

In conclusion, I would reiterate the claim that Spanish mysticism is now perhaps more free than ever to stand on its own—that is, this great spiritual era is no longer part of the nineteenth-century ecclesiastical-political program of building a Catholic fortress against secular modernity but is rather seen as a way for exploring some of the deepest aspects of our relation to God. Ignatius, Teresa, John of the Cross, as well as the many other mystics treated here, offer us an invitation to take up, once again, something that can be considered integral to a fully lived human life—the task of searching for a deeper consciousness of the presence of God. The teaching of these mystical voices of Spain corroborates the Gospel message: "Seek first the kingdom of God."

Bibliography

SECTION I. SOURCES

A. Collections

Místicos franciscanos españoles. Edited by Juan Bautista Gomis. 3 vols. Biblioteca de Autores Cristianos, Sección 4: Ascética y mística 38, 44, 46. Madrid: Biblioteca de Autores Cristianos, 1948–49.

Místicos franciscanos españoles. Edited by Pedro M. Cátedra et al. 2 vols. Madrid: Biblioteca de Autores Cristianos, 1998.

Monumenta historica societatis Jesu. Madrid: Gabriel López del Horno, 1894–.

Monumenta Ignatiana (MI). Four Series.

Series I: *S. Ignatii . . . Epistolae et Instructiones.* 12 vols. Madrid: Gabriel López del Horno, 1903–11.

Series II: *Exercitia spiritualia et Directoria exercitiorum spiritualium (1540–1599).* 2 vols. Rome: Institutum Historicum Societatis Jesu, 1955–69.

Series III: *Constitutiones et Regulae Societatis Jesu.* 4 vols. Rome, 1934–48.

Series IV: *Fontes narrativi de S. Ignatio et de Societatis Jesu initiis* (FN). 4 vols. Rome, 1943–60.

B. Translation Collections

Arenal, Electa, and Stacey Schlau. *Untold Sisters: Hispanic Nuns in Their Own Works.* Albuquerque: University of New Mexico Press, 1989.

Payne, Steven. *The Carmelite Tradition.* Spirituality in History. Collegeville, MN: Liturgical Press, 2011.

Pond, Kathleen. *The Spirit of the Spanish Mystics: An Anthology of Spanish Religious Prose from the Fifteenth to the Seventeenth Century.* New York: P. J. Kenedy & Sons, 1958.

C. Spanish Authors (Alphabetical by First Name)

1. ALPHONSO RODRIGUEZ (1538–1616)

Translation

Esercitio de Perfettione e di Virtù composto dal R. P. Alfonso Rodriguez . . . . Venice: Andrea Poleti, 1722.

2. ANA DE SAN AGUSTÍN (1555–1624)

Relaciones. Elizabeth Teresa Howe, *The Visionary Life of Madre Ana de San Agustín.* Woodbridge, Suffolk: Tamesis, 2004.

3. ANA DE SAN BARTOLOMÉ (1549–1626)

Obras Completas de la Beata Ana de San Bartolomé. Edited by Julián Urkiza. 2 vols. Rome: Edizioni Teresianum, 1981–85.

4. BALTASAR ALVAREZ (1533–1580)

Escritos espirituales. Edited by Camilo M. Abad. Barcelona: Flors, 1961.

Translation

Sur l'oraison de repos et de silence. Mesnil-sur-l'Estrée: Éditions Arfuyen, 2010.

5. BERNABÉ DE PALMA (ca. 1469–1532)

Via Spiritus de Bernabé de Palma; Subida de Monte Sión de Bernardino de Laredo. Edited by Teodoro H. Martín. Colección Clásicos de Espiritualidad. Madrid: Biblioteca de Autores Cristianos, 1998.

6. BERNARDINO DE LAREDO (1480–1540)

Subida del Monte Sión. Edited by Alegría Alonso González et al. Madrid: Fundación Universitaria Española, 2000.

Translation

The Ascent of Mount Sion. Translated by E. Allison Peers. New York: Harper & Bros., 1950.

7. CECILIA DEL NACIMIENTO (1570–1646)

Obras completas de Cecilia del Nacimiento. Edited by José Diaz Cerón. Madrid: Editorial de Espiritualidad, 1970.

Translation

Cecilia del Nacimiento: Journeys of a Mystical Soul in Poetry and Prose. Edited and translated by Kevin Donnelly and Sandra Sider. Toronto: Centre for Reformation and Renaissance, 2012.

8. DIEGO DE ESTELLA (1524–1578)

Meditaciones devotísimas del amor de Dios. In *Místicos franciscanos españoles,* edited by Juan Bautista Gomis, 3:59–367. 3 vols. Biblioteca de Autores Cristianos, Sección 4: Ascética y mística 38, 44, 46. Madrid: Biblioteca de Autores Cristianos, 1948–49.

Translation

Meditations on the Love of God from the Meditationes Devotísimas del Amor de Dios of R. P. F. Diego de Estella. Translated by Julia Pember. London: Sheed & Ward, 1940.

9. DIEGO DE JESÚS (1570–1621)

Apuntamientos y advertiencias en tres discorsos . . . . In *Obras del Místico Doctor San Juan de la Cruz,* edited by Gerardo de San Juan de la Cruz, 3:465–502. 3 vols. Toledo: Viuda e Hijos de J. Peláez, 1914.

10. FRANCISCO DE OSUNA (1492–1540)

Tercer abecedario espiritual de Francesco de Osuna. Edited by Saturnino López Santidrián. In *Místicos franciscanos españoles,* edited by Pedro M. Cátedra et al. 2 vols. Madrid: Biblioteca de Autores Cristianos, 1998.

Translation

The Third Spiritual Alphabet. Translated by Mary E. Giles. Classics of Western Spirituality. New York: Paulist Press, 1981.

11. GARCÍA DE CISNEROS (1455–1510)

García Jiménez de Cisneros: Obras Completas. Edited by Cipriano Baraut, OSB. 2 vols. Montserrat: Monastery of Montserrat, 1965.

Translation

Book of the Exercises of the Spiritual Life. Translated by E. Allison Peers. Montserrat: Monastery of Montserrat, 1929.

12. GREGORIO LÓPEZ (1542–1596)

La vida que Hizo el Siervo de Dios Gregorio Lopez en algunos lugares de Nueva España. Mexico City, 1613.
Declaración del Apocalypsis. Edited by Alvaro Huerga. Madrid: Fundación Universitaria Española, 1999.

Translation

Doyle, Canon F. C. *The Life of Gregorio Lopez.* London: R. Washbourne, 1876.

13. IGNATIUS OF LOYOLA (ca. 1491–1556)

Diario espiritual. In *Obras completas de San Ignacio de Loyola,* edited by Victoriano Larrañaga, 1:625–792. Madrid: Biblioteca de Autores Cristianos, 1947.
Ejercicios Espirituales: Comentario pastoral. Edited by Luis González and Ignacio Iparraguirre. Madrid: Biblioteca de Autores Cristianos, 1965.
Obras completas de San Ignacio de Loyola. Edited by Ignacio Iparraguirre and Cándido de Dalmases. 4th ed. Madrid: Biblioteca de Autores Cristianos, 1982.

Translations

Ignatius of Loyola: The Spiritual Exercises and Selected Works. Translated by George E. Ganss et al. Classics of Western Spirituality. New York: Paulist Press, 1991.
The Spiritual Exercises of St. Ignatius: Based on Studies in the Language of the Autograph. Translated by Louis J. Puhl. Chicago: Loyola University Press, 1951.
Letters of St. Ignatius of Loyola. Selected and translated by William J. Young. Chicago: Loyola University Press, 1959.

Saint Ignatius of Loyola: Personal Writings. Translated and edited by Joseph A. Munitiz and Philip Endean. London: Penguin Books, 1996.

Saint Ignatius of Loyola: The Constitutions of the Society of Jesus. Translated by George E. Ganss. St. Louis: Institute of Jesuit Sources, 1970.

Remembering Iñigo: Glimpses of the Life of Saint Ignatius of Loyola–The Memoriale of Luis Gonçalves da Câmara. Translated by Alexander Eaglestone and Joseph A. Munitiz. St. Louis: Institute of Jesuit Sources, 2004.

Spiritual Diary. In Antonio T. de Nicolás, *Ignatius de Loyola: Powers of Imagining. A Philosophical Hermeneutic of Imagining through the Collected Works of Ignatius de Loyola*, 189–238. Albany: State University of New York Press, 1986.

14. JOANA DE JESUS (1617–1681)

Joana de Fátima Gonçalves Pita do Serrado, *Ancia/Anxiousness in Joana de Jesus (1617–1681): Historical and Philosophical Approaches.* Ph.D. dissertation. University of Groningen, 2014.

15. JOHN OF THE CROSS (JUAN DE LA CRUZ) (1542–1591)

Vida y Obras de San Juan de la Cruz. Edited by Crisógono de Jesús, Matias del Niño Jesús, and Lucinio del SS. Sacramento. 5th ed. Madrid: Biblioteca de Autores Cristianos, 1964.

Translations

The Collected Works of Saint John of the Cross. Translated by Kieran Kavanaugh and Otilio Rodriguez. Rev. ed. Washington, DC: ICS Publications, 1991.

The Complete Works of Saint John of the Cross, Doctor of the Church. Translated by E. Allison Peers. 3 vols. London: Burns & Oates, 1935. Reprint, Westminster, MD: Newman Press, 1964.

Poems of St. John of the Cross. Translated by Roy Campbell. New York: Pantheon Books, 1956.

16. JOSÉ DE JESÚS MARÍA (QUIROGA) (1562–1626)

Apología mística. In Fortunato Antolín, *Primeras Biografías y Apologías de San Juan de la Cruz*, 125–322. Salamanca: Junta de Castilla y León, 1991.

17. JOSEPHUS A SPIRITU SANCTO, THE ANDALUSIAN (1667–1736)

P. Fr. Ioseph a Spiritu Sancto, Cursus Theologiae Mystico-Scholasticae. Edited by Fr. Anastasius of St. Paul. 5 vols. Bruges: C. Beyaert, 1924–34.

18. JUAN DE AVILA (1499–1569)

Translation

Audi filia–Listen, O Daughter. Translated and introduced by Joan Frances Gormley. Classics of Western Spirituality. New York: Paulist Press, 2006.

19. JUAN DE LOS ANGELES (ca. 1536–1609)

Obras místicas de Juan de los Angeles. Edited by Jaime Sala and G. Fuentes. 2 vols. Madrid: Nueva Biblioteca de Autores Españoles, 1912, 1917.
Manual de vida perfecta. In *Místicos franciscanos españoles,* edited by Juan Bautista Gomis, 3:479–681. 3 vols. Biblioteca de Autores Cristianos, Sección 4: Ascética y mística 38, 44, 46. Madrid: Biblioteca de Autores Cristianos, 1948–49.

Translation

The Loving Struggle between God and the Soul by Fray Juan de los Angeles (1532–1609). Translated by Eladia Gómez-Posthill. London: Saint Austin Press, 2000.

20. JUANA DE LA CRUZ (1481–1534)

El Conhorte: Sermones de una mujer, La Santa Juana (1481–1584). Edited by Inocente García de Andrés. 2 vols. Madrid: Fundación Universitaria Española, 1999.

Translation

Mother Juana de la Cruz, 1481–1534: Visionary Sermons. Translated by Ronald E. Surtz and Jessica A. Boon. Tempe: Arizona Center for Medieval and Renaissance Studies, 2016.

21. LUIS DE GRANADA (1504–1588)

Guia de pecadores. Edited by Alvaro Huerga. Madrid: Fundación Universitaria Española, 1994.
Libro de la oración y meditación. Madrid: Ediciones Palabra, 1979.

22. LUIS DE LEÓN (1527–1593)

Obras Completas Castellanas de Fray Luis de León. Edited by Felix García. 2nd ed. corrected and augmented. Madrid: Biblioteca de Autores Cristianos, 1951.
Poesias. Edited by Angelo Custodio Vega. Barcelona: Editorial Planeta, 1970.

Translations

The Names of Christ. Translated by Manuel Durán and William Kluback. Classics of Western Spirituality. New York: Paulist Press, 1984.
Lyrics of Luis de León. With English renderings by Aubrey F. G. Bell. London: Burns, Oates & Washbourne, 1928.
The Unknown Light: The Spanish Poems of Fray Luis de León. Introduction and translation by Willis Barnstone. Albany: State University of New York Press, 1979.

23. LUIS DE LA PUENTE (1554–1624)

Obras escogidas del V.P. Luis de la Puente. Edited by P. Camilo María Abad. Madrid: Biblioteca de Autores Españoles,1958.

Translations

Meditations on the mysteries of our holy faith, together with a treatise on mental prayer. 6 vols. London, 1852.
A Treatise on Mental Prayer. London: Burns, Oates & Washbourne, 1929.
Of Familiar Intercourse with God in Prayer . . . (From the "Spiritual Guide"). Treatise I. London: Burns, Oates & Washbourne, 1932.

24. LUISA DE CARVAJAL (1566–1614)

Elizabeth Rhodes, *This Tight Embrace: Luisa de Carvajal y Mendoza (1566–1614).* Reformation Texts with Translation (1350–1650): Women of the Reformation 2. Milwaukee: Marquette University Press, 2000.

25. MARÍA DE AGREDA (1602–1665)

Mística Ciudad de Dios: Vida de la Virgen María. 7 vols. Barcelona: P. Riera, 1860.

Translation

The Mystical City of God. 4 vols. South Chicago, IL: Theopolitan, 1914. Reprint, Albuquerque, NM: Corcoran, 1949.

26. MARÍA DE SAN JOSÉ (1548–1603)

Escritos espirituales. Edited by Simeón de la Sagrada Familia. Rome: Postulación General O.C.D., 1979.

Translation

Book for the Hour of Recreation. Translated by Alison Weber. Chicago: University of Chicago Press, 2002.

27. MARÍA DE SANTO DOMINGO (1486–1524)

Translation

Giles, Mary E. *The Book of Prayer of Sor María of Santo Domingo: A Study and Translation.* Albany: State University of New York Press, 1990.

28. MARÍA VELA Y CUERTO (1561–1617)

Translation

Keyes, Frances Parkinson. *The Third Mystic of Avila: The Self Revelation of Maria Vela, a Sixteenth Century Spanish Nun.* New York: Farrar, Straus & Cudahy, 1960.

29. MARIANA DE SAN JOSÉ (1568–1638)

Madre Mariana de San José: Obras Completas. Edited by Jesús Diez Rastrilla. Madrid: Biblioteca de Autores Cristianos, 2014.

30. NICOLAS DE JESÚS MARÍA (ca. 1590–1655)

Phrasium mysticae theologiae V. P. Fr. Joannis de Cruce . . . elucidatio. In *Opera mystica V. ac Mystici doctoris F. Iohannis a Cruce.* Cologne: Gualtieri, 1639.

31. PEDRO DE ALCÁNTARA (1499–1562)

Translation

Treatise on Prayer and Meditation. Translated by Dominic Devas. Westminster, MD: Newman Press, 1949.

32. ROSE OF LIMA (1586–1617)

Hansen, Leonardo. *Vida admirabile de Santa Rosa de Lima*. Translated and edited by Jacinto Parra. Vergara: El Santísimo Rosario and Lima, Centro Catolico, 1895.

33. TERESA OF AVILA
(TERESA DE JESÚS) (1515–1582)

Obras Completas de Santa Teresa de Jesús: Edición Manual. Edited by Efrén de la Madre de Dios and Otger Steggink. Madrid: Biblioteca de Autores Cristianos, 1986.

Translation

The Collected Works of St. Teresa of Avila. Translated by Kieran Kavanaugh and Otilio Rodriguez. 3 vols. Washington, DC: ICS Publications, 1976–85.
The Collected Letters of St. Teresa of Avila. Translated by Kieran Kavanaugh. 2 vols. Washington, DC: ICS Publications, 2001.
Complete Works of St. Teresa of Jesus. Translated and edited by E. Allison Peers. 3 vols. London and New York: Sheed & Ward, 1944–46.
The Life of Saint Teresa of Avila by Herself. Translated by J. M. Cohen. London: Penguin Books, 1957.

34. TERESA DE CARTAGENA (ca. 1420–CA. 1470)

Translation

The Writings of Teresa de Cartagena. Translated by Dayle Seidenspinner-Núñez. Rochester: Boydell & Brewer, 1998.

35. TOMAS DE JESÚS (1564–1627)

Opera Omnia. 2 vols. Cologne, 1684.
Ven. P. Thomas a Jesu. *De contemplatione acquisita (Opus ineditum) et*

Via brevis et plana orationis mentalis. Edited by P. Eugenius a Sto. Joseph. Milan: Tipografia S. Lega Eucharistica, 1922.

Translation

Trattato della contemplazione divina. Introduction and translation by Elisabetta Zambruno. Milan: Edizioni Glossa Srl, 2015.

SECTION II. SECONDARY WORKS

Acebal Luján, Mariano. "Pierre d'Alcántara (saint)." DS 12:1489–95.

Ackermann, Jane. "Stories of Elijah and Medieval Carmelite Identity." *History of Religions* 35 (1995): 124–47.

Adnès, Pierre. "Larmes." DS 9:287–303.

———. "Mystique B. XVIe–XXe siècles." DS 10:1919–39.

———. "Toucher, Touches." DS 15:1073–98.

———. "Visions." DS 16:949–1002.

Adolfo de la Madre de Dios et al. "Espagne, III: L'Age d'Or." DS 4:1127–78.

Ahlgren, Gillian T. W. "Ecstasy, Prophecy, and Reform: Catherine of Siena as a Model for Holy Women of Sixteenth-Century Spain." In *The Mystical Gesture: Essays on Medieval and Early Modern Spiritual Culture in Honor of Mary E. Giles,* edited by Robert Boenig, 53–65. Burlington, VT: Ashgate, 2000.

———. *Entering Teresa of Avila's "Interior Castle": A Reader's Companion.* New York: Paulist Press, 2005.

———. "Negotiating Sanctity: Holy Women in Sixteenth-Century Spain." *Church History* 64 (1995): 373–87.

———. *Teresa of Avila and the Politics of Sanctity.* Ithaca, NY: Cornell University Press, 1996.

Alamo, Mateo. "Cisneros (Garcia ou Garzias de)." DS 2:910–21.

Alcalá, Angel. "Maria de Cazalla: The Grievous Price of Victory." In *Women of the Inquisition: Spain and the New World,* edited by Mary E. Giles, 98–118. Baltimore: Johns Hopkins University Press, 1999.

———, ed. *The Spanish Inquisition and the Inquisitorial Mind.* Atlantic Studies on Society in Change 49. New York: Columbia University Press, 1987.

Alvarez, Tomás. *See* Cruz, Tomás de la

Andía, Ysabel de. "San Juan de la Cruz y la 'Teología Mística' de 'San Dionisio.'" In *Actas del Congreso Internacional Sanjuanista: Avila, 23–28 de Septiembre de 1991,* 3:97–125. 3 vols. N.p.: Junta de Castilla y León, Consejería de Cultura y Turismo, 1993.

Andrés Martín, Melquíades. "Alumbrados, Erasmians, 'Lutherans,' and Mystics: The Risk of a More 'Intimate' Spirituality." In *The Spanish Inquisition and the Inquisitorial Mind,* edited by Angel Alcalá, 457–94. Atlantic Studies on Society in Change 49. New York: Columbia University Press, 1987.

———. "La espiritualidad de fray Luis de León." In *Fray Luis de León: Historia, Humanismo y Letras,* edited by Victor García de la Concha and Javier San José Lera, 224–39. Salamanca: Ediciones Universidad, 1986.

———. *Historia de la mística de la Edad de Oro en España y América.* Madrid: Biblioteca de Autores Cristianos, 1994.

———. *Los recogidos: Nueva visión de la mística española (1500–1700).* Madrid: Fundación Universitaria Española, 1975.

———. *La teología española en el siglo XVI.* 2 vols. Biblioteca de Autores Cristianos, Serie Maior 13, 14. Madrid: Biblioteca de Autores Cristianos, 1977.

Andrews, Frances. *The Other Friars: Carmelite, Augustinian, Sack and Pied Friars in the Middle Ages.* Rochester, NY: Boydell, 2006.

Antolín, Fortunato. *Primeras Biografías y Apologías de San Juan de la Cruz.* Salamanca: Junta de Castilla y León, 1991.

Aschenbrenner, George. "Consciousness Examen." *Review for Religious* 31 (1972): 13–21.

Astigarraga, Juan Luis, et al., eds. *Concordancias de los escritos de San Juan de la Cruz.* Rome: Teresianum, 1990.

———. *Concordancias de los escritos de Santa Teresa de Jesús.* 2 vols. Rome: Editoriales O.C.D., 2000.

Bache, Christopher M. "A Reappraisal of Teresa of Avila's Supposed Hysteria." *Journal of Religion and Health* 24 (1985): 300–315.

Baird, Robert. "When Can I Free Myself and Fly? Luis de León and the Question of Mysticism." (Unpublished).

Balthasar, Hans Urs von. "Action and Contemplation." In Balthasar, *Explorations in Theology.* Volume 1, *The Word Made Flesh*, 227–40. San Francisco: Ignatius Press, 1988.

———. "St. John of the Cross." In Balthasar, *The Glory of the Lord: A Theological Aesthetics.* Volume 3, *Studies in Theological Style: Lay Styles*, 105–71. San Francisco: Ignatius Press, 1986.

Bara Bancel, Silvia. "Le Escuela Mística Renana y *Las Moradas* de Santa Teresa." In *Las Moradas del Castillo Interior de Santa Teresa de Jesús: Actas del IV Congreso Internacional Teresiano en Avila, 2–9 Septiembre 2013,* edited by Francisco Javier Sancho Fermín and Rómolo Cuartas Londoño, 179–219. Burgos: Monte Carmelo, 2014.

Barnstone, Willis. *The Poetics of Ecstasy: Varieties of ekstasis from Sappho to Borges.* New York: Holmes & Meier, 1983.

Barthes, Roland. *Sade, Fourier, Loyola.* New York: Hill & Wang, 1976.

Barton, Marcella Biro. "Saint Teresa of Avila: Did She Have Epilepsy?" *Catholic Historical Review* 68 (1982): 581–98.

Baruzi, Jean. *Saint Jean de la Croix et le problème de l'expérience mystique.* 2 vols. Paris: Félix Alcan, 1924.

———. "St. Jean de la Croix et le problème de la valeur noétique de l'expérience mystique." *Bulletin de la Société française de Philosophie* 25 (1925): 25–88.

Bataillon, Marcel. *Erasme et l'Espagne,* edited by Daniel Devoto and Charles Amiel. 3 vols. Geneva: Jérôme Millon, 1991.

Baumann, Theodore. "Die Berichte über die Vision des heiligen Ignatius bei La Storta." *Archivum Historicum Societatis Jesu* 27 (1958): 181–208.

"Benedictine of Stanbrook Abbey." *Mediaeval Mystical Tradition and Saint John of the Cross.* London: Burns & Oates, 1954.

Bertaud, Émile. "Hortus, Hortulus, Jardin spiritual." DS 7:766–84.

Bilinkoff, Jodi. *The Avila of Saint Teresa: Religious Reform in a Sixteenth-Century City.* Ithaca, NY: Cornell University Press, 1989.

———. "Francisco Losa and Gregorio López: Spiritual Friendship and Identity Formation on the New Spain Frontier." In *Colonial Saints: Discovering the Holy in the Americas*, edited by Allan Greer and Jodi Bilinkoff, 115–28. New York: Routledge, 2003.

———. "A Spanish Prophetess and Her Patrons: The Case of María de Santo Domingo." *Sixteenth Century Journal* 23 (1992): 21–34.

Blais, Donald. "Contextualizing Teresa: Vida 20.1: Are the Phenomena Identical?" *Studies in Spirituality* 12 (2002): 141–46.

Blommestijn, Hein. "The Dark Night in John of the Cross: The Transformational Process." *Studies in Spirituality* 10 (2000): 228–41.

Blommestijn, Hein, Jos Huls, and Kees Waaijman. *The Footprints of Love: John of the Cross as a Guide in the Wilderness.* Fiery Arrow Collection 3. Leuven: Peeters, 2000.

Blommestijn, Hein, and Kees Waaijman. "L'homme spirituel à l'Image de Dieu selon Saint Jean de la Croix." In *Juan de la Cruz, Espíritu de Llama: Estudios con ocasión del cuarto centenario de su muerte (1591–1991)*, edited by Otger Steggink, 623–56. Vacare Deo 10. Studies in Spirituality Supplement 1. Kampen: Kok Pharos, 1991.

Boon, Jessica A. "Mother Juana de la Cruz: Marian Visions and Female Preaching." In *A New Companion to Hispanic Mysticism*, edited by Hilaire Kallendorf, 127–48. Brill's Companions to the Christian Tradition 19. Leiden: Brill, 2010.

—————. *The Mystical Science of the Soul: Medieval Cognition in Bernardino de Laredo's Recollection Method.* Toronto: University of Toronto Press, 2012.

Bord, André. *Les amours chez Jean de la Croix.* Beauchesne Religions 24. Paris: Beauchesne, 1998.

—————. *Jean de la Croix en France.* Beauchesne Religions 21. Paris: Beauchesne, 1993.

—————. *Mémoire et espérance chez Jean de la Croix.* Bibliothèque de spiritualité 8. Paris: Beauchesne, 1971.

Boyle, Marjorie O'Rourke. *Loyola's Acts: The Rhetoric of the Self.* New Historicism 36. Berkeley: University of California Press, 1997.

Bremond, Henri. *Histoire littéraire du sentiment religieux en France depuis la fin des guerres de religion jusqu'à nos jours.* 5 vols. Grenoble: Jérôme Millon, 2006.

Brenan, Gerald. *St. John of the Cross: His Life and Poetry.* Cambridge: Cambridge University Press, 1973.

Brodrick, James. *The Progress of the Jesuits (1556–79).* New York: Longmans, Green, 1947.

Brown, Judith C. *Immodest Acts: The Life of a Lesbian Nun in Renaissance Italy.* Studies in the History of Sexuality. New York: Oxford University Press, 1986.

Bruno, Fr. *St. John of the Cross.* New York: Sheed & Ward, 1932.

Buckley, Michael. "Ecclesial Mysticism in the *Exercises.*" *Theological Studies* 56 (1995): 441–63.

—————. "The Structure of the Rules for Discernment." In *The Way of Ignatius Loyola: Contemporary Approaches to the Spiritual Exercises,* edited by Philip Sheldrake, 219–37. St. Louis: Institute of Jesuit Sources, 1991.

Burke, Gregory. "Fr. Jerome Gracián: A Heroic Follower of St. Teresa." *Mount Carmel: A Review of the Spiritual Life* 63 (2015): 49–57.

Cabassut, A. "Blessure d'amour." DS 1:1724–29.

Calvert, Laura. *Francisco de Osuna and the Spirit of the Letter.* North Carolina Studies in the Romance Languages and Literatures 133. Chapel Hill: University of North Carolina Department of Romance Languages, 1973.

Camelot, P. T. "Action et contemplation dans la tradition chrétienne." *La vie spirituelle* 78 (1958): 272–302.

Campos, Julio. "Marie de Jésus (d'Agreda)." DS 10:508–13.

Cargnoni, Costanzo. "Houses of Prayer in the History of the Franciscan Order." In *Franciscan Solitude,* edited by André Cirino and Josef Raischl, 211–64. St. Bonaventure, NY: Franciscan Institute, 1995.

Carrera, Elena. *Teresa of Avila's Autobiography: Authority, Power and the Self in Mid-Sixteenth-Century Spain.* London: Legenda, 2005.

Carroll, Eamon R. "The Saving Role of the Human Christ for St. Teresa." In *Centenary of St. Teresa*, 133–52. Carmelite Studies 3. Washington, DC: ICS Publications, 1984.

Castro, Manuel de. "Jean des Anges." DS 8:259–64.

Certeau, Michel de. *The Mystic Fable: The Sixteenth and Seventeenth Centuries.* 2 vols. Religion and Postmodernism. Chicago: University of Chicago Press, 1992, 2015.

Charmot, F. *L'union au Christ dans l'action selon saint Ignace.* Paris: Bonne Presse, 1959.

Christian, William A., Jr. *Apparitions in Late Medieval and Renaissance Spain.* Princeton: Princeton University Press, 1981.

Coelho, Mary. "St. Teresa of Avila's Transformation of the Symbol of the Interior Castle." *Ephemerides Carmelitanae* 38 (1987): 109–25.

Coemans, C. "La letter du P. C. Aquaviva sur l'oraison." *Revue d'ascétique et de mystique* 17 (1936): 313–21.

Cognet, Louis. *La spiritualité moderne.* Volume 1, *L'essor, 1500–1650.* Histoire de la spiritualité chrétienne 3.2. Paris: Aubier, 1966.

Colahan, Clark. "María de Jesús Agreda: The Sweetheart of the Inquisition." In *Women in the Inquisition: Spain and the New World*, edited by Mary E. Giles, 155–70. Baltimore: Johns Hopkins University Press, 1999.

———. *The Visions of Sor María de Agreda: Writing, Knowledge, and Power.* Tucson: University of Arizona Press, 1994.

Collings, Ross. *John of the Cross.* Way of the Christian Mystics 10. Collegeville, MN: Liturgical Press, 1990.

Connors-Nelson, Catherine. "Touched by the God of Grace: The *Anfechtung* of Luther and the Dark Night of John of the Cross." *Studies in Spirituality* 9 (1999): 109–39.

Constable, Giles. "The Interpretation of Mary and Martha." In Constable, *Three Studies in Medieval Religious and Social Thought*, 3–141. Cambridge: Cambridge University Press, 1995.

Copeau, J. Carlos. "The Constitutions of the Society of Jesus: The Rhetorical Component." *Studies in Spirituality* 14 (2004): 199–208.

Coreth, Emerich. "In Actione Contemplativus." *Zeitschrift für katholische Theologie* 76 (1954): 55–82.

Corteguera, Luis R. "Visions and the Ascent of the Soul in Spanish Mysticism." In *Looking Beyond: Visions, Dreams, and Insights in Medieval Art & History*, edited by Colum Hourihane, 255–63. Index of Christian Art: Occasional Papers 11. Princeton: Index of Christian Art, 2010.

Corteguera, Luis R., and Sherry Velasco. "Authority in the Margin: Re-Examining the Autograph Letters of Sor María de Agreda and Philip IV of Spain." In *Women's Voices and the Politics of the Spanish Empire*, edited by Jennifer L. Eich, Jeanne Gillespie, and Lucia G. Harrison, 235–62. New Orleans: University Press of the South, 2008.

Crisógono de Jesús Sacramentado. *The Life of St. John of the Cross.* London: Longmans, 1958.

Cruz, Tomas de la (Alvarez). "L'Extase chez Saint Thérèse d'Avila." DS 4:2151–60.

———. "Humanité du Christ, IV: L'École Carmélitaine." DS 7:1097–1100.

———. *St. Teresa of Avila: 100 Themes on Her Life and Work.* Washington, DC: ICS Publications, 2011.

Cugno, Alain. *Saint John of the Cross: Reflections on Mystical Experience.* New York: Seabury, 1982.

Culligan, Kevin. "Mary and Martha Working Together: Teresa of Avila's *Meditations on the Song of Songs.*" In *Seeing the Seeker: Explorations in the Discipline of Spirituality. Festschrift for Kees Waaijman on the Occasion of His 65th Birthday*, edited by Hein Blommestijn et al., 315–29. Studies in Spirituality Supplement 19. Leuven: Peeters, 2008.

De contemplatione in Schola Teresiana. Ephemerides Carmeliticae 13. Rome: Teresianum, 1962.

Derville, André. "Paroles intérieures." DS 12:252–57.

Dicken, E. W. Trueman. *The Crucible of Love: A Study of the Mysticism of St. Teresa of Jesus and St. John of the Cross.* New York: Sheed & Ward, 1963.

Diez, Miguel Angel. "Thomas de Jésus (Díaz Sánchez Dávila)." DS 15:833–44.

Di Fonzo, L. "Fratri Minori." DIP 4:823–911.

Dinzelbacher, Peter. *"Revelationes."* Typologie des sources du Moyen Âge occidental 57. Turnhout: Brepols, 1991.

———. *Vision- und Visionsliteratur im Mittelalter.* Monographien zur Geschichte des Mittelalters. Stuttgart: Hiersemann, 1981.

DiSalvo, Angelo J. *The Spiritual Literature of Recollection in Spain (1500–1620): The Reform of the Inner Person.* Texts and Studies in Religion 84. Lewiston, NY: Edwin Mellen, 1999.

Domínguez, Freddy. "From Saint to Sinner: Sixteenth-Century Perceptions of 'La Monja de Lisboa.'" In *A New Companion to Hispanic Mysticism*, edited by Hilaire Kallendorf, 297–320. Brill's Companions to the Christian Tradition 19. Leiden: Brill, 2010.

Doyle, Dominic. "Changing Hopes: A Comparative Study of the Theological Virtue of Hope in Thomas Aquinas, John of the Cross, and Karl Rahner." *Irish Theological Quarterly* 77 (2012): 18–36.

———. "From Triadic to Dyadic Soul: A Genetic Study of John of the Cross on the Anthropological Basis of Hope." *Studies in Spirituality* 21 (2011): 219–41.

Dudon, Paul. "Les leçons d'oraison de P. Balthasar Alvarez." *Revue d'ascétique et de mystique* 2 (1921): 36–57.

Dupuy, Michel. "Nuit (Ténèbre)." DS 11:519–26.

Durán, Manuel. *Luis de León.* New York: Twayne, 1971.

Dúran López, Fernando. "Religious Autobiography." In *A New Companion to Hispanic Mysticism,* edited by Hilaire Kallendorf, 15–38. Brill's Companions to the Christian Tradition 19. Leiden: Brill, 2010.

Egan, Harvey D. "Affirmative Way." In *The New Dictionary of Catholic Spirituality,* edited by Michael Downey, 16–17. Collegeville, MN: Liturgical Press, 1993.

———. *Ignatius Loyola the Mystic.* Way of the Christian Mystics. Collegeville, MN: Liturgical Press, 1987.

Egan, Keith J. "The Biblical Imagination of John of the Cross in *The Living Flame of Love.*" In *Juan de la Cruz, Espíritu de Llama: Estudios con ocasión del cuarto centenario de su muerte (1591–1991),* edited by Otger Steggink, 507–21. Vacare Deo 10. Studies in Spirituality Supplement 1. Kampen: Kok Pharos, 1991.

———. "Contemplation in the 'Spiritual Canticle': The Program of Dark Night: Education for Beauty." In *Carmel and Contemplation: Transforming Human Consciousness,* 241–66. Carmelite Studies 8. Washington, DC: ICS Publications, 2000.

———. The Spirituality of the Carmelites," In *Christian Spirituality: High Middle Ages and Reformation,* edited by Jill Raitt et al., 50–62. World Spirituality 17. New York: Crossroad, 1987.

Egido, Teófanes. "The Historical Setting of St. Teresa's Life," In *Spiritual Direction,* edited by John Sullivan, 122–82. Carmelite Studies 1. Washington, DC: ICS, 1980.

Eich, Jennifer L., Jeanne Gillespie, and Lucia G. Harrison, eds., *Women's Voices and the Politics of the Spanish Empire.* New Orleans: University Press of the South, 2008.

Elisée de la Nativité. "Antoine du Saint-Esprit." DS 1:717–18.

Elliot, John H. *Imperial Spain 1469–1716.* London: Penguin, 2002.

Endean, Philip. "The Spiritual Exercises." In *The Cambridge Companion to the Jesuits,* edited by Thomas Worchester, 52–67. Cambridge Companions to Religion. Cambridge: Cambridge University Press, 2008.

————. "'The Strange Style of Prayer': Mercurian, Cordeses, and Alvarez." In *The Mercurian Project: Forming Jesuit Culture 1573–1580*, edited by Thomas M. McCoog, 351–97. St. Louis: Institute of Jesuit Sources, 2004.

Etchegoyen, Gaston. *L'amour divin: Essai sur les sources de sainte Thérèse.* Bibliothèque de l'École des hautes études hispaniques 4. Paris: De Boccard, 1923.

Fabre, Pierre-Antoine. "The Writings of Ignatius of Loyola as a Seminal Text." In *A Companion to Ignatius of Loyola: Life, Writings, Spirituality, Influence,* edited by Robert Aleksander Maryks, 103–22. Brill's Companions to the Christian Tradition. Leiden: Brill, 2014.

Fedewa, Marilyn H. *María of Agreda: Mystical Lady in Blue.* Albuquerque: University of New Mexico Press, 2009.

Fernandez, Quirino. "Lopez (Grégoire), eremite, 1542–1596." DS 9:996–99.

Fernández-Armesto, Felipe. "Cardinal Cisneros as a Patron of Printing." In *God and Man in Medieval Spain: Essays in Honour of J. R. L. Highfield,* edited by Derek W. Lomaz and David Mackenzie, 149–68. Westminster: Aris & Phillips, 1989.

Fidèle de Ros, Father. *Un inspirateur de sainte Thérèse: Le frère Bernardin de Laredo.* Études de théologie et d'histoire de la spiritualité 11. Paris: Vrin, 1948.

————. *Un maître de sainte Thérèse: Le père François d'Osuna. Sa vie, son oeuvre, sa doctrine spirituelle.* Paris: Beauchesne, 1936.

————. "La vie et oeuvre de Jean des Anges." In *Mélanges offerts au R. P. Cavallera,* 405–23. Toulouse: Bibliothèque de l'Institut Catholique, 1948.

FitzGerald, Constance. "Impasse and Dark Night." *Living with the Apocalypse,* edited by Tilden Edwards, 93–116. San Francisco: Harper & Row, 1984.

Fortunato de Jesús Sacramentado. "Images et contemplation, IV: Dans l'école Carmélitaine." DS 7:1490–1503.

————. "Joseph de Jésus-Marie (Quiroga)." DS 8:1354–59.

Franco, Jean. *Plotting Women: Gender and Representation in Mexico.* New York: Columbia University Press, 1989.

Freitas Carvalho, José Adriano de. "Traditions, Life Experiences and Orientations in Portuguese Mysticism (1515–1630)." In *A New Companion to Hispanic Mysticism,* edited by Hilaire Kallendorf, 39–70. Brill's Companions to the Christian Tradition 19. Leiden: Brill, 2010.

Freitas Carvalho, José Adriano de, and Maria de Lourdes Belchior. "Portugal (16e–18 siècles)." DS 12:1958–73.

Frohlich, Mary. *The Intersubjectivity of the Mystic: A Study of Teresa of Avila's "Interior Castle."* American Academy of Religion Academy Series 83. Atlanta: Scholars Press, 1993.

Gabriel de Sainte-Marie-Madeleine. "Carmes Déchaussés, II: École mystique Thérésienne (Carmes Déchaussés)." DS 2:171–209.

Gallagher, Timothy M. *Discerning God's Will: An Ignatian Guide to Decision Making.* New York: Crossroad, 2009.

———. *The Discernment of Spirits: An Ignatian Guide to Everyday Living.* New York: Crossroad, 2005.

García de la Concha, Victor, and Javier San José Lera, eds. *Fray Luis de León: Historia, Humanismo y Letras.* Salamanca: Ediciones Universidad, 1986.

Garrigou-Lagrange, Réginald. *Christian Perfection and Contemplation according to St. Thomas Aquinas and St. John of the Cross.* St. Louis: B. Herder, 1951.

Gavrilyuk, Paul L., and Sarah Coakley, eds. *The Spiritual Senses: Perceiving God in Western Christianity.* Cambridge: Cambridge University Press, 2012.

Giles, Mary E. "Spanish Visionary Women and the Paradox of Performance." In *Performance and Transformation: New Approaches to Late Medieval Spirituality*, edited by Mary A. Suydam and Joanna E. Ziegler, 273–97. New York: St. Martin's Press, 1999.

Girón-Negrón, Luis M. "Dionysian Thought in Sixteenth-Century Spanish Mystical Theology." *Modern Theology* 24 (2008): 693–707.

Graziano, Frank. *Wounds of Love: The Mystical Marriage of St. Rose of Lima.* New York: Oxford University Press, 2004.

Green, Deirdre. *Gold in the Crucible: Teresa of Avila and the Western Mystical Tradition.* Shaftesbury: Element Books, 1989.

Greer, Allan. "Iroquois Virgin: The Story of Catherine Tekakwitha in New France and New Spain." In *Colonial Saints: Discovering the Holy in the Americas*, edited by Allan Greer and Jodi Bilinkoff, 115–28. New York: Routledge, 2003.

Greer, Allan, and Jodi Bilinkoff, eds. *Colonial Saints: Discovering the Holy in the Americas.* New York: Routledge, 2003.

Groult, Pierre. *Les mystiques des Pays-Bas et la littérature espagnole du seizième siècle.* Louvain: Librairie Universitaire, 1927.

Guibert, Joseph de. *The Jesuits: Their Spiritual Doctrine and Practice. A Historical Study.* Translated by William J. Young. Chicago: Institute of Jesuit Sources, 1964.

———. "Mystique Ignatienne: A propos du 'Journal spirituel' de S. Ignace de Loyola." *Revue d'ascétique et de la mystique* 19 (1938): 3–22, 113–40.

———. *La spiritualité de la Compagnie de Jésus: Esquisse historique.* Rome: Institutum Historicum Societatis Jesu, 1953.

Guillet, Jacques, et al. "Discernement des esprits." DS 3:1222–91.

Gutiérrez, David. "León (Luis de)." DS 9:634–43.

Guy, Alain. "Fray Luis de León et le mysticism." In *Santa Teresa y la literatura mística Hispánica*, edited by Manuel Criado de Val, 521–26. Madrid: EDI, 1984.

———. *Le pensée de Fray Luis de León: Contribution à l'étude de la philosophie espagnole au XVIe siècle.* Paris: Vrin, 1943.

Haas, Adolf. "The Mysticism of St. Ignatius according to His *Spiritual Diary*." In *Ignatius of Loyola: His Personality and Spiritual Heritage, 1556–1996. Studies on the 400th Anniversary of His Death,* edited by Friedrich Wulf, 164–99. St. Louis: Institute of Jesuit Sources, 1977.

Haas, Alois M. ". . . ausserhalb Gottes ist alles eng': Johannes' vom Kreuz 'Appetit' nach Gott." In *Aufgang: Jahrbuch für Denken, Dichten, Musik.* Volume 2, *Sehnsucht* (Stuttgart: Kohlhammer, 2005): 121–41.

———. "Die dunkle Nacht der Sinne und des Geistes: Mystische Leiderfahrung nach Johannes vom Kreuz." In *Die Dunkle Nacht der Sinne: Leiderfahrung und christliche Mystik*, edited by Gotthard Fuchs, 108–25. Düsseldorf: Patmos, 1989.

———. "Mors Mystica: Ein mystologisches Motiv." In Haas, *Sermo mysticus: Studien zu Theologie und Sprache der deutschen Mystik*, 392–480. Dokimion 4. Freiburg, Schweiz: Universitätsverlag, 1979.

Hadot, Pierre. *Philosophy as a Way of Life: Spiritual Exercises from Socrates to Foucault.* Oxford: Blackwell, 1995.

Haliczer, Stephen. *Between Exaltation and Infamy: Female Mystics in the Golden Age of Spain.* Oxford: Oxford University Press, 2002.

Hamilton, Alastair. "The *Alumbrados*: *Dejamiento* and Its Practioners." In *A New Companion to Hispanic Mysticism*, edited by Hilaire Kallendorf, 103–24. Brill's Companions to the Christian Tradition 19. Leiden: Brill, 2010.

———. *Heresy and Mysticism in Sixteenth-Century Spain: The Alumbrados.* Toronto: University of Toronto Press, 1992.

Hardy, Richard P. *John of the Cross: Man and Mystic.* Washington, DC: ICS Publications, 2015.

Hatzfeld, Helmut. "The Influence of Ramon Lull and Jan van Ruysbroeck on the Spanish Mystics." *Traditio* 4 (1946): 337–94.

Hausherr, Irénée. *The Name of Jesus.* Cistercian Studies 44. Kalamazoo: Cistercian Publications, 1978.

Hermann, Christian. "Settlements: Spain's National Catholicism." In *Handbook of European History, 1400–1600: Late Middle Ages, Renaissance, and Reformation*, edited by Thomas A. Brady, Heiko A.

Oberman, and James D. Tracy, 2:491–522. 2 vols. Grand Rapids: Eerdmans, 1996.

Hernandez, E. "Alvarez (Balthasar)." DS 1:405–6.

Hildner, David J. *Poetry and Truth in the Spanish Works of Fray Luis de León*. Colección Támesis: Monografías 151. London: Tamesis Books, 1992.

Honings, Bonifatius. "La contemplazione secondo Filippo della SS. Trinità." In *De contemplatione in Schola Teresiana*, 691–713. Ephemerides Carmeliticae 13. Rome: Teresianum, 1962.

Howe, Elizabeth Teresa. "Heeding the 'Madre': Ana de San Agustín and the Voice of Santa Teresa." In *The Heirs of St. Teresa of Avila*, edited by Christopher C. Wilson, 45–58. Carmelite Studies 9. Washington, DC: ICS Publications, 2006.

Howells, Edward. "Early Modern Reformations." In *The Cambridge Companion to Christian Mysticism*, edited by Amy Hollywood and Patricia Z. Beckman, 114–34. Cambridge: Cambridge University Press, 2012.

———. "Is Darkness a Psychological or a Theological Category in the Thought of John of the Cross?" In *The Renewal of Mystical Theology: Essays in Memory of John N. Jones (1964–2012)*, edited by Bernard McGinn, 140–61. New York: Crossroad-Herder, 2017.

———. *John of the Cross and Teresa of Avila: Mystical Knowing and Selfhood*. New York: Crossroad, 2002.

———. "'O guiding night!': Darkness as the Way to God in John of the Cross's Mysticism." (Unpublished).

Huerga, Alvaro. *Historia de los Alumbrados*. 4 vols. Madrid: Fundación Universitaria Española, 1978–88.

———. "Louis de Grenade." DS 9:1043–54.

Huot de Longchamp, Max. *Lectures de Jean de la Croix: Essai d'anthropologie mystique*. Théologie historique 62. Paris: Beauchesne, 1981.

———. "Les mystiques catholiques et la Bible." In *Le temps des Réformes et la Bible*, edited by Guy Bedouelle and Bernard Roussel, 587–612. Bible de tous les temps 5. Paris: Beauchesne, 1989.

Inge, William Ralph. *Christian Mysticism: Considered in Eight Lectures Delivered before the University of Oxford*. London: Methuen, 1899.

Jotischky, Andrew. *The Carmelites and Antiquity: Mendicants and Their Pasts in the Middle Ages*. Oxford: Oxford University Press, 2005.

———. *The Perfection of Solitude: Hermits and Monks in the Crusader States*. University Park: Pennsylvania State University Press, 1995.

Kallendorf, Hilaire, ed. *A New Companion to Hispanic Mysticism*. Brill's Companions to the Christian Tradition 19. Leiden: Brill, 2010.

Kamen, Henry. *Inquisition and Society in Spain in the Sixteenth and Seventeenth Centuries.* Bloomington: Indiana University Press, 1985.

Kavanaugh, Kieran. "Blessed Anne of St. Bartholomew." In *The Heirs of St. Teresa of Avila*, edited by Christopher C. Wilson, 59–71. Carmelite Studies 9. Washington, DC: ICS Publications, 2006.

Knuth, Elizabeth. "The Gift of Tears in Teresa of Avila." *Mystics Quarterly* 20 (1994): 131–42.

Kokkaravalayil, Sunny. "The Principle and Foundation of the *Spiritual Exercises* of St. Ignatius of Loyola and the Jesuit Constitution." *Studies in Spirituality* 18 (2008): 229–44.

Koppedrayer, K. I. "The Making of the First Iroquois Virgin: Early Jesuit Biographies of the Blesssed Kateri Tekakwitha." *Ethnohistory* 40 (1993): 277–306.

Lanzetta, Beverly J. "Wound of Love: Feminine Theosis and Embodied Mysticism in Teresa of Avila." In *The Participatory Turn: Spirituality, Mysticism, Religious Studies,* edited by Jorge N. Ferrer and Jacob H. Sherman, 225–44. Albany: State University of New York Press, 2008.

Lavin, Irving. *Bernini and the Unity of the Visual Arts.* 2 vols. Franklin Jasper Walls Lectures 1975. New York: Oxford University Press, 1980.

Lépée, Marcel. "St. Teresa of Jesus and the Devil." In *Satan*, edited by Bruno de Jésus Marie, O.C.D., 97–102. New York: Sheed & Ward, 1952.

Lobkowicz, Nikolaus. *Theory and Practice: History of a Concept from Aristotle to Marx.* International Studies of the Committee on International Relations. Notre Dame, IN: University of Notre Dame Press, 1967.

López-Baralt, Luce. "Teresa of Jesus and Islam: The Simile of the Seven Concentric Castles of the Soul." In *A New Companion to Hispanic Mysticism*, edited by Hilaire Kallendorf, 175–99. Brill's Companions to the Christian Tradition 19. Leiden: Brill, 2010.

López Santidrián, Saturnino. "Introducción." In *Tercer abecedario espiritual de Francisco de Osuna*, 5–82. Madrid: Biblioteca Autores Cristianos, 1998.

———. "Recueillement, II: Dans la spiritualité classique espagnole." DS 13:255–67.

Louis-Marie. "Diego de Jesús." DS 3:873–74.

Luta, Mary. "A Marriage Well Arranged: Teresa of Avila and Fray Jerónimo Gracián." *Studia Mystica* 10 (1989): 32–46.

Lynch, John. *Spain 1516–1598: From Nation State to World Empire.* Cambridge, MA: Blackwell, 1992.

Macca, V., et al. "Carmelitane, Suore." DIP 2:398–423.

———. "Carmelitane Scalze, Monache." DIP 2:423–54.

———. "Carmelitani Scalzi." DIP 2:523–602.

Maréchal, Joseph. *Études sur la psychologie des mystiques,* vol. 2. Paris: Desclée, 1937.

Maritain, Jacques. *Distinguish to Unite: Or, The Degrees of Knowledge.* New York: Charles Scribner's Sons, 1959.

Marno, David. "Attention and Indifference in Ignatius's *Spiritual Exercises.*" In *A Companion to Ignatius of Loyola: Life, Writings, Spirituality, Influence,* edited by Robert Aleksander Maryks, 232–47. Brill's Companions to the Christian Tradition. Leiden: Brill, 2014.

Márquez, Antonio. *Los alumbrados: Orígenes y filosofía (1525–1559).* 2nd ed. Madrid: Taurus, 1980.

———. "De mística luisiana: ser o no ser." In *Fray Luis de León: Historia, Humanismo y Letras,* edited by Victor García de la Concha and Javier San José Lera, 287–98. Salamanca: Ediciones Universidad, 1986.

Martínez Llamas, Enrique. *Santa Teresa de Jesús y la Inquisición Española.* Madrid: Editorial de Espiritualidad, 1972.

Maryks, Robert Aleksander, ed. *A Companion to Ignatius of Loyola: Life, Writings, Spirituality, Influence.* Brill's Companions to the Christian Tradition. Leiden: Brill, 2014.

Mateos, François. "Espagne, V: Pays de langue espagnole: Amerique du sud." DS 4:1192–1203.

Matthew, Iain. *The Impact of God: Soundings from St. John of the Cross.* London: Hodder & Stoughton, 2010.

McCann, Leonard Albert. *The Doctrine of the Void.* Toronto: Basilian Press, 1955.

McGinn, Bernard. "Catherine of Siena: Apostle of the Blood of Christ." *Theology Today* 48 (2001): 329–42.

———. *The Essential Writings of Christian Mysticism.* New York: Random House, 2006.

———. "'Evil-Sounding, Rash, and Suspect of Heresy': Tensions between Mysticism and Magisterium in the History of the Church." *Catholic Historical Review* 90 (2004): 193–212.

———. "'One Word Will Contain within Itself a Thousand Mysteries': Teresa of Avila, the First Woman Commentator on the Song of Songs." *Spiritus* 16 (2016): 21–40.

———. "Three Forms of Negativity in Christian Mysticism." In *Knowing the Unknowable: Science and Religions on God and the Universe,* edited by John Bowker, 99–121. Library of Modern Religion 2. London: I. B. Tauris, 2009.

———. "True Confessions: Augustine and Teresa of Avila on the Mystical Self." In *Teresa of Avila: Mystical Theology and Spirituality in the Carmelite Tradition,* edited by Peter Tyler and Edward Howells, 9–29. London: Routledge, 2017.

———. "Visio dei: Seeing God in Medieval Theology and Mysticism." In *Envisaging Heaven in the Middle Ages*, edited by Carolyn Muessig and Ad Putter, 15–33. Studies in Medieval Religion and Culture 6. London: Routledge, 2007.

———. "Visions and Visualizations in the Here and Hereafter." *Harvard Theological Review* 98 (2005): 227–46.

———. "Women Reading the Song of Songs in the Christian Tradition." In *Scriptural Exegesis: The Shapes of Culture and the Religious Imagination. Essays in Honour of Michael Fishbane*, edited by Deborah A. Green and Laura S. Lieber, 281–96. Oxford: Oxford University Press, 2009.

McGlynn, Michael. "Silence and Ineffability as Cognition in San Juan de la Cruz' *Coplas del Mismo Hechas sobre un Éxtasis de Alta Contemplación*." *Studies in Spirituality* 21 (2011): 193–217.

McGreal, Wilfrid. *At the Fountain of Elijah: The Carmelite Tradition.* Maryknoll, NY: Orbis Books, 1999.

McIntosh, Mark J. *Discernment and Truth: The Spirituality and Theology of Knowledge.* New York: Crossroad, 2004.

McKendrick, Geraldine, and Angus MacKay. "Visionaries and Affective Spirituality in the First Half of the Sixteenth Century." In *Cultural Encounters: The Impact of the Inquisition in Spain and the New World,* edited by Mary Elizabeth Perry and Anne J. Cruz, 93–104. Berkeley: University of California Press, 1991.

McManamon, John M. *The Text and Contexts of Ignatius Loyola's "Autobiography."* New York: Fordham University Press, 2013.

McNight, Kathryn Joy. *The Mystic of Tunja: The Writings of Madre Castillo, 1671–1742.* Amherst: University of Massachusetts Press, 1997.

Meersemann, Gilles. "A propos de deux écrits de spiritualité attribués à saint Thomas." *Revue Thomiste* 35 (1930): 560–70.

Meissner, W. W. *Saint Ignatius of Loyola: The Psychology of a Saint.* New Haven: Yale University Press, 1992.

Melchior de Sainte-Marie. "Joseph du Saint-Esprit (l'andaluo)." DS 8:1397–1402.

———. "Doctrina Josephi a Spiritu Sancto de contemplazione infusa." In *De contemplatione in Schola Teresiana*, 714–57. Ephemerides Carmeliticae 13. Rome: Teresianum, 1962.

Mieth, Dietmar. *Die Einheit von Vita Activa und Vita Contemplativa in den deutschen Predigten und Traktaten Meister Eckharts und bei Johannes*

Tauler: Untersuchungen zur Struktur des christlichen Lebens. Studien zur Geschichte der katholischen Moral-theologie 15. Regensburg: Pustet, 1969.

Molinar, Jose María de la Cruz. *Historia de la literatura mística en España.* Burgos: "El Monte Carmelo," 1961.

Morel, Georges. *Le sens de l'existence selon Saint Jean de la Croix.* 3 vols. Paris: Aubier, 1961.

Morietti, Roberto. "Philippe de la Trinité." DS 12:1325–28.

Moriones, Ildefonso. "Jérôme de la Mère de Dieu (Gracian)." DS 8:920–28.

———. "Nicolás de Jésus-Marie," DS 11:286–87.

Mujica, Barbara. "Cecilia del Nacimiento: Un alma inflamando del amor." In Mujica, *Women Writers of Early Modern Spain: Sophia's Daughters*, 99–115. New Haven: Yale University Press, 2004.

———. "Paul the Enchanter: Saint Teresa's Vow of Obedience to Gracián." In *The Heirs of St. Teresa of Avila*, edited by Christopher C. Wilson, 21–44. Carmelite Studies 9. Washington, DC: ICS Publications, 2006.

———. *Teresa de Avila: Lettered Woman.* Nashville: Vanderbilt University Press, 2009.

Murphy, John J. "St. John of the Cross and the Philosophy of Religion: Love of God and the Conceptual Parameters of a Mystical Experience." *Mystics Quarterly* 22 (1996): 163–86.

Myers, Kathleen Ann. "'Redeemer of America': Rose of Lima (1586–1617), the Dynamics of Identity, and Canonization." In *Colonial Saints: Discovering the Holy in the Americas*, edited by Allan Greer and Jodi Bilinkoff, 251–75. New York: Routledge, 2003.

Myers, Kathleen A., and Amanda Powell, eds., *Wild Country out in the Garden: The Spiritual Journals of a Colonial Mexican Nun.* Bloomington: Indiana University Press, 1998.

Nagy, Piroska. *Les don des larmes au Moyen Âge: Un instrument spirituel en quête d'institution (Ve–XIIIe siècle).* Bibliothèque Albin Michel. Paris: Albin Michel, 2000.

Nevin, Winifred. *Heirs of St Teresa of Avila.* Milwaukee: Bruce, 1959.

Newman, Barbara. *From Virile Woman to WomanChrist: Studies in Medieval Religion and Literature.* Philadelphia: University of Pennsylvania Press, 1995.

Nicolau, Miguel. "La Puente (Louis de), jésuite, 1554–1624." DS 9:265–76.

Nuth, Joan. "*Acatamiento*: Living in an Attitude of Affectionate Awe—An Ignatian Reflection on the Unitive Way." *Spiritus* 10 (2010): 173–91.

O'Brien, Timothy. "'Con Ojos Interiores': Ignatius of Loyola and the Spiritual Senses." *Studies in Spirituality* 26 (2016): 263–81.

Oechslin, R. L. *Louis of Granada.* St. Louis: Herder, 1962.

Ofilada Mina, Macario. "Between Semiotics and Semantics: An Epistemological Exploration of Spanish Mysticism and Literature and Its Contribution to Spirituality in the Academy." *Studies in Spirituality* 22 (2012): 69–88.

———. "The True Truth (Book of Life 21.9): Teresian Comprehension of Mystical Experience." *Studies in Spirituality* 25 (2015): 223–46.

O'Malley, John. "Early Jesuit Spirituality: Spain and Italy." In *Christian Spirituality III: Post-Reformation and Modern,* edited by Louis Dupré and Don E. Saliers, in collaboration with John Meyendorff, 3–27. World Spirituality 18. New York: Crossroad, 1989.

———. *The First Jesuits.* Cambridge, MA: Harvard University Press, 1993.

———. "Was Ignatius Loyola a Church Reformer? How to Look at Early Modern Catholicism." *Catholic Historical Review* 77 (1991): 177–93.

Ong, Walter J. "St. Ignatius' Prison-Cage and the Existentialist Situation." In Ong, *The Barbarian Within and Other Fugitive Essays and Studies,* 242–59. New York: Macmillan, 1954.

Orcibal, Jean. "Une formule de l'amour extatique de Platon à Saint Jean de la Croix et au Cardinal de Bérulle." In *Mélanges offerts à Etienne Gilson, de l'Académie française,* 447–63. Toronto: Pontifical Institute of Mediaeval Studies, 1959.

———. "Le role de l'intellect possible chez Jean de la Croix: Ses sources scolastiques et Nordiques." In *La mystique rhénane: Colloque de Strasbourg, 16–19 mai 1961,* 235–79. Paris: Presses universitaires de France, 1963.

———. *Saint Jean de la Croix et les mystiques Rhéno-flamands.* Présence du Carmel 6. N.p.: Desclée de Brouwer, 1966.

O'Reilly, Terence. *From Ignatius Loyola to John of the Cross: Spirituality and Literature in Sixteenth-Century Spain.* Collected Studies 484. Aldershot: Variorum, 1995.

Ortega Costa, Milagros. "Spanish Women in the Reformation." In *Women in Reformation and Counter-Reformation Europe,* edited by Sherrin Marshall, 89–119. Bloomington: Indiana University Press, 1989.

Ortiz Lottman, Maryrica. "The Gardens of Teresa of Avila." In *A New Companion to Hispanic Mysticism,* edited by Hilaire Kallendorf, 323–42. Brill's Companions to the Christian Tradition 19. Leiden: Brill, 2010.

Pacho, Eulogio. *Apogeo de la mística cristiana: Historia de la espirituali-dad clásica española, 1450–1650.* Burgos: Monte Carmelo, 2008.

————. "El 'Gemido Pacifico de la Esperanza'; Síntesis definitiva del pensamiento sanjuanista." *Studies in Spirituality* 6 (1996): 152–67.

————. *San Juan de la Cruz y sus escritos.* Madrid: Ediciones Cristian-dad, 1969.

————. *Vértice de la poesía y de la mística: El "Cántico Espiritual" de San Juan de la Cruz.* Burgos: Editorial Monte Carmelo, 1983.

Papa, Joseph T. *A Phenomenological Analysis of St. Ignatius of Loyola's Rules for the Discernment of Spirits.* Doctoral Dissertation, Pontifical Athenaeum of St. Anselm, 2007.

Pastore, Stefania. *Un'eresia spagnola: Spiritualità conversa, alumbradismo e Inquisizione (1449–1559).* Florence: Olschki, 2004.

Paul VI, Pope. Apostolic Letter "Multiformis Sapientia Dei," as avail-able on line at http://www.vatican.va/holy_father/paul_vi/apost_letters/documents/hf_p-vi_apl.

Payne, Stanley G. *Spanish Catholicism: An Historical Overview.* Madison: University of Wisconsin Press, 1984.

Payne, Steven. "The Influence of John of the Cross in the United States: A Preliminary Survey." In *John of the Cross: Conferences and Essays by Members of the Institute of Carmelite Studies and Others,* 167–95. Car-melite Studies 6. Washington DC: ICS Publications, 1992.

————. *John of the Cross and the Cognitive Value of Mysticism: An Analysis of Sanjuanist Teaching and Its Philosophical Implications for Contem-porary Discussions of Mystical Experience.* New Synthese Historical Library 37. Dordrecht: Kluwer, 1990.

Peers, E. Allison. *Handbook to the Life and Times of St. Teresa and St. John of the Cross.* Westminster, MD: Newman Press, 1954.

————. "Mysticism in the Poetry of Fray Luis de León." In Peers, *St. Teresa of Jesus and Other Essays and Addresses,* 153–73. London: Faber & Faber, 1953.

————. *Studies of the Spanish Mystics.* 3 vols. New York: Macmillan, 1927–36. Revised edition, New York: Macmillan, 1951.

Pepin, Fernande. *Noces de feu: Le symbolisme nuptial du "Cantico espiri-tual" de Saint Jean de la Croix à la lumière du "Canticum Canticorum."* Recherches: Theologie 9. Paris: Desclée, 1972.

Perrin, David Brian. *Canciones entre el Alma y el Esposo of Juan de la Cruz: A Hermeneutical Interpretation.* San Francisco: Catholic Schol-ars Press, 1996.

————. *For Love of the World: The Old and New Self of John of the Cross.* San Francisco: Catholic Scholars Press, 1997.

Pietro della Madre di Dio. "La Sacra Scrittura nelle Opere di Teresa di Gesu." *Rivista di Vita Spirituale* 18 (1964): 41–102.

Pinard de la Boullaye, Henry. "Sentir, Sentimiento, Sentido dans le style de Saint Ignace." *Archivum Historicum Societatis Jesu* 25 (1956): 416–30.

Plattig, Michael. "Die 'Dunkle Nacht' als Gotteserfahrung: Aspekte und Anregungen für gegenwartsbezogene Spiritualität." *Studies in Spirituality* 4 (1994): 165–205.

———. "Vom Trost der Tränen: Ignatius von Loyola und die Gabe der Tränen." *Studies in Spirituality* 2 (1992): 148–99.

Poutrin, Isabelle. *La voile et la plume: Autobiographie et sainteté féminine dans l'Espagne moderne.* Bibliothèque de la Casa de Velázquez 11. Madrid: Casa de Velázquez, 1995.

Rahner, Hugo. *Ignatius the Theologian.* New York: Herder & Herder, 1968.

———. "Die Mystik des hl. Ignatius und der Inhalt der Vision von La Storta." *Zeitschrift für Aszese und Mystik* 10 (1935): 202–20.

———. *The Spirituality of St. Ignatius Loyola: An Account of Its Historical Development.* 1953. Reprint, Chicago: Loyola University Press, 1980.

Rahner, Karl. "Being Open to God as Ever Greater." In Rahner, *Theological Investigations.* Volume 7, *Further Theology of the Spiritual Life,* 25–46. New York: Herder & Herder, 1971.

———. "The Ignatian Mysticism of Joy in the World." In Rahner, *Theological Investigations,* 3:277–93. Baltimore: Helicon, 1967.

———. *Ignatius of Loyola Speaks.* South Bend, IN: St. Augustine's Press, 2013.

———. "The Immediate Experience of God in the Spiritual Exercises of Saint Ignatius of Loyola." In *Karl Rahner in Dialogue: Conversations and Interview 1965–1982,* edited by Paul Imhof and Hubert Biallowons, 174–81. New York: Crossroad, 1986.

———. "The Logic of Concrete Individual Knowledge in Ignatius of Loyola." In *The Dynamic Element in the Church,* 84–170. Quaestiones disputatae 12. New York: Herder & Herder, 1964.

Rayez, André. "Gaultier (René)." DS 6:144–47.

Redworth, Glyn. "A New Way of Living? Luisa de Carvajal and the Limits of Mysticism." In *A New Companion to Hispanic Mysticism,* edited by Hilaire Kallendorf, 273–95. Brill's Companions to the Christian Tradition 19. Leiden: Brill, 2010.

Reiser, William. "The *Spiritual Exercises* in a Religiously Pluralistic World." *Studies in Spirituality* 10 (2010): 135–57.

Reypens, Léonce. "Ame (son fond, ses puissances, et sa structure d'après les mystiques)." DS 1:460–63.

Rhodes, Elisabeth. "What's in a Name: On Teresa of Avila's Book." In *The Mystical Gesture: Essays on Medieval and Early Modern Spiritual Culture in Honor of Mary E. Giles,* edited by Robert Boenig, 79–106. Aldershot: Ashgate, 2000.

Roberto de S. Teresa di Gesú. "La contemplazione infusa nel ven. P. Giovanni di Gesú Maria (Sampedro)." In *De contemplatione in Schola Teresiana*, 650–90. Ephemerides Carmeliticae 13. Rome: Teresianum, 1962.

Ricard, Robert. "Deux traits de l'expérience mystique de Saint Ignace." *Archivum Historicum Societatis Jesu* 25 (1956): 431–36.

———. "Fray Luis de León et le problème du nom." In *Études sur Sainte Thérèse*, edited by Robert Ricard and Nicole Pélisson, 187–94. Collection Études hispaniques: Série Littérature 3. Paris: Centre de Recherches Hispaniques, 1968.

———. "L'influence des 'Mystiques du Nord' sur les spirituels Portugais du XVIe et XVIIe siècle." In *La mystique rhénane*, 219–33. Paris: Presses universitaires de France, 1963.

———. "La tradition dionysienne en Espagne après saint Jean de la Croix: Luis de la Puente, s.j." *Revue d'ascétique et de mystique* 45 (1969): 409–24.

Roy, Louis. "Expérience du silence de Dieu chez Jean de la Croix." *Prêtre et Pasteur* 115 (2012): 79–86.

Ruiz Jurado, Manuel. "Rodriguez (Alphonse), jésuite, 1538–1616." DS 13:853–60.

Saggi, L. "Carmelitani." DIP 2:460–76.

Saint-Joseph, Lucien Marie de. "The Devil in the Writings of St. John of the Cross." In Bruno de Jésus Marie, O.C.D., *Satan*, 84–96. New York: Sheed & Ward, 1952.

———. "S. Jean de la Croix." DS 8:408–47.

Salazar, J. A. "Beaterio." DIP 1:1153–54.

Sanmartín Bastida, Rebeca. *La representación de las místicas: Sor María de Santo Domingo en su contexto europeo.* Santander: Real Sociedad Menéndez Pelayo, 2012.

Sanson, Henri. *L'esprit humain selon Saint Jean de la Croix.* Publications de la Faculté des lettres d'Alger 2/22. Paris: Presses universitaires de France, 1953.

Saranyana, Josep-Ignasi. "Análisis doctrinal de l'Tratado del Apocalypsi' de Gregorio López (d. 1596 en México), publicado en Madrid in 1678." In *Storia e figure dell'Apocalisse fra '500 e '600*, edited by Roberto Rusconi, 225–40. Rome: Viella, 1996.

Schineller, J. Peter. "The Pilgrim Journey of Ignatius: From Soldier to Laborer in the Lord's Vineyard and Its Implications of Apostolic Lay Spirituality." *Studies in the Spirituality of Jesuits* 31/4 (September 1999).

Schoot, Henk J. M. *Christ the 'Name' of God: Thomas Aquinas on Naming Christ.* Leuven: Peeters, 1993.

———. "Friars in Negative Theology: Thomas Aquinas and Luis de León." In *The Myriad Christ: Plurality and the Quest for Unity in Contemporary Christology,* edited by T. Merrigan and J. Haers, 331–47. Bibliotheca Ephemeridum theologicarum Lovaniensium 152. Leuven: Peeters, 2000.

Schreiner, Susan. *Are You Alone Wise? The Search for Certainty in the Early Modern Era.* Oxford Studies in Historical Theology. New York: Oxford University Press, 2011.

Sclafert, Clément. "L'allégorie de la bûche enflammée dans Hugues de Saint-Victor et dans Saint Jean de la Croix." *Revue d'ascétique et de mystique* 33 (1957): 242–63 and 361–86.

Scott, Lewis. "Balthasar Alvarez and the Prayer of Silence." *Spirituality Today* 41 (1989): 112–42.

Serrado, Joana de Fátima Gonçalves Pita do. *Ancias/Anxiousness in Joana de Jesus (1617–1681): Historical and Philosophical Approaches.* Ph.D. Dissertation, University of Groningen, 2014.

Sheldrake, Philip, ed. *The Way of Ignatius Loyola: Contemporary Approaches to the Spiritual Exercises.* St. Louis: Institute of Jesuit Sources, 1991.

Short, William J. "From Contemplation to Inquisition: The Franciscan Practice of Recollection in Sixteenth-Century Spain." In *Franciscans at Prayer,* edited by Timothy J. Johnson, 449–74. Leiden: Brill, 2007.

Sieben, Hermann Josef, and Aimé Solignac. "Ivresse spirituelle." DS 7:2312–37.

Silos, Leonardo R. "Cardoner in the Life of St. Ignatius." *Archivum Historicum Societatis Jesu* 33 (1964): 3–43.

Simeón de la Sagrada Familia. "Joseph du Saint-Joseph (le portugais)." DS 8:1395–97.

Slade, Carole. "Saint Teresa's *Meditaciones sobre los Cantares*: The Hermeneutics of Humility and Enjoyment." *Religion and Literature* 18 (1986): 27–43.

———. *St. Teresa of Avila: Author of a Heroic Life.* Berkeley: University of California Press, 1995.

Sluhovsky, Moshe. *Believe Not Every Spirit: Possession, Mysticism and Discernment in Early Modern Catholicism.* Chicago: University of Chicago Press, 2007.

————. "Loyola's *Spiritual Exercises* and the Modern Self." In *A Companion to Ignatius Loyola: Life, Writings, Spirituality, Influence*, edited by Robert A. Maryks, 216–31. Brill's Companions to the Christian Tradition. Leiden: Brill, 2014.

Smet, Joachim. *The Carmelites: A History of the Brothers of Our Lady of Mount Carmel*. 4 vols. Darien, IL: Carmelite Spiritual Center, 1975–85.

————. *Cloistered Carmel*. Rome: Institutum Carmelitanum, 1987.

Solignac, Aimé. "Multilocation." DS 10:1837–40.

————. "Vie active, vie contemplative, vie mixte." DS 16:592–623.

Solignac, Aimé, and Lin Donnet. "Marthe et Marie." DS 10:664–73.

Staring, Adrianus. "Nicolai Prioris Generalis Ordnis Carmelitarum Ignea Sagitta." *Carmelus* 9 (1962): 237–307.

Steggink, Otger. "Carmelitani Scalzi, II: Spiritualità." DIP 2:476–501.

————. "Esperienza e teologia nella storia della mistica Cristiana: Teresa di Gesù, donna e mistica, di fronte alla teologia e ai teologi." In *Sentieri illuminati dallo Spirito: Atti del Congresso internazionale di mistica*, 243–68. Rome: Edizioni O.C.D, 2006.

————. "Jerónimo Gracián und die 'Perfectistas': Eine spanische Auseinandersetzung mit der Mystik des Nordens." *Studies in Spirituality* 2 (1992): 200–208.

Stein, Edith. *The Science of the Cross: A Study of St. John of the Cross*. Chicago: Regnery, 1960. German original, 1940–41.

Strina, Giovanni Maria. "Jean de Jésus-Marie (le calagurritain)." DS 8:576–81.

Surgy, P. de. "La source de l'échelle d'amour chez saint Jean de la Croix." *Revue d'ascétique et de mystique* 27 (1951): 18–40, 237–59, and 327–46.

Surtz, Ronald E. *The Guitar of God: Gender, Power, and Authority in the Visionary World of Mother Juana de la Cruz (1481–1534)*. Philadelphia: University of Pennsylvania Press, 1990.

————. *Writing Women in Late Medieval and Early Modern Spain: The Mothers of Saint Teresa of Avila*. Philadelphia: University of Pennsylvania Press, 1995.

Swietlicki, Catherine. *Spanish Christian Cabala: The Works of Luis de León, Santa Teresa de Jesús, and San Juan de la Cruz*. Columbia: University of Missouri Press, 1986.

Tar, Jane. "Flying through the Empire: The Visionary Journeys of Early Modern Nuns." In *Women's Voices and the Politics of the Spanish Empire*, edited by Jennifer L. Eich, Jeanne Gillespie, and Lucia G. Harrison, 235–62. New Orleans: University Press of the South, 2008.

Tavard, George H. *Poetry and Contemplation in St. John of the Cross.* Athens: Ohio University Press, 1988.

Tellechea Idigoras, José Ignacio. *Ignatius of Loyola: The Pilgrim Saint.* Edited and translated by Michael Buckley. Chicago: Loyola University Press, 1994.

Theophilus, Father. "Mystical Ecstasy according to St. Teresa." In *St. Teresa of Avila: Studies in Her Life, Doctrine and Times,* edited by Father Thomas and Father Gabriel, 139–53. London: Burns & Oates, 1963.

Thompson, Colin P. "Dangerous Visions: The Experience of Teresa of Avila and the Teaching of John of the Cross." In *Angels of Light? Sanctity and the Discernment of Spirits in the Early Modern Period,* edited by Clare Copeland and Jan Machielsen, 53–73. Studies in Medieval and Reformation Traditions 164. Leiden: Brill, 2013.

———. *The Poet and the Mystic: A Study of the Cántico Espiritual of San Juan de la Cruz.* Oxford Modern Languages and Literature Monographs. Oxford: Oxford University Press, 1977.

———. Review of *Luis de León, The Names of Christ,* translated by Manuel Durán and William Kluback. *New Blackfriars* 66 (1985): 201–2.

———. *St. John of the Cross: Songs in the Night.* Washington, DC: Catholic University of America Press, 2003.

———. *The Strife of Tongues: Fray Luis de León and the Golden Age of Spain.* Cambridge: Cambridge University Press, 1988.

Thurston, Herbert. "Maria Coronel de Agreda." In Thurston, *Surprising Mystics,* 122–32. Chicago: Henry Regnery, 1955.

Toft, Emily. "Cecilia del Nacimiento: Mystic in the Tradition of John of the Cross." In *The Mystical Gesture: Essays on Medieval and Early Modern Spiritual Culture in Honor of Mary E. Giles,* edited by Robert Boenig, 169–84. Aldershot: Ashgate, 2000.

Toner, Jules J. *A Commentary on Saint Ignatius' Rules for the Discernment of Spirits: A Guide to the Principles and Practice.* St. Louis: Institute of Jesuit Sources, 1982.

———. *Discerning God's Will: Ignatius of Loyola's Teaching on Christian Decision Making.* St. Louis: Institute of Jesuit Sources, 1991.

Tracy, David. *The Analogical Imagination: Christian Theology and the Culture of Pluralism.* New York: Crossroad, 1981.

Turner, Denys. *The Darkness of God: Negativity in Christian Mysticism.* Cambridge: Cambridge University Press, 1995.

Tyler, Peter. *The Return of the Mystical: Ludwig Wittgenstein, Teresa of Avila, and the Christian Mystical Tradition.* London: Continuum, 2011.

———. *St. John of the Cross.* London: Continuum, 2014.

———. *Teresa of Avila: Doctor of the Soul.* London: Bloomsbury, 2013.

———. "Teresa of Avila's Transformative Strategies on Embodiment in *Meditations on the Song of Songs.*" In *Sources of Transformation: Revitalising Christian Spirituality,* edited by Edward Howells and Peter Tyler, 135–45. London: Continuum, 2010.

Tyler, Peter, and Edward Howells, eds., *Teresa of Avila: Mystical Theology and Spirituality in the Carmelite Tradition.* London and New York: Routledge, 2017.

Tylus, Jane. "Between Two Fathers: Teresa of Avila and Mystical Autobiography." In *Writing and Vulnerability in the Late Renaissance,* edited by Jane Tylus, 54–79. Stanford: Stanford University Press, 1993.

Underhill, Evelyn. *Mysticism.* 3rd ed. New York: E. P. Dutton, 1961.

Veale, Joseph. "Dominant Orthodoxies." *Milltown Studies* 30 (1992): 43–65.

———. "Saint Ignatius Asks: Are You Sure You Know Who I Am?" *Studies in the Spirituality of Jesuits* 33/4 (September 2001).

———. "Saint Ignatius Speaks about Ignatian Prayer." *Studies in the Spirituality of Jesuits* 28/2 (March 1996).

Vilnet, Jean. *Bible et mystique chez saint Jean de la Croix.* Études carmélitaines. Bruges: Desclée de Brouwer, 1949.

Waaijman, Kees. "Allí me Hirió: Estudio sobre la poesía 'Super Flumina Babilonis' de Juan de la Cruz." *Studies in Spirituality* 3 (1993): 200–212.

Weber, Alison. "María de San José (Salazar): Saint Teresa's 'Difficult' Daughter." In *The Heirs of St. Teresa of Avila,* edited by Christopher C. Wilson, 1–20. Carmelite Studies 9. Washington, DC: ICS Publications, 2006.

———. "Spiritual Administration: Gender and Discernment in the Carmelite Reform." *Sixteenth Century Journal* 31 (2000): 123–46.

———. *Teresa of Avila and the Rhetoric of Femininity.* Princeton: Princeton University Press, 1990.

———. "The Three Lives of the *Vida*: The Uses of Convent Autobiography." In *Women, Texts and Authority in the Early Modern Spanish World,* edited by Marta V. Vicente and Luis R. Corteguera, 107–25. Women and Gender in the Early Modern World. Aldershot: Ashgate, 2003.

Weintraub, Karl Joachim. *The Value of the Individual: Self and Circumstance in Autobiography.* Chicago: University of Chicago Press, 1978.

Wilhelmsen, Elizabeth. *Cognition and Communication in John of the Cross.* Frankfurt am Main: P. Lang, 1985.

———. *Knowledge and Symbolization in Saint John of the Cross.* Frankfurt am Main: P. Lang, 1993.

Williams, Rowan. "The Deflections of Desire: Negative Theology in Trinitarian Disclosure." In *Silence and the Word: Negative Theology and Incarnation*, edited by Oliver Davies and Denys Turner, 115–35. Cambridge: Cambridge University Press, 2002.

———. *Teresa of Avila.* Outstanding Christian Thinkers. London: Geoffrey Chapman, 1991.

———. "Teresa, the Eucharist, and the Reformation." In *Teresa of Avila: Mystical Theology and Spirituality in the Carmelite Tradition*, edited by Peter Tyler and Edward Howells, 67–76. London: Routledge, 2017.

Wilson, Christopher C., ed. *The Heirs of St. Teresa of Avila.* Carmelite Studies 9. Washington, DC: ICS Publications, 2006.

———. "Taking Teresian Authority to the Front Lines: Ana de San Bartolomé and Ana de Jesús in Art of the Spanish Netherlands." In *The Heirs of St. Teresa of Avila*, edited by Christopher C. Wilson, 72–106. Carmelite Studies 9. Washington, DC: ICS Publications, 2006.

Wlusek, Stephen. "The Foundations of John of the Cross' Spiritual Theology in the Thought and Writings of Pseudo-Dionysius." *Studies in Spirituality* 18 (2008): 195–213.

Wojtyla, Karol (Pope John Paul II). *Faith according to St. John of the Cross.* San Francisco: Ignatius Press, 1981.

Wolf, Hubert. *The Nuns of Sant'Ambrogio: The True Story of a Convent Scandal.* New York: Alfred A. Knopf, 2015.

Worchester, Thomas, ed. *The Cambridge Companion to the Jesuits.* Cambridge: Cambridge University Press, 2008.

Zagano, Phylis. "The Ignatian Mystic." In *The Renewal of Mystical Theology: Essays in Memory of John N. Jones,* edited by Bernard McGinn, 109–30. New York: Crossroad-Herder, 2017.

Zambruno, Elisabetta. *Tra filosofia e mistica: Tommaso di Gesù.* Collana di testi mistici 16. Vatican City: Libreria Editrice Vaticana, 2009.

Index of Subjects

Index of Names

470

Index of Scripture References (Vulgate)